D0087704

PART 9 Editing for Word Choice

PART 10 Sentence Punctuation

PART 11 Mechanics and Spelling

PART 12 Guide for Multilingual Writers

PART 13 Further Resources for Learning

The McGraw-Hill Handbook

Second Edition

Catalyst 2.0

The Online Learning Center for *The McGraw-Hill Handbook* **(http://www.mhhe.com/mhhb2)** provides full coverage of writing, researching, and editing, featuring diagnostic quizzes that help students assess their knowledge of usage, grammar, punctuation, mechanics, and spelling. A list of print and online resources in 30 disciplines provides a starting point for student research projects. "How to Use This Book" tutorials teach students to locate information in the textbook with ease.

The site features all the resources of Catalyst 2.0, the premiere online tool for writing, research, and editing.

To access premium Catalyst content, please go to the Online Learning Center for *The McGraw-Hill Handbook, Second Edition* at http://www.mhhe.com/mhhb2 and click on the "Enter Catalyst 2.0" graphic shown below in the middle of the home page.

Catalyst 2.0 features interactive tutorials on document design and visual rhetoric, guides for avoiding plagiarism and evaluating sources, electronic writing tutors for composing a range of essays, and more than 4,500 exercises with feedback in grammar, usage, and punctuation.

The McGraw-Hill Handbook

Second Edition

Elaine P. Maimon
Governors State University

Janice H. Peritz
Queens College,
City University of New York

Kathleen Blake Yancey
Florida State University

With notes for multilingual students
and *Guide for Multilingual Writers* by
Maria Zlateva, Boston University

Boston Burr Ridge, IL Dubuque, IA Madison, WI New York
San Francisco St. Louis Bangkok Bogotá Caracas Kuala Lumpur
Lisbon London Madrid Mexico City Milan Montreal New Delhi
Santiago Seoul Singapore Sydney Taipei Toronto

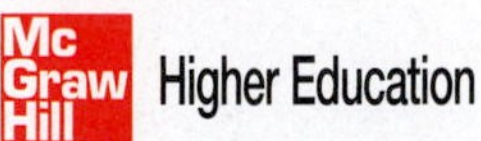

Mc Graw Hill Higher Education

This book is printed on acid-free paper.

1 2 3 4 5 6 7 8 9 0 DOW / DOW 0 9

Hardcover
ISBN-13: 978-0-07-338381-1
MHID: 0-07-338381-3

Softcover
ISBN-13: 978-0-07-730074-6
MHID: 0-07-730074-2

Vice President and Editor in Chief: *Michael Ryan*
Publisher: *David S. Patterson*
Senior Sponsoring Editor: *Christopher Bennem*
Director of Development: *Dawn Groundwater*
Development Editor: *Anne Kemper*
Executive Marketing Manager: *Allison Jones*
Market Development Manager: *Molly Meneely*
Lead Production Editor: *Brett Coker*
Manuscript Editor: *Barbara Armentrout*
Lead Designer: *Cassandra Chu*
Interior and Cover Designer: *Maureen McCutcheon*
Art and Photo Editor: *Sonia Brown*
Production Supervisors: *Randy Hurst, Richard DeVitto*
Lead Media Project Manager: *Ron Nelms*
Composition: *9/11 New Century Schoolbook by Thompson Type*
Printing: *45# Pub Matte Thin Bulk by R.R. Donnelley & Sons*

Cover images: *(from top to bottom) © Visual Landscape; © Philadelphia Museum of Art / CORBIS; © NASA / Roger Ressmeyer / CORBIS; Nevros / Folio, Inc; © Jon Hicks / CORBIS*

Credits: The credits section for this book begins on page C-1 and is considered an extension of the copyright page.

Library of Congress Cataloging-in-Publication Data
Maimon, Elaine P.
[New McGraw-Hill handbook]
The McGraw-Hill handbook / Elaine Maimon, Janice Peritz, Kathleen Yancey. —2nd ed.
p. cm.
Originally published as: 1st ed.The new McGraw-Hill handbook, c2007
Includes bibliographical references and index.
ISBN-13: 978-0-07-338381-1 (alk. paper)
ISBN-10: 0-07-338381-3 (alk. paper)
1. English language—Rhetoric—Handbooks, manuals, etc. 2. Academic writing—Handbooks, manuals, etc. 3. Report writing—Handbooks, manuals, etc. I. Peritz, Janice. II. Yancey, Kathleen Blake, 1950- III. Title.

PE1408.M3364 2009
808'.042—dc22 2008047891

The Internet addresses listed in the text were accurate at the time of publication. The inclusion of a Web site does not indicate an endorsement by the authors or McGraw-Hill, and McGraw-Hill does not guarantee the accuracy of the information presented at these sites.

www.mhhe.com

Contents

PART 1 ■ Writing and Designing Texts

PART 2 ▪ Common Assignments across the Curriculum

PART 3 ■ Researching

PART 4 ▪ Documenting across the Curriculum

PART 5 ▪ Writing beyond College

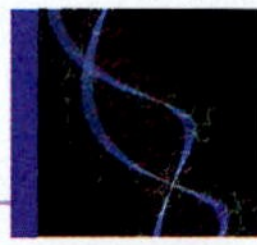

PART 6 ▪ Grammar Basics

PART 7 ▪ Editing for Grammar Conventions

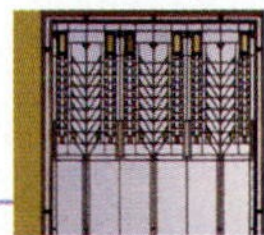

PART 8 ▪ Editing for Clarity

PART 9 ■ Editing for Word Choice

PART 10 ▪ Sentence Punctuation

PART 11 ▪ Mechanics and Spelling

PART 13 ▪ Further Resources for Learning

Preface

As we wrote the first edition of *The McGraw-Hill Handbook,* our students were always on our minds. We knew that today's students' perspectives on college life were different from those of previous generations of students, and so were their expectations. Most college students today have never known a world without the Internet. Advances in technologies ensure that they are constantly connected to a wealth of information on almost any topic, as well as to one another. Raised on the Web, television, and advertising, they are highly attuned to visual images. At the same time, students with careers and families are entering, and reentering, academia with their own rich set of experiences and expectations. More than ever before, today's students represent an abundance of linguistic and cultural backgrounds, needing a variety of approaches to writing and editing at the college level. Multitasking at unprecedented levels, they need a handbook they can rely on in all their courses: whether that means learning about revision in their English composition class, preparing PowerPoints for a speech course, or looking for help with integrating sources into a history assignment.

Students are different,

the tools are different,

but the goals are the same:

writing well and succeeding in college and beyond.

As students change, so, too, do the tools that students use for writing and research. Research occurs online via databases and the Web, and the greatest challenges students face are not in finding sources, but in choosing and evaluating the most appropriate sources and using them effectively in their projects. Word processing, presentation software, and writing for the Web have increased the importance of visuals and design in writing. Many composition courses make use of digital technologies such as electronic portfolios or blogs and use Blackboard or other course-management systems to foster student collaboration and online peer review.

Even though the occasions, tools, and audiences for writing seem more varied than ever, the fundamental goals of composition courses persist. Instructors strive to produce students who can think critically, recognize rhetorical situations, communicate clearly and effectively, write in a variety of genres, and edit their own work. Students must be discerning and ethical researchers, acknowledging the contributions of others and documenting sources appropriately. And composition courses still aim to build writing skills that students will carry with them into their other courses, their work in the community, and their professional lives. In response to these goals—suggested by the WPA Outcomes Statement for First-Year Composition (reproduced on pp. xxxii–xxxiii) and those of many colleges and universities—*The McGraw-Hill Handbook* pays new attention to commonly identified outcomes for composition to help students track their progress and understand how they may be assessed.

Today's students need a handbook with state-of-the-art, accessible resources on writing, researching, editing, and design—a handbook they can rely on for all their academic writing.

In revising this text, we have dedicated ourselves to making *The McGraw-Hill Handbook* an even stronger, more current, and more versatile resource for achieving excellence in the ever-changing environments that students encounter in college.

Features of *The McGraw-Hill Handbook*

Specific, student- and instructor-tested features of *The McGraw-Hill Handbook* equip today's students with tools for learning, writing, researching, and editing. The book also provides students and teachers with access to powerful online resources.

A Ready Resource

The second edition of *The McGraw-Hill Handbook* meets the needs of busy students with new, quickly accessible features that make it an even more convenient reference tool.

***New* Resources for Writers: Identifying and Editing Common Problems foldout**

This handy reference presents easy access to fixes for the most common errors students make when editing for clarity, word choice, grammatical conventions, and correctness (punctuation, mechanics, and spelling). On the back of this foldout, students will find **Quick Reference for Multilingual Writers,** a chart offering help with the most common problems that affect Generation 1.5 students and English language learners alike.

***New* Resources for Writers foldouts for documenting in MLA and APA style**

These foldouts reflect the most recent changes to these two styles of citation. On the front of each foldout, **Identifying and Documenting Sources,** flowcharts help guide students to the correct model citations in the text. On the reverse side, each panel includes visual guidelines for citing sources, showing where students can find the bibliographic information for a book, periodical article, Web site, selection from an online database (MLA), or online article with Digital Object Identifier (APA).

***New* Resources for Writers: Discipline-Specific Resources and World Map foldout**

Since research forms a vital part of college writing, this pull-out section includes up-to-date information on reference works and resources from a variety of disciplines. More reliable than a Google search, this listing of academically vetted sources provides students with a quick-reference guide to the places online and in the library where research might reasonably start. A revised, full-color map of the world is found on the back of the foldout.

***New* attention to key writing outcomes**

Writing Outcomes boxes at the beginning of each section indicate where students can find key material that will help them master aspects of writing such as rhetorical knowledge, the writing process, and critical thinking. Based on the Writing Program Administrators Outcomes Statement for First-Year Composition (reproduced on pp. xxxii–xxxiii), this feature helps students find the support they need to address the key issues in their writing on which they are likely to be assessed.

***New* checklists for self-assessment**

These checklists on topics such as editing for style and avoiding plagiarism help students evaluate their own work and reflect on processes for improving their writing.

***New* online interactive tutorials**

The handbook offers important guidance for students throughout college and beyond, and these online guides help students get the most out of this valuable resource. Brief visual overviews to using the text accompany interactive quizzes that help students become more familiar with it.

A Resource for Writing

The McGraw-Hill Handbook recognizes the importance of critical thinking and academic writing in first-year composition.

Guidelines for the most common college writing assignments
Part 2: Common Assignments across the Curriculum gives students step-by-step advice on writing the three most commonly assigned types of papers (informative, interpretive, and argumentative essays), as well as guidance on other common assignments including personal essays, case studies, lab reports, in-class essay exams, oral presentations with PowerPoint, and multimedia assignments. Eight full student papers appear in this section as models.

A focus on critical thinking and effective writing across the curriculum
Although instructors in various disciplines may approach subject matter differently, thinking critically and writing logically are underlying expectations across the curriculum. For this reason, Part 2 begins with a chapter on the connections among critical reading, thinking, and writing.

More sample papers and samples of writing than any other handbook
The McGraw-Hill Handbook provides plentiful samples of student and professional writing for a variety of purposes—to inform, interpret, and argue—from a wide range of disciplines. The writing process chapters follow the development of a student essay from conception to final draft; the document design chapter contains a student's reflective essay from an electronic portfolio; the common assignments chapters include eight student papers; and the MLA and APA documentation chapters each feature a complete student research report.

This edition includes four *new* sample student papers:

- Reflective essay from an electronic portfolio
- Informative report in the social sciences
- Interpretive analysis in the sciences
- Argument paper in the social sciences

***New* Expanded coverage of argument and visual argument**
The second edition further equips students for success in this important genre, with fuller treatment of the classical appeals, fallacies, counterarguments, and the classical, Toulmin, and Rogerian structures of argument. New material on visual argument in Chapter 10: Arguments invites students to recognize the persuasive visual messages that surround them and help them to use those techniques in their own arguments.

New visual rhetoric icon complements integrated coverage of visual rhetoric
This image appears throughout the text and in the table of contents on pages v–xxi. It guides students and instructors to sections dealing with the use of visuals—a complete listing also appears in the Quick Guide to Key Resources at the back of the book. *The McGraw-Hill Handbook* includes a section on learning in a multimedia world in Chapter 1: Learning across the Curriculum and a chapter on finding and creating effective visuals in Part 3: Researching. Coverage is also integrated throughout the text, particularly in Part 1: Writing and Designing Texts. In addition, the book itself includes visuals drawn from various disciplines, time periods, and cultures.

New updated coverage of today's technologies
Today's students have more opportunities to write than ever before, including *Facebook* and *MySpace* pages, e-mail and texting, chat rooms and blogs. The text gives updated advice on using online tools for learning; practical suggestions for using electronic resources to collaborate and revise; a chapter on designing papers and preparing print and electronic portfolios; advice for writing scannable résumés; and TextConnex boxes with advice on technology and useful links throughout the text.

Preparation for writing at work and in the community
Part 5: Writing beyond College demonstrates how writing in college prepares students for success in the professional world. Special topics include applying for internships, producing résumés, service learning, and creating brochures and newsletters. In addition, Writing beyond College boxes throughout the book illustrate the variety of writing situations students are likely to encounter outside college.

A Resource for Researching

The McGraw-Hill Handbook helps students navigate the complexities of research today.

New updated and expanded coverage of MLA, APA, and CSE documentation
Part 4: Documenting across the Curriculum now conforms to the seventh edition of the *MLA Handbook for Writers of Research Papers* (2009), the *APA Style Guide to Electronic References* (2007), and the seventh edition of the *CSE Manual for Authors, Editors, and Publishers* (2006). (The text also includes up-to-date coverage of *Chicago Manual of Style* documentation.) This expanded section contains 120 MLA citation models and 69 APA citation models.

New Source Smart boxes
Appearing throughout Part 3: Researching, these boxes offer students tips on researching wisely. Topics include creating a research

strategy, conducting interviews, avoiding plagiarism, and integrating sources via summary, paraphrase, and quotation.

***New* expanded sections on integrating sources and avoiding plagiarism**
In Chapter 21: Working with Sources and Avoiding Plagiarism, more examples and guidelines give students additional advice on using sources effectively in their papers. Thorough explanation of acceptable and unacceptable paraphrases, summaries, and quotations enables students to avoid accidental plagiarism. An expanded overview of copyright, plagiarism, and fair use appears in Chapter 20: Plagiarism, Copyright, and Intellectual Property.

***New* expanded sections on how to evaluate and use online sources appropriately**
Chapter 18: Evaluating Sources now includes an examination of the reliability of three Web sites. These guidelines help students conduct Web research wisely. Chapter 21 helps students draw on a full range of media in their writing, with examples that include blog entries and audio podcasts.

***New* discussion of annotated bibliography**
Chapter 21 includes a sample annotated bibliography. The text shows students how to complete this common research assignment, enabling them to assess and track their sources.

A unique chapter on finding and creating effective visuals
Chapter 17: Finding and Creating Effective Visuals includes discussions of why and when students should—or should not—use images to reinforce a point and gives them practical advice on displaying information visually.

A Resource for Editing

The McGraw-Hill Handbook helps today's students see how grammar fits into the writing process, so they can learn to become effective editors of their own work.

Grammar in the context of editing
Most of the chapters in Parts 7–11, which cover the conventions of English grammar, usage, punctuation, and mechanics, are structured first to teach students to identify a particular problem and then to edit to eliminate the problem in a way that strengthens their writing.

Identify and Edit boxes
These boxes appear in key style, grammar, and punctuation chapters. They give students (especially visual learners) strategies for identifying their most serious sentence problems and are especially useful for quick reference.

✓ ***New* Common Issues icon**
This new icon appears throughout the text and in the table of contents, highlighting sections that discuss students' most common difficulties with grammar, style, word choice, punctuation, and mechanics. These sections are listed in the Quick Guide to Key Resources at the back of the book and referenced, for quick consultation, on the Resources for Writers: Identifying and Editing Common Problems foldout.

***New* interactive online Test Yourself diagnostic quizzes**
Now online, these interactive diagnostics provide immediate feedback to students to let them know where they need improvement, and where to find help in those areas. They help students gauge their own strengths and weaknesses on the conventions of grammar, style, punctuation, and mechanics. Two new quizzes cover the MLA and APA documentation styles.

Practice exercises
Practice exercises throughout the book include content from subjects across the curriculum that students are likely to encounter in their first-year courses. For students who need additional practice, *Catalyst 2.0* offers more than 4,500 exercises with immediate explanatory feedback in response to incorrect answers.

A Resource for Learning

The McGraw-Hill Handbook is unique in the amount of support it provides students to help them meet the challenges of learning in college.

A guide for success in college through writing
Chapter 1: Learning across the Curriculum introduces students to the new territory of college and to college writing. In this unique section, we define concepts such as *discipline* and explain how to use writing as a tool for learning. New tips in Chapter 1 help students set priorities, take notes, and succeed in all their courses.

Abundant resources for multilingual writers
The McGraw-Hill Handbook offers non-native speakers of English extensive support for learning and writing in college. Chapter 1 advises multilingual students on how to use writing to deal with their unique challenges. Numerous For Multilingual Students boxes throughout the book and Part 12, a three-chapter Guide for Multilingual Writers (prepared by Maria Zlateva, Director of ESL at Boston University), provide targeted advice on every stage of the writing process. A separate index for multilingual writers follows the main index. A complete list of all the For Multilingual Students boxes also appears in the Quick Guide to Key Resources at the back of the book. The Quick Reference for Multilingual Writers foldout offers handy grammar tips in a convenient format.

New **attention to Generation 1.5 of English language learners**
Chapter 1c: Learning in a Multilingual World now addresses both traditional ESL students and members of Generation 1.5, who have marginal proficiency in English as well as one or more other languages.

Further Resources for Learning
The innovative final section of the book, Part 13: Further Resources for Learning, provides students with a variety of aids—a timeline of world history, a glossary of selected terms from across the curriculum, a map of the world, and a directory of print and online discipline-specific resources—that will come in handy for students in a wide variety of courses.

Charting the Territory boxes
These boxes provide students with examples of how requirements and conventions vary across the curriculum. They present relevant information on such topics as informative assignments in different disciplines and the function of the passive voice in scientific writing.

A Resource for Technology

Online Learning Center (www.mhhe.com/mhhb2)

Throughout *The McGraw-Hill Handbook*, Web references in the margin let students know where they can find additional resources on the text's comprehensive Web site. Access to the site—which is powered by *Catalyst 2.0*, an online resource for writing, research, and editing—is free with every copy of *The McGraw-Hill Handbook*. The site includes the following resources for students:

- Interactive tutorials on document design and visual rhetoric
- Guides for avoiding plagiarism and evaluating sources
- Electronic writing tutors for composing informative, interpretive, and argumentative papers
- Over 4,500 exercises with feedback in grammar, usage, and punctuation

Additional Options Online

Connect Composition for *The McGraw-Hill Handbook*
This online premium companion to the text provides students and instructors with:

- **Interactive exercises and assignments keyed to the chapters of the text** which allow students to practice the material in the text and submit assignments online.
- **Online diagnostics and study plans** which allow students to test themselves and find where they might need help; Connect Composition will then suggest a course of study including video instruction, practice exercises, and a post-test.
- **Online tools for administering peer review** in a flexible, easy-to-use electronic format that help students throughout the process of inventing, drafting, and revising their work.
- **Live, online tutors** via Net Tutor that offer students help with their writing when instructors or writing centers might not be available.
- **Numerous additional interactive resources for writing and research,** including interactive writing tutors, as well as tutorials for visual rhetoric and avoiding plagiarism.

Connect Composition Plus: *The McGraw-Hill Handbook Online*
This interactive, economical alternative to the print text includes all of the features contained in Connect Composition *plus:*

- **All the content of the full handbook online,** optimized for online reading—with material broken out in easy-to-read chunks of information, and with interactive elements integrated contextually throughout.
- **A state-of-the-art search portal** which allows students to explore the whole text using numerous digital navigational tools including text and advanced text search options, hyperlinked indexes and table of contents, interactive Resources for Writers pages for help with the most common problems, and multimedia quick links that offer instant access to all of the text's multimedia instruction in one place.
- **Over 100 Ask the Author video segments** integrated throughout the digital text, providing students with instant-access multimedia guidance on the most commonly asked questions about writing, researching, editing, and designing their work.
- **An economical price** providing students access to the interactive text for approximately half the price of the print text.

Visit ShopMcGraw-Hill.com to purchase registration codes for this exciting new product. Or contact English@mcgraw-hill.com.

CourseSmart
Learn Smart. Choose Smart.

CourseSmart is a new way for faculty to find and review eTextbooks. It's also a great option for students who are interested in accessing their course materials digitally and saving money. CourseSmart offers thousands of the most commonly adopted textbooks across hundreds of courses from a wide variety of higher education publishers. It is the only place for faculty to review and compare the full text of a textbook online, providing immediate access without the environmental impact of requesting a print exam copy. At CourseSmart, students can save up to 50% off the cost of a print book, reduce their impact on the environment, and gain access to powerful Web tools for learning including full text search, notes and highlighting, and e-mail tools for sharing notes among classmates.

Mc Graw Hill tegrity campus

Tegrity Campus is a service that makes class time available all the time by automatically capturing every lecture in a searchable format for students to review when they study and complete assignments. With a simple one-click start and stop process, you capture all computer screens and corresponding audio. Students replay any part of any class with easy-to-use browser-based viewing on a PC or Mac.

Educators know that the more students can see, hear, and experience class resources, the better they learn. With Tegrity Campus, students quickly recall key moments by using Tegrity Campus's unique search feature. This search helps students efficiently find what they need, when they need it across an entire semester of class recordings. Help turn all your students' study time into learning moments immediately supported by your lecture.

To learn more about Tegrity, watch a two-minute Flash demo at http://tegritycampus.mhhe.com.

WPA Outcomes Statement for First-Year Composition

Adopted by the Council of Writing Program Administrators (WPA), April 2000. For further information about the development of the Outcomes Statement, please see http://comppile.tamucc.edu/ WPAoutcomes/continue.html

For further information about the Council of Writing Program Administrators, please see http://www.wpacouncil.org

A version of this statement was published in WPA: Writing Program Administration 23.1/2 (fall/winter 1999): 59-66

Introduction

This statement describes the common knowledge, skills, and attitudes sought by first-year composition programs in American postsecondary education. To some extent, we seek to regularize what can be expected to be taught in first-year composition; to this end the document is not merely a compilation or summary of what currently takes place. Rather, the following statement articulates what composition teachers nationwide have learned from practice, research, and theory. This document intentionally defines only "outcomes," or types of results, and not "standards," or precise levels of achievement. The setting of standards should be left to specific institutions or specific groups of institutions.

Learning to write is a complex process, both individual and social, that takes place over time with continued practice and informed guidance. Therefore, it is important that teachers, administrators, and a concerned public do not imagine that these outcomes can be taught in reduced or simple ways. Helping students demonstrate these outcomes requires expert understanding of how students actually learn to write. For this reason we expect the primary audience for this document to be well-prepared college writing teachers and college writing program administrators. In some places, we have chosen to write in their professional language. Among such readers, terms such as "rhetorical" and "genre" convey a rich meaning that is not easily simplified. While we have also aimed at writing a document that the general public can understand, in limited cases we have aimed first at communicating effectively with expert writing teachers and writing program administrators.

These statements describe only what we expect to find at the end of first-year composition, at most schools a required general education course or sequence of courses. As writers move beyond first-year composition, their writing abilities do not merely improve. Rather, students' abilities not only diversify along disciplinary and professional lines but also move into whole new levels where expected outcomes expand, multiply, and diverge. For this reason, each statement of outcomes for first-year composition is followed by suggestions for further work that builds on these outcomes.

Rhetorical Knowledge

By the end of first year composition, students should

- Focus on a purpose
- Respond to the needs of different audiences
- Respond appropriately to different kinds of rhetorical situations
- Use conventions of format and structure appropriate to the rhetorical situation
- Adopt appropriate voice, tone, and level of formality

- Understand how genres shape reading and writing
- Write in several genres

Faculty in all programs and departments can build on this preparation by helping students learn

- The main features of writing in their fields
- The main uses of writing in their fields
- The expectations of readers in their fields

Critical Thinking, Reading, and Writing

By the end of first year composition, students should

- Use writing and reading for inquiry, learning, thinking, and communicating
- Understand a writing assignment as a series of tasks, including finding, evaluating, analyzing, and synthesizing appropriate primary and secondary sources
- Integrate their own ideas with those of others
- Understand the relationships among language, knowledge, and power

Faculty in all programs and departments can build on this preparation by helping students learn

- The uses of writing as a critical thinking method
- The interactions among critical thinking, critical reading, and writing
- The relationships among language, knowledge, and power in their fields

Processes

By the end of first year composition, students should

- Be aware that it usually takes multiple drafts to create and complete a successful text
- Develop flexible strategies for generating, revising, editing, and proof-reading
- Understand writing as an open process that permits writers to use later invention and re-thinking to revise their work
- Understand the collaborative and social aspects of writing processes
- Learn to critique their own and others' works
- Learn to balance the advantages of relying on others with the responsibility of doing their part
- Use a variety of technologies to address a range of audiences

Faculty in all programs and departments can build on this preparation by helping students learn

- To build final results in stages
- To review work-in-progress in collaborative peer groups for purposes other than editing
- To save extensive editing for later parts of the writing process
- To apply the technologies commonly used to research and communicate within their fields

Knowledge of Conventions

By the end of first year composition, students should

- Learn common formats for different kinds of texts
- Develop knowledge of genre conventions ranging from structure and paragraphing to tone and mechanics
- Practice appropriate means of documenting their work
- Control such surface features as syntax, grammar, punctuation, and spelling

Faculty in all programs and departments can build on this preparation by helping students learn

- The conventions of usage, specialized vocabulary, format, and documentation in their fields
- Strategies through which better control of conventions can be achieved [http://www.wpacouncil.org/positions/outcomes.html, accessed 10/17/2008]

Supplements to *The McGraw-Hill Handbook*

***Instructor's Manual* (available online in printable format) (www.mhhe.com/mhhb2)**
Deborah Coxwell Teague, Florida State University; Dan Melzer, California State University, Sacramento; Lynette Reini-Grandell, Normandale Community College

***MLA Quick Reference Guide* (ISBN 0-07-730080-7)**
Carol Schuck, Ivy Tech Community College
This handy card features the basic guidelines for MLA citation in a convenient, portable format.

***APA Quick Reference Guide* (ISBN 0-07-730076-9)**
This handy card features the basic guidelines for APA citation in a convenient, portable format.

Partners in Teaching: Instructor Resource Portal for Composition
(www.mhhe.com/englishcommunity)
McGraw-Hill is proud to partner with many of the top names in the field to build a *community of teachers helping teachers. Partners in Teaching* features up-to-date scholarly discourse, practical teaching advice, and community support for new and experienced instructors.

***The McGraw-Hill Exercise Book* (ISBN 0-07-326032-0)**
Santi Buscemi, Middlesex College and Susan Popham, University of Memphis
This workbook features numerous sentence-level and paragraph-level editing exercises, as well as exercises in research, documentation, and the writing process.

***The McGraw-Hill Exercise Book for Multilingual Writers* (ISBN 0-07-326030-4)**
Maggie Sokolik, University of California, Berkeley
This workbook features numerous sentence-level and paragraph-level editing exercises tailored specifically for multilingual students.

***The McGraw-Hill Writer's Journal* (ISBN 0-07-326031-2)**
Lynée Gaillet, Georgia State University
This elegant journal for students includes quotes on writing from famous authors, as well as advice and tips on writing and the writing process.

Dictionary and Vocabulary Resources

***Merriam-Webster's Collegiate® Dictionary,* Eleventh Edition (ISBN 978-0-877-79808-8)**
The new edition of America's best-selling dictionary merges print, CD-ROM, and online formats to deliver unprecedented accessibility and flexibility. Fully revised content features more than 225,000 clear and precise definitions and more than 10,000 new words and meanings. Includes an easy-to-install Windows/ Macintosh CD-ROM and a free one-year subscription to the Collegiate Web site.

***The Merriam-Webster Dictionary* (Paperback) (ISBN 978-0-877-79930-6)**
This completely revised edition of the best-selling dictionary of all time covers the core vocabulary of everyday life.

***The Merriam-Webster Thesaurus* (Paperback). (ISBN 978-0-877-79637-4)**
The new edition of this classic thesaurus features over 150,000 synonyms, antonyms, and related and contrasted words.

***Merriam-Webster's Notebook Dictionary.* (ISBN 978-0-8777-9650-3)**
This handy, quick-reference word resource is conveniently designed for three-ring binders. Includes definitions for 40,000 words.

***Merriam-Webster's Notebook Thesaurus* (ISBN 978-0-8777-9671-8)**
Conveniently designed for three-ring binders, this quick-reference compendium provides synonyms, related words, and antonyms for over 100,000 words.

***Merriam-Webster's Dictionary and Thesaurus* (ISBN 978-0-8777-9851-4)**
This incredible new addition to the Merriam-Webster family features two essential references in one handy volume. 60,000 alphabetical dictionary entries integrated with more than 13,000 thesaurus entries.

***Merriam-Webster's Vocabulary Builder* (ISBN 978-0-877-79910-8)**
Introducing 3,000 words and including quizzes to test progress, this excellent resource will help students improve their vocabulary skills.

***Merriam-Webster's Dictionary of Basic English* (ISBN 978-0-8777-9605-3)**
Over 33,000 entries offer concise, easy-to-understand definitions. More than 10,000 word-use examples, over 400 black-and-white

illustrations, word histories, abbreviations, and proper names make this a great resource for multilingual students.

Acknowledgments

When we wrote *The McGraw-Hill Handbook,* we started with the premise that it takes a campus to teach a writer. It is also the case that it takes a community to write a handbook. This text has been a major collaborative effort for all three of us. And over the years, that ever-widening circle of collaboration has included reviewers, editors, librarians, faculty colleagues, and family members.

Let us start close to home. Mort Maimon brought to this project his years of insight and experience as a writer and as a secondary and post-secondary English teacher. Gillian Maimon, a first-grade teacher, a PhD candidate, and a writing workshop leader, and Alan Maimon, a journalist who is expert in using every resource available to writers, inspired and encouraged their mother in this project. Elaine also drew inspiration from her young granddaughters, Dasia and Madison Stewart and Annabelle Elaine Maimon, who already show promise of becoming writers. Rudy Peritz and Lynne Haney reviewed drafts of a number of chapters, bringing to our cross-curricular mix the pedagogical and writerly perspectives of, respectively, a law professor and a sociologist. Jess Peritz, a recent college graduate, was consulted on numerous occasions for her expert advice on making examples both up-to-date and understandable. David, Genevieve, and Matthew Yancey—whose combined writing experience includes the fields of biology, psychology, medicine, computer engineering, mathematics, industrial engineering, and information technology—helped with examples as well as with their understandings of writing both inside and outside of the academy.

At Governors State University, Diane Dates Casey, dean of Library Science and Academic Computing, provided research support, while Executive Assistant Penny Purdue gave overall encouragement. At Arizona State University West, Beverly Buddee, executive assistant to the provost, worried with us over this project for many years. Our deepest gratitude goes to Lisa Kammerlocher and Dennis Isbell for the guidelines on critically evaluating Web resources in Chapter 18, as well as to Sharon Wilson. Thanks, too, go to C. J. Jeney and Cheryl Warren for providing assistance. ASU West professors Thomas McGovern and Martin Meznar shared assignments and student papers with us. In the chancellor's office at the University of Alaska Anchorage, Denise Burger, and Christine Tullius showed admirable support and patience.

Several colleagues at Queens College and elsewhere not only shared their insights on teaching and writing, but also gave us valuable classroom materials to use as we saw fit. Our thanks go to Fred

Buell, Stuart Cochran, Nancy Comley, Ann Davison, Joan Dupre, Hugh English, Sue Goldhaber, Marci Goodman, Steve Kruger, Eric Lehman, Norman Lewis, Charles Molesworth, Beth Stickney, Amy Tucker, and Stan Walker. We are also grateful to Jane Collins, Jane Hathaway, Jan Tecklin, Christine Timm, Scott Zaluda, Diane Zannoni, and Richard Zeikowitz. The Queens College librarians also gave us help with the researching and documentation chapters, and we thank them, especially Sharon Bonk, Alexandra DeLuise, Izabella Taler, and Manny Sanudo.

We give special thanks to the students whose papers we include in full: Rajeev Bector, Diane Chen, Sam Chodoff, McKenna Doherty, Josh Feldman, Audrey Galeano, Josephine Hearn, Esther Hoffman, Carlos Jasperson, Ignacio Sanderson, Mark Shemwell, Jon Paul Terrell, and Ken Tinnes. We also acknowledge the following students who allowed us to use substantial excerpts from their work: Ilona Bouzoukashvili, Lara Deforest, Baz Dreisinger, Sheila Foster, Jacob Grossman, Jennifer Koehler, Holly Musetti, and Umawattie Roopnarian.

Our thanks also go to Judy Williamson and Trent Batson for contributing their expertise on writing and computers as well as for sharing what they learned from the Epiphany Project. We are grateful to Harvey Wiener and the late Richard Marius for their permission to draw on their explanations of grammatical points in *The McGraw-Hill Handbook.* We also appreciate the work of Andras Tapolcai, who collected many of the examples used in the documentation chapters, and the contributions of Maria Zlateva of Boston University; Karen Batchelor of City College of San Francisco; and Daria Ruzicka for their work on Part 12: A Guide for Multilingual Writers and on the For Multilingual Students boxes that appear throughout the text. Thanks to Charlotte Smith of Adirondack Community College for her help on several sections of the book. Thanks also go to librarians Debora Person, University of Wyoming, and Ronelle K. H. Thompson, Augustana College, who provided us with helpful comments on Part 3: Researching. Our colleague Don McQuade has inspired us, advised us, and encouraged us throughout the years of this project.

Within the McGraw-Hill organization, many wonderful people have been our true teammates. Tim Julet believed in this project initially and signed us on to what has become a major life commitment. From 1999, Lisa Moore, first as executive editor for the composition list, then as publisher for English, and now as publisher for special projects in Art, Humanities, and Literature, has creatively, expertly, and tirelessly led the group of development editors and in-house experts who have helped us find the appropriate form to bring our insights as composition teachers to the widest possible group of students. We have learned a great deal from Lisa. Thanks also to

Christopher Bennem, who had the unenviable job of filling Lisa's shoes as sponsoring editor. Crucial support also came from Beth Mejia, editorial director; David Patterson, publisher for English; Dawn Groundwater, director of development for English; and Molly Meneely, market development manager. This book has benefited enormously from three extraordinary development editors: Anne Kemper, development editor; Carla Samodulski, senior development editor; and David Chodoff, senior development editor. All were true collaborators; as the chapters on editing show, the book has benefited enormously from their care and intelligence. Other editorial kudos go out to Meredith Grant, Drew Henry, Karen Herter, Bruce Thaler, Joanna Imm, Judy Voss, Sarah Caldwell, Laura Olson, Elsa Peterson, Aaron Zook, Karen Mauk, Steven Kemper, Anne Stameshkin, and Margaret Farley for their tireless work on this project. Thanks as well to Paul Banks, Andrea Pasquarelli, Todd Vaccaro, Alex Rohrs, and Manoj Mehta, without whom there would be no *Catalyst 2.0.* Chanda Feldman and Brett Coker, lead project managers, monitored every detail of production; Cassandra Chu, lead designer, supervised every aspect of the striking text design and cover; and Robin Mouat and Sonia Brown, art editors, were responsible for the stunning visuals that appear throughout the book. Allison Jones, executive marketing manager; and Ray Kelley, Paula Radosevich, Byron Hopkins, Barbara Siry, and Brian Gore, field publishers, have worked tirelessly and enthusiastically to market *The McGraw-Hill Handbook.* Jeff Brick provided valuable promotional support. We also appreciate the hands-on attention of McGraw-Hill senior executives Mike Ryan, editor-in-chief of the Humanities, Social Sciences, and World Languages group; and Steve Debow, president of the Humanities, Social Sciences, and World Languages group.

Finally, many, many thanks go to the reviewers who read this text, generously shared their perceptions, and had confidence in us as we shaped this book to address the needs of their students. We wish to thank the following instructors:

Content Consultants and Reviewers

Angela Albright, North West Arkansas Community College

Regina Alston, North Carolina Central University

Don Bennett, Jacksonville State University

Doug Branch, Southwest Tennessee Community College, Macon

Ashlee Brand, Cuyahoga Community College

Carolyn Briggs, Marshalltown Community College

Christy Burns, Jacksonville State University

Licia Calloway, The Citadel

Yvonne Cassidy, Alfred State College

Constance Chapman, Clark Atlanta University

April Childress, Greenville Technical College

P.J. Colbert, Marshalltown Community College

Aniko Constantine, Alfred State College

Julia Cote, Houston Community College

Darin Cozzens, Surry Community College

Nancy Davies, Miami Dade College

Syble Davis, Houston Community College

Michael Day, Northern Illinois University

Anne Dearing, Hudson Valley Community College

Tony Diaz, Houston Community College

Carlton Downey, Houston Community College

Nancy Enright, Seton Hall University

Mary Evans, Hudson Valley Community College

Kari Fisher, Normandale Community College

Lloren Foster, Hampton University

Grace Giorgio, University of Illinois, Champaign

Sam Goldstein, Daytona State College

Nate Gordon, Kishwaukee College

Susan Grimland, Collin College

Mickey Hall, Volunteer State Community College

Scott Hathaway, Hudson Valley Community College

Jeannine Horn, Houston Community College

Gloria Horton, Jacksonville State University

Vicki Houser, Northeast State Technical Community College

Billy Hug, Jacksonville State University

Ned Huston, Eastern Illinois University

Jeffrey Ihlenfeldt, Harrisburg Area Community College

Helen Jackson, Houston Community College

Sandy Jordan, Houston Community College

Lori Kanitz, Oral Roberts University

Sandra Gollin Kies, Benedictine University

Ellen Laird, Hudson Valley Community College

Mary Lang, Wharton County Junior College

Debbie Rudder Lohe, Washington University

Linda Macri, University of Maryland

Teri Maddox, Jackson State Community College

Gretchen McCroskey, Northeast State Technical College

Susan McDermott, Hudson Valley Community College

Heather McDonald, Daytona State College

Elizabeth Metzger, University of South Florida, Tampa

Susan Miller, University of Utah, Salt Lake City

Chester Mills, Southern University, New Orleans

Sean Mitsein, St. Cloud State University

Jennifer Mooney, Wharton County Junior College

Thomas Moretti, University of Maryland

Marguerite Newcomb, University of Texas, San Antonio

Sandra Offiah-Hawkins, Daytona State College

David Pates, Normandale Community College

John Pleimann, Jefferson College

Maria Plochocki, Bergen Community College

Peggy Porter, Houston Community College

Roberta Proctor, Palm Beach Community College, Lake Worth

Teresa P. Reed, Jacksonville State University

Joseph Register, Harrisburg Area Community College

Terrie Relf, San Diego City College

Cindy Renfro, Houston Community College

Diane Russo, University of New Haven

Deborah Ryals, Pensacola Junior College

Vicki Sapp, Tarrant County College

John Schaffer, Blinn College

Grace Sikorski, Anne Arundel Community College

Beverly Stroud, Greenville Technical College

Linda Tetzlaff, Normandale Community College

Tammy Townsend, Jones County Junior College

Christopher Twiggs, Florida Community College

April Van Camp, Indian River Community College

Lash Keith Vance, University of California, Riverside

Philip Wedgeworth, Jones County Junior College

Carolyn West, Daytona State College

Editorial Board of Advisors

Connie Adair, Marshalltown Community College

Alan Ainsworth, Houston Community College

Deborah Coxwell-Teague, Florida State University

Heather Eaton, Daytona State College

Kitty Ellison, Howard University

Holly French, Bossier Parish Community College

Ellen Laird, Hudson Valley Community College

Shellie Michael, Volunteer State Community College

Kathleen Moore, University of California, Riverside

Michael Ronan, Houston Community College

Linda Strahan, University of California, Riverside

Freshman Composition Symposia

Every year McGraw-Hill conducts Freshman Composition Symposia, which are attended by instructors from across the country. These events are an opportunity for editors from McGraw-Hill to gather information about the needs and challenges of instructors teaching the Freshman Composition course. They also offer a forum for the attendees to exchange ideas and experiences with colleagues they might not have otherwise met. The feedback we have received has been invaluable and has contributed—directly or indirectly—to the development of *The McGraw-Hill Handbook* and its supplements.

Ellen Arnold, Coastal Carolina University

Tony Atkins, University of North Carolina, Wilmington

Edith Baker, Bradley University

Evan Balkan, Community College of Baltimore

Carolyn Barr, Broward Community College

Laura Basso, Joliet Junior College

Linda Bergmann, Purdue University

Karen Bilda, Cardinal Stritch University

Carol Bledsoe, Florida Gulf Coast University

Kimberly Bovee, Tidewater Community College

Charley Boyd, Genesee Community College

Charlotte Brammer, Samford University

Amy Braziller, Red Rocks Community College

Bob Broad, Illinois State University

Cheryl Brown, Towson University

Liz Bryant, Purdue University, Calumet-Hammod

JoAnn Buck, Guilford Technical Community College

Monica Busby, University of Louisiana, Lafayette

Jonathan Bush, Western Michigan University

Steve Calatrello, Calhoun Community College

Susan Callendar, Sinclair Community College

Diane Canow, Johnson County Community College

Richard Carpenter, Valdosta State University

Sandy Clark, Anderson University

Keith Comer, University of Canterbury

Jennifer Cooper, University of Texas, Arlington

Deborah Coxwell-Teague, Florida State University

Mary Ann Crawford, Central Michigan University

Susan Jaye Dauer, Valencia Community College

Michael Day, Northern Illinois University

Rosemary Day, Central New Mexico Community College

Michel de Benedictis, Miami-Dade College

Anne Dearing, Hudson Valley Community College

Nancy DeJoy, Michigan State University

Christy Desmet, University of Georgia

Brock Dethier, Utah State University

Carlton Downey, Houston Community College

Robert Eddy, Washington State University

Anthony Edgington, University of Toledo

Dan Ferguson, Amarillo College

Bonnie Finkelstein, Montgomery County Community College

Steve Fox, Indiana University–Purdue University, Indianapolis

Sherrin Frances, San Jacinto College, Pasadena

Elaine Fredericksen, University of Texas, El Paso

Karen Gardiner, University of Alabama, Tuscaloosa

Judith Gardner, University of Texas, San Antonio

Elizabeth Gassel, Darton College

Joanna Gibson, Texas A&M University

Lois Gilmore, Bucks County Community College

Chuck Gonzalez, Central Florida Community College, Ocala

John Gooch, University of Texas, Dallas

Cathy Gorvine, Delgado Community College

Frank Gunshanan, Daytona State College

Emily Gwinn, Glendale Community College

Audley Hall, North West Arkansas Community College

Carolyn Handa, University of Alabama, Tuscaloosa

Rebecca Heintz, Polk Community College

Dedria Humphries, Lansing Community College

Kim Jameson, Oklahoma City Community College

Nanette Jaynes, Wesleyan College

Theodore Johnston, El Paso Community College

Peggy Jolly, University of Alabama, Birmingham

Joseph Jones, University of Memphis

Rebecca Kajs, Anne Arundel Community College

Pam Kannady, Tulsa Community College

Shelley Kelly, College of Southern Nevada

Elizabeth Kessler, University of Houston

Kirk Kidwell, Michigan State University

Roxanne Kirkwood, Marshall University

Sandra Lakey, Pennsylvania College of Technology

William Lennertz, Santiago Canyon College

Tom Lovin, Southwestern Illinois College

Heidi Marshall, Florida Community College

Denise Martone, New York University

Barry Mauer, University of Central Florida

Michael McCready, University of Mississippi

Sharon McGee, Southern Illinois University, Edwardsville

Janice McIntire-Strasburg, St. Louis University

Patrick McLaughlin, Lakeland Community College

Shellie Michael, Volunteer State Community College

John Miles, University of New Mexico

Susan Miller, Santa Fe Community College

Susan Miller-Cochran, North Carolina State University, Raleigh

Jennifer Nelson, College of Southern Nevada

Donna Nelson-Beene, Bowling Green State University

Lindee Owens, University of Central Florida

Matthew Parfitt, Boston University

Irvin Peckham, Louisiana State University

Chere Peguesse, Valdosta State University

Bruce Peppard, El Camino College

Rich Peraud, St. Louis Community College, Meramec

David Peterson, University of Nebraska, Omaha

Helen Frances Poehlman, Blinn College

Susan Popham, University of Memphis

Mara Rainwater, Keiser University

Christa Raney, University of North Alabama

Beverly Reed, College of Dupage

Patricia Reid, University of Toledo

David Reinheimer, Southeast Missouri State University

Mandi Riley, Florida A&M University

Dixil Rodriguez, Tarrant County College

Denise Rogers, University of Louisiana

Lou Ethel Rolliston, Bergen Community College

Shirley Rose, Purdue University

Kathleen Ryan, University of Montana

Mary Sauer, Indiana University–Purdue University, Indianapolis

Mark Saunders, Front Range Community College

Matthew Schmeer, Johnson County Community College

Jane Schreck, Bismark State College

Carol Schuck, Ivy Tech Community College

Marc Scott, New Mexico State University

Susan Sebok, South Suburban College

Wendy Sharer, East Carolina University

E. Stone Shiflet, Capella University

Patrick Slattery, University of Arkansas

Beverly Slaughter, Brevard Community College, Melbourne

James Sodon, St. Louis Community College, Florissant Valley

Ann Spurlock, Mississippi State

Wayne Stein, University of Central Oklahoma

Kip Strasma, Illinois Central College

Beverly Stroud, Greenville Technical College

Paul Tanner, Utah Valley University

Todd Taylor, University of North Carolina

William Thelin, University of Akron

Gordon Thomas, University of Idaho

Donna Thomsen, Johnson & Wales University

Martha Tolleson, Collin College

Pauline Uchmanowicz, State University of New York, New Paltz

Frank Vaughn, Campbell University

Stephanie Venza, Brookhaven College

Philip Virgen, Wilbur Wright College

Judy Welch, Miami-Dade College

Christina Wells, Northern Virginia Community College

Jeff Wiemelt, Southeastern Louisiana University

John Ziebell, College of Southern Nevada

Supplements Team

Preston Allen, Miami Dade College

Santi Buscemi, Middlesex College

Deborah Coxwell Teague, Florida State University

Thomas Dinsmore, University of Cincinnati, Clermont College

Lynée Gaillet, Georgia State University

Dan Melzer, California State University, Sacramento

Susan Popham, University of Memphis

Lynette Reini-Grandell, Normandale Community College

Carol Schuck, Ivy Tech Community College

Maggie Sokolik, University of California, Berkeley

Technology Consultants

Cheryl Ball, Illinois State University

Dene Grigar, Washington State University

Elizabeth Nist, Anoka-Ramsey Community College

Donna Reiss, Tidewater Community College

Rich Rice, Texas Tech University

Heather Robinson, City University of New York, York College

James Sodon, St. Louis Community College, Florissant Valley

ESL Consultants

Karen Batchelor, City College of San Francisco

Cherry Campbell, University of California, Los Angeles

Christine T. Francisco, City College of San Francisco

Candace A. Henry, Westmoreland Community College

Maria Zlateva, Boston University

Design and Cover Reviewers

Yvonne Cassidy, Alfred State College

Constance Chapman, Clark Atlanta University

April Childress, Greenville Technical College

Aniko Constantine, Alfred State College

Julia Cote, Houston Community College

Michael Day, Northern Illinois University

Anne Dearing, Hudson Valley Community College

Nancy Rosenberg England, University of Texas, Arlington

Mary Evans, Hudson Valley Community College

Holly French, Bossier Parish Community College

Jeannine Horn, Houston Community College

Gloria Horton, Jacksonville State University

Sandy Jordan, University of Houston

Lori Kanitz, Oral Roberts University

Mary Lang, Wharton County Junior College

Chester Mills, Southern University, New Orleans

Jennifer Mooney, Wharton County Junior College

Thomas Moretti, University of Maryland

Sandra Offiah-Hawkins, Daytona State College

Terrie Leigh Relf, San Diego City College

John Schaffer, Blinn College

Linda Tetzlaff, Normandale Community College

Christopher Twiggs, Florida Community College, Jacksonville

Focus Group and Seminar Participants

Joyce Adams, Brigham Young University

Jeannette Adkins, Tarrant County Community College

Jim Allen, College of Dupage

Sonja Andrus, Collin College

Marcy Bauman, Lansing Community College

Sue Beebe, Texas State University, San Marcos

Candace Bergstrom, Houston Community College

Bruce Bogdon, Houston Community College

Barbara Bonallo, Miami-Dade College

Sarah Bruton, Fayetteville Tech Community College

Joe Bryan, El Paso Community College

Alma Bryant, University of South Florida

Lauryn Angel Cann, Collin College

Diane Carr, Midlands Technical College

Lucia Cherciu, Dutchess Community College

Regina Clemens Fox, Arizona State University

Terry Cole, Laguardia Community College

Keith Comer, University of Canterbury

Genevieve Coogan, Houston Community College

Dagmar Corrigan, University of Houston

Marla DeSoto, Glendale Community College

Debra Dew, University of Colorado, Colorado Springs

Erika Dieters, Moraine Valley Community College

Michael Donnelly, Ball State University

Marilyn Douglas-Jones, Houston Community College

Carlton Downey, Houston Community College

Lisa Dresdner, Norwalk Community College

Heather Eaton, Daytona State College

George Edwards, Tarrant County Community College

Richard Enos, Texas Christian University

Nancy Enright, Seton Hall University

Paula Eschliman, Richland College

Karin Evans, College of Dupage

Jennie Fauls, Columbia College–Chicago

Africa Fine, Florida Atlantic University

Stacha Floyd, Wayne County Community College

John Freeman, El Paso Community College

Casey Furlong, Glendale Community College

Karen Gardiner, University of Alabama, Tuscaloosa

Mary Lee Geary, Front Range Community College

Ruth Gerik, University of Texas, Arlington

Phyllis Gooden, Atlantic International University, Chicago

Lisa Gordon, Columbus State Community College

Jay Gordon, Youngstown State University

Steffen Guenzel, University of Alabama, Tuscaloosa

John Hagerty, Auburn University

Jonathan Hall, Rutgers University, Newark

Dustin Hanvey, Pasadena Area Community College

Bryant Hayes, Bernard M. Baruch College

Shawn Hellman, Pima Community College

Maren Henry, University of West Georgia

Kevin Hicks, Alabama State University

Brandy James, University of West Georgia

Peggy Jolly, University of Alabama, Birmingham

Nicole Khoury, Arizona State University

Jessica Kidd, University of Alabama, Tuscaloosa

Lindsay Lewan, Arapahoe Community College

Victoria Lisle, Auburn University

Colleen Lloyd, Cuyahoga Community College

Margaret Lowry, University of Texas, Arlington

Andrew Manno, Raritan Valley Community College

Shirley McBride, Collin College

Dan Melzer, California State University, Sacramento

Erica Messenger, Bowling Green State University

Joyce Miller, Collin College

Dorothy Minor, Tulsa Community College

Webster Newbold, Ball State University

Gordon O'Neal, Collin College

Maryann Perlman, Wayne County Community College

Joann Pinkston-McDuffie, Daytona State College

Deborah Prickett, Jacksonville State University

Roberta Proctor, Palm Beach Community College, Lake Worth

Helen Raica-Klotz, Saginaw Valley State University

Sharon Roberts, Auburn University

Cassanda Robison, Central Florida Community College

Michael Ronan, Houston Community College

Jane Rosencrans, J.S. Reynolds Community College

Mark Saunders, Front Range Community College

Mary Beth Schillacci, Houston Community College

Shelita Shaw, Moraine Valley Community College

Jenny Sheppard, New Mexico State University

Michelle Sidler, Auburn University

Jean Sorensen, Grayson County College

Cathy Stablein, College of Dupage

Wayne Stein, University of Central Oklahoma

Martha Tolleson, Collin College

Saundra Towns, Bernard M. Baruch College

George Trail, University of Houston

Bryon Turman, North Carolina A&T University

Christopher Twiggs, Florida Community College

Kathryn Valentine, New Mexico State University

Kevin Waltman, University of Alabama

Maryann Whitaker, University of Alabama, Tuscaloosa

Joseph White, Fayetteville Tech Community College

Virginia Wicher, Tarrant County Community College

Reginald Williams, Daytona State College

Elizabeth Woodworth, Auburn University, Montgomery

Elaine P. Maimon

Janice H. Peritz

Kathleen Blake Yancey

About the Authors

Elaine P. Maimon is president of Governors State University in the south suburbs of Chicago, where she is also professor of English. Previously she was chancellor of the University of Alaska Anchorage, provost (chief campus officer) at Arizona State University West, and vice president of Arizona State University as a whole. In the 1970s, she initiated and then directed the Beaver College writing-across-the-curriculum program, one of the first WAC programs in the nation. A founding executive board member of the National Council of Writing Program Administrators (WPA), she has directed national institutes to improve the teaching of writing and to disseminate the principles of writing across the curriculum. With a PhD in English from the University of Pennsylvania, where she later helped to create the Writing Across the University (WATU) program, she has also taught and served as an academic administrator at Haverford College, Brown University, and Queens College.

Janice Haney Peritz is an associate professor of English who has taught college writing for more than thirty years, first at Stanford University, where she received her PhD in 1978, and then at the University of Texas at Austin; Beaver College; and Queens College, City University of New York. From 1989 to 2002, she directed the Composition Program at Queens College, where in 1996, she also initiated the college's writing-across-the-curriculum program and the English department's involvement with the Epiphany Project and cyber-composition. She also worked with a group of CUNY colleagues to develop The Write Site, an online learning center, and more recently directed the CUNY Honors College at Queens College for three years. Currently, she is back in the English department doing what she loves most: full-time classroom teaching of writing, literature, and culture.

Kathleen Blake Yancey is the Kellogg W. Hunt Professor of English and director of the Graduate Program in Rhetoric and Composition at Florida State University. She is past president of the Council of Writing Program Administrators (WPA), past chair of the Conference on College Composition and Communication (CCCC), and past president of the National Council of Teachers of English (NCTE). In addition, she co-directs the Inter/National Coalition on Electronic Portfolio Research. She has directed several institutes focused on electronic portfolios and on service learning and reflection, and with her colleagues in English education, she is working on developing a program in new literacies. Previously, she has taught at UNC Charlotte and at Clemson University, where she directed the Pearce Center for Professional Communication and created the Class of 1941 Studio for Student Communication, both of which are dedicated to supporting communication across the curriculum.

The way the butterfly in this image emerges on a computer screen, as if from a cocoon of written text, suggests the way writers transform words and visuals into finished works through careful planning, drafting, revision, and design.

PART 1

I like to do first drafts at night, when I'm tired, and then do the surgical work in the morning when I'm sharp.
—Alex Haley

Writing and Designing Texts

1 Learning across the Curriculum

1a Use writing to learn as you learn to write.

College is a place for exploration. You will travel through many courses, participating in numerous conversations—oral and written—about nature, society, and culture. As you navigate your college experience, use this book as your map and guide.

- As a map, this text will help you understand different approaches to knowledge and see how your studies relate to the larger world of learning.
- As a guide, this text will help you write everything from notes to exams to research papers.

www.mhhe.com/ mhhb2

For discipline-related resources, go to **Learning > Links across the Curriculum**

1. Studying the world through a range of academic disciplines

Each department in your college represents a specialized territory of academic study, or area of inquiry, called a **discipline.** A discipline has its own history, terminology, issues, and subgroups. The discipline of sociology, for example, is concerned with the conditions,

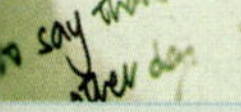

WRITING OUTCOMES

Part 1: Writing and Designing Texts

This section will help you answer questions such as:

Rhetorical Knowledge

- How do I respond appropriately to different writing situations? **(2b–h)**
- What type of visuals will help my writing achieve its purpose? **(3d)**

Critical Thinking, Reading, and Writing

- What is a thesis statement, and how do I think of one? **(3b)**
- How do I provide constructive feedback on my classmates' work? **(5a)**

Processes

- What are the components of the writing process? **(2a)**
- How can technology help me in the writing process? **(4a, 5b, 5c, 6b)**

Knowledge of Conventions

- How can I write effective, organized paragraphs? **(4c)**
- What aspects of document design can help my writing communicate more effectively? **(6c)**

CHARTING the TERRITORY

Getting the Most from a Course

When you take a course, your purpose is not just to amass information. Your purpose is also to understand the kinds of questions people who work in the discipline ask.

- In an art history class, for example, you might ask how a work relates to an artist's life and times.
- In a math class, you might ask about the practical applications of a particular concept.

patterns, and problems of people in groups and societies. Sociologists collect, analyze, and interpret data about groups and societies; they also debate the data's reliability and various interpretations in journals, books, conferences, and classrooms.

Your college curriculum is likely to include distribution requirements that will expose you to a range of disciplines. You may be asked to take one or two courses in the humanities (the disciplines of literature, music, and philosophy, for example), the social sciences (sociology, economics, and psychology, for example), and the natural sciences (physics, biology, and chemistry, for example). When you write in each discipline—taking notes, writing papers, answering essay-exam questions—you will join the academic conversation, deepen your understanding of how knowledge is constructed, and learn to see and think about the world from different vantage points.

2. Using writing as a tool for learning

One goal of this handbook is to help you create well-researched and interesting texts. As you go from course to course, however, remember that writing itself is a great aid to learning. Think of the way a simple shopping list helps your memory once you get to the store, or recall the last time you were asked to keep the minutes of a meeting. Because of your heightened attention, you undoubtedly knew more about what happened at that meeting than did anyone else who attended it. Writing helps you remember, understand, and create.

www.mhhe.com/mhhb2
For more on learning in college, go to
Learning

- **Writing aids memory.** From taking class notes (*see Figure 1.1 on p. 4*) to jotting down ideas for later development, writing ensures that you will be able to retrieve important information. Many students use an informal outline for lecture notes (*see Figure 1.1*) and then go back to fill in the details after class. Write down ideas inspired by your course work—in any form or order. These ideas can be the seeds for a research project or other critical inquiry.

www.mhhe.com/mhhb2
For activities to help strengthen your use of writing as a tool for learning, go to
Learning > Writing to Learn Exercises

3/17
MEMORY

3 ways to store memory
1. sensory memory —everything sensed
2. short term memory STM —15-25 sec.
   —stored as meaning
   —5-9 chunks
3. long term memory LTM —unlimited
   —rehearsal
   —visualization
* If long term memory is unlimited, why do we forget?
Techniques for STM to LTM
   —write, draw, diagram
   —visualize
   —mnemonics

FIGURE 1.1 Lecture notes. Jotting down the main ideas of a lecture and the questions they raise helps you become a more active listener.

- **Writing sharpens observations.** When you record what you see, hear, taste, smell, and feel, you increase the powers of your senses. Note the smells during a chemistry experiment, and you will more readily detect changes caused by reactions.
- **Writing clarifies thought.** Carefully reading your own early drafts helps you pinpoint what you really want to say. The last paragraph of a first draft often becomes the first paragraph of the next draft.
- **Writing uncovers connections.** Maybe a character in a short story reminds you of your neighbor, or an image in a poem makes you feel sad. Writing down the reasons you make connections like these can help you learn more about the work and, possibly, more about yourself.
- **Writing improves reading.** When you read, taking notes on the main ideas and drafting a brief summary of the writer's points sharpen your reading skills and help you retain what you have read. Writing a personal reaction to the reading enhances your understanding. (*For a detailed discussion of critical reading and writing, see Chapter 7.*)
- **Writing strengthens argument.** In the academic disciplines, an argument is not a fiery disagreement but rather

a path of reasoning to a position. When you write an argument, you work out the connections between your ideas—uncovering both flaws that force you to rethink your position and new connections that make your position stronger. Writing also requires you to consider your audience and the objections they might raise. *(For a detailed discussion of argument, see Chapter 10.)*

3. Taking responsibility for reading, writing, and research

The academic community assumes that you are an independent learner, capable of managing your workload without supervision. For most courses, the course syllabus will be the primary guide to what is expected of you, serving as a contract between you and your instructor. It will tell you what reading you need to do in advance of each class, when tests are scheduled, and when papers or stages of papers (for example, topic and research plan, draft, and final paper) are due. Use the syllabus to map out your weekly schedule for reading, research, and writing. *(For tips on how to schedule a research paper, see Chapter 15.)*

www.mhhe.com/mhhb2
For more on study skills, go to
Learning > Study Skills Tutor

If you are collaborating with a group on a project, plan a series of meetings well in advance to avoid schedule conflicts. Also make time for your solo projects, away from the distractions of phones, e-mail, and visitors. You will be much more efficient if you work in shorter blocks of concentrated time than if you let your reading and writing drag on for hours filled with interruptions.

4. Recognizing that writing improves with practice

Composition courses are extremely valuable in helping you learn to write at the college level, but your development as a writer does not end there. Writing in all your courses, throughout your academic career, will enable you to mature as a writer while preparing you for more writing after college.

Exercise 1.1 Examining a syllabus

Refer to the syllabus for your writing class and answer the following questions:

1. How can you get in touch with your instructor? When should you contact him or her?
2. How much is class participation worth in your overall course grade?
3. What happens if you turn in a paper late?
4. How are final course grades determined? Is there a final exam or culminating project?

Tips

LEARNING in COLLEGE

Study Skills

Whether academic pursuits are a struggle or come easily to you, whether you are fresh out of high school or are returning to school after many years, college is a challenge. Here are a few hints and strategies for taking on some of the challenges you will encounter.

- **Make the most of your time by setting clear priorities.** Deal with surprises by saying "no," getting away from it all, taking control of phone and e-mail interruptions, and leaving slack in your schedule to accommodate the unexpected.
- **Recognize how you prefer to learn.** *Tactile learners* prefer hands-on learning that comes about through touching, manipulating objects, and doing things. *Visual learners* like to see information in their mind, favoring reading and watching over touching and listening. *Auditory learners* favor listening as the best approach. Work on improving your less-preferred learning styles.
- **Evaluate the information you gather.** Consider how authoritative the source is, whether the author has any potential biases, how recent the information is, and whether anything important is missing from the research. In college, critical thinking is essential.
- **Take good notes.** The central feature of good note taking is listening and distilling important information—not writing down everything that is said.
- **Build reading and listening skills.** When you read, identify the main ideas, prioritize them, think critically about the arguments, and explain the writer's ideas to someone else. Listen actively: focus on what is being said, pay attention to nonverbal messages, listen for what is not being said, and take notes.
- **Improve your memory.** Rehearsal is the key strategy in remembering information. Repeat the information, summarize it, associate it with other memories, and above all, think about it when you first come across it.

Source: Based on Robert S. Feldman, *P.O.W.E.R. Learning: Strategies for Success in College and Life,* 2nd ed., New York: McGraw-Hill, 2003.

1b Explore ways of learning in a multimedia world.

More people than ever are using electronic media to write in school, social situations, and the workplace. Composition today includes such diverse activities as sending a text message to a friend, posting a

LEARNING in COLLEGE

Dealing with Stress

Whether you are fresh out of high school or graduated years ago, college is a challenge. It helps to develop responses to the stress that often results.

- **Make flexible schedules.** Schedules help you control your time and avoid procrastination by breaking big projects into manageable bits. Be sure to leave room for the unexpected so that the schedule itself does not become a source of stress.
- **Take care of yourself.** Eating healthful food, exercising regularly, and getting plenty of sleep are well-known stress relievers. Some people find meditation to be very effective.
- **Reach out for support.** If you find it difficult to cope with stress, seek professional help. Colleges have trained counselors on staff as well as twenty-four-hour crisis lines.

photo on a social-networking site like *Facebook*, and adding an original video to a content-sharing site like *YouTube*. These sites are part of Web 2.0, a "second generation" of Internet sites and tools that foster user creativity and community. Their growth has led many more people to write for different purposes and audiences: to stay in touch with friends or to develop a research project with an international colleague. Today's college writers read and compose verbal, audio, and visual texts.

Although you probably have used digital communication tools in social situations, bear in mind that academic and professional writing requires greater formality. For example, an e-mail to your instructor or employer should contain standard capitalization, punctuation, and spelling (use *you* and *through*, not *u* and *thru*). (*For more on this topic, see Chapter 29 and the box on p. 12.*)

1. Becoming aware of the persuasive power of images

As a student, you will be analyzing images as well as creating them. We live in a world in which images—in advertising, in politics, in books and classrooms—join with words as tools of persuasion as well as instruction. Images, like words, require careful, critical analysis. A misleading graph (*see Figure 1.2, p. 8*) or an altered photograph can easily distort your perception of a subject. The ability not only to understand visual information but also to evaluate its credibility is an essential tool for learning and writing. (*For details on evaluating visuals, see Chapter 7: Reading, Thinking, Writing, pp. 121–37.*)

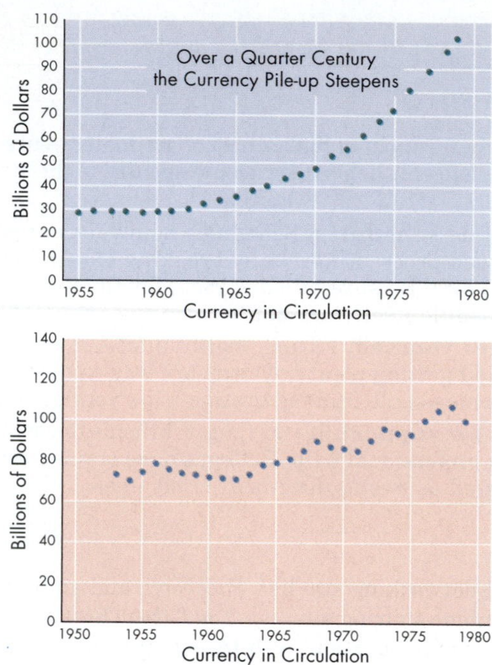

FIGURE 1.2 A misleading graph. The graph on top, which appeared in a 1979 article in the *Wall Street Journal*, shows a dramatic and accelerating increase in currency in circulation in the United States between 1953 and 1979. As a measure of the purchasing power of the individual Americans who held the currency, however, the graph is misleading because it fails to take inflation into account. The second graph, corrected for inflation (based on the dollar's purchasing power in 1979), reveals a generally steady but far less dramatic rate of increase.

Exercise 1.2 Recognizing misleading images

Conduct a Web search using the keywords "misleading images" and "misleading charts," and collect examples of three different types of misleading visuals. Be prepared to share your examples with the class.

2. Making effective use of multimedia elements

Technology allows you to include images and other nonverbal elements in your writing to convey certain ideas more efficiently or powerfully. You can create these elements yourself or import them from other sources and place them where you want them. Always cite the source of any elements from another source. (*See Chapters 20–21 for*

FIGURE 1.3 New Orleans immediately after Hurricane Katrina (top) and one year later (bottom).

information on how to do so.) The source credits for this book begin at the back on page C-1.

A photo or diagram or chart can contain information that adds details or makes relationships clearer. In a project for a geography course, for example, photographs like the ones above (*Figure 1.3*) can illustrate at a glance the effects of a hurricane and the scale of recovery.

A graph (*see Figure 1.4, p. 10*) can effectively illustrate important trends for a history assignment. A timeline, like the one in the Further Resources for Learning section at the end of this book, can help your readers grasp the relationships among important events.

If you can post your text online or deliver it as an electronic file to be read on the computer, you can include an even greater variety of media. You could supplement a musical passage, for example, with a link to an audio file. You could supplement a paper about political speeches for an American Government course with a link to a video clip of a politician giving a speech.

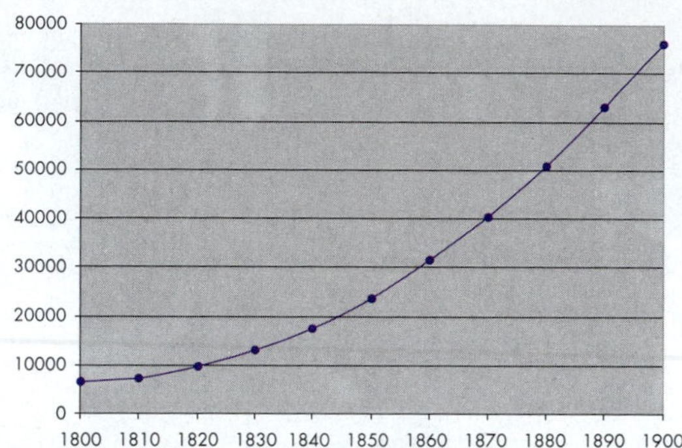

FIGURE 1.4 A line graph showing trends over time. To learn how to create a graph like this one, see Figure 17.2.

www.mhhe.com/mhhb2

For an interactive tutorial on using visuals, go to

Writing > Visual Rhetoric Tutorial > Visualizing Data

Presentation software such as PowerPoint allows you to integrate audio and visual features into oral or stand-alone presentations. Effects such as animation can enliven your presentation, but avoid using multimedia elements in a merely decorative manner.

(For details on creating effective visuals, see Chapter 3: Planning and Shaping the Whole Essay; Chapter 4: Drafting Paragraphs and Visuals; and Chapter 5: Revising and Editing. For information on creating oral and multimedia presentations, see Chapter 13: Oral Presentation, and Chapter 14: Multimedia Writing. For help with finding appropriate visuals, see Chapter 17: Finding and Creating Effective Visuals.)

Exercise 1.3 Deciding when to use visuals

1. Decide whether each of the following would be best presented as a visual, as written text, or as both. For those that call for a visual, which type of visual would you use?
   a. Instructions for constructing a birdhouse
   b. An inventory of the different species of birds that appear in your yard during a one-month period
   c. A description of a songbird's call
   d. A discussion of how a bird's wings enable it to fly
   e. A proposal on ways to protect endangered songbirds from predation by cats
2. Go to the Further Resources for Learning section at the end of this book; read the entry for the term *Aristotelian* in the glossary of Selected Terms from across the Curriculum (*p. FR-18*); and note the entry for Aristotle on the Timeline of World

History (*p. FR-3*). How does the timeline help you place the term in historical context? What can you learn from the timeline about significant developments in geometry, theater, physics, and religion that occurred within a few hundred years of Aristotle's lifetime?

3. Taking advantage of online and other electronic tools for learning

Technology now makes it possible to transcend the constraints of the clock, the calendar, and the car and to engage in educational activities 24/7, or twenty-four hours a day, seven days a week. Different electronic tools work best for different purposes (*see the TextConnex box below*).

www.mhhe.com/mhhb2
For more about online learning resources, go to
Learning > Additional Links on Learning

- **E-mail.** E-mail is one of the most frequently used forms of written communication in the world today. In some classes, you can use e-mail to communicate with your professor, other students, or a consultant in your school's writing center.
- **Instant messaging.** Instant messaging (IM) can be used to further your learning in much the same way as e-mail. Some instructors may encourage you to contact them in this way, but otherwise, use IM sparingly in an academic setting. Like other technologies, it can distract you from work.

TEXTCONNEX

Digital Communication Tools: Best Uses

	PEER REVIEW	GROUP PROJECT	FORMAL CONVERSATION	INFORMAL CONVERSATION	QUICK QUESTION	EXTENDED DISCUSSION
E-mail	X	X	X	X	X	X
Instant message/ Chat	X	X		X	X	
Text message				X	X	
Listserv		X	X	X	X	X
Blog	X	X		X		X
Wiki	X	X				X

This table shows the most appropriate academic uses of six electronic communication tools.

TEXTCONNEX

Netiquette

The term *netiquette* combines the words *Internet* and *etiquette* to form a new word that stands for good manners online. Here are some netiquette guidelines:

- **Remember that most forms of electronic communication can be reproduced.** Avoid saying anything you would not want attributed to you or forwarded to others. Do not forward another person's words without consent.
- **Remember that you are interacting with real humans,** not machines, and practice kindness, patience, and good humor.
- **Use words economically,** and edit carefully. Readers become impatient and their eyes tire when they encounter all lowercase letters or text that lacks appropriate punctuation.
- **Bear in mind that without cues such as facial expressions, body language, and vocal intonation, your message can easily be misunderstood.** Be extra careful about humor that could be misread as sarcasm. Misunderstandings can escalate quickly into *flaming*, the sending of angry, inflammatory posts that use heated language.
- **Avoid ALL CAPS.** Typing in all caps is considered shouting.
- **Always seek permission to use other people's ideas,** and acknowledge them properly.
- **Never copy other people's words and present them as your own.** This practice, known as *plagiarism*, is always wrong. (*See Part 4: Documenting across the Curriculum, for help with citing Internet sources.*)
- **Limit e-mails to a single topic and use accurate subject headers. Include a sufficient portion of the previous text** when responding to an e-mail, or use a dash to keep the conversation flowing and to provide context. **Include your name and contact information at the end of every e-mail you send.**
- **When sending text messages, use abbreviations in moderation.** Keep messages brief, but do not use so many abbreviations and emoticons that your meaning is obscured.

- **Course Web sites.** Your instructor may have a Web site for your course. If so, check it for late-breaking announcements, the course syllabus, assignments (and their due dates), and course-related links as well as other Web resources. For course Web sites that are part of Web-based software offered by companies like Blackboard, see "Using Web-based course software" on page 14.

- **Networked classrooms and virtual classrooms.** Some colleges and instructors use **networked classrooms** in which each student works at one of a network of linked computers. Instructors can post daily assignments and discussion topics, and students might be assigned to work collaboratively on a writing project. Computers and the Internet also make it possible for students to engage in distance learning—from almost anywhere in the world—in classes conducted entirely online in **virtual classrooms.** Because you are interacting in writing rather than in spoken discussion, you can more easily save ideas and comments and use them in the first draft of a paper.
- **Blogs.** A **blog** is a continually updated site that features dated entries with commentary on a variety of topics, links to Web sites the authors find interesting, and (sometimes) a way for readers to add comments. These readers, as well as the blog's author, may or may not be experts on the topics. (*For information on assessing a blog's credibility, see Chapter 18, pp. 289–98.*) Students sometimes use blogs to summarize and reflect on readings. A class blog may allow students to comment on one another's drafts. Faculty also may use blogs as sites for sharing assignments, where students can access them at any time and ask for clarification via comments. (*See Chapter 14, pp. 244–47.*)
- **Podcasts.** Instructors may record their lectures as downloadable audio or video **podcasts,** making them available to the class for repeated listening or viewing on a computer or an MP3 player. Popular radio shows, television shows, and newspapers frequently include podcasts; the *New York Times*, for example, has a print book review section and a podcast of reviews. Reputable podcasts, such as these, are important sources for research projects.
- **Text messages.** Texting is especially useful for very short messages, and its abbreviations can be used in class notes to make note-taking faster. Abbreviations and emoticons (combinations of characters that look like images, such as :-)) should not be used in more formal writing situations.
- **Videos.** Outside school and in some college classes, many students and instructors create short videos, which they may post on video sharing sites such as *YouTube*. Although compositions usually have a specific intended audience, many Web sites allow these texts to be viewed by anyone with Internet access. When students create their own videos, they become better prepared to analyze the informative and persuasive videos that surround us today.

TEXTCONNEX

Web 2.0

The Machine Is Us/ing Us— This video by Michael Wesch of Kansas State University shows some defining features of Web 2.0 <http://mediatedcultures.net/mediatedculture.htm>

- **Social networking sites.** Sometimes students use **social networking sites** (like *MySpace* and *Facebook*) to discuss writing projects, conduct surveys, and locate experts. Postings may be private, from person to person; or public, from one person to many. Be careful what you post on these sites, as this information is potentially public and visible to prospective employers.
- **Wikis.** A **wiki** comprises interlinking Web pages created collaboratively, which form databases of information. Because multiple people create and edit pages on the site, college students and instructors often use wikis to create collaborative projects. The popular online encyclopedia *Wikipedia* is not always accurate because almost anyone can create or edit its content. The content of some other, more reliable wikis is created and monitored by experts. Always learn enough about a wiki to assess its reliability (*see Chapter 18: Evaluating Sources, pp. 289–98*).
- **Virtual environments.** Some college students and instructors use virtual spaces for group projects. These include graphic **virtual worlds** such as Second Life, as well as older text-based technologies such as MUDs (multiuser dimensions) and MOOs (object-oriented multiuser dimensions). (*See Chapter 16: Finding and Managing Print and Online Sources, p. 280.*)

4. Using Web-based course software

Many colleges offer some kind of course management software (CMS) like Blackboard. Although these programs vary, they typically include common features that students can access at any time via a password-protected course Web page. "Distribution" features allow instructors to present the course syllabus, assignments, and readings. "Contribution" features promote class participation and communication. These features may include e-mail systems; bulletin boards and chat rooms for class discussions; and folders where students can post their work to be read and commented upon by classmates and the instructor. **Chat rooms** are online spaces that permit real-time communication. All participants in a chat see the text of the others as they type. Often the CMS will save a transcript of the chat for future reference.

Some CMS platforms include tools for **peer review,** in which students comment on one another's writing at specific stages in the writing process. Specialized software, like the writing environment in the *Catalyst* Web site that accompanies this book, makes peer review an efficient and accessible learning tool.

If your course has a home page, take time at the beginning of the semester to become familiar with its features—as well as any related course requirements. (*For more on chat rooms, see Chapter 3: Planning and Shaping the Whole Essay, p. 33 and p. 41.*)

www.mhhe.com/mhhb2

To explore *Catalyst*, go to **Home**

Exercise 1.4 Using *Catalyst*

Go to *Catalyst*, the Web site that supports this text. Once you have entered the student home page, explore the site's five resource areas: Learning, Writing, Research, Editing, and More Resources. If you have a personal digital assistant (PDA), you can download a reference version of the grammar and documentation portions of this handbook from the site. Indicate where you would look for help with the following:

1. Choosing a topic to research
2. Deciding if a sentence you have written has a comma splice
3. Evaluating the source of some demographic data about your town
4. Searching for online sources for a psychology paper
5. Writing an interpretive paper about a short story
6. Developing a thesis for a paper
7. Avoiding plagiarism when you make use of sources in a research paper

1c Use strategies for learning in a multilingual world.

To some extent, all college students navigate multiple cultures and languages. The language of anthropology, for example, probably sounds strange and new to most students. In college, students who know two or more languages have an advantage over those who know only English. Multilingual students are able to contribute insights about other cultures and often have interesting career opportunities in our rapidly globalizing world.

This book uses the term *multilingual* to address students from varied cultural, national, and linguistic backgrounds. You may be an international student learning to speak and write English. You may have grown up speaking standard American English at school and another language or dialect at home. Perhaps your family has close ties to another part of the world. You may have moved between the United States and another country more than once. If you came to the United States at a young age, you may read and write English better than you do your parents' native language. You may speak a blended language such as "Spanglish," a mixture of English and Spanish.

Because the way we talk influences the way we write, blended and other nonstandard forms of English often appear in college students' writing. There is no single "correct" English, but there is a type typically used in academic contexts. Academic language is formal, with an expanded vocabulary as well as complex grammar patterns and culturally specific usage patterns. Learning to read and write academic English may pose special challenges to multilingual students, but the learning strategies discussed in this section can help you meet those challenges.

1. Becoming aware of cultural differences in communication

If you are familiar with at least two languages and cultures, you already know that there is more than one way to interact politely and effectively with other people. Your classmates may pride themselves on being direct, but you may think that they sound almost impolite in their enthusiasm to make a point. They may consider themselves to be explicit and precise; you may wonder why they are explaining things attentive people should be able to figure out on their own.

Colleges in the United States emphasize openly exchanging views, clearly stating opinions, and explicitly supporting judgments with examples, observations, and reasons. You may be concerned about an accent or about the fine points of grammar or pronunciation. Don't worry. Gather up your confidence and join the conversation. In some cultures, asking a question indicates that the student has not done the homework or has not been paying attention. In contrast, instructors in the United States generally encourage students to ask questions and participate in class discussion. Students who need advice can approach the instructor or fellow students outside class.

During the first few sessions of a class, observe how students show their interest through body language. Usually, American students are expected to sit up straight, look at the instructor, and take notes. Note your classmates' posture, their facial expressions, and the gestures they make. Do they raise their hands to ask a question?

Do they wait until the end of class and speak with the instructor privately?

Just as students are not all the same, neither are instructors. Does the instructor tell students to ask their questions after class? Another good way to learn an instructor's preferences is to visit his or her office hours and ask questions.

Instructors in the United States often ask students to form small groups to discuss an issue or solve a problem. All the members of such a group are expected to contribute to the conversation and offer ideas. Students usually speak and interact much more informally in these groups than they do with the instructor in class. (For example, you would not raise your hand before speaking in a small group.)

In every class, students must read and think critically. You will be asked to question the statements in the textbook or the author's reasons for writing. You will also be expected to write about what you have read and share your opinions.

2. Using reading, writing, and speaking to learn more about English

To develop your fluency in English, get into the habit of reading, writing, and speaking in English every day.

- **Keep a reading and writing notebook.** Write down thoughts, comments, and questions about the reading assignments in your courses. Try to put ideas from the readings into your own words (and note the source). Make a list of new words and phrases that you find in your reading or that you overhear. Many of them may be **idioms,** words and phrases that have a special meaning not always included in a simple dictionary definition. Go over these lists with a tutor, a friend, or your writing group.
- **Write a personal journal or blog.** Using English to explore your thoughts, feelings, and questions about your studies and your life in college will help make you feel more at home in the language.
- **Join a study group.** Most college students can benefit from belonging to a study group. When you get together and discuss an assignment, you often understand it better. Study groups also provide opportunities to practice some of those new words on your list.
- **Write letters in English.** Letters are a good way to practice the informal style used in conversation. Write to out-of-town acquaintances who do not speak your first language. Write a letter to the college newspaper. You can also write brief notes either on paper or through e-mail to instructors, tutors, librarians, secretaries, and other native speakers of English.

www.mhhe.com/mhhb2

For access to online dictionaries and thesauri, go to

Learning > Dictionaries and Thesauri

3. Using learning tools that are available for multilingual students

The following reference books can also help you as you write papers for your college courses. You can purchase them in your college's bookstore or find copies in the reference room of your college's library.

ESL dictionary A good dictionary designed especially for second-language students can be a useful source of information about word meanings. Ordinary dictionaries frequently define difficult words with other difficult words. In the *American Heritage Dictionary,* for example, the word *haze* is defined as "atmospheric moisture, dust, smoke, and vapor suspended to form a partially opaque condition." An ESL dictionary defines it more simply as "a light mist or smoke."

Do not confuse ESL dictionaries with bilingual, or "translation," dictionaries. Translation dictionaries frequently oversimplify word meanings. So too do abridged dictionaries that do not indicate shades of meaning.

Like all standard English dictionaries, an ESL dictionary includes instructions for its use. These instructions explain the abbreviations used in the entries. They also list the special notations used for words classified as slang, vulgar, informal, nonstandard, or other categories worthy of special attention. In the ESL/Learner's Edition of the *Random House Webster's Dictionary of American English* (1997), you will find "pig out" as the sixth entry under the word *pig*:

> **Pig out** (no obj) Slang. to eat too much food: *We pigged out on pizza last night.*

The entry tells you that "pig out" does not take a direct object ("no obj") and that its use is very informal ("Slang"), appropriate in talking with classmates but not in writing formal texts. You will hear a great deal of slang on your college campus, on the radio, and on TV. Make a list of slang phrases, and look them up later. If you don't find them listed in your standard or ESL dictionary, check for them in a dictionary of American slang.

The dictionary will help you with spelling, syllabication, pronunciation, definitions, word origins, and usage. The several meanings of a word are arranged first according to part of speech and then from most common to least common meaning. Examine the entry for the word *academic* in the ESL/Learner's Edition:

> **ac·a·dem·ic** /ˌækəˈdɛmɪk/ *adj.* **1.** (before a noun) of or relating to a school, esp. one for higher education: *an academic institution.* **2.** Of or relating to school subjects that teach general intellectual skills rather than specific job skills: *academic subjects like English and mathematics.* **3.** Not practical or

directly useful: *Whether she wanted to come or not is an academic question because she's here now.*—*n.* (count) **4.** A student or teacher at a college or university—**ac'a·dem'i·cal·ly,** *adv.*

Note that nouns are identified as count or noncount, indicating whether you can place a number in front of the noun and make it plural. You can say "Four academics joined the group," so when *academic* is used as a noun, it is a count noun. *Honesty* is a noncount noun.

When you look up words or phrases in the dictionary, add them to your personal list. Talk about the list with classmates. They will be happy to explain particular, up-to-date uses of the words and phrases you are learning.

Thesaurus Look up a word in a thesaurus to find other words with related meanings. The thesaurus can help you expand your vocabulary. However, always look up synonyms in a dictionary before using them because all synonyms differ slightly in meaning.

Dictionary of American idioms As explained earlier, an idiom is an expression that is peculiar to a particular language and cannot be understood by looking at the individual words. "To catch a bus" is an idiom.

Desk encyclopedias You will find one-volume encyclopedias on every subject from U.S. history to classical or biblical allusions in the reference room of your college's library. You may find it useful to look up people, places, and events that are new to you, especially if the person, place, or event is referred to often in U.S. culture.

Exercise 1.5 Using learning tools

Choose one of the following statements and use one of the learning tools discussed in this section to determine what any unfamiliar terms or concepts in the statement mean.

1. "Like those typical New Deal liberals, Smith wants to remake the way we do things in this hospital!"
2. "I need to get the straight dope on that situation before I can proceed."
3. "I plan to sign up for another tour of duty in the Navy."
4. "Let's not pour any more money down that rat hole."
5. "We need to protect our rights under the Fourteenth Amendment."

2 Understanding Writing Assignments

No matter what your course of study, writing assignments help you learn about a topic and demonstrate what you have learned. They will be an important part of your college experience. Understanding what is being asked of you as a writer is a critical ingredient in your success.

2a Recognize that writing is a process.

www.mhhe.com/mhhb2
For help with the writing process, go to **Writing > Writing Tutors**

Words do not flow effortlessly from the pens—or keyboards—of even the most experienced writers. As you begin working on a project, remember that writing is a process, a series of manageable activities that result in a finished product. Although **writing processes** vary in scope and sequence from writer to writer and assignment to assignment, these activities should be part of every lengthy writing project:

- **Understand the assignment** (Chapter 2). Begin by analyzing the assignment so you are clear about your **writing situation:** your topic and purpose as well as the audience you will address, the tone you will take, and the genre—or type of writing—you will produce. Note other important details about deadline, length, and format.
- **Generate ideas and plan your approach** (Chapter 3). Give yourself time to explore your topic, using a variety of brainstorming techniques. Decide on a working thesis that will help you focus your first draft, and sketch an informal or a formal plan for the sequence of your ideas.
- **Draft paragraphs and visuals** (Chapter 4). Use paragraph development as a way of moving your writing forward. Use various strategies such as description and comparison to develop and shape your ideas. Consider when visuals such as tables and graphs will be an efficient way to present data and support your ideas. After you draft the body of your composition, develop an effective introduction and conclusion.
- **Revise, edit, and proofread** (Chapter 5). Develop your first draft and tailor it for your readers in one or more subsequent drafts. Analyze the overall development from paragraph to paragraph; then look at individual paragraphs, sentences, and words. Use revising and editing checklists in this process.
- **Design your document** (Chapter 6). A clear, uncluttered format will make your text more appealing to readers. Lists and headings may help them see the structure of longer documents.

WRITING beyond COLLEGE

Writing Skills in College and Beyond

The writing that you do in college is excellent preparation for your professional life, even if you do not choose a career in academia. Business leaders say that strong writing skills are an essential component of job performance, and the amount of writing increases with job advancement. The skills you develop by responding to college writing assignments—analyzing the writing situation, gathering information, generating ideas, drafting unified and coherent paragraphs, and revising and editing with your audience in mind—will serve you well after graduation.

Exercise 2.1 Exploring your writing process

Learn about yourself as a writer by telling the story of your writing experiences. The following questions will help you write a brief narrative.

1. How were you taught to write in school? Were you encouraged to explore ideas and use your imagination, or was the focus primarily on writing correct sentences? Did you struggle with writing assignments, or did they come easily to you? Have you ever written for pleasure, not just in response to a school assignment?
2. Describe the writing process you use for academic papers. Does your process vary according to the assignment? If so, how? Do you engage in all the activities described on page 20? If not, which ones do you skip? Which activities are the most difficult for you? Why? Which are the easiest? Why?

LEARNING in COLLEGE

Understanding Assignments

It is often helpful to talk with the instructor after receiving and looking over a new assignment. It is far better to ask for clarification before you begin an assignment than to have to start over, or to turn in something that does not fulfill the requirements.

2b Understand the writing situation.

Writers respond to **writing situations.** When you write a lab report for a science class, create a flyer for a candidate for student government, or send an e-mail inviting a friend for coffee, you shape the communication (**message**) to suit the purpose, audience, and context. The results for each situation will differ. All communication arises because something is at stake (the **exigence**). The **audience** receives the message. Audience members may be friendly or hostile to the writer's message, and their cultures and backgrounds will influence their reactions. Your **purpose** may be to inform them or to move them to action. **Context** includes the means of communication, current events, and the environment in which the communication takes place. See an illustration of how these elements are related in Figure 2.1:

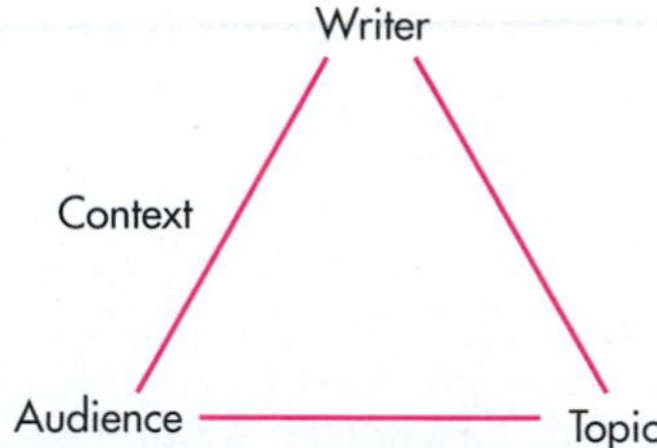

FIGURE 2.1 Elements of a writing situation.

CHECKLIST

Understanding the Writing Situation

Ask yourself these questions as you approach a writing assignment.

Topic *(see 2c)*

- ☐ What are you being asked to write about?
- ☐ Have you narrowed your topic to a question that interests you?
- ☐ What kind of visuals, if any, would be appropriate for this topic?
- ☐ What types of sources will help you explore this topic? Where will you look for them?
- ☐ What genre or format would suit this assignment? *(see 2e)*

Purpose *(see 2d)*

- ☐ What do you want your writing to accomplish? Are you trying to inform, analyze, or argue? (What key words in your assignment indicate the purpose?)

CHECKLIST *(continued)*

- ☐ Do you want to intensify, clarify, complicate, or change your audience's assumptions or opinions?

Audience and Tone *(see 2f and 2g)*

- ☐ What are your audience's demographics (education level, social status, gender, cultural background, and language)? How diverse is your audience?
- ☐ What does your audience know about the topic at hand?
- ☐ What common assumptions and different opinions do these audience members bring to the issue? Are they likely to agree with you, or will you have to persuade them?
- ☐ What is your relationship to them?
- ☐ What sort of voice would appeal to this audience: informal, entertaining, reasonable, or forceful? Why?

Context *(see 2h)*

- ☐ Does your topic deal with issues of interest to the public or to members of an academic discipline?
- ☐ What have other writers said recently about this topic?
- ☐ How much time do you have to complete the assignment?
- ☐ What is the specified number of pages?
- ☐ What medium are you using (print essay, video podcast, Web site, presentation software)?

2c Find an appropriate topic.

Many college writing assignments allow students to find a topic of interest to them within the framework of the course. Here is an example:

ASSIGNMENT Visit a local photography exhibit or check out the photography archives in the library. Choose one or more photographs to analyze, and discuss the role of the photographer. Consider the formal elements of the photograph(s) as well as the social context.

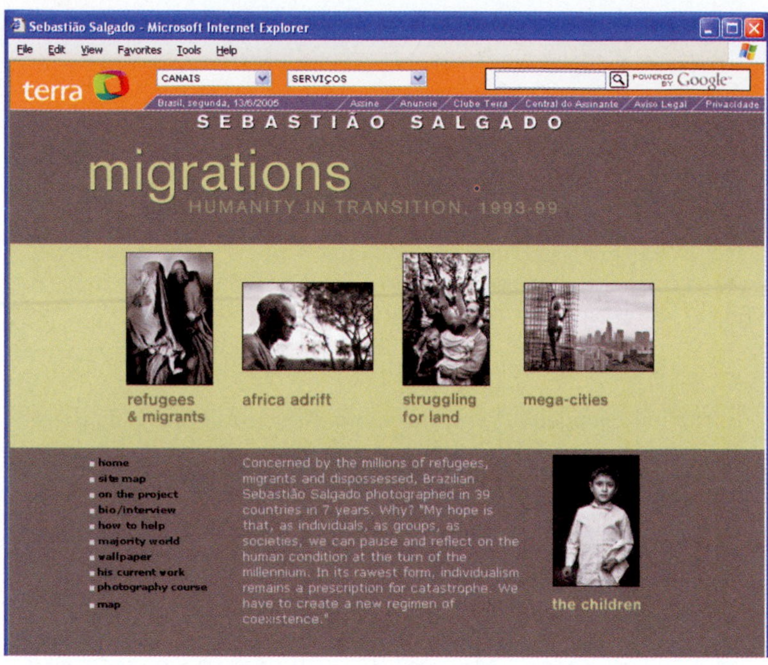

FIGURE 2.2 The Web site for a photography exhibit. Diane Chen found this Web site about Sebastião Salgado's exhibit *Migrations:*

After locating some photography exhibits in her area, reading a few reviews of them, and exploring information about them on the Web, Diane Chen selected an exhibit called *Migrations: Humanity in Transition* (*Figure 2.2*) because of its relevance to her family's immigrant history. (We will follow Diane Chen's work on this assignment from start to finish in the following chapters. *For guidelines on analyzing photographs, see Chapter 14, pp. 228–31.*) A topic does not need to have personal relevance to be intellectually interesting, of course. A student with an interest in science who is assigned to write about one factor in the decline of the Roman Empire might focus on the epidemics that ravaged the Roman population. Someone interested in military history might focus instead on the instability caused by a succession of military emperors who seized power by force.

1. Finding a manageable topic

Thinking of questions on a topic will help you generate interesting ideas. Play the "I wonder/They say/I think" game:

- **I wonder:** Starting with the subject matter of the course or the assignment, list concepts and issues that you wonder about.

- **They say:** Reviewing your class notes, course reading, online discussion-group postings, and scholarly bibliographies, see what topics and issues others in the field say are important. Jot down relevant information, ideas, and issues.
- **I think:** Choosing an item or two that you have listed, figure out what you think about it, giving your curiosity free rein. Connect your interests to what you are learning in the course.

2. Narrowing your topic

When choosing a topic, consider whether it is narrow enough to fit your assignment. A topic such as Thomas Jefferson's presidency would be appropriate for a book-length treatment but could not be covered in adequate detail in an essay. Consider the following examples:

BROAD TOPICS	NARROW TOPICS
Sports injuries	The most common types of field injuries in soccer and how to administer emergency care
Reading problems	Approaches to treating dyslexia in middle-school students

The following strategy can help you narrow your subject area:

1. Browse your course texts and class notes to find topics and then ask specific questions about the topics. Use the "five *w*'s and an *h*" strategy by asking about the *who, what, why, when, where,* and *how* of a topic (*see Chapter 3, p. 36*). See the box on the bottom of page 26 for examples of questions.
2. Make sure that you are posing a challenging question that will interest your readers. An appropriate question cannot be answered with a simple yes or no, a dictionary-like definition, or a handful of well-known facts.
3. Speculate about the answer to your question, which will give you a hypothesis to work with during the research process. A **hypothesis** is a speculation, or guess, that you must test and revise as you explore your topic.

Exercise 2.2 Narrowing a topic

Narrow the topics below to make them appropriate for a composition of approximately ten double-spaced pages.

1. For a course in criminal justice: crime-prevention programs
2. For a psychology course: studies on memory
3. For a nutrition course: obesity in the United States

4. For a film course: filmmaking in the 1990s
5. For a history course: Civil War battles

2d Be clear about the purpose of your assignment.

If your instructor has provided a written description of the assignment, look for key terms that might give you a clue about the composition's **purpose.** Are you expected to inform, interpret, or argue? Each of these purposes is linked to a common writing assignment found in many different disciplines.

- In an **informative report,** the writer's purpose is to pass on what he or she has learned about a topic or issue. The following terms are often associated with the task of informing:

  Classify   Illustrate   Report   Survey

  EXAMPLE A psychology student might *survey* recent research about the effects on adolescents of violence in video games.

  EXAMPLE A business major might *illustrate* the theory of supply-side economics with an example from recent history.

- An **interpretive analysis** explores the meaning of written documents, cultural artifacts, social situations, or natural

CHARTING the TERRITORY

Posing Discipline-Specific Questions

The particular course you are taking defines a range of questions that are appropriate within a given discipline. Here are examples of the way your course would help define the questions you might ask if, for example, you were writing about Thomas Jefferson:

U.S. history: How did Jefferson's ownership of slaves affect his public stance on slavery?

Political science: To what extent did Jefferson's conflict with the courts redefine the balance of power among the three branches of government?

Art history: What architectural influences do you see at work in Jefferson's design for his home at Monticello?

CHARTING the TERRITORY

Writing to Express: Personal Essays

Another purpose for writing is to express thoughts and feelings about personal experiences. Your first writing assignment for college—the essay required by the Admissions Department as part of your college application form—probably had this purpose. The personal essay is one of the most literary kinds of writing and therefore is often assigned in English composition courses. (*For more on personal essays and writing with an expressive purpose, see Chapter 11, pp. 212–16.*)

events. The following terms often appear when the purpose is interpreting:

Analyze Compare Explain Reflect

EXAMPLE A philosophy student might *explain* the allegory of the cave in Plato's *Republic.*

EXAMPLE A science student might *analyze* satellite images in order to make weather predictions.

- An **argument** proves a point or supports an opinion through logic and concrete evidence. The following terms usually indicate that the purpose of a paper is to argue a position:

Agree Assess Defend Refute

EXAMPLE A political science student might *defend* the electoral college system.

EXAMPLE A nutrition student might *refute* the claims of low-carb weight-loss diets.

Exercise 2.3 Identifying the purpose

For each of the following assignments, state whether the primary task is to inform, interpret, or argue a position.

1. Defend or refute the claim that the colonies would inevitably have declared independence no matter how Britain had responded to their demands.
2. Explain the Declaration of Independence as a product of the European Enlightenment.
3. Survey and classify the variety of ways in which Americans responded to the Declaration of Independence and the outbreak of the Revolutionary War.

2e Use the appropriate genre.

When you know your composition's purpose, you can select a genre that supports that purpose. **Genre** simply means kind of writing. Poems, stories, and plays are genres of literature, and audiences have different expectations for each. Most of the writing you will be asked to produce in college will be nonfiction, that is, writing about real events, people, and things for the purpose of argument, information, or interpretation. Within nonfiction, however, there are many additional genres of writing such as letters, brochures, case studies, lab reports, and literary analyses. Some types of writing, like the case study, are common in a particular field such as sociology. Understanding the genre that an assignment calls for is an important step in successfully fulfilling it. If you are supposed to be writing a description of a snake for a field guide, you will not be successful if you write a poem—even a very good poem—about a snake.

Some Common Genres of Writing

Letters	Profiles	Brochures
Memoirs	Proposals	Case studies
Essays	Instructions	
Reviews	Reports	

Sometimes an assignment will specify a genre. For example, you may be asked to write a report (an informative genre), a comparative analysis (an interpretive genre), or a critique (an argumentative genre). In other instances you might be asked to select the genre yourself. Make sure the one you choose—whether it be a multimedia presentation or a researched essay—is appropriate to the purpose of your assignment.

Some genres have very specific conventions for formatting and design. Whether you need to follow the formatting conventions and documentation style recommended by the Modern Language Association (MLA), the American Psychological Association (APA), the editors of *The Chicago Manual of Style,* the Council of Science Editors (CSE), or some other authority will depend largely on the disciplinary context of your writing. Your instructor will typically let you know which style you should use. You can find coverage of the MLA, APA, Chicago, and CSE styles in Part 4: Documenting across the Curriculum. (*For more on when to use a specific documentation style for a discipline, see Chapter 22: Writing the Paper, pp. 337–40.*)

If you are unfamiliar with the conventions of a particular genre, seek out examples from your instructor or college writing center. Many genres of academic writing are covered in Part 2: Common Assignments across the Curriculum; additional genres are covered in Part 5: Writing beyond College.

2f Ask questions about your audience.

Whether we realize it or not, most of us are experts at adjusting what we say to suit the audience we are addressing. In everyday conversation, for example, your description of a car accident would be different if you were talking to a young child instead of an adult. For most college assignments, your instructor is your primary audience, but he or she also represents a larger group of readers who have an interest or stake in your topic. Consider *why* your topic might interest your audience as you answer the following questions (*see also the checklist on p. 22*):

1. **Are your readers specialists, or are they members of a general audience?** How much prior knowledge and specialized vocabulary can you assume your audience has? An education professor, for example, might ask you to write for a general audience of your students' parents. You can assume that they have a general knowledge of your subject but that you will need to explain concepts such as "authentic assessment" or "content standards." If you were presenting to a specialist audience of school principals, you would not need to define these common terms from within the discipline.

   Consider, for example, how audience accounts for the differences in these two passages about snakes:

   > Many people become discouraged by the challenge of caring for a snake which just grows and grows and grows. Giant pythons can get bigger than their owners, eat bunnies, and need large cages, plus it's hard to find pet sitters for them when you go out of town.
   >
   > —DANA PAYNE, Woodland Park Zoo Web site

   > The skull of *Python m. bivittatus* is very highly ossified, with dense bone and complex sutures. Like other snakes, it has lost the upper temporal bar, jugal, squamosal, and epipterygoid. A bony interorbital septum is present.
   >
   > —SUSAN EVAN, NSF Digital Library at UT Austin

   The first passage, written for a general audience, gives practical advice in simple, nontechnical language and with a humorous tone. The second passage focuses on physical details of primary interest to other scientists who study snakes and uses technical language and a serious tone.

2. **Are the demographics** (age, gender, sexual orientation, ethnicity, cultural background, religion, group membership) **of your audience relevant to your presentation?** What experiences, assumptions, interests, opinions, and attitudes might your audience members have in common? What are

WRITING beyond COLLEGE

Purposes and Genres

The common purposes of academic writing are also the common purposes for most genres of communication that you will encounter outside college. (*See Part 5: Writing beyond College.*)

- A blog presents an individual's interpretation of world events.
- A brochure can inform its reader about a particular subject.
- A grant proposal argues for an allocation of funds or other resources.

their needs? Will any of your ideas be controversial? Background information can help you build rapport with your audience and anticipate any objections they may have, especially when you are writing an argument. In some high-stakes situations, writers may use interviews or questionnaires to gather information about their audience. More typically, writers use peer review to gauge audience reactions and make adjustments (*see Learning in College: An Audience of Your Peers on p. 31*).

2g Determine the appropriate tone.

The identity, knowledge level, and needs of your audience will determine the tone of your composition. In speech, the sentence "I am surprised at you" can express anger, excitement, or disappointment depending on your tone of voice. In writing, your content, style, and word choice communicate **tone.**

Consider the differences in tone in the following passages on the subject of a cafeteria makeover:

SARCASTIC "I am special," the poster headline under the smirking face announces. Well, good for you. And I'm specially glad that cafeteria prices are up because so much money was spent on motivational signs and new paint colors.

SERIOUS Although the new colors in the cafeteria are electric and clashing, color in general does brighten the space and distinguish it from the classrooms. But the motivational posters are not inspiring and should be removed.

Tips LEARNING in COLLEGE

An Audience of Your Peers

In some courses, you may have the opportunity to get feedback on your drafts from a peer audience—classmates with similar levels of expertise in the course content. Comments from readers can help you see where passages are unclear, paragraphs need more detail, and sentences delight or offend. Audiences are not monolithic: opinions vary; individuals react to and notice different things. Look for recurring comments and themes among the responses. You may want to address those issues before submitting your paper to its final audience.

The tone in the first passage is sarcastic and obviously intended for other students. An audience of school administrators probably would not appreciate the slang or the humor. The second passage is more serious and respectful in tone while still offering a critique.

For most college writing, your tone should reflect seriousness about the subject matter and purpose, as well as respect for your readers. You can indicate your seriousness by stating information accurately, presenting reasonable arguments and interpretations, dealing fairly with opposing views, and citing sources for your ideas. Unless you are writing a personal essay, the topic, not yourself or your feelings, should be the center of attention.

Writing with sincerity and authority does not mean being condescending or pompous to readers, as in the following examples:

CONDESCENDING	Along with many opportunities, obstacles exist that have restricted the amount of foreign direct investment, as I already explained to you.
POMPOUS	It behooves investors to cogitate over the momentousness of their determinations.

These sentences use a more appropriate tone for college writing:

APPROPRIATE	Along with many opportunities, obstacles exist that have restricted the amount of foreign direct investment, as noted earlier.
APPROPRIATE	Investors should consider the consequences of their decisions.

(*For more on appropriate language, see Chapter 48.*)

Exercise 2.4 Analyzing audience and tone

Find an article from one of the following sources and rewrite a paragraph in the article for the specified audience.

1. An article on a diet or exercise that appears in a magazine for teenagers (30- to 40-year-old adults)
2. An article on a celebrity's court trial that appears in a supermarket tabloid (the audience of a highly respected newspaper such as the *New York Times* or the *Wall Street Journal*)
3. A discussion of clinical depression from a psychology journal (your classmates)

2h Consider the context.

The context, or surrounding circumstances, influences how an audience receives your communication. Your assignment goes a long way toward establishing the context in which you write. Your instructor probably has specified a length, due date, and genre. Medium also affects writing: an assignment asking you to create a Web site requires different decisions on your part from one asking you to write a print essay. If you create a Web site, you have the option of including audio and video, for example.

Context also involves broader conversations about your topic. Your course gives you background on what others in the discipline have said and what issues have been debated. Current events, on campus and in society as a whole, provide a context for public writing. You may wish, for example, to e-mail the student newspaper in response to a new school policy or on an issue of general concern.

2i Meet early to discuss coauthored projects.

In many fields, **collaborative writing** is essential. Here are some suggestions to help you make the most of this activity:

- Working with your partners, decide on ground rules, including meeting times, deadlines, and ways of reconciling differences, whether by majority rule or some other method. Is there an interested and respected third party you can consult if the group's dynamics break down?
- Divide the work fairly so that everyone has a part to contribute to the project. Each group member should do some researching, drafting, revising, and editing.
- In your personal journal, record, analyze, and evaluate the intellectual and interpersonal workings of the group as you see and experience them.

Tips LEARNING in COLLEGE

For Coauthoring Online

Computer networks make it easy for two or more writers to coauthor texts. Wikis allow writers to contribute to a common structure and edit one another's work. Most courseware (such as Blackboard) includes chat rooms and public space for posting and commenting on drafts. Word-processing software also allows writers to make tracked changes in files. (*See Chapter 5, pp. 76–79 for more on peer review.*)

If your group meets online, make sure that you save a transcript of the discussion. If you exchange ideas via e-mail, you will automatically have a record of how the piece developed and how well the group worked together. Archive these transcripts and e-mails into designated folders. In all online communications, be especially careful with your tone. Without the benefit of facial expression and tone of voice, readers can easily misinterpret critical comments.

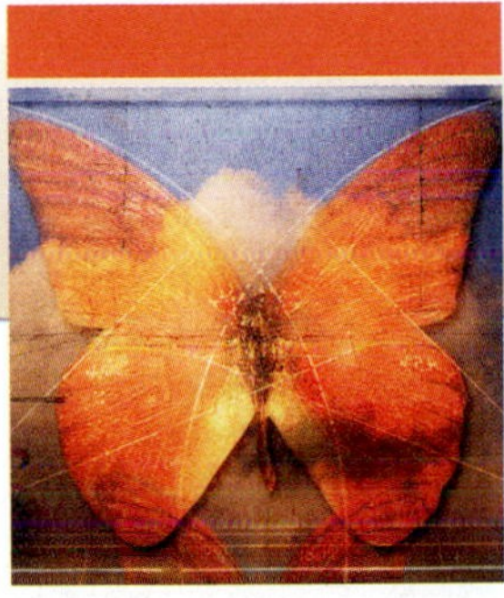

3 Planning and Shaping the Whole Essay

This chapter will help you get started on writing the first draft of your composition. It offers strategies for exploring your topic, developing a thesis, and planning a preliminary structure. These strategies are useful at the beginning of the writing process, but you may also need to return to them at a later stage of your project, especially if you find yourself staring at a blank screen. Writing is a messy business, and planning, drafting, revising, and designing rarely proceed in a straight line; writers often need to circle back to an earlier stage.

3a Explore your ideas.

The following strategies, sometimes called **invention techniques** or **prewriting activities,** are designed to get you thinking and writing about your topic. Remember that what you write at this stage is for your eyes only—no one will be judging your work. You can do much

www.mhhe.com/mhhb2
For help generating ideas, go to
Writing > Paragraph/Essay Development > Prewriting

CHECKLIST

Activities for Exploring Your Ideas

- ☐ Freewrite. (*3a1*)
- ☐ List. (*3a2*)
- ☐ Cluster. (*3a3*)
- ☐ Question. (*3a4*)
- ☐ Review your notes and annotations. (*3a5*)
- ☐ Keep a journal. (*3a6*)
- ☐ Browse in the library. (*3a7*)
- ☐ Search the Internet. (*3a8*)
- ☐ Exchange ideas. (*3a9*)

TEXTCONNEX

Invisible Writing

If you find your mind wandering when you freewrite, or if you find it hard to resist the urge to stop and reread what you have written, try turning down the brightness and contrast on your monitor or using white as your font color. (Highlight the document and select black when you are done.)

of your exploratory writing in a **journal** (print or electronic), which is simply a place to record your thoughts on a regular basis. (*For more on journals, see p. 39.*) Your class notes constitute a type of academic journal, as do the notes you take on your reading and research.

As you explore, turn off your internal critic and generate as much material as possible. Later you can select the best ideas from what you produce. We will witness this process by following the development of student Diane Chen's composition.

1. Freewriting

To figure out what you are thinking, try **freewriting.** Just write whatever occurs to you about a topic. If nothing comes to mind, then write "nothing comes to mind" until you think of something else. The

For MULTILINGUAL STUDENTS

Using Another Language to Explore Ideas

Consider exploring your topic using your native language. You won't have to worry about grammar, spelling, or vocabulary, so these issues won't interfere with your creative thought. Once you have some ideas, it is best to work with them in English.

trick is to keep pushing forward without stopping. Do not worry about spelling, punctuation, or grammar rules as you freewrite. Your objective is to explore ideas freely and to "loosen up" in the same way that a jogger does before a long run.

Once you have some ideas down on paper, you might try doing some **focused freewriting.** Begin with a point or a specific question. You might explore more deeply one of the ideas or questions that you discovered while freewriting. The following is a portion of Diane Chen's freewriting about her photography paper:

> I want to talk about what it's like to look at all these pictures of people suffering, but to also admire how beautifully the photographs have been composed. Those two things feel like they shouldn't go together. But it's also what makes the photographs so great—because you're feeling two different emotions at the same time. It makes it harder to stop looking at what it is he's trying to show us.

You can see ideas beginning to take shape that Diane might be able to use in her paper. She needed several sessions of general freewriting, however, before she was able to reach this point.

2. Listing

Another strategy is to **brainstorm** by starting with a topic and listing the words, phrases, images, and ideas that come to mind. Later, you can review this list and highlight the items you would like to explore. When you brainstorm in this way, don't worry about whether the individual thoughts or ideas are "right." Just get them down on paper or into an electronic file.

Once you have composed a fairly lengthy list, go through it looking for patterns and connections. If you have written your list on paper, highlight or connect related ideas. If you have typed them into a document, group related material together. Move apparently extraneous material or ideas to the end of the list or to a separate page.

Now zero in on the areas of most interest, and add any new ideas that occur to you. Arrange the items into main points and subpoints if necessary. Later, this material may form the basis of an outline for your paper.

Here is part of a list that Diane Chen produced for her paper about a photography exhibit:

> **Migrations—still photographs, dynamic subject**
> **why migrate/emigrate?**
> **my family—hope of a better life**
> **fear & doubt in new places; uprooting**
> **beautiful photos but horrible reality**
> **Sebastião Salgado as photojournalist**
> **black & white pictures**
> **strong vertical & horizontal lines**
> **lighting choices are meaningful**

TEXTCONNEX

Digital Tools for Exploring Ideas

Some students use a separate file on a word processor to record ideas, which can then be copied and pasted into a draft. Others use Web sites, such as bubbl.us (http://www.bubbl.us), that allow individuals and groups to generate ideas and link them in a visual cluster. This cluster can be e-mailed to one or more recipients.

3. Clustering

Having something down in writing enables you to look for categories and connections. **Clustering,** sometimes called **mapping,** is a brainstorming technique that generates categories and connections from the beginning. To make an idea cluster, do the following:

- Write your topic in the center of a piece of paper, and draw a circle around it.
- Surround the topic with subtopics that interest you. Circle each, and draw a line from it to the center circle.
- Brainstorm more ideas. As you do so, connect each one to a subtopic already on the sheet, or make it a new subtopic of its own.

Web sites such as bubbl.us allow you to use this technique on the computer, alone or in groups (*see the box above*). As she explored her ideas about the Sebastião Salgado exhibit, Diane Chen prepared the cluster that appears in Figure 3.1 on the next page.

4. Questioning

Asking questions is a good way to explore a topic further. The journalist's five *w*'s and an *h* (*who? what? where? when? why?* and *how?*) can help you find specific ideas and details. For example, here are some questions that would apply to the photography exhibit:

- Who is the photographer, who are his subjects, and who is his audience?
- What is the photographer's attitude toward his subjects?
- Where were these pictures shot and first published?
- When did these events take place?
- Why are the people in these pictures migrating?
- How did I react to these images?

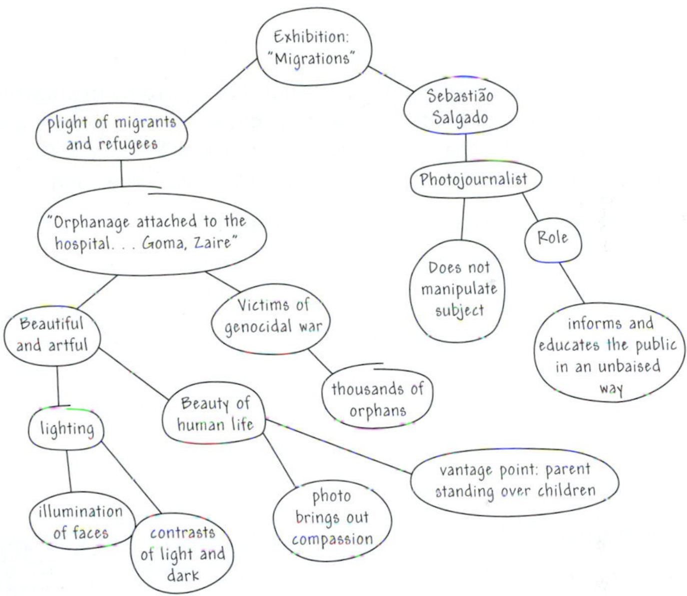

FIGURE 3.1 Diane Chen's cluster about the Salgado exhibit.

CHARTING the TERRITORY

Different Questions Lead to Different Answers

Always consider what questions make the most sense in the context of the course you are taking.

- **Sociology:** A sociologist might ask questions about the ways recent immigrants interact with more established immigrants from the same country.
- **History:** A historian might ask how and why immigration to the United States has changed over the past century.
- **Economics:** An economist might wonder what effect refugees have on the economy of their host country.

TEXTCONNEX

Blogging as a Writing Process Tool

As a site for invention, a blog provides space for your notes. It also can function as a research notebook in which you link to online sources and record your own ideas, and it allows you to ask readers questions about issues you encounter in an assignment. (*For more on blogs, see Chapter 14: Multimedia Writing, pp. 244–47.*)

Another questioning technique is looking at a topic dramatically, as an action (*what*) with actors (*who*), a scene (*where*), a time period (*when*), means (*how*), and a purpose (*why*). Also take note of the problems or questions your professor poses to get class discussion going.

5. Reviewing your notes and annotations

If your assignment involves reading one or more texts or researching multiple sources, review your notes and annotations. (*For details on annotating, see Chapter 7. For details on researching and keeping a research journal, see Chapter 21.*) If you are writing about something you have observed, review any notes or sketches you have made. These immediate comments and reactions are some of your best sources for ideas. Look for patterns.

CHARTING the TERRITORY

Varieties of Notes

Here are some examples of the different kinds of notes you might take when preparing paper assignments for courses in two different disciplines:

- **For a paper on conflict resolution** among four-year-olds for a course in human development, you observe and record the play activities of one child during several play periods in a preschool class. Your careful written observations will help you understand principles in the course text and may later contribute to a case study (*see Chapter 11*).
- **For an article on journalistic styles** for a news reporting class, you read an account of the same event in the *New York Times*, the *Arizona Republic*, and *Time* magazine, annotating each with notes on its style and point of view. Analyzing the treatment of the same story in different publications will help you identify stylistic differences.

6. Keeping a journal or notebook

You may find it helpful to go beyond note taking and start recording ideas and questions inspired by your classes or your exploratory writing in a journal. For example, you might write about connections between what has happened in your personal life and your academic subjects, connections among your subjects, or ideas touched on in class that you would like to know more about. Jotting down one or two thoughts at the end of class and taking a few minutes later in the day to explore those ideas at greater length will help you build a store of writing ideas.

> Prof. says some Civil War photographers posed the corpses on the battleground. Does that change the meaning or value of their work? Did their audiences know they did this, and if so, what did they think of the practice?

For MULTILINGUAL STUDENTS

Private Writing in English

Multilingual students can also use a journal to develop fluency in thinking and writing in English. Keep in mind that no one will be correcting your work, so you can focus on writing as much as possible. You can also use your journal to collect and comment on idioms and to express your thoughts on your experience as a multilingual student.

Exercise 3.1 Keeping an academic journal

Start a print or electronic journal and write in it daily for at least two weeks. Using your course work as a springboard, record anything that comes to mind, including personal reactions and memories. At the end of the two weeks, reread your journal and write about the journal-keeping experience. Does your journal contain any ideas or information that might be useful for the papers you are writing? Has the journal helped you gain any insight into your courses or your life as a student?

7. Browsing in the library

Your college library is filled with ideas—and it can provide inspiration when you need to come up with your own. Sometimes it helps to take a break: leave your study carrel, stretch your legs, and browse the bookshelves. You can also explore online resources via your library's Web site. Keep careful track of the sources of compelling ideas so that you will be able to provide proper credit if you use them in your writing. Using others' ideas without acknowledging them is plagiarism.

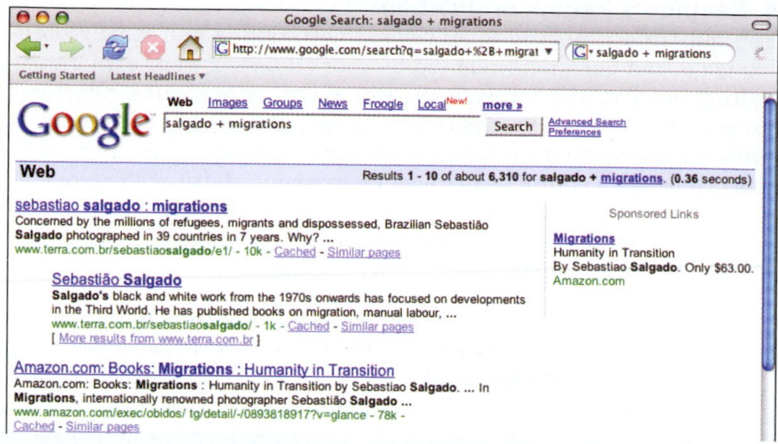

FIGURE 3.2 Initial results of an Internet search. This screen shows the first three results of Diane Chen's search on *Google*.

(*See Chapter 21: Working with Sources and Avoiding Plagiarism, pp. 314–32.*) (*For help with library research, see Chapter 16: Finding and Managing Print and Online Sources, pp. 259–80.*)

8. Searching the Internet

Type keywords related to your topic into a search engine such as *Google,* and visit several sites on the list that results. (*See Chapter 16: Finding and Managing Print and Online Sources, pp. 259–80.*) When Diane Chen searched *Google* using the keywords "Salgado" and "migrations," for example, she got the results in Figure 3.2.

Evaluate information from the Web with a critical eye, as Web sites are not screened for reliability. Keyword searches of library resources are more likely to yield accurate information. (*See Chapter 18: Evaluating Sources, pp. 289–98.*)

9. Exchanging ideas in person or online

Seek out opportunities to talk about your writing with your classmates, friends, and family.

- Visit your college writing center to discuss your work in progress.
- Brainstorm within your peer response group, if your instructor has set up such groups. Come prepared with ideas and information about your topic to get the discussion started.
- Contact graduate students and professionals with expertise in your discipline and discuss with them their approaches to writing assignments.

Online tools that are available to writers offer additional ways for you to collaborate with others on your papers. Discuss your assignments by exchanging e-mail. Especially if your course has a class Web site, you might exchange ideas in chat rooms. Other options include instant messaging (IM), text messaging, and virtual environments. You also might use a blog to exchange ideas and drafts with your classmates (*See the TextConnex box on p. 38*).

Writing e-mail When you work on papers with classmates, use e-mail in the following ways:

- To check out your understanding of the assignment
- To ask each other useful questions about ideas and topics
- To share your freewriting, listing, and other exploratory writing
- To respond to each other's ideas

Chatting about ideas You can also use online chats as well as other virtual spaces to share ideas. Your instructor may include **chat room** activities, where you go into virtual rooms to work on assignments in small groups or visit and interact with classes at other colleges.

You can also exchange ideas in virtual worlds such as *Second Life* (secondlife.com). Instant messaging (IM) also permits real-time online communication. Exchanging ideas with other writers via IM can help you clarify your thinking on a topic. In the exchange in Figure 3.3, for example, two students share ideas about work.

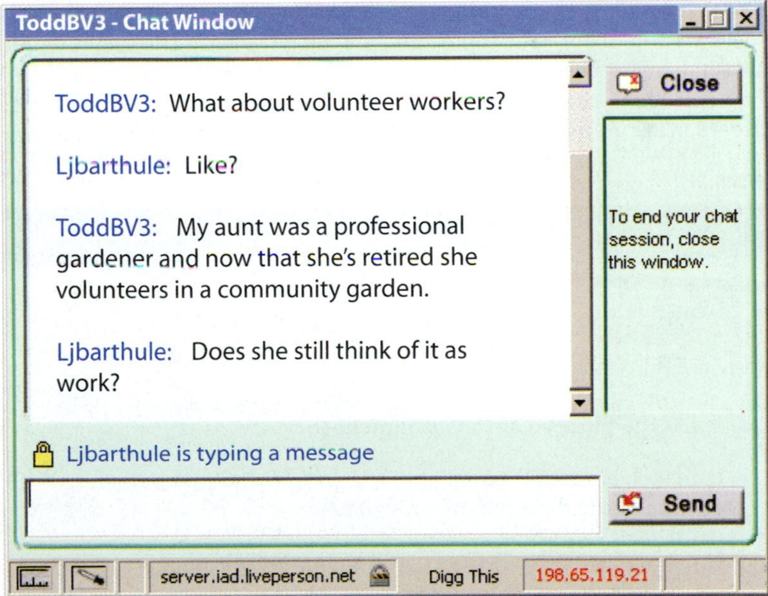

FIGURE 3.3 **Exchanging ideas in an online discussion.**

TEXTCONNEX

Exchanging Text Messages

Text messaging—the exchange of brief messages between cell phones—can be a helpful tool. You can text your ideas for an assignment to a classmate (or, with permission, your instructor) for response. Although you can employ abbreviations commonly used in texting for speedier note taking, *never* use such shorthand in assignments.

Exercise 3.2 Generating ideas

For a paper that you are currently writing or a topic you are interested in, brainstorm by listing, clustering, freewriting, questioning, and searching the Internet or browsing in the library. Be sure to put your responses in writing, even if your instructor will not be reading your work. If possible, exchange ideas with classmates, either in person or online. Write a summary of what techniques worked best for you and why.

www.mhhe.com/mhhb2
For help with developing a thesis, go to
Writing > Paragraph/Essay Development > Thesis/Central Idea

3b Decide on a thesis.

The **thesis** is the central idea of your paper. It should communicate a specific point about your topic and suit the purpose of the assignment. As you explore your topic, ideas for your thesis will begin to emerge. You can focus these ideas by drafting a preliminary, or working, **thesis statement,** which can be one or more sentences long. As you

CHECKLIST

A Strong Thesis

A strong thesis does the following:

- ☐ It fits the purpose of the assignment.
- ☐ It makes a specific point about the topic and gives readers a sense of the direction of your paper.
- ☐ It asserts something that could make a difference in what

draft and revise your paper, you may revise or even change your thesis several times.

1. Making sure your thesis fits the purpose of the assignment

All theses are arguments in the sense that they make an assertion about a topic. But there are different kinds of assertions or theses: a thesis for an informative or interpretive paper usually previews the paper's content or expresses the writer's insight, while a thesis for an argument takes a position on a debatable issue or recommends an action. (*For information on assignment purposes, see 2d, p. 26.*)

THESIS TO INFORM The exhibit *Migrations* offers images of the world's poor people.

THESIS TO INTERPRET Sebastião Salgado's photographs ask us to understand the pain and suffering that refugees experience.

THESIS TO ARGUE Military intervention by the United States and other nations can prevent further increases in the number of refugees.

For MULTILINGUAL STUDENTS

State Your Thesis Directly

In U.S. academic and business settings, readers expect writers to state the main idea right away. Some other cultures may use an indirect style, telling stories and giving facts but not stating the central idea in an obvious way. When assessing a writing situation, consider your readers' expectations and values.

2. Making sure that your thesis is specific

Avoid thesis statements that simply announce your topic, state an obvious fact about it, or offer a general observation:

ANNOUNCEMENT

I will discuss the photography exhibit *Migrations* by Sebastião Salgado. [*What is the writer's point about the photography exhibit?*]

STATEMENT OF FACT

The exhibit of photographs by Sebastião Salgado is about people in migration. [*This information does not make a specific point about the exhibit.*]

GENERAL OBSERVATION

Sebastião Salgado's photographs of people in migration are beautiful and informative. [*This point could apply to many photographs. What makes these photographs special?*]

By contrast, a specific thesis signals a focused, well-developed paper.

SPECIFIC

Like a photojournalist, Salgado brings us images of newsworthy events, but he goes beyond objective reporting, imparting his compassion for refugees and migrants.

In this example, the thesis expresses the writer's particular point—Salgado's intention to move the viewer.

> ***Note:*** A thesis statement can be longer than one sentence (if necessary) to provide a framework for your main idea. All of the sentences taken together, though, should build to one specific, significant point that fits the purpose of your assignment. (Some instructors may prefer that you limit your thesis statements to one sentence.)

3. Making sure your thesis is significant

A significant thesis makes an assertion that could change what readers know, understand, or believe. A topic that makes a difference to you is much more likely to make a difference to your readers. When you are looking for possible theses, be sure to challenge yourself to develop one that you care about.

Exercise 3.3 Evaluating thesis statements

Evaluate the thesis statements that accompany each of the following assignments. If the thesis statement is inappropriate or weak, explain why and suggest how it could be stronger.

1. *Assignment:* For a social ethics course, find an essay by a philosopher on a contemporary social issue, and argue either for or against the writer's position.
   Thesis: In "Active and Passive Euthanasia," James Rachels argues against the standard view that voluntary euthanasia is always wrong.
2. *Assignment:* For an economics course, find an essay on the gap between rich and poor in the United States, and argue either for or against the writer's position.
   Thesis: George Will's argument that economic inequality is healthy for the United States depends on two false analogies.

Finding a Thesis through Questioning

Think of the thesis as an answer to a question. In the following examples, the topic of the thesis is in italics and the assertion about that topic is underlined.

QUESTION What did Alfred Stieglitz contribute to the art of photography?

THESIS *Alfred Stieglitz's struggle to promote photography as an art* involved starting a journal, opening a gallery, and making common cause with avant-garde modernist artists.

QUESTION What makes a photograph significant?

THESIS *The significance of a photograph* depends on both its formal and its documentary features.

QUESTION Is Susan Sontag right that photography obstructs critical thinking?

THESIS *Susan Sontag's critique of photography* is unconvincing, partly because it assumes that most people are visually unsophisticated and thoughtlessly voyeuristic.

3. *Assignment:* For a nutrition course, report on recent research on an herbal supplement.
   Thesis: Although several researchers believe that echinacea supplements may help reduce the duration of a cold, all agree that the quality and the content of these supplements vary widely.
4. *Assignment:* For a literature course, analyze the significance of setting in a short story.
   Thesis: William Faulkner's "A Rose for Emily" is set in the fictional town of Jefferson, Mississippi, a once-elegant town that is in decline.
5. *Assignment:* For a history course, describe the factors that led to the fall of the Achaemenid Empire.
   Thesis: Goverments that attempt to build far-flung empires will suffer the same fate as the Achaemenids.

Exercise 3.4 Thinking about your own thesis statements

Identify the thesis statements in two of your recent papers, and evaluate how well they meet the criteria for thesis statements given in the checklist on page 42. Freewrite about the process of arriving at a thesis in those papers: Did you start drafting your paper with a preliminary thesis? If not, would a working thesis have made it easier or harder to produce a first draft? At what point did you arrive at the final thesis? Did your thesis change over the course of several drafts?

3c Plan a structure that suits your assignment.

Many writers feel that they are more efficient when they know in advance how to develop their thesis and where to fit the information they have gathered. For some, that means organizing their notes into a sequence that makes sense. Others prefer to sketch out a list of ideas in a rough outline; still others prefer to prepare a formal outline.

Every paper needs the following components:

- A beginning, or **introduction,** that hooks the reader and usually states the thesis
- A middle, or **body,** that develops the main idea of the paper in a series of paragraphs—each making a point that is supported by specific details
- An ending, or **conclusion,** that gives the reader a sense of completion, often by offering a final comment on the thesis

1. Deciding on an organizational scheme

Give some thought to how you will lay out the body of the paper, using one or a combination of the following organizational schemes:

- **Chronological organization:** A chronological organization takes the reader through a series of events while explaining their significance to the thesis. A text that walks the reader scene by scene through a movie or play employs a chronological scheme, as does a biography or a case study. A survey of the literature for an informative report might also proceed chronologically, from the earliest to the most recent articles on a topic.
- **Problem-solution organization:** The problem-solution scheme is an efficient way to present a rationale for change. For example, an argument paper for a U.S. government course could explain the problems with electronic voting devices and then describe solutions for overcoming each difficulty.
- **Thematic organization:** A thematic structure takes the reader through a series of examples that build from simple to complex, from general to specific, or from specific to general. For example, in her paper about the *Migrations* exhibit, Diane Chen begins with a general discussion of Salgado's work and then focuses on one specific photograph.

TEXTCONNEX

Using Presentation Software as a Writing Process Tool

Presentation-software slides provide a useful tool for exploring and organizing your ideas before you start drafting. The slides also give you another way to get feedback from peer reviewers and others. Here are the steps to follow:

- Well before a paper is due, create a very brief, three- to five-slide presentation—with visuals if appropriate—that previews the key points you intend to make in the paper.
- Present the preview to an audience—friends, other students in the class, perhaps even the course instructor—and ask for suggestions for improvement.

2. Deciding on a type of outline

www.mhhe.com/mhhb2
For more on outlines, go to
Writing > Paragraph/Essay Development > Outlines

It is not essential to have an outline before you begin drafting, but a scratch outline can help you get started and keep you moving forward. After you have a first draft, outlining what you've written can help you spot organizational problems or places where the support for your thesis is weak.

A **scratch outline** is a simple list of points, without the levels of subordination that are found in more complex outlines. Scratch outlines are useful for briefer papers. Here is a scratch outline for Diane Chen's paper on the *Migrations* exhibit:

1. Photojournalism should be factual and informative, but it can be beautiful and artful too, as Salgado's *Migrations* exhibit illustrates.
2. The exhibit overall—powerful pictures of people uprooted, taken in 39 countries over 7 years. Salgado documents a global crisis: over 100 million displaced due to war, resource depletion, overpopulation, natural disasters, extreme poverty.
3. Specific picture—"Orphanage"—describe subjects, framing, lighting, emotions it evokes.
4. Salgado on the purpose of his photographs. Quote.

www.mhhe.com/mhhb2
For help with outlining, go to
Writing > Outlining Tutor

A **formal outline** classifies and divides the information you have gathered, showing main points, supporting ideas, and specific details by organizing them into levels of subordination. You may be required to include a formal outline for some assignments.

Formal outlines come in two types. A formal **topic outline** uses single words or phrases; a formal **sentence outline** states every idea in sentence form. Because the process of division always results in at least two parts, in a formal outline every I must have a II; every A, a B; and so on. Also, items placed at the same level must be of the same kind; for example, if I is London, then II can be New York City but not the Bronx or Wall Street. Items at the same level should also be grammatically parallel; for example, if A is "Choosing Screen Icons," then B can be "Creating Away Messages" but not "Away Messages."

Here are two outlines for Diane Chen's paper on the *Migrations* exhibit, a formal topic outline first, followed by a formal sentence outline:

FORMAL TOPIC OUTLINE

Thesis: Like a photojournalist, Salgado brings us images of newsworthy events, but he goes beyond objective reporting, imparting his compassion for refugees and migrants.

I. Sophistication of Salgado's photographs
II. Power of "Orphanage attached to the hospital" photo
    A. Three infant victims of Rwanda War
        1. Label: abstract statistics
        2. Photo: making abstractions real
    B. Documentary vividness and dramatic contrasts of black and white
        1. Black-and-white stripes of blankets
        2. White eyes and dark blankets
        3. Faces
            a. Heart-wrenching look of baby on left
            b. Startled look of baby in center
            c. Glazed and sickly look of baby on right
    C. Intimate vantage point
        1. A parent's perspective
        2. Stress on innocence and vulnerability
III. Salgado's ability to illustrate big issues with intimate images

FORMAL SENTENCE OUTLINE

Thesis: Like a photojournalist, Salgado brings us images of newsworthy events, but he goes beyond objective reporting, imparting his compassion for refugees and migrants.

I. The images in *Migrations,* an exhibit of his work, suggest that Salgado does more than simply point and shoot.
II. Salgado's photograph "Orphanage attached to the hospital at Kibumba, Number One Camp, Goma, Zaire" illustrates the power of his work.
    A. The photograph depicts three infants who are victims of the war in Rwanda.
        1. The label indicates that there are 4,000 orphans in the camp and 100,000 orphans overall.
        2. The numbers are abstractions that the photo makes real.
    B. Salgado's use of black and white gives the photo a documentary feel, but he also uses contrasts of light and dark to create a dramatic image of the babies.

      1. The vertical black-and-white stripes of the blanket direct viewers' eyes to the infants' faces and hands.
      2. The whites of the infants' eyes stand out against the darkness of the blankets.
      3. The camera's lens focuses sharply on the babies' faces, highlighting their expressions.
         a. The baby on the left has a heart-wrenching look.
         b. The baby in the center has a startled look.
         c. The baby on the right has a glazed and sunken look and appears to be near death.
   C. The vantage point of this photograph is one of a parent standing directly over his or her child.
      1. The infants seem to belong to the viewer.
      2. The photo is framed so that the babies take up the entire space, consuming the viewer with their innocence and vulnerability.
III. Salgado uses his artistic skill to get viewers to look closely at painful subjects, illustrating a big, complex topic with a collection of intimate, intensely moving images.

Tips LEARNING in COLLEGE

Formatting Rules for Formal Outlines

- Place the thesis statement at the beginning of the outline. It should not be numbered.
- Start the outline with the first body paragraph. Do not include the introduction or conclusion.
- For a topic outline, capitalize the first word of each new point and all proper nouns. Do not use periods to end each point.
- For a sentence outline, capitalize and punctuate each item as you would any sentence.
- Different styles of numbers and letters indicate levels of generality and importance, as in the examples on pages 48–49. Use capital Roman numerals (I, II, III) for each main point, capital letters (A, B, C) for each supporting idea, arabic numbers (1, 2, 3) for each specific detail, and lowercase letters (a, b, c) for parts of details. Place a period and a space after each number or letter.
- Indent consistently. Roman numerals should line up under the first letter in the thesis statement. Capital letters should line up under the first letter of the first word of the main point, and so on. See the example on page 48 for a model of outline format.

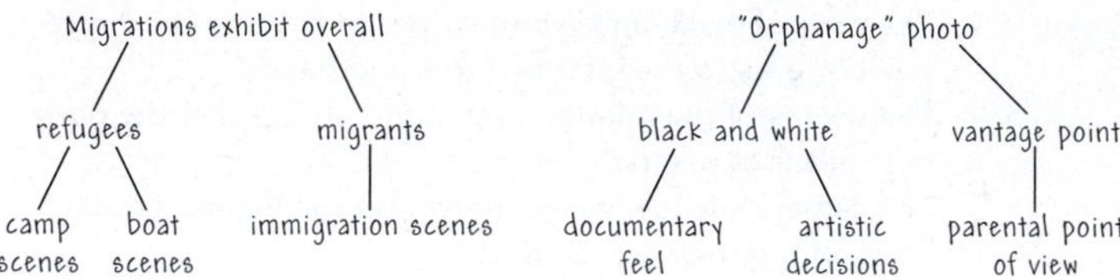

A **tree diagram** is a nonlinear method of planning your paper's organization. In a tree diagram (*see Figures 3.4 and 3.5*), you can see the relationship between topics and subtopics, but the sequence of topics is not specified. Tree diagrams are useful when you want to group ideas but prefer to make decisions about their sequence as you draft.

TEXTCONNEX

Formatting an Outline

Most word-processing software has a feature that will indent and number your outline automatically. Spend a little time investigating this feature before you attempt to set up a numbered outline so that the program can help rather than hinder your efforts.

Exercise 3.5 Shaping notes into an outline

Arrange the following items into a properly formatted formal topic outline, with several levels of subordination.

thesis: used with supervision, instant messaging can offer adolescents many advantages
build social ties
strengthen existing friendships
maintain long-distance relationships
chat with several friends simultaneously
extend social network
meet friends' friends
talk to new classmates
explore identity
create an online persona
pick screen icon
create screen name
experiment with multiple personas
adopt public screen name
assume private or secret screen name

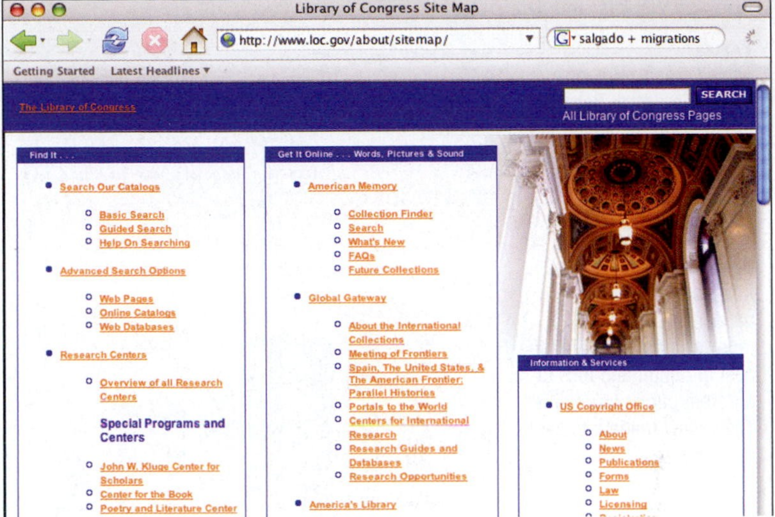

FIGURE 3.5 A site map. Site maps such as this one for the Library of

Exercise 3.6 Reflecting on your own work: Outlining

Generate an outline for one of your current assignments—before or after you write your first draft—and freewrite about your experiences. Were you able to generate an outline before you started drafting paragraphs? If so, did you stick with your outline, or did you deviate from it? What kind of outline are you most comfortable with? If you were not able to create an outline before you started drafting, why not?

3d Consider using visuals.

Visuals such as tables, charts, and graphs can clarify complex data or ideas. Effective visuals are used for a specific purpose, not for decoration, and each type of visual illustrates some kinds of material better than others. For example, compare the table and the line graph on page 52. Both present similar types of data, but does one strike you as clearer or more powerful than the other?

When you use photographs or illustrations, always credit your source, and be aware that most photographs and illustrations are protected by copyright. If you plan to use a photograph as part of a Web page, for example, you will usually need to obtain permission from the copyright holder. (*The credit information for most illustrations in this book appears in the Credits list at the back of the book.*)

Types of Visuals and Their Uses

Tables

Tables organize precise data for readers. Because the measurements in the example include decimals, it would be difficult to plot them on a graph.

Emissions from Waste (Tg CO_2 Eq.)

Gas/Source	1990	1995	2000	2001	2002	2003	2004	2005
CH_4	**185.8**	**182.2**	**158.3**	**153.5**	**156.2**	**160.5**	**157.8**	**157.4**
Landfills	161.0	157.1	131.9	127.6	130.4	134.9	132.1	132.0
Wastewater treatment	24.8	25.1	26.4	25.9	25.8	25.6	25.7	25.4
N_20	**6.4**	**6.9**	**7.6**	**7.6**	**7.7**	**7.8**	**7.9**	**8.0**
Domestic wastewater treatment	6.4	6.9	7.6	7.6	7.7	7.8	7.9	8.0
Total	**192.2**	**189.1**	**165.9**	**161.1**	**163.9**	**168.4**	**165.7**	**165.4**

Note: Totals may not sum due to independent rounding.
SOURCE: U.S. Environmental Protection Agency. *Inventory of U.S. Greenhouse Gas Emissions and Sinks: 1996-2005*. U.S. Environmental Protection Agency, 15 Apr. 2008. Web. 9 June 2008. p. 8-1.

Bar Graphs

Bar graphs highlight comparisons between two or more variables, such as the cost of tuition and fees at different public universities. They allow readers to see relative sizes quickly.

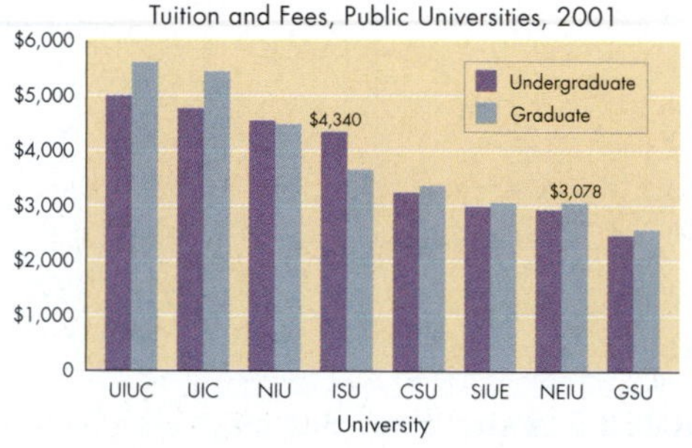

Pie Charts

Pie charts show the size of parts in relation to the whole. The segments must add up to 100% of something; differences in segment size must be significant; and there should not be too many segments.

Sources of Contamination Resulting in Warnings Posted Statewide in Year 2000 (Based on Beach Mile Days)

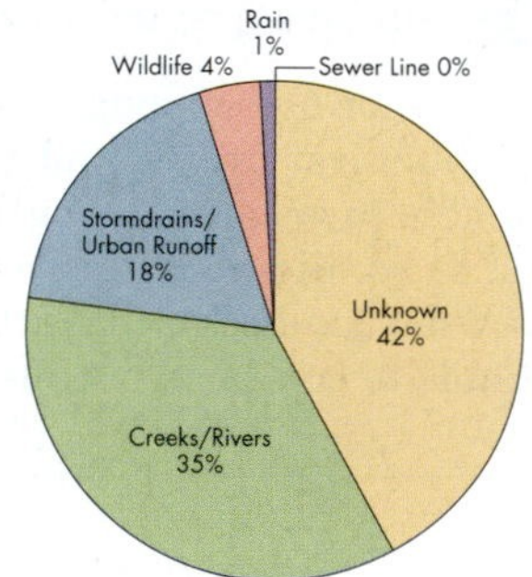

Line Graphs

Line graphs show changes in one or more variables over time. The example shows three sources of nitrous oxide emissions over a sixteen-year period.

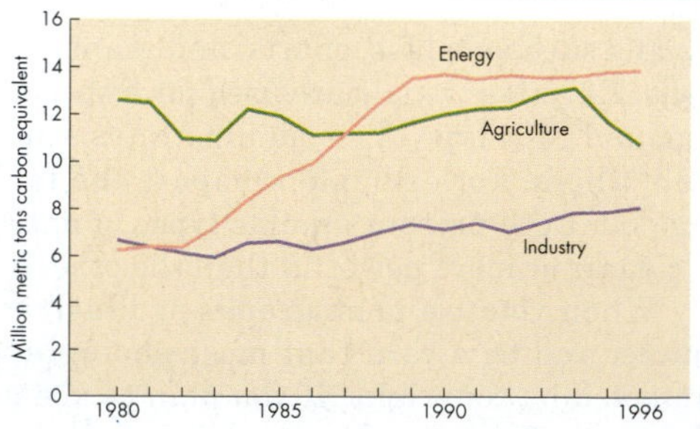

Diagrams
Diagrams show processes or structures visually. Common in technical writing, they include time lines, organization charts, and decision trees. The example shows the factors involved in the decision to commit a burglary.

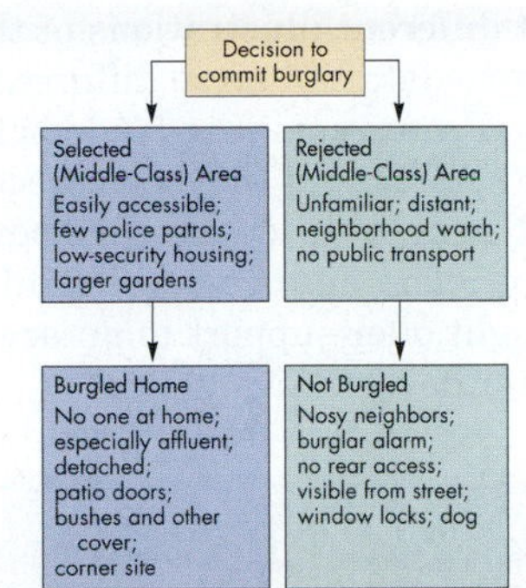

Photos
Photos can reinforce your point by showing readers what your subject actually looks like or how it has been affected. This image could support a portrayal of Kurt Cobain as a talented but conflicted artist.

Maps
Maps highlight locations and spatial relationships, and they show relationships between ideas. This one shows the size of Hurricane Frances when it struck the United States in 2004.

Illustrations
Like photographs, illustrations make a point dramatically. (*See p. 192 for more about this image.*)

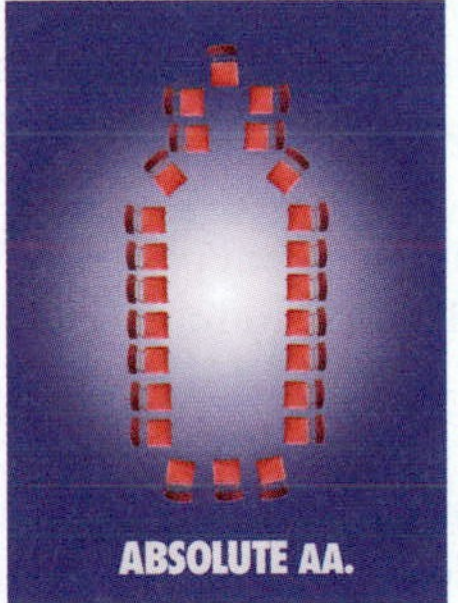

A complete directory of visual rhetoric resources in this text appears in the back of the book following the Index for Multilingual Writers.

Note that different illustrations of the same subject or charts depicting the same data can serve different purposes. The satellite image of Hurricane Frances on page 53 depicts the storm's size and the region affected; the photos of the area affected by Hurricane Katrina (*p. 9 in Chapter 1*) convey the destructive power of the storm and the progress of recovery. The map serves an informative purpose, whereas the photos might offer support to an argument about funding rebuilding efforts after devastating storms.

TEXTCONNEX

Preparing Pie Charts

Several types of computer programs allow you to create pie charts. When you insert a pie chart in PowerPoint 2007, for example, you will see a premade slide. Change the title and size of each section by deleting the text in the spreadsheet that is displayed along with the pie chart and typing in your own numbers and category labels.

Caution: Because the use of visual elements is more accepted in some fields than in others, you may want to ask your instructor for advice before planning to include visuals in your composition.

Exercise 3.7 Using visuals

For each of the following kinds of information, decide which type of visual would be most effective. (You do not need to prepare the visual itself.)

1. For an education paper, show the percentage of teaching time per week devoted to math, language arts, science, social studies, world languages, art, music, and physical education using a ______________________.
2. For a business paper, show the gross domestic product (GDP) for ten leading industrial countries over a five-year period using a ______________________.
3. For a criminal justice paper, compare the incidence of three different types of crime in one precinct during a three-month period using a ______________________.
4. For a health paper, chart the number of new cases of AIDS in North America and Africa over a ten-year period in order to show which continent has had the greater increase using a ______________________.

4 Drafting Paragraphs and Visuals

Except during an exam, you will usually refine your essay by working through several drafts. (*See Chapter 5: Revising and Editing, for an example of a paper in successive drafts.*) Think of your first draft as an attempt to discover a beginning, a middle, and an end for what you have to say. Avoid putting pressure on yourself to make it perfect the first time through.

This chapter offers strategies for developing paragraphs, the building blocks of a composition. It will also help you decide when to use visuals to present information and what kinds of visuals suit different purposes. In Chapter 5, we will look at strategies for revising your work. Keep in mind, though, that you may move back and forth between drafting and revising.

4a Use electronic tools for drafting.

www.mhhe.com/mhhb2

For more on drafting and revising, go to

Writing > Paragraph/Essay Development > Drafting and Revising

If you did not set up a folder for your paper as you were researching and generating ideas, be sure to do so now. Use the following tips:

1. **Save your work.** Always protect your drafts from power surges and other acts of technological treachery. Save often, and make backups.
2. **Label revised drafts with different file names.** Use a different file name for each successive version of your paper. For example, Diane Chen saved drafts of her paper as Migrations1, Migrations2, Migrations3, and so on.
3. **Print hard copies early and often.** If you save and print the original, you can feel free to experiment.

TEXTCONNEX

Using Hypertext as a Writing Process Tool

A variety of links in your essays can help you during the writing process. For example, you might include a link to additional research, to a source that refutes an argument, or to interesting information that is not directly relevant to the primary subject. These links can help you refer to supplemental material without undermining the coherence of the text. If a reader of an early draft—an instructor or a colleague—thinks the linked material should be in the essay itself, you can include it in the next draft.

LEARNING in COLLEGE

Avoiding Writer's Block

Do not put off writing the first draft. If you find it difficult to get started, consider the tips below.

1. **Resist the temptation to be a perfectionist.** The poet William Stafford said, "There's no such thing as writer's block for writers whose standards are low enough." Reserve your high standards for the revising and editing stages of your paper. For your first draft, do not worry about getting the right word, the stylish phrase, or even the correct spelling.
2. **Take it "bird by bird."** Writer Anne Lamott counsels students to break down writing assignments into manageable units and then make a commitment to finishing each unit in one session. She passes along her father's advice to her brother, who had procrastinated on a report about birds and was frozen by the enormity of the project: "Bird by bird, buddy. Just take it bird by bird."
3. **Start anywhere.** If you are stuck on the beginning, pick a section where you have a clearer sense of what you want to say. You can go back later and work out the transitions. Writers often compose the introduction after drafting a complete text.
4. **Generate more ideas.** If you are drawing a blank, you may need to do more reading, research, or brainstorming. Be careful, though, not to use reading and research as a stalling tactic.
5. **Set aside time and work in a quiet place.** Make sure you have somewhere you can work undisturbed for at least half an hour at a stretch.

www.mhhe.com/mhhb2

For more on paragraph unity, go to

Writing > Paragraph/Essay Development > Unity

4b Write focused paragraphs.

A **paragraph** is a set of sentences that develop an idea or example in support of the thesis. In academic papers, paragraphs are usually four or more sentences long, allowing for the detailed development of your ideas. Paragraphs break the text into blocks for your readers, allowing them to see how your essay builds step by step. A paragraph indent of one-half inch is typical in academic writing. In business writing and publishing, a line space above the paragraph serves instead. When writing for the Web, use very short paragraphs, and place links at the ends of paragraphs to ensure readers read all of the text.

1. Focusing on one main point or example

In a strong paragraph, the sentences form a unit that explores one main point or elaborates on one main example. When you are drafting, start a new paragraph when you introduce a new reason that supports your thesis, a new step in a process, or a new element in an analysis. New paragraphs also signal shifts in time and place, changing speakers in dialogue, contrasts with earlier material, and changes in level of emphasis. The paragraphs in your first draft may not all be perfectly unified, and you will likely need to revise for paragraph unity later on (*see Chapter 5: Revising and Editing*). However, bear in mind as you draft that a paragraph develops a main point or example.

The paragraph in the following example focuses on a theory that the writer will refer to later in his essay. The main idea is highlighted:

> Current thinking on the topic of loss and mourning rests on foundations constructed by the British psychiatrist John Bowlby. Using examples from animal and human behavior, Bowlby (1977) posited "attachment theory" as a means of understanding the powerful bonds between humans and the disruption that comes when the bonds are jeopardized or destroyed. The bonds are formed because of a need for security and safety, are developed early in life, are long enduring, and are directed toward a few special individuals. In normal maturation, the child becomes ever more independent, moving away from the figure of attachment, and returning periodically for safety and security. If the bonds are threatened, the individual will try to restore them through crying, clinging, or other types of coercion; if they are destroyed, withdrawal, apathy, and despair will follow.
>
> —JONATHAN FAST, "After Columbine: How People Mourn Sudden Death"

The main idea is introduced in the highlighted sentences.

Details of attachment theory are developed in the rest of the paragraph.

2. Signaling the main idea of your paragraph with a topic sentence

A **topic sentence** can be a helpful starting point as you draft a paragraph. In the paragraph below, the topic sentence (highlighted) provides the writer with a launching point for a series of details:

> The excavation also revealed dramatic evidence for the commemorative rituals that took place after the burial. Four cattle had been decapitated and their skulls symbolically placed in a ditch enclosing the burial pit. In the soil above the skulls archaeologists found the butchered bones of at least 250 slaughtered cattle, evidence for a huge ceremonial feast. Clearly this was an expensive way to commemorate a leader. Indeed, the huge quantity of meat suggests that the entire tribe may have gathered at the grave to take part in a ritual feast. Perhaps this was one way the bonds between scattered communities were strengthened.
>
> —DAMIAN ROBINSON, "Riding into the Afterlife"

The topic sentence announces that the paragraph will focus on a certain kind of evidence.

Sometimes the sentences in a paragraph will lead to a unifying conclusion, a form of topic sentence, as in this example:

> Table 1 presents the 15 mechanisms for gaining prestige that were reported for girls and for boys. There were few differences in the avenues to prestige between those in public and private high schools, particularly for girls. Avenues to prestige for girls that focus on their physical attributes, such as attractiveness, popularity with boys, clothes, sexual activity, and participation in sports, were more prominent in public schools than in private schools. In private schools the avenues more indicative of personality attributes, such as general sociability, having a good reputation/virginity, and participating in school clubs/government and cheerleading, were more prominent. Contrary to what parents may expect, avenues considered to be more negative, such as partying and being class clown, appeared more prevalent in private schools than in public schools. However, only clothes remained a significantly more important route to prestige for girls in public schools compared to girls in private schools once controls were introduced for region, size of community, year of graduation, and gender of respondent. Thus, taken together, type of high school had little effect on the ways in which girls accrued prestige in high school.
>
> —J. Jill Suitor, Rebecca Powers, and Rachel Brown, "Avenues to Prestige among Adolescents"

If a topic sentence would simply state the obvious, it can be omitted. In the following example, it is not necessary to state that the paragraph is about Igor Stravinsky's early life:

> Stravinsky was born in Russia, near St. Petersburg, grew up in a musical atmosphere, and studied with Nikolai Rimsky-Korsakov. He had his first important opportunity in 1909, when the great impresario Sergei Diaghilev heard his music.
>
> —Roger Kamien, *Music: An Appreciation*

Exercise 4.1 Paragraph unity

Underline the topic sentences in the following paragraphs. If there is no topic sentence, state the main idea.

1. Based on the results of this study, it appears that a substantial amount of bullying by both students and teachers may be occurring in college. Over 60% of the students reported having observed a student being bullied by another student, and

over 44% had seen a teacher bully a student. More than 6% of the students reported having been bullied by another student occasionally or very frequently, and almost 5% reported being bullied by a teacher occasionally or very frequently, while over 5% of the students stated that they bullied students occasionally or very frequently.

—MARK CHAPELL ET AL., "Bullying in College by Students and Teachers"

2. ARS [the Agricultural Research Service] launched the first areawide IPM [Integrated Pest Management] attacks against the codling moth, a pest in apple and pear orchards, on 7,700 acres in the Pacific Northwest. Other programs include a major assault against the corn rootworm on over 40,000 acres in the Corn Belt, fruit flies in the Hawaiian Islands, and leafy spurge in the Northern Plains area. In 2001, an areawide IPM project began for fire ants in Florida, Mississippi, Oklahoma, South Carolina, and Texas on pastures using natural enemies, microbial pesticides, and attracticides.

—ROBERT FAUST, "Integrated Pest Management Programs Strive to Solve Agricultural Problems"

4c Write paragraphs that have a clear organization.

The sentences in your final draft need to be clearly related to one another. As you are drafting, make connections among your ideas and information as a way of moving your writing forward. One way to make your ideas work together is to organize them using one of the common organizational schemes for paragraphs. (*For advice on using repetition, pronouns, and transitions to relate sentences to one another, see Chapter 5.*)

1. Developing a chronological or spatial organization

The sentences in a paragraph with a **chronological organization** describe a series of events, steps, or observations as they occur in time: this happened, then that, and so on. The sentences in a paragraph with a **spatial organization** present details as they appear to a viewer: from top to bottom, outside to inside, east to west, and so on. In the following example, the authors use a chronological organization to describe how they found research subjects for their study:

First step

Recruitment of students with ADHD and their teachers occurred through two mechanisms. The first mechanism

> involved making initial contact with school systems and/or principals to determine potential interest for participation. Contacts were made with administrators (principals, special education directors, or superintendents) from school systems in the Boston suburban area. Approximately half of the contacted school systems expressed initial interest in participating. The principal investigator described the study at faculty meetings at the schools within each system to solicit the participation of teachers. To protect against potential confounds (i.e., differences between teachers who agreed and did not agree to participate), all teachers in each school had to agree to participate for the school to be included in the study. Approximately 85% of schools agreed to participate after hearing the project described.
>
> —Ross Greene et al., "Are Students with ADHD More Stressful to Teach?"

Result of first step

Second step

Result of second step

You can see an example of spatial organization in paragraphs 5–7 of Diane Chen's student paper about Sebastião Salgado, on pages 102–03.

2. Developing a general-to-specific organization

As we have seen, paragraphs often start with a general topic sentence that states the main idea and then proceed with specifics that elaborate on that idea. The general topic sentence can include a question that the paragraph then answers or a problem that the paragraph goes on to solve. A variation of the general-to-specific organization includes a **limiting sentence** that seems to oppose the main idea. This structure allows you to bring in a different perspective on the main idea but then go on to defend it with specific examples, as in this paragraph:

> Parents do not have the moral right to make decisions for their children simply because of their status as parents. This idea may seem to go against our basic understanding of how families should operate. However, there are a number of actual cases that illustrate the weaknesses in the argument for absolute parental rights. [*The following paragraphs present a series of examples.*]
>
> —Sheila Foster, "Limiting Parental Rights," student paper

General topic sentence

Limiting sentence

Specifics

3. Developing a specific-to-general organization

Putting the general topic sentence at the end of the paragraph, preceded by the specific details leading up to that general conclusion, is especially effective when you are preparing your reader for a revelation. The following example is a variation on this organization;

the paragraph begins and ends with general statements that offer an interpretive framework:

> Even the subtlest details of Goya's portrait convey tension between revealing and concealing, between public and private personae. Dona Josefa's right eye avoids our gaze while her left eye engages it. Half of her ear is revealed while half is obscured by her hair. Above the sitter's arms, her torso faces us directly; her legs, however, turn away from us toward the left. The closed fan that Dona Josefa holds atop her stomach, pointed toward her enclosed womb, seems a mere trapping of formality in an otherwise informal setting. The fan reminds viewers that though we intrude on a private domain, Dona Josefa remains aware that she is indeed receiving company. Thus while our glimpse of her is, in many ways, an intimate one, Goya never allows us to forget that through the act of portraiture, this private self is being brought into the social sphere—and that our voyeurism has not gone unnoticed.
>
> —BAZ DREISINGER, "The Private Made Public: Goya's *Josefa Castilla Portugal de Garcini y Wanasbrok*," student paper

Introductory general statement

Specific details

Concluding general statement

4. Developing other organizational schemes

Many other methods of organizing paragraphs are available. These include the problem-solution scheme, in which the topic sentence defines an issue and the rest of the paragraph presents a solution (*discussed in Chapter 3, p. 46, as it applies to entire essays*). Other schemes include simple to complex, most familiar to least familiar, and least important to most important.

Exercise 4.2 Paragraph organization

Go back to the paragraphs in Exercise 4.1 (*pp. 58–59*) and identify the organizational strategy used in each one.

4d Develop ideas and use visuals strategically.

When you develop ideas, you give your writing texture and depth as well as provide support for your thesis. Depending on the purpose of your text, you may use a few of these strategies or a mix of all of them. Photographs and other kinds of visuals can also support your ideas. Keep in mind, though, that visuals should always serve the overall purpose of your work. (*See 3d, pp. 51–54, for more on types of visuals and their purposes.*)

www.mhhe.com/mhhb2
For more information on developing paragraphs, go to **Writing > Paragraph Patterns**

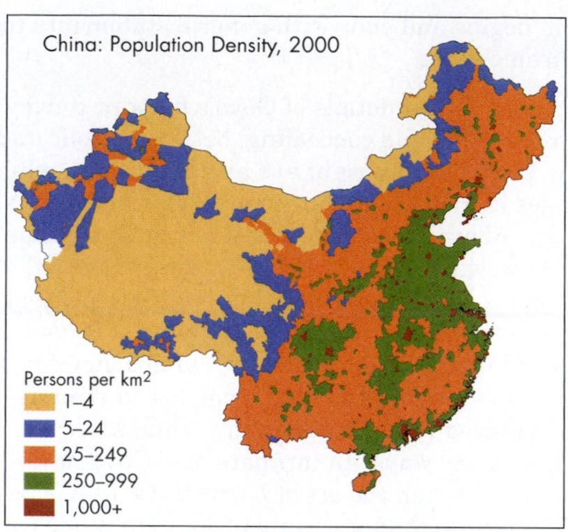

FIGURE 4.1 Visuals that illustrate. This map illustrates the population densities in various regions of China in the year 2000.

1. Illustration

To appeal to readers, you often have to show as well as tell. Detailed examples (and well-chosen visuals—see Figure 4.1) can make abstractions more concrete and generalizations more specific, as the following paragraph shows:

> As Rubin explains, "for much of the Accord era, the ideal-typical family . . . was composed of a 'stay-at-home-mom,' a working father, and dependent children. He earned wages; she cooked, cleaned, cared for the home, managed the family's social life, and nurtured the family members" (97). Just such an arrangement characterized my grandmother's married life. My grandmother, who had four children, stayed at home with them, while her husband went off to work as a safety engineer. Sadly, when he died, she was left with nothing. She needed to support herself, yet had no work experience, no credit, and little education. But even though society frowned on her for seeking employment, my grandmother eventually found a clerical position—a low-level job with few perks.
>
> —JENNIFER KOEHLER, "Women's Work in the United States: The 1950s and 1990s"

www.mhhe.com/mhhb2

For help with the use of illustration, go to

Writing > Writing Tutors > Exemplification

Caution: Although any image you choose to include in your paper will be illustrative, images should not function merely as decoration. Ask yourself whether each image you are considering truly adds information to your text.

FIGURE 4.2 Visuals that narrate. Using images that narrate can be a powerful way to reinforce a message or portray events you discuss in your paper. Images like this one help tell one of many stories about the war in Iraq.

2. Narration

When you narrate, you tell a story. (*See Figure 4.2 for an example of a narrative visual.*) The following paragraph comes from a personal essay on the goods that result from "a lifetime of production":

> My dad changed too. He had come to that job feeling—as I do now—that everything was still possible. He'd served his time in the air force during the Korean War. Then, while my mother worked as a secretary to support them, he earned a college degree courtesy of the GI Bill. After graduation, my father painted houses for a season until he was offered a position scheduling the production of corrugated board. He took it, though he has told me that he never planned to stay. It was not something he envisioned as his life's work. I try to imagine what it is like suddenly to look up from a stack of orders and discover that the job you started one December day has watched you age.
>
> —MICHELLE M. DUCHARME, "A Lifetime of Production"

Notice that Ducharme begins with two sentences that state the topic and point of her narration. Then, using the past tense, she recounts in chronological sequence some key events that led to her father's taking a job in the box manufacturing business.

www.mhhe.com/mhhb2
For help with use of narration, go to
Writing > Writing Tutors > Narration

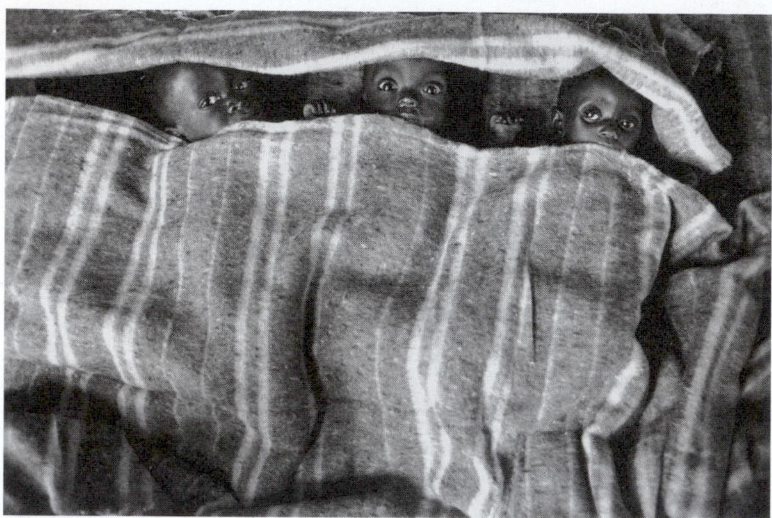

FIGURE 4.3 Visuals that describe. Pay attention to the effect your selection will have on your paper. This photograph by Sebastião Salgado appeals to the viewer's emotions, evoking sympathy for the refugee children's plight.

www.mhhe.com/mhhb2
For help with the use of description, go to
Writing > Writing Tutors > Description

3. Description

To make an object, a person, or an activity vivid for your readers, describe it in concrete, specific words that appeal to the senses of sight, sound, taste, smell, and touch. In the following example, Diane Chen describes her impression of the photograph in Figure 4.3:

> The vertical black-and-white stripes of the blanket direct our eyes to the infants' faces and hands, which are framed by a horizontal white stripe. The whites of their eyes in particular stand out against the darkness created by the shell of the blankets. The camera's lens also seems to be in sharper focus on the faces than on the blankets, again drawing our attention to the babies' expressions.
>
> —DIANE CHEN, "The Caring Eye of Sebastião Salgado," student paper

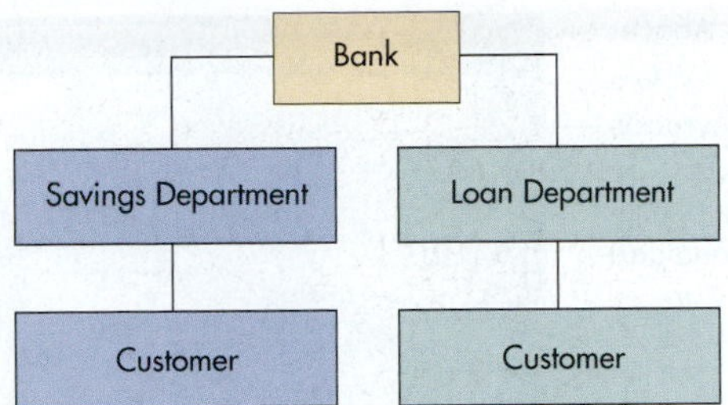

FIGURE 4.4 Visuals that classify or divide. An image can help you make the categories in or parts of complex systems or organizations easier to understand. The image shown here, for example, helps readers comprehend the structure of a business.

4. Classification

Classification is a useful way of grouping individual entities into identifiable categories (*see Figure 4.4*). Classifying occurs in all academic disciplines and often appears with its complement—**division,** which breaks a whole entity into its parts. **Analysis** interprets the meaning and importance of these parts.

www.mhhe.com/mhhb2
For help with the use of classification, go to
Writing > Writing Tutors > Classification

> [M]ost of America's traditional, routinized manufacturing jobs will disappear. So will routinized service jobs that can be done from remote locations, like keypunching of data transmitted by satellite. Instead, you will be engaged in one of two broad categories of work: either complex services, some of which will be sold to the rest of the world to pay for whatever Americans want to buy from the rest of the world, or person-to-person services, which foreigners can't provide for us because (apart from new immigrants and illegal aliens) they aren't here to provide them.
>
> Complex services involve the manipulation of data and abstract symbols. Included in this category are insurance, engineering, law, finance, computer programming, and advertising. Such activities now account for almost 25 percent of our GNP, up from 13 percent in 1950. They have already surpassed manufacturing (down to about 20 percent of GNP). Even *within* the manufacturing sector, executive, managerial, and engineering positions are increasing at a rate almost three times that of total manufacturing employment. Most of these jobs, too, involve manipulating symbols.
>
> —Robert Reich, "The Future of Work"

To make his ideas clear, Reich first classifies future work into two broad categories: complex services and person-to-person services. Then in the next paragraph, he develops the idea of complex services in more detail, in part by dividing that category into more specific—and familiar—categories like engineering and advertising.

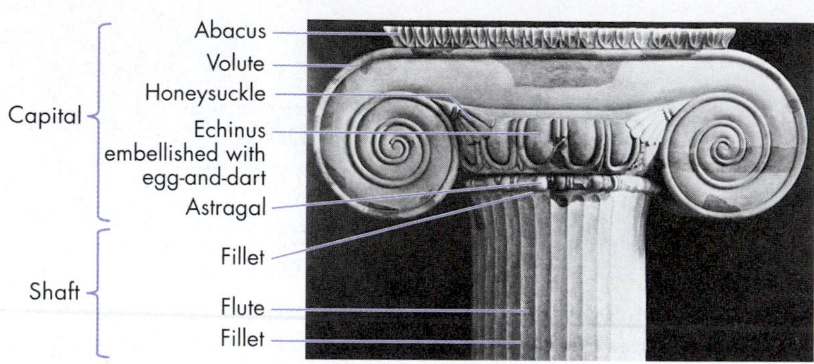

FIGURE 4.5 Visuals that define. Visuals can be extremely effective when used to support a written definition or to identify parts of a whole. This image uses labels and leader lines to identify the characteristics of an Ionic column, an example of one of the five orders of classical architecture.

www.mhhe.com/mhhb2
For help with the use of definition, go to
Writing > Writing Tutors > Definition

5. Definition

You should define any concepts that the reader must understand to follow your ideas. (*See Figure 4.5 for an example of the use of a visual to define.*) Interpretations and arguments often depend on one or two key ideas that cannot be quickly and easily defined. In the following example, John Berger defines "image," a key idea in his televised lectures on the way we see things:

> An image is a sight which has been recreated or reproduced. It is an appearance, or a set of appearances, which has been detached from the place and time in which it first made its appearance and preserved—for a few moments or centuries. Every image embodies a way of seeing. Even a photograph. For photographs are not, as is often assumed, a mechanical record. Every time we look at a photograph, we are aware, however slightly, of the photographer selecting that sight from an infinity of other possible sights. This is true even in the most casual family snapshot. The photographer's way of seeing is reflected in his choice of subject.
>
> —JOHN BERGER, *Ways of Seeing*

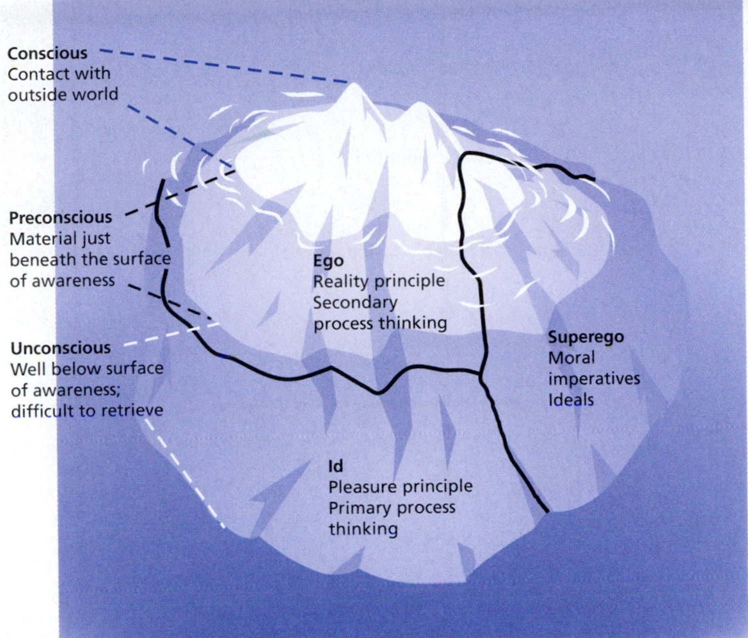

FIGURE 4.6 Visuals as analogies. Visual analogies operate in the same way as written analogies. This figure uses the image of an iceberg to illustrate Freud's theory of the unconscious. The portion of the iceberg below the surface of the water represents the preconscious and unconscious mind.

6. Analogy

An **analogy** compares topics that at first glance seem quite different (*see Figure 4.6*). A well-chosen analogy can make unfamiliar or technical information seem more commonplace and understandable.

> The human eye provides a good starting point for learning how a camera works. The lens of the eye is like the *lens* of the camera. In both instruments the lens focuses an image of the surroundings on a *light-sensitive surface*—the *retina* of the eye and the *film* in the camera. In both, the light-sensitive material is protected within a light-tight container—the *eyeball* of the eye and the *body* of the camera. Both eye and camera have a mechanism for shutting off light passing through the lens to the interior of the container—the *lid* of the eye and the *shutter* of the camera. In both, the size of the lens opening, or *aperture*, is regulated by an *iris diaphragm*.
>
> —Marvin Rosen, *Introduction to Photography*

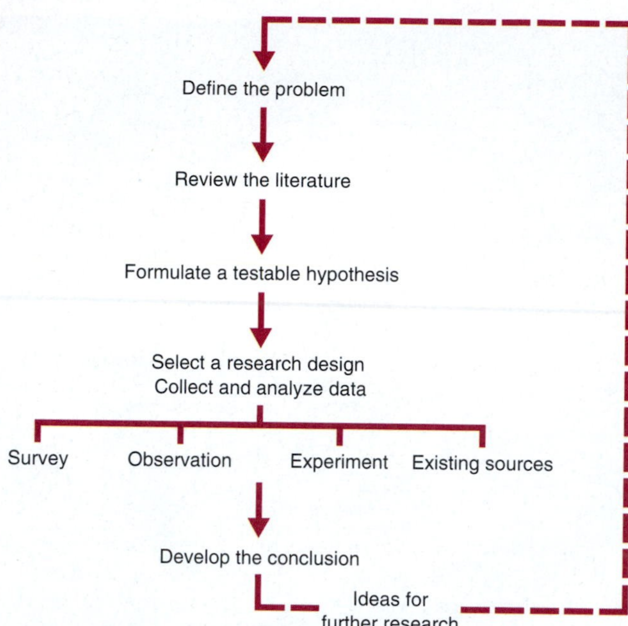

FIGURE 4.7 Visuals that show a process. Flow charts and diagrams are especially useful when illustrating a process. This one shows the scientific method used in disciplines throughout the sciences and social sciences.

www.mhhe.com/mhhb2
For help with describing a process, go to
Writing > Writing Tutors > Process Analysis

7. Process

To explain how to do something or show readers how something is done, you use process analysis (*see Figure 4.7*), explaining each step of the process in chronological order, as in the following example:

> To end our Hawan ritual of thanks, *aarti* is performed. First, my mother lights a piece of camphor in a metal plate called a *taree*. Holding the taree with her right hand, she moves the fire in a circular, clockwise movement in front of the altar. Next, she stands in front of my father and again moves the fiery *taree* in a circular, clockwise direction. After touching his feet and receiving his blessing, she attends to each of us children in turn, moving the fire in a clockwise direction before kissing us, one by one. When she is done, my father performs his *aarti* in a similar way, and then my sister and I do ours. When everyone is done, we say some prayers and sit down.
>
> —U. Roopnarian, "Family Rituals," student paper

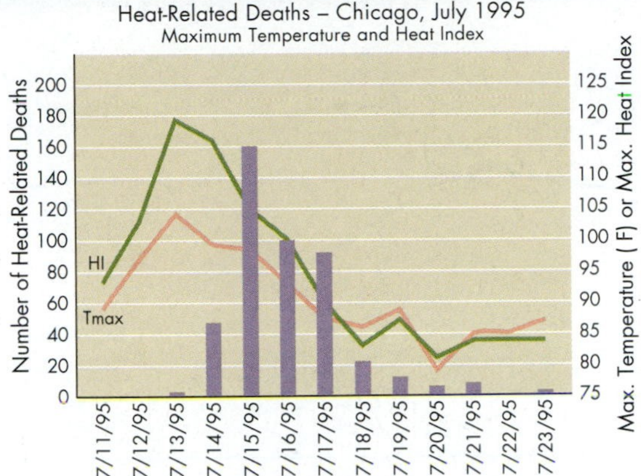

This graph tracks maximum temperature (Tmax), heat index (HI), and heat-related deaths in Chicago each day from July 11 to 23, 1995. The orange line shows maximum daily temperature, the green line shows the heat index, and the bars indicate number of deaths for the day.

FIGURE 4.8 Visuals that show cause and effect. Visuals can provide powerful evidence when you are writing about causes and effects. Although graphs like this one may seem self-explanatory, you still need to analyze and interpret them for your readers.

www.mhhe.com/mhhb2
For more information on how to work with visuals, go to
Writing > Visual Rhetoric Tutorial > Understanding Images

8. Cause and effect

Use a cause-and-effect strategy when you need to trace the causes of some event or situation, to describe its effects, or both (*see Figure 4.8*). In the following example, Rajeev Bector explains the reasons for a character's feelings and actions in a short story:

www.mhhe.com/mhhb2
For help analyzing cause and effect, go to
Writing > Writing Tutors > Causal Analysis

> Given the differences between Mrs. Chestny's and her son's values, as well as the oppressiveness of Mrs. Chestny's racist views, we can understand why Julian struggles to "teach" his mother "a lesson" (185) throughout the entire bus ride. Goffman would point out that "each individual is engaged in providing evidence to establish a definition of himself at the expense of what can remain for the other" (29). But in the end, neither character wins the contest. Julian's mother loses her sense of self when she is pushed down to the ground by a "colored woman" wearing a hat identical to hers (187). Faced with his mother's breakdown, Julian feels his own identity being overwhelmed by "the world of guilt and sorrow."
>
> —Rajeev Bector, "The Character Contest in Flannery O'Connor's 'Everything That Rises Must Converge,'" student paper

> ***Caution:*** When you use graphs or other visuals to summarize numeric data or show possible causal relationships, be sure to discuss the visuals in the body of your text.

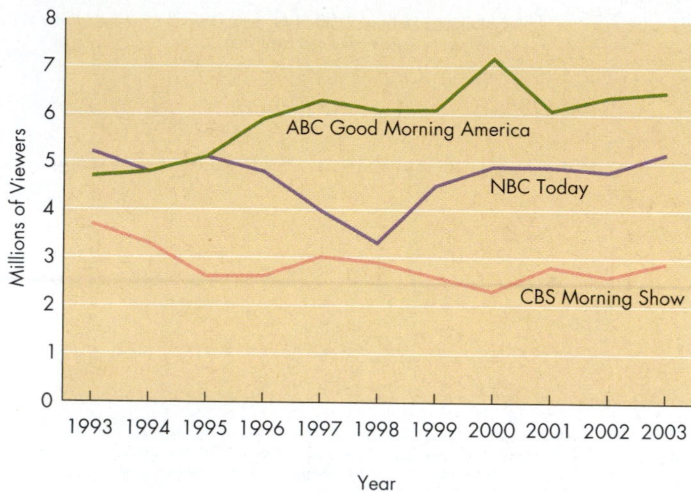

FIGURE 4.9 Visuals that compare and contrast. Graphs and charts are effective ways of comparing parallel sets of data. This line graph tracks the population of viewers for the three most popular morning shows over ten years.

www.mhhe.com/mhhb2

For help with the use of comparison and contrast, go to

Writing > Writing Tutors > Comparison/Contrast

9. Comparison and contrast

When you *compare*, you explore the similarities and differences among various items. When used with the term *contrast*, however, *compare* has a narrower meaning: "to spell out key similarities." *Contrast* always means "to itemize important differences." (*See Figure 4.9.*)

In the following example, the student writer uses a **subject-by-subject** pattern to contrast the ideas of two social commentators, Jeremy Rifkin and George Will:

> Rifkin and Will have different opinions about unemployment due to downsizing and the widening income gap between rich and poor. Rifkin sees both the decrease in employment and the increase in income disparity as evils that must be immediately dealt with lest society fall apart: "If no measures are taken to provide financial opportunities for millions of Americans in an era of diminishing jobs, then . . . violent crime is going to increase" (3). Will, on the other hand, seems to believe that both unemployment and income differences are necessary to the health of American society. Will writes, "A society that chafes against stratification derived from disparities of talents will be a society that discourages individual talents" (92). Apparently, the society that Rifkin wants is just the kind of society that Will rejects.
>
> —JACOB GROSSMAN, "Dark Comes before Dawn," student paper

Notice that Grossman comments on Rifkin first and then turns to his second subject, George Will. To ensure paragraph unity, he begins with a topic sentence that mentions both subjects.

In the following paragraph, the student writer organizes her comparison of two photographs **point by point** rather than subject by subject. Instead of saying everything about Smith's picture before commenting on the Associated Press (AP) photo, the writer moves back and forth between the two images as she makes and supports two points: first, that the images differ in figure and scene and second, that they are similar in theme.

> Divided by an ocean, two photographers took pictures that at first glance seem absolutely different. W. Eugene Smith's well-known *Tomoko in the Bath* and the less well-known AP photo *A Paratrooper Works to Save the Life of a Buddy* portray distinctively different settings and people. Smith brings us into a darkened room where a Japanese woman is lovingly bathing her malformed child, while the AP staff photographer captures two soldiers on the battlefield, one intently performing CPR on his wounded friend. But even though the two images seem as different as women and men, peace and war, or life and death, both pictures show something similar: a time of suffering. It is the early 1970s—a time when the hopes and dreams that modernity promoted are being exposed as deadly to human beings. Perhaps that is why the bodies in both pictures seem humbled. Grief pulls you down onto your knees. Terror impels you to crawl along the ground.
>
> —ILONA BOUZOUKASHVILI, "On Reading Photographs," student paper

Exercise 4.3 Developing ideas

Experiment with the development strategies just discussed— illustration, narration, description, classification, definition, analogy, process, cause and effect, and comparison and contrast—in a paper you are currently drafting. Are some strategies inappropriate to your assignment? Have you combined any of the strategies in a single paragraph?

4e Integrate visuals effectively.

If you decide to use a table, chart, diagram, or photograph, keep this general advice in mind:

1. **Number and label tables and other figures** consecutively throughout your paper: Table 1, Table 2, and so on. Do not abbreviate *Table*. *Figure* may be abbreviated as *Fig*.

www.mhhe.com/mhhb2
For an interactive tutorial on using visuals, go to
Writing > Visual Rhetoric Tutorial > Document Design

2. **Refer to the visual element in your text** before it appears, placing the visual as close as possible to the text in which you state why you are including it. If your project contains many visuals or complex tables, you may want to group them in an appendix. Always refer to a visual by its label: for example, "See Fig. 1."
3. **Give each visual a title or caption** that clearly explains what the visual shows. A visual with its caption should be clear without the discussion in the text, and the discussion of the visual in the text should be clear without the visual itself.
4. **Include explanatory notes below the visuals.** If you want to explain a specific element within the visual, use a superscript *letter* (not a number) both after the specific element and before the note. The explanation should appear directly beneath the graphic, not at the foot of the page or at the end of your paper. Do not use your word processor's Insert/Footnote commands to create the footnote because the program will put the note in the wrong place.
5. **Credit sources for visuals.** If you use a visual element from a source, be sure to credit the source. Unless you have specific guidelines to follow, you can use the word *Source*, followed by a colon and complete documentation of the source, including the author, title, publication information, and page number if applicable.

Note: The Modern Language Association (MLA) and the American Psychological Association (APA) provide guidelines for figure captions and crediting sources of visuals that differ from the previous guidelines (*see Chapter 23: MLA Documentation Style, pp. 341–90, and Chapter 24: APA Documentation Style, pp. 391–410*).

www.mhhe.com/mhhb2
For more information on crafting introductions, go to
Writing > Paragraph/Essay Development > Introductions

4f Craft an introduction that establishes your purpose.

As you begin your first draft, you may want to skip the introduction and start by writing the body of your paper. After your paper has taken shape, you can then go back and sketch out the main ideas for your introduction.

For most types of compositions, your opening paragraph or paragraphs will include your thesis statement. If your thesis has changed in the course of writing your first draft, adjust it as necessary.

An introduction that begins with broad assertions and then narrows the focus to conclude with the thesis is called a **funnel opener.** If your purpose is analytic, however, you may prefer to build up to your thesis, placing it near the end of the paper. Some types of writing, such as narratives, may not require an explicitly stated thesis if the main idea is obvious without it.

Focus on presenting the main ideas of your introduction in a way that will hook readers. Because the introduction establishes your credibility, avoid either understating or overstating your authority ("I'm not completely sure about this, but . . ."; "As an expert on the topic, I think . . ."). Instead, encourage readers to share your view of the topic's importance. An introduction that begins by referring to the paper title or that baldly states "The purpose of my essay is . . ." could benefit from a more creative approach. Here are some opening strategies:

- Tell a brief story related to the question your thesis answers.
- Begin with a relevant and attention-getting quotation.
- Begin with a paraphrase of a commonly held view that you immediately question.
- State a working hypothesis.
- Define a key term, but avoid the tired opener that begins "According to the dictionary. . . ."
- Pose an important question.

The following paragraphs from an informative essay begin with an attention-getting fact, followed by a definition of key terms, a key question, and a working hypothesis:

> Every year huge rotating storms packing winds greater than 74 miles per hour sweep across tropical seas and onto shorelines—often devastating large swaths of territory. When these roiling tempests—called hurricanes in the Atlantic and the eastern Pacific oceans, typhoons in the western Pacific and cyclones in the Indian Ocean—strike heavily populated areas, they can kill thousands and cause billions of dollars of property damage. And nothing, absolutely nothing, stands in their way.
>
> But must these fearful forces of nature be forever beyond our control? My research colleagues and I think not. Our team is investigating how we might learn to nudge hurricanes onto more benign paths or otherwise defuse them. Although this bold goal probably lies decades in the future, we think our results show that it is not too early to study the possibilities.
>
> —Ross N. Hoffman, "Controlling Hurricanes"

The following paragraphs from an analytical essay begin with a vivid quotation that illustrates a commonly held view. The writer then calls that view into question:

> "Loathsome hordes, dark swarms of worms that emerge from the narrow crevices of their holes when the sun is high,

TEXTCONNEX

Web Sites: Beginnings, Middles, and Ends

If you are creating a Web site, remember that readers may enter it in the "middle" and never find the "end." Web sites simply do not have the kind of linear structure that papers do, and readers tend to want information in short chunks rather than in lengthy paragraphs. However, readers visiting a Web site still expect to be able to go to an introductory page, or **home page,** that makes the overall purpose and contents of the site clear. Make sure that your home page loads quickly—in under ten seconds or less. Provide clear navigational links on every page of the site, and always include one link that returns the user to the home page.

preferring to cover their villainous faces with hair rather than their private parts and surrounding areas with clothes." So wrote the sixth-century British churchman Gildas, lamenting the depredations of Pictish and other Scotland-based barbarian "butchers" a century earlier following Rome's abandonment of its British provinces in A.D. 410. This characterization of the Picts as illiterate, uncivilized, scantily clothed, and promiscuous heathens has clung to them to the present day. Although over the past half century scholars have regarded the cleric Gildas as a somewhat biased commentator, most haven't tended to see the Picts as outstandingly civilized either.

Now, however, one of the most detailed surveys of their art has revealed that these archetypal barbarians actually developed a deep knowledge of the Bible and of some aspects of Roman classical literature. . . .

—DAVID KEYS, "Rethinking the Picts"

www.mhhe.com/mhhb2
For more information on conclusions, go to **Writing > Paragraph/Essay Development > Conclusions**

4g Conclude by answering "So what?"

Your closing makes a final impression and motivates the reader to think further. You should not merely repeat the main idea, nor should you introduce a completely new topic. Instead, remind readers of the paper's significance (without overstating it) and satisfy those who might be asking, "So what?" Here are some common strategies for concluding a paper effectively:

- Refer to the story or quotation you used in your introduction.
- Answer the question you posed in your introduction.
- Summarize your main point.
- Call for some action on your reader's part.

- Present a powerful image or forceful example.
- Suggest some implications for the future.

The following conclusion refers to a quotation used in the introduction on pages 73–74 as it summarizes the main point:

> Burghead, the current excavations at Tarbat, and new art-history research demonstrate the extraordinary diversity and sophistication of Dark Age Pictish culture. Even if the Picts had once been scantily clothed "butchers," as Gildas and others no doubt perceived them, they evolved into something quite different.
>
> —David Keys, "Rethinking the Picts"

If your paper is brief—five hundred words or fewer—a few concluding sentences may be enough to satisfy the reader. You might also end a brief paper with a powerful supporting point and vivid image. A short composition presenting two sides of the argument over whether cell phones make us more secure concludes with a quotation supporting the pro–cell phone side:

> "If you are left to your own, what would you think about?" said Kenneth J. Gergen, a professor of psychology at Swarthmore College, and author of *The Saturated Self*. "You have to have other voices, reports and news. The best decisions are made in a whole set of dialogues."
>
> —Ken Belson, "Saved, and Enslaved, by the Cell"

Exercise 4.4 Analyzing introductions and conclusions

Find an essay that has an introduction or a conclusion that engaged you and one with an introduction or conclusion that failed to draw you in. What strategies did the successful essay employ? What strategies could the writer of the unsuccessful essay have used? Next look at the introduction and conclusion of an essay you are currently writing. Do these paragraphs use any of the strategies discussed in this section? If not, try one of these strategies when you revise.

For MULTILINGUAL STUDENTS

Special Features of Introductions and Conclusions

U.S. readers expect introductory paragraphs to tackle the topic directly. Therefore, avoid offering long background explanations or making broad generalizations. Readers expect the concluding paragraph to revisit the thesis and, for complex papers, to summarize the main points. Bringing the text to an orchestrated close gives the reader a final opportunity to grasp your message.

5 Revising and Editing

Once you have a draft, you can approach it with a critical eye. In the **revising** stage, you review the whole composition and its parts, adding, deleting, and moving text as necessary. After you are satisfied with the substance of your paper, **editing** begins. When you edit, you polish sentences so that you say what you want to say as effectively as possible.

This chapter focuses on revising and includes a complete student essay in several drafts. It also introduces the concepts and principles of editing, which are covered in much greater detail in Parts 6 through 12.

5a Get comments from readers.

Asking actual readers to comment on your draft is the best way to get fresh perspectives on your writing. (Be sure that your professor allows this kind of collaboration.)

1. Trying peer review

Whether it is required or optional, online or face-to-face, **peer review** is a form of **collaborative learning** that involves reading and critiquing your classmates' work while they review yours. Consider including some of your peers' responses with your final draft so that your teacher knows you have taken the initiative to work with other writers.

Help your readers help you by asking them specific questions. The best compliment readers can pay you is to take your work seriously enough to make constructive suggestions. When you share a draft with readers, provide responses to the following questions:

- **What is the assignment?** Readers need to understand your purpose and audience.
- **How close is the project to being finished?** Help readers understand where you are in the writing process and how to assist you in taking the next step.
- **What steps do you plan to take to complete the project?** If readers know your plans, they can either question the direction you are taking or give you more specific advice, for example, additional sources that you might consult.
- **What kind of feedback do you need?** Do you want readers to summarize your main points so you can determine whether you have communicated them clearly? Do you want to know what readers were thinking and feeling as they read or heard your draft? Do you want a response to the logic of your argument or the development of your thesis?

LEARNING in COLLEGE

Re-Visioning Your Paper

Revising is a process of "re-visioning"—of looking at your work through the eyes of your audience. Here are some tips for getting a fresh perspective on your paper:

1. **Get feedback from other readers.** Candid, respectful feedback can help you discover the strong and weak areas of your paper. See "Responding to readers" below and the box on page 78 for advice on making use of readers' reactions to your drafts.
2. **Let your draft cool.** Whenever possible, try to schedule a break between drafting and revising. A good night's sleep, a movie break, or some physical exercise will help you view your paper more objectively.
3. **Read your paper aloud.** Some people find that reading aloud helps them hear their paper the way their audience will.
4. **Use revising and editing checklists.** The checklists on pages 82, 93, 94–95, and 99 will assist you in evaluating your paper systematically.

Reading other writers' drafts will help you view your own work more objectively, and comments from readers will help you see your own writing as others see it. As you gain more objectivity, you will become more adept at revising your work. The approaches that you see your classmates taking to the assignment will broaden your perspective and give you ideas for new directions in your own writing.

The writing environment in the *Catalyst* Web site that accompanies this book can make it easier for you to obtain and review comments from your readers. Many Web-based tools such as *Google Docs* enable groups to share, edit, and revise their work online.

2. Responding to readers

Consider and evaluate your readers' suggestions, but remember that you are under no obligation to do what they say. One reader may like a particular sentence; a second reader may suggest that you eliminate the very same sentence. Is there common ground? Yes. Both readers stopped at that sentence. Ask yourself why—and whether you want readers to pause there. You are the one who is ultimately responsible for your paper, so make decisions accordingly.

5b Use resources available on your campus, on the Internet, and in your community.

You can call on a number of different resources outside the writing classroom for feedback on your paper.

www.mhhe.com/mhhb2

For links to online resources on writing, go to

Writing > Writing Web Links

CHECKLIST

Giving Feedback

- ☐ **Focus on strengths as well as weaknesses.** Let writers know what parts of their paper are strongest so that they can retain those sections and use them as models to improve weaker sections. Do not withhold constructive criticism, or you will deprive the writer of an opportunity to improve the paper.
- ☐ **Be specific.** Give examples to back up your general reactions.
- ☐ **Be constructive.** Phrase negative reactions to help the writer see a solution. Instead of saying that an example is a bad choice, explain that you did not understand how the example was connected to the main point and suggest a way to clarify the connection.
- ☐ **Ask questions.** Jot down any questions that occur to you as you read. Ask for clarification, or note an objection that other readers might make.

See also: Checklist—Revising Your Draft for Content and Organization, on page 82.

Receiving Feedback

- ☐ **Resist being defensive.** Keep in mind that readers are discussing your paper, not you, and their feedback offers a way for you to see your paper differently. Be respectful of their time and efforts. Remember that you, not your reviewers, are in charge of decisions about your paper.
- ☐ **Ask for more feedback if you need it.** Some students may be hesitant to share all their reactions, and you may need to do some coaxing.

1. Using the campus writing center

Tutors in the campus writing center can read and comment on drafts of your work. They can also help you find and correct problems with grammar, punctuation, and mechanics.

2. Using online writing labs, or OWLs

Most OWLs present information about writing that you can access anytime, including lists of online resources. OWLs with tutors on staff can be useful in the following ways:

For MULTILINGUAL STUDENTS

Peer Review

Respectful peer review will challenge you to view your writing critically and present ideas to a diverse audience. It also will show you that many of your errors are quite common; it will improve your ability to detect mistakes and decide what to correct first. Your unique perspective can help native speakers improve their writing, as they can help you with the subtleties of English idioms.

- You can submit a draft by e-mail for feedback. OWL tutors will return your work, often within forty-eight hours.
- OWLs may post your paper in a public access space where you will receive feedback from more than just one or two readers.
- You can read papers online and learn how others are handling writing issues.

You can learn more about what OWLs have to offer by checking out the following Web sites:

- *Purdue University's Online Writing Lab* (*Figure 5.1 on p. 80*) http://owl.english.purdue.edu
- *Writing Labs and Writing Centers on the Web* (you can visit almost fifty OWLs) http://owl.english.purdue.edu/internet/owls/writing-labs.html

3. Working with experts and instructors

In addition to sharing your work with peers in class, through e-mail, or in online environments, you can use e-mail to consult your instructor or other experts. Your instructor's comments on an early draft are especially valuable, but remember, it is your responsibility to address the issues your instructor raises and to revise your work.

5c Use electronic tools for revising.

Even though word-processing programs can make a first draft look finished, it is still a first draft. Check below the surface for problems in content, structure, and style. Move paragraphs around, add details, and delete irrelevant sentences. Print out a copy of your draft to see the big picture—your paper as a whole.

Become familiar with the revising and editing tools in your word-processing program.

www.mhhe.com/mhhb2

For help with revising, go to

Writing > Paragraph/Essay Development > Drafting and Revising

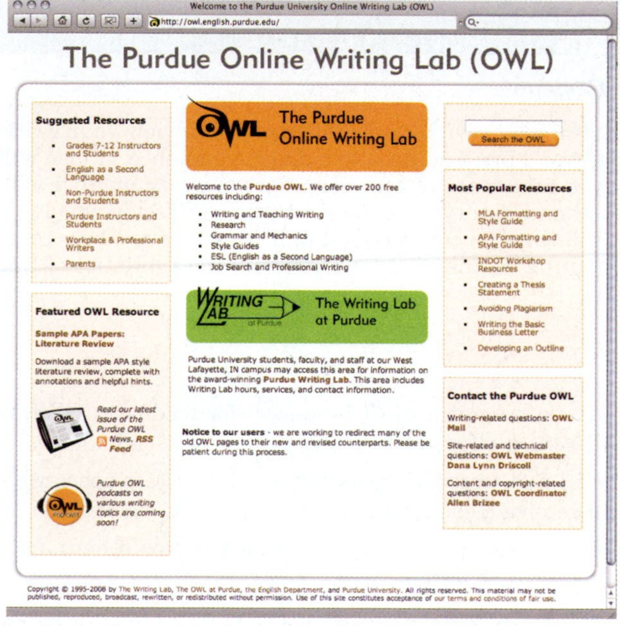

FIGURE 5.1 The Purdue Online Writing Lab.
http://owl.english.purdue.edu/

- **Comments:** Many word-processing programs have a Comments feature (*see Figure 5.2*) that allows you to add notes to sections of text. This feature is very useful for giving feedback on someone else's draft. Some writers use it to make notes to themselves.
- **Track Changes:** The Track Changes feature (*see Figure 5.3*) allows you to edit a piece of writing while maintaining the original text. You can judge whether a suggested edit has improved the paper. If you change your mind, you can restore the deleted text. When collaborating with another writer, take care to delete comments and to accept or reject all changes before turning in a paper to your instructor. You can preserve a record of the edits by saving the Track Changes version as a seperate file.

5d Focus on the purpose of your writing.

As you revise your paper, consider your purpose. Is your primary purpose to inform, to interpret, or to argue? (*For more on assignment purposes, see Chapter 2, pp. 26–27.*)

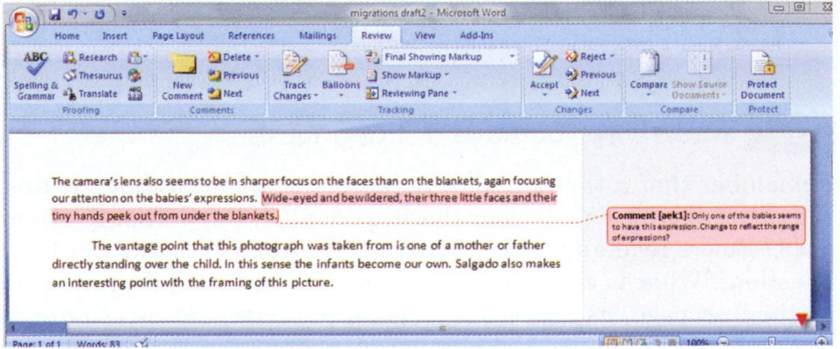

FIGURE 5.2 Using Microsoft Word 2007's Comments feature.

Clarity about your purpose is especially important when an assignment calls for interpretation. A description is not the same as an interpretation. With this principle in mind, Diane Chen read over the first draft of her paper on the *Migrations* photography exhibit. Here is part of her description of the photograph she chose to discuss in detail:

FIRST DRAFT

The photograph is black and white, as are the others in the show. The faces of the babies are in sharp focus while the blanket is a bit defocused. Light, which is essential to photography, is disseminated from a single source coming from the upper left-hand corner of the picture. The light source is not too bright as to bathe the babies in light, but just bright enough to illuminate their faces, which have expressions of interest and puzzlement. Perhaps they are wondering who Salgado is or what is that strange contraption he is holding.

Keeping her purpose in mind, Chen realized that she needed to discuss the significance of her observations—to interpret the details and offer an analysis. She wanted to show her readers how the formal elements of the photograph functioned. Her revision clarifies this interpretation.

REVISION

The orphanage photograph is shot in black and white, as are the other images in the show, giving it a documentary feel that emphasizes the truth of the situation. But Salgado's choice of black-and-white photography is also an artistic decision. He uses the contrasts of light and dark to create a dramatic image of the three babies.

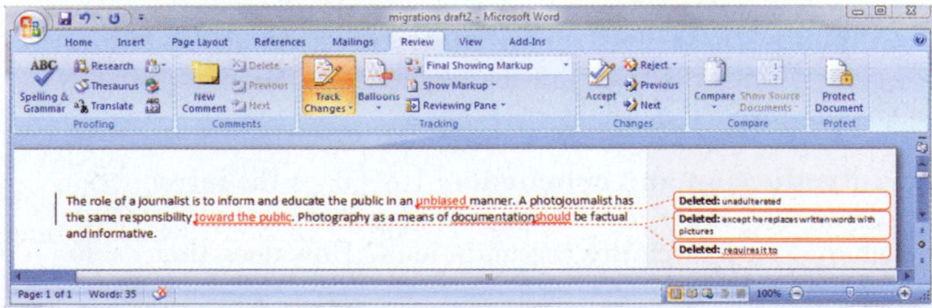

FIGURE 5.3 Showing revisions with Track Changes.

The vertical black-and-white stripes of the blanket direct our eyes to the infants' faces and hands, which are framed by a horizontal white stripe . . .

www.mhhe.com/mhhb2

For help developing a strong thesis, go to

Writing > Paragraph/Essay Development > Thesis/Central Idea

5e Make sure you have a strong thesis.

Remember that a thesis makes an assertion about a topic. It links the *what* and the *why*. Is your thesis evident on the first page of your draft? Before readers get very far along, they expect an answer to the question, "What is the point of all this?" If you do not find the point on the first page, its absence is a signal to revise, unless you are deliberately waiting until the end to reveal your thesis. (*For more on strong theses, see Chapter 3, pp. 42–46.*)

CHECKLIST

Revising Your Draft for Content and Organization

- ☐ **Purpose:** What is the purpose of the text, and how clearly does the writing communicate it? What aspects of the text convey the purpose? What would make it more apparent?
- ☐ **Thesis:** What is the thesis? Is it clear and specific, and does it appear early in the draft? If not, is there a reason for withholding it? What revisions would make the thesis clearer?
- ☐ **Audience:** How does the approach—including evidence and tone—appeal to the intended audience? How might the composition appeal to this audience more effectively?
- ☐ **Structure:** How does the order of the key points support the thesis, and would another order do so more effectively? Do any sections not support the thesis, and if so, which ones? How might overly long or short sections be revised?
- ☐ **Paragraphs:** How might the development, unity, and coherence of each paragraph be improved?
- ☐ **Visuals:** Do visuals communicate the intended meaning clearly and without unnecessary clutter? How might they be improved?
- ☐ **Introduction and conclusion:** How does the introduction draw the reader in? What main idea does it convey? What changes might clarify the main idea? How does the conclusion answer the "So what?" question?

When Diane Chen looked over the first draft of her paper, she decided that she needed to strengthen her thesis statement. She had included two sentences that could serve as a thesis, and it wasn't clear which one was to be the central idea of her paper:

POSSIBLE THESIS

[A] photograph taken with an aesthetic awareness does not debase the severity of war and worldwide suffering.

POSSIBLE THESIS

Whether capturing the millions of refugee tents in Africa that seem to stretch on for miles or the disheartened faces of small immigrant children, Salgado brings an artistic element to his pictures that suggests he does so much more with his camera than just point and shoot.

Chen decided to change her introduction to sharpen the focus on one main idea:

FINAL THESIS Like a photojournalist, Salgado brings us images of newsworthy events, but he goes beyond objective reporting, imparting his compassion for refugees and migrants to the viewer.

(*To compare Diane's first and second drafts, see p. 100 and pp. 101–102.*)

Tips LEARNING in COLLEGE

Selecting a Title

Your essay title should engage your readers' interest and prepare them for the thesis of your paper. The title should not simply state a broad topic ("Lake Superior Zooplankton") but rather should indicate your angle on that topic ("Changes in the Lake Superior Crustacean Zooplankton Community"). Here are some suggestions for strengthening your title:

1. Include a phrase that communicates the purpose of your paper.
   - Alcohol Myopia Theory: A Review of the Literature
   - From Palm to iPhone: A Brief History of PDAs
2. Use a question to indicate that your paper weighs different sides of an argument.
   - Does the Patriot Act Strengthen America?
   - Performance-Based Funding for the Arts: Wise Fiscal Policy or Unwise Gamble?
3. Use a quotation and/or a play on words or a vivid image.
   - Much Ado about "Noting": Perception in Shakespeare's Comedy
   - Many Happy Returns: An Inventory Management Success Story
   - A Fly Trapped in Amber: On Investigating Soft-Bodied Fossils

Readers need to see a statement of the main idea on the first page, but they also expect the writer to return to the thesis near the end. Here is Diane Chen's restatement of her thesis from the end of her revised draft:

> Salgado uses his skills as an artist to get us not only to look at these difficult subjects, but also to feel compassion for them. He is able to bring a story as big and complex as the epic displacement of the world's people to us through a collection of intimate and intensely moving images. As he says in his introduction to the exhibit catalog, "We hold the key to humanity's future, but for that we must understand the present. We cannot afford to look away" (15).

Exercise 5.1 Revising thesis statements

Examine some of your recent papers to see whether the thesis is clearly stated. Is the thesis significant? Can you follow the development of this idea throughout the paper? Does the version of your thesis in the conclusion answer the "So what?" question?

5f Review the structure of your project as a whole.

Does your draft have a beginning, a middle, and an end, with bridges between those parts? When you revise, you can refine and even change this structure so that it supports what you want to say more effectively.

One way to review the structure is by outlining your first draft. (*For help with outlining, see Chapter 3, pp. 47–51.*) Try listing the key points in sentence form; whenever possible, use sentences that actually appear in the draft. Ask yourself if the key points are arranged effectively or if another arrangement would work better. The following structures are typical ways of organizing papers:

- **Informative:** Sets out the key parts of a topic.
- **Exploratory:** Begins with a question or problem and works step by step to discover or explain an answer or a solution.
- **Argumentative:** Presents a set of linked reasons plus supporting evidence.

5g Revise your composition for paragraph development, paragraph unity, and coherence.

As you revise, examine each paragraph, asking yourself what role it plays—or should play—in the paper as a whole. Keeping this role in mind, check the paragraph for development and unity. You should also check each paragraph for coherence—and consider whether all the paragraphs taken together contribute to the paper as a whole.

1. Paragraph development

Paragraphs in academic papers are usually about a hundred words long. Consider dividing any that exceed two hundred words or that are especially dense. When paragraphs are short for no apparent stylistic reason, you may need to develop them or combine them with other paragraphs. Would more information make the point clearer? Perhaps a term should be defined. Do generalizations need to be supported with examples?

Note how this writer developed one of her draft paragraphs, adding details and examples to clarify her points and make a more effective argument.

FIRST DRAFT

A 1913 advertisement for Shredded Wheat illustrates Kellner's claim that advertisements sell self-images. The ad suggests that serving Shredded Wheat will give women the same sense of accomplishment as gaining the right to vote.

REVISION

According to Kellner, "advertising is as concerned with selling lifestyles and socially desirable identities . . . as with selling the products themselves" (193). A 1913 ad for Shredded Wheat shows how the selling of self-images works. At first glance, this ad seems to be promoting the women's suffrage movement. In big, bold letters, "Votes for Women" is emblazoned across the top of the ad. But a closer look reveals that the ad is for Shredded Wheat cereal. Holding a piece of the cereal in her hand, a woman stands behind a large bowlful of Shredded Wheat biscuits that is made to look like a voting box. The text claims that "every biscuit is a vote for health, happiness and domestic freedom." Like the rest of the advertisement, this claim suggests that serving Shredded Wheat will give women the same sense of accomplishment as gaining the right to vote.

—Holly Musetti, "Targeting Women," student paper

2. Paragraph unity

To check for **unity,** identify the paragraph's topic sentence (*see p. 57*). Everything in the paragraph should be clearly and closely connected to the topic sentence. In particular, check very long paragraphs (over two hundred words) for unity. Items unrelated to the topic sentence should be deleted or developed into separate paragraphs. Another option is to revise the topic sentence.

www.mhhe.com/mhhb2
For help developing paragraph unity, go to
Writing > Paragraph/Essay Development > Unity

Compare the first draft of the following paragraph with its revision, and note how the addition of a topic sentence (in bold in the revision) makes the paragraph more clearly focused and therefore easier for the writer to revise further. Note also that the writer deleted ideas that did not directly relate to the paragraph's main point (underlined in the first draft):

FIRST DRAFT

Germany is ranked first on worldwide production levels. Automobiles, aircraft, and electronic equipment are among Germany's most important products for export. As the standard of living of the citizens of what was formerly East Germany increases due to reunification, their purchasing power and productivity will increase. A major problem is that east Germany is not as productive or efficient as west Germany, and so it would be better if less money were invested in the east. Germany is involved in most global treaties that protect business interests, and intellectual property is well protected. A plus for potential ventures and production plans is its highly skilled workforce. Another factor that indicates that Germany will remain strong in the arena of productivity and trade is its physical location in the world. "Its terrain and geographical position have combined to make Germany an important crossroads for traffic between the North Sea, the Baltic, and the Mediterranean. International transportation routes pass through all of Germany," thus utilizing a comprehensive and efficient network of transportation, both on land and over water ("Germany," 1995, p. 185). Businesses can operate plants in Germany and have no difficulties transporting goods and services to other parts of the country. Generally, private enterprise, government, banks, and unions cooperate, making the country more amenable to negotiations for business entry or joint ventures.

REVISION

For many reasons, Germany is attractive both as a market for other nations and as a location for production. As the standard of living of the citizens of what was formerly East Germany increases because of reunification, their purchasing power and productivity increase. Intellectual property is well protected, and Germany is involved in most global treaties that protect business interests. Germany's highly skilled workforce is another plus for potential ventures and production plans. Generally, private enterprise, government, banks, and unions cooperate, making the country amenable to negotiations for business entry or joint ventures. Germany also has an excellent physical location that makes it an "important crossroads for traffic between the North Sea, the Baltic, and the Mediterranean" ("Germany," 1995, p. 185). Equally important, a comprehensive and efficient transportation system allows businesses to operate plants in Germany and easily transport their goods and services to other parts of the country and the world.

—JENNIFER KOEHLER, "Germany's Path to Continuing Prosperity"

3. Coherence

A coherent paragraph flows smoothly, with an organization that is easy to follow and with each sentence clearly related to the next. (*See Chapter 4, pp. 59–61, for tips on how to develop well-organized paragraphs.*) You can improve the **coherence** both within and among the paragraphs in your draft by using repetition, pronouns, parallel structure, and transitions.

www.mhhe.com/mhhb2
For help writing coherent paragraphs, go to
Writing > Paragraph/Essay Development > Coherence

Use repetition to emphasize the main idea Repeating key words helps your readers stay focused on the topic of your paper and reinforces your thesis. In the example that follows, Rajeev Bector opens his paper with a paragraph that uses repetition (highlighted) to define a key term central to his essay:

> Sociologist Erving Goffman believes that every social interaction establishes our identity and preserves our image, honor, and credibility in the hearts and minds of others. Social interactions, he says, are in essence "character contests" that occur not only in games and sports but also in our everyday dealings with strangers, peers, friends and even family members. Goffman defines character contests as "disputes [that] are sought out and indulged in (often with glee) as a means of establishing where one's boundaries are" (29). Just such a contest occurs in Flannery O'Connor's short story "Everything That Rises Must Converge."
>
> —RAJEEV BECTOR, "The Character Contest in Flannery O'Connor's 'Everything That Rises Must Converge,'" student paper

(*To see Bector's complete essay, turn to p. 167 in Chapter 9: Interpretive Analyses.*)

Use pronouns to avoid unnecessary repetition Too much repetition can make your sentences sound clumsy and your paragraphs seem monotonous. Use pronouns to stand in for nouns where needed, and to form connections between sentences.

In the next paragraph, Diane Chen uses pronouns (highlighted) to create smooth-sounding sentences that hold the paragraph together:

> Salgado uses his skills as an artist to get us not only to look at these difficult subjects, but also to feel compassion for them. He is able to bring a story as big and complex as the epic displacement of the world's people to us through a collection of intimate and intensely moving images. As he says in his introduction to the exhibit catalog, "We hold the key to humanity's future, but for that we must understand the present. We cannot afford to look away."

Use parallel structure to emphasize connections Parallel structure helps to form connections within and between the sentences of your paragraph. In the following sentence, for example, the three clauses are grammatically parallel, each consisting of a pronoun (P) and a past-tense verb (V):

P - V P - V P - V

► **We came, we saw, and we conquered.**

Within paragraphs, two or more sentences can have parallel structures, as in the following example:

► **Because the former West Germany lived through a generation of prosperity, its people developed high expectations of material comfort. Because the former East Germany lived through a generation of deprivation, its people developed a disdain for material values.**

Too much parallelism can seem repetitive, though, so save this device for ideas that you can pair meaningfully. (*For more information on editing for parallelism in your writing, turn to Chapter 42: Faulty Parallelism.*)

Use transitional words and phrases One-word **transitions** and **transitional expressions** link one idea to another, helping readers understand your logic. (*See the box on p. 89 for a list of common transitional expressions.*) Compare the following two paragraphs, the first version without transitions and the second, revised version with transitions (in bold type):

FIRST DRAFT

Glaser was in a position to affect powerfully Armstrong's career and his life. There is little evidence that the musician submitted to whatever his business manager wanted or demanded. Armstrong seemed to recognize that he gave Glaser whatever power the manager enjoyed over him. Armstrong could and did resist Glaser's control when he wanted to. That may be one reason why he liked and trusted Glaser as much as he did.

TRANSITIONAL EXPRESSIONS

- **To show relationships in space:** above, adjacent to, against, alongside, around, at a distance from, at the . . . , below, beside, beyond, encircling, far off, forward, from the . . . , in front of, in the rear, inside, near the back, near the end, nearby, next to, on, over, surrounding, there, through the . . . , to the left, to the right, up front
- **To show relationships in time:** afterward, at last, before, earlier, first, former, formerly, immediately, in the first place, in the interval, in the meantime, in the next place, in the last place, later on, latter, meanwhile, next, now, often, once, previously, second, simultaneously, sometime later, subsequently, suddenly, then, therefore, third, today, tomorrow, until now, when, years ago, yesterday
- **To show addition or to compare:** again, also, and, and then, besides, further, furthermore, in addition, last, likewise, moreover, next, too
- **To give examples that intensify points:** after all, as an example, certainly, clearly, for example, for instance, indeed, in fact, in truth, it is true that, of course, specifically, that is
- **To show similarities:** alike, in the same way, like, likewise, resembling, similarly
- **To show contrasts:** after all, although, but, conversely, differ(s) from, difference, different, dissimilar, even though, granted, however, in contrast, in spite of, nevertheless, notwithstanding, on the contrary, on the other hand, otherwise, still, though, unlike, while this may be true, yet
- **To indicate cause and effect:** accordingly, as a result, because, consequently, hence, since, then, therefore, thus
- **To conclude or summarize:** finally, in brief, in conclusion, in other words, in short, in summary, that is, to summarize

REVISION

Clearly, Glaser was in a position to affect powerfully Armstrong's career and his life. **However,** there is little evidence that the musician submitted to whatever his business manager wanted or demanded. **In fact,** Armstrong seemed to recognize that he gave Glaser whatever power the manager enjoyed over him. When he wanted to, Armstrong could and did resist Glaser's control, and that may be one reason why he liked and trusted Glaser as much as he did.

—ESTHER HOFFMAN, "Louis Armstrong and Joe Glaser"

(*To see Hoffman's complete essay, turn to pp. 379–90 in Chapter 23: MLA Documentation Style.*)

Use coherence strategies to show how paragraphs are related

You can also use repetition, pronouns, parallelism, and transitions to show how paragraphs are related to one another. In addition, you can use **transitional sentences** both to refer to the previous paragraph and at the same time to move your essay on to the next point. Lengthy essays may contain short transitional paragraphs to bridge two topics that are developed in some detail. Notice how the first sentence at the beginning of the second paragraph below, from Diane Chen's paper about Sebastião Salgado, both refers to the babies described in the previous paragraph and serves as a topic sentence for the second paragraph.

> The vertical black-and-white stripes of the blanket direct our eyes to the infants' faces and hands, which are framed by a horizontal white stripe. The whites of their eyes in particular stand out against the darkness created by the shell of the blankets. The camera's lens also seems to be in sharper focus on the faces than on the blankets, again focusing our attention on the babies' expressions.
>
> Each baby has a different response to the camera. The baby on the left returns our gaze with a heart-wrenching look. The baby in the center, whose eyes are open extra-wide, appears startled and in need of comforting. But the baby on the right, whose eyes are glazed and sunken, doesn't even notice the camera. We glimpse death in that child's face.

Exercise 5.2 Revising paragraphs

Revise the paragraphs below to improve their unity, development, and coherence.

1. Vivaldi was famous and influential as a virtuoso violinist and composer. Vivaldi died in poverty, having lost popularity in the last years before his death. He had been acclaimed during his lifetime and forgotten for two hundred years after his death. Many composers suffer that fate. The baroque revival of the 1950s brought his music back to the public's attention.
2. People who want to adopt an exotic pet need to be aware of the consequences. Baby snakes and reptiles can seem fairly easy to manage. Lion and tiger cubs are playful and friendly. They can seem as harmless as kittens. Domestic cats can revert to a wild state quite easily. Adult snakes and reptiles can grow large. Many species of reptiles and snakes require carefully controlled environments. Big cats can escape. An escaped lion or tiger is a danger to itself and to others. Most exotic animals need professional care. This kind of care is available in zoos and wild-animal parks. The best environment for an exotic animal is the wild.

Exercise 5.3 Writing well-developed, coherent paragraphs

Using the strategies for paragraph development and coherence discussed in section 5g, write a paragraph for one of the following topic sentences. Working with two or more classmates, decide where your paragraph needs more details or improved coherence.

1. Awards shows on television often fail to recognize creativity and innovation.
2. Most people learn only those aspects of a computer program that they need to use every day.
3. First-year students who also work can have an easier time adjusting to the demands of college life than nonworking students.
4. E-mail messages that circulate widely can be broken down into several categories.

5h Revise visuals.

www.mhhe.com/mhhb2 For more on using visuals, go to Writing > Visual Rhetoric Tutorial > Visualizing Data

Review your visuals during the revision stage to eliminate what scholar Edward Tufte calls **chartjunk,** or distracting visual elements. The "Revising Visuals" Checklist on page 93 presents Tufte's suggestions for editing visuals so that your readers will focus on your data rather than your "data containers."

5i Edit sentences.

www.mhhe.com/mhhb2 For additional help with editing, go to Editing

Parts 7, 8, and 9 of this handbook address editing for grammar conventions, clarity, and word choice. The section that follows gives you an overview of editing concerns and techniques.

1. Editing for grammar conventions

Sometimes writers construct a sentence or choose a word form that does not follow the rules of standard written English. In academic writing, these kinds of errors are distracting to readers and can obscure your meaning.

DRAFT
Photographs of illegal immigrants being captured by the United States border patrol, of emotional immigrants on the plane to their new country, and of villagers fleeing rebel gangs. [*This is a sentence fragment because it lacks a verb. It also omits the writer's point about these images.*]

EDITED SENTENCE
Photographs of illegal immigrants being captured by the United States border patrol, of emotional immigrants on the plane to their new country, and of villagers fleeing rebel gangs exemplify the range of migration stories.

Professional editors use abbreviations and symbols to note errors in a manuscript; a list of common ones can be found at the back of this book. Your instructor and other readers may use these abbreviations and symbols, and you may find it helpful to learn them as well.

DRAFT

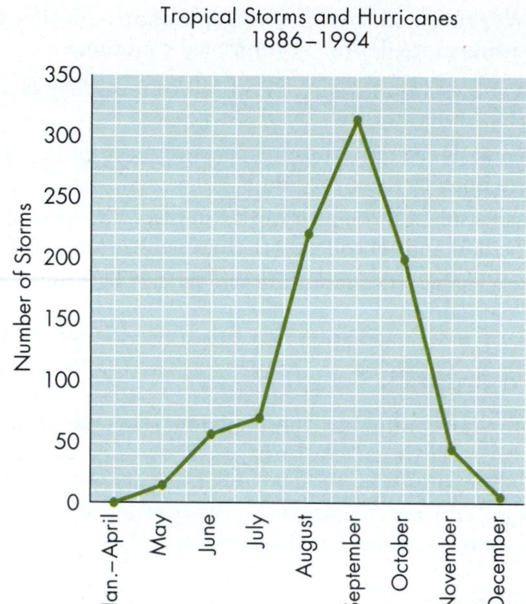

REVISION

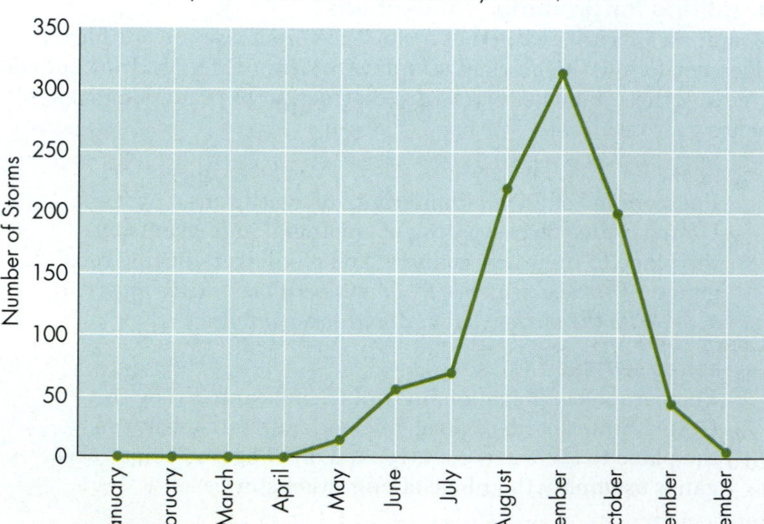

FIGURE 5.4 **Eliminating distortion in a line graph.**

CHECKLIST

Revising Visuals

- ☐ **Are grid lines needed in tables?** Eliminate grid lines or, if the lines are needed for clarity, lighten them. Tables should not look like nets, with every number enclosed in a box. Vertical rules are needed only when space is extremely tight between columns.
- ☐ **Are there unnecessary three-dimensional renderings?** Cubes and shadows can distort the information in a visual. For most charts, including pie charts, a flat image makes it easier for readers to compare parts.
- ☐ **Is data labeled clearly?** Avoid abbreviations and legends, if possible.
- ☐ **Does each visual have an informative title?**
- ☐ **Do bright colors focus attention on the key data?** If you are including a map, use muted colors over large areas, and save strong colors for emphasis.
- ☐ **Do pictures distract from the visual's purpose?** Clip art and other decorative elements seldom make data more interesting, nor do they make it appear more substantial.
- ☐ **Are data distorted?** Look out for and correct distortions of the data. In the draft version of the graph in Figure 5.4 (*on the facing page*), eight months of the year are plotted separately, with the months of January, February, March, and April grouped together. This creates a misleading impression of hurricane activity by month. The revision corrects this distortion.

2. Editing for clarity

Concentrate on sentence style. Some of your sentences, though grammatically correct, can probably be improved. A volley of short, choppy sentences, for example, distracts readers from what you have to say, whereas an unbroken stream of long, complicated sentences is likely to dull their senses. Also vary sentence openings and structure. In the example that follows, notice how the revised version connects ideas for readers and, consequently, is easier to read.

DRAFT My father was a zealous fisherman. He took his fishing rod on every family outing. He often spent the whole outing staring at the water,

CHECKLIST

Editing Sentences and Words

The online diagnostic "Test Yourself" quizzes that accompany this handbook, as well as the exercises and Checklists in Parts 7 through 12, can help you determine which conventions give you trouble. To create a personalized editing checklist, fill in the boxes next to your trouble spots in the list that follows. For examples of the most common errors in student writing, see the foldout section at the beginning of Part 6.

1. **Editing for grammar conventions** (*Part 7*): Does the paper contain any of these common errors? Note and correct any sentences that contain errors.

- ☐ Sentence fragments (*Chapter 32, pp. 514–25*)
- ☐ Comma splices (*Chapter 33, pp. 526–37*)
- ☐ Run-on sentences (*Chapter 33, pp. 526–37*)
- ☐ Subject-verb agreement problems (*Chapter 34, pp. 538–53*)
- ☐ Incorrect verb forms (*Chapter 35, pp. 553–77*)
- ☐ Inconsistent verb tenses (*Chapter 35, pp. 553–77*)
- ☐ Pronoun-antecedent agreement problems (*Chapter 36, pp. 588–93*)
- ☐ Incorrect pronoun forms (*Chapter 36, pp. 577–99*)
- ☐ Misused adjectives or adverbs (*Chapter 37, pp. 599–612*)
- ☐ Other: ______________________________

2. **Editing for clarity** (*Part 8*): Does the paper contain any of the following common causes of unclear sentences? Note sections that could be clearer.

- ☐ Wordiness (*Chapter 38, pp. 614–22*)
- ☐ Missing words (*Chapter 39, pp. 622–27*)
- ☐ Mixed constructions (*Chapter 40, pp. 628–31*)

- ☐ Confusing shifts (*Chapter 41, pp. 631–39*)
- ☐ Faulty parallelism (*Chapter 42, pp. 639–47*)
- ☐ Misplaced or dangling modifiers (*Chapter 43, pp. 647–54*)
- ☐ Problems with coordination and subordination (*Chapter 44, pp. 655–64*)
- ☐ Other: ______________________________

3. **Editing for word choice** (*Part 9*):

- ☐ How can I revise to avoid slang, biased language, clichés, or other inappropriate usages? (*Chapter 48, pp. 691–98*)
- ☐ Where and how might the choice of words be more precise? (*Chapter 49, pp. 698–709*)
- ☐ Does the paper misuse any commonly confused words (for example, *advice* vs. *advise*) or use any nonstandard expressions (for example, *could of*)? (*Chapter 50, pp. 709–18*)

If you are in the process of developing fluency in English, consult Part 12: Guide for Multilingual Writers for more advice.

waiting for a nibble. He went to the kitchen as soon as he got home. He usually cleaned and cooked the fish the same day he caught them.

REVISED A zealous fisherman, my father took his fishing rod on every family outing. He would often spend the whole afternoon by the shore, waiting for a nibble, and then hurry straight to the kitchen to clean and cook his catch.

You should also condense and focus sentences that are wordy and that lack a clear subject and a vivid verb. Rephrase sentences beginning with *it is, there is,* or *there are* (**expletive constructions**) to begin with the subject and a stronger verb. (Change *There are five cats in the house* to *Five cats reside in the house.*)

DRAFT Although both vertebral and wrist fractures cause deformity and impair movement, hip fractures, which are one of the most devastating consequences of osteoporosis, significantly increase the risk of death, since 12%–30% of patients with a hip fracture die within one year after the fracture, while the mortality rate climbs to 40% for the first two years post fracture.

REVISED Hip fractures are one of the most devastating consequences of osteoporosis. Although vertebral and wrist fractures cause deformity and impair movement, hip fractures significantly increase the risk of death. Within one year after a hip fracture, 12%–20% of the injured die. The mortality rate climbs to 40% after two years.

DRAFT *There are stereotypes* from the days of a divided Germany that must be dealt with.

REVISED *Stereotypes* formed in the days of a divided Germany *persist* and must be dealt with.

TEXTCONNEX

The Pros and Cons of Grammar Checkers and Spell Checkers

Grammar checkers and spell checkers can help you spot some errors, but they miss many others and may even flag correct sentences. Consider the following example:

► **Thee neighbors puts there cats' outsider.**

A spelling and grammar checker did not catch the five real errors in the sentence. (Correct version: *The neighbors put their cats outside.*) The software also flagged the following grammatically correct and eloquent sentence by Alice Walker and suggested the nonsense substitution below.

WALKER'S SENTENCE

► **Consider, if you can bear to imagine it, what might have been the result if singing, too, had been forbidden by law.**

GRAMMAR CHECKER'S SUGGESTION

► **Consider, if you can bear to imagine it, law if singing, too, had forbid what might have been the result.**

If you are aware of your program's limitations, then you can make some use of it as you edit your manuscript. Be sure, however, to review the manuscript carefully yourself.

3. Editing for word choice

Finding precisely the right word and putting that word in the best place is an important part of revision. Different disciplines and occupations have their own terminologies. The word *significant,* for example, has a mathematical meaning for the statistician and a different meaning for the literary critic. When taking courses in a discipline, you should use its terminology accurately. Whenever you are unsure of a word's denotation (its exact meaning), consult a dictionary.

As you review your draft, look for general terms that might need to be made more specific:

DRAFT Foreign direct investment (FDI) in Germany will probably remain low because of several *factors.* [Factors *is a general word. To get specific, answer the question, what factors?*]

REVISED Foreign direct investment (FDI) in Germany will probably remain low because of *high labor costs, high taxation, and government regulation.*

Your search for more specific words can lead you to a dictionary and a thesaurus. A dictionary gives the exact definition of a word, its history (etymology), and the parts of speech it belongs to. A thesaurus provides its synonyms, words with the same or nearly the same meaning. (*For more on using a dictionary and a thesaurus, see Chapter 47.*)

One student used both a thesaurus and a dictionary as aids in revising the following sentence:

DRAFT Malcolm X had a special kind of power.

A thesaurus listed *influence* as a synonym for *power,* and *charisma* as a special kind of influence. In the dictionary, the writer found that *charisma* means a "divinely conferred" power and has an etymological connection with *charismatic,* a term used to describe ecstatic Christian experiences like speaking in tongues. *Charisma* was exactly the word she needed to convey both the spiritual and the popular sides of Malcolm X:

REVISED Malcolm X had charisma.

As you edit for word choice, make sure that your tone is appropriate for academic writing (*see Chapter 2, p. 30*) and that you have avoided biased language, such as the use of *his* to refer to women as well as men:

BIASED
Every student who wrote *his* name on the class list had to pay a copying fee in advance and pledge to attend every session.

REVISED AS PLURAL

Students who wrote *their* names on the class list had to pay a copying fee in advance and pledge to attend every session.

REVISED TO AVOID PRONOUNS

Every student who signed up for the class had to pay a copying fee in advance and pledge to attend every session.

REVISED WITH *HIS* OR *HER*

Every student who wrote *his or her* name on the class list had to pay a copying fee in advance and pledge to attend every session.

(*See Chapter 48: Appropriate Language for advice on editing to eliminate biased language.*)

Exercise 5.4 Editing sentences

Type the following sentences into your word processor and activate the grammar and spell-checker feature. Copy the sentence suggested by the software, and then write your own edited version of the sentence.

1. Lighting affects are sense of the shape and texture of the objects depict.
2. A novelist's tells the truth even though he invent stories and characters.
3. There are the question of why bad things happen to good people, which story of Job illustrate.
4. A expensive marketing campaign is of little value if the product stinks.
5. Digestive enzymes melt down the nutrients in food so that the body is able to put in effect a utilization of those nutrients when the body needs energy to do things.

5j Proofread carefully before you turn in your composition.

Once you have revised your paper at the composition, paragraph, and sentence levels, give your work one last check to make sure that it is free of typos and other mechanical errors.

Many writers prefer to **proofread** when their work is in its final format. Even if you are submitting an electronic version of your project, it is still a good idea to proofread a printed version. Placing a ruler under each line can make it easier to focus. You can also start at the end and proofread your way backward to the beginning, sentence by sentence.

CHECKLIST

Proofreading

- ☐ Have you included your name, the date, your professor's name, and the paper title? (*See Chapters 23–26 for the formats to use for MLA, APA, Chicago, and CSE style.*)
- ☐ Are all words spelled correctly? Be sure to check the spelling of titles and headings. (*See Chapter 63: Spelling.*)
- ☐ Have you used the words you intended, or have you substituted words that sound like the ones you want but have a different spelling and meaning, such as *too* for *to*, *their* for *there*, or *it's* for *its*? (*See Chapter 50: Glossary of Usage.*)
- ☐ Are all proper names capitalized? Have you capitalized titles of works correctly, and either italicized them or put them in quotation marks, as required? (*See Chapter 57: Capitalization, and Chapter 60: Italics and Underlining.*)
- ☐ Have you punctuated your sentences correctly? (*See Part 10.*)
- ☐ Are sources cited correctly? Double-check all source citations and the works-cited or reference list. (*See Chapters 23–26.*)
- ☐ Have you checked anything you retyped—for example, quotations, data tables—against the original?

5k Learn from one student's revisions.

In this section we will look at several drafts of Diane Chen's paper on the *Migrations* photography exhibit. The photograph that she is discussing appears in the final version of her paper, on page 103.

1. First draft, with revision comments

In Chapter 2, we saw Diane Chen choose the exhibit of photographs by Sebastião Salgado as the topic for a paper (*see 2c, pp. 23–24*). In Chapter 3, we saw her explore this topic (*see 3a, pp. 33–42*), develop a working thesis (*see 3b, pp. 42–45*), and plan her organization (*see 3c, pp. 46–50*). Here is Diane Chen's first draft, along with notes about general and paragraph-level concerns that she received at her school's writing center.

Consider using a title that is related to your thesis.

Sebastião Salgado
Migrations: Humanity in Transition

The role of a photojournalist is to inform and educate the public in an unbiased manner. Photography as a means of documentation requires it to be factual and informative. However, a photograph taken with an aesthetic awareness does not debase the severity of war and worldwide suffering.

Why is this artistic element significant?

In a recent exhibition of Sebastião Salgado's work entitled, "Migrations: Humanity in Transition," the noted photographer displayed his documentation of the plight of migrants and refugees through beautiful and artful photographs. Whether capturing the millions of (OK?) refugee tents in Africa that seem to stretch on for miles or the disheartened faces of small immigrant children, Salgado brings an artistic element to his pictures that suggests he does so much more with his camera than just point and shoot.

Is this phrase appropriate? Does this apply to all three faces?

So many photographs in Salgado's show are certain to impress and touch the viewers with their subject matter and sheer beauty. However, "Orphanage attached to the hospital at Kibumba, Number One Camp, Goma, Zaire," was my favorite photograph. It depicts three apparently newborn or several month old babies, who are victims of the genocidal war in Rwanda, arranged neatly in a row, wrapped in a mass of stripe-patterned clothes or blankets. Wide-eyed and bewildered, their three little faces and their tiny hands peek out from under the blankets. The whites of their eyes stand out against the darkness created by the shell of the blankets.

Excellent descriptions but tie them to analyses.

The photograph is black and white, as are the others in the show. The faces of the babies are in sharp focus while the blanket is a bit defocused. Light, which is essential to photography, is disseminated from a single source coming from the upper left-hand corner of the picture. The light source is not too bright as to bathe the babies in light, but just bright enough to illuminate their faces, which have expressions of interest and puzzlement. Perhaps they are wondering who Salgado is or what is that strange contraption he is holding. The lighting also creates contrasts of light and dark in the peaks and valleys created by the folds in the blanket.

Do the details that follow support this idea?

What I find most impressing (ive) in this picture is Salgado's ability to find the beauty of human life amidst the ugliness of warfare. The vantage point that this photograph was taken from is one of a mother or father directly standing over the child. In this sense the infants become our own. Salgado also makes an interesting point with the framing of this picture. The babies and the blanket occupy the entire photo. The beauty of the infants consumes the viewer. It is unclear if any part of this composition was posed. Logically, a true photojournalist would not manipulate his subject but photograph it as is.

Point is not related to paragraph.

meaning?

What is it?

Perhaps such aesthetic consciousness is necessary in order for the audience to even be able to look at the photographs. Hardly anyone enjoys looking at gruesome or explicit pictures, an issue newspaper editors have to grapple with in every copy. As art, Salgado's photographs transport us in grand and abstract way. As a photojournalist, Salgado needs to tell it like it is. Finding the right balance between the two means atracting the eye of the viewer while conveying a strong message. Salgado never lets us forget that it is after all, refugee camps and remnants of bloody tribal gang warfare that we are looking at. Beauty needs to accompany truth for it to be bearable.

Diane,
Your paper is full of great observations about the Salgado picture, but I wasn't sure of your thesis. There seemed to be one at the end of the first paragraph and another at the end of the second. A clear thesis would give you a focus for discussing the significance of your observations. I look forward to reading the next draft.
Seth

2. Second draft, with edits

For her second draft, Chen revised her introduction and sharpened her thesis statement. She changed the focus of her essay somewhat, from the beauty of the picture to the way that the picture forces the viewer to look closely into the babies' faces and feel compassion for them. She also tightened the focus of her descriptive paragraphs so that the details in each one served her analytic purpose. After revising her paper overall, she edited her second draft.

The Caring Eye of Sebastião Salgado

Photographer Sebastião Salgado spent seven years ~~of his life~~traveling along migration routes to city slums and refugee camps~~, and migration routes~~ in order to document the lives of people uprooted from their homelands. A selection of his photographs can be seen in the exhibit, ~~"~~*Migrations: Humanity in Transition*.~~"~~ Like a photojournalist, Salgado brings us images of newsworthy events, but he goes beyond objective reporting, imparting his compassion for refugees and migrants to the viewer.

~~So m~~Many of the photographs in Salgado's show are certain to ~~impress and~~ touch ~~the~~ viewers~~ with their subject matter and sheer beauty~~. Whether capturing the thousands~~millions~~ of refugee tents in Africa that seem to stretch on for miles or the disheartened faces of ~~small~~ immigrant children, ~~Salgado brings an artistic element to his pictures that~~the images in *Migrations* suggests that ~~he~~ Salgado does so much more with his camera than ~~just~~ point and shoot.

Salgado's photograph of the most vulnerable of these refugees illustrates the power of his work. "Orphanage attached to the hospital at Kibumba, Number One Camp, Goma Zaire~~,~~" (Fig. 1) depicts three ~~apparently newborn or several month old babies~~infants~~,~~ who are victims of the genocidal war in neighboring Rwanda. The label for the photograph reveals ~~tells us~~ that there were 4,000 orphans at this camp and an estimated 100,000 Rwandan orphans overall. Those numbers are mind-numbing abstractions, but this picture is not.

The orphanage photograph is shot in black and white, as are the others in the show, ~~and provides the audience with~~giving it a ~~very~~ documentary~~, newspaper type of~~ feel that emphasizes that this is a real~~, newsworthy~~ situation ~~that we need to be aware of~~ deserving our attention. But Salgado's choice of black-and-white photography is also an artistic decision. He uses the contrasts of light and dark to create a dramatic image of the three babies.

The vertical black-and-white stripes of the blanket direct our eyes to the infants' faces and hands, which are framed by a horizontal white stripe. The whites of their eyes in particular stand out against the darkness created by the shell of the blankets. The camera's lens also seems to be in sharper focus on the faces than on the blankets, again focusing our attention on the babies' expressions. Each baby has a different response to the camera. The center baby, with his or her extra-wide eyes, appears startled and in need of comforting. The baby to the right is oblivious to the camera and in fact seems to be starving or ill. The healthy baby on the left returns our gaze.

Diane Chen 4/24/08 9:22 AM
Comment: Reorganize—move from left to right across the picture for a more dramatic conclusion. (... [6])

The vantage point of~~that~~ this photograph~~ was taken from~~ is one of a ~~mother or father~~parent ~~directly~~ standing directly over his or her~~the~~ child. In this sense the infants become our own. Salgado also ~~makes an interesting point with the framing of~~frames this picture strategically. The babies in their blanket consumes the entire space, so that their innocence and vulnerability consumes the viewer.

Salgado uses his skills as an artist to get us ~~not only~~ to look at these difficult subjects~~, but also to feel compassion for them~~. He is able to bring a story as big and complex as the epic displacement of the world's people to us through a collection of intimate and intensely moving images. As he says in his introduction to the exhibit catalog, "We hold the key to humanity's future, but for that we must understand the present. We cannot afford to look away."

Diane Chen 4/24/08 9:22 AM
Comment: Add citation to work cited.

3. Final draft

After editing her paper, Chen printed it out, proofread it, corrected some minor errors, and then printed the final version, which is reprinted below. (Chen formatted her paper using the MLA style. The version here, however, does not reflect all the MLA conventions for page breaks, margins, and line spacing. For details on the proper formatting of a paper in MLA style, see Chapter 23 and the sample that begins on p. 379.)

Diane Chen
Professor Bennet
Art 258: History of Photography
5 December 2009

The Caring Eye of Sebastião Salgado

Chen identifies the topic and then states her thesis.

Photographer Sebastião Salgado spent seven years traveling along migration routes to city slums and refugee camps in order to document the lives of people uprooted from their homelands. A selection of his photographs can be seen in the exhibit *Migrations: Humanity in Transition*. Like a photojournalist, Salgado brings us images of newsworthy events, but he goes beyond objective reporting, imparting his compassion for refugees and migrants to the viewer.

Chen provides background about the exhibit.

Many of the photographs in Salgado's show are certain to touch viewers. Whether capturing the thousands of refugee tents in Africa that seem to stretch on for miles or the disheartened faces of immigrant children, the images in *Migrations* suggest that Salgado does so much more than point and shoot.

Chen first references the photo that illustrates her main point.

Salgado's photograph of the most vulnerable among these refugees illustrates the power of his work. "Orphanage attached to the hospital at Kibumba, Number One Camp, Goma, Zaire" (see fig.1) depicts three infants who are victims of the genocidal war in neighboring Rwanda. The label for the photograph reveals that there were 4,000 orphans at this camp and an estimated 100,000 Rwandan orphans overall. Those numbers are mind-numbing abstractions, but this picture is not.

The fourth paragraph focuses on the image.

The orphanage photograph is shot in black and white, as are the others in the show, giving it a documentary feel that emphasizes that this is a real situation deserving our attention. But Salgado's choice of black-and-white photography is also an artistic decision. He uses the contrasts of light and dark to create a dramatic image of the three babies.

Chen describes the photograph in the next three paragraphs, using a spatial organization.

The vertical black-and-white stripes of the blanket direct our eyes to the infants' faces and hands, which are framed by a horizontal white stripe. The whites of their eyes in particular stand out against the darkness created by the shell of the blankets. The camera's lens also seems to be in sharper focus on the faces than on the blankets, again focusing our attention on the babies' expressions.

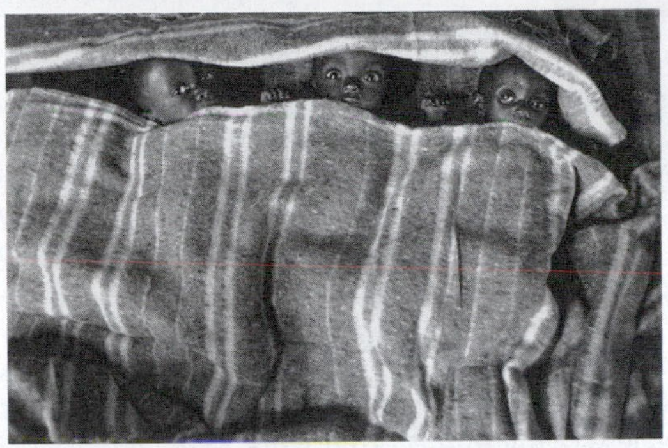

Fig.1. Sebastião Salgado, *Migrations,* "Orphanage attached to the hospital at Kibumba, Number One Camp, Goma, Zaire."

Each baby has a different response to the camera. The baby on the left returns our gaze with a heart-wrenching look. The baby in the center, whose eyes are open extra-wide, appears startled and in need of comforting. But the baby on the right, whose eyes are glazed and sunken, doesn't even notice the camera. We glimpse death in that child's face.

The vantage point of this photograph is one of a parent standing directly over his or her child. In this sense the infants become our own. Salgado also frames this picture strategically. The babies in their blanket consume the entire space, so that their innocence and vulnerability consume the viewer.

Salgado uses his skills as an artist to get us to look closely at these difficult subjects. He is able to bring a story as big and complex as the epic displacement of the world's people to us through a collection of intimate and intensely moving images. As he says in his introduction to the exhibit catalog, "We hold the key to humanity's future, but for that we must understand the present. We cannot afford to look away" (15).

The concluding paragraph restates the thesis; the paper ends with a compelling quotation.

——————————[new page]——————————

Work Cited

Salgado, Sebastião. *Migrations.* New York: Aperture, 2000. Print.

The work-cited entry appears on a new page, listing the source of the quotation used to end the essay.

6 Designing Academic Papers and Preparing Portfolios

One of your crucial writing tasks is to format your text so that readers can "see" your ideas clearly. The focus of this chapter is on designing academic papers. (*Advice on designing multimedia presentations and Web sites is in Chapter 14: Multimedia Writing, and advice on designing brochures, newsletters, résumés, and other documents is in Part 5: Writing beyond College.*)

In your writing classes, as well as in other courses and in your professional life, you may be called on to compile a **portfolio,** a collection of your writing and related work. This chapter offers guidelines for designing print and electronic portfolios that showcase your work effectively.

www.mhhe.com/mhhb2

For links to information on document and Web design, go to

Writing > Writing Web Links > Annotated Links on Design

6a Consider audience and purpose when making design decisions.

Effective design decisions take into account your purpose for writing as well as the needs of your audience. If you are writing an informative paper for a psychology class, your instructor—your primary audience—will probably prefer that you follow the guidelines provided by the American Psychological Association (APA). If you are writing a lab report for a biology or chemistry course, you will very likely need to follow a well-established format and use the documentation style recommended by the Council of Science Editors (CSE) to cite any sources you use. A history paper might call for use of the Chicago style. Interpretive papers for language and literature courses usually use the style recommended by the Modern Language Association (MLA). In any paper, however, your goal is to enhance the content of your text, not decorate it. (*For help with these documentation styles, see Chapters 23–26.*)

6b Use the tools available in your word-processing program.

Most word-processing programs give you a range of options for editing, sharing, and, especially, designing documents. For example, if you are using Microsoft Word 2007, you can access groups of commands by clicking on the various tabs at the top of the screen. Figure 6.1 on the facing page shows the Home tab, which contains basic formatting and editing commands. You can choose different typefaces; add bold, italic, or underlined type; insert numbered or bulleted lists, and so on. Other tabs allow you to add boxes and drawings to your text, make comments, and change the page layout.

Many word-processing programs are organized differently. Some include menus of commands on toolbars instead of on tabs. Take

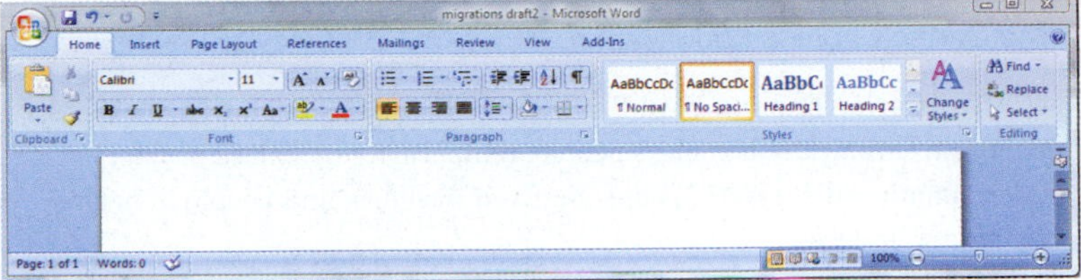

FIGURE 6.1 Formatting tools in a word-processing program.

some time to learn the different formatting options available in your program.

6c Think intentionally about design.

For any print or online document that you create, whatever its purpose or audience, apply the same basic **document design** principles:

- Organize information for readers.
- Choose typefaces and use lists and other graphic options to make your text readable and to emphasize key elements.
- Format related design elements consistently.
- Use headings to organize long papers.
- Use restraint.
- Meet the needs of readers with disabilities.

A sample page from a student's report on a local food bank, which includes information that she gathered while serving as a volunteer, illustrates these principles. The content in Figure 6.2 on page 106 is not presented effectively because the author has not adhered to these principles. By contrast, the same material in Figure 6.3 on page 107 is clearer and easier for readers to understand because of its design.

www.mhhe.com/mhhb2
For more on designing your paper, go to
Writing > Visual Rhetoric Tutorial > Document Design

1. Organizing information for readers

You can organize information visually and topically by grouping related items using boxes, indents, headings, spacing, and lists. These variations in text appearance help readers scan, locate important information, and dive in when they need to know more about a topic. If a color printer is available to you and your instructor allows you to use color in your paper, then it can serve this purpose as well. Use color with restraint, and remember that colors may look different on screen and in print. Also consider readers with disabilities (*see p. 111*).

You can also use **white space,** areas of a document that do not contain type or graphics, to help organize information for your readers. Generous margins and plenty of white space above headings and around other elements make text easier to read. Use white space to divide your document into chunks of related information.

Emphasis wrong: Title of report is not as prominent as the heading within the report.

The Caring Express Food Bank

The Caring Express Food Bank serves a varied population of clients, including chronically homeless people, temporarily homeless people, recent immigrants, elderly people on fixed incomes, and people in need of temporary services.

Margins are not wide enough, making the page look crowded.

Bar chart is not introduced in the text and does not have a caption.

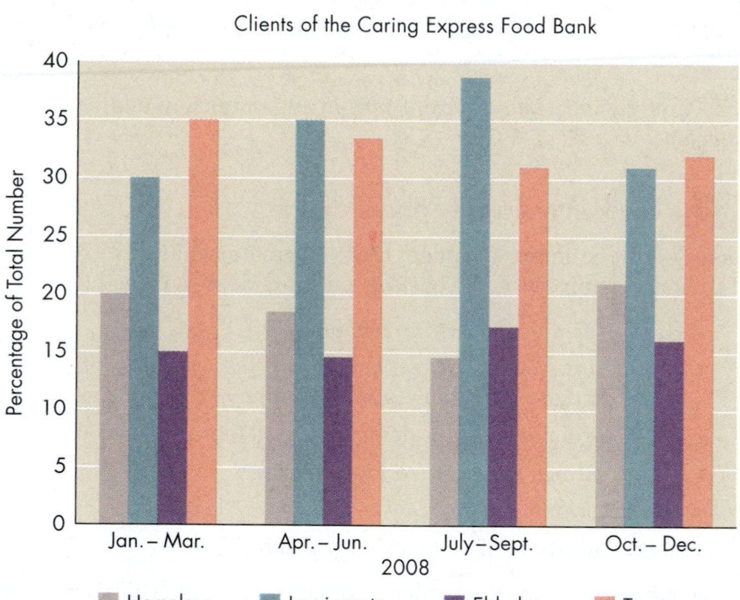

While the number of homeless, both temporary and permanent, that Caring Express assisted in 2008 decreased during the summer months, the number of immigrant workers increased. The percentage of elderly people and people in need of temporary services remained fairly stable throughout the year.

Description of procedure is dense, not easy to follow.

How Caring Express Helps Clients

When new clients come to Caring Express, a volunteer fills out a **form** with their **address** (if they have one), their **phone number**, their **income,** their **employment situation,** and the help they are receiving, if any, from the local department of human services. Clients who do not live in Maple Valley are referred to a food bank or outreach program in their area. Clients who qualify check off the food they need from a list, and then that food is packed and distributed to them.

Use of bold type and different typeface for no reason.

FIGURE 6.2 Example of a poorly designed report.

The Caring Express Food Bank

The Caring Express Food Bank serves a varied population of clients, including chronically homeless people, temporarily homeless people, recent immigrants, elderly people on fixed incomes, and people in need of temporary services. As Figure 1 shows, while the number of homeless, both temporary and permanent, that Caring Express assisted in 2008 decreased during the summer months, the number of immigrant workers increased. The percentage of elderly people and people in need of temporary services remained fairly stable throughout the year.

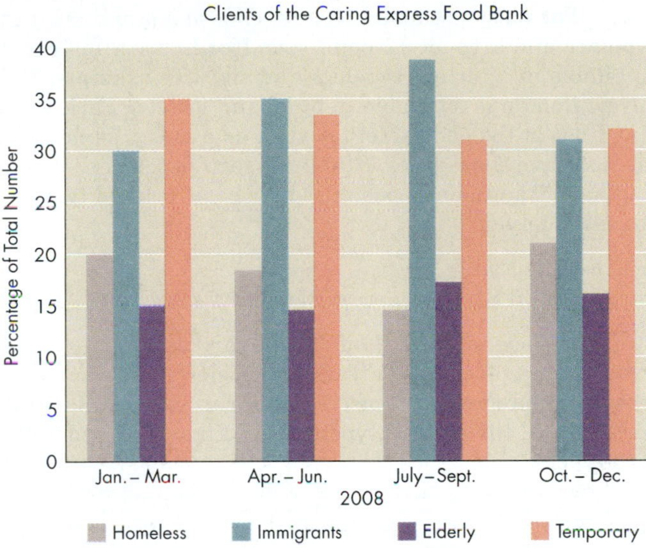

Clients of the Caring Express Food Bank

Percentage of Total Number

0 5 10 15 20 25 30 35 40

Jan. – Mar. Apr. – Jun. July – Sept. Oct. – Dec.

2008

Homeless Immigrants Elderly Temporary

Figure 1. Percentage of clients in each group during 2008

How Caring Express Helps Clients

When new clients come to Caring Express, the volunteers follow this procedure:

1. The volunteer fills out a form with the client's address (if he or she has one), phone number, income, and employment situation.
2. Clients who do not live in Maple Valley are referred to a food bank or outreach program in their area.
3. Clients who qualify check off the food they need from a list.
4. The food is packed and distributed to them.

Title is centered and in larger type than text and heading.

Bar chart is introduced and explained.

White space above and below figure sets it off.

Caption explains figure.

Heading is subordinate to title.

Procedure is explained in a numbered list. Writer uses parallel structure for list entries.

FIGURE 6.3 Example of a well-designed report.

In the résumé on page 466, Laura Amabisca uses white space to group her experience into different categories, such as education, work experience, and internship. This makes her résumé easy to evaluate in the sixty seconds or so that a prospective employer may first look at it.

You should also introduce any visuals within your text and position them so that they appear near—but never before—this text reference. Strive for a pleasing balance between visuals and other text elements; don't try to cram too many visuals onto one page.

2. Using type style and lists to make your text readable and to emphasize key elements

Typefaces are designs that have been established by printers for the letters in the alphabet, numbers, punctuation marks, and special characters. For most academic papers, choose a standard, easy-to-read typeface and a 10- or 12-point size. **Fonts** are all of the variations available in a certain typeface and size (for example, 12-point Times New Roman is available in **bold** and *italics*). Serif typefaces have tiny lines at the ends of letters such as n and y; sans serif typefaces do not have these lines. Standard serif typefaces such as the following have traditionally been used for basic printed text because they are easy to read:

Times New Roman　　Courier
Bookman Old Style　　Palatino

Sans serif typefaces such as the following are used for headings because they offer a pleasing contrast, or for electronic documents because they are more readable onscreen. (Norms may be changing. For example, Calibri, the default typeface in Microsoft Word 2007, is a sans serif typeface.)

Calibri
Arial
Verdana

Generally, if a document's main portion is in a sans serif typeface, headings should be in serif typeface, and vice versa.

Many typefaces available on your computer are known as *display fonts,* for example:

Curlz　　Old English
Lucinda Sans　　*Monotype Corsiva*

These should be used rarely, if ever, in academic papers, on the screen, or in presentations. They can be used effectively in other kinds of documents, however, such as brochures, fliers, and posters.

Elements of type allow you to organize content. You can emphasize a word or phrase in your text by selecting it and making it **bold,** *italicized,* or underlined. Numbered or bulleted lists help you

LEARNING in COLLEGE

Margins, Spacing, Type, and Page Numbers

Here are a few basic guidelines for formatting academic papers.

- **First page:** In a paper that is no longer than five pages, you can usually place a header with your name, your professor's name, your course and section number, and the date on the first page, preceding the text. (*See the final draft of Diane Chen's paper on p. 102.*) If your paper exceeds five pages, page one is usually a title page. (*For an example of a title page for a paper written in APA style, see the first page of Audrey Galeano's paper on p. 412.*)
- **Type:** Select a common typeface, or font, such as Calibri, Times New Roman, or Bookman, and choose a 12-point size.
- **Margins:** Use one-inch margins on all four sides of your text. Adequate margins make your paper easier to read and give your instructor room to write comments and suggestions.
- **Margin justification:** Line up, or justify, the lines of your document along the left margin but not along the right margin. Leaving a "ragged-right"—or uneven—right margin enables you to avoid odd spacing between words.
- **Spacing:** Always double-space your paper unless you are instructed to do otherwise, and indent the first line of each paragraph five spaces. Use the ruler at the top of your screen to set this indent automatically. (Many business documents are single spaced, with an extra line space between paragraphs, which are not indented.) Allow one space after periods, question marks, exclamation points, commas, semicolons, and colons. Add a space before and after an ellipsis mark. Do not allow extra space before or after dashes, hyphens, apostrophes within words, quotation marks, parentheses or brackets, or a mark that is immediately followed by another mark, such as a comma followed by a quotation mark. (*For more on these punctuation marks, see Part 10.*)
- **Page numbers:** Place page numbers in the upper or lower right-hand corner of the page. Some documentation styles require a header next to the page number—see Chapters 23–26 for the requirements of the style you are following.

cluster larger amounts of related information and make the material easier for readers to navigate and understand. You can use a numbered list to display steps in a sequence, present checklists, or suggest recommendations for action. Use parallel structure in your list (give entries the same grammatical form, as in the examples on page 110). Introduce your list with a complete sentence followed by a colon, and put a period at the end of each entry only if the entries are complete sentences. (*For more on parallel structure, see Chapter 42, pp. 637–45.*)

Putting information in a box emphasizes it and also makes it easier for readers to find if they need to refer to it again. Most word-processing programs offer several ways to enclose text within a border or box.

3. Formatting related design elements consistently

In design, simplicity, contrast, and consistency matter. If you emphasize an item by putting it in italic or bold type or in color, or if you use a graphic element such as a box to set it off, consider repeating this effect for similar items to give your document a unified look. Even a simple horizontal line can be a purposeful element in a long document when used consistently to help organize information.

4. Using headings to organize long papers

In short papers, headings are usually not necessary. In longer papers, though, they can help you organize complex information. (*For headings in APA style, see Chapter 25, p. 411.*)

Effective headings are brief and descriptive. Make sure that your headings are consistent in grammatical structure as well as formatting:

Phrases beginning with *-ing* words
Handling Complaints
Fielding Inquiries

Nouns and noun phrases
Complaints
Customer Inquiries

Questions
How Do I Handle Complaints?
How Do I Field Inquiries?

Imperative sentences
Handle Complaints Calmly and Politely
Field Inquiries Efficiently

Headings at different levels can be in different forms. If you have not already done so, preparing a formal topic outline will help you decide what your main points and second-level points are and where headings should go. (*For help with topic outlines, see Chapter 3, pp. 47–51.*) You might center all first-level headings—which correspond to the main points in your outline—and put them in bold type. If you have second-level headings—your supporting points—you might align them at the left margin and underline them.

LEARNING in COLLEGE

Standard Headings and Templates

Some types of papers, such as lab reports and case studies, have standard headings, such as Introduction, Abstract, and Methods and Materials (*see Chapter 8, pp. 148–54*). Word-processing programs allow you to create *templates,* or preformatted styles, that establish the structure and settings for the document and apply them automatically. If you frequently write papers that require formatting—lab reports, for example—consider creating a template.

First-Level Heading

Second-Level Heading
Third-Level Heading

If a heading falls at the very bottom of a page, move it to the top of the next page.

5. Using restraint

If you include too many graphics, headings, bullets, boxes, or other elements in a document, you risk making it "noisy." Certain typefaces and fonts have become standard because they are easy on the eye. Variations from these standard fonts are jarring. Bold or italic type, underlining, or any other graphic effect should not continue for more than one or two sentences at a time.

6. Meeting the needs of readers with disabilities

If your potential audience might include the vision- or hearing-impaired, follow these guidelines:

- **Use a large, easily readable font:** The font should be 14 point or larger. Use a sans serif font such as Arial, as readers with poor vision find these fonts easier to read. Make headings larger than the surrounding text (rather than relying on a change in font, bold, italics, or color to set them apart).
- **Use ample spacing between lines:** The American Council of the Blind recommends a line spacing of 1.5.
- **Use appropriate, high-contrast colors:** Black text on a white background is best. If you use color for text or visuals, put light material on a dark background and dark material on a light background. Use colors from different families

(such as yellow on purple). Also, avoid red and green because colorblind readers may have trouble distinguishing them.

- **Include narrative descriptions of all visuals:** Describe each chart, map, photograph, or other visual. Indicate the key information and the point the visual makes, so that users of screen-reader software will be able to follow your meaning.
- **If you include audio or video files in an electronic document, provide transcripts:** Also include narrative description of what is happening in the video.

For further information, consult the American Council of the Blind (http://acb.org/accessible-formats.html), Lighthouse International (http://www.lighthouse.org/print_leg.htm), and the American Printing House for the Blind (http://www.aph.org/edresearch/lpguide.htm).

6d Compile a print or an electronic portfolio that presents your work to your advantage.

Students, job candidates, and professionals are often asked to collect their writing in a portfolio. Although most portfolios consist of a collection of papers in print form, many students create electronic writing portfolios incorporating a variety of media.

Portfolios, regardless of medium, share at least three common features:

- They are a *collection* of work.
- They offer a *selection*—or subset—of a larger body of work.
- Once assembled, they are introduced, narrated, or commented on by a document that offers the writer's *reflection* on his or her work.

As with any type of writing, both print and electronic portfolios serve a purpose and address an audience. For example, you may be asked to prepare a "showcase" or "best-work" portfolio to demonstrate writing proficiency to a prospective employer. Or you might be asked to create a portfolio that documents how your writing has improved during a course, for a grade. You also might use a portfolio to assess your own work and set new writing goals.

1. Assembling a print portfolio

Course requirements vary, so always follow the guidelines your instructor provides. Nevertheless, when creating a print writing portfolio, you will usually need to engage in the five activities in the following Checklist box.

CHECKLIST

Assembling a Print Portfolio

- ☐ Gather all your written work.
- ☐ Make appropriate selections.
- ☐ Arrange the selections.
- ☐ Include a reflective essay or letter.
- ☐ Polish your portfolio.

Gathering your writing To organize your portfolio, create a list, or inventory, of the writing that you might include. For a writing course, you may need to provide your exploratory writing, notes, and comments from peer reviewers, as well as all your drafts for one or more of the papers you include. Make sure that all of your materials have your name on them and that your final draft is error free.

Reviewing your written work and making selections Keep the purpose of the portfolio in mind as well as the criteria that will be used to evaluate it. If you are assembling a presentation portfolio, select your best work. If you are demonstrating your improvement (a process portfolio), select papers that show your development and creativity, such as the exploratory writing, peer comments, and drafts for a particular paper.

If no criteria have been provided, consider the audience for the portfolio when deciding which selections will be most appropriate. Who will read it and what qualities will they be seeking?

Tips LEARNING in COLLEGE

Process Portfolios

If you include multiple drafts in your portfolio, you might use one or more of the following strategies to demonstrate improvement:

- Use a highlighter to note changes you made from one draft to the next.
- Annotate changes to explain why you made them.
- Choose two texts, completed at different times, to demonstrate how your writing has improved over the course of a term or year.

Arranging the selections deliberately If you have not been told how to organize your portfolio (for example, chronologically), you can think of it as if it were a single text and decide on an arrangement that will serve your purpose. Does it make sense to organize your work from weakest to strongest? From less important to more important? How will you determine importance?

Whatever arrangement you choose, explain your rationale for it to your audience. You can include this information in a letter to the reader, in a brief introduction, or via annotations in your table of contents.

Writing a reflective essay or letter The reflective statement may take the form of an essay or a letter, depending on your purpose and the assignment. Sometimes, the reflective essay will be the last item in a portfolio so that the reader can review all of the work first and then read the writer's interpretation. Or a reflective letter can open the portfolio. Either way, the reflective text lets you explain something about your writing or about yourself as a writer. Common topics in the reflective text include the following:

- How you developed various papers
- Which papers you believe are particularly strong and why
- What you learned as you worked on these assignments
- Who you are now as a writer

Follow the stages of the writing process in preparing your reflective essay or letter. Once you have completed it, you can assemble all of the components of your portfolio in a folder.

Polishing your portfolio In the process of writing the reflective letter or essay, you might discover a better way to arrange your work, or as you arrange your portfolio, you might want to review all your work again. Do not be surprised if you find yourself repeating some of these tasks. As with any writing, a portfolio will also improve if it is revised based on peer review.

Most students learn about themselves and their writing as they compile their portfolios and write reflections on their work. The process not only makes them better writers, it helps them learn how to demonstrate their strengths as well.

2. Preparing an electronic portfolio

For some courses or professional purposes, you will need to present your work in an electronic format. For example, an education student might be required to provide an electronic portfolio of lesson plans, class handouts, and other instructional materials. Electronic portfolios can be saved on CD or DVD, or published on the Web.

The process of creating an electronic portfolio differs somewhat from that of creating a print portfolio. Digital portfolios allow you to include different kinds of texts, such as audio files and video clips; they can be connected to other texts using hyperlinks; and their success depends on the use of visual elements. See the Checklist box below for the essential steps.

CHECKLIST

Creating an Electronic Portfolio

- ☐ Gather all your written work and audio, video, and visual texts.
- ☐ Make selections and consider connections.
- ☐ Decide on an arrangement, navigation, and presentation.
- ☐ Include a reflective essay or letter.
- ☐ Test your portfolio for usability.

Gathering your written work as well as your audio, video, and visual texts Depending on your assignment and purpose, you will need to make up to four inventories:

- A verbal inventory, consisting of your written work (Be sure to scan in any handwritten work that is not provided as a digital text.)
- An audio inventory (examples: speeches, music, podcasts)
- A video inventory (examples: movie clips, videos you have created)
- A visual inventory (examples: photographs, drawings)

The most important—and typical—components of an electronic portfolio tend to be the verbal and visual texts. Visuals can help you think about the images you will want to use to describe your work. One writer, for instance, might use images of everyday life in two countries to coordinate with texts in two languages in her portfolio.

Selecting appropriate texts and making connections among them Choose works from your inventory based on your portfolio's purpose and the criteria for evaluation. Consider relationships among your selections as well as external materials. These connections should reveal something about you and your writing. Ultimately, they will become the links that help the reader navigate your digital portfolio. Internal links connect one piece of your writing to another. For instance, you might link an earlier draft to a later one or link a PowerPoint presentation to a paper on the same topic. External links connect the reader to related files external to the portfolio but relevant to it. For instance, if you collaborated with a colleague or classmate on a project, you might link to that person's electronic portfolio.

Deciding on arrangement, navigation, and presentation As in a print portfolio, your work can be arranged in a variety of ways including in chronological order or order of importance. Once you have decided on a basic arrangement, help your reader navigate through the portfolio. As you plan, create a flowchart that shows each item in your portfolio and how it is linked to others. (*For sample Web site plans, see Chapter 14, p. 239.*) After you have planned your site's structure, add hyperlinks to your documents. Many word-processing programs have a Hyperlink function. Make the link text descriptive of the destination (a link reading "Résumé" should lead to your résumé).

One very simple, intuitive method for helping readers navigate the portfolio is a table of contents with links to the text for each item. You might then provide links from each final draft to exploratory writing, drafts in progress, and comments from peer reviewers. Alternatively, you might decide to make the table of contents part of an introductory page that also gives information about you and explains the course. You might open with a reflective letter embedded with links that take readers to your written work and other texts. The portfolio in Figure 6.4 on the facing page features a menu of links that appears on each page, as well as links in the reflective text.

Consider how the opening screen will establish your purpose and appeal to your audience, and what kind of guidance you will provide for the reader. Choose colors, images for the front page and successive pages, and typefaces that visually suggest who you are as a writer and establish a tone appropriate for your purpose. (For example, some typefaces and themes suggest a more serious tone, while others are more lighthearted.)

Writing a reflective text As in a print portfolio, the reflective text explains to readers what the writer wants them to know about the selections. A digital environment, however, offers you more possibilities for presenting this reflection. You can make it highly visual; for example, you might have it cascade across a series of screens. Another option would be to link to an audio or video file in which you talk directly to the reader.

Process & Product

Reflections

Home
Essays
Reflections
Process & Product
Audience & Genre
Evidence & Analysis
Who is Ken Tinnes?
External Links

Throughout this semester, one of my main goals for this course was to be able to learn how to effectively create and utilize a detailed outline to assist with my writing process in order to ensure good organizational skills. The essay from this semester in which I was best able to achieve this goal was the research project. Due to the abundance of sources, as well as the mere size of the assignment, I knew I would need any organizational help I could get.

Before I could begin writing my paper, or even working on an outline for it, I needed to decide what exactly I wanted to write about, and how I would approach that topic specifically. To do this, I created a thesis statement for my essay. I read and revised my thesis numerous times on my own. I also looked to some of my peers from my dorm floor to revise my thesis as well. After establishing an accurate and detailed thesis summarizing and introducing the content of my essay, I was ready to research and prewrite.

Throughout the entire writing process for the research paper, I was focused on the structure of my essay. When I would find new sources, I would try to automatically classify the topic of that source, and cite it in my outline wherever I found it to be most appropriate. I tried to establish some of my transitions, and extract the exact quotes or information I would be using in my essay. By doing this, I was able to see the progression of my paper before it was even written. I didn't have to worry about rearranging my essay after it had already been written. That was extremely helpful, as there is nothing I find to be more difficult than rearranging full paragraphs, while trying to maintain a rhythmic flow to my paper.

As I wrote my paper, I tried my best to stick to the outline. If I came up with fresh ideas as I was writing, I would put them into my outline first, so that I would know where they would best fit inside my paper. By doing this, I was able to avoid many of the problems I experienced in some of my earlier writings. By filtering everything through my outline first, I was able to think of an intelligent way to convey my information. I would write my main arguments for each source and thought contained in my paper, so that I was able to reconstruct them until they were perfect. In doing this, I created what I like to think of as the most elaborate and detailed passages that I have ever written.

By writing these passages in my outline first, rather than my essay, I was able to avoid the disorganization that comes with a rush of thoughts, and focus on the sole goal of establishing thorough theses and arguments that would have a greater chance of being fully and accurately conveyed by my audience.

Home > Reflections > Process & Product >

© 2006 Ken Tinnes Contact Me

FIGURE 6.4 A reflective essay from a student's electronic portfolio.

Testing your electronic portfolio before sharing it with the intended audience Make sure your portfolio works—both conceptually and structurally—before releasing it. You should navigate all the way though your portfolio yourself and ask a friend to do so from a different machine. Sometimes links fail to work, or files stored on one machine do not open on another, so this step is very important. In addition, another person may have comments or suggestions about the portfolio's structure or the content of your reflective text. Ultimately, this feedback will help you make the portfolio easy to use.

Auguste Rodin's sculpture The Thinker *evokes the psychological complexity of human thought and suggests the spirit of critical inquiry common to all disciplines across the curriculum.*

PART 2

Anybody who is involved in working across the disciplines is much more likely to have a lively mind and a lively life.

—MARY FIELD BELENKY

Common Assignments across the Curriculum

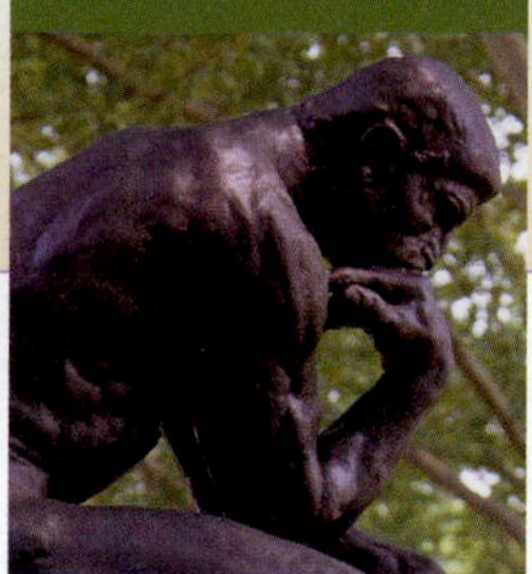

7 Reading, Thinking, Writing: The Critical Connection

The exchange of ideas in every discipline happens as scholars read and respond to one another's work. This chapter introduces you to the process of critical reading as a way of getting intellectually involved with your studies. In this context, the word *critical* means thoughtful. When you read critically, you recognize the literal meaning of the text, make inferences about implicit or unstated meanings, and then make your own judgments in response.

It is now easier than ever to obtain information in a variety of ways, so you need to be able to "read" critically not just written texts, but visuals, sounds, video, and spoken texts as well.

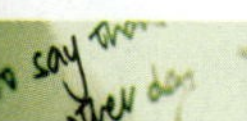

WRITING OUTCOMES

Part 2: Common Assignments

This section will help you answer questions such as:

Rhetorical Knowledge

- How can I argue persuasively? **(10c)**
- How can I keep my audience interested in my oral presentation? **(13b)**
- What should I *not* put on my blog or social networking page? **(14f)**

Critical Thinking, Reading, and Writing

- How do I analyze printed text and images? **(7b–d)**
- How can annotation and summary help me with reading assignments? **(7d)**
- How can I defend my paper against counterarguments? **(10c)**

Processes

- What is the best way to prepare for essay exams? **(12a)**
- How can I use presentation software (such as PowerPoint) effectively? **(13b, 14d)**
- What steps should I take in planning my Web site? **(14e)**

Knowledge of Conventions

- What is a review of the literature, and where do such reviews appear? **(8d)**
- What special design principles apply to Web sites? **(14e)**

CHECKLIST

Reading Critically

- ☐ **Preview** the piece before you read it.
- ☐ **Read** the selection for its topic and point.
- ☐ **Analyze** the who, what, and why of the piece by **annotating** it as you reread it and **summarizing** what you have read.
- ☐ **Synthesize** through making connections.
- ☐ **Evaluate** what you have read.

7a Recognize that critical reading is a process.

Critical reading is a process. As with writing, you will find yourself moving back and forth among the steps in this process.

Critical readers don't just read; they reread. The writer Ray Bradbury claims that he read Herman Melville's *Moby Dick* eighty to ninety times before he understood it well enough to write the screenplay for John Huston's movie adaptation. Your goals for reading (from simply checking a fact to undertaking a full-scale evaluation of a text) will determine how much time you need to spend.

Writing at every stage of the critical reading process also helps to deepen your involvement with the text. If you are reading a book that you own, write in it as you read, highlighting key ideas and terms and noting your questions or objections. If you are reading a library book, a Web page, or a nonprint text, keep notes in a journal—paper or electronic—to help you remember what you have read and reflect on its significance. Some writers use a double-column notebook, with one column for notes about the text and the other column for their own reactions and ideas. (*See the TextConnex box on p. 130 for other tips on annotating electronic texts.*)

7b Preview the text or visual.

Critical reading begins with **previewing:** looking over the text's author and publication information and quickly scanning its contents to gain a context for understanding and evaluating it.

If the text is a possible source for a paper, you will also need to determine whether it is a **primary source** or a **secondary source**—that is, whether it is a firsthand (primary) account of an event or research or someone else's (secondary) interpretation of that firsthand account. Research reports in the sciences are primary sources; textbooks and encyclopedia articles are secondary sources. Original works of art, literature, theater, film, and music are also primary sources; critical analyses and reviews are secondary sources.

1. Asking questions as you preview a written text

As you preview a text, ask questions to get a sense of the topics and to help you judge the credibility of the evidence and arguments the piece presents.

CHECKLIST

www.mhhe.com/mhhb2
For more on evaluating sources, go to
Research > CARS Source Evaluation Tutor

Previewing a Written Text

Author

- ☐ Who wrote this piece?
- ☐ What are the author's credentials and occupation?
- ☐ Who is the author's employer?
- ☐ What are the author's interests and values?

Purpose

- ☐ What do the title and first and last paragraphs tell you about the purpose of this piece?
- ☐ Do the headings and visuals provide clues to the purpose of the piece?
- ☐ What might have motivated the author to write the piece?
- ☐ Will the main purpose be to inform, to interpret, to argue, or something else (to entertain or to reflect, for instance)?

Audience

- ☐ Whom is the author trying to inform or persuade?
- ☐ Does the vocabulary give you a sense of the kind of knowledge the author expects his or her audience to have?

Content

- ☐ What do the title and headings tell you about the piece?
- ☐ Does the first paragraph include the main point?
- ☐ Do the headings give you the gist of the piece?
- ☐ Does the conclusion tell you what the author is trying to inform you about, interpret for you, or argue?
- ☐ What do you already know and think about the topic?

Context

- ☐ Is the publication date (or most recent update for a Web site) current? Does the date matter?
- ☐ What kind of publication is it? Is it a book, an article in a periodical or library database, a Web site, or something else?
- ☐ Where and by whom was the piece published? If it was published electronically, was it posted by the author or by an organization with a special interest?

2. Asking questions as you preview a visual

You can use most of the previewing questions for written texts to preview visuals. Here are some additional questions you should ask:

- In what context does the visual appear? Was it intended to be viewed on its own or as part of a larger work? Is it part of a series of images (for example, a graphic novel, a music video, or a film)?
- What does the visual depict? What is the first thing you notice in the visual? Is its literal meaning immediately clear, or do you need to spend time looking at it to figure it out?
- Does the visual represent a real event, person, or thing (a news photo, a portrait), or is it fictional (an illustration in a story)?
- Is the visual accompanied by audio or printed text?

www.mhhe.com/mhhb2
For an interactive tutorial on analyzing visuals, go to
Writing > Visual Rhetoric Tutorial > Understanding Images

A preview of Figure 7.1 (on the next page) might produce these answers:

- **In what context does the visual appear?** This public service advertisement appeared in several publications targeted to college students. As the Peace Corps logo in the lower right-hand corner indicates, the ad was produced by the Peace Corps to recruit volunteers.

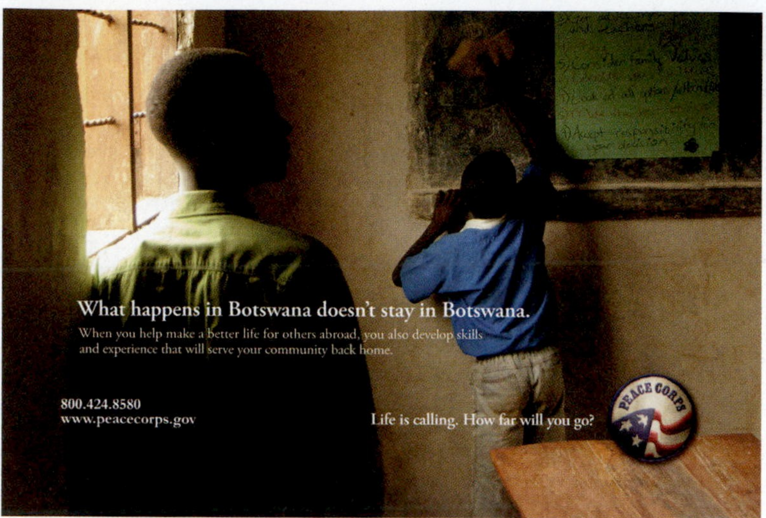

FIGURE 7.1 Peace Corps advertisement. The text superimposed on this photograph reads: **What happens in Botswana doesn't stay in Botswana.** When you help make a better life for others abroad, you also develop skills and experience that will serve your community back home. Life is calling. How far will you go?

- **What does the visual depict? What is the first thing you notice in the visual?**

  The scene is a bare school room in Botswana. (*Look at the foldout Resources for Writers: World Map in* Part 13: Further Resources, *to find Botswana in Africa.*) As sun streams from a window, one young man in the foreground looks on as a younger boy erases a blackboard. On the blackboard, a handwritten poster appears with points of advice, for example, "Accept responsibility for your decision."
- **Is it a representation of a real event, person, or thing, or is it fictional?** The scene represents the reality of African children in need of the Peace Corps' help.
- **Is the visual accompanied by audio or printed text?**

  Bold text appears in the center of the image, followed by smaller print directly addressed to the viewer. The phone number and Web address for the Peace Corps are printed in the lower left, and another appeal to the viewer, followed by the Peace Corps logo, is printed in the lower right.

LEARNING in COLLEGE

Evaluating Context in Different Kinds of Publications

- **For a book:** What is the publisher's reputation? University presses, for example, are very selective and usually publish scholarly works. Vanity presses—which require authors to pay to publish their work—are not selective at all.
- **For an article in a periodical:** Look at the list of editors and their affiliations. What do you know about the journal, magazine, or newspaper in which this writing appears? Are the articles that appear in it reviewed by experts in a particular field before they are published?
- **For a Web site:** Who created the site? A Web site named for a political candidate, for example, may actually have been put on the Web by his or her opponents. (*See the Checklist box, Using the CARS Checklist to Evaluate Web Sites, in Chapter 18: p. 297.*)

The meaning of this image is not immediately clear from a preview. We will need to read it more closely to grasp its message fully.

7c Read and record your initial impressions.

A first reading is similar to a first draft—your primary purpose is to get a sense of the whole. Identify what the text is about and the main point the writer makes about the topic. Note difficult passages to come back to, as well as interesting ideas. Look up any unfamilar terms. Record your initial impressions:

- If the written text or image is an argument, what opinion does it express? Were you persuaded by it?
- Did you have an emotional response to the text or image? Were you surprised, amused, or angered by anything in it?
- What was your initial sense of the writer or speaker?
- What key ideas did you take away from the work?

Exercise 7.1 Preview and first reading of an essay

On the following pages is an essay that appeared in the *Village Voice,* a weekly journal of opinion and commentary published in New York City.

1. Preview the essay, using the questions in the Checklist on pages 122–23.
2. Read through the essay in one sitting, then record your initial impressions, using the questions in 7c (*above*).

Misguided Multiculturalism

Nat Hentoff

An American-history requirement hallows ethnocentrism just as everyone else is embracing internationalism and preparing students to become citizens of the world.

—Joanne Reitano,
history professor and
chair of the Community
College Caucus, *New
York Post*, May 28 [2000]

Both my parents were immigrants from Russia. In my neighborhood, Yiddish was a first and second language. I grew up in the depths of the Great Depression. There were weeks when my father came home with $5 or less. My mother walked blocks to save a few cents on food.

I went to public school. Some of my friends were sent to the yeshiva—an Orthodox Jewish religious school—but my parents, having experienced the vicious, pervasive anti-Semitism in the Old Country, wanted me to learn what America was all about.

At Boston Latin School and Northeastern University—a working-class college—I took classes that taught a great deal about the fundamental rights and liberties that had to be fought for during this still "unfinished American revolution," as Thurgood Marshall called it. These were required courses, and inspired my lifelong involvement in civil rights and civil liberties.

This is a personal prelude to an intense controversy over a proposed four-year master plan for the City University of New York by CUNY's Board of Trustees, which will be voted on by the New York State Board of Regents in September. The leading, and impassioned, advocate of the part of the plan that I'm focusing on here is Herman Badillo, chairman of CUNY's Board of Trustees.

A key element in the plan is its 5
call for a core curriculum, including a required course in American history—which is already in place in the state university system. A number—not all—of the faculty members on the various campuses vigorously object. Some say trustees have no business meddling in what should be the prerogative of the faculty. Others call the very idea of a required course in American history absurd. "The assumption," says professor Joanne Reitano, "is that our immigrant students need to be taught what it means to be an American."

Over the years, I have given classes in this city's public schools, from elementary grades through high school. And as a reporter, I have spent considerable time in other classrooms. As is the case throughout the country—from failing schools to the prestigious high schools—the teaching of American history, with few exceptions, is cursory, scattered, and superficial.

It's just as bad in most colleges. A recent survey by the American Council of Trustees and Alumni (David Broder's column, *The*

Washington Post, July 2) reveals "historical illiteracy" about this country across the board—even among students at Amherst, Williams, Harvard, Duke, and the University of Michigan. Moreover, "none of the 55 elite colleges and universities (as rated by *U.S. News & World Report*) requires a course in American history before graduation." As for high schools, Broder notes, a report by the National Assessment of Educational Progress disclosed that "fully 57 percent of the high school seniors failed to demonstrate a basic level of understanding of American history and institutions—the lowest category in the test."

The foremothers of women's liberation, Susan B. Anthony and Elizabeth Cady Stanton, as well as civil rights leaders like Frederick Douglass and Malcolm X, used the First Amendment as an essential weapon; but how many Americans, including students, know the embattled history of free speech in this nation?

Also neglected in the vast majority of secondary schools and colleges is the history of the American labor movement—its fight against repression in the 19th century and well into this century.

10 When teaching, I have found interest among a wide array of students in the story of why we have a Fourth Amendment—British officials' random, often savage searches of the colonists' homes and businesses to look for contraband. As Supreme Court Justice William Brennan told me, the resultant fury of those initial Americans was a precipitating cause of the American Revolution.

I told that story and others about resistance to discrimination, and worse, throughout American postrevolutionary history to a large group of predominantly black and Hispanic high school students in Miami a couple of years ago.

Before I started, one of their teachers told me, "Don't be upset if they don't pay attention. What they're mostly interested in is clothes and music."

After more than an hour, there was a standing ovation. Not for me, but because they had discovered America—its triumphs and failures. Talking to some of them later, I was told they'd heard none of those stories in school.

Multiculturalism is a welcome development in American education so long as some of its college courses do not exalt one particular culture and history over others. Then, it is indeed ethnocentric. But to understand where you came from, you also have to understand where you are now. You have to know how the society you live in works, and that requires a full-scale knowledge of its history—from its guiding principles to what still has to be done to make them real. For everybody.

Justice William Brennan said: 15
"We do not yet have justice, equal and practical, for the members of minority groups, for the criminally accused, for the displaced persons of the technological revolution, for alienated youth, for the urban masses, for the unrepresented consumer—for all, in short, who do not take part of the abundance of American life. . . . Ugly inequities continue to mar the face of our nation. We are surely

nearer the beginning than the end of the struggle."

To do something about that, CUNY students should know the strategies, successes, and failures of widely diverse Americans who have been part of that struggle. For insisting on core American history courses, Herman Badillo should be cheered, not scorned.

From the *Village Voice*,
July 19–25, 2000

Exercise 7.2 Preview and first reading of an essay

Find an article that interests you in a newspaper or magazine, preview it using the Checklist's questions in 7b, then read through it in one sitting and record your initial impressions using the questions in 7c.

Exercise 7.3 First reading of a visual

Spend some time looking at the image and text for the Peace Corps ad on page 124. Record your responses to the following questions:

1. Did you have an emotional response to the ad?
2. What opinion, if any, did you have of the Peace Corps before you read the ad? Has your opinion changed in any way as a result of the ad?
3. What key ideas does the ad attempt to present?
4. If you recognize the slogan the ad references, what do you think is the impact of its use here? Is it effective? Why or why not?

7d Reread using annotation and summary to analyze and interpret.

Once you understand the literal, or surface, meaning of a text, dig deeper by analyzing and interpreting it. To **analyze** a text is to break it down into significant parts and examine how those parts relate to each other. We analyze a text to **interpret** it and come to a fuller understanding of its meanings.

1. Using annotation and summary

Annotation and **summary** can help with analysis and interpretation.

Annotation To annotate a text, read through it slowly and carefully while asking yourself the *who*, *what*, *how*, and *why* questions. As you read, underline or make separate notes about words, phrases, and sentences that strike you as significant or puzzling, and write down your questions and observations.

EXAMPLE OF AN ANNOTATED PASSAGE

Introductory paragraphs from "Misguided Multiculturalism" by Nat Hentoff

Both my parents were immigrants from Russia. In my neighborhood, Yiddish was a first and second language. I grew up in the depths of the Great Depression. There were weeks when my father came home with $5 or less. My mother walked blocks to save a few cents on food.

Childhood story—establishes his personal experience of multicultural issues.

I went to public school. Some of my friends were sent to the yeshiva—an Orthodox Jewish religious school—but my parents, having experienced the vicious, pervasive anti-Semitism in the Old Country, wanted me to learn what America was all about.

At Boston Latin School and Northeastern University—a working-class college—I took classes that taught a great deal about the fundamental rights and liberties that had to be fought for during this still "unfinished American revolution," as Thurgood Marshall called it. These were required courses, and inspired my lifelong involvement in civil rights and civil liberties.

Essential?

Supreme Court.

Would they inspire every-one?

This is a personal prelude to an intense controversy over a proposed four-year master plan for the City University of New York by CUNY's Board of Trustees, which will be voted on by the New York State Board of Regents in September. The leading, and impassioned, advocate of the part of the plan that I'm focusing on here is Herman Badillo, chairman of CUNY's Board of Trustees.

=introduction Smooth transi-tion to the real argument.

EXAMPLE OF A NOTEBOOK ENTRY

"Misguided Multiculturalism," by Nat Hentoff: Intro paragraphs

Starts by discussing his own background, telling us about his childhood and his education:
—Son of Russian immigrants, grew up poor
—Spoke Yiddish (bilingual upbringing)
—Parents wanted him to "learn what America was all about"
—Took mandatory courses about U.S. rights and liberties in school

Long build-up before he gets to the real subject of his article: a proposal to make American history course mandatory at a university in New York. Is his story really relevant?

2. Questioning the text

Analysis and interpretation require a thorough understanding of the who, what, how, and why of a text:

- **What is the writer's *stance*, or attitude toward the subject?** Does the writer appear to be objective, or does the writer seem to have personal feelings about the subject?
- **What is the writer's *voice*?** Is it that of a reasonable judge, an enthusiastic preacher, or a reassuring friend? Does the writer seem to be speaking *at, to,* or *with* the audience?

- **What assumptions does the writer seem to be making about the audience?** Does the writer assume a readership of specialists or a general audience? Does the writer assume that the reader agrees with him or her, or does the writer try to build agreement? Does the writer seem to have chosen examples and evidence with a certain audience in mind?
- **What is the author's primary purpose?** Is the purpose to present findings, offer an objective analysis, or argue for a particular action or opinion?
- **How does the author develop ideas?** What kind of support does the author rely on? Does the writer define key terms? Include supporting facts? Provide logical reasons?
- **Does the text appeal to emotions?** Does the writer use words, phrases, clichés, images, or examples that are emotionally charged?
- **Is the text fair?** Does the author consider opposing ideas, arguments, or evidence and do so fairly?
- **Is the evidence strong?** Does the author provide sufficient evidence? What are his or her assumptions? Where is the argument strongest and weakest?
- **Is the text effective?** How do your assumptions and views affect your reading? Has the text challenged or changed your beliefs on this subject?
- **How do the ideas in this text relate to those in other texts?**

Visuals too can be subjected to critical analysis, as the annotations a reader made on the Peace Corps ad indicate (*Figure 7.2 on p. 131.*)

TEXTCONNEX

Annotating Electronic Text

Unless a copyright notice prohibits it, you can download an electronic file for your own use in order to annotate it. Write on a printout of the file, or insert your comments directly in the file using a contrasting typeface or color or the Comments feature of your word-processing program. Record full source information in case you need to find or cite the original. (*See Chapter 21, p. 321.*)

Composition of the photograph like Vermeer's paintings of sunlight illuminating an indoor scene. Subtle appeal to students of art history?

Reference to Las Vegas slogan, "What happens here stays here." Secrets of Las Vegas (superficial fun) stay there because of shame. Working with the Peace Corps in Botswana illuminates your life—and the world (another reference to the sunlight?)

The boy is reaching up to erase or wash something from the blackboard. An older boy watches—also "reaching"? A poster covering part of the board lists principles valuable in Botswana and in the United States.

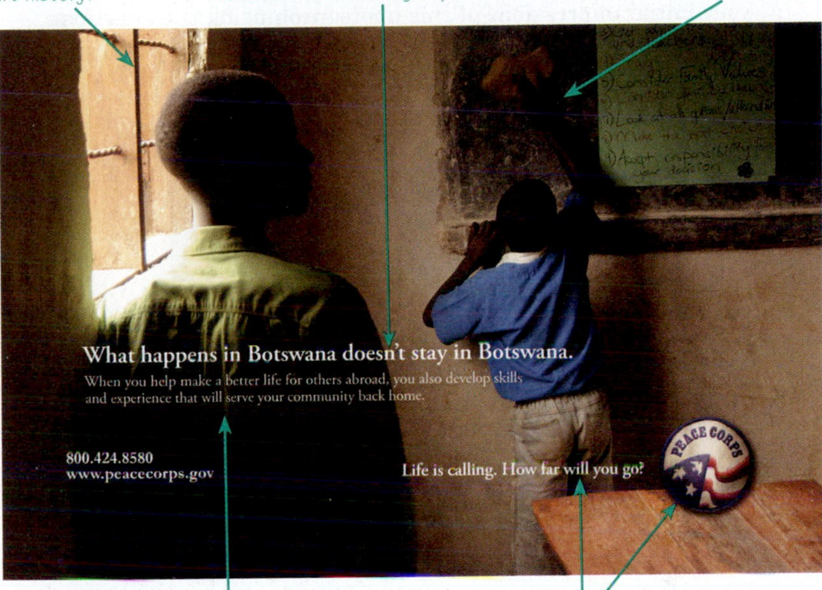

What happens in Botswana doesn't stay in Botswana.
When you help make a better life for others abroad, you also develop skills and experience that will serve your community back home.
800.424.8580
www.peacecorps.gov
Life is calling. How far will you go?
PEACE CORPS

Smaller print emphasizes the What Happens message above. Elaborates on win/win opportunity of the Peace Corps vs. likelihood of losing games in Las Vegas.

The Peace Corps logo combines the globe with the American flag—a global view of patriotism. How far will you go geographically and personally?

FIGURE 7.2 An annotated image.

Exercise 7.4 Analyzing an essay

Reread "Misguided Multiculturalism" on pages 126–28. Annotate it or take separate notes as you read, and analyze it to determine how its parts work together. Add your own interpretations of Hentoff's statements.

Exercise 7.5 Analyzing an article

Reread the article you selected for Exercise 7.2, analyzing it with annotations or in separate notes.

Exercise 7.6 Analyzing a visual

1. Add to the annotated analysis of the Peace Corps ad in Figure 7.2 on page 131, focusing on the text as well as the photograph.
2. The photograph shown in Figure 7.3 below was taken during the January 30, 2005 elections in Iraq. It shows Kurdish women waiting to vote in the city of Kirkuk. First, preview and record your initial impressions of this photograph using the questions in 7b and 7c. Then analyze and annotate it, either directly on the page or on a separate sheet of paper.

FIGURE 7.3 **Women voting in Kirkuk, Iraq, January 30, 2005.**

Summary A **summary** conveys the basic content of a text. When you summarize, your goal is to communicate the text's main points in your own words, without saying what you think of it. A summary of an essay or article typically runs about one paragraph in length. Even when you are writing a fuller summary of a longer work, you should always use the fewest words possible. Clarity and brevity are important. A summary should never be longer than the original work.

A summary requires simplification, but avoid misrepresenting a writer's points by *oversimplifying* them. Consider this summary of the main point of the Hentoff essay (*from pp. 126–28*).

OVERSIMPLIFIED SUMMARY

> A U.S. history course should be required because college students are ignorant.

Although Hentoff does point to a general lack of knowledge about U.S. history among college students, a more accurate summary would indicate *why* Hentoff feels an understanding of U.S. history is important.

Here is a summary of Hentoff's essay that Ignacio Sanderson wrote as he was working on the paper that appears at the end of this chapter:

THOUGHTFUL SUMMARY

In his essay "Misguided Multiculturalism," Nat Hentoff defends a proposal to require all students of the City University of New York to take an American history course. Hentoff begins by noting that he is the son of immigrants from Russia. He goes on to discuss his upbringing and education and how the courses he took in American civics inspired his "lifelong involvement in civil rights and civil liberties" (29). In addition to pointing out how valuable the study of American history was to his own career, Hentoff notes that most college students, even at schools like Duke and Harvard, do not know much about U.S. history. Hentoff acknowledges that multiculturalism is a worthwhile value, but stipulates, "You have to know how the society you live in works, and that requires a full-scale knowledge of its history" (30). While multiculturalism is important, a basic knowledge of U.S. history is essential.

Note: Summaries are especially useful in research as a tool for recording various sources' points of view. A good summary can help you avoid plagiarism as well, because a central characteristic of a summary is that it is expressed in your own words. *(For more on summary, as well as paraphrase and quotation—two other methods of incorporating ideas—see Chapter 21: Working with Sources and Avoiding Plagiarism, pp. 322–28.)*

Exercise 7.7 Summarizing

Evaluate these summaries of passages from the Peace Corps ad (*p. 124*) and "Misguided Multiculturalism" (*pp. 126–28*). Indicate the problem with each faulty summary, and suggest how it should be revised.

1. The Peace Corps ad describes Botswana.
2. In "Misguided Multiculturalism," Nat Hentoff argues that everyone should have an education like his.
3. In paragraph 7 of "Misguided Multiculturalism," Hentoff argues that U.S. college and high school students have little knowledge about U.S. history.

Exercise 7.8 Summarizing

If your word-processing program has a feature like "AutoSummarize," use it to generate a summary of one of your own academic papers. Then identify and describe any problems with the computer-generated summary.

Exercise 7.9 Summarizing

1. Summarize the content and message of the Peace Corps ad (*p. 124*).
2. Summarize the article you selected for Exercise 7.2.
3. Summarize the photograph of Iraqi Kurdish women voting in Figure 7.3 (*p. 132*).

Tips

LEARNING in COLLEGE

Writing a Critical Response Paper

- Summarize the main idea of the text fairly and accurately recognizing its strengths as well as its weaknesses.
- Use your course readings to help formulate an approach to your analysis.
- Narrow your focus to one or two key points rather than responding to every point in the text.
- Use facts as well as personal experience to support your points. Avoid phrases such as "I feel" or "In my opinion."
- Avoid derogatory comments and labels such as "stupid."
- Document the text and any additional sources, using the documentation style required by your instructor. (*See Part 4: Documenting across the Curriculum for guidelines.*)

7e Synthesize your observations in a critical response paper.

To **synthesize** means to bring together, to make something out of different parts. In the last stage of critical reading, you pull your analysis, interpretation, and summary together into a coherent whole. Often this synthesis takes the form of a critical response paper.

A **critical response paper** typically begins with a summary of the text, followed by a thesis. The thesis should encapsulate your response to the text. Here are some possible thesis statements in response to Hentoff's "Misguided Multiculturalism":

POSSIBLE THESIS

Hentoff effectively argues that people need a knowledge of U.S. history to live in the United States and that a required U.S. history course is necessary to give people this knowledge.

POSSIBLE THESIS

Hentoff makes valid points about the necessity and importance of learning about U.S. history, but he underestimates the negative impact a required course would have on immigrants and first- and second-generation Americans.

The rest of the response paper should elaborate on your thesis, supporting it with evidence from the text, your other reading, any related research, and your relevant personal experience.

In the following critical response paper, Ignacio Sanderson synthesizes his reading of Nat Hentoff's "Misguided Multiculturalism" with his own experience.

Ignacio Sanderson

Professor Blackwell

English 99-B

15 March 2009

Critical Response to "Misguided Multiculturalism"
by Nat Hentoff

Multiculturalism is one of the most hotly debated topics in higher education today. As the son of an immigrant to the United States, I take this debate personally. The question of what makes an "American education" strikes a chord in me.

The same is true for Nat Hentoff, as he explains in his article "Misguided Multiculturalism." Hentoff first notes that he is the son of immigrants from Russia. He goes on to discuss his upbringing and education and how the courses he took in American civics inspired his "lifelong involvement in civil rights and civil liberties" (29).

Hentoff then defends a proposal by the City University of New York's Board of Trustees to introduce a mandatory American history course for all the university's students. In addition to pointing out how valuable the study of American history was to

Hentoff's argument summarized.

his own career, Hentoff notes that most college students, even at schools like Duke and Harvard, do not know much about U.S. history. He complains that students are ignorant about the history of the Bill of Rights and the American labor movement. Hentoff acknowledges that multiculturalism is a worthwhile value but stipulates, "You have to know how the society you live in works, and that requires a full-scale knowledge of its history" (30). While multiculturalism is important, a basic knowledge of U.S. history is essential.

Thesis statement

I have experienced the transition from one culture to another firsthand. Although I agree with Hentoff that it is crucial to learn about American history if you want to be an American, requiring an American history course of everyone sends the wrong message to immigrants and first- and second-generation Americans. It tells such people that there is only one important history university students should know: American history.

Objection to Hentoff's argument.

Hentoff is clearly sensitive to the charge of "ethnocentrism,"or the placing of one culture or ethnicity above all others. In the article, however, he seems to want to have it both ways: he supports a multicultural, non-ethnocentric curriculum, but also a required American history course. These goals are incompatible, however. Making all students take a course in the history of one society to the exclusion of those of other societies is inevitably ethnocentric.

Consideration of Hentoff's response to the objection.

Hentoff tries to answer this objection by pointing out that an American history course might reveal to students the history of discrimination—and the fight against it—in this country. He implies that, even if requiring the course is ethnocentric, the content of the course would not have to be ethnocentric propaganda. That may be true, but Hentoff does not know what the course will cover. He discusses the history he would like students to learn, but offers no evidence that faculty members will teach it. Unless there is a set syllabus for the course, however, there is no guarantee that students will be exposed to a balanced account of U.S. history.

Nat Hentoff's heart is in the right place. It is important for all Americans to know how the United States became the country it is today. This knowledge would be better gained by people acting individually, though, rather than within the context of mandated classes. Students should have the right to manage for themselves the complex task of becoming American.

Conclusion reinforces Sanderson's point.

---------------------------------[new page]-------------------------------------

Work Cited

Hentoff, Nat. "Misguided Multiculturalism." *Village Voice* 19 July 2000: 29–30. Print.

Works-Cited list follows MLA style and begins on a new page.

Exercise 7.10 Writing a critical response to an article

Using the analysis that you prepared in Exercise 7.5 and the summary that you wrote in Exercise 7.9.2, write a critical response to the article you selected for Exercise 7.2.

Exercise 7.11 Writing a critical response to a visual

1. Using the analysis that you prepared in Exercise 7.6 and the summary you wrote in Exercise 7.9.1, write a critical response to the Peace Corps ad (*p. 124*).
2. Using the analysis that you prepared in Exercise 7.6.2 and the summary you wrote in Exercise 7.9.3, describe your personal reaction to the photograph of Iraqi women voting in Figure 7.3 (*p. 132*).

8 Informative Reports

Imagine what the world would be like without records of what others have learned. Fortunately, we have many sources of information to draw on, including informative reports.

8a Understand the assignment.

An **informative report** passes on what someone has learned about a topic or issue; it teaches. An informative report gives you a chance to do the following:

- Learn more about an issue that interests you.
- Make sense of what you have read, heard, and seen.
- Teach others in a clear and unbiased way what you have learned.

(For examples of the types of informative reports assigned in college, see pp. 141 and 150.)

CHARTING the TERRITORY

Informative Reports

Informative reports are commonly written by members of the humanities, social sciences, and natural sciences disciplines, as these examples indicate.

- In a published article, an anthropologist surveys and summarizes information from archeological, historical, and ethnographic sources relating to warfare among the indigenous peoples of the American Southwest.
- For an encyclopedia of British women writers, a professor of literature briefly recounts the life and works of Eliza Fenwick, a recently rediscovered eighteenth-century author.
- In an academic journal for research biologists, two biochemists summarize the findings of more than two hundred recently published articles on defense mechanisms in plants.

For an interactive tutorial on writing informative reports, go to **Writing > Writing Tutors > Informative Reports**

8b Approach writing an informative report as a process.

1. Selecting a topic that interests you

The major challenge of writing informative reports is engaging the reader's interest. Selecting a topic that interests you makes it more likely that your report will interest your readers.

Connect what you are learning in one course with a topic you are studying in another course or with your personal experience. For example, one student, John Terrell, majored in political science and aspired to a career in international relations. For his topic, he decided to investigate how one Muslim organization was pursuing human rights for women. (*Terrell's paper begins on p. 141.*)

2. Considering what your readers know about the topic

Assume that your readers have some familiarity with the topic area but that most of them do not have clear, specific knowledge of your particular topic. In his paper on Sisters in Islam, Terrell assumes that his readers probably have seen images of Afghan women in burqas.

3. Developing an objective stance

When writers have an **objective stance,** they do not take sides. They present ideas and facts fairly and emphasize the topic, not the writer. (By contrast, when writers are **subjective,** they let readers know their views.) A commitment to objectivity gives an informative report its authority.

4. Composing a thesis that summarizes your knowledge of the topic

An informative thesis typically states an accepted generalization or reports the results of the writer's study. Before you decide on a thesis, review the information you have collected. Compose a thesis statement that summarizes the goal of your paper and forecasts its content. (*For more on thesis statements, see Chapter 3: Planning and Shaping the Whole Essay, pp. 42–46.*)

www.mhhe.com/mhhb2
For more help with developing a thesis, go to
Writing > Paragraph/Essay Development > Thesis/Central Idea

In his paper about Sisters in Islam (SIS), Terrell develops a general thesis that he supports in the body of his paper with information about how the group does its work:

> Based in Malaysia, SIS has developed three key ways to promote women's rights within the context of the Muslim religion and its holy book, the Qur'an.

Notice how the phrase "three key ways" forecasts the body of Terrell's report. We expect to learn something about each of the three key ways, and the report is structured to give us that information, subtopic by subtopic.

5. Providing context in your introduction

Informative reports usually begin with a relatively simple introduction to the topic and a straightforward statement of the thesis. Provide some relevant context or background, but get to your specific topic as quickly as possible and keep it in the foreground. (*For more on introductions, see Chapter 4: Drafting Paragraphs and Visuals, pp. 72–74.*)

6. Organizing your paper for clarity by classifying and dividing information

Develop ideas in an organized way, by classifying and dividing information into categories, subtopics, or the stages of a process. (*For more on developing your ideas, see Chapter 4: Drafting Paragraphs and Visuals, pp. 61–72.*)

www.mhhe.com/mhhb2

For more on using patterns of development, go to

Writing > Paragraph Patterns

7. Illustrating key ideas with examples

Use specific examples to help readers understand your most important ideas. In his paper on Sisters in Islam, Terrell provides many specific examples, including pertinent quotations from the Qur'an, a discussion of the attempt to establish the Domestic Violence Act, and descriptions of SIS educational programs. Examples make his report interesting as well as educational. (*For more on using examples, see Chapter 4: Drafting Paragraphs and Visuals, p. 62.*)

8. Defining specialized terms and spelling out unfamiliar abbreviations

Explain specialized terms with a synonym or a brief definition. For example, Terrell provides a synonym and a brief description of the term *sharia* in the third paragraph of his informative report on Sisters in Islam. (*For more on definition, see Chapter 4: Drafting Paragraphs and Visuals, p. 66.*) Unfamiliar abbreviations like SIS (Sisters in Islam) and NGO (non-governmental organization) are spelled out the first time they are used, with the abbreviation in parentheses.

www.mhhe.com/mhhb2

For more information on conclusions, go to

Writing > Paragraph/Essay Development > Conclusions

9. Concluding by answering "so what?"

Conclude with an image that suggests the information's value or sums it all up. Remind readers of your topic and thesis, and then answer the "So what?" question.

At the end of his report on Sisters in Islam, Terrell answers the "So what?" question by contrasting press stereotypes of the status of women in Islam with the more complex and encouraging view his paper presents.

> But their efforts show that the situation of women in Islamic countries is actually much more complex and encouraging than many recent newspaper images and stories have led us to believe.

(*Also see information on conclusions in Chapter 4: Drafting Paragraphs and Visuals, pp. 74–75.*)

LEARNING in COLLEGE

Informative Reports in the Social Sciences

Informative reports in the social sciences examine a wide range of behavioral and social phenomena, such as consumer spending, courtship rituals, political campaign tactics, and job stress.

Some Types of Informative Reports in the Social Sciences

- *Research reports* describe the process and results of research conducted by the author(s).
- *Reviews of the literature* synthesize the published work on a particular topic (*see 8d*).

Documentation Styles

- APA (*see Chapter 24*) and Chicago (*see Chapter 25*)

8c Write informative reports on social science research.

In the informative report that follows, John Terrell reports what he has learned about a Muslim non-governmental organization dedicated to promoting women's rights. Notice how Terrell provides a context for his topic, cites various sources (using the APA documentation style), divides the information into subtopics, and illustrates his ideas with examples, all hallmarks of a clear, carefully developed paper. The annotations in the margin of this paper point out specific aspects of the informative report. (*For details on the proper formatting of a paper in APA style, see Chapter 24 and the sample paper that begins on p. 412.*)

www.mhhe.com/mhhb2
For another sample of informative writing, go to
Writing > Writing Samples > Informative Paper

Sample student informative report

Sisters Redefining the Divine

John Terrell

Political Science 252 Contemporary Issues: Human Rights

Professor Paul

December 20, 2008

--------------------------------[new page]--------------------------------------

Following APA style, Terrell includes a separate title page. He does not include an abstract, however, because his instructor did not require one for this assignment.

Sisters Redefining the Divine

Topic introduced.

The rights of women in Islamist and majority-Muslim nations have recently become an issue of concern and contention. Images of women in burqas, along with news stories describing forced marriages, public executions by flogging, and virtual house arrest for women without chaperones have led many Americans to assume that Muslim women have no rights and no way to change that situation. But that is not the whole picture. In many parts of the Islamic world, non-governmental organizations (NGOs) are working hard to make sure that women and their interests have a political voice. Sisters in Islam (SIS) is just such an organization. Based in Malaysia, SIS has developed three key ways to promote women's rights within the context of the Muslim religion and its holy book, the Qur'an.

First use of unfamiliar abbreviation spelled out.

Thesis stated.

First way—introduces subtopic.

Source information summarized.

One way that SIS works to promote women's rights is to show how those rights are rooted in the origins of Islam and the Qur'an. Members note that women fought side by side with the prophet Muhammad in the early struggle to establish Islam's rule and point out that allowing some degree of choice in marriage, permitting divorce, and granting inheritance rights for women were revolutionary concepts when Muslims first introduced them to the world 1,400 years ago (Othman, 1997). Furthermore, they argue that the Qur'an mandates "the principles of equality, justice and freedom" and does not specifically prohibit women from assuming leadership roles or contributing to public service. But they also recognize that the revolutionary possibilities of Islam were curtailed when a small group of men claimed "exclusive control over the interpretation of the Qur'an" (Sisters in Islam, 2007).

Voices of Muslim women are important to this topic so are quoted directly.

Source named in signal phrase.

According to Coleman (2006), the Qur'an contains almost 80 sections on legal issues, but neither it nor the secondary texts and oral traditions of Islam contain instruction on everyday matters. To make matters even more complex, the Qur'an includes many seemingly contradictory passages. Its statements on polygamy are a prime example. One verse in the text says, "Marry those women who are lawful for you, up to two, three, or four, but only if you can treat them equally," while a later verse reads, "No matter how you try you will never be able to treat your wives equally." In the early years following the death of the prophet Muhammad, legal scholars were called upon to examine issues in need of clarification. They were also encouraged to apply independent thinking and then make non-binding rulings. This practice lasted until the 11th century, at which time Sunni religious scholars consolidated legal judgments into strict schools of thought and placed a ban on independent interpretation. The result was *sharia,* or Muslim law. Over the next nine hundred years, this approach to the law changed little. In application, however, sharia does vary according to regional traditions. In Tunisia, for example, taking more than one wife is banned altogether, while India provides few restrictions upon polygamy (Women Living under Muslim Laws, 2003). Likewise, rules concerning dress and moral codes vary from state to state, with headscarves for women being obligatory in Iran and optional in Egypt.

Example given for clarity and interest.

Unfamiliar term defined.

National diversity in applying sharia accounts for the second way that SIS promotes women's rights within the framework of Islam: they focus their work for change on one country, Malaysia. Before 1957, Malaysia was a British colony with a court system divided between the federal and the local levels. Local Islamic leaders were allowed to establish courts to preside over cases of family law, while most other legal matters went to the federal courts. After Malaysia gained independence, Article 3 of its constitution named Islam as the state religion, although a clause in the same article guaranteed non-Muslims the right to practice their faiths (Mohamad, 1988). The court system, however, remained the same, meaning that the 60 percent of the population who are Muslim are still subject to local Islamic family courts, while the 40 percent who do not follow Islam are not (U.S. Department of State, 2005).

Second way—introduces subtopic.

Source given for data.

Objective stance: first person (I) avoided with APA style.

Malaysia's legal system complicates the work of SIS, as the 1995 campaign to pass a domestic violence act shows. In matters of violence against women, Muslim family law provides little legal recourse. The usual response by Islamic judges is to send the woman home to reconcile with her husband. So in 1995 the SIS campaigned to pass the Domestic Violence Act, which aimed to provide basic legal protections for women. After a vigorous lobbying campaign, the law was passed. Yet the response from Malaysia's Islamic religious establishment was to say that the law would only apply to non-Muslims (Othman, 1997). Even though this interpretation of the law has not been successfully reversed, SIS continues to work on family law reform, submitting to the government memoranda and reports on such issues as divorce, guardianship, and polygamy. In 2005, for example, SIS and five other NGOs formed a Joint Action Group on Gender Equality (JAG) and prepared a memorandum requesting a review and withdrawal of parts of a bill that was intended to improve the Islamic Family Law Act of 1984. While praising the new requirement that in cases of contracting polygamous marriages, both the existing and future wives must be present in the court, JAG (2005) objected to other parts of the bill such as a change in wording that would make it easier for men to practice polygamy; instead of having to show that the new marriage was both "just and necessary," the men would only have to show that it was "just or necessary."

Example given for clarity and interest.

Third way—introduces subtopic.

Although advocating for changes in the law is certainly important, SIS has developed another key way of promoting women's rights: public research-backed education. Using surveys and interviews, the group began a pilot research project in 2004 on the impact of polygamy on the family institution; that research project has recently gone national. As its Web site documents, SIS also sponsors numerous public lectures and forums on such issues as Islam and the political participation of women, the challenges of modernity, the use of fatwa, and the emergence of genetic engineering. There are also seminars and workshops for specific

Examples given for clarity and interest.

groups such as single parents, study sessions with visiting writers, and a rich array of printed material, including newspaper columns that answer women's questions as well as pamphlets on such concerns as family planning, Qur'an interpretation, and domestic violence. Clearly SIS takes a very public approach to reform, an approach that Zainah Anwar (2004), the executive director, contends is necessary to ensure that Islam does not "remain the exclusive preserve of the *ulama* [traditionally trained religious scholars]."

Quotation integrated into writer's sentence.

Instead of waiting patiently for Islamic scholars and judges to work issues out in closed sessions, SIS has developed an activist approach to reform. So it is not surprising that its key ways of effecting change sometimes get as much criticism from conservative Islamists as the proposed changes themselves do (Anwar, 2004). It remains to be seen whether SIS, along with other NGOs working for human rights in Muslim countries, will succeed in moderating what they see as harmful expressions of their faith. But their efforts show that the situation of women in Islamic countries is actually much more complex and encouraging than many recent newspaper images and stories have led us to believe.

Interpretation provided without biased opinion.

Point and purpose restated in conclusion.

---------------------------------[new page]---------------------------------

References

References list follows APA style and begins on a new page.

Anwar, Z. (2004, September-October). Sisters in Islam: A voice for everyone. *Fellowship Magazine*. Retrieved from http://www.forusa.org/fellowship/sept-oct-04/anwar.html

Coleman, I. (2006, January-February). Women, Islam, and the new Iraq. *Foreign Affairs*. Retrieved from http://www.foreignaffairs.org/20060101faessay85104/isobel-coleman/women-islam-and the-new-iraq.html

Joint Action Group on Gender Equality. (2005, December). Memorandum to Ahli Dewan Negara to review the Islamic Family Law (Federal Territories) (Amendment) Bill

2005. Retrieved from http://www.sistersinislam.org.my/memo/08122005.htm

Mohamad, M. (1988). Islam, the secular state, and Muslim women in Malaysia. Retrieved November 15, 2008, from http://www.wluml.org/english/pubsfulltst.shtml?cmd[87]=i-87-2615

Othman, N. (1997). Implementing women's human rights in Malaysia. *Human Rights Dialogue, 1*(9). Retrieved from http://www.cceia.org/resources/publications/dialogue/1_09/articles/567.html

Sisters in Islam. (2007). Mission. Retrieved December 10, 2008, from http://sistersinislam.org.my/mission.htm

U.S. Department of State. Bureau of Democracy, Human Rights, and Labor. (2005, November 8). *Malaysia: International Religious Freedom Report 2005*. Retrieved from http://www.state.gov/g/drl/rls/irf/2005/51518.htm

Women Living under Muslim Laws. (2003). Knowing our rights: Women, family, laws, and customs in the Muslim world. Retrieved December 12, 2008, from http://www.wluml.org/english/pubsfulltst.shtml?cmd[87]=i-87-16766

8d Write reviews of the literature to summarize current knowledge in a specific area.

In upper-division courses in the social and natural sciences, instructors sometimes assign a special kind of informative report called a **review of the literature.** Here the term *literature* refers to published research reports, and the term *review* means that you need to survey others' ideas, not evaluate them or argue for your opinion. A review presents an organized account of the current state of knowledge in a specific area, an account that you and other researchers can use to figure out new projects and directions for research. A review of the literature may also be a subsection within a research report.

The following paragraph is an excerpt from the review of the literature section in an article by psychologists investigating the motivations for suicide:

> One source of information about suicide motives is suicide notes. International studies of suicide notes suggest that women and men do not differ with regard to love versus achievement

> motives. For example, in a study of German suicide notes, Linn and Lester (1997) found that women and men did not differ with regard to relationship versus financial or work motives. In a study of Hong Kong suicide notes, Ho, Yip, Chiu, and Halliday (1998) reported no gender or age differences with regard to interpersonal problems or financial/job problems. Similarly, in a UK study, McClelland, Reicher, and Booth (2000) found that men's suicide notes did not differ from women's notes in terms of mentioning career failures. In fact, in the UK study relationship losses were reported more often in men's than in women's suicide notes.
>
> —Canetto and Lester, *Journal of Psychology,* September 2002

8e Write informative reports in the sciences to share discoveries.

Reading and writing play a role at each stage of scientific inquiry. Scientists observe phenomena and record their findings in notebooks. They ask questions about their observations, read related work by other scientists, and compose hypotheses that explain the observations. To prove or disprove their hypotheses, they conduct experiments, carefully documenting their procedures and findings. Finally, they write research reports to share their work with other scientists.

8f Write lab reports to demonstrate understanding.

As a college student, you may be asked to demonstrate your scientific understanding by showing that you know how to perform and report on an experiment designed to verify some well-established fact or principle. In advanced courses, you may get to design original experiments as well. (*An example of a student lab report can be found on pp. 150–54.*)

> ***Note:*** When scientists report the results of original experiments designed to provide new insight into issues on the frontiers of scientific knowledge, they go beyond informative reporting to interpretive analysis of the significance of their findings.

Lab reports usually include the following sections: Abstract, Introduction, Methods and Materials, Results, Discussion, Acknowledgments, and References. Begin drafting the report, section by section, while your time in the lab is still fresh in your mind.

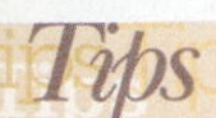

LEARNING in COLLEGE

Informative Reports in the Sciences

Informative reports in the sciences examine a wide range of natural and physical phenomena, such as plant growth, weather patterns, animal behavior, chemical reactions, and magnetic fields.

Some Types of Informative Reports in the Sciences

- *Lab reports* describe experiments, following the steps of the scientific method.
- *Research reports* describe the process and results of research conducted by the author(s). Research reports are more extensive than lab reports.
- *Reviews of the literature* synthesize the published work on a particular topic. (*See 8d, pp. 146–47 for an explanation and example.*)

Documentation Styles

- CSE name-year style, citation-name style, and citation-sequence style (*see Chapter 26*).

Throughout your report, use passive voice to describe objects of study, which are more important than the experimenter ("the mixture *was heated* for 10 minutes"). Use the present tense to state established knowledge ("the rye seed *produces*"), but use the past tense to describe your own results and the work of prior researchers ("Kurland *reported*").

Follow the scientific conventions for abbreviations, symbols, and numbers. See if your textbook includes a list of accepted abbreviations and symbols. Use numerals for dates, times, pages, figures, tables, and standard units of measurement. Spell out numbers between one and nine that are not part of a series of larger numbers.

1. Abstract

An abstract is a one-paragraph summary (about 250 words) of your lab report. It answers the following questions: What methods were used in the experiment? What variables were measured? What were the findings? What do the findings imply?

2. Introduction

In the introduction, state your topic, summarize prior research, and present your hypothesis. Sometimes you will include a review of the literature (*see pp. 146–47*).

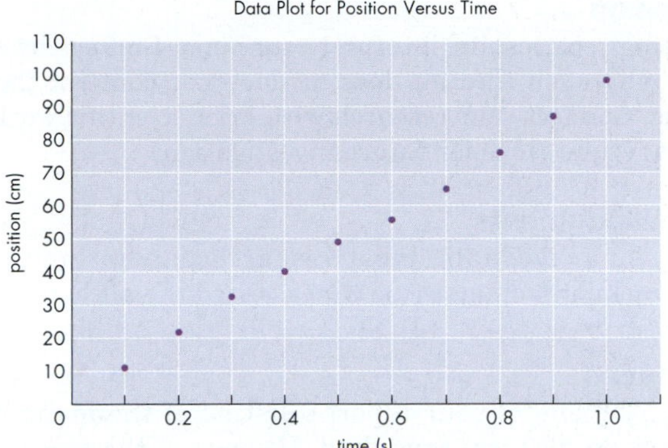

FIGURE 8.1 The distance traveled by a paper airplane plotted in 0.1 second intervals.

3. Methods and materials

Select the details that other scientists will need to replicate the experiment. Using the past tense, recount in chronological order what was done with specific materials.

4. Results

In this section, tell your reader about the results that are relevant to your hypothesis, especially those that are statistically significant. Results may be relevant even if they are different from what you expected.

You might summarize results in a table or graph. For example, the graph in Figure 8.1 above, which plots the distance (in centimeters, *y*-axis) a glider traveled over a period of time (in seconds, *x*-axis), was used to summarize the results of an engineering assignment.

Every table and figure you include in a lab report must be mentioned in the text. Point out the relevant patterns the figure displays. If you run statistical tests on your findings, be careful not to make the tests themselves the focus of your writing. Also refrain from interpreting why things happened the way they did.

Note: Like the terms *correlated* and *random*, the term *significant* has a specific statistical meaning for scientists and should therefore be used in a lab report only in relation to the appropriate statistical tests.

5. Discussion

In discussing your results, interpret your major findings by explaining how and why each finding does or does not confirm the original hypothesis. Connect your research with prior scientific work and look ahead to new questions for future investigation.

6. Acknowledgments

In professional journals, most research papers include a brief statement acknowledging those who assisted the author or authors.

7. References

Include at the end of your report a listing of the manuals, books, and journal articles you consulted. Use one of the citation formats developed by the Council of Science Editors (CSE style), unless your instructor prefers another citation format.

Sample student lab report

Orientation by Sight in Schooling and Nonschooling Fish

Josephine Hearn

Biology 103

May 5, 2008

Lab partners: Tracy Luckow, Bryan Mignone, Darcy Langford

Experiment summarized.

Abstract

This experiment examined the tendency of schooling and of nonschooling fish to orient by sight toward conspecifics. Schooling species did orient toward conspecifics by sight and nonschooling species did not show any preference, indicating that schooling fish show a positive phototaxis toward conspecifics.

CSE citation-sequence style: superscript numeral indicates source in references list.

Introduction

Vision has been established as the primary method by which many schooling fish maintain a close proximity to one another. Olfaction, sound, and water pressure are secondary factors in schooling[1].This experiment tested this theory, specifically, to determine whether schooling fish orient by sight toward conspecifics, whether schooling fish orient toward conspecifics more readily in the presence of a nonschooling species than of another schooling species, and whether schooling fish orient toward conspecifics more readily than nonschooling fish do. It was predicted that schooling fish would show a positive phototaxis to conspecifics, and that nonschooling fish would demonstrate no definite taxis movement toward conspecifics; furthermore, schooling fish would orient toward conspecifics more readily in an environment with nonschooling fish than in one with other schooling fish; finally, strongly schooling fish would more readily orient to conspecifics than would less strongly schooling fish.

Background information provided: earlier study, scope and hypothesis of current experiment.

The hypothesis was tested by placing two species in an aquarium, one species at each end of the tank, with a test fish belonging to one of the two species in the center of the tank allowed to orient by sight toward either species.

Methods and materials

Observations were made of 5 species of fish: *Brachydanio* sp. (zebra danios), *Barbus tetrazona* (tiger barbs), *Xiphophorus maculatus* (swordtails), *Hyphessobrycon* sp. (tetras), and *Cichlasoma nigrofasciatum* (juvenile convict cichlids). The species were ranked according to the schooling behavior exhibited, determined by recording the time each species spent schooling. Criteria for ranking were the proximity of conspecifics to one another and the tendency to move together. Barbs were ranked as the species with the strongest schooling tendency, followed closely by tetras, then danios, swordtails, and cichlids. Cichlids were considered a nonschooling species. The top 2 ranking species, barbs and tetras, and the last ranking species, cichlids, were selected for this experiment.

As illustrated in Figure 1, three cylinders were placed inside a filled 10-gallon aquarium surrounded by a dark curtain to prevent the entry of light from the sides[2]. Plexiglas cylinders were used to keep species separated and able to orient to each other by sight alone. The 2 outermost cylinders contained 4 each of 2 different species. A test fish, belonging to either of those species, was placed in the central cylinder. The water temperature was uniformly 22°C and remained so throughout the experiment.

Figure introduced (appears on p. 152).

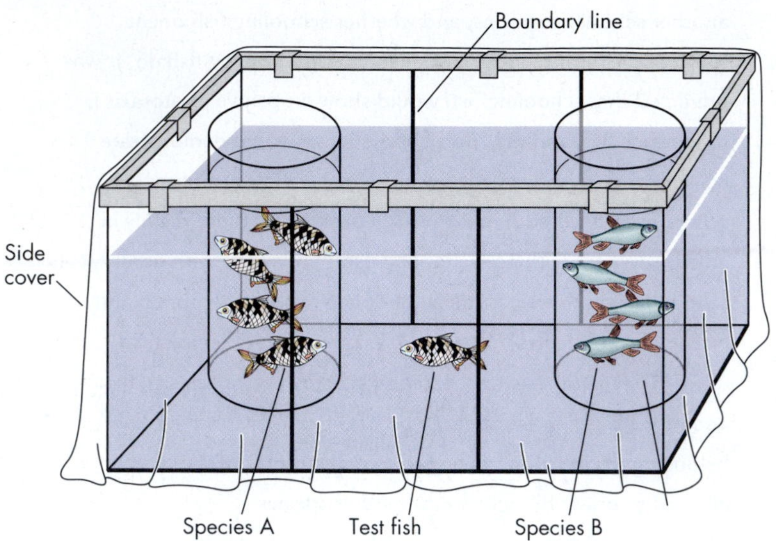

Figure 1 Test tank used to study orientation behavior (from Glase JC; Zimmerman MC, Waldvogel JA[2]).

Specifics about how the experiment was conducted.

When all cylinders were in place, the central cylinder was lifted out of the tank, allowing the test fish to move freely. Over the course of one minute, the time that the test fish spent on the side with conspecifics was recorded. The procedure was repeated with all possible combinations of the 3 species, and 5 replicates of each combination.

Results

Outcome of the experiment summarized.

Figure 2 shows the results for each of the three species for all of the trials. As predicted, the mean time out of one minute spent on the conspecifics side is higher for the barbs and tetras than for the cichlids. Figure 3 compares the mean times for each of the schooling species when the test fish were with the other schooling species or with the nonschooling species. The mean times for the schooling species are higher when the test fish was with other schooling species than with the nonschooling species.

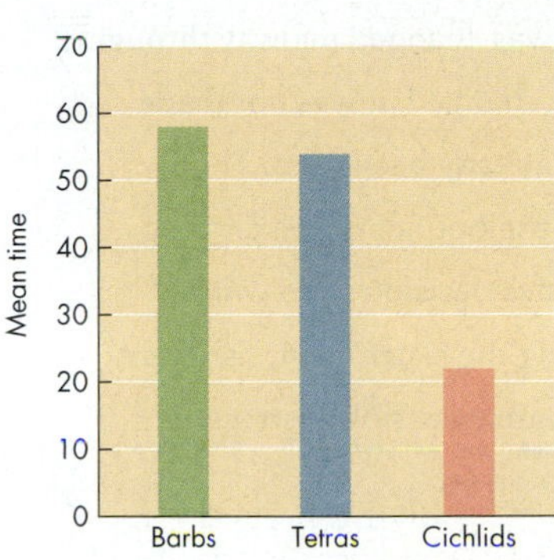

Figure 2 Mean time spent with conspecifics.

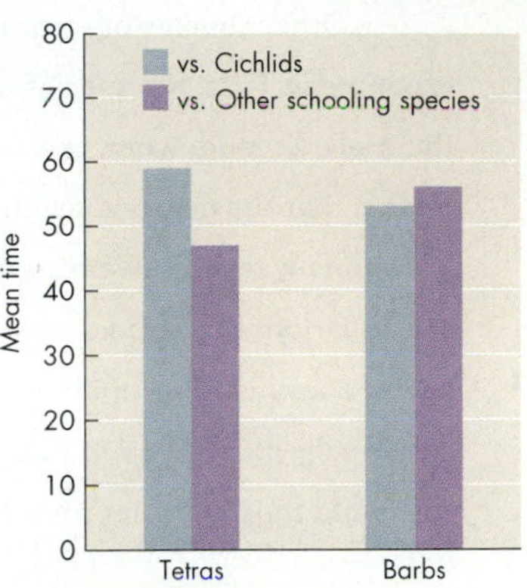

Figure 3 Comparison of mean times.

Discussion

The hypothesis that schooling fish would orient more readily than nonschooling fish to conspecifics was supported. It was shown that barbs and tetras, both schooling fish, spent nearly the entire time on the side with their own species, whereas the cichlids divided their time almost equally between the 2 sides. This result supports the theory that schooling fish orient to each other visually[1]. Furthermore, the barbs, the species with stronger schooling tendencies, showed more orientation than the tetras, the species with weaker schooling tendencies.

Barbs and tetras did not orient more or less readily to conspecifics depending on whether it was the other schooling species or the nonschooling species present in the tank. This indicates that schooling fish are neither attracted to other species of schooling fish nor repelled by nonschooling fish; however, because of the limited data, this subject deserves more investigation. An experiment should be conducted in which schooling fish are placed in a tank with the choice to orient either toward another schooling species or toward a nonschooling species, neither of which are conspecifics to the test fish.

Results of the experiment interpreted and flaws described.

Other sources of error may have affected the results of this experiment. First, the species of tetra was changed midway through the trials. Second, when test fish were changed, it was not made certain that the new test fish had not already been used. Third, occasionally test fish were so close to the boundary line dividing the aquarium that it became a subjective decision as to which side the test fish was on. Fourth, during the experiment, fish were continually moved in and out of the water, possibly distressing them and thus affecting their ability to orient.

——————————————[new page]——————————————

References list follows CSE citation-sequence style and begins on a new page.

References

1. Burgess JW, Shaw E. Development and ecology of fish schooling. Oceanus. 1979; 22(2):11–17.
2. Glase JC, Zimmerman MC, Waldvogel JA. Investigations in orientation behavior [Internet]. Association for Biology Laboratory Education (US); c1997 [cited 2008 Apr 28]. Available from: Association for Biology Laboratory Education at http://www.zoo.utoronto.ca/able/volumes/vol-6/1-glase/1-glase.htm

8g Write informative reports on events or findings in the humanities.

In the humanities, informative papers are used primarily to report on an event or finding in one of the humanities disciplines (for example, art, literature, history, philosophy, music, theater, and film). Unlike informative reports in the sciences, informative reports in the humanities may sometimes include subjective responses—your reaction to the event—in addition to specific details that support your points.

In the following example, a journalist explains the recent work of an artist who combines music, video, and readings in live performance.

LEARNING in COLLEGE

Informative Reports in the Humanities

Informative reports in the humanities describe the ideas, stories, and values of people past and present. Topics could include archeological discoveries, accounts of musical performances, and historical findings about art patronage.

Some Types of Informative Reports in the Humanities

- *Concert, theater, or film reports* describe the elements of a single performance or series of performances.
- *Book reports* describe the plot, characters, setting, and themes of a novel or summarize a nonfiction work.

Documentation Styles

- MLA (*see Chapter 23*) and Chicago (*see Chapter 25*)

Sample informative piece

The Sample Life

CARLY BERWICK

Paul D. Miller, a.k.a. DJ Spooky that Subliminal Kid, straddles hip-hop, club culture, and silent film

A young boy danced in the aisle to the DJ's pounding beats until his well-coiffed mother ushered him back to his seat in Lincoln Center's Alice Tully Hall. Behind a series of turntables and computers, Paul D. Miller, a.k.a. DJ Spooky that Subliminal Kid, warmed up his audience for *TransMetropolitan*, a night of music, videos, and readings he likened to a 1960s happening. Later that week, Miller performed *Rebirth of a Nation*, his live remix of D. W. Griffith's 1915 silent film *Birth of a Nation*, which presents the Ku Klux Klan as the saviors of a South overrun by unruly free blacks. Using the computer to edit and project the movie across three screens, Miller cut and grouped scenes from the nearly three-hour film into repeated gestures, as Robert Johnson's blues echoed beneath rhythmic violin chords Miller created on the computer.

For more than ten years, Miller, a 33-year-old writer, artist, and DJ, has been making the case that sampling and remixing—taking existing sounds or images and

DJ Spooky and Ryuichi Sakamoto during the premiere of *TransMetropolitan*.

reconfiguring them into new ones, like collage—are the way we experience the world today. Originally from Washington, D.C., Miller says sampling provides a "seamless consolidation of cultural patterns." His performance of *TransMetropolitan* at Lincoln Center, for example, brought together writers and musicians from Sri Lanka, Pakistan, England, and Brooklyn. Moreover, he says, our invisible networks of technological communication link us more powerfully than the visible ones. As examples, he lists standard time and wireless Internet networks. "Software," he adds, "has changed all of our cultural patterns."

Films help people respond to certain often-repeated cues. Miller thinks *Birth of a Nation,* one of Hollywood's first blockbusters, "has conditioned people's responses" to race, he says. By reframing the movie, Miller allows contemporary audiences to examine racist gestures established 90 years ago and their persistence in contemporary culture. Miller showed posters and stills from his video, a looped DVD projection, at New York's Paula Cooper Gallery earlier this year, where the prints sold for $1,500 and the edition of five videos was priced at around $10,000.

Miller's music tends to be accessible, with arcane allusions and provocative samples supported by a driving beat. He started working as a DJ to "pay rent," he says, and his desire for people to enjoy the music comes through. "I look at myself as straddling hip-hop, club culture, and the metaphysics of text," says Miller—as he simultaneously scans the paper and answers his cell phone—a relentlessly multitasking interpreter of the wide wired world.

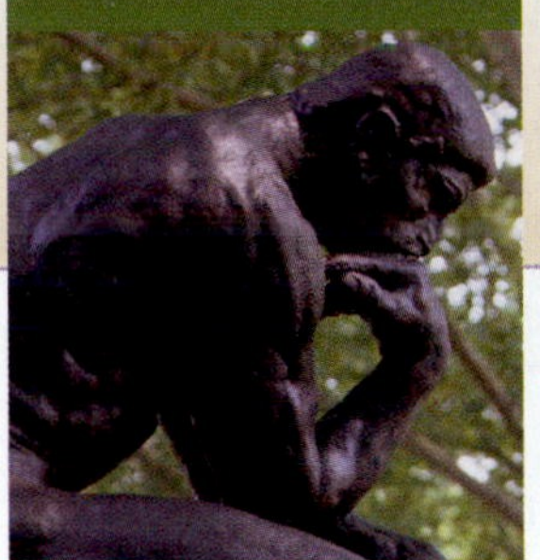

9 Interpretive Analyses and Writing about Literature

Interpretation involves figuring out a way of understanding a written document, literary work, cultural artifact, social situation, or natural event and presenting your understanding so that it is meaningful and convincing to readers.

9a Understand the assignment.

When an assignment asks you to compare, explain, analyze, discuss, or do a reading of something, you are expected to study that subject closely. An interpretive analysis moves beyond simple description and examines or compares particular items for a reason: to enhance your reader's understanding of people's conditions, actions, beliefs, or desires.

9b Approach writing an interpretive analysis as a process.

www.mhhe.com/mhhb2

For an interactive tutorial on writing interpretive analyses, go to

Writing > Writing Tutors > Interpretive Analysis

Writing an interpretive analysis typically begins with critical reading. (*See Chapter 7: Reading, Thinking, Writing: The Critical Connection for a discussion of how to read texts and visuals critically.*)

1. Discovering an aspect of the subject that is meaningful to you

Think about your own feelings and experiences while you read, listen, or observe. Connecting your own thoughts and experiences to what you are studying can help you develop fresh interpretations.

2. Developing a thoughtful stance

Think of yourself as an explorer. Be thoughtful, inquisitive, and open-minded. You are exploring the possible meaning of something. When you write your paper, invite readers to join you on an intellectual journey, saying, in effect, "Come, think this through with me."

3. Using an intellectual framework

To interpret your subject effectively, use a relevant perspective or an intellectual framework. For example, the basic elements of a work of fiction, such as plot, character, and setting, are often used to analyze stories. Sigmund Freud's theory of conscious and unconscious forces in conflict might be applied to people, poems, and historical periods. In his analysis of Flannery O'Connor's

WRITING beyond COLLEGE

Interpretive Analyses

You can find interpretive analyses like the following in professional journals like *PMLA* (*Publications of the Modern Language Association*) as well as popular publications like the *New Yorker* and the *Atlantic*:

- A cultural critic contrasts the way AIDS and cancer are talked about, imagined, and therefore treated.
- Two geologists analyze photos of an arctic coastal plain taken from an airplane and infer that the effects of seismic activity vary according to the type of vegetation in the area.
- A musicologist compares the revised endings of two pieces by Beethoven to figure out what makes a work complete and finished.

story "Everything That Rises Must Converge," Rajeev Bector uses sociologist Erving Goffman's ideas about "character contests" to interpret the conflict between a son and his mother. (*Bector's analysis begins on p. 167.*)

No matter what framework you use, analysis often entails taking something apart and then putting it back together by figuring out how the parts make up a cohesive whole. Because the goal of analysis is to create a meaningful interpretation, the writer should treat the whole as more than the sum of its parts and recognize that determining meaning is a complex problem with multiple solutions.

www.mhhe.com/**mhhb2**

For more help with developing a thesis, go to

Writing > Paragraph/Essay Development > Thesis/Central Idea

4. Listing, comparing, questioning, and classifying to discover your thesis

To figure out a thesis, it is often useful to explore separate aspects of your subject. For example, if you are analyzing literature, you might consider the plot, the characters, the setting, and the tone before deciding to focus your thesis on how a character's personality drives the plot to its conclusion. If you are comparing two subjects, you would look for and list points of likeness and difference. Can you find subtle differences in aspects that at first seem alike? Subtle similarities in aspects that at first seem very different? The answers to these questions might help you figure out your thesis.

As you work on discovering your thesis, try one or more of the following strategies:

- Take notes about what you see or read, and if it helps, write a summary.

- Ask yourself questions about the subject you are analyzing, and write down any interesting answers. Imagine what kinds of questions your instructor or classmates might ask about the artifact, document, performance, or event you are considering. In answering these questions, try to figure out the thesis you will present and support.
- Name the class of things to which the item you are analyzing belongs (for example, memoirs). Then identify important parts or aspects of that class (for example, scene, point of view, turning points).

5. Making your thesis focused and purposeful

To make a point about your subject, focus on one or two questions that are key to understanding it. Resist the temptation to describe everything you see.

FOCUSED THESIS

In O'Connor's short story, plot, setting, and characterization work together to reinforce the impression that racism is a complex and pervasive problem.

Although you want your point to be clear, you also want to make sure that your thesis anticipates the "So what?" question and sets up an interesting context for your interpretation. Unless you relate your specific thesis to some more general issue, idea, or problem, your interpretive analysis may seem pointless to readers. (*For more on developing your thesis, see Chapter 3: Planning and Shaping the Whole Essay, pp. 42–46.*)

6. Introducing the general issue, a clear thesis or question, and relevant context

www.mhhe.com/mhhb2
For more on crafting introductions, go to
Writing > Paragraph/Essay Development > Introductions

In interpretive analyses, the introduction often requires more than one paragraph to do the following:

- Identify the general issue, concept, or problem at stake. You can also present the intellectual framework that you are applying.
- Provide relevant background information.
- Name the specific item or items you will focus on in your analysis (or the items you will compare).
- State the thesis you will support and develop or the main question(s) your analysis will answer.

You need not do these things in the order listed. Sometimes it is a good idea to introduce the specific focus of your analysis before presenting either the issue or the background information. Even though you may begin with a provocative statement or an example designed to capture your readers' attention, make sure that your introduction does the four things it needs to do. (*For more on introductions, see Chapter 4: Drafting Paragraphs and Visuals, pp. 72–74.*)

For example, the following is the introductory paragraph from a paper on the development of Margaret Sanger's and Gloria Steinem's feminism that was written for a history class:

> In our male-dominated society, almost every woman has experienced some form of oppression. Being oppressed is like having one end of a rope fastened to a pole and the other end fastened to one's belt: it tends to hold a woman back. But a few tenacious and visionary women have fought oppression and have consequently made the lives of others easier. Two of these visionary women are Margaret Sanger and Gloria Steinem. As their autobiographical texts show, Sanger and Steinem felt compassion for women close to them, and that compassion not only shaped their lives but also empowered them to fight for changes in society.

In one paragraph, the student identifies her composition's general issue (the feminist struggle against oppression), introduces the items to be compared (two autobiographical texts), and in the last sentence, states her main point or thesis. Her readers now need additional background information about Sanger and Steinem that will give them a context for the two texts that are being compared.

7. Planning your paper so that each point supports your thesis

After you pose a key question or state your thesis in the introduction, work point by point to answer the question and support your interpretive thesis. From beginning to end, readers must be able to follow your train of thought and see how each point you make is related to your thesis. (*For more on developing your ideas, see Chapter 3: Planning and Shaping the Whole Essay, pp. 46–51.*)

9c Write interpretive papers in the humanities.

Writers in the humanities analyze literature, art, film, theater, music, history, and philosophy. In Part 1, we followed a student's analysis of a photograph through several drafts. In this chapter we look at some examples of literary analysis. The following ideas and practices are useful in writing interpretive papers in the humanities:

- **Base your analysis on the work itself.** Works of art affect each of us differently, and any interpretation has a subjective element. There are numerous critical theories about the significance of art. However, the possibility

Tips LEARNING in COLLEGE

Interpreting in the Visual Arts

Interpreting a painting is similar to interpreting a literary work or any other work of art. For example, your interpretation of this 1965 painting by Andy Warhol, titled *Campbell's Soup Can (Tomato)*, would likely reflect your personal reaction to the work as well as what you know about the artist and his times, but it would have to be grounded in a discussion of details of the work itself. What is the subject of the painting? How has the artist rendered it? How closely does it resemble an actual soup can? What does the painting suggest about the relationship between fine art and popular culture?

of different interpretations does not mean that all interpretations are equally valid. Your reading of the work needs to be grounded in details from the work itself.

- **Consider how the concepts you are learning in your course apply to the work you are analyzing.** If your course focuses on the formal elements of art, for example, you might look at how those elements function in the painting you have chosen to analyze. If your course focuses on the social context of a work, you might look at how the work shares or subverts the belief system and worldview that was common in its time.
- **Use the present tense when writing about the work and the past tense when writing about its history.** Use the present tense to talk about the events that happen within a work: *In Aristophanes's plays, characters frequently* ***step*** *out of the scene and* ***address*** *the audience directly.* Use the present tense as well to discuss decisions made by the work's creator: *In his version of the Annunciation, Leonardo* ***places*** *the Virgin outside, in an Italian garden.* Use the past tense, however, to relate historical information about the work or creator: *Kant* ***wrote*** *about science, history, criminal justice, and politics as well as philosophical ideas.*

QUESTIONS for ANALYZING POETRY

Speaker and Tone

How would you describe the speaker's voice? Is it that of a parent or a lover, an adult or a child, a man or a woman? What is the speaker's tone—is it stern or playful, melancholy or elated, nostalgic or hopeful?

Connotations

Although both *trudge* and *saunter* mean "walk slowly," their connotations (associative meanings) are very different. What feelings or ideas do individual words in the poem connote?

Imagery

Does the poem conjure images that appeal to any of your senses—for example, the shocking feeling of a cold cloth on feverish skin or the sharp smell of a gas station? How do the images shape the mood of the poem? What ideas do they suggest?

Figurative Language

Does the poem use **simile** to directly compare two things using *like* or *as* (*his heart is sealed tight like a freezer door*)? Does it use **metaphor** to implicitly link one thing to another (*his ice-hard heart*)? How does the comparison enhance meaning?

Sound, Rhythm, and Meter

What vowel and consonant sounds recur through the poem? Do the lines of the poem resemble the rhythms of ordinary speech, or do they have a more musical quality? Consider how the sounds of the poem create an effect.

Structure

Notice how the poem is organized into parts or stanzas, considering spacing, punctuation, capitalization, and rhyme schemes. How do the parts relate to one another?

Theme

What is the subject of the poem? What does the poet's choice of language and imagery suggest about his or her attitude toward that subject?

www.mhhe.com/mhhb2
For another sample of interpretive writing, go to
Writing > Writing Samples > Interpretive Paper

9d Write a literary interpretation of a poem.

The poet Edwin Arlington Robinson defined poetry as "a language that tells us, through a more or less emotional reaction, something that cannot be said." Although literary analysis can never tell us exactly what a poem is saying, it can help us think about it more deeply.

First read the complete poem without stopping, and then note your initial thoughts and feelings. What is your first sense of the subject of the poem? What ideas and images does the poem suggest?

Reread the poem several times, paying close attention to the rhythms of the lines (reading aloud helps) and the poet's choice of words. Think about how the poem develops. Do the last lines represent a shift from or fulfillment of the poem's opening? Look for connections among the poem's details, and think about their significance. The questions in the box on page 162 may help guide your analysis.

Use the insights you gain from your close reading to develop a working thesis about the poem. In the student essay that begins on page 164, McKenna Doherty develops a thesis about the poem "Testimonial," reprinted below. Doherty's analysis is based on her knowledge of other poems by Rita Dove and her attempt to discover the theme of this particular work. She focuses on how four poetic devices give the theme its emotional impact.

Testimonial

RITA DOVE

Back when the earth was new
and heaven just a whisper,
back when the names of things
hadn't had time to stick;

back when the smallest breezes
melted summer into autumn,
when all the poplars quivered
sweetly in rank and file . . .

the world called, and I answered.
Each glance ignited to a gaze.
I caught my breath and called that life,
swooned between spoonfuls of lemon sorbet.

I was pirouette and flourish,
I was filigree and flame.
How could I count my blessings
when I didn't know their names?

Back when everything was still to come,
luck leaked out everywhere.
I gave my promise to the world,
and the world followed me here.

Sample student analysis of a poem

Rita Dove's "Testimonial": The Music of Childhood

Rita Dove rarely uses obvious, rigid rhyme schemes or strict metrical patterns in her poetry, and her subtle use of language often obscures both the subject and themes of her poetry. However, careful analysis of her work is rewarding, as Dove's poems are dense with ideas and figurative language. Her poem "Testimonial" is a good example of this complexity. Although the poem seems ambiguous on first reading, repeated readings reveal many common and cleverly used poetic techniques that are employed to express a common literary theme: the difference between adult knowledge and childhood innocence.

Central subject of paper identified.

The first two lines refer to a time when "the earth was new / and heaven just a whisper." At first, these lines appear to refer to the Biblical origins of earth and heaven; however, the title of the poem invites us to take the poem as a personal account of the speaker's experience. The time when "the earth was new" could refer to the speaker's youth. Youth is also the time of life when heaven is "just a whisper," since matters of death and religion are not present in a child's awareness. Thus, Dove's opening lines actually put the reader in the clear, familiar context of childhood.

Examples provided to illustrate theme.

The lines that follow support the idea that the poem refers to youth. Dove describes the time period of the poem as "when the names of things / hadn't had time to stick" (lines 3–4). Children often forget the names of things and are constantly asking their parents, "What is this? What is that?" The names of objects do not "stick" in their minds. The second stanza, describing a scene of trees and breezes, seems childlike in its sensitivity to nature, particularly to the change of seasons. The trees swaying "sweetly in rank and file" (8) suggest an innocent, simplistic worldview, in which everything, even the random movement of trees in the wind, occurs in an orderly, nonthreatening fashion.

More examples given and interpreted.

Notice that Dove does not state "when I was a child" at the beginning of the poem. Instead, she uses poetic language—alliteration, rhyme, uncommon words, and personification—to evoke the experience of childhood. Figurative language may make the poem more difficult to understand on first reading, but it ultimately makes the poem more personally meaningful.

Writer presents four poetic techniques, which she explains in the following paragraphs.

In line 12, "swooned between spoonfuls of lemon sorbet" not only evokes the experience of childhood, a time when ice cream might literally make one swoon, but the alliteration of "swooned," "spoonfuls," and "sorbet" also makes the poem musical. Dove also uses alliteration in lines 14, 15, and 18. This conventional poetic technique is used relatively briefly and not regularly. The alliteration does not call attention to itself—the music is quiet.

"Testimonial" also uses the best known poetic technique: rhyme. Rhyme is used in many poems—what is unusual about its use in this poem is that, as with alliteration, rhyme appears irregularly. Only a few lines end with rhyming words, and the rhymes are more suggestive than exact: "whisper" and "stick" (2 and 4), "gaze" and "sorbet" (10 and 12), "flame" and "names" (14 and 16), and "everywhere" and "here" (18 and 20). These rhymes, or consonances, stand out because they are isolated and contrast with the other, unrhymed lines.

Dove occasionally uses words that children would probably not know, such as "swooned" (12), "sorbet" (12), "pirouette" (13), "flourish" (13), and "filigree" (14). These words suggest the central theme, which is underscored in the final question of the stanza when the narrator of the poem asks, "How could I count my blessings / when I didn't know their names?" The adult words emphasize the contrast between the speaker's past innocence and present knowledge.

The poem ends with the mysterious lines, "I gave my promise to the world / and the world followed me here" (19–20). The

Analysis of poem concluded with interpretation of entire poem.

world is personified, given the characteristics of a man or woman capable of accepting a promise and following the speaker. As with the opening lines, these final lines are confusing if they are taken literally, but the lines become clearer when one considers the perspective of the speaker. It is as if the speaker has taken a journey from childhood to adulthood. Just as the speaker has changed during the course of this journey, so too has the world changed. The childhood impressions of the world that make up the poem—the sorbet, the trees swaying in the breeze—do not last into adulthood. The speaker becomes a different person, an adult, and the world also becomes something else. It has "followed" the speaker into adulthood; it has not remained static and unchanging.

Paper concluded briefly, neatly.

In "Testimonial," Dove presents a vision of childhood so beautifully, so musically, that we can experience it with her, if only for the space of a few lines.

------------------[new page]------------------

Works-Cited list follows MLA style and begins on a new page.

Work Cited

Dove, Rita. "Testimonial." *Literature: Approaches to Fiction, Poetry, and Drama*. Ed. Robert DiYanni. New York: McGraw-Hill, 2004. 738. Print.

9e Write a literary interpretation of a work of fiction.

A literary analysis paper is an opportunity to look beyond the plot of a short story or novel and develop a better understanding of it. You may want to read the work, or key sections of it, more than once. The questions in the box on pages 169–70 may help guide your analysis.

The field of literary criticism offers various strategies for analyzing fiction, including formalist theories, reader response theory, and postmodern theories. However, it is also possible to apply the insights offered by other disciplines to your literary analysis paper. In the essay that begins on the next page, Rajeev Bector, a sociology major, applies a theory that he learned in a sociology course to his analysis of a short story.

Sample student analysis of a short story

The Character Contest in Flannery O'Connor's
"Everything That Rises Must Converge"

Sociologist Erving Goffman believes that every social interaction establishes our identity and preserves our image, honor, and credibility in the hearts and minds of others. Social interactions, he says, are in essence "character contests" that occur not only in games and sports but also in our everyday dealings with strangers, peers, friends, and even family members. Goffman defines character contests as "disputes [that] are sought out and indulged in (often with glee) as a means of establishing where one's boundaries are" (29). Just such a contest occurs in Flannery O'Connor's short story "Everything That Rises Must Converge."

Key idea that provides intellectual framework.

As they travel from home to the Y, Julian and his mother, Mrs. Chestny, engage in a character contest, a dispute we must understand in order to figure out the story's theme. Julian is so frustrated with his mother that he virtually "declare[s] war on her," "allow[s] no glimmer of sympathy to show on his face," and "imagine[s] various unlikely ways by which he could teach her a lesson" (O'Connor 185, 186). But why would Julian want to hurt his mother, a woman who is already suffering from high blood pressure?

Question posed.

Julian's conflict with Mrs. Chestny results from pent-up hostility and tension. As Goffman explains, character contests are a way of living that often leaves a "residue": "Every day in many ways we can try to score points and every day we can be shot down" (29). For many years, Julian has had to live under his racist mother's authority, and every time he protested her racist views he was probably shot down because of his "radical ideas" and "lack of practical experience" (O'Connor 184). As a result, a residue of defeat and shame has accumulated that fuels a fire of rebellion against his mother. But even though Julian rebels against his mother's racist views, it does not mean that he is not

Interpretation organized point by point: first point.

a racist himself. Julian does not realize that in his own way, he is as prejudiced as his mother. He makes it "a point" to sit next to blacks, in contrast to his mother, who purposely sits next to whites (182). They are two extremes, each biased, for if Julian were truly fair to all, he would not care whom he sat next to.

"We" indicates thoughtful stance, not Bector's personal feelings.

When we look at the situation from Mrs. Chestny's viewpoint, we realize that she must maintain her values and beliefs for two important reasons: to uphold her character as Julian's mother and to act out her prescribed role in society. Even if she finds Julian's arguments on race relations and integration valid and plausible, Mrs. Chestny must still refute them. If she did not, she would lose face as Julian's mother—that image of herself as the one with authority. By preserving her self-image, Mrs. Chestny shows that she has what Goffman sees as key to "character": some quality that seems "essential and unchanging" (28).

Second point.

Besides upholding her character as Julian's mother, Mrs. Chestny wants to preserve the honor and dignity of her family tradition. Like an actor performing before an audience, she must play the role prescribed for her—the role of a white supremacist. But her situation is hopeless, for the role she must play fails to acknowledge the racial realities that have transformed her world. According to Goffman, when a "situation" is "hopeless," a character "can gamely give everything . . . and then go down bravely, or proudly, or insolently, or gracefully or with an ironic smile on his lips" (32). For Mrs. Chestny, being game means trying to preserve her honor and dignity as she goes down to physical defeat in the face of hopeless odds.

Third point.

Thesis.

Conclusion: main point about Julian and his mother related to larger issue of racism.

Given the differences between Mrs. Chestny's and her son's values, as well as the oppressiveness of Mrs. Chestny's racist views, we can understand why Julian struggles to "teach" his mother "a lesson" (185) throughout the entire bus ride. Goffman would point out that "each individual is engaged in providing evidence to establish a definition of himself at the expense of what can remain for the other" (29). But in the end, neither character wins the contest. Julian's mother loses her sense of self when she is pushed to the ground by a "colored woman" wearing a hat identical to hers (187). Faced with his mother's breakdown, Julian feels his own identity being overwhelmed by "the world of guilt and sorrow" (191).

————————————————[new page]————————————————

Works-Cited list follows MLA style and begins on a new page.

Works Cited

Goffman, Erving. "Character Contests." *Text Book: An Introduction to Literary Language*. Ed. Robert Scholes, Nancy Comley, and Gregory Ulmer. New York: St. Martin's, 1988. 27–33. Print.

O'Connor, Flannery. "Everything That Rises Must Converge." *Fiction*. Ed. R. S. Gwynn. 2nd ed. New York: Addison, 1998. 179–91. Print.

QUESTIONS for ANALYZING FICTION

Characters

What are the relationships among the characters? What do the characters' thoughts, actions, and speech reveal about them? What changes take place among or within the characters?

Point of View

Is the story told by a character speaking as "I" (first-person point of view), or by a third-person narrator, who lets the reader know what one (or none) or all of the characters are thinking? How does point of view affect your understanding of what happens in the story?

Plot

What do these particular episodes in the characters' lives reveal? What did you think and feel at different points in the story? What kinds of changes take place over the course of the story?

Setting

What is the significance of the story's setting (its time and place)? What associations does the writer make with each location? How does the social context of the setting affect the characters' choices and attitudes?

QUESTIONS for ANALYZING FICTION (*continued*)

Language

Fiction writers, like poets, use figurative language and imagery to meaningful effect (*see the box "Questions for Analyzing Poetry" on p. 162*). Are there patterns of imagery and metaphor in the story? What significance can you infer from these patterns?

Theme

What sense of the story's significance can you infer from the elements above? Are there any passages in the work that seem to address the theme directly?

9f Write a literary interpretation of a play.

When we interpret a play, we need to imagine the world of the play—the setting and costumes, the delivery of lines of dialogue, and the movement of characters in relation to one another. Like a poem or story, a play is best read more than once.

Like poetry, drama is meant to be spoken, and the sound and rhythm of its lines are significant. Like fiction, drama unfolds through characters acting in a plot. As in both genres, imagery and figurative language work to convey emotions and meaning. Review the questions for analyzing poetry and fiction (*see pp. 162 and 169–70*), and consider the questions in the box below when analyzing a play.

In the following paper, Sam Chodoff uses dialogue to analyze the theme of honor as it applies to the characters in Shakespeare's *Hamlet*.

QUESTIONS for ANALYZING DRAMA

Dialogue

What does the dialogue reveal about the characters' thoughts and motivations? How do the characters' words incite other characters to action?

Stage Directions

Do the stage directions include references to any objects that may serve as dramatic symbols? How might costume directions suggest mood or symbolize such concepts as freedom, repression, or chivalry, for example? Do the directions call for any music or sounds to add to the atmosphere of the work?

Sample student analysis of a play

Honor in Shakespeare's *Hamlet*

In the world of Shakespeare's *Hamlet*, actions, not motives, are the measure of a character's honor. Good actions bestow honor; evil actions withdraw it. Not all characters in the play, however, are equally equipped to know one from the other. The main characters receive divine enlightenment about what is right and wrong, but the minor characters have to rely on luck, making choices without divine assistance.

Key term—"honor"—defined.

Characters fall into one of three categories of honor determined by where their actions fall on the spectrum between good and evil. Hamlet and Fortinbras represent extreme good; Claudius represents extreme evil. These characters have been enlightened by heaven, and their actions are based on this divinely granted knowledge. In the middle of the spectrum are all the other characters, who have chosen a path based on their own, not divine, knowledge, and for whom honor is a matter of luck.

Fig. 1. Hamlet confronted by his father's ghost as his mother looks on amazed, engraving from John and Josiah Boydell, *Boydell's Shakespeare Prints* (Mineola: Dover, 2004) 73. Print.

Illustration of a scene discussed in the paper.

As Hamlet storms into the palace in anger, seeking revenge for the death of his father, Claudius reassures Gertrude, telling her, "Do not fear our person. / There's such divinity doth hedge a king / That treason can but peep to what it would, / Acts little of his will" (4.5.122-25). Claudius knows that by killing his brother and usurping his throne, he has forfeited any chance to be the rightful king, and behind his façade, he struggles with his own guilt, knowing that heaven will remain closed to him while he still holds the "effects for which [he] did the murder" (3.3.54). Meanwhile, unbeknownst to Claudius, heaven has, through the ghost of Hamlet's father, commanded Hamlet to avenge his father's murder and restore a rightful king to the throne, as shown in fig. 1. This reveals that Claudius is on the lowest end of the honor spectrum, that his honor is false, a mere pretense of honor with nothing but evil underneath. His actions show that an honorable life remains unattainable when the appearance of honor is the only goal, and that, in Hamlet's words, "one may smile, and smile, and be a villain" (1.5.108).

First of three examples to illustrate the categories of honor.

Hamlet and Fortinbras, on the other hand, have been shown by heaven the conflict that they must resolve and are left to do that task without any further divine aid. The engraving in fig. 1 shows Hamlet recoiling at the sight of the ghost. This image emphasizes the way this supernatural contact literally and metaphorically sets Hamlet apart from his mother. With a clear duty whose virtue is unquestionable, the honor of Hamlet and Fortinbras is assured as long as they pursue and complete their objective. The last scene shows that they have achieved this goal, as Fortinbras gives orders to pay tribute to Hamlet: "Let four captains / Bear Hamlet like a soldier to the stage, / . . . and for his passage / The soldier's music and the rite of war / Speak loudly for him" (5.2.400-01, 403-05). While the bodies of the other characters are ignored, Hamlet's is treated with ceremony. This disparity in how the characters are treated confirms that Hamlet and Fortinbras have been placed at the highest end of the honor spectrum, and it shows that the many grave mistakes they both have made (resulting in the death of many innocent people) will be forgiven because the mistakes were made in pursuit of a divine objective. This idea of honor was acceptable in Shakespeare's day, as illustrated in a treatise by Sir William Segar in 1590: "God . . . would give victory to him that justly

Second example given.

Points illustrated with quotations from the play.

adventured his life for truth, honor, and justice. . . . the trial by Arms is not only natural, but also necessary and allowable" (qtd. in Corum 153).

Other characters in *Hamlet* are not privy to the true nature of the world and are forced to make decisions without heaven's help. The level of honor these characters attain is determined by luck; with their limited knowledge of good and evil, right and wrong, these characters often act dishonorably. When Rosencrantz and Guildenstern are summoned before the king and asked to spy on Hamlet, they respond positively, saying, "[W]e both obey, / And here give up ourselves in the full bent / To lay our service freely at your feet / To be commanded" (2.2.29-32). In their ignorance, they accept Claudius as the rightful king and thus unintentionally align themselves with the evil he represents, losing any honor they might have gained. Other characters are similarly tricked into obeying Claudius.

Third example given.

Luck can go both ways, however, and several characters end up well, even in the absence of a divine messenger. For example, Horatio chooses from the very beginning to follow Hamlet and not only survives but also attains honor. His honor, though, is by no means assured; there are many instances in which he could have acted differently. He could quite easily have gone to Claudius with the news of the ghost, an act which, while perfectly natural, would have left him devoid of honor.

Another example given of the third category of honor, to strengthen claim.

We would like to think that, by adhering to virtues, we can control how we will be judged. In *Hamlet*, we are shown a world in which lives are spent in the struggle between good and evil, often without clear guidance. But those who have lived honorably are rewarded with a place in heaven, the "undiscover'd country" (3.1.79) that every character both fears and desires. Only those characters either chosen by heaven to be honorable or who by luck become honorable reach paradise, while others burn in hell or wait in purgatory (Greenblatt 51). Very few people in Hamlet's world will be granted a place in heaven.

Essay concluded concisely.

——————————[new page]——————————

Works-Cited list follows MLA style and begins a new page.

Works Cited

Corum, Richard. *Understanding Hamlet: A Student Casebook to Issues, Sources, and Historical Documents.* Westport, CT: Greenwood, 1998. Print.

Greenblatt, Stephen. *Hamlet in Purgatory*. Princeton: Princeton UP, 2001. Print.

Shakespeare, William. *Hamlet*. Ed. Harold Jenkins. Arden Edition of the Works of William Shakespeare. London: Methuen, 1982. Print.

9g Write case studies and other interpretive analyses in the social sciences.

Social scientists are trained observers and recorders of the behavior of individuals and groups in specific situations and institutions. They use writing not only to see clearly and remember precisely what they observe but also to interpret its meaning, as in this passage from a textbook by anthropologist Conrad Kottak.

Rituals at McDonald's (excerpt)

CONRAD KOTTAK

Each day, on the average, a new McDonald's restaurant opens somewhere in the world. The number of McDonald's outlets today far surpasses the total number of all fast-food restaurants in the United States in 1945. McDonald's has grown from a single hamburger stand in San Bernardino, California, into today's international web of thousands of outlets. Have factors less obvious to American natives than relatively low cost, fast service, and taste contributed to McDonald's success? Could it be that natives—in consuming the products and propaganda of McDonald's—are not just eating but experiencing something comparable in certain respects to participation in religious rituals? To answer this question, we must briefly review the nature of ritual.

[Religious] [r]ituals . . . are formal—stylized, repetitive, and stereotyped. They are performed in special places at set times. Rituals include liturgical orders—set sequences of words and actions laid down by someone other than the current performers. Rituals also convey information about participants and their cultural traditions. Performed year after year, generation after generation, rituals translate messages, values, and sentiments into action. Rituals are social acts. Inevitably, some participants are more strongly committed than others are to the beliefs on which the rituals are founded. However, just by taking part in a joint public act, people signal that they accept an order that transcends their status as mere individuals.

For many years, like millions of other Americans, I have occasionally eaten at McDonald's. Eventually I began to notice certain ritual-like aspects of Americans' behavior at these fast-food restaurants. Tell your fellow Americans that going to McDonald's is similar in some ways to going to church, and their bias as natives will reveal itself in laughter, denials, or questions about your sanity. Just as football is a game and *Star Trek* is "entertainment," McDonald's, for natives, is just a place to eat. However, an analysis of what natives do at McDonald's will reveal a very high degree of formal, uniform behavior by staff members and customers alike. It is particularly interesting that this invariance in word and deed has developed without any theological doctrine. McDonald's ritual aspect is founded on 20th-century technology, particularly automobiles, television, work away from home, and the short lunch break. It is striking, nevertheless, that one commercial organization should be so much more successful than other businesses, the schools, the military, and even many religions in producing behavioral invariance. Factors other than low cost, fast service, and the taste of the food—all of which are approximated by other chains—have contributed to our acceptance of McDonald's and adherence to its rules. . . .

In this passage, Kottak based many of his conclusions on his observations of the way people behave at McDonald's restaurants. When social scientists conduct a systematic study of people's behavior in groups or institutions, they report on and interpret their observations in **case studies**. Anthropologists, for example, often spend extended periods living among and observing the people of one society or group and then report on their findings in a kind of case study called an *ethnography*.

Accurate observations are essential starting points for a case study, and writing helps researchers make clear and precise observations. Here are some things to consider as you undertake a case study assignment.

1. Choosing a topic that raises a question

In doing a case study, your purpose is to connect what you see and hear with issues and concepts in the social sciences. Choose a topic and turn it into a research question. Write down your hypothesis—a tentative answer to your research question—as well as some categories of behavior or other things to look for in your field research.

2. Collecting data

Make a detailed and accurate record of what you observe and when and how you observed it. Whenever you can, count or measure, and take down word for word what is said. Use frequency counts—the number of occurrences of specific, narrowly defined instances of behavior. If you are observing a classroom, for example, you might count the number of teacher-directed questions asked by several children. Your research methodologies course will introduce you to many ways to quantify data. Graphs like Figure 9.1 can help you display and summarize frequency data.

3. Assuming an unbiased stance

In a case study, you are presenting empirical findings, based on careful observation. Your stance is that of an unbiased observer.

4. Discovering meaning in your data

As you review your notes, try to uncover connections, identify inconsistencies, and draw inferences. For example, ask yourself why a subject behaved in a specific way, and consider different explanations

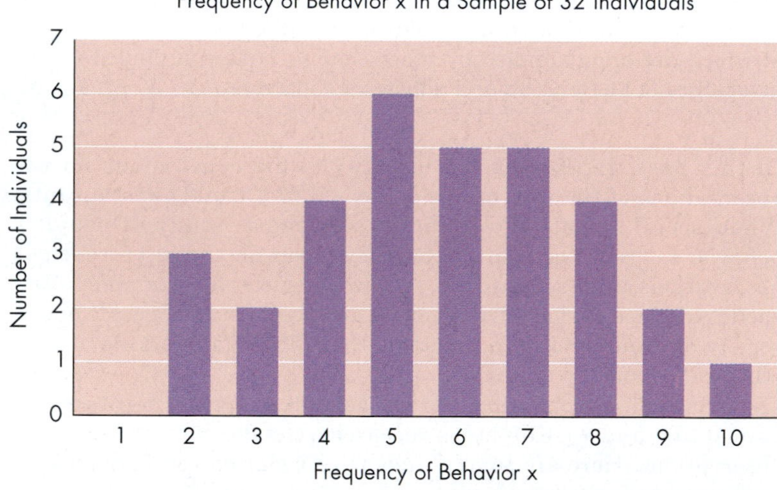

FIGURE 9.1 Graphing frequency data. Column graphs like this one can be useful for summarizing behavioral observations. The numbers on the horizontal axis represent the frequency, or number of occurrences, of a particular behavior. (An example might be the number of teacher-directed questions a student asks during a class). The vertical axis represents the number of individuals at each frequency. In this case, three individuals exhibited the behavior twice, two exhibited it three times, and so forth.

for the behavior. You will also need to draw upon the techniques for quantitative analysis that you learn in a statistics course.

5. Presenting your findings in an organized way

There are two basic ways to present your findings in the body of a case study. (1) **As stages of a process:** A student studying gang initiation organized her observations chronologically into appropriate stages. If you organize your study this way, be sure to transform the minute-by-minute history of your observations into a pattern with distinctive stages. (2) **In analytic categories:** A student observing the behavior of a preschool child used the following categories from the course textbook to present his findings: motor coordination, cognition, and socialization.

> ***Note:*** Develop your stages or categories while you are making your observations. In your paper, be sure to illustrate your stages or categories with material drawn from your observations—with descriptions of people, places, and behavior, as well as with telling quotations.

CHARTING the TERRITORY

Case Studies

You may be asked to write case studies in a number of social science and science disciplines.

- **In sociology:** You may be asked to analyze a small group to which you have belonged or belong now. In this case, your study will address such issues as the group's norms and values, stratification and roles, and cultural characteristics. Your audience will be your professor, who will want to see how your observations reflect current theories on group norms.
- **In nursing:** You may note details of your care of a patient that corroborate or differ from what you have been taught to expect. Your audience is the supervising nurse, who is interested in your interactions with the patient.
- **In education:** As a student teacher, you may closely observe and write about one student in the context of his or her socioeconomic and family background. Your audience will be your supervising teacher, who seeks more insight into students' behavior.

6. Including a review of the literature, statement of your hypothesis, and description of your methodology in your introduction

The introduction presents the framework, background, and rationale for your study. Begin with the topic, and review related research, working your way to the specific question that your study addresses. Follow that with a statement of your hypothesis, accompanied by a description of your **methodology**—how, when, and where you made your observations and how you recorded them.

7. Discussing your findings in the conclusion

The conclusion of your case study should answer the following three questions: Did you find what you expected? What do your findings show, or what is the bigger picture? Where should researchers working on your topic go now?

9h Write interpretive analyses in the sciences.

Many research papers in the sciences, like those in the social sciences, are interpretive as well as informative. As mentioned in Chapter 8, for example, interpretation is a crucial aspect of lab reports describing the results of original experiments designed to create new scientific knowledge.

Scientists, however, may also be called upon to analyze trends and make predictions in papers that do not follow the lab or research report model. In the following example, Josh Feldman interprets historical data about hurricanes to see whether they reveal trends in weather patterns.

Sample student interpretive paper in the sciences

Keeping an Eye on the Storms

Gripping facts in the introduction engage reader's attention.

On August 29, 2005, Hurricane Katrina struck the Gulf Coast of the United States. It was among the deadliest storms in American history, responsible for the deaths of close to 2,000 people, and caused tens of billions of dollars in damage[1]. (See Figure 1.) The images of Katrina's devastation in New Orleans, across Mississippi, in Florida, and beyond horrified people around the world. Alarmingly, though, there is reason to fear that the years ahead could bring even more hurricanes as powerful, or indeed more powerful, than Katrina. And while we generally think of hurricanes as natural phenomena over which we have no

Figure 1 Katrina's winds tear the roof off a building outside New Orleans. (from Thompson, I[2])

control, evidence suggests that humans may in fact be contributing to an increase in the number of deadly hurricanes. The effects of global warming may mean that we will soon see more hurricanes, and ones of greater strength, approaching our shores.

Thesis stated.

To understand why powerful hurricanes may become increasingly common, it is necessary to understand a key fact about hurricane formation: hurricanes depend on warm water. Typically, a hurricane forms only in water that is 80° or warmer[3]. The longer a hurricane remains over warm water, the stronger it becomes. As Katrina moved over the Gulf of Mexico, for example, surface waters there were unusually warm[4]. This is one reason Katrina was such a powerful storm when it made landfall.

The relationship between hurricanes and warm water also connects hurricanes to global warming. The United Nations' Intergovernmental Panel on Climate Change concluded that the evidence of global warming, in the air and in the oceans, was "unequivocal." They also stated the most likely explanation for this warming was human release of greenhouse gases like carbon dioxide into the atmosphere[5].

Authoritative source cited.

Figure 2 shows the global average sea surface temperature from 1860 to 2000. Each line on the graph represents a different

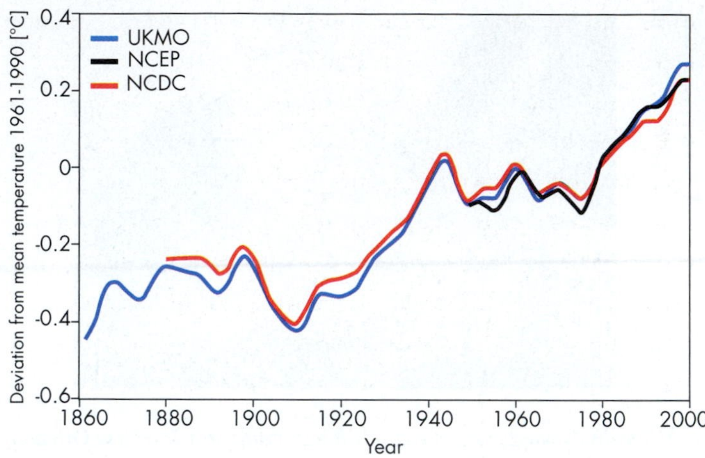

Figure 2 The change in sea surface temperature from 1860 to 2000 (from Intergovernmental Panel on Climate Change[6])

source for this data. The red line shows data from the United States Climatic Data Center; the blue line, data from the United Kingdom Met Office; and the black line, data from the United States National Center for Environmental Prediction[6]. Each line shows that sea surface temperatures are rising, with notable acceleration in the last decades of the 20th century, when human-produced global warming accelerated. Overall, average sea surface temperatures have risen roughly 1 ° Fahrenheit over the last century[4].

Use of statistics establishes authority.

Prediction made.

Again, hurricanes require warm water for their formation and strength. It stands to reason that as waters across the globe become warmer, there will be more and more opportunities for hurricanes to form and gain power. An article published online by the Pew Center on Global Climate Change states the point clearly: "[Global warming] clearly has created circumstances under which powerful storms are more likely to occur at this point in history (and in the future) than they were in the past[4]." While people often think of global warming in terms of melting ice and unseasonable warmth, it has consequences for every facet of the natural world—including creating oceanic conditions that make hurricanes more likely.

Indeed, humans may already be witnessing the effects of their carbon dioxide production on storm formation. Kerry Emanuel of the Massachusetts Institute of Technology conducted a study that showed that hurricane strength has been on the rise in recent decades. Specifically, Emanuel found a 50% increase in hurricane power and duration since the 1970s[7]. As humans continue to pour carbon dioxide and other greenhouse gases into the atmosphere, there is little reason to believe this trend will be reversed in the near future.

Evidence for prediction.

In the aftermath of Katrina, government, the media, and Americans across the country debated what could be done to prevent similar disasters in the future. These discussions largely focused on infrastructure, preparedness, and emergency services. However, it would be wrong to overlook the human role in creating hurricanes in the first place. While there is no scientific link between global warming and Katrina specifically, science does suggest that global warming might make storms like Katrina more common. Working to ensure that there is never another Katrina should also mean working to reduce human effects on the Earth's atmosphere.

Issue of global warming placed in context of broader debate about hurricanes.

Conclusion stated succinctly.

------------------------------------[new page]----------------------------------

References

Reference list follows CSE ciatation-sequence style and begins on a new page.

1. Knabb RD, Rhome JR, Brown DP. Tropical cyclone report Hurricane Katrina 23–30 August 2005 [Internet]. Miami (FL): National Hurricane Center (US); c2005 Dec 20 [updated 2006 Aug 10; cited 2008 Apr 29]. Available from: http://www.nhc.noaa.gov/pdf/TCR-AL122005_Katrina.pdf
2. Thompson, I. High winds blow the roof off Backyard Barbeque in Kenner, LA. Dallas Morning News [Internet]. 2005 Aug 29 [cited 2008 Apr 29]. Available from: http://www.dallasnews.com/s/dws/spe/2006/pulitzer

3. Brain M, Freudenrich C. How hurricanes work [Internet]. Atlanta (GA): HowStuffWorks; c2000 Aug 29 [cited 2008 Apr 29]. Available from: http://science.howstuffworks.com/hurricane8.htm
4. Pew Center on Global Climate Change. Katrina and global warming [Internet]. Arlington (VA): Pew Center on Global Climate Change; [cited 2008 Apr 29]. Available from: http://www.pewclimate.org/specialreports/katrina.cfm
5. Rosenthal E, Revkin AC. Science panel calls global warming "unequivocal." New York Times [Internet]. 2007 Feb 3 [cited 2008 Apr 29]. Available from: http://www.nytimes.com/2007/02/03/science/earth/03climate.html?scp=4&59=global+warming&st=nyt
6. Intergovernmental Panel on Climate Change. Globally averaged sea-surface temperature, according to three data centres: The UK Met Office (UKMO), the US National Center for Environmental Prediction (NCEP), and the US National Climatic Data Center (NCDC) [Internet]. Berlin (Germany): German Advisory Council on Climate Change; c2006 [cited 2008 Apr 29]. Available from: http://www.wbgu.de/wbgu_sn2006_en/wbgu_sn2006_en_voll_2.html
7. Roach, J. Is global warming making hurricanes worse? National Geographic News [Internet]. Washington (DC): National Geographic Society; 2005 Aug 4 [cited 2008 Apr 29]. Available from: http://news.nationalgeographic.com/news/2005/08/0804_050804_hurricanewarming.html

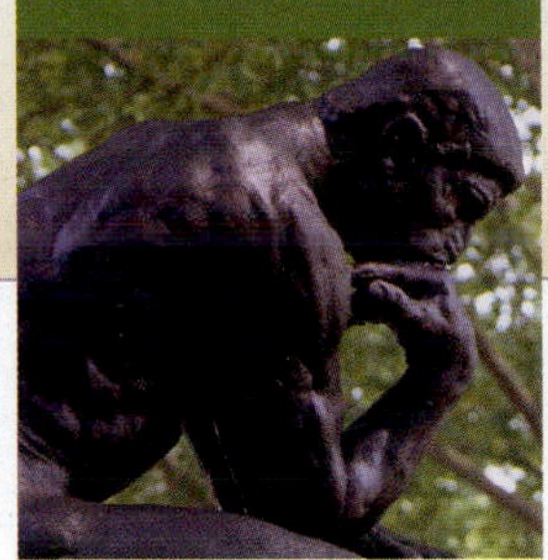

10 Arguments

In the college classroom and in reasoned debate outside the classroom, an **argument** is a path of reasoning aimed at developing an assertion on an issue under debate. In this chapter, we look at how to construct an argument. Arguments often respond to the thinking of others, so we first look at how to evaluate an argument.

10a Understand the assignment.

In college, reasoned positions matter more than opinions based on personal feelings, and writing arguments is a way to form reasoned positions. When you write an argument paper, your purpose is not to win but to take part in a debate by stating and supporting your position on an issue. In addition to position papers, written arguments appear in various forms, including critiques, reviews, and proposals.

- **Critiques:** Critiques address the question "What is true?" A critique fairly summarizes another's position before either refuting or defending it. *Refutations* either expose the reasoning of the position as inadequate or present evidence that contradicts the position. In his response to Nat Hentoff's article "Misguided Multiculturalism" in Chapter 7, Ignacio Sanderson attempts to refute Hentoff's claims by identifying weaknesses in Hentoff's reasoning (*pp. 135–37*). Matt Shadwell's essay "Person of the Year" (*pp. 201–06*) refutes *Time* magazine's choice of "You" for this annual distinction. *Defenses* clarify the author's key terms and reasoning, present new arguments to support the position, and show that criticisms of the position are unreasonable or unconvincing.
- **Reviews:** Reviews address the question "What is good?" In a review, the writer evaluates an event, artifact, practice, or institution, judging by reasonable principles and criteria. Dale Jamieson's essay on pages 207–08 is an example of a review.
- **Proposals, or policy papers:** Proposals, sometimes called policy papers, address the question "What should be done?" They are designed to cause change in the world. Readers are encouraged to see the situation in a specific way, and to take action. The Council for Biotechnology's argument about genetically modified foods (*see pp. 209–12*) is an example of a proposal.

WRITING beyond COLLEGE

Arguments

Arguments are central to American democracy and its institutions of higher learning because they help create the common ground that is sometimes called public space. Fields inside and outside of the academy value reason and welcome arguments such as the following:

- The board of a national dietetic association publishes a position statement identifying obesity as a growing health problem that dieticians should be involved in preventing and treating.
- An art critic praises a museum's special exhibition of modern American paintings for its diversity and thematic coherence.
- A sociologist proposes four policies that he claims will improve the quality of life and socioeconomic prospects of people living in inner-city neighborhoods.

10b Learn how to evaluate verbal and visual arguments.

Three common ways to analyze verbal and visual arguments are (1) to concentrate on the type of reasoning the writer is using; (2) to question the logical relation of a writer's claims, grounds, and warrants, using the Toulmin method; and (3) to examine the ways an argument appeals to its audience.

1. Recognizing types of reasoning

Writers of arguments may use either inductive or deductive reasoning. When writers use **inductive reasoning,** they do not prove that the statements that make up the argument are true; instead they convince reasonable people that the argument's validity is probable by presenting **evidence** (facts and statistics, anecdotes, and expert opinions). When writers use **deductive reasoning,** they claim that a conclusion follows necessarily from a set of assertions, or **premises**—if the premises are true and the relationship between them is valid, the conclusion must be true.

Consider the following scenarios.

Inductive reasoning A journalism student writing for the school paper makes the following claim:

> As Saturday's game shows, the Buckeyes are on their way to winning the Big Ten title.

Reasoning inductively, the student presents a number of facts—her evidence—that support her claim but do not prove it conclusively:

FACT 1	With three games remaining, the Buckeyes have a two-game lead over the second-place Badgers.
FACT 2	The Buckeyes' final three opponents have a combined record of 10 wins and 17 losses.
FACT 3	The Badgers lost their two star players to season-ending injuries last week.
FACT 4	The Buckeyes' last three games will be played at home, where they are undefeated this season.

A reader would evaluate this student's argument by judging the quality of her evidence, using the criteria listed in the box on page 186.

Inductive reasoning is a key feature of the **scientific method.** Scientists gather data from experiments, surveys, and careful observations to formulate hypotheses that explain the data. Then they test their hypotheses by collecting additional information.

Deductive reasoning The basic structure of a deductive argument is the **syllogism.** It contains a **major premise,** or general statement; **minor premise,** or specific case; and conclusion, which follows when the general statement is applied to the specific case. Suppose the journalism student were writing about great baseball teams and made the following argument:

MAJOR PREMISE	Any baseball team that wins the World Series more than 25 times in 100 years is one of the greatest teams in history.
MINOR PREMISE	The New York Yankees have won the World Series more than 25 times in the past 100 years.
CONCLUSION	The New York Yankees are one of the greatest baseball teams in history.

This is a deductive argument: if the relationship between its premises is valid and both premises are true, the conclusion must be true. The conclusion must follow from the premises. For example, it is not accurate to say: "The train is late. Jane is late. Therefore, Jane must be on the train." However, if the train is late and Jane is on the train, Jane must be late.

If the logical relationship between the premises is valid, a reader must evaluate their truth. Do you think, for example, that the number of World Series wins is a proper measure of a team's greatness? If not,

Tips LEARNING in COLLEGE

Assessing Evidence in an Inductive Argument

- **Is it accurate?** Make sure that any facts presented as evidence are correct and not taken out of context.
- **Is it relevant?** Check to see if the evidence is clearly connected to the point being made.
- **Is it representative?** Make sure that the writer's conclusion is supported by evidence gathered from a sample that accurately reflects the larger population (for example, it has the same proportion of men and women, older and younger people, and so on). If the writer is using an example, make sure that the example is typical and not a unique situation.
- **Is it sufficient?** Evaluate whether there is enough evidence to satisfy questioning readers.

you could claim that the major premise is false and does not support the conclusion.

Deductive reasoning predominates in mathematics and philosophy and some other humanities disciplines. However, you should be alert to both types of reasoning in all your college courses and in your life.

2. Using the Toulmin method to analyze arguments

Philosopher Stephen Toulmin's analysis of arguments is based on claims (assertions about a topic), grounds (reasons and evidence), and warrants (assumptions or principles that link the grounds to the claims).

Consider the following sentence from an argument by a student:

> The death penalty should be abolished because if it is not abolished, innocent people could be executed.

This example, like all logical arguments, has three facets:

CLAIM	The death penalty should be abolished.
GROUNDS	Innocent people could be executed (related stories and statistics).
WARRANT	It is not possible to be completely sure of a person's guilt.

1. **The argument makes a claim.** Also known as a *point* or a *thesis*, a **claim** makes an assertion about a topic. A strong claim responds to an issue of real interest to its audience, in terms that are clear and precise. It also allows for some uncertainty by including qualifying words such as *might* or *possibly,* or a

description of circumstances under which the claim is true. A weak claim is merely a statement of fact or a statement that few would argue with. Personal feelings are not debatable and thus are not an appropriate claim for an argument.

WEAK CLAIMS The death penalty is highly controversial.
The death penalty makes me sick.

2. **The argument presents grounds for the claim. Grounds** consist of the reasons and evidence (facts and statistics, anecdotes, and expert opinion) that support the claim. As grounds for the claim in the example, the student would present stories and statistics related to innocent people being executed. The box below should help you assess the evidence supporting a claim.
3. **The argument depends on assumptions that link the grounds to the claim.** When you analyze an argument, be aware of the unstated assumptions, or **warrants,** that underlie both the claim and the grounds that support it. The warrants underlying the example argument against the death penalty include the idea that it is wrong to execute innocent people and that it is not possible to be completely sure of a person's guilt. Warrants differ from discipline to discipline and from one school of thought to another. If you were studying the topic of bullfighting and its place in Spanish society in a sociology course, for example, you would probably make different arguments with different warrants than would the writer of a literary analysis of Ernest Hemingway's book about bullfighting, *Death in the Afternoon.* You might argue that bullfighting serves as a safe outlet for its fans' aggressive feelings. Your warrant would be

TYPES of EVIDENCE for CLAIMS

- **Facts and statistics:** Relevant, current facts and statistics can be persuasive support for a claim. People on different sides of an issue can interpret the same facts and statistics differently, however, or can cite different facts and statistics to prove their point.
- **Anecdotes:** An anecdote is a brief narrative used as an illustration to support a claim. Stories appeal to the emotions as well as to the intellect and can be very effective. Be especially careful to check anecdotes for logical fallacies (*see pp. 188–90*).
- **Expert opinion:** The views of authorities in a given field can also be powerful support for a claim. Check that the expert cited has proper credentials.

that sports can have socially useful purposes. A more controversial warrant would be that it is acceptable to kill animals for entertainment.

As you read the writing of others and as you write yourself, look for unstated assumptions. What does the reader have to assume to accept the reason and evidence in support of the claim? Hidden assumptions sometimes show **bias,** positive or negative inclinations that can manipulate unwary readers. Assumptions also differ across cultures.

3. Analyzing appeals

Arguments support claims by way of three types of appeals to readers, categorized by the Greek words **logos** (logic), **pathos** (emotions), and **ethos** (character).

- **Logical appeals** offer facts, including statistics, as well as reasoning, such as the inductive and deductive arguments on pages 184–86.
- **Emotional appeals** engage an audience's feelings and invoke beliefs that the author and audience share.
- **Ethical appeals** present authors as fair and trustworthy, and they provide the testimony of experts.

Most arguments draw on all three appeals. A proposal for more nutritious school lunches might cite statistics about childhood obesity (a logical appeal). The argument might address the audience's sense of fairness by stating that all children deserve nourishing meals (an emotional appeal). It might quote a doctor explaining that healthful food aids concentration (an ethical appeal). When writing an argument, tailor the type and content of appeals to the appropriate audience. Administrators would appreciate logical appeals about the affordability of nutritious lunches.

4. Avoiding fallacies

In their enthusiasm to make a point, writers sometimes commit **fallacies,** or mistakes in reasoning. Fallacies also can be understood as misuses of the three appeals. Learn to identify fallacies when you read and to avoid them when you write.

Logical fallacies involve errors in the inductive and deductive reasoning processes discussed above:

- **Non sequitur:** A conclusion that does not logically follow from the evidence presented or one that is based on irrelevant evidence.

EXAMPLE Students who default on their student loans have no sense of responsibility. [*Students who default on loans could be faced with high medical bills or prolonged unemployment.*]

Generalizing based on evidence is an important tactic of argument. However, the evidence must be relevant. Non sequiturs also stem from dubious assumptions.

- **False cause or post hoc:** An argument that falsely assumes that because one thing happens after another, the first event was a cause of the second event.

EXAMPLE I drank green tea and my headache went away; therefore, green tea makes headaches go away. [*How do we know that the headache did not go away for another reason?*]

Although writers frequently describe causes and effects in argument, fallacies result when they oversimplify complex relationships.

- **Self-contradiction:** An argument that contradicts itself.

EXAMPLE No absolute statement can be true. [*The statement itself is an absolute.*]

- **Circular reasoning:** An argument that restates the point rather than supporting it with reasonable evidence.

EXAMPLE The wealthy should pay more taxes because taxes should be higher for people with higher incomes. [*Why should wealthy people pay more taxes? The rest of the statement does not answer this question; it just restates the position.*]

Claims must be backed with evidence, which is missing here.

- **Begging the question:** A form of circular reasoning that assumes the truth of a questionable opinion.

EXAMPLE The president's poor relationship with the military has weakened the armed forces. [*Does the president really have a poor relationship with the military?*]

Some claims contain assumptions that must be proven first. The author of the above claim must first support the assertion that the president has a poor relationship with the military.

- **Hasty generalization:** A conclusion based on inadequate evidence.

EXAMPLE It took me over an hour to find a parking spot downtown. Therefore, the city should build a new parking garage. [*Is this evidence enough to prove this very broad conclusion?*]

- **Sweeping generalization:** An overly broad statement made in absolute terms. When about a group of people, a sweeping generalization is a **stereotype.**

EXAMPLE College students are carefree. [*What about students who work to put themselves through school?*]

Legitimate generalizations must be based on evidence that is accurate, relevant, representative, and sufficient (*see the box on p. 186*).

- **Either/or fallacy:** The idea that a complicated issue can be resolved by resorting to one of only two options when in reality there are additional choices.

EXAMPLE Either the state legislature will raise taxes or our state's economy will falter. [*Are these really the only two possibilities?*]

Frequently, arguments consider different courses of action. Authors demonstrate their fairness by addressing a range of options.

Ethical fallacies undermine a writer's credibility by showing lack of fairness to opposing views and lack of expertise on the subject of the argument.

- **Ad hominem:** A personal attack on someone who disagrees with you rather than on the person's argument.

EXAMPLE The district attorney is a lazy political hack, so naturally she opposes streamlining the court system. [*Even if the district attorney usually supports her party's position, does that make her wrong about this issue?*]

This fallacy stops debate by ignoring the real issue.

- **Guilt by association:** Discrediting a person because of problems with that person's associates, friends, or family.

EXAMPLE Smith's friend has been convicted of fraud, so Smith cannot be trusted. [*Is Smith responsible for his friend's actions?*]

This tactic undermines an opponent's credibility and is based on a dubious assumption: if a person's associates are untrustworthy, that person is also untrustworthy.

- **False authority:** Presenting the testimony of an unqualified person to support a claim.

EXAMPLE As the actor who plays Dr. Fine on *The Emergency Room,* I recommend this weight-loss drug because . . . [*Is an actor qualified to judge the benefits and dangers of a diet drug?*]

Although expert testimony can strengthen an argument, the person must be an authority on the subject in question. This fallacy frequently underlies celebrity endorsements of products.

Emotional fallacies stir readers' sympathy at the expense of their reasoning.

- **False analogy:** A comparison in which a surface similarity masks a significant difference.

EXAMPLE Governments and businesses both work within a budget to accomplish their goals. Just as business must focus on the bottom line, so should government. [*Is the goal of government to make a profit? Does government instead have other, more important goals?*]

Analogies can enliven an argument and deepen an audience's understanding of a subject, provided the things being compared actually are similar.

- **Bandwagon:** An argument that depends on going along with the crowd, on the false assumption that truth can be determined by a popularity contest.

EXAMPLE Everybody knows that Toni Morrison is preoccupied with the theme of death in her novels. [*How do we know that "everybody" agrees with this statement?*]

- **Red herring:** An argument that diverts attention from the true issue by concentrating on something irrelevant.

EXAMPLE Hemingway's book *Death in the Afternoon* is unsuccessful because it glorifies the brutal sport of bullfighting. [*Why can't a book about a brutal sport be successful? The statement is irrelevant.*]

5. Reading visual arguments

Like written arguments, visual arguments support claims with reasons and evidence, rely on assumptions, and may contain fallacies. They make logical appeals, such as a graph of experimental data; emotional appeals, such as a photograph of a hungry child; and ethical appeals, such as a corporate logo (*see p. 188*). Like all written works, visual arguments are created by an author for an audience and to achieve a purpose, within a context. (*See Chapter 2, pp. 21–23.*)

Recall that Toulmin's system analyzes arguments based on the claims they make, the grounds (evidence and reasons) for those claims, and the warrants (underlying assumptions) that connect the grounds with the claims. (*See the explanation of Toulmin analysis on pp. 186–88.*) While these elements function similarly in verbal and visual arguments, unstated assumptions play a larger role in visual arguments because claims and grounds often are not stated explicitly.

Consider an example of Toulmin analysis of an image. A photograph of a politician with her family members makes a claim (She is a good public servant) and implicitly offers grounds (because she cares for her family). The warrant is that a person's family life indicates how she will perform in office. This may be a non sequitur (*see p. 188*).

Advertisements combine text and images to promote a product or message to an audience in a social context. They use the resources of visual design: type of image, position, color, light and shadows, fonts, and white space. (*See the questions on previewing a visual in Chapter 7, pp. 123–24 and the discussion of design in Chapter 6, pp. 105–12.*) The public-service ad below was developed by the nonprofit advocacy group Adbusters.

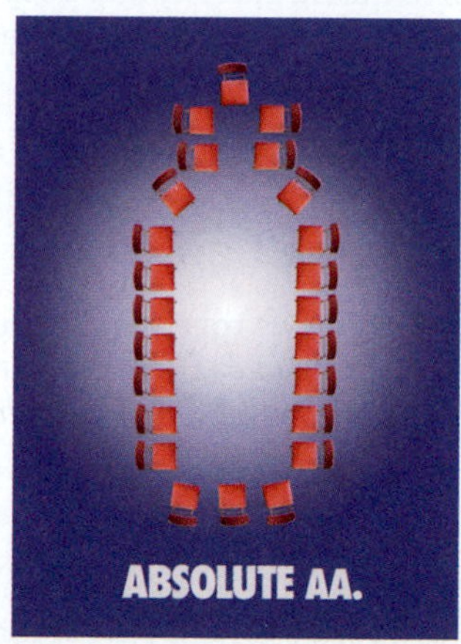

The ad's text and design evoke a popular series of ads for a brand of vodka. Its uncluttered design focuses the viewer's attention on the shape of a bottle, the outline of which consists of chairs. The text at the bottom refers to AA: Alcoholics Anonymous. By association, the text and images in this public-service ad remind readers that liquor can lead to alcoholism (and then to AA). In contrast with those it spoofs, this ad evokes an unexpected threat, creating a powerful emotional appeal.

What claims do you think this ad makes? One might be "alcohol is dangerous." The evidence is supplied by the reader's prior knowledge about alcoholism. The argument's assumptions include familiarity with both the original liquor campaign and the initials "AA" for Alcoholics Anonymous.

Fallacies frequently occur in visual arguments. For example, celebrity endorsements of products rely on our respect for the celebrity's character. However, an athlete's endorsement of a particular type of car is an example of false authority, unless she also happens to be an expert on cars. (*See p. 191.*)

CHECKLIST

Reading Visual Arguments Critically

Review the questions for previewing a visual from Chapter 7, pages 123–24, and add the following:

- ☐ What can you tell about the visual's creator or sponsor?
- ☐ What seems to be the visual's purpose? Is a product or message promoted?
- ☐ Who do you think is the intended audience? What aspects of the visual suggest this audience? How?
- ☐ How do aspects of design such as size, position, color, and shape affect the visual's message?
- ☐ What is the effect of any text, audio, or video that accompanies the visual?

10c Approach writing your own argument as a process.

Selecting a topic that you care about will give you the energy to think matters through and make cogent arguments. Of course, you will have to go beyond your personal emotions about an issue to make the most convincing case. You will also have to empathize with potential readers who may disagree with you about a subject that is important to you.

www.mhhe.com/mhhb2

For an interactive tutorial on writing arguments, go to

Writing > Writing Tutors > Arguments

1. Figuring out what is at issue

Before you can take a position on a topic like air pollution or population growth, you must figure out what is at issue. Ask questions about your topic. Are there indications that all is not as it should be? Have things always been this way, or have they changed for the worse? From what different perspectives—economic, social, political, cultural, medical, geographic—can problems like world food shortages be understood? Do people interested in the topic disagree about what is true, what is good, or what should be done?

Based on your answers to such questions, identify the issues your topic raises. Then decide which of those issues is most important, interesting, and appropriate to write about in response to your assignment.

2. Developing a reasonable stance that negotiates differences

When writing arguments, you want your readers to respect your intelligence and trust your judgment. By getting readers to trust your character, you build **ethos.** Conducting research on your issue can make you well informed; reading other people's views and thinking critically about them can enhance your thoughtfulness. Pay attention to the places where you disagree with other people's views, but also note what you have in common—topical interests, key questions, or underlying values. (*For more on appeals to your audience, see p. 198.*)

Avoid language that may promote prejudice or fear. Misrepresentations of other people's ideas are out of place, as are personal attacks on their character. Write arguments to open minds; do not slam doors shut. (*See the box on blogs on p. 195.*)

Trying out different perspectives can also help you figure out where you stand on an issue. (*Also see the next section on stating your position.*) Make a list of the arguments for and against a specific position; then compare the lists and decide where you stand. Does one set of arguments seem stronger than the other? Do you want to change or qualify your initial position?

3. Making a strong claim

A successful argument requires a strong, engaging, arguable thesis. As noted in the section on the Toulmin model of argument, personal feelings and accepted facts cannot serve as an argument's thesis because they are not debatable (*see 10b, pp. 186–87*).

PERSONAL FEELING, NOT A DEBATABLE THESIS

I feel that developing nations should not suffer food shortages.

ACCEPTED FACT, NOT A DEBATABLE THESIS

Food shortages are increasing in many developing nations.

TEXTCONNEX

Blogs

Blogs frequently function as vehicles for public debate. For example, the online editions of many newspapers include blogs, which invite readers to comment on the news of the day and to present dissenting opinions. While online debate can be freewheeling, it is important to search for common ground with your readers. (*For more on blogs, see Chapter 14, pp. 244–47.*)

Looking at blogs can help you learn about an issue or find common counterarguments to your position. (*See Chapter 16, pp. 278–80.*) However, evaluate blogs carefully before using them as support for an argument (*see Chapter 18, pp. 291–98*). Many blogs rely heavily on personal opinion, and some may not receive careful editing for factual accuracy.

DEBATABLE THESIS

> Current food shortages in developing nations are in large part due to climate change and the use of food crops in biofuels.

In proposals and policy papers, the thesis presents a solution in terms of the writer's definition of the problem. The logic behind a thesis for a proposal can be stated like this:

> Given these key variables and their underlying cause, one solution to the problem would be . . .

Because this kind of thesis is both complex and qualified, you will often need more than one sentence to state it clearly. You will also need numerous well-supported arguments to make it creditable. Readers will finally want to know that the proposed solution will not cause worse problems than it solves.

4. Supporting and developing your claim

A strong, debatable thesis needs to be supported and developed with sound reasoning and carefully documented evidence. You can think of an argument as a dialogue between writer and readers. A writer states a debatable thesis, and one reader wonders, "Why do you believe that?" Another reader wants to know, "But what about this factor?" Writers need to anticipate readers' questions and answer them by presenting reasons that are substantiated with evidence and by refuting opposing views. They should also be sure to define any abstract terms, such as *freedom*, that figure importantly in their arguments. In his critique of *Time* magazine's choice of "You" for Person of the

Year, Matt Shadwell presents the magazine's definition of Person of the Year and sets out to prove that "You" does not meet these criteria (*pp. 201–06*).

Usually, a well-developed argument paper includes more than one type of reason and one kind of evidence. Besides generalizations based on empirical data or statistics, it often includes authoritative reasons based on the opinions of experts and ethical reasons based on the application of principle. In his paper, Shadwell presents facts about the passivity of *YouTube* users, citing the percentage who contribute information at only 0.07 percent. He also quotes an expert commentator, Frank Rich, who points out that Internet users prefer sites about celebrities to sites that focus on world events (*see p. 204*). In addition, he presents the anecdotal example of an average user, demonstrating that her actions are far from revolutionary. As you conduct research for your argument, note evidence—facts, examples or anecdotes, and expert testimony—that can support each argument for or against your position. Demonstrate your trustworthiness by properly quoting and documenting the information you have gathered from your sources.

Also build your credibility by paying attention to **counterarguments,** substantiated claims that do not support your position. Consider whether a reader could reasonably draw different conclusions from your evidence or disagree with your assumptions. Use the following strategies to take the most important ones into account:

- Qualify your thesis in light of the counterargument by including a word such as *most, some, usually,* or *likely:* "Students with credit cards *usually* have trouble with debt" recognizes that some do not.
- Add to the thesis a statement of the conditions for or exceptions to your position: "Businesses *with over five hundred employees* will save money using the new process."
- Choose one or two counterarguments and refute their truth or their importance.

Introduce a counterargument with a signal phrase like, "Others might contend . . ." (*See Part 3: Researching, p. 330 for a discussion of signal phrases.*) Refute a counterargument's validity by questioning the author's interpretation of the evidence or the author's assumptions. Shadwell refutes the counterargument that passive users of the Internet should be honored as "Person of the Year." He also suggests that the editors of *Time* have assumed that all Internet users create content, and he shows this is not the case.

www.mhhe.com/mhhb2

For more help with creating an outline, go to

Writing > Paragraph/Essay Development > Outlines

5. Creating an outline that includes a linked set of reasons

Arguments are most effective when they present a chain—a linked set—of reasons. Shadwell presents evidence first and builds to his thesis at the end of his critique. Although there are multiple ways to order an argument, your outline should include the following parts (arranged below according to **classical structure**):

- An introduction to the topic and the debatable issue, establishing your credibility and seeking common ground with your readers
- A thesis stating your position on the issue
- A point-by-point account of the reasons for your position, including evidence (facts, examples, authorities) to substantiate each major reason
- A fair presentation and refutation of one or two key counterarguments
- A response to the "So what?" question. Why does your argument matter? If appropriate, include a call to action.

If you expect your audience to disagree with you, consider using a **Rogerian structure**:

- An introduction to the topic and the debatable issue
- An attempt to reach common ground by naming values you share and providing a sympathetic portrayal of your readers' (opposing) position
- A statement of your position and presentation of supporting evidence
- A conclusion that restates your view and suggests a compromise or synthesis

(*See p. 198 for information on Rogerian argument.*)

6. Appealing to your audience

You want your readers to see you as *reasonable, ethical,* and *empathetic*—qualities that promote communication among people who have differences. You display the quality of your logos, ethos, and pathos by the way that you argue for what you believe. (*For more on the classical appeals, see p. 188.*)

Logical appeals include giving reasons and supplying evidence for your position; you also establish your logos when you avoid fallacies. (*For more on fallacies, see pp. 188–91.*) Ethical appeals demonstrate that you are sincere and fair-minded; you build ethos by respecting those who do not share your viewpoint and by avoiding sarcasm and biased language. Emotional appeals show that you care deeply about your thesis and seek to win the hearts of your audience; you may infuse your argument with pathos by relating a compelling anecdote, a memorable quotation, or a concrete description.

When you read your argument, pay attention to the impression you are making. Ask yourself these questions:

- Would a reasonable person be able to follow the logic of the reasons and evidence I offer in support of my thesis?
- Have I presented myself as ethical and fair? What would readers who have never met me think of me after reading what I have to say?
- Have I expressed my feelings about the issue? Have I sought to arouse the reader's feelings?

www.mhhe.com/mhhb2
For more on crafting introductions, go to
Writing > Paragraph/Essay Development > Introductions

7. Emphasizing your commitment to dialogue

To promote dialogue with readers, look for common ground—beliefs, concerns, and values you share with those who disagree with you and those who are undecided. Sometimes called **Rogerian argument** after the psychologist Carl Rogers, the common-ground approach is particularly important in your introduction, where it can build bridges with readers who might otherwise become too defensive or annoyed to read further. For example, Dale Jamieson opens his review of a book on Charles Darwin (*p. 207*) by acknowledging the controversy over Darwin's theories. (*See p. 197 for the structure of a Rogerian argument.*)

Keep the dialogue open throughout your essay by maintaining an objective tone and acknowledging opposing views. If possible, point out ways in which your position would be advantageous for both sides (a **win-win solution**). At the end of your argument, leave a favorable impression by referring again to common ground.

8. Concluding by restating your position and emphasizing its importance

Bring your argument to a close by restating your position. The version of your thesis that you present in your conclusion should be more complex and qualified than in your introduction, to encourage readers to appreciate your argument's importance. Readers may not agree with you, but they should know why the issue and your argument matter.

9. Using visuals in your argument

Consider including visuals that support your argument's purpose. Each should relate directly to your argument as a whole or to a point within it. For example, Matt Shadwell takes the cover of *Time* magazine as the subject of his argument, refuting its message. (*See p. 202.*) Visuals also may provide evidence: a photograph can illustrate an example, and a graph can present statistics that support an argument.

Visual evidence makes emotional, logical, and ethical appeals. The Absolute AA ad on page 192 makes an emotional appeal by substituting a warning against alcoholism for the expected commercial message. The graph of Amazon deforestation rates in Audrey Galeano's paper (*Chapter 24: APA Documentation Style, p. 415*) makes a logical appeal by presenting evidence that supports her claim. It also demonstrates the depth of her research (building her ethos).

Consider how your audience is likely to react to your visuals. Nonspecialists will need more explanation of charts, graphs, and other visuals. When possible, have members of your target audience review your argument and visuals. Help them interpret your visuals with specific captions that describe each visual and how it supports your argument. Mention each image in your text. Make sure charts and graphs are free of distortion or chartjunk (*see Chapter 5: Revising and Editing, p. 91*). Also acknowledge any data from other sources and obtain permission when needed. (*See also Chapter 17: Finding and Creating Visuals, pp. 281–89.*)

10. Reexamining your reasoning

After you have completed the first draft of your paper, take time to reexamine your reasoning. Step outside yourself and assess your argument objectively. Peer review is also an essential tool for developing critical thinking and writing skills. Use the checklist "Self/Peer Review of Argument" on page 200 to assess your own arguments and those of your classmates.

For MULTILINGUAL STUDENTS

Learning about Cultural Differences through Peer Review

U.S. culture encourages writing direct and explicit arguments, while some other cultures do not. When you share your work with peers born and raised in the United States, you may learn that the vocabulary or the style of presentation you have used makes it difficult for them to understand your point. They may want you to be more direct. Ask your peers to suggest different words and approaches. Then decide whether their suggestions will make your ideas more accessible to others.

CHECKLIST

Self/Peer Review of Argument

- ☐ **What makes the thesis strong and arguable?**
- ☐ **Does the essay give a sufficient number of reasons to support its thesis, or does it need one or two more?**
- ☐ **Are the reasons and evidence suitable for the purpose and audience?**
- ☐ **Does the argument contain mistakes in logic?** Refer to pages 188–90 to check for logical fallacies.
- ☐ **How does the essay develop each reason it presents in support of the thesis?** Is the reason clear? Where are its key terms defined? Is the supporting evidence sufficient? Does the argument quote or paraphrase from sources accurately and document them properly? (*For more on quoting, paraphrasing, and documenting sources, see Part 3: Researching, and Part 4: Documenting across the Curriculum.*)
- ☐ **How does the essay address at least one significant counterargument?** How does it treat opposing views?
- ☐ **In what way does each visual support the thesis?** How are the visuals tailored to the audience?
- ☐ **Are logical and emotional appeals consistent?**

www.mhhe.com/mhhb2
For more samples of argument papers, go to
Writing > Writing Samples > Argument Papers

10d Construct arguments to address issues in the social sciences

In the following critique, Matt Shadwell argues that the editors of *Time* magazine made a poor choice in designating "You" as Person of the Year. As you read Shadwell's argument, notice how he defines criteria of accomplishment and then shows that "You" does not fit those standards. In critiquing the *Time* magazine cover, he is also criticizing the passivity of Internet users, refuting the cover's basic claim that "You" are actively engaged in a "flat" world through surfing and blogging.

> ***Note:*** For details on the proper formatting of a paper in APA style, see Chapter 24 and the sample paper that begins on page 412.

Sample student argument paper

Person of the Year

Matt Shadwell

Communications 110

Professor Bianco

March 11, 2008

Following APA style, Shadwell includes a separate title page. His instructor did not require an abstract for this assignment.

------------------------------[new page]------------------------------------

Time magazine's Persons of the Year have ranged from celebrities, politicians, religious leaders, and humanitarians to more inclusive or abstract selections such as "the American Soldier," "the Peacemakers," and "Endangered Earth." The rationale for selection has varied as widely as the character of its "persons." The Man of the Year in 1938, Adolf Hitler, was chosen for the singular power of his personality and the scale of his terrifying accomplishments; on the other hand, "U.S. Scientists" were named collectively in 1960 for affecting "the life of every human presently inhabiting the planet" through a long list of breakthroughs including the discovery of DNA. In its eighty-year retrospective of this annual cover story, *Time* states that the recognition is "bestowed by the editors on the person or persons who most affected the news and our lives, for good or ill, and embodied what was important about the year." It is therefore baffling to consider *Time's* 2006 honoree, "You" (see Figure 1).

Lively beginning inviting readers to consider other Person of the Year choices, including those selected for evil accomplishments.

Topic introduced

According to the 2006 Person of the Year cover story, the world's boundaries have been broken and its people have united via the Internet. People are flocking to social networking and content-sharing sites like *MySpace* and *YouTube* to broadcast programming and information to millions worldwide. Access to potentially enormous audiences is simpler and more widely available than ever, and *Time's* editors admiringly note that people are finding more uses for this broad public forum every day. Lev Grossman (2006), author of the cover story, wrote:

> [W]ho are these people? Seriously, who actually sits down after a long day at work and says, I'm not going to watch *Lost* tonight. I'm going to turn on my computer and

Figure 1 Cover of *Time* announcing Person of the Year, December 25, 2006. *Note:* Hochstein, A., & Jones-Glasshouse, S. (2006, December 25). *Time.* Retrieved from http://www.time.com/time/covers/0,16641,20061225,00.html

Presents *Time* magazine's position fairly via an engaging quote.

> make a movie starring my pet iguana. I'm going to mash up 50 Cent's vocals with Queen's instrumentals? I'm going to blog about my state of mind or the state of the nation or the steak-frites at the new bistro down the street? Who has that time and energy and passion? The answer is, you do. (para. 3)

Poses key question about article's claim.

Since *Time* is honoring "You" for this achievement, it seems worthwhile to question who precisely the magazine's editors are referring to. In conferring responsibility for this revolution in the control and flow of information, does *Time* mean to honor each and every person in the world who surfed the Internet in 2006, or just the comparatively small number of computer savvy individuals who produced mass quantities of text, film, music, etc. online? At the beginning of "What Is the 1% Rule," Charles Arthur (2006) wrote that "if you get a group of 100 people online then one will create content, 10 will 'interact' with it (commenting or offering improvements) and the other 89 will just view it" (para. 1). To illustrate the "One Percent Rule," examine the statistics of uploading and downloading content on *YouTube*. According to Antony Mayfield (2006), *YouTube's* hundreds of millions of daily downloads (passive viewings) outnumber its uploads (posting of content) by a margin of 1,538 to 1. That means that the percentage of users on *YouTube* who contribute information is about 0.07 percent—a good deal less than the One Percent Rule would predict. "You" would therefore seem a rather generous way to describe a relatively small number of people.

Presents factual evidence to support point.

Alternatively, one might suppose the magazine truly wishes to honor the vast numbers of passive users as well. This, too, seems ill-conceived. Consider a typical Internet user. He or she accesses the Web daily, visiting sites such as *YouTube* on a regular basis. On social networking sites such as *MySpace* and *Facebook*, the user maintains a profile to stay in touch with friends, occasionally adding photos, sending out notices, or posting entries on a blog. Sites like these offer a degree of self-expression through personalized page designs (including music, images, and sometimes video); they also typically allow users to control access to their sites, enabling them to designate certain features or their profile at large as either public, private, or selectively public (meaning only visitors designated as "friends" can look at the features).

Presents and refutes counter-argument.

As novel as such activities may seem to the tens of millions of people who visit such sites daily, it is difficult to see how pasting a *YouTube* video on a *MySpace* profile deserves recognition for "seizing the reins of the global media, for founding and framing the new digital democracy, for working for nothing and beating the pros at their own game" (Grossman, 2006). If *Time* means to include everyone who uses the Internet in their profile, then the editors are simply congratulating people for becoming more eager consumers of an emerging technological market. This is like honoring "Cable TV Viewers" for changing the face of television, or "Hybrid Car Buyers" for revolutionizing the auto industry.

One wonders if the magazine isn't actually expressing wonder over the technology itself, much as it did when it honored "the Computer" in 1982. Since the Internet itself is nothing new, one can only assume *Time*'s editors are terrifically impressed by new applications of existing technology. Web sites such as *YouTube* or *Google Video*, which essentially are do-it-yourself video outlets, are visited by millions of viewers every day; but is their content as significant or groundbreaking as the *Time* article seems to claim, or do such sites and their content exist mostly to entertain? Some have argued that the availability of footage from the Iraq war typifies the potential informative power of online video sites. Certainly, in an era in which the Pentagon limits media access to military funerals (Tapper, 2007), and official reports of civilian casualties remain haphazard (and often contradictory), one can argue for the value of access to footage taken by American soldiers and Iraqi civilians in the war zone. Unfortunately, access to information does not necessarily equal interest. *The New York Times* columnist Frank Rich (2006) wrote that a typical Internet search showed that "Britney Spears Nude on Beach" received over a million hits by *YouTube's* visitors, while "Iraq" clips were viewed by a little over twenty thousand users. It would seem, then, that online media exists primarily for entertainment. And it is difficult to see how watching fifteen-second clips of *I Love Lucy* or montages of Rocky Marciano's knockout punches changes the world for better or worse.

Compelling critique of *Time's* editors for being swayed by novelty of new Internet applications.

Uses expert testimony to support critique.

Likewise, *Time*'s assertion that *YouTube* serves as a powerful mirror into the life of the typical American seems overstated. Grossman claimed that "[y]ou can learn more about how Americans live just by looking at the backgrounds of *YouTube* videos—those rumpled bedrooms and toy-strewn basement recreation rooms—than you could from 1,000 hours of network television" (Grossman, 2006, para. 5). Is it revelatory to learn that many people keep messy homes? Also, it must be remembered that an individual's control over content can prevent these glimpses

Refutes *Time's* secondary argument that *YouTube* videos reveal 21st century lives.

into people's everyday lives from being truly spontaneous or accurate. The person behind the camcorder controls what he or she wants us to see.

Finally, it should be noted that while the Internet has certainly made more information instantly available than ever before, in many countries this access falls under government control. In China, for example, search engines such as *Google* have been forced to purge links to any Web sites disapproved of by the government. As a result, it is difficult for the typical Chinese Internet user to find information about Tibet, student protests, or dissident groups such as Falun Gong (Thompson, 2006, para. 5). In the United States, legislation such as the Child Online Protection Act of 1998 has sought to punish online providers of sexually explicit material (ACLU, 2007). Though such laws have been repeatedly struck down by the Supreme Court due to First Amendment concerns, many Web sites, including *MySpace* and *YouTube*, voluntarily police content that its administrators or users identify as explicit or otherwise objectionable. How can one accept the claim that "You" have taken control of the flow of information when governments and service providers still have ultimate power over what is and isn't seen?

Refutes claim that "You" are in control of information.

It would be difficult to identify single figures who dominated the events of 2006; rather, the continuing conflicts in Iraq and Afghanistan, the deepening diplomatic crises surrounding the nuclear ambitions of North Korea and Iran, and the sudden reversals of political fortunes in Washington all involved numerous individuals, many of them anonymous, slogging through complex issues that are difficult to characterize in a simple way. Perhaps this is the best explanation for *Time* magazine's baffling choice for Person of the Year . It does seem, however, that the rationale for the selection lacks reason, clarity, or meaning. For good or ill, a Person of the Year should actually have accomplished something significant. *Time*'s "You" has not really done so.

Establishes common ground: acknowledges the difficulty of selecting a Person of the Year.

Full statement of thesis refuting the choice.

Underlines the critique's importance: *Time's* choice misleads readers.

References list begins on a new page and is formatted according to APA style.

-----------------------------[new page]-----------------------------------

References

American Civil Liberties Union. (2007, March 22). *ACLU victorious in defense of online free speech* [Press release]. Retrieved from http://www.aclu.org/freespeech/internet/29138prs20070322.html

Arthur, C. (2006, July 20). What is the 1% rule? *Guardian Unlimited*. Retrieved from http://guardian.co.uk

Grossman, L. (2006, December 13). Time's person of the year: you. *Time*. Retrieved from http://www.time.com/time/magazine/article/0,9171,1569514,00.html

Hochstein, A., & Jones-Glasshouse, S. (2006, December 25). *Time*. Retrieved from http://www.time.com/time/covers/0,16641,20061225,00.html

Mayfield, A. (2006, July 17). 0-60% in under 18 months: *YouTube* dominates online video. *Open*. Retrieved from http://open.typepad.com/open/2006/07/index.html

Rich, F. (2006, December 24). Yes, you are the person of the year. *The New York Times*. Retrieved from http://nytimes.com

Tapper, J. (2007, November 14). Pentagon limits media coverage of funerals. *ABC News Online*. Retrieved from http://abcnews.go.com

Thompson, C. (2006, April 23). Google's China problem (and China's Google problem). *New York Times Magazine*. Retrieved from http://www.nytimes.com

Time's person of the year, 1927–2006. (2007, November 8). *Time*. Retrieved from http://www.time.com

www.mhhe.com/mhhb2

For online resources in various disciplines, go to

Learning > Links across the Curriculum

10e Construct arguments to address issues in the humanities.

Reviews are arguments in the sense that they involve making principled claims about a specific book or performance. The following review essay by philosopher Dale Jamieson evaluates arguments in a book by another philosopher, James Rachels, and then evaluates the merits of the book overall.

Sample review essay

The Morality of Species

Dale Jamieson

[A review of] *Created from Animals: The Moral Implications of Darwinism.* By James Rachels. Oxford: Oxford University Press, 1990. 245 pp. $19.95 cloth.

Poor Charles Darwin. For fundamentalists he is the Great Satan, for Social Darwinists the Great Liberator, and for academics, the stuff of dissertations, books, and careers. The sickly gentleman from Downe is roundly loved, hated, reviled, and admired, mostly for bad reasons, by people who never read his books or misread them when they do. Like Matisse, who sometimes claimed forgeries as his own original artworks, Darwin was not always a good judge of what he brought forth: he thought that Spencer was "by far the greatest living philosopher in England: perhaps equal to any that have lived."

In this brilliant but readable book, James Rachels has done much in a few pages to recover the historical Darwin. Although only the first chapter is explicitly about Darwin, his spirit infuses the entire book. Rachels brings out the broadly consequentialist nature of Darwin's moral thinking, and quotes several remarkable passages in which Darwin looks forward to an age in which moral sympathy is "extended to all sentient beings" (p. 165). The Darwin that emerges is not just a biologist cum philosopher. He is also a curious boy, a casual student, an opponent of slavery, and a defender of science. One vignette is especially revealing. Shortly after Darwin's marriage to the devout Emma Wedgewood, who would be his wife for more than forty years, she wrote urging him to reconsider his views about religion. After Darwin's death this letter was found among his papers. Scrawled on the bottom were the words: "When I am dead, know how many times I have kissed and cried over this."

Rachels's first chapter, "Darwin's Discovery," vividly captures the spirit of Darwin's life and work. "How Evolution and Ethics Might Be Related" is a critical but sympathetic discussion of post-Darwinian attempts to connect evolution and ethics. Nodding toward Hume, Rachels rejects deductivist views about what the connection might be but goes on to claim that "Darwinism undermines traditional morality" (p. 97). Chapter three asks, "Must a Darwinian Be Skeptical about Religion?" Yes, is Rachels's answer. Although there is no logical incompatibility between Darwinism and theism, Darwinism "undermines religious belief by removing some of the grounds that previously supported it" (p. 127). "How Different Are Humans from Other Animals?" argues that although some humans are quite different from other animals, the differences are matters of degree rather than kind: "Darwinism leads inevitably to the abandonment of the idea of human dignity and the substitution of a different sort of ethic"

(p. 171). The final chapter, "Morality without the Idea That Humans Are Special," outlines that ethic. It is a view that Rachels calls "moral individualism" and it implies the rejection of speciesism in all its forms.

People who make their living fighting over arguments and texts will find much to quarrel with in Rachels's book. No doubt scholars have found other ways of reading Darwin. Not all moral philosophers will be enamored of Rachels's "moral individualism." I myself would have liked to hear more about the relation of "undermining," and I somehow missed the move from the claim that the value of a life is the value that it has to its subject, to the claim that "the more complex their lives are, the greater the objection to destroying them" (p. 209). Nor is it clear how much weight the distinction between differences of degree and differences of kind can bear: contemplate the difference between the bald and the hirsute. In its treatment of texts, claims, and arguments this book is very good, but Rachels's real accomplishment lies elsewhere.

What Rachels has given us is a framework (a "narrative," as a postmodernist might say) that makes sense of much of the debate in recent moral philosophy, especially in such areas as medical and environmental ethics. What we are witnessing, more than a century after the publication of Darwin's *Origin*, is moral change occasioned by the belated impact of the Darwinian perspective.

Rachels describes moral change in the following way. In the first stage a moral outlook "is supported by a world-view in which everyone . . . has confidence" (p. 221). In the second stage the world-view begins to break up. According to Rachels the "old morality" of human uniqueness and dignity was supported by a world-view with the earth at its center, a specially created home for humans who were made in God's image, with animals given to humans to use as they please. Although this world-view was under attack long before Darwin, it was he who struck the death blow by showing that humans and animals are both products of purposeless natural processes, and indeed are kin. According to Rachels we are now in the third stage of moral change, in which the old morality is no longer taken for granted. It is widely agreed that it requires defense. The fourth stage is one in which a new morality emerges, one that is at home with our best understandings of ourselves and our relation to the world. If Rachels is right, much of this new morality is implicit in Darwin's own thought.

Rachels has given us an important book that provides a new perspective on what we are doing in moral philosophy. It is well written, well argued, and well researched. It deserves a very wide readership.

10f Construct arguments to address issues in the sciences.

Scientists are called upon to evaluate the research of others and to argue for changes in policy. In the following essay by the Council for Biotechnology Information, the authors argue that biotech crops offer a solution to a looming crisis in food production.

Sample policy paper

Growing More Food*

COUNCIL FOR BIOTECHNOLOGY INFORMATION

The world's population more than doubled in the last half century and topped 6 billion in 1999.[1] Each year, it is adding about 73 million people—a population nearly the size of Vietnam's. By 2030, it is projected to reach around 8 billion, and nearly all of that increase is expected to occur in developing countries,[2] which are also expected to see higher incomes and rapid urbanization.

At the same time, the world's hungry and chronically malnourished remain at about 840 million people, despite global pledges and national efforts to improve food security.

These trends mean the world will have to double its food production and also improve food distribution over the next quarter century.[3] These pose staggering challenges for the world's farmers: Much of the world's land suitable for farming is already cultivated and natural resources are under pressure. Soil degradation is widespread, agriculture has already razed 20 to 30 percent of the world's forest areas[4] and water tables in many areas are falling. Agriculture consumes about 70 percent of the fresh water people use every year and, at the current consumption rate, two out of three people will live in water-stressed conditions by 2025.[5]

By 2050, some 4.2 billion people may not have their daily basic needs met.[6]

These projections and complex challenges facing the world's future food supply are prompting international food and agricultural experts and policymakers—including the U.N. Food and Agriculture Organization and the World Health Organization—to call plant biotechnology a critical tool to help feed a growing population in the 21st century.

Governments need to develop policies to ensure greater investment in research and regulatory oversight that's needed to manage the health, environmental and socioeconomic issues associated with biotechnology, according to the Human Development Report 2001, an annual report commissioned by the U.N. Development Programme.[7]

Biotechnology: An eco-efficient option

World crop productivity could increase by as much as 25 percent[8] through the use of biotechnology to grow plants that resist pests and diseases, tolerate harsh growing conditions and delay ripening to reduce spoilage, according to the Consultative Group on International Agricultural Research (CGIAR). All this could be achieved on existing farmland and customized to meet local needs.

*The documentation style used in this paper is that which appeared in the original and does not correspond fully to any of the styles discussed elsewhere in the handbook (*see Part 4: Documenting across the Curriculum*).

Biotechnology also offers the possibility for scientists to design "farming systems that are responsive to local needs and reflect sustainability requirements," said Calestous Juma, director of the Science, Technology and Innovation Program at the Center for International Development and senior research associate at the Belfer Center for Science and International Affairs, both at Harvard University.[9]

Scientists are developing crops that resist diseases, pests, viruses, bacteria and fungi, all of which reduce global production by more than 35 percent at a cost estimated at more than $200 billion a year.[10] For instance, test fields in Kenya are growing sweet potato varieties that are resistant to a complex set of viruses that can wipe out three-fourths of Kenyan farmers' harvest.

In the United States, crops with built-in insect protection and that tolerate a specific herbicide have helped farmers improve yields and reduce costs. In 2000, direct benefit to growers of insect resistant corn, cotton and potatoes exceeded $300 million, according to the Environmental Protection Agency.[11]

In a study to be released in 2002, the National Center for Food and Agricultural Policy quantified biotechnology's benefits for U.S. farmers through 44 case studies that covered 30 different crops, including papaya, citrus, soybeans and tomatoes. For instance, it found that herbicide tolerant soybeans helped farmers reduce their annual production costs by $15 an acre, which totals $735 million across 49 million acres. Virus-resistant papaya is credited with saving Hawaii's papaya industry, which produces 53 million pounds of the fruit valued at $17 million a year.[12]

Biotechnology: Getting the most from poor growing conditions

Scientists are developing crops that can tolerate extreme conditions, such as drought, flood and harsh soil. For instance, researchers are working on a rice that can survive long periods under water [13] as well as rice and corn that can tolerate aluminum in soil. [14]

A tomato plant has been developed to grow in salty water that is 50 times higher in salt content than conventional plants can tolerate and nearly half as salty as seawater.[15] About a third of the world's irrigated land has become useless to farmers because of high levels of accumulated salt.

Biotech crops "could significantly reduce malnutrition, which still affects more than 800 million people worldwide, and would be especially valuable for poor farmers working marginal lands in sub-Saharan Africa," the Human Development Report stated.

Technology in a seed

While the Green Revolution kept mass starvation at bay and saw global cereal production double as a result of improved crop varieties, fertilizers, pesticides and irrigation, its benefits bypassed such regions as sub-Saharan Africa. The new hybrids needed irrigation and chemical inputs that farmers there couldn't afford.

In contrast, the benefits of biotechnology are passed on through a seed or plant cutting, so that farmers anywhere around the world can easily adopt the technology. That's why biotechnology is particularly attractive to scientists and rural development experts in poor countries where most of the people farm for a living.

Biotech crops are "tailor-made for Africa's farmers, because the new technology is packaged in the seed, which all farmers know how to handle," said Florence Wambugu, a Kenyan plant scientist who helped develop a virus-resistant sweet potato.[16]

Agreeing with Wambugu, the International Society of African Scientists issued a statement in October 2001 calling plant biotechnology a "major opportunity to enhance the production of food crops."[17]

Notes

[1] United Nations Population Fund (UNFPA), "Population Numbers and Trends," <www.unfpa.org/modules/briefkit/05.htm>.

[2] International Food Policy Research Institute, "World Food Prospects: Critical Issues for the Early Twenty-First Century," October 1999, p. 9.

[3] United Nations Population Fund (UNFPA), "State of World Population 2001 Report," November 7, 2001, <www.unfpa.org/swp/swpmain.htm>.

[4] "New Study Reveals That Environmental Damage Threatens Future World Food Production," World Resources Institute, February 14, 2001, <www.wri.org/press/page_agroecosystems.html>.

[5] Global Environment Outlook, 2000—UN Environment Programme, <www.unep.org/geo2000/>.

[6] "State of World Population 2001 Report," United Nations Population Fund (UNFPA), November 7, 2001, <www.unfpa.org/swp/swpmain.htm>.

[7] "The Human Development Report 2001," United Nations Development Programme, July 2001, <www.undp.org/>.

[8] Prakash, C.S., (October 4, 2001). In a media presentation sponsored by the American Medical Association (AMA), cited Consultative Group on International Agricultural Research (CGIAR) as source. See <www.ama-assn.org> media briefings.

[9] Calestous, Juma, director of the Science, Technology and Innovation Program at the Center for International Development and senior research associate at the Belfer Center for Science and International Affairs, "Appropriate Technology for Sustainable Food Security—Modern Biotechnology," both at Harvard University, *2020 Focus 7,* International Food Policy Research Institute (IFPRI). August 2001.

[10] Krattiger, Anatole, "Food Biotechnology: Promising Havoc or Hope for the Poor?" Proteus, 2000.

[11] "Bt Plant-Pesticides Biopesticides Registration Action Document—Executive Summary," United States Environmental Protection Agency, <www.epa.gov/pesticides/biopesticides/otherdocs/bt_brad2/1 overview.pdf>.

[12] Gianessi, Leonard, (October 4, 2001). "The Potential for Biotechnology to Improve Crop Pest Management in the United States," In a media presentation sponsored by the American Medical Association (AMA). See www.ncfap.org and <www.ama-assn.org> media briefings.

[13] "Food in the 21st Century: From Science to Sustainable Agriculture," CGIAR, p. 36, <www.worldbank.org/html/cgiar/publications/shahbook/shahbook.pdf>.

[14] "Food in the 21st Century: From Science to Sustainable Agriculture," CGIAR, p. 36, <www.worldbank.org/html/cgiar/publications/shahbook/shahbook.pdf>

[15] Owens, Susan, "Genetic engineering may help to reclaim agricultural land lost due to salination," *European Molecular Biology Organization (EMBO) Reports 2001,* Vol. 2/No. 10, p. 877–879, <www.embo-reports.oupjournals.org/cgi/content/full/2/10/877>.

[16] "Biotech 'Tailor-Made' for Africa, Researcher Tells Tufts Conference," Council for Biotechnology Information, Washington, D.C., November 19, 2001 <index.asp?id=1156&redirect=con1309mid17%2E.html>.

[17] "Position Statement on Agricultural Biotechnology Applications in Africa and the Caribbean," International Society of African Scientists, <www.monsantoafrica.com/reports/ISAS/ISAS.html>.

11 Personal Essays

The personal essay is a literary form. Like a poem, a play, or a story, it should feel meaningful to readers and relevant to their lives. A personal essay should speak in a distinctive voice and be both compelling and memorable.

11a Understand the assignment.

When you write a personal essay, you are exploring your experiences, clarifying your values, and composing a public self. The focus, however, does not need to be on you. You might write a personal

WRITING beyond COLLEGE

Personal Essays

Doctors, social workers, nutritionists—as well as novelists—publish memoirs and personal essays based on their life's work.

- Gloria Ladson-Billings, a teacher, reflects on her experience in the classroom to figure out what makes teachers successful.
- Oliver Sacks, a neurologist, writes about his experiences with people whose perceptual patterns are impaired and about what it means to be fully human.

essay about a tree in autumn, a trip to Senegal, an encounter with a stranger, or an athletic event. The real topic is how these objects and experiences have become meaningful to you.

When we read a personal essay, we expect to learn more than the details of the writer's experience; we expect to see the connections between that experience and our own. You may decide to intensify, clarify, or complicate the reader's sense of things. But no matter what you intend, your point is likely to be more effective if it is not stated directly. The details you emphasize, the words you choose, and the characters you create all communicate your point implicitly without turning it into "the moral of the story."

1. The personal essay as conversation

Personal essayists usually use the first person (*I* and *we*) to create a sense that the writer and reader are engaged in the open-ended give-and-take of conversation. How you appear in this conversation—shy, belligerent, or friendly, for example—will be determined by the details you include in your essay, as well as the connotations of the words you use. Consider how Meghan Daum represents herself in relation to both computer-literate and computer-phobic readers in the following excerpt from her personal essay "Virtual Love," which appeared in a 1997 issue of the *New Yorker*:

> The kindness pouring forth from my computer screen was bizarrely exhilarating, and I logged off and thought about it for a few hours before writing back to express how flattered and "touched"—this was probably the first time I had ever used that word in earnest—I was by his message.
>
> I am not what most people would call a computer person. I have no interest in chat rooms, news groups, or most Web sites. I derive a palpable thrill from sticking a letter in the United States mail.

TEXTCONNEX

Personal Writing and Social Networking Web Sites

In addition to the personal essays you write for class, you may use Web sites like *Facebook* and *MySpace* for personal expression and autobiographical writing. Remember that these sites are networked, so you do not always know who is reading your information. Strangers, including prospective employers, often view people's profiles and make judgments.

Besides Daum's conversational stance, notice the emotional effect of her remark on the word *touched* and her choice of words connoting excitement: *pouring forth, exhilarating,* and *palpable thrill.*

2. The personal essay as a link between one person's experience and a larger issue

To demonstrate the significance of a personal essay to its readers, writers usually connect their individual experience to a larger issue. Here, for example, are the closing lines of Daum's essay on "virtual love":

> The world had proved to be too cluttered and too fast for us, too polluted to allow the thing we'd attempted through technology ever to grow on the earth. PFSlider and I had joined the angry and exhausted living. Even if we met on the street, we wouldn't recognize each other, our particular version of intimacy now obscured by the branches and bodies and falling debris that make up the physical world.

Notice how Daum relates the disappointment of her failed Internet romance with "PFSlider" to a larger social issue: the general contrast between cyberspace and material realities. Her point, however, is quite surprising; most people do not think of cyberspace as more "intimate"—or touching—than their everyday, earthly world of "branches and bodies."

11b Approach writing a personal essay as a process.

Shaping your private personal writing into a personal essay for a public audience can be challenging. The following suggestions should help.

1. Keeping a journal or a writer's notebook where you can practice putting your experience into words

Record your observations about meaningful objects (houses, photographs, personal treasures), memorable incidents and experiences (an encounter with a stranger, coming to the United States, winning and losing), and distinctive situations (living arrangements, social cliques, neighborhood conflicts) in a journal.

2. Thinking about the broader meaning of your topic when planning the focus of your essay

Readers will appreciate the significance of your individual experience only if you connect it with something more social or general. For example, if you are writing about a turning point in your life, think of your experience as a metaphor for what we gain and what we lose as we grow and change.

3. Structuring your essay like a story

There are three common ways to narrate events and reflections:

- **Chronological sequence** uses an order determined by clock time; what happened first is presented first, followed by what happened second, then third, and so on.
- **Emphatic sequence** uses an order determined by the point you want to make; for emphasis, events and reflections are arranged from either least to most important or from most to least important.
- **Suspenseful sequence** uses an order determined by the emotional effect the writer wants the essay to have on the reader. To keep the reader hanging, the essay may begin in the middle of things with a puzzling event, then flash back or go forward to clear things up. Some essays may even begin with the end—with the insight achieved—and then flash back to recount how the writer came to that insight.

4. Letting details tell your story

The story takes shape through details. The details you emphasize, the words you choose, and the characters you create communicate the point of your essay.

Consider, for example, the following passage by Gloria Ladson-Billings:

> Mrs. Harris, my third-grade teacher, was quite a sharp dresser. She wore beautiful high-heeled shoes. Sometimes she switched to flats in the afternoon if her feet got tired, but every morning began with the click, click, click of her high heels as she greeted us up and down the rows. I wanted

> to dress the way Mrs. Harris did. I didn't want to wear old-lady comforters like Mrs. Benn's and I certainly didn't want to wear worn-out loafers like those of my first-grade teacher, Miss Schwartz. I wanted to wear beautiful, shiny, high-heeled shoes like Mrs. Harris's. That was the way a teacher should look, I thought.

Ladson-Billings uses details to make her idea of a good teacher come alive for the reader. At one level—the literal—the "click, click, click" refers to the sound of Mrs. Harris's shoes. At another level, it represents the glamorous teacher. At the most figurative level, the "click, click, click" evokes the feminine kind of power that the narrator both longs for and admires.

5. Using the present tense strategically

When writers tell stories about themselves, they often use the *past tense,* as if the experience were over and done with ("once upon a time"). This choice makes sense, but the *present tense* creates a sense of immediacy and helps make an essay vivid and memorable. Notice how the student writer of the following passage puts the reader inside the young girl's head by purposefully changing from the past to the present tense:

> As I was learning the switchboard, I caught my Dad watching me out of the corner of his eye. Hmm, I hope he doesn't think that I'm going to give him the satisfaction of not doing a good job. Yes, he's deprived me of my beach days with Joey. But I am on display here. And the switchboard is so vital to this office!

If they have good reason to do so, writers of personal essays may also sometimes take liberties with certain other conventions of grammar and style. Be sure you understand any rules you may be stretching, however, and if you are writing a personal essay for a class assignment, be sure your instructor will accept the results. Some instructors, for example, might object to the shift from past to present tense in the paragraph above (*see Chapter 41: Confusing Shifts*). Some also might object to the last two sentences in the paragraph because they begin with coordinating conjunctions (*but* and *and*).

12 Essay Exams

If you spend some time now thinking about what you are expected to do in an essay exam, you may feel less stress the next time you are faced with one.

12a Prepare to take an essay exam.

As you prepare for the exam, consider the specific course as your writing context and the course's instructor as your audience. The best preparation for any exam is to learn the course material. Review your notes and readings. Think about how your instructor approached and presented the course material.

- What questions or problems did your instructor explicitly or implicitly address?
- What frameworks did your instructor use to analyze topics?
- What key terms did your instructor repeatedly use during lectures and discussions?

Essay exams are designed to test your knowledge, not just your memory. Make up some essay questions that require you to:

- **Explain** what you have learned in a clear, well-organized way. (*See question 1 in the box on p. 218.*)
- **Connect** what you know about one topic with what you know about another topic. (*See question 2 in the box on p. 218.*)
- **Apply** what you have learned to a new situation. (*See question 3 in the box on p. 218.*)
- **Interpret** the causes, effects, meanings, value, or potential of something. (*See question 4 in the box on p. 218.*)
- **Argue** for or against some controversial statement about what you have learned. (*See question 5 in the box on p. 218.*)

12b Approach essay exams strategically.

1. Planning your time

At the beginning of the exam period, quickly look through the whole exam, and determine how much time to spend on each part or question. You will want to move as quickly as possible through the questions that have lower point values and spend the bulk of your time responding to the questions that are worth the greatest number of points.

CHARTING the TERRITORY

Essay Exam Questions across the Curriculum

During finals week, you may be asked to respond to essay questions like the following:

1. Discuss the power of the contemporary presidency as well as the limits of that power. [*from a political science course*]
2. Compare and contrast the treatment of labor supply decisions in the economic models proposed by Greg Lewis and Gary Becker. [*from an economics course*]
3. Describe the observations that would be made in an alpha-particle scattering experiment if (a) the nucleus of an atom were negatively charged and the protons occupied the empty space outside the nucleus and (b) the electrons were embedded in a positively charged sphere. [*from a chemistry course*]
4. Examine the uses of caesura and enjambment in the following poem, and analyze their effect on the poem's rhythm. [*from a literature course*]
5. In 1800, was Thomas Jefferson a dangerous radical? Be sure to define your key terms and to support your position with evidence from specific events, documents, and so on. [*from an American history course*]

2. Responding to short-answer questions by showing the significance of the information

The most common type of short-answer question is the identification question: Who or what is X? In answering questions of this sort, present just enough information to show that you understand X's significance within the context of the course. For example, if you are asked to identify "Judith Loftus" on an American literature exam, don't just write "character who knows Huckleberry Finn is a boy." Instead, craft one or two sentences that identify Loftus as a character Huckleberry Finn encounters while he is disguised as a girl; by telling Huck how she knows that he is not a girl, Loftus complicates the reader's understanding of gender.

3. Responding to essay questions tactically

Keep in mind that essay questions usually ask you to do something specific with a topic. Begin by determining precisely what you are being asked to do.

Before you write anything, read the question—all of it—and circle the key words:

> Explain two ways in which Picasso's *Guernica* evokes war's terrifying destructiveness.

To answer this question, focus on two of the painting's features, such as coloring and composition, not on Picasso's life.

4. Using the question itself to structure your response

Usually, you will be able to transform the question itself into the thesis of your answer. If you are asked to agree/disagree with the Federalists' characterization of Thomas Jefferson in the election of 1800, you might begin with the following thesis:

> In the election of 1800, the Federalists characterized Jefferson as a dangerous radical. Although Jefferson's ideas were radical for the times, they were not dangerous to the republic.

Take a minute or two to list evidence for each of your main points, and then write the essay.

5. Drafting the essay

As you write, observe the relevant discipline's conventions of form and style. Using your notes, state your thesis and develop a paragraph for each point in your list. Leave space between lines to make additions and corrections after your draft is complete. If you get stuck trying to think of a term or fact, briefly describe it and go on; the specific words may come to you later. Conclude by succinctly stating how you have supported your thesis.

6. Checking your work

Leave a few minutes to read quickly through your completed answer. Is your thesis consistent with what you ended up writing? Is each point well supported? Also look for words you might have omitted or key sentences that make no sense. You can usually cross out incorrect words and sentences and make corrections neatly above the original line of text. Above all, ensure the essay demonstrates your knowledge of the subject.

Sample essay test responses

A student's response to an essay question in an art appreciation course begins on the following page. Both the question (*below*) and the student's notes (*p. 220*) are provided.

QUESTION

> Both of these buildings (Figure 1 and Figure 2) feature dome construction. Identify the buildings, and discuss the differences in the visual effects created by the different dome styles.

FIGURE 1

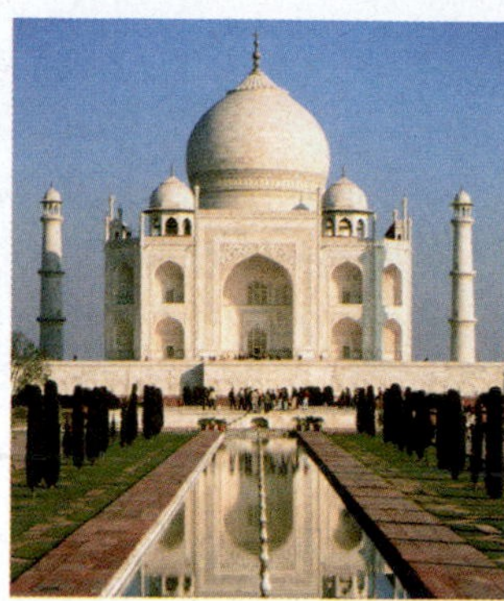

FIGURE 2

STUDENT'S NOTES

Fig 1: Pantheon. Plain outside—concrete, can barely see dome. Dramatic inside—dome opens up huge interior space. Oculus to sky: light, air, rain. Coffered ceiling.
Fig 2: Taj Mahal. Dramatic exterior—dome set high, marble, reflecting pool, exterior lines go up. Inside not meant to be visited.

STUDENT'S ANSWER

Answers identification question and states thesis.

The Pantheon (Figure 1) and the Taj Mahal (Figure 2) are famous for their dome construction. The styles of the domes are dramatically different, however, resulting in dramatically different visual effects.

Key points supported by details.

Uses specialized terms from course.

The Pantheon, which was built by the Romans as a temple to the gods, looks very plain on the exterior. The dome is barely visible from the outside, and it is made of a dull grey concrete. Inside the building, however, the dome produces an amazing effect. It opens up a huge space within the building, unobstructed by interior supports. The sides of the dome are coffered, and those recessed rectangles both lessen the weight of the dome and add to its visual beauty. Most dramatically, the top of the dome is open to the sky, which allows sun or rain to pour into the building. This opening is called the oculus, meaning "eye" (to or of Heaven).

Sets up comparison.

Key point supported by details.

Overall comparison as a brief conclusion.

The Taj Mahal, which was built by a Muslim emperor of India as a tomb for his wife, is the complete opposite of the Pantheon—dazzling on the outside and plain on the inside. The large central dome is set up high on the base so that it can be seen from far away. It is made of white marble, which reflects light beautifully. The dome is surrounded by other structures that frame it and draw attention to its exterior—a long reflecting pond and four minarets. Arches and smaller domes on the outside of the building repeat the large dome's shape. Because the Taj Mahal's dome is tall and narrow, however, it does not produce the kind of vast interior space of the shorter, squatter Pantheon dome. Indeed, the inside of the Taj Mahal is not meant to be visited. Unlike the Pantheon, the dome of the Taj Mahal is intended to be admired from the outside.

13 Oral Presentations

Preparing an oral presentation, like preparing any text, is a process. Consider your audience and purpose as you choose the focus and level of your topic. Gather information, decide on the main idea of your presentation, think through the organization, and choose visuals that support your points.

13a Plan and shape your oral presentation.

1. Considering the interests, background knowledge, and attitudes of your audience

Find out as much as you can about your listeners before you prepare the speech. What does the audience already think about your topic? Do you want to intensify your listeners' commitment to what they already think, provide new and clarifying information, provoke more analysis and understanding of the issue, or change what they believe about something?

If you are addressing an unfamiliar audience, ask the people who invited you to fill you in on the audience's interests and expectations. It is also possible to adjust your speech once you get in front of your audience, making your language more or less technical, for instance, or adding more examples to illustrate points.

2. Working within the allotted time

Gauge how many words you speak a minute by reading a passage aloud at a conversational pace (about 120–150 words a minute is ideal). Be sure to time your presentation when you practice it.

13b Draft your presentation with the rhetorical situation in mind.

www.mhhe.com/mhhb2

For more on crafting introductions, go to

Writing > Paragraph/Essay Development > Introductions

1. Making your opening interesting

A strong opening both puts the speaker at ease and gains the audience's attention and confidence. Try out several approaches to your introduction during rehearsal, to see which get the best reactions. Stories, brief quotations, striking statistics, and surprising statements are attention getters. Or craft an introduction that lets your listeners know what they have to gain from your presentation—for example, new information or new perspectives on a subject of common interest.

2. Making the focus and organization of your presentation explicit

Select two or three ideas that you most want your audience to hear—and to remember. Preview the content of your presentation in a statement such as "I intend to make three points about fraternities on campus," and then list the three points.

The phrase "to make three points" signals a topical organization. Other common organizational patterns include chronological organization (*at first, later, in the end*), causal organization (*because of that, then this follows*), and problem-solution organization (*given the situation, then this set of proposals*). A question-answer format also works well, either as an overall strategy or as part of another organizational pattern.

3. Being direct

What your audience hears and remembers has as much to do with how you say your message as it does with what you say. Use a direct, simple style.

- Choose basic sentence structures.
- Repeat key terms.
- Pay attention to the rhythm of your speech.
- Don't be afraid to use the pronouns *I, you,* and *we.*

Notice how applying these principles transforms the following written sentence into a group of sentences appropriate for oral presentation:

WRITTEN

> Although the claim that the position of the stars can help people predict the future has yet to be substantiated by either an ample body or an exemplary piece of empirical research, advocates of astrology persist in pressing the claim.

ORAL

> Your sign says a lot about you. So say advocates of astrology. But what evidence do we have that the position of the stars helps people predict the future? Do we have lots of empirical research or even one really good study? The answer is, "Not yet."

www.mhhe.com/mhhb2
For an interactive tutorial on using PowerPoint, go to
Writing > PowerPoint Tutorial

4. Using visual aids: Posters and presentation software

Slides, posters, objects, video clips, and music help make your focus explicit. Avoid oversimplifying your ideas to fit them on a slide, and make sure the images, videos, or music fit your purpose and audience.

When preparing a poster presentation, keep the poster simple with a clear title, bullets listing your key points, and images that support your purpose. Ensure text can be read from several feet away. (*For more on design principles, see Chapter 6: Designing Academic Papers and Preparing Portfolios, pp. 105–12.*)

Presentation software such as PowerPoint can help you stay focused while you are speaking. The twelve PowerPoint slides in Figure 13.1 below and on page 224 offer advice on how to design

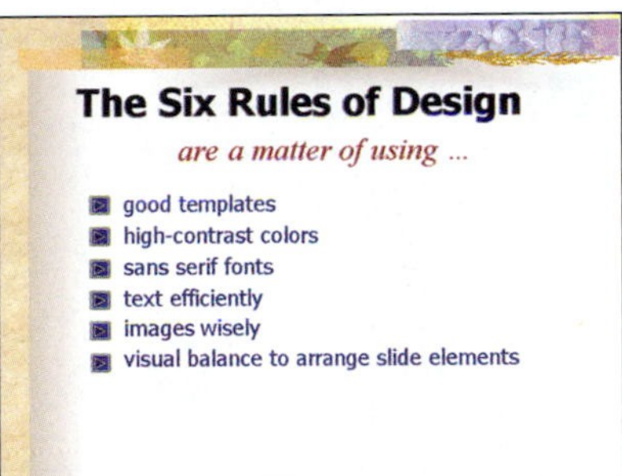

FIGURE 13.1 A sample PowerPoint presentation with advice on designing effective presentation slides.

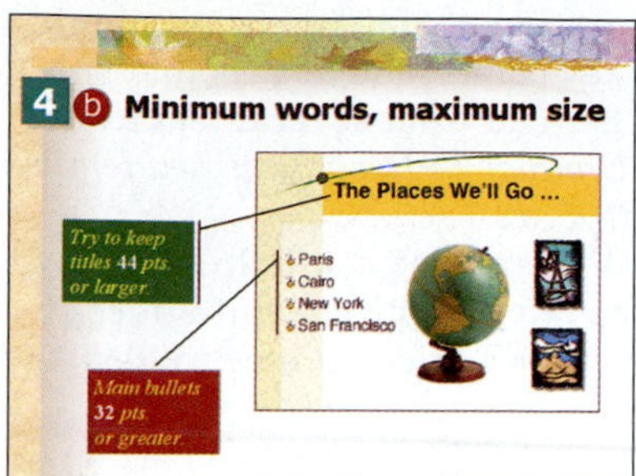

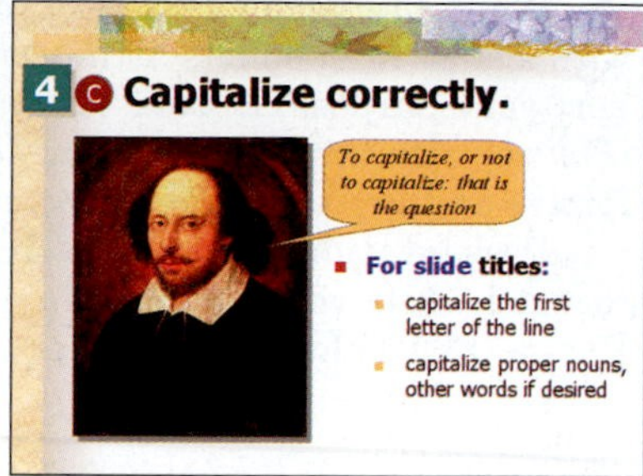

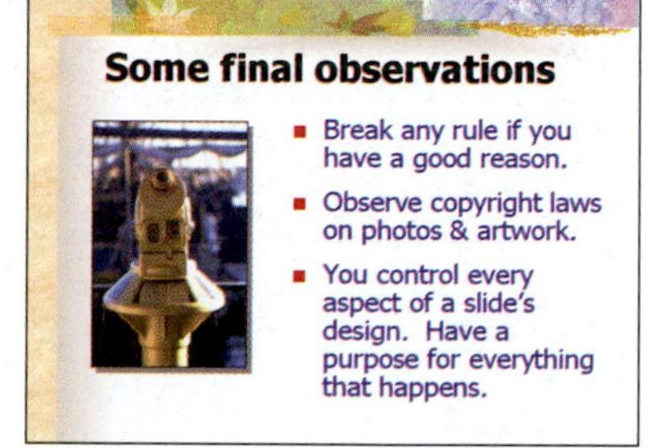

FIGURE 13.1 ***(continued)***

effective slides for a presentation. (*For more on using presentation software see Chapter 14: Multimedia Writing, pp. 232–37*)

5. Concluding memorably

Try to make your ending truly memorable: return to that surprising opener, play with the words of your opening quotation, look at the initial image from another angle, or reflect on the story you have told. Use signal phrases such as "in conclusion" or "let me end by saying," if necessary. Keep your conclusion short to maintain the audience's attention.

TEXTCONNEX

Webcasts

Webcasts allow you to reach audiences anywhere in the world with an Internet connection. When you present a speech online, multimedia elements become even more important, particularly if your audience will not be able to see you. (*See Chapter 14: Multimedia Writing, pp. 232–37.*) Practice your presentation to ensure that you can access all necessary files easily. If your image will be broadcast, practice speaking into the camera or Webcam.

13c Prepare for your presentation.

1. Deciding whether to use notes or a written script

To be an effective speaker, make eye contact with your listeners; monitor their responses; and adjust what you say accordingly. For most occasions, it is inappropriate to write out everything you want to say and then read it word for word. Speak from an outline or notecards, and write out only those parts of your presentation where precise wording counts, such as quotations.

In some scholarly or formal settings, precise wording may be necessary, especially if your oral presentation is to be published or if your remarks will be quoted by others. Sometimes the setting for your presentation may be so formal or the audience may be so large that a script feels necessary. In such instances, do the following:

- Triple-space the typescript of your text.
- Avoid carrying sentences over from one page to another.
- Mark your manuscript for pauses, emphasis, and the pronunciation of proper names.

2. Rehearsing, revising, and polishing

Practice your presentation aloud. Adjust transitions that don't work, points that need further development, and sections that are too long.

After you have settled on the content of your speech and can project it comfortably, focus on polishing the style of your delivery. Video yourself or ask your friends to watch and listen to your rehearsal. Check that your body posture is straight but relaxed, that your voice is loud and clear, and that you are making eye contact around the room. Time your final rehearsals, adding or cutting as necessary. If an on-site rehearsal is not possible, at least be sure to arrive at your presentation well in advance.

3. Accepting nervousness as normal

The adrenaline surge you feel before a presentation can invest your talk with positive energy. Practice and revise your presentation until it flows smoothly, and make sure that you have a strong opener to get you through the first, most difficult moments of a speech. Remember that other people cannot always tell that you are nervous.

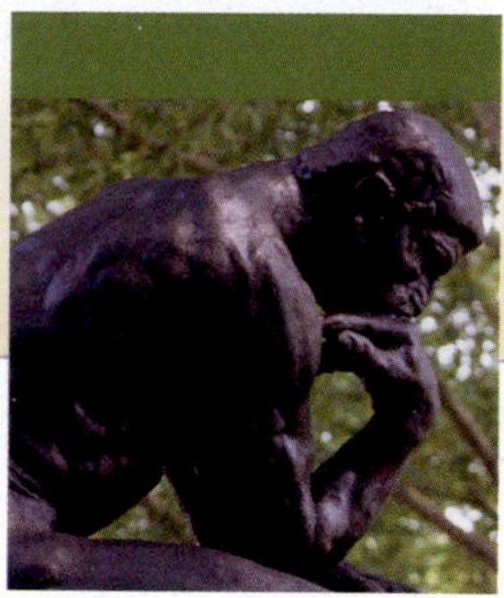

14 Multimedia Writing

Multimedia writing combines words with images, video, or audio into a single composition. The most common form of multimedia writing—discussed in many chapters of this book—is a combination of words and still visuals such as photographs, maps, charts, or graphs. Another form is an oral presentation with any kind of visual support, from a diagram on a blackboard to a PowerPoint slide show (*see Chapter 13: Oral Presentations*). Digital technology also allows writers to create works that combine written words with sound, video, and animation. You probably have used social networking Web sites such as *Facebook* and *MySpace*, which let users integrate text, images, and other multimedia elements.

Like any form of composition, multimedia writing allows you to convey a message to a particular audience for a particular purpose: to inform, to interpret, or to persuade. A video or audio segment—like a photograph, map, or chart—must support the purpose of the writing in a way that is appropriate to the audience.

14a Learn about the tools for creating multimedia texts.

Multimedia writing can take a variety of forms and can be created with a variety of software tools. Here are a few options:

- Most word processors allow you to integrate still visuals with text in a single document, and many also make it possible to create a composition that permits readers to connect to various files—including audio, image, and video. (*See 14b and 14c.*)

- Most presentation software packages similarly allow you to accompany a presentation with audio and video files as well as still visuals. (*See 14d.*)
- A variety of programs and Web-based tools allow you to create your own **Web pages** and **Web sites,** which can include a wide range of multimedia features. (*See 14e.*)
- You can create a **weblog** (**blog**), on which, in addition to your written entries, you can post your multimedia files and links to files on other blogs and Web sites. You also can collaborate with other writers on a **Wiki**. (*See 14f.*)

14b Combine text and images with a word-processing program to analyze images.

Two types of assignments you might be called on to write are image analyses and imaginary stories.

1. Composing image analyses

You may be called on to analyze a single image, such as a painting from a museum. In this case, your two tasks are to describe the picture as carefully as possible, using adjectives, comparisons, and words that help the reader focus on the picture and the details that compose it; and to analyze the *argument* the picture seems to be making.

Exercise 14.1 Image interpretations

1. In a local museum or on a museum Web site, find a painting created by an artist whose work is new to you. (Some examples of museum Web sites include http://www.moma.org/collection/ for the Museum of Modern Art (New York), http://www.artic.edu/aic/ for the Art Institute of Chicago, and http://www.louvre.fr/louvrea.htm for the Louvre in Paris.) Or you may wish to write about Breughel's *Fall of Icarus* on page 229.

   Take notes on your response to the painting, and write an initial analysis of it. As you do, consider the following:

   - Who or what is in the painting?
   - If there are people in the painting, are they active or passive? Rich or poor? Old or young?

- Are the people central to the painting, or are they peripheral? If peripheral, what is the painting's central focus?
- How does the artist represent the subjects of the painting—in other words, what does the artist's presentation of people, objects, buildings, or landscapes say about his or her attitude toward them?
- What in your own experience may be affecting your response? What personal associations do you make with the subject of the painting? How might your own position—for example, as a student, daughter or son, member of a political party—influence the way you interpret the painting?

Now read a short biography of the artist in a book or on the Web, and add that information to your analysis. Point out whether and how the biographical information either reinforces your interpretation or leads you to alter it.

2. Find an image in a current newspaper or magazine. First outline two possible arguments that the picture might be making. Then decide which is the more likely of the two arguments, and explain why.

---

2. Imagining stories

Sometimes a writer tries to imagine the story behind an evocative photograph. Often that story is as much an expression of the writer as it is a statement about the photograph.

Some photographs, like the one in Figure 14.1, taken on September 11, 2001, by photojournalist Thomas Hoepker, connect private life and public events. On the morning of the catastrophe, Hoepker drove across New York City's East River from Manhattan to Brooklyn, with the intention of shooting a panoramic view of the burning World Trade Center towers. He took this photo of five young people who, in the photographer's opinion, "didn't seem to care." When David Plotz, deputy editor of the online magazine *Slate*, saw the photo, he disagreed and called for a response from any of the people in the photograph <http://www.slate.com/id/2149508>. Walter Sipser, one of the photograph's subjects, wrote to *Slate*, saying, "We were in a profound state of shock" <http://www.slate.com/id/2149578>. What do you think?

If you have read W. H. Auden's poem "Musée des Beaux Arts" (*on p. 230*) or seen the painting described in the poem, Breughel's *Fall of Icarus* (*shown in Figure 14.2*), you may see a telling comparison between Hoepker's interpretation of the reaction of the photographic subjects to 9/11 and the response of those who observed "a boy falling

FIGURE 14.1 ***New York City, September 11, 2001.*** © Thomas Hoepker/ Magnum.

out of the sky." Compare the composition of Hoepker's photo with Breughel's painting (*Figure 14.2*). Hoepker himself wondered about "the devious lie of a snapshot" <http://slate.com/id/2149675>. In light of Sipser's remarks, what might Hoepker mean by that?

FIGURE 14.2 **Pieter Breughel's *Fall of Icarus* (ca 1554–1555).** Only Icarus's legs can be seen in the water between the closest boat and the shore.

Musée des Beaux Arts

W. H. Auden

About suffering they were never wrong,
The Old Masters; how well they understood
Its human position; how it takes place
While someone else is eating or opening a window or just walking dully along;
How, when the aged are reverently, passionately waiting
For the miraculous birth, there always must be
Children who did not specially want it to happen, skating
On a pond at the edge of the wood:
They never forgot
That even the dreadful martyrdom must run its course
Anyhow in a corner, some untidy spot
Where the dogs go on with their doggy life and the torturer's horse
Scratches its innocent behind on a tree.
In Breughel's Icarus, for instance: how everything turns away
Quite leisurely from the disaster; the ploughman may
Have heard the splash, the forsaken cry,
But for him it was not an important failure; the sun shone
As it had to on the white legs disappearing into the green
Water; and the expensive delicate ship that must have seen
Something amazing, a boy falling out of the sky,
Had somewhere to get to and sailed calmly on.

Exercise 14.2 Photographic stories

1. Find one photograph from at least fifty years ago in a magazine or book, on a Web site, or in a family collection. (The Library of Congress's online repository is an excellent source <http://www.loc.gov/rr/print/catalog.html>.) For the photograph, create two short, specific stories and one more general story. Explain the "logic" of each story using evidence from the photograph. As you look for stories, ask yourself these questions:

   - Who or what is in the photograph?
   - How is the photograph composed? What first draws your attention?
   - If you think of the photograph as having a center, where would it be, and what would be in it?
   - If you think of the photograph as being divided into quadrants, what is in each one?

- What emotional reaction do you have to the photograph?
- If the photograph is in color, how is color used? What does it contribute to the photograph? If the photograph is in black and white, what effect does that have on you?
- What details in the picture evoke a mood?
- What is left out of the photograph and why? Can you imagine other items or people who, if included, would help tell a different story?
- Is the photograph about a short, specific story, a longer story, or both kinds of stories?
- How might your own position—for example, as a student, daughter or son, member of a political party—influence your view of the photo?

2. Take several photographs that allow for rich interpretations. Choose two of the photos and interpret them. Bring them to class, and ask two classmates to provide you with a story for each. Do their stories match yours? Do their stories seem more interesting than yours? Why or why not?

14c Use a word-processing program to create a hypertext essay.

Writers create **hypertext essays** using word-processing software, Web-development software, blogs, or wikis. **Links** in a document take the reader to other **files,** including text, image, audio, and video files. Links can take several forms:

- **Internal links** connect from one place to another in the same document, or to other files stored on the writer's computer or a storage device (CD, DVD, or flash drive).
- **External links** connect to Web sites or files on the Internet.

As with any evidence, however, a multimedia file must be relevant to the audience and purpose of the essay. It can either complement the essay's verbal claims or, like a good chart or graph, support the claims directly. For example, in a political science project on inaugural addresses, you might include links to video files of several presidents delivering their inaugural addresses. These links might simply complement your thesis, or they might provide direct evidence for an important point about, say, a particular president's style of delivery. However, unless your assignment includes specific directions to emphasize linked material as evidence, think of it as supplemental to your written claims.

If you have never created a hypertext essay, start small, with a limited set of links that all clearly serve your audience and purpose. Create internal links to the full information about works on your works-cited page, to any assignments that are related to your current topic, to tangential material that you collected while working on the essay and that provides additional context, or to a file in which you raise additional questions about your topic. Create external links to works on your topic written by your classmates or to background material on the Web.

> ***Caution:*** When you revise your hypertext essay, make sure all links are relevant and function correctly. Also, if your essay includes internal links to files on your computer, be sure to include those files with the essay file when you submit it to your instructor.

Exercise 14.3 Hypertext essays

1. Construct a hypertext essay in which you use links to create puns or jokes. In other words, compose the text; then insert links that let you talk back to your own points, as well as link to puns, jokes, and visuals on the Web.
2. Create a hypertext essay in which you use five links to connect your piece with some personal experience relevant to it or to connect it with relevant information about another assignment you are working on. For example, if you are writing about changes in agricultural societies, you might include links to your own experience with agriculture, from growing up on a farm to buying groceries in a store. You might also link to material you are studying in an economics class or an ancient history class.

14d Use presentation software to create multimedia presentations.

Presentation software makes it possible to incorporate audio, video, and animation into a talk. It can also be used to create multimedia compositions that viewers can go through on their own.

www.mhhe.com/mhhb2
For an interactive tutorial on using PowerPoint, go to
Writing > PowerPoint Tutorial

1. Using presentation software for an oral presentation

Presentation slides that accompany a talk should identify major points and display information in a visually effective way.

TEXTCONNEX

Using Storyboards

Artists, directors, and Web designers use storyboards—traditionally, comic-strip-like sketches of major changes in a scene sequence—to preview different sequences of visual elements.

Storyboarding can help you organize a hypertext essay (*14c*), a slide presentation (*14d*), a Web site (*14e*), or an electronic portfolio (*Chapter 6, pp. 114–17*). Sketch the elements of your document or presentation—some writers use an index card for each slide or screen—and rearrange them until you find a logical sequence. Consider how users will navigate based on the document's purpose (*see 14e, p. 237*). Your sketches should include the basic text and design for each slide or screen as well, including design elements that will be common to all slides or screens.

Remember that slides support your talk; they do not replace it. Limit the amount of information on each slide to no more than fifty words, and plan to show each slide for about one minute. Use bulleted lists and phrases rather than full sentences. Make fonts large enough to be seen by your audience: titles should be in 44-point type or larger, subheads in 32-point type or larger. High-contrast color schemes and sufficient blank space between slide elements will also increase the visibility of your presentation.

For a talk in a science course you might want to include only a single image and a set of key terms on each slide. For a talk about the writers Langston Hughes and Ralph Ellison you might use a slide like the one in Figure 14.3 (*p. 234*) to summarize their similarities and differences.

(*For more on preparing and presenting oral presentations, see Chapter 13: Oral Presentations, pp. 221–26.*)

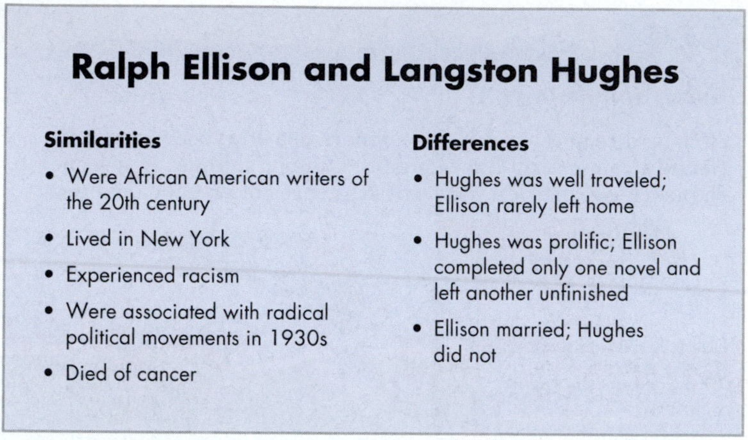

Ralph Ellison and Langston Hughes

Similarities	Differences
• Were African American writers of the 20th century	• Hughes was well traveled; Ellison rarely left home
• Lived in New York	• Hughes was prolific; Ellison completed only one novel and left another unfinished
• Experienced racism	• Ellison married; Hughes did not
• Were associated with radical political movements in 1930s	
• Died of cancer	

FIGURE 14.3 A slide for a presentation on Ralph Ellison and Langston Hughes.

2. Using presentation software to create an independent composition

With presentation software, you can also create compositions that run on their own or at the prompting of the viewer. This capability is especially useful in distance learning settings, in which students attend class and share information electronically.

3. Preparing a slide presentation

The following guidelines apply.

Decide on a slide format You should begin thinking about slides while you plan what you are going to say. As you decide on the words for your talk or independent composition, you will think of visuals that support your points, and as you work out the visuals, you are likely to see additional points you can make—and adjust your presentation as a result. Every aspect of your slides—such as fonts, images, and animations—should support your purpose and appeal to your audience. Never use multimedia elements for mere decoration.

Before you create your slides, establish their basic appearance. What background color will they have? What typeface or typefaces? What design elements, such as borders and rules? Will the templates provided by the software suit your talk? Can you modify a template to suit your needs? The format you establish will be the canvas for all your slides—it needs to complement, not distract from, the images and text you intend to display.

FIGURE 14.4 The collapse of the Tacoma Narrows Bridge. The dramatic collapse of the bridge was captured on film, and some of the footage is available in video files.

Incorporate images into your presentation Include images when appropriate. To summarize quantitative information, you might use a chart or graph. To show geographical relationships, you would likely use a map. You can also add photographs that illustrate your points. In all cases, select appropriate, relevant images that support your purpose.

www.mhhe.com/mhhb2
For more on designing documents, go to
Writing > Writing Web Links > Document and Web Design

Incorporate relevant audio, video, and animation Slides can also include audio files, recording background information for each slide in an independent composition. Or for a presentation on music, you can insert audio files to show how a type of music has developed over time.

Slides can also include video files and animated drawings and diagrams. A video clip of the collapse of the Tacoma Narrows Bridge in violently high winds on November 7, 1940, for example (*see Figure 14.4*), might help illustrate a presentation on bridge construction. An animated diagram of the process of cell division could help illustrate a presentation on cellular biology. If you are using audio, video, or animation files that belong to others, cite the source. If you plan to make your presentation publicly available online, obtain permission to use these items from the copyright holder. (*For more on finding and citing multimedia, see Chapter 17, Finding and Creating Effective Visuals, pp. 281–89.*)

Incorporate hypertext links A presenter might use an internal link within a slide sequence to jump to another slide that illustrates or explains a particular point or issue. For instance, for a presentation on insects, you might include a hyperlink to a slide about insects specific to the part of the country in which you live, complete with an image of one of them. You can also create external links to resources on the Web. Be careful not to rely too much on external links, however, because they can undermine the coherence of a presentation. External links can also take a long time to load.

> ***Caution:*** If you plan to make external links part of your presentation, make sure that you have a functioning Web browser on your computer and that a fast connection to the Internet is available where you will be giving the presentation. If possible, run through your presentation on site so your external links are cached.

4. Reviewing a slide presentation

Once you have the text of your presentation in final form and the multimedia elements in place, you should carefully review your slides to make sure they work together coherently.

- **Check how slides in your software's slide sorter window move one to the next.** Do you have an introductory slide? Do you need to add transitional effects that reveal the content of a slide gradually or point by point? Some transitions permit audio: would that support your purpose? Use transitional effects to support your rhetorical situation. Do you have a concluding slide?
- **Make sure that the slides are consistent with the script of the talk you plan to deliver.** If the slides are to function as an independent document, do they include enough introduction, an adequate explanation, and a clear conclusion?
- **Check the arrangement of your slides.** Try printing them and spreading them out over a large surface, rearranging them if necessary, before implementing needed changes on the computer.
- **Be sure the slides have a unified look.** For example, do all the slides have the same background? Do all use the same typefaces in the same way? Are headers and bullets consistent?

Exercise 14.4 Presentation slides

1. Choose three key terms related to multimedia, and define them in a three- to five-slide presentation for your class. In doing so, use any two of the features of presentation slides discussed in this section, and write a one-page reflection about why you chose those terms and those presentation features.
2. Draft a preview of a paper you are working on in an eight-slide presentation. Share this preview with your classmates in an eight-minute talk. Then ask them to tell you (a) what they think your main purpose is, (b) what worked well in the presentation, and (c) what you should consider changing when you write the paper.

14e Create a Web site.

www.mhhe.com/mhhb2
For more on designing Web sites, go to
Writing > Writing Web Links > Document and Web Design

Thanks to Web editing software, it is now almost as easy to create a Web site and post it on the Internet as it is to write a paper using word-processing software. Many Web-based businesses like Google provide free server space for hosting sites and offer tools for creating Web pages. Many schools also make server space available for student Web sites.

To be effective, a Web site must be well designed and serve a well-defined purpose for its audience. In creating a Web site, plan the site, draft its content and select its visuals, and then revise and edit as you would for any other composition. (*See Chapters 3–5 in Part 1: Writing and Designing Texts, for more on these stages.*) The following sections offer guidelines for composing a Web site.

1. Planning a structure for your site

Like most paper documents, a Web site can have a linear structure, where one page leads to the next, and so on. Because of the hyperlinked nature of this medium, however, a site can also be organized in a hierarchy or with a number of pages that connect to a central page, or hub, like the spokes of a wheel. The diagrams in Figure 14.5 on page 239 illustrate the hierarchical and hub structures. To choose the structure that will work best for your site, consider how you expect visitors to use it. Visitors intrigued by the topic of Tyler County's historic buildings will probably want to explore. Visitors to a caregiver resources site will probably be looking to find specific information quickly. The structure of a site should accommodate its users' needs.

To determine your site's structure, try mapping the connections among its pages by arranging them in a storyboard. Represent each page with an index card and rearrange the pages on a flat surface, experimenting with possible configurations. Or use sticky notes on a whiteboard and draw arrows among them. How will readers navigate

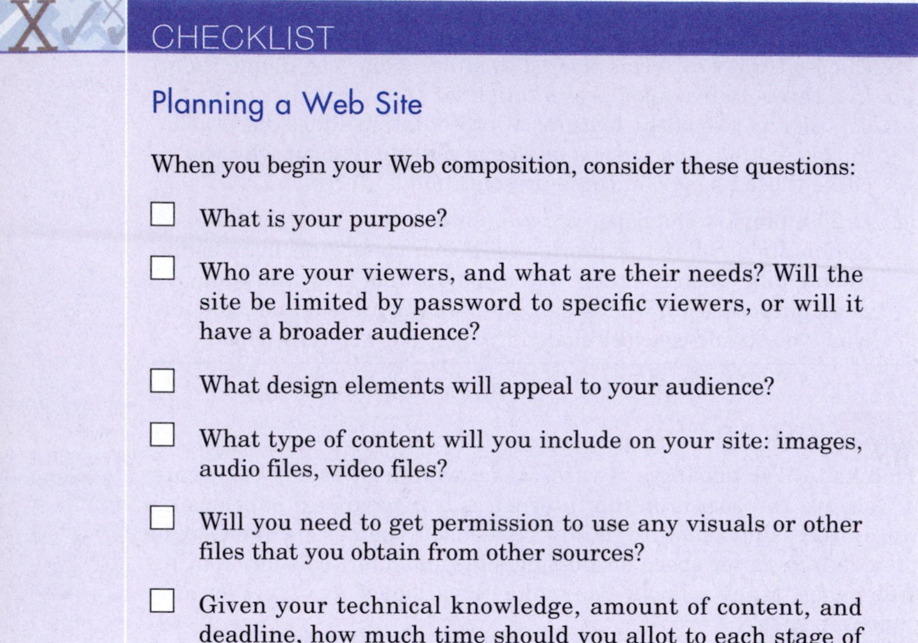

CHECKLIST

Planning a Web Site

When you begin your Web composition, consider these questions:

- ☐ What is your purpose?
- ☐ Who are your viewers, and what are their needs? Will the site be limited by password to specific viewers, or will it have a broader audience?
- ☐ What design elements will appeal to your audience?
- ☐ What type of content will you include on your site: images, audio files, video files?
- ☐ Will you need to get permission to use any visuals or other files that you obtain from other sources?
- ☐ Given your technical knowledge, amount of content, and deadline, how much time should you allot to each stage of building your site?
- ☐ Will the site be updated, and if so, how frequently?

through the site? (*See the box on p. 233.*) Also begin planning the visual design of your site. For consistency, establish a template page, including background color and fonts. Choose a uniform location for material that will appear on each page, such as site title, page title, navigation links, and your contact information. (*See pp. 240–41 on designing a site with a unified look.*)

2. Gathering content for your site

The content for a Web site usually consists of written work along with links and graphics. Depending on your topic and purpose, you might also provide audio files, video files, and even animations.

There are some special requirements for written content that appears on a Web site:

- Usually readers neither expect nor want lengthy text explanations. Instead, they want to find the link or information they are looking for within a few seconds.
- Readers prefer short paragraphs ("chunks"), so the text for each topic or point should fit on one page. Avoid long passages that require readers to use the scroll bar.

Hierarchical Structure

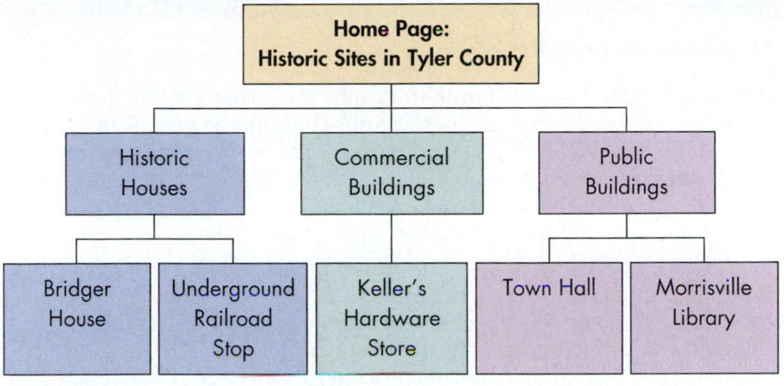

Hub Structure

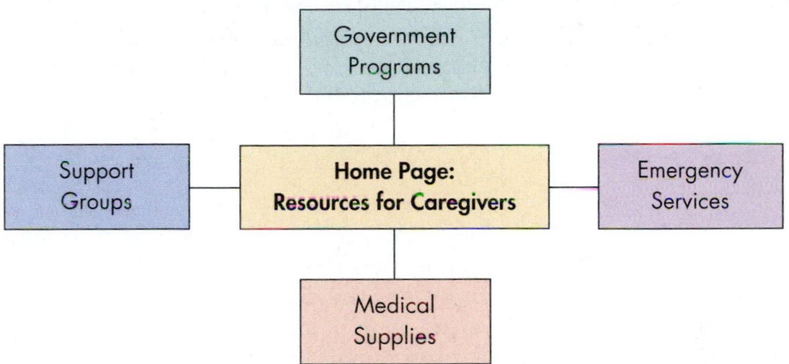

FIGURE 14.5 **Hub and hierarchical structures compared.**

- Use links to connect your interests with those of others and to provide extra sources of relevant and credible information. Make links part of your text and give them descriptive names, such as "Support Groups." Place links at the end of a paragraph so readers don't navigate away in the middle.

As you prepare your written text, gather any graphics, photographs, and audio and video files that you plan to include. Some sites allow you to download images; and some images, including many of the historical photographs available through the Library of Congress, are in the public domain. Another useful site for visual, audio, and video files is *Creative Commons* (http://search.creativecommons.org), which directs you to material licensed for specific types of use. Check the license of the material to see what is permitted.

TEXTCONNEX

Understanding Web Jargon

JPEG and **GIF:** Formats for photographs and other visuals that are recognized by browsers. Photographs that appear on a Web site should be saved in JPEG (pronounced *"jay-peg"*) format, which stands for Joint Photographic Experts Group. The file extension is .jpg or .jpeg. Clip art should be saved as GIF files (Graphics Interchange Format, pronounced like *gift* without the *t.*)

HTML/XML: Hypertext markup language/extensible markup language. These languages tag or code text so that your browser can rebuild a document from the compressed files that travel through the Internet. It is not necessary to learn HTML or XML to publish on the Web. Programs such as FrontPage, PageMill, Dreamweaver, Nvue, and Mozilla provide a WYSIWYG (what you see is what you get) interface for creating Web pages. Most word-processing programs also have a "Save as HTML" option.

URL: Uniform resource locator or Web address. When you type or paste a URL into your Web browser, you are sending a request through your browser to another computer, asking it to transfer data to your computer.

Always cite material that you do not generate yourself. If your Web text will be public, request permission for use of any material not in the public domain unless the site says permission is not needed. Check for a credit in the source, and if the contact information of the creator is not apparent, e-mail the sponsor of the site and ask for it. (*For citation formats see Part 4: Documenting across the Curriculum.*)

3. Designing Web pages to capture and hold interest

On good Web sites, you will find such easy-to-follow links as "what you'll find here," FAQs (frequently asked questions), or "list of those involved." In planning the structure and content of your site, keep your readers' convenience in mind.

4. Designing a readable site with a unified look

The design of your site should suit its purpose and intended audience: a government site to inform users about copyright law will present an uncluttered design that focuses attention on the text. A university's **home page** might feature photographs of young people and sun-drenched lawns to entice prospective students. Readers generally appreciate a site with a unified look. "Sets" or "themes" are readily available at free graphics sites offering banners, navigation buttons, and other design

Web Resources for Site Design and Construction

- *Webmonkey* <http://www.webmonkey.com>
- *Web Guide: Designing a Web Page* <http://people.depauw.edu/djp/webguide/designwebpage.html>
- *American Council of the Blind*—information about creating Web pages for people with disabilities <http://acb.org/accessible-formats.html/>

elements. You can also create visuals with a graphics program or scan your personal art and photographs. Design your home page to complement your other pages, or your readers may lose track of where they are in the site—as well as their interest in staying.

- Use a design template (*see p. 238*) to keep elements of page layout consistent across the site.
- Align items such as text and images. (In Figure 14.8 on page 243, note that the heading "Library Highlights" lines up on the left with the icons below it.)
- Consider including a site map, a Web page that serves as a table of contents for your entire site. (*See Chapter 3, p. 51.*)
- Select elements such as buttons, signs, animations, sounds, and backgrounds with a consistent design suited to your purpose and audience.
- Use colors that provide adequate contrast, white space, and sans serif fonts that make text easy to read. Pages that are too busy are not visually compelling. (*For more on design, see Chapter 6: Designing Academic Papers and Preparing Portfolios, pp. 105–12.*)
- Limit the width of your text; readers find wide lines of text difficult to process.
- Leave time to find appropriate image, audio, and video files created by others, and to obtain permission to use them.

The two Web pages shown in Figure 14.6 (*on the following page*) illustrate some of these design considerations.

5. Designing a Web site that is easy to access and navigate

Help readers find their way to the areas of the site that they want to visit. Make it easy for them to take interesting side trips if they would like to without wasting their time or losing their way.

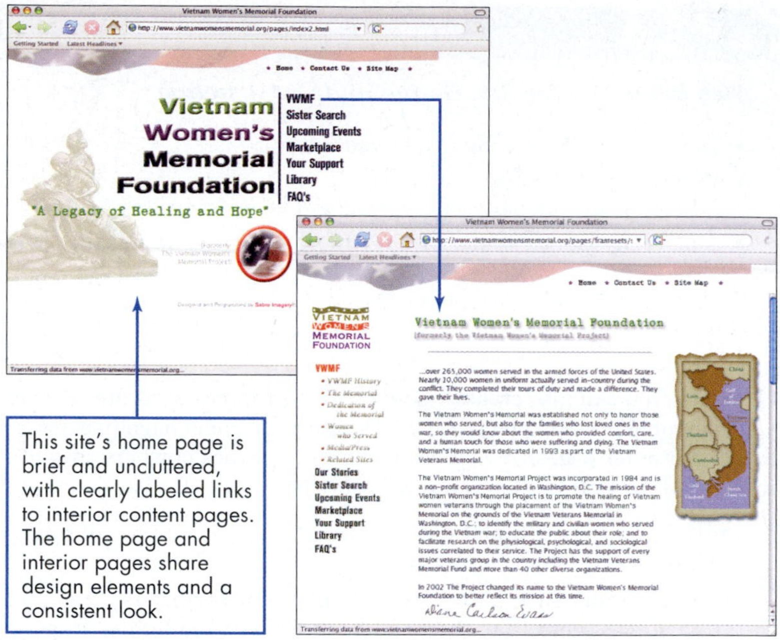

FIGURE 14.6 The home page and an interior page from the Web site of the Vietnam Women's Memorial Foundation.

- **Identify your Web site on each page, and provide a link to the home page.** Remember that people will not always enter your Web site through the home page. Give the title of the site on each page, and provide an easy-to-spot link to your home page.
- **Provide a navigation bar on each page.** A **navigation bar** can be a simple line of links that you copy and paste at the top or bottom of each page. For example, on the Web page from Governors State University shown in Figure 14.7, visitors can choose from three rows of links in the navigation bar at the top of the page.
- **Use graphics that load quickly.** Limit the size of your images to no more than 40 kilobytes, so that they will load quickly.
- **Use graphics judiciously.** Your Web site should not depend on graphics alone to make its message clear and interesting. Graphics should reinforce your purpose. For example, the designers of the Library of Congress Web site (*see Figure 14.8*) use icons, such as musical notation and a map, to help visitors navigate the site. Avoid clip art, which often looks unprofessional.

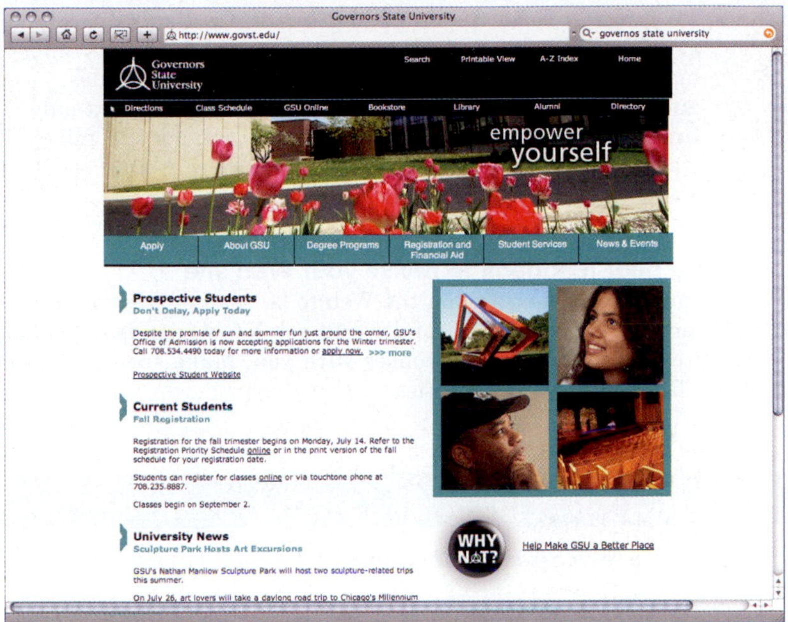

FIGURE 14.7 Governors State University home page.

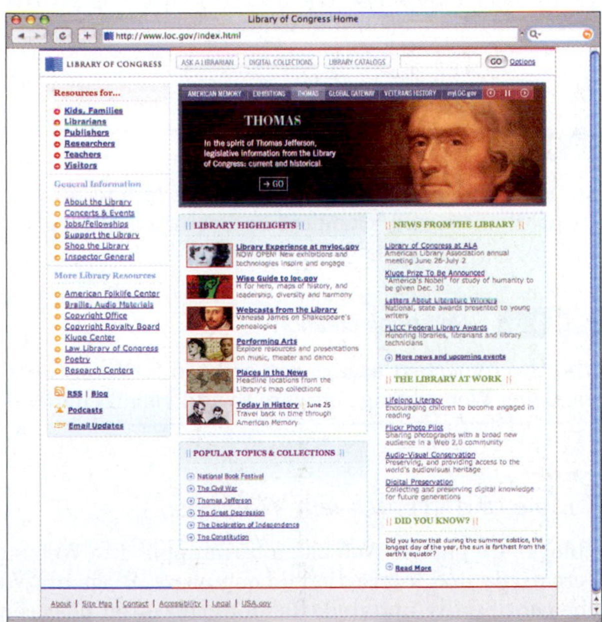

FIGURE 14.8 The home page of the Library of Congress Web site.

- **Be aware of the needs of visitors with disabilities.** Provide alternate ways of accessing visual or auditory information. Include text descriptions of visuals, media files, and tables (for users of screen-reader software or text-only **browsers**). All audio files should have captions and full transcriptions. (*See Chapter 6, Designing Academic Papers and Preparing Portfolios, pp. 111–12.*)

6. Using peer feedback to revise your Web site

Before publishing your site on the Web to be read by anyone in the world, proofread your text carefully, and ask a few friends to look at your site and share their responses with you. Make sure your site reflects favorably on your abilities.

For MULTILINGUAL STUDENTS

Designing a Web Site Collaboratively

If you are asked to create a Web site as part of a class assignment, arrange to work with a partner or a small group. Periodically, you can invite peers to check over the writing you contribute and make suggestions. At the same time, you will be able to provide the project with the benefit of your multicultural viewpoint.

Exercise 14.5 Web site critique

Choose an example of a well-designed Web site and an example of one that is poorly designed. Compare and contrast aspects of the two designs.

Exercise 14.6 Web page creation

Convert the two hypertext essays you created for Exercise 14.3 into Web pages, using Web editing software to add visual elements.

14f Create and interact with Weblogs.

Weblogs (blogs) are part of Web 2.0, a term applied to Web sites that facilitate creativity and interaction among users. Blogs are Web sites that can be continually updated. Readers can often post comments on entries. Some blogs provide a space where a group of writers can discuss one another's work and ideas.

TEXTCONNEX

Blog Resources

Blogs 101—The New York Times—Directory of blogs by topic <http://www.nytimes.com/ref/technology/blogs_101.html>

Technorati—Search engine for blogs <http://www.technorati.com>

In schools, classes have used blogs to discuss issues, organize work, compile portfolios, and gather and store material and commentary. Figure 14.9 depicts a blog for an English class at Queens College. Here, instructor Jason Tougow and his students discuss the title of their upcoming conference.

Blogs have become important vehicles for public discussion and commentary. For example, most presidential campaigns in 2008 maintained blogs on their Web sites, and many conventional news sources, like the *New York Times*, link to their own blogs on their Web sites. Compared to other types of publications and academic writing, blogs have an informal tone that combines information, entertainment, and personal opinion.

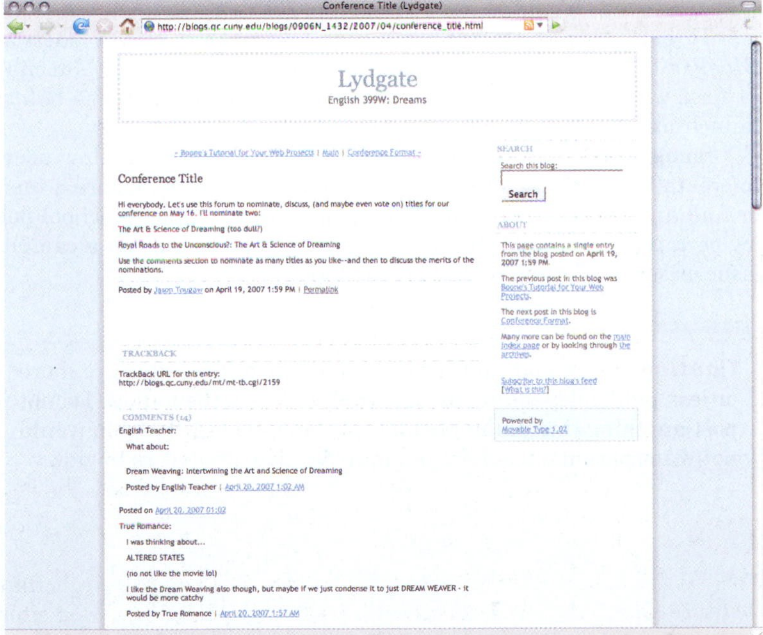

FIGURE 14.9 The blog for Jason Tougow's English course. Here, a student comments on the instructor's post.

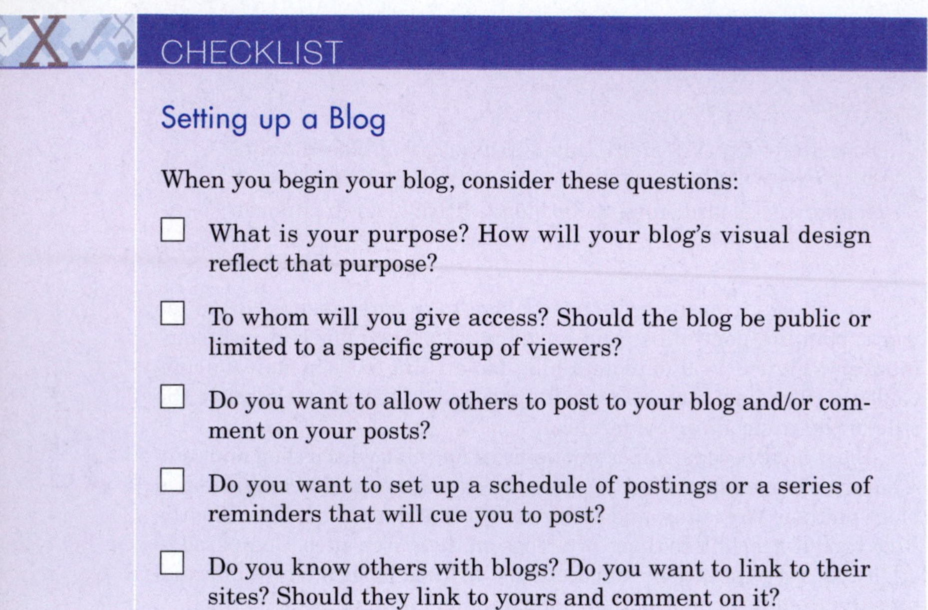

CHECKLIST

Setting up a Blog

When you begin your blog, consider these questions:

- ☐ What is your purpose? How will your blog's visual design reflect that purpose?
- ☐ To whom will you give access? Should the blog be public or limited to a specific group of viewers?
- ☐ Do you want to allow others to post to your blog and/or comment on your posts?
- ☐ Do you want to set up a schedule of postings or a series of reminders that will cue you to post?
- ☐ Do you know others with blogs? Do you want to link to their sites? Should they link to yours and comment on it?

To begin blogging, set up a blog site with a server such as *Blogger* (blogger.com) or *Word Press* (wordpress.com). You may at first want to confine yourself to a very specific purpose before launching into wide-ranging commentary.

Some social networking sites such as *MySpace* also allow users to create blogs. These sites can sometimes be used to explore a topic or find an expert on a particular subject. For example, if school policy permits it you might informally survey your friends on a campus issue or set up a group to discuss the topic.

Caution: Blogs and profiles on social networking sites are more or less public depending on the level of access they allow. Do not post anything (including photographs and videos) that you would not want parents, teachers, and prospective employers to view.

TEXTCONNEX

Wikis

A wiki is another kind of Web-interfaced database that can be updated easily. While a blog typically is managed by one person, a wiki allows multiple writers to post and edit content. Thus, wikis are useful spaces for collaborative authoring and research compilation.

One well-known wiki is the online encyclopedia *Wikipedia* (*see Chapter 18, p. 266*). Many instructors do not consider *Wikipedia* a credible source for papers because anyone can create or edit its content. Changes are not reviewed by experts before appearing on the site. Because the information provided isn't always correct, confirm it with another source. Some other wikis, such as *Citizendium*, rely on experts in a discipline to write and edit articles.

Exercise 14.7 Blogs

1. Examine a variety of blogs, and identify their purpose and audience. How do features of the visual design and the writing support the purpose?
2. Create your own blog with three of your classmates, and use it as a peer-review forum for your next paper assignment. How does this kind of peer review compare with a face-to-face review?
3. Choose a current-events blog to read for several days, and then post a comment on an issue. If the blog author or another reader responds to your comment, write in your print or electronic journal or blog about the resulting exchange.
4. Using the questions for previewing text and visuals in Chapter 7 (*pp. 122–24*), write a short rhetorical analysis of a blog.

Interplanetary probes help astronomers research the far reaches of the solar system. Voyager 2 sent this image of Saturn's rings to Earth.

PART 3

For all knowledge and wonder (which is the seed of knowledge) is an impression of pleasure in itself.
—FRANCIS BACON

Researching

15 Understanding Research

Your campus or neighborhood library provides valuable resources for almost any kind of research. These include not just books, magazines, and journals but access to specialized online databases and the expert guidance of a research librarian.

Doing research in the twenty-first century includes the library but is not limited to it. The Internet provides direct access in seconds to an abundance of information. This ease of access, however, can be treacherous. The results of Internet searches can sometimes provide an overwhelming flood of sources, many of them of questionable legitimacy.

The goal of Part 3 of this book is to help you learn about the research process. Chapters 15–22 provide tips for skillfully navigating today's research landscape, managing the information you discover within it, and using that information to write research papers.

15a Understand primary and secondary research.

Academic inquiry calls for both primary and secondary research. **Primary research** involves working in a laboratory, in the field, or with an archive of raw data, original documents, or authentic artifacts to

WRITING OUTCOMES

Part 3: Researching

This section will help you answer questions such as:

Rhetorical Knowledge

- What writing situation does my assignment specify? **(15c)**

Critical Thinking, Reading, and Writing

- What are primary and secondary research? **(15a, 19)**
- How can I tell if my sources are worth including? **(18)**
- How do I present my ideas along with those of my sources? **(21c–e)**

Processes

- How can I think of a topic for my research paper? **(15d)**
- How do I plan my research project? **(15e)**
- When and how should I use visuals in my research paper? **(17)**

Knowledge of Conventions

- What is an annotated bibliography, and how do I create one? **(21b)**
- When and how should I use paraphrases, summaries, and quotations? **(21c, e)**

make firsthand discoveries. (*For more information on primary research, see Chapter 19, pp. 299–306*). **Secondary research** involves looking at what other people have learned and written about a field or topic.

Your college research writing might require primary research, secondary research, or some combination of the two. For example, a research project for an education course might ask you to observe and document the behavior of children in a classroom and then to analyze your findings based on the work of child development specialists.

Knowing how to identify facts, interpretations, and evaluations is key to conducting good secondary research:

- **Facts** are objective. Like your body weight, facts can be measured, observed, or independently verified in some way.
- **Interpretations** spell out the implications of facts. Are you as thin as you are because of your genes—or because you exercise every day? The answer to this question is an interpretation.
- **Evaluations** are debatable judgments about a set of facts or a situation. Attributing a person's thinness to genes is an interpretation, but the assertion that "one can never be too rich or too thin" (credited to Wallis Simpson and Babe Paley) is an evaluation.

Once you are up-to-date on the facts, interpretations, and evaluations in a particular area, you will be able to design a research project that adds to this knowledge. Usually, what you will add is your *perspective* on the sources you found and read:

- Given all that you have learned about the topic, what strikes you as important or interesting?
- What patterns do you see, or what connections can you make between one person's work and another's?
- Where is the research going, and what problems still need to be explored?

TEXTCONNEX

Types of Sources

- *Research 101—The Basics* <http://www.lib.washington.edu/uwill/research101/basic00.htm>: This page from the University of Washington site discusses the difference between primary and secondary research sources, as well as the difference between popular and scholarly periodicals.
- *Research Papers: Resources* <http://owl.english.purdue.edu/workshops/hypertext/ResearchW/resource.html>: From The Purdue Online Writing Lab, offers guidelines for finding primary and secondary sources.

CHARTING the TERRITORY

Classic and Current Sources

Classic sources are well-known and respected older works that have made such an important contribution to a discipline or a particular area of research that contemporary researchers use them as touchstones for further research in that area. Current research is up to date but has not yet met the test of time. In many fields, sources published within the past five years are considered current. However, sources on topics related to medicine, recent scientific discoveries, or technological change must be much more recent to be considered current. Many disciplines also have key reference texts—discipline-specific encyclopedias and dictionaries, for example. These can usually direct you to classic sources.

15b Recognize the connection between research and college writing.

In one way or another, research informs all college writing. But some assignments require more rigorous and systematic research than others. These **research project** assignments offer you a chance to go beyond your course texts—to find and read both classic and current material on a specific issue. A research paper constitutes your contribution to the ongoing conversation about a specific issue.

When you are assigned to write a research paper for any of your college courses, the project may seem overwhelming at first. If you break the project into phases, however, and allow enough time for each phase, you should be able to manage your work and write a paper that contributes to the academic conversation.

15c Understand the research assignment.

Consider the rhetorical situation of the research project as you would any other piece of writing. Think about your paper's audience, purpose, and scope. (*See Chapter 2: Understanding Writing Assignments.*)

1. Audience

Although your *audience* will most likely include only your instructor and perhaps your fellow students, thinking critically about their needs and expectations will help you plan a research strategy and create a schedule for writing your paper.

WRITING beyond COLLEGE

Audience in Research Writing

Ask yourself the following questions about your audience. If your instructor approves, use your imagination to think about alternative audiences for your research—for example, a local school board for a paper about an education issue, the members of a state legislature for a paper about an environmental issue, or the readers of a newspaper's editorial page for a paper on a political issue.

- What does my audience already know about this subject? How much background information and context will I need to provide? (Your research should include *facts*.)
- Might my audience find my paper controversial or challenging? How should I accommodate and acknowledge different perspectives and viewpoints? (Your research should include *interpretations*, and you will need to balance opposing interpretations.)
- Do I expect my audience to take action based on my research? (Your research should include *evaluations*, carefully supported by facts and interpretations, that demonstrate clearly to members of your audience why they should adopt a particular course of action or point of view.)

2. Purpose

Your *purpose* for writing a research paper might be *informative*—to educate your audience about an unfamiliar subject or point of view (*see Chapter 8: Informative Reports, p. 137*). It might be *interpretive*—to reveal the meaning or significance of a work of art, a historic document, or a scientific study (*see Chapter 9: Interpretive Analyses, p. 157*). It might instead be *persuasive*—that is, to convince your audience, with logic and evidence, to accept your point of view on a contentious issue or to act on the information in your paper (*see Chapter 10: Arguments, p. 183*).

3. Scope

A project's scope includes the expected length, the deadline, and any other requirements such as number and type of sources. Most research assignments call for a mix of classic and current sources that address a range of viewpoints. Are primary sources appropriate? Should you include visuals, and is any type specified? Select a topic that will allow you to meet the assignment's scope. It might be difficult to find sufficient and appropriate sources if your topic is very current or specialized.

Tips LEARNING in COLLEGE

Keywords Indicating Purpose in Research Assignments

Review your assignment for keywords that signal its purpose. Here are some examples.

- **Informative:** *explain, describe, compare, review*
- **Interpretive:** *analyze, compare, explain, interpret*
- **Persuasive:** *assess, justify, defend, refute, determine*

Sample Informative Research Assignments

- **History:** Describe the relationship between abolitionism and the women's suffrage movement prior to the Civil War.
- **Biology:** Explain the impact of zebra mussels on native fauna in a lake.

Sample Interpretive Research Assignments

- **History:** Interpret the *Declaration of Sentiments*—issued at the first women's rights convention in 1848—as a response to the *Declaration of Independence*.
- **Biology:** Analyze the results of recent studies of lakes infested with zebra mussels.

Sample Persuasive Research Assignments

- **History:** Defend or refute this statement: "The women's movement and the civil rights movement have long cooperated based on a historically rooted shared agenda."
- **Biology:** Determine the least invasive way to remove zebra mussels from a local ecosystem, and create an implementation plan for doing so.

For more on narrowing your topic, go to Writing > Paragraph/Essay Development > Thesis/Central Idea

15d Choose an interesting research question for critical inquiry.

Approach your assignment in a spirit of critical inquiry. *Critical* in this sense does not mean "skeptical," "cynical," or even "urgent." Rather it refers to a receptive but reasonable and discerning frame of mind. Choosing a topic that interests you will help make the results of your inquiry meaningful to you and your readers.

1. Choosing a question with personal significance

Begin with the wording of the assignment, analyzing the project's required audience, purpose, and scope. (*See section 15c.*) Then browse through the course texts and your class notes, looking for a match between your interests and topics, issues, or problems in the subject area.

For example, suppose you have been assigned to write a seven- to ten-page report on some country's global economic prospects, for a business course. If you have recently visited Mexico, you might find it interesting to explore that country's prospects.

2. Making your question specific

The more specific your question, the more your research will have direction and focus. To make a question more specific, use the "five *w*'s and an *h*" strategy by asking about the *who, what, why, when, where,* and *how* of a topic (*see Chapter 3, pp. 36–37*).

After you have compiled a list of possible research questions, choose one that is relatively specific, or rewrite a broad one to make it more specific and therefore answerable within the scope of the assignment. For example, as Audrey Galeano developed a topic for a research paper on the impact of globalization for an anthropology course, she rewrote the following broad question to make it answerable:

TOO BROAD	How has globalization affected the Amazon River Basin?
ANSWERABLE	How has large-scale agriculture in the Amazon Basin affected the region's indigenous peoples?

(*Galeano's finished paper appears at the end of Chapter 24: APA Documentation Style, pp. 412–22*)

CHARTING the TERRITORY

Typical Lines of Inquiry in Different Disciplines

Research topics and questions—even when related to a single broad issue—differ from one discipline to another. The following examples show the distinctions:

History: How did India's experience of British imperialism affect its response to globalization?

Marketing: How do corporations develop strategies for marketing their products to an international consumer audience?

Political Science: Why did many nations of Europe agree to unite, creating a common currency and an essentially "borderless" state called the European Union, or E.U.?

Anthropology: What is the impact of globalization on the world's indigenous cultures?

Try to rephrase a broad question as a statement, then add the word *because* or *by* at the end, and fill in the blank with possible answers. For example, if your broad question is "How has globalization affected the Amazon Basin?" restate it as "Globalization has affected the Amazon Basin by ________" and give a few precise reasons. Here are some examples Audrey Galeano considered:

> Globalization has affected the Amazon Basin by ________
>
> > . . . overwhelming traditional forms of music, dress, and expression with global pop culture.
> > . . . encouraging the construction of roads that make the region more accessible.

3. Finding a challenging question

If a question can be answered with a simple yes or no, a dictionary-like definition, or a textbook presentation of information, you should choose another question or rework the simple one to make it more challenging and interesting.

NOT CHALLENGING	Has economic globalization contributed to the destruction of the Amazon rain forest?
CHALLENGING	How can agricultural interests and indigenous peoples in the Amazon region work together to preserve the environment while creating a sustainable economy?

4. Speculating about answers

Sometimes it can be useful to speculate on the answer to your research question so that you have a **hypothesis** to work with during the research process. Do not forget, however, that a hypothesis is a tentative answer that must be tested and revised against the evidence you turn up in your research. Be aware of the assumptions embedded in your hypothesis or research question. Consider, for example, the following hypothesis:

HYPOTHESIS	The global market for agricultural products will destroy the Amazon rain forest.

This hypothesis assumes that destructive farming practices are the only possible response in the Amazon to global demand. But assumptions are always open to question. Researchers must be willing to adjust their ideas as they learn more about a topic.

As the above example demonstrates, your research question must allow you to generate testable hypotheses. Assertions about your personal beliefs or feelings do not make testable hypotheses.

Exercise 15.1 Answerable, challenging questions

For each of the following broad topics, create at least three answerable, challenging questions.

1. Internet access is becoming as important as literacy in determining the livelihood of a nation's people.
2. Genetically modified organisms (GMOs) and biotechnology are controversial approaches to addressing the world's food problems.
3. The problem of terrorism requires a multilateral solution.

15e Create a research plan.

www.mhhe.com/mhhb2
For resources to start your research, go to
Research > Discipline Specific Resources

Your research will be more productive if you create both a general plan and a detailed schedule immediately after you receive your assignment. A general plan will ensure that you understand the full scope of your assignment. A detailed schedule will help you set priorities and meet your deadlines. To develop a general plan of research, answer the following questions:

- Do I understand exactly what my instructor expects?
- Is the purpose of my paper fundamentally informative, interpretive, or persuasive? Do I have a choice?
- If the topic is assigned: What do I already know about this topic?
- If the specific topic is open: What idea-generation techniques can I use to help me discover a topic?
- Will collaboration be allowed?
- Will I need to conduct primary as well as secondary research? If so, what general arrangements do I anticipate needing to make?
- How many and what kinds of sources am I expected to consult? (*See Chapters 16–18 for information on finding and evaluating sources.*)
- What citation style does my instructor want me to use? What are the expectations for the final presentation format of my research? (*See Part 4: Documenting across the Curriculum.*)

Exercise 15.2 Research schedule

Adapt this worksheet to create a research schedule whenever you have a research assignment. If you use a PDA, type in this schedule and set reminders or alarms for key dates (such as completing library

SOURCE SMART

Planning Your Search

Your research plan should include where you expect to find your sources. For example, you may have to visit the library to view print material that predates 1980; you will need to consult a subscription database online or at the library for recent scientific discoveries; historical documents may require archival research; and you may need to conduct field research, such as interviewing fellow students. Set priorities to increase your efficiency in each location (library, archive, online).

research, completing a first draft, or conferring with the campus writing center).

Task	Date
Phase I:	
Complete a general plan for research.	________
Decide on a topic and a research question.	________
Consult reference works and reference librarians.	________
List relevant **keywords** for online searching (*see Chapter 16, pp. 266–67*).	________
Compile a **working bibliography** (*see Chapter 21, pp. 314–18*).	________
Sample some of the items in the bibliography.	________
Make arrangements for primary research (if necessary).	________
Phase II:	
Locate, read, and evaluate selected sources.	________
Take notes; write summaries and paraphrases.	________
Cross-check notes with working bibliography.	________
Conduct primary research (if necessary).	________
Find and create visuals.	________
Confer with instructor or writing center (optional).	________
Develop thesis and outline or plan organization of paper.	________
Phase III:	
Write first draft.	________
Decide which primary and secondary resource materials to include.	________

Peer review (optional).	______
Revise draft.	______
Conference with instructor or writing center (optional).	______
Perform final revision and editing.	______
Create in-text citations as well as Works-Cited or References list.	______
Proofread and check spelling.	______
Due Date	______

16 Finding and Managing Print and Online Sources

The amount of information available in the library and on the Internet is vast. Usually, a search for useful sources entails three activities:

- Collecting keywords from reference works
- Using library databases
- Finding material in the library and on the Web

16a Use the library in person and online.

Librarians know what is available at your library and how to get material from other libraries. They can also show you how to access the library's computerized book catalog, periodical databases, and electronic resources or how to use the Internet to find information relevant to your research project. At many schools, reference librarians are available for online chats at any time, and some take queries via text message. Your library's Web site may have links to subscription databases or important reference works available on the Internet, as shown in Figure 16.1 on the next page.

In addition, **help sheets** or online tutorials at most college libraries give the location of both general and discipline-specific periodicals and noncirculating reference books, along with information about the book catalog, special databases, indexes, Web resources, and library policies.

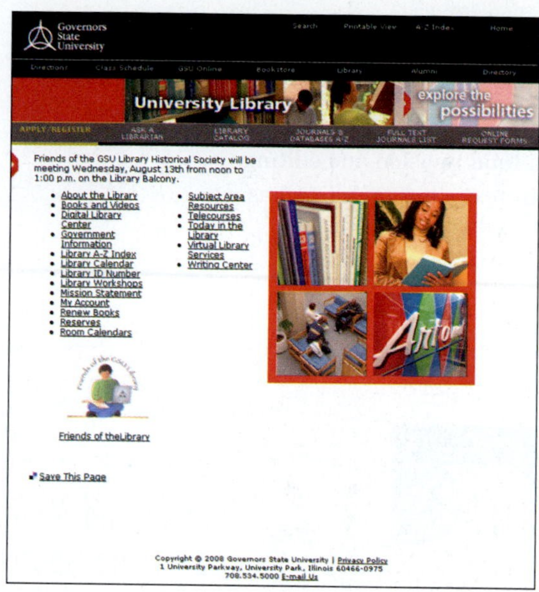

FIGURE 16.1 Linking to online resources from a college library's Web site. This page from the Web site of Governors State University Library provides links to a variety of Web-based reference sources.

www.mhhe.com/mhhb2

For more information on and links to library resources, go to **Research > Using the Library**

16b Consult various kinds of sources.

You should always review more than one source, and usually more than one kind of source: general and specialized, books and articles, print and online. Chances are, you will consult more sources during your research than you will cite in your final project. Your assignment may specify how many print and electronic sources you

SOURCE SMART

Organizing Your Sources

List your sources alphabetically. For each, include citation information (*see p. 315*), key points, and relevance to your topic. Does the source support or detract from your claim? Is it an early source or a later one? Does it agree or disagree with other sources you have read? Do other sources reference this one? You might color-code your list to indicate related ideas across sources. Include useful quotations and their page numbers. (*For instructions on preparing a formal annotated bibliography and an example, see Chapter 21: Working with Sources and Avoiding Plagiarism, p. 319.*)

are expected to look at and cite. Some types of sources available to you are summarized in the following sections.

CHECKLIST

Finding Library Resources

Make it a point to tour your library when you begin college. Your library also may have online tutorials describing its resources. Be sure to do the following:

- ☐ Locate the reference desk and note its hours. (Reference books cannot be checked out, so you will need to schedule time to consult them while the library is open.) Collect any help sheets.
- ☐ Set up an account and a password to use the online catalog. Find out how to link to the catalog from a computer in your dorm or home. Also locate the library's card catalog if it has one.
- ☐ Locate the library's **stacks** (the shelves where it stores its collections of books). To get books from closed stacks, you have to request them and have them brought to you by a library employee.
- ☐ Learn your library's interlibrary loan policies.
- ☐ Learn about the library's **reserve service,** which lets professors set aside books and articles for students to consult for limited times, or post them electronically, ensuring their availability to everyone in the class.
- ☐ Locate your library's photocopying machines, computer terminals, printers, and other helpful devices.
- ☐ Locate and learn to use any online databases to which the library subscribes. These provide access to journal articles as well as newspapers and magazines often dating back to the 1980s. Older sources may be on microform or microfiche. Learn the location of the machines that allow you to read them.
- ☐ Find out about any multimedia resources or primary sources available online or at the library.

1. General reference works

General reference works provide overview information about a variety of topics. General encyclopedias (such as *Encyclopaedia Britannica*), for example, include entries for anything from the history of the alphabet to the science of zoology. Other general reference works include dictionaries, annuals, almanacs, biographical encyclopedias, and world atlases. They can introduce you to the basic concepts and vocabulary of a subject, giving you a source of **keywords** to use in online searches for more specialized sources. (*The basics of keyword searches are covered in section 16d.*)

2. Specialized reference works

Specialized reference works provide specific information relevant to particular disciplines. A discipline-specific encyclopedia of philosophy, for example, would have entries on important philosophers, major approaches to philosophy, and the meaning of significant philosophical terms. Other specialized reference works include discipline-specific biographical encyclopedias, almanacs, dictionaries, and bibliographies. These can also provide an overview of a topic as well as keywords.

3. Books

Most of the books you use will be in the library in printed form. Some books, however, are available online, including reports by think tanks, government agencies, and research groups. Some Web sites (such as Project Gutenberg, http://www.gutenberg.org/) provide the complete texts of classic works of literature that are no longer under copyright (*see Chapter 20, pp. 306–14*).

4. Periodical articles

Periodicals include newspapers and magazines from around the world, scholarly and technical journals (some of which may be available through online databases as well as in print), and Web-only publications.

5. Web sites

Many special-interest groups, government and academic organizations, and businesses maintain Web sites that provide information about policies, products, or particular points of view.

6. Other online sources

Online discussion groups, virtual environments, news groups, chat rooms, social networking sites, and blogs can sometimes provide access to people knowledgeable about a particular subject who can help guide your research. (Be careful, though; you can also encounter many unqualified people with suspect views in these environments.)

For MULTILINGUAL STUDENTS

Researching a Full Range of Sources

Your mastery of a language other than English can sometimes give you access to important sources. Even if you find researching in English challenging, it is important to broaden your search as soon as you can to include a range of print and Internet resources written in English.

7. Primary print sources

Primary print resources include government documents (the text of a law, for example); census data; pamphlets; maps; the original text of literary works; and the original manuscripts (or facsimiles) of literary works, letters, and personal journals, among many others. You can find these in your library, in special collections at other libraries, in government offices, and online.

8. Primary nonprint sources

In addition to written works, primary sources also include such nonprint items as works of art, video and audio recordings, sound archives, photographs, and the artifacts of everyday life.

9. Other primary sources

Other primary sources include a researcher's records from experiments or field research. These may include interviews, field notes, surveys, and the results of observation and laboratory experiments.

Exercise 16.1 Finding information at your library

Choose anyone born between 1900 and 1950 whose life and accomplishments interest you. You could select a politician, a film director, a rock star, a Nobel Prize–winning economist—*anyone.* At your library, find at least one of each of the following resources with information about or relevant to this person:

- A directory of biographies
- An article in a pre-1990 newspaper
- An article in a scholarly journal
- An audio or video recording, a photograph, or a work of art
- A printout of the search results of your library's electronic catalog
- A printout of an article obtained via a subscription database
- An obituary (if your subject has died)
- A list of your subject's accomplishments, including, for example, prizes received, books published, albums released, or movies made

LEARNING in COLLEGE

Popular or Scholarly?

The audience for and purpose of a source, especially a publication, determine whether it should be considered *scholarly* or *popular*. You may begin your inquiry into a research topic with popular sources, but to become fully informed, you need to delve into scholarly sources.

Popular sources:

- Are widely available on newsstands and in retail stores.
- Are printed on magazine paper with a color cover.
- Accept advertising for a wide range of popular consumer goods or are themselves advertised.
- Are published by a commercial publishing house or media company (such as Time Warner, Inc.).
- Include a wide range of topics in each issue, from international affairs to popular entertainment.
- Usually do not contain bibliographic information.
- If online, have a URL that likely ends in .com.

Scholarly sources:

- Are usually found in academic libraries, not on newsstands.
- List article titles and authors on the cover.
- Have few advertisements.
- Are published by scholarly or nonprofit organizations, often in association with a university press.
- Focus on discipline-specific topics.
- Include articles with extensive citations and bibliographies.
- Include articles mostly by authors who are affiliated with colleges, museums, or other scholarly institutions.
- Are **refereed** (which means, in the case of a scholarly journal, that each article has been reviewed, commented on, and accepted for publication by other scholars in the field).
- If online, have a URL that likely ends in .edu or .org.

16c Use printed and online reference works for general information.

Reference works provide an overview of a subject area and typically are less up to date than the specialized knowledge found in academic journals and scholarly books. If your instructor approves, you may start your research by consulting a general or discipline-specific

Tips LEARNING in COLLEGE

Refining Keyword Searches

Although search engines vary, the following advice should work for many.

Group words together. Put quotation marks or parentheses around the phrase you are looking for—for example, "Dixieland jazz." This tells the search engine to find only sites with those two words in sequence.

Use Boolean operators.

AND (+)	Use AND or + when you need sites with both of two or more words: **Armstrong + Glaser.**
OR	Use OR if you want sites with either of two or more terms: **jazz OR "musical improvisation."**
NOT (–)	Use NOT or – in front of words that you do not want to appear together in your results: **Armstrong NOT Neil.**

Use truncation plus a "wildcard." For more results, combine part of a keyword with an asterisk (*) used as a wildcard: **music*** (for "music," "musician," "musical," and so forth).

Search the fields. Some search engines permit you to search within fields, such as the title field of Web pages or the author field of a library catalog. Thus **TITLE + "Louis Armstrong"** will give you all items that have "Louis Armstrong" in their title.

encyclopedia, but for college research you should explore your topic in greater depth. Often, the list of references at the end of an encyclopedia article can lead you to useful sources on your topic.

Reference books do not circulate, so plan to take notes or make photocopies of pages you may need to consult later. Check your college library's home page for access to online encyclopedias.

Here is a list of some other kinds of reference materials available in print, on the Internet, or both:

ALMANACS

- *Almanac of American Politics*
- *Information Please Almanac*
- *World Almanac*

BIBLIOGRAPHIES

- *Bibliographic Index*
- *Bibliography of Asian Studies*

- *Books in Print*
- *MLA International Bibliography*

BIOGRAPHIES

- *African American Biographical Database*
- *American Men and Women of Science*
- *Dictionary of American Biography*
- *Dictionary of Literary Biography: Chicano Writers*
- *Dictionary of National Biography*
- *Webster's New Biographical Dictionary*
- *Who's Who*

DICTIONARIES

- *American Heritage Dictionary of the English Language*
- *Concise Oxford Dictionary of Literary Terms*
- *Dictionary of American History*
- *Dictionary of Philosophy*
- *Dictionary of the Social Sciences*
- *Oxford English Dictionary* (*OED*)

16d Understand keywords and keyword searches.

Most online research—whether in your library's catalog, in a specialized database, or on the Web—requires an understanding of **keyword searches.** In the context of online searching, a **keyword** is a term (or terms) you enter into a **search engine** (searching software) to find sources—books, journal articles, Web sites—that have information about a particular subject.

TEXTCONNEX

Wikipedia

The online encyclopedia *Wikipedia* offers information on almost any subject and can be a starting point for research. However, you should evaluate its content critically. Volunteers (who may or may not be experts) write *Wikipedia's* articles, and almost any user may edit any article. Although the site has some mechanisms to help it maintain accuracy, you should check any findings with another source (and cite that source, if you use the information).

To hone in on your subject, you often need to refine your initial search term. The "Learning in College" box on page 265 describes a variety of techniques for doing so that work in most search engines. Many search engines also have an advanced search feature that can help with the refining process.

16e Use print indexes and online databases to find articles in journals and other periodicals.

1. Periodicals

Newspapers, magazines, and scholarly journals that are published at regular intervals are classified as **periodicals.** The articles in scholarly and technical journals, written by experts and based on up-to-date research and information, are usually more detailed and reliable than articles in popular newspapers and magazines. Ask your instructor or librarian which periodicals are considered important in the discipline you are studying.

2. Indexes and Databases

Articles published in periodicals are cataloged in general and specialized **indexes.** Indexes are available on subscription-only online **databases,** as print volumes, and possibly on CD-ROMs. If you are searching for articles that are more than twenty years old, you may use print indexes or an appropriate electronic index. Print indexes can be searched by author, subject, or title. Electronic databases can also be searched by date and keyword and will provide you with a list of articles that meet your search criteria. (Some allow you to restrict your search to peer-reviewed scholarly journals.) Each entry in the list will include the information you need to find and cite the article. Depending on the database, you may also be able to see an abstract of each article, or even its full text. Once you find a relevant result, use its subject headings as keywords in future search queries. (*See the box "Learning in College: Formats for Database Information," on p. 274.*)

When selecting a database, consult its description on your library's site (often labeled "Info") to see the types of sources included, subjects covered, and number of periodicals included from each subject area. Would your topic be best served by a general database or one that is discipline specific? Should you focus on a particular type of periodical, such as newspapers? Also consider the time period each database spans.

Citation indexes, another type of database, indicate what other scholars have said about specific articles and books. They can help you assess a source's relevance, reliability, and position in current debates in the field.

The TextConnex box on pages 271–72 lists some of the major online databases and service providers, and Figures 16.2, 16.3, and 16.4 on pages 268–70 illustrate a search on one of them, ProQuest. Keep in mind that not all libraries subscribe to all databases.

Caution: When you refer to the full text of an article that you retrieved from a subscription database service, your citation must include the date on which you retrieved the article, the name of the database, and information about the publication in which the article appeared.

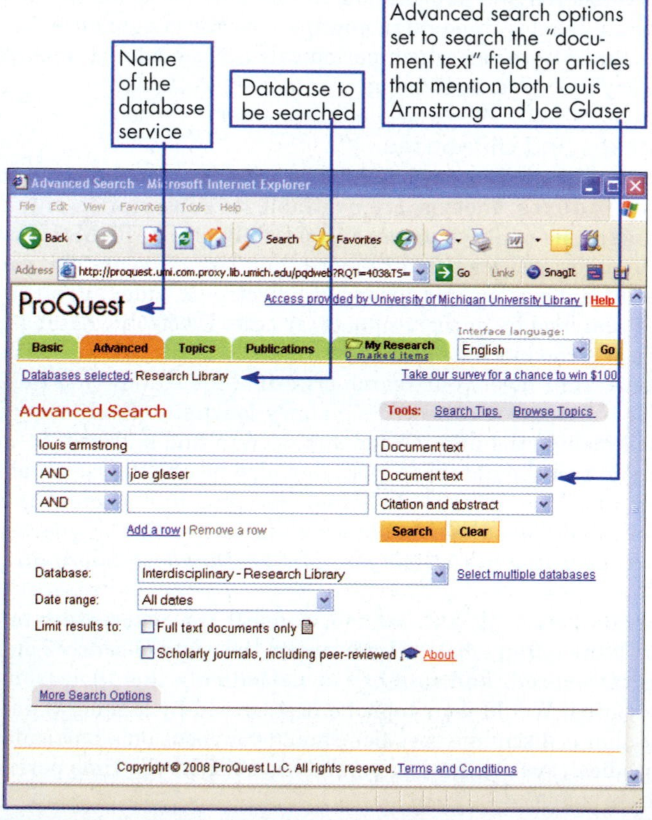

FIGURE 16.2 **ProQuest's Advanced Search page.** Image published with permission of ProQuest Information and Learning Company. Further reproduction is prohibited without permission.

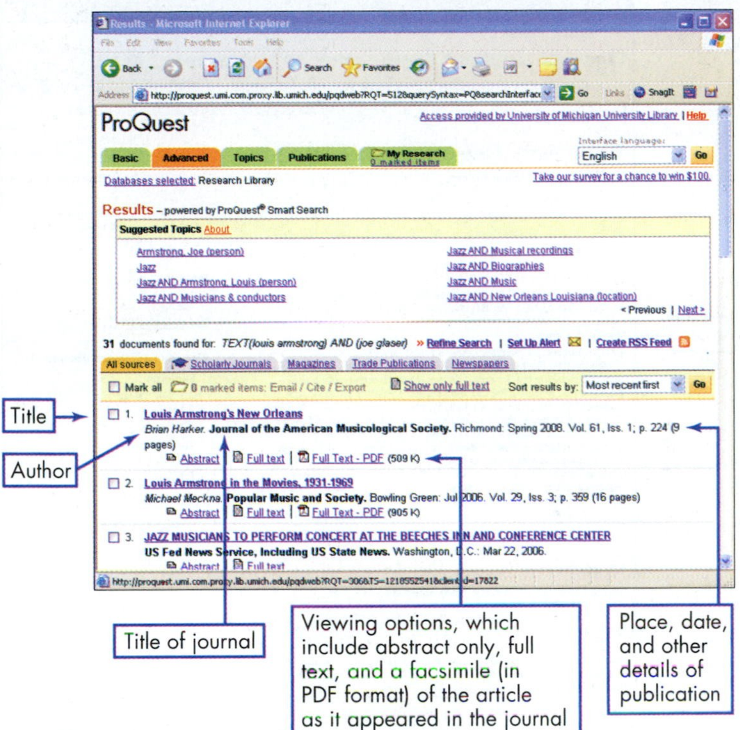

FIGURE 16.3 Partial results of the search started in Figure 16.2. Image published with permission of ProQuest Information and Learning Company. Further reproduction is prohibited without permission.

16f Use search engines and subject directories to find sources on the Internet.

To find information that has been published in Web pages, you will need to use an Internet search engine. Because each searches the Web in its own way, you will probably use more than one. Each search engine's home page provides a link to advice on using the search engine efficiently as well as help with refining a search. Look for a link labeled "search help," "about us," or something similar.

Some Internet search engines provide for specialized searches—for images, for example (*see Chapter 17*). *Google* offers *Google Book Search*, which can help you find and view books on your topic. *Google Scholar* locates only scholarly sources in response to a search term. At this point it offers incomplete information, and you should not rely on it alone.

Many Internet search engines also include sponsored links—links that a commercial enterprise has paid to have appear in response to specific search terms. These are usually clearly identified.

www.mhhe.com/mhhb2
For more information on and links to Internet resources, go to
Research > Using the Internet

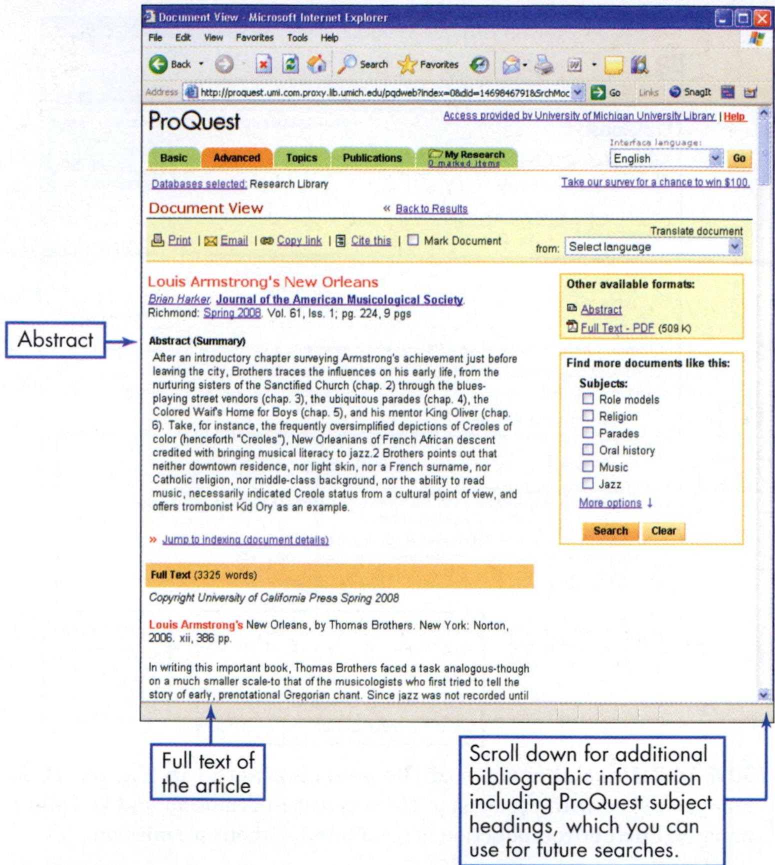

FIGURE 16.4 The abstract and the beginning of the full text of an article selected from results in Figure 16.3. Image published with permission of ProQuest Information and Learning Company. Further reproduction is prohibited without permission.

Internet keyword searches usually need to be carefully worded to provide relevant results. For example, a search of *Google* using the keywords *louis armstrong* (*Figure 16.5*) yields a list of more than 3,810,000 Web sites, a staggering number of links, or **hits.** Altering the keywords to make them more specific narrows the results significantly (*Figure 16.6 on p. 273*). (*See also the box on p. 265.*)

In addition to keyword searches, many Internet search engines offer a **subject directory,** a listing of broad categories. Clicking through this hierarchy of choices eventually brings you to a list of sites related to a specific topic.

(*Text continues on p. 272.*)

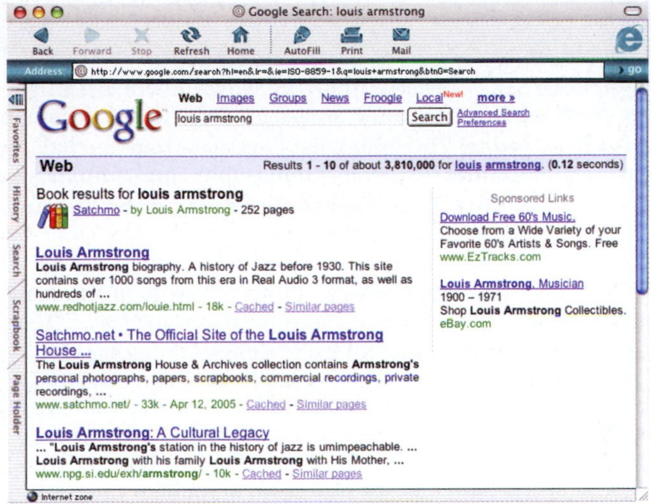

FIGURE 16.5 A keyword search in *Google*. An initial search using the keywords *louis armstrong* yields more than three million hits.

Some Online Subscription Databases

- ***ABC-CLIO:*** This service offers access to two history-related databases. *America: History and Life* covers the United States and Canada from prehistory to the present. *Historical Abstracts* addressess the rest of the world from 1450 to the present.
- ***Lexis-Nexis Academic:*** Updated daily, this online service provides full-text access to around 6,000 newspapers, professional publications, legal references, and congressional sources.
- ***EBSCOhost:*** This service's *Academic Search Premier* database provides full-text coverage for more than 8,000 scholarly publications and indexes articles in all academic subject areas.
- ***ERIC:*** This database lists publications in the area of education.
- ***Factiva:*** This database offers access to the Dow Jones and Reuters news agencies, including newspapers, magazines, journals, and Web sites.
- ***General Science Index:*** This index is general (rather than specialized). It lists articles by biologists, chemists, and other scientists.
- ***GDCS:*** Updated monthly, the *Government Documents Catalog Service (GDCS)* contains records of all publications printed by the United States Government Printing Office since 1976.

- ***GPO Access:*** This service of the U.S. Government Printing Office provides free electronic access to government documents.
- ***Humanities Index:*** This index lists articles from journals in language and literature, history, philosophy, and similar areas.
- ***InfoTrac Web:*** This Web-based service searches bibliographic and other databases such as the *General Reference Center Gold, General Business File ASAP,* and *Health Reference Center.*
- ***JSTOR:*** This archive provides full-text access to journals in the humanities, social sciences, and natural sciences.
- ***MLA Bibliography:*** Covering from 1963 to the present, the *MLA Bibliography* indexes journals, dissertations, and serials published worldwide in the fields of modern languages, literature, literary criticism, linguistics, and folklore.
- ***PAIS International:*** Produced by the Public Affairs Information Service, this database indexes literature on public policy, social policy, and the general social sciences from 1972 to the present.
- ***Periodical Abstracts:*** This database indexes more than 2,000 general and academic journals covering business, current affairs, economics, literature, religion, psychology, and women's studies from 1987 to the present.
- ***ProQuest:*** This service provide access to dissertations; many newspapers and journals, including many full-text articles back to 1996; information on sources in business, general reference, the social sciences, and humanities back to 1986; and a wealth of historical sources back to the nineteenth century.
- ***PsycInfo:*** Sponsored by the American Psychological Association (APA), this database indexes and abstracts books, scholarly articles, technical reports, and dissertations in the area of psychology and related disciplines.
- ***Social Science Index:*** This index lists articles from such fields as economics, psychology, political science, and sociology.
- ***WorldCat:*** This is a catalog of books and other resources available in libraries worldwide.

Some Web sites provide content-specific subject directories designed for research in a particular field. These sites are often reviewed or screened and are excellent starting points for academic research.

Other online tools can help you organize sources and keep track of your Web research. Save the URLs of promising sites to your browser's Bookmarks or Favorites. Your browser's history function can allow you to retrace your steps if you forget how to find a particular site. The box on page 279 includes additional online resources.

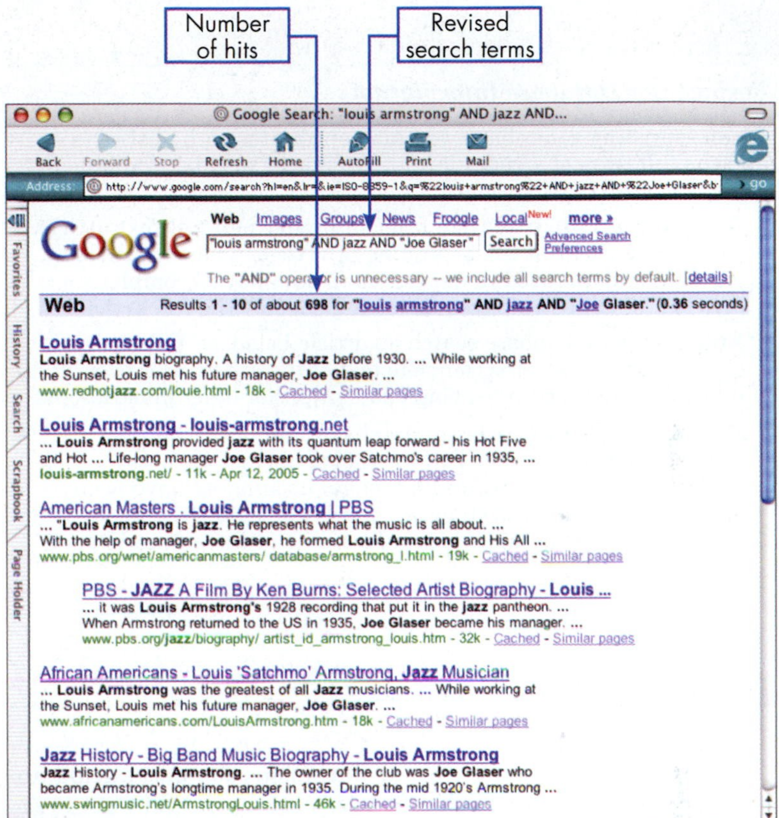

FIGURE 16.6 Refining the search. Putting quotes around *louis armstrong,* adding *jazz*, and adding *joe glaser* (Armstrong's longtime manager) reduces the number of hits to an almost manageable 698, as opposed to Figure 16.5's three million. (Note that the AND operator could have been omitted because *Google* treats terms by default as if they were joined by AND.)

Exercise 16.2 Finding information online

Look at the sample research topics listed in the "Charting the Territory" box on page 255, and conduct a keyword search for each on at least three search engines. Experiment with the phrasing of each keyword search, and compare your results with those of other classmates.

EXAMPLE What is the impact of globalization on the world's indigenous cultures?

"indigenous culture" AND globalization

Tips LEARNING in COLLEGE

Formats for Database Information

When searching a database, you may encounter both abstracts and the full texts of articles. Full-text articles may be available in either PDF or HTML format.

- **Abstract:** An **abstract** is a brief summary of a full-text article. Abstracts appear at the beginning of articles in some scholarly journals and are used in databases to summarize complete articles. If an abstract sounds useful, consult the full article.
- **Full text:** In a database search an article listed as "full text" comes with a link to the complete text of the article. However, it may not include accompanying photographs or other illustrations.
- **PDF** and **HTML:** Articles in databases and other online sources may be in either PDF or HTML format (or both). HTML (Hypertext Markup Language) documents have been formatted to read as Web pages. PDF (Portable Document Format) documents appear as a facsimile of the original page.

16g Use your library's online catalog or card catalog to find books.

In addition to searching library databases for periodicals and searching the Internet for relevant information, you will want to find books on your topic to explore it in depth. Books in most libraries are shelved by **call numbers,** a series of unique identifying numerals based on the Library of Congress classification system. In this system, books on the same topic have similar call numbers and are shelved together. Browsing the shelves near one source, therefore, can lead you to similar works. Some libraries use the Dewey Decimal system of call numbering, which classifies knowledge in divisions of 10 from 000 to 990. Whichever system your library uses, you will need the call number to locate the book on the library's shelves. When consulting a library catalog, be sure to jot down (or print out) the call numbers of books you want to consult. Some archives and specialized libraries use card catalogs. Cards usually are filed by author, title, and subject based on *Library of Congress Subject Headings* (*LCSH*).

You can conduct a keyword search of most online library catalogs by author, by title, or by subject (*Figure 16.7*). A search of the term *Louis Armstrong* by author would produce a list of works by Louis Armstrong; a search by title would produce a list of works with the words *Louis Armstrong* in the title; and a search by subject would

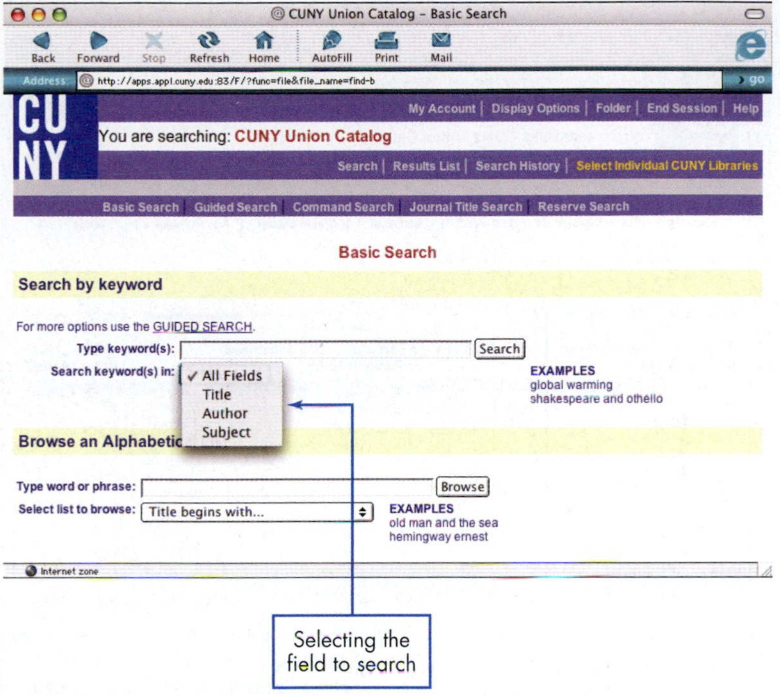

Courtesy of Libraries of The City University of New York. Microsoft® Internet Explorer screen shot reprinted with permission from Microsoft Corporation.

FIGURE 16.7 The opening search page of the online library system of the City University of New York (CUNY).

produce a list of works that are all or partly about Louis Armstrong. Subject terms appear in the *LCSH,* which provides a set of key terms that you can use in your search for sources. Keyword searches of many catalogs also include publisher, notes, and other fields.

The results of a keyword search of a library's online catalog will provide a list composed mostly of books. In the examples that follow of a search of the City University of New York Library's online catalog, notice that under the column "Format" other kinds of media that match a keyword subject search may be listed; you can alter the terms of a search to restrict the formats to a specific medium.

Figures 16.8 and 16.9 (*pp. 276–77*) show the results of experimenting with different keywords on the topic of jazz in general and Louis Armstrong in particular. Figure 16.8, a subject search using only the keyword *jazz,* resulted in too many hits to be practical. Figure 16.9, a subject search using the key term *Louis Armstrong,* produced a workable number.

In addition to searching the catalog, consult reference works to find books relevant to your topic. Bibliographies, such as the *MLA*

(*Text continues on p. 278.*)

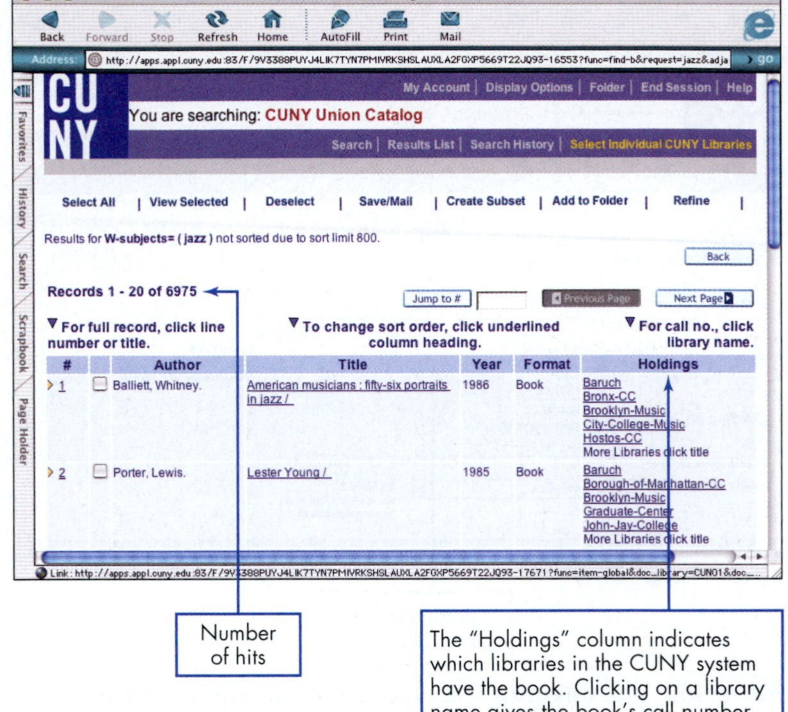

FIGURE 16.8 Searching an online catalog. Using the word *jazz* as a keyword in a subject search produces 6,975 sources.

LEARNING in COLLEGE

Cautions for Researching Online

In Chapter 18, we will consider ways to evaluate the usefulness and credibility of information you find on the Web. Here are some general cautions:

- The URL (Web address) is always subject to change.
- Topics are not usually covered in depth online. For depth and context, consult library databases for sources such as books and articles.
- Learn how to structure a keyword search to retrieve information relevant to you.

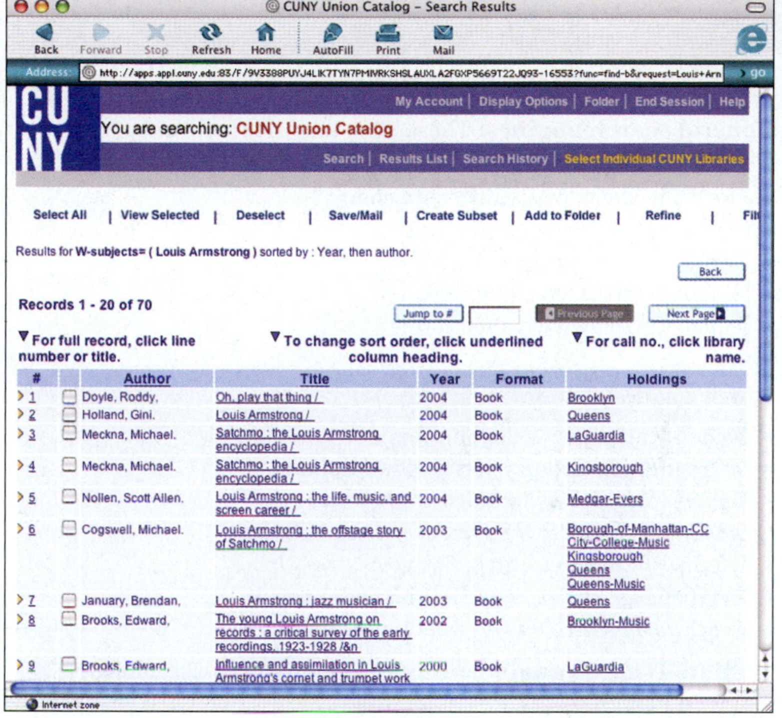

Courtesy of Libraries of The City University of New York. Microsoft® Internet Explorer screen shot reprinted with permission from Microsoft Corporation.

FIGURE 16.9 Changing a search term. A keyword search using the search term *Louis Armstrong* produces 70 results, a manageable number.

Bibliography, and review indexes, such as *Book Review Index*, can direct you to promising sources.

16h Take advantage of printed and online government documents.

The U.S. government publishes an enormous amount of information and research every year, most of which is available online. The *Monthly Catalog of U.S. Government Publications* and the *U.S. Government Periodicals Index* are available as online databases. The Government Printing Office's own Web site, *GPO Access* <http://www.gpoaccess.gov/>, is an excellent resource for identifying and locating federal government publications. Other online government resources include:

- *FedWorld Information Network* (maintained by the National Technical Information Service) <http://www.fedworld.gov/>

TEXTCONNEX

Popular Internet Search Engines

General search engines: These sites allow for both category and keyword searches.

- *AltaVista* <http://www.altavista.com>
- *Google* <http://www.google.com>
- *Live Search (Microsoft)* <http://www.msn.com>
- *Vivisimo* <http://vivisimo.com>
- *Yahoo!* <http://www.yahoo.com>

Meta search engines: These sites search several different search engines at once.

- *Dogpile* <http://www.dogpile.com>
- *Internet Public Library* <http://www.ipl.org>
- *Ixquick* <http://www.ixquick.com>
- *Librarian's Index to the Internet* <http://lii.org>
- *Library of Congress* <http://loc.gov>
- *MetaCrawler* <http://www.metacrawler.com>
- *WebCrawler* <http://www.webcrawler.com>

Mediated search engines: These sites have been assembled and reviewed by people who sometimes provide annotations and commentary about topic areas and specific sites.

- *About.com* <http://www.about.com>
- *Looksmart* <http://search.looksmart.com/>

- *FirstGov* (the "U.S. Government's Official Web Portal") <http://firstgov.gov/>
- *The National Institutes of Health* <http://www.nih.gov>
- *U.S. Census Bureau* <http://www.census.gov>

16i Explore online communication.

The Internet provides access to communities with common interests and varying levels of expertise on different subjects. Carefully evaluate information from these sources (*see Chapter 18: Evaluating Sources, pp. 289–98*). Discussion lists (electronic mailing lists), Usenet news groups, blogs, and social networking sites are the most common communities. Various forums of synchronous communication in which people interact in real time exist as well. Before participating in any forums, observe the way members interact. Online forums can help you with research in the following ways:

- You can get an idea for a paper by finding out what topics interest and concern people and what people think about almost any topic.
- You can zero in on a very specific or current topic.
- You can query an expert in the field about your topic via e-mail or a social networking site.

Caution: The level of expertise among the people who participate in online forums and the scholarly seriousness of the forums themselves vary widely. Look for scholarly forums by way of your library or department Web site, and consider whether participants' claims appear reasonable. (*See also Chapter 18: Evaluating Sources, pp. 289–98.*)

Discussion lists (electronic mailing lists) are networked e-mail conversations on particular topics. Lists can be open (anyone can join) or closed (only certain people, such as members of a particular class or group, can join). If the list is open, you can subscribe by sending a message to a computer that has list-processing software installed on it.

Unlike lists, **Usenet news groups** are posted to a *news server,* a computer that hosts the news group and distributes postings to

TEXTCONNEX

Online Tools for Research

- ***Zotero*** <http://www.zotero.org>: Compatible with the Mozilla Firefox browser (version 2.0 and higher), this program automatically saves citation information for online text and images via your browser. It creates formatted references in multiple styles and helps you organize your sources by assigning tags (categories based on keywords) to them.
- ***Del.icio.us*** <http://www.del.icio.us>: This site allows you to create an online collection of Web links. You can access this list from any computer, and you can organize its entries by assigning tags.
- ***DiRT*** (*Digital Research Tools*) <http://digitalresearchtools.pbwiki.com/>: This site links to online tools that help researchers in the humanities and social sciences perform many tasks, such as collaborating with others, finding sources, and visualizing data.

participating servers. Postings are not automatically distributed by e-mail; you must subscribe to read them.

Podcasts are downloadable audio or video recordings, updated regularly. The Smithsonian provides reliable podcasts on many topics (http://www.si.edu/podcasts). **RSS** (Really Simple Syndication) **feeds** deliver the latest content from continually updated Web sites to your browser or home page. You can use RSS feeds to keep up with information on your topic, once you identify relevent Web sites.

Interactively structured Web sites provide another medium for online communication. **Social networking sites** help people form online communities. **Blogs** (*see Chapter 14*) can be designed to allow readers to post their own comments and queries. Blogs can convey the range of positions on a topic under debate. However, many blog postings consist of unsupported opinion, and they may not be monitored closely for accuracy. **Wikis,** sites designed for online collaboration, allow people both to comment on and to modify one another's contributions. When evaluating information from a wiki, check to see who can update content and whether experts review the changes. If content is not monitored by identified experts, it is safest to check your findings with another source. (*See the box on* Wikipedia *on p. 266.*).

Synchronous communication includes **chat rooms** organized by topic, where people can carry on real-time discussions. **Instant messaging (IM)** links only people who have agreed to form a conversing group. Other formats include virtual worlds such as *Second Life*, multiuser dimensions (MUDs), and object-oriented multiuser dimensions (MOOs). These can be used for collaborative projects.

TEXTCONNEX

Discussion Lists and News Groups

Check the following Web sites for more information about discussion lists and news groups:

- *Tile.net: The Reference to Internet Discussion and Information Lists* <http://tile.net/lists>: Allows you to search for discussion lists by name, description, or domain.
- *Google Groups* <http://www.google.com>: Allows you to access, create, and search news groups.
- *Newsreaders.com* <http://www.newsreaders.com/guide/news.html>: Explains why you would want a newsreader and how to use one.
- *Harley Hahn's Master List of Usenet Newsgroups* <http://www.harley.com/usenet>: A master list of Usenet news groups with descriptions. Search by category or keyword.

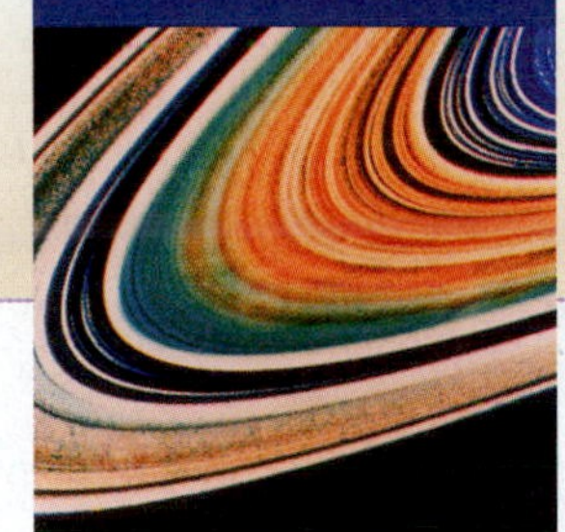

17 Finding and Creating Effective Visuals

Visuals often serve as support for a writer's thesis, sometimes to enhance an argument and other times to constitute the complete argument. A relief organization, for example, might post a series of compelling visuals on its Web site to persuade potential donors to contribute money following a catastrophic event.

For some writing situations, you will be able to prepare or provide your own visuals. You may, for example, provide your own sketch of an experiment, or, as the authors of the lab report in Chapter 8 have done, create bar graphs from data that you have collected (*see section 8f, p. 153*). In other situations, however, you may decide to create a visual from data that you have found in a source, or you may search in your library or on the Internet for a visual to use.

> ***Caution:*** Whether you are using data from a source to create an image or incorporating an image created by someone else into your project, you must give credit to the source of the data or image. Furthermore, if you plan to publish a visual you have selected from a source on a Web site or in another medium, you must obtain permission to use it from the copyright holder, unless the source specifically states that such use is allowed.

17a Find quantitative data and display the data visually.

www.mhhe.com/mhhb2

For resources to begin your search, go to

Research > Discipline Specific Resources

Research writing in many disciplines—especially in the sciences, social sciences, business, math, engineering, and other technical fields—often requires reference to quantitative information. That information generally has more impact when it is displayed visually in a chart, graph, or map than as raw numbers alone. Pie charts, for instance, show percentages of a whole. Bar graphs are often used to compare groups over time. Line graphs also show trends over time, such as the impact of wars on immigration rates and population movements. These ways of showing information are also tools of analysis. (*For examples of graphs and charts and situations in which to use them, see pp. 52–53 in Chapter 3, the box on p. 286, and pp. 69–70 in Chapter 4.*)

1. Finding existing graphs, charts, and maps

www.mhhe.com/mhhb2

For an interactive tutorial, go to

Writing > Visual Rhetoric

As you search for print and online sources (*see Chapter 16*), take notes on useful graphs, charts, or maps that you can incorporate (with proper acknowledgment) into your paper. Some you may find

CHECKLIST

Deciding When to Use an Image in Your Paper

Consider these questions as you look for visuals:

- ☐ What contribution will each image make to the text?
- ☐ What contribution will the set of images make to the text?
- ☐ How many images will you need?
- ☐ Where will each image appear in the text?
- ☐ Does the audience have enough background information to interpret the image in the way you intend?
- ☐ If not, is their additional information you should include in the text?
- ☐ What information needs to be in the caption?
- ☐ Have you reviewed your own text (and perhaps asked a colleague to review it, as well) to see how well the image is "working"—in terms of appropriateness, location, and context?

in online sources. If an image is available in print only, you may be able to use a scanner to print and digitize it. The graph in Figure 17.1 comes from the National Hurricane Center Web site. It shows the position of Hurricane Jeanne on September 23, 2004, and Jeanne's predicted path for the next five days, along with predicted wind speed and intensity.

SOURCE SMART

Citing Data

Make citations of data specific. Indicate the report and page number or Web address(es) where you found the information, as well as any other elements required by your documentation style. If you analyze the data, refer to any analysis in the source before presenting your own interpretation.

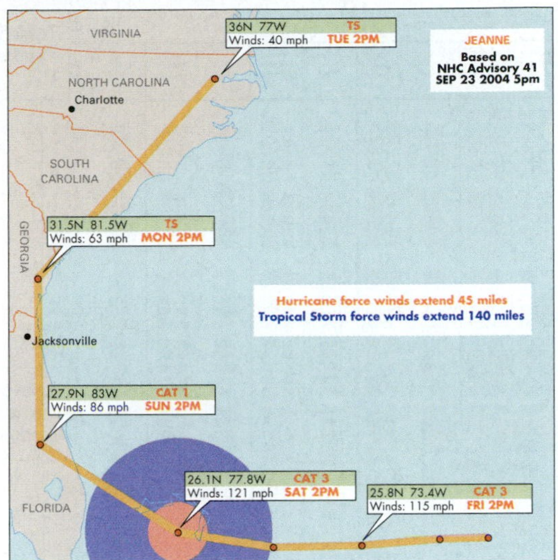

FIGURE 17.1 A map showing the projected path and intensity of Hurricane Jeanne.

2. Creating visuals from quantitative data

Sometimes you may find data presented in writing or in tables that would be effective in your paper as a chart or graph. You can use the data to create a visual using the graphics tools available in spreadsheet or other software.

For example, suppose you were writing a paper on population trends in the United States in the nineteenth century and wanted to illustrate the country's population growth during that period with a line graph. For population data, you might go to the Web site of the U.S. Census Bureau, which provides a wealth of quantitative historical information about the United States, all of it in the public domain. Most Census data, however, appears in tables like the one at the top of Figure 17.2 on the next page. As the figure shows, if you transfer data from such a table to a spreadsheet program or some word-processing programs, you can use the program to create a graph.

3. Displaying the data accurately

Display data in a way that is consistent with your purpose and not misleading to viewers. For example, scholar Nancy Kaplan has pointed out distortions in a graph from a National Endowment for the Arts report on reading practices (*Figure 17.3 on p. 285*). The NEA graph presents the years 1988 to 2004, showing a sharp decline in reading. However, the source for the graph, the National Center for Educational Statistics (NCES), presents a less alarming picture in Figure 17.4. (*See p. 285 to compare these two graphs.*)

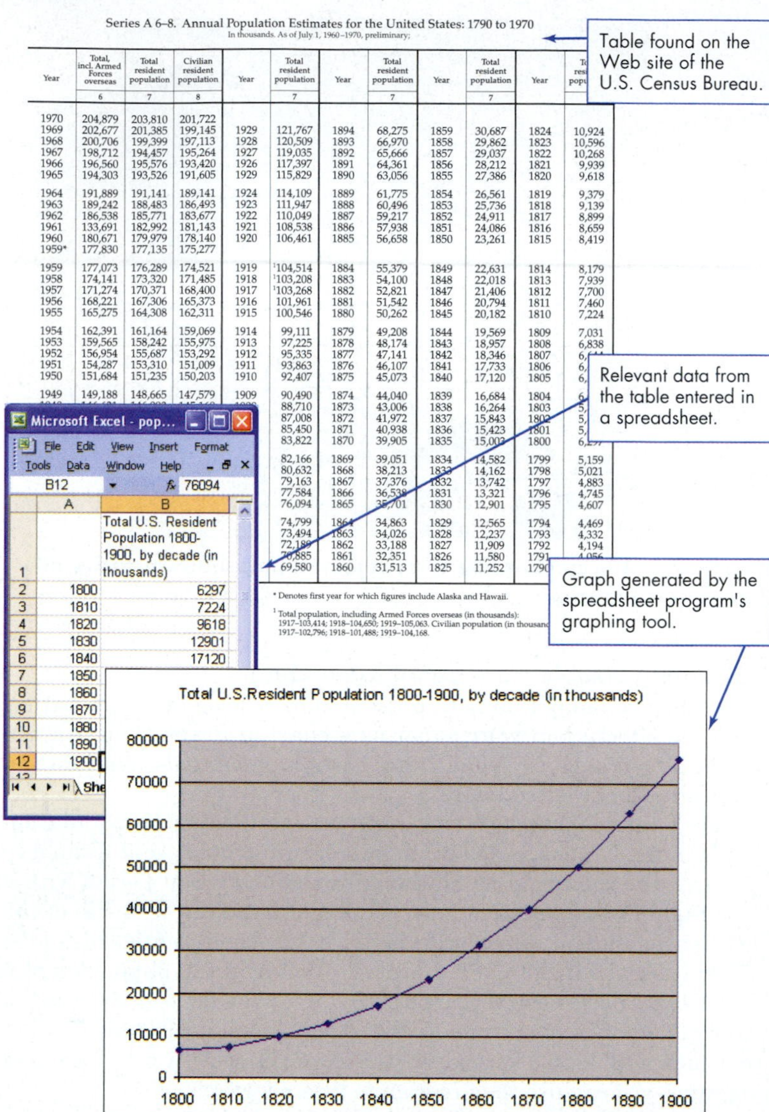

Series A 6–8. Annual Population Estimates for the United States: 1790 to 1970
In thousands. As of July 1, 1960–1970, preliminary;

Year	Total, incl. Armed Forces overseas	Total resident population	Civilian resident population	Year	Total resident population	Year	Total resident population	Year	Total resident population	Year	[illegible]
	6	7	8		7		7		7		
1970	204,879	203,810	201,722								
1969	202,677	201,385	199,145	1929	121,767	1894	68,275	1859	30,687	1824	10,924
1968	200,706	199,399	197,113	1928	120,509	1893	66,970	1858	29,862	1823	10,596
1967	198,712	194,457	195,264	1927	119,035	1892	65,666	1857	29,037	1822	10,268
1966	196,560	195,576	193,420	1926	117,397	1891	64,361	1856	28,212	1821	9,939
1965	194,303	193,526	191,605	1929	115,829	1890	63,056	1855	27,386	1820	9,618
1964	191,889	191,141	189,141	1924	114,109	1889	61,775	1854	26,561	1819	9,379
1963	189,242	188,483	186,493	1923	111,947	1888	60,496	1853	25,736	1818	9,139
1962	186,538	185,771	183,677	1922	110,049	1887	59,217	1852	24,911	1817	8,899
1961	133,691	182,992	181,143	1921	108,538	1886	57,938	1851	24,086	1816	8,659
1960	180,671	179,979	178,140	1920	106,461	1885	56,658	1850	23,261	1815	8,419
1959*	177,830	177,135	175,277								
1959	177,073	176,289	174,521	1919	[1]104,514	1884	55,379	1849	22,631	1814	8,179
1958	174,141	173,320	171,485	1918	[1]103,208	1883	54,100	1848	22,018	1813	7,939
1957	171,274	170,371	168,400	1917	[1]103,268	1882	52,821	1847	21,406	1812	7,700
1956	168,221	167,306	165,373	1916	101,961	1881	51,542	1846	20,794	1811	7,460
1955	165,275	164,308	162,311	1915	100,546	1880	50,262	1845	20,182	1810	7,224
1954	162,391	161,164	159,069	1914	99,111	1879	49,208	1844	19,569	1809	7,031
1953	159,565	158,242	155,975	1913	97,225	1878	48,174	1843	18,957	1808	6,838
1952	156,954	155,687	153,292	1912	95,335	1877	47,141	1842	18,346	1807	[illegible]
1951	154,287	153,310	151,009	1911	93,863	1876	46,107	1841	17,733	1806	[illegible]
1950	151,684	151,235	150,203	1910	92,407	1875	45,073	1840	17,120	1805	[illegible]
1949	149,188	148,665	147,579	1909	90,490	1874	44,040	1839	16,684	1804	[illegible]
					88,710	1873	43,006	1838	16,264	1803	[illegible]
					87,008	1872	41,972	1837	15,843	1802	[illegible]
					85,450	1871	40,938	1836	15,423	1801	[illegible]
					83,822	1870	39,905	1835	15,003	1800	[illegible]
					82,166	1869	39,051	1834	14,582	1799	5,159
					80,632	1868	38,213	1833	14,162	1798	5,021
					79,163	1867	37,376	1832	13,742	1797	4,883
					77,584	1866	36,538	1831	13,321	1796	4,745
					76,094	1865	35,701	1830	12,901	1795	4,607
					74,799	1864	34,863	1829	12,565	1794	4,469
					73,494	1863	34,026	1828	12,237	1793	4,332
					72,189	1862	33,188	1827	11,909	1792	4,194
					70,885	1861	32,351	1826	11,580	1791	[illegible]
					69,580	1860	31,513	1825	11,252	1790	[illegible]

* Denotes first year for which figures include Alaska and Hawaii.

[1] Total population, including Armed Forces overseas (in thousands): 1917–103,414; 1918–104,650; 1919–105,063. Civilian population (in thousand[illegible] 1917–102,796; 1918–101,488; 1919–104,168.

FIGURE 17.2 Using a spreadsheet program to create a graph from data in a table.

The NCES graph indicates that reading levels have fluctuated little from 1971 to 2004. In addition, the NEA graph is not consistent in its units: the period 1984 to 1988 takes up the same amount of space as 1988 to 1990. In selectively displaying and distorting data, the NEA graph stacks the deck to argue for the existence of a reading crisis.

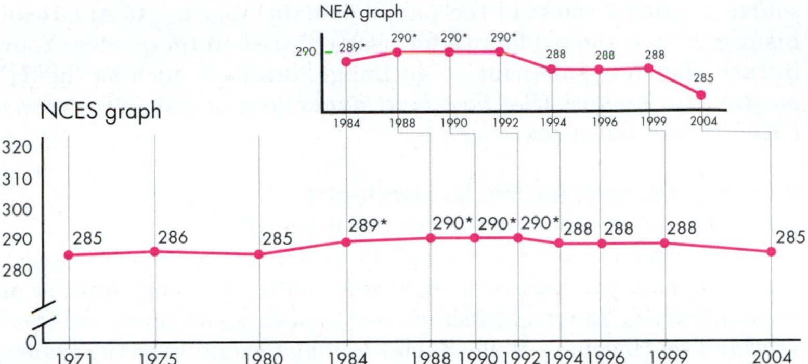

FIGURE 17.3 NEA graph: A distorted display of reading practices indicates a decline.

FIGURE 17.4 NCES graph: An accurate display of reading practices shows only mild fluctuations.

Avoid intentionally or unintentionally distorting data. Do not use photo-editing software to alter photographs. Plot the axes of line and bar graphs so that they do not misrepresent data. (*See Chapter 5, pp. 91–93.*)

17b Search for appropriate images in online and print sources.

Photographs, pictures of artwork, drawings, diagrams, and maps can provide visual support for many kinds of papers, particularly in the humanities (English and other languages, philosophy, music, theater, and other performing arts). As with a display of quantitative data, you might choose an image from a source to use in your paper, or you might create one. If you were preparing a report comparing the way corporations are organized, for example, you might use organization charts that appear in corporate reports. Alternatively, you might use your word processor's drawing features to create your own organization charts based on information you find in the corporate reports. When using an image from another source, be sure to cite it correctly. If the image will appear on a public Web site, ask the copyright holder for permission.

1. Search online image collections and subscription databases

Several libraries and other archival institutions maintain collections of images online. The Library of Congress, for example, is a rich source of images (most in the public domain) relating to American history. Follow the guidelines for usage posted on these sites. Your library also may subscribe to an image database such as the *AP Multimedia Archive*. *(See the "TextConnex" box on page 288 for the URLs of these image collections.)*

www.mhhe.com/ mhhb2
For a selection of search engines, go to
Research > Additional Links on Research

2. Using a search engine to conduct a keyword search for images on the Internet

Many search engines have the ability to search the Web for images alone. Suppose you were writing a paper on the northern frontier of Roman Britain. You might include a map of England separated from Scotland by Hadrian's Wall. Such an image would help the reader understand the relationship between these different territories. To find an appropriate image you could conduct an image search on

CHECKLIST

What Kind of Chart or Graph Should I Use?

In deciding on the kind of chart or graph to use, consider these questions:

- ☐ What information do you want to show, and why?
- ☐ What options do you have for displaying the information?
- ☐ How much context do you want to include, and why?
- ☐ How many charts or graphs might you need?
- ☐ How detailed should each one be, and why?
- ☐ Will your visual serve to analyze the future, or will it report on the past?
- ☐ How dynamic does the chart or graph need to be?
- ☐ What information will you leave out or minimize, and how important is that loss?
- ☐ What other information—an introduction, an explanation, a summary, an interpretation—will your readers need to make sense of the chart or graph?

(See also Chapter 3, pp. 52–53.)

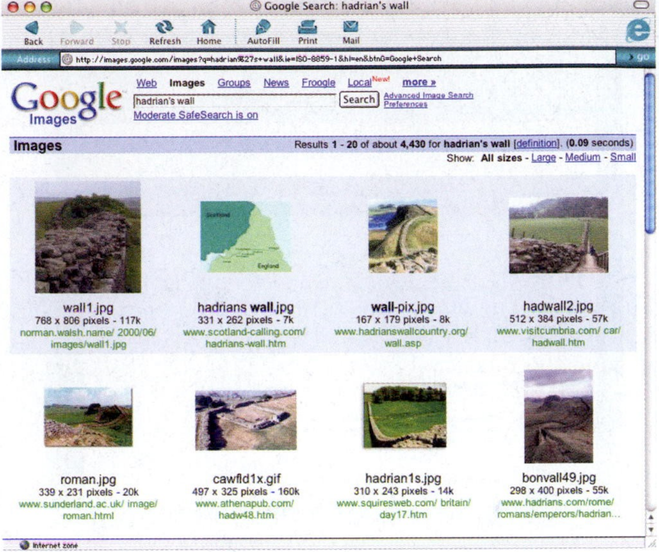

FIGURE 17.5 An image search on *Google*. A search using the term *Hadrian's Wall* brings up pictures of the wall itself, as well as maps of its location and other images, some relevant and some not.

Google by clicking on the Images option, and entering the keyword *Hadrian's Wall,* as shown in Figure 17.5.

Image- and media-sharing sites such as *Flickr* and *YouTube* can provide sources for multimedia projects. Read the information on the site carefully to see what uses are permitted.

The *Creative Commons* site (www.creativecommons.org) lets you search for material with a *Creative Commons* license. Such a license, shown in Figure 17.6 on the next page, states permitted uses of the content. The material shown can be reproduced or altered for noncommercial purposes, as long as it is cited.

Assume that copyright applies to material on the Web unless the site says otherwise. If your project will be published or placed on a public Web site, you must obtain permission to use this material. (*See Chapter 20: Plagiarism, Copyright, and Intellectual Property, pp. 306–14*).

Caution: The results of Internet image searches need to be carefully evaluated for relevance and reliability. (*See Chapter 18: Evaluating Sources, pp. 290–98.*) Make sure you record proper source information as well.

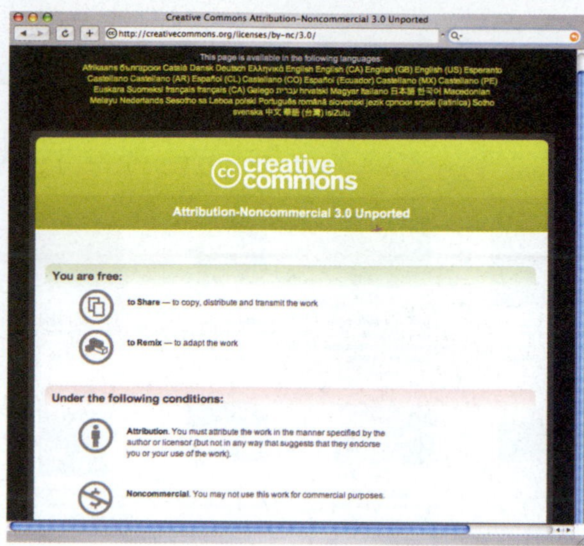

FIGURE 17.6 Creative Commons license. This page shows the terms of use for a particular online work.

TEXTCONNEX

Some Online Image Collections

Art Institute of Chicago <http://www.artic.edu/aic/index.html>: Selected works from the museum's collection

Library of Congress <http://www.loc.gov/>

National Archives Digital Classroom <http://www.archives.gov/digital_classroom/index.html>: Documents and photographs from American history

National Aeronautics and Space Administration <http://www.nasa.gov/vision/universe/features/index.html>: Images and multimedia features on space exploration

National Park Service Digital Image Archive <http://photo.itc.nps.gov/storage/images/index.html>: Thousands of public-domain photographs of U.S. national parks

New York Public Library <www.nypl.org/digital/>

Schomburg Center for Research in Black Culture <www.nypl.org/research/sc/sc.html>

VRoma: A Virtual Community for Teaching and Learning Classics <http://www.vroma.org/>: Images and other resources related to ancient Rome

3. Scanning images from a book or journal

You can use a scanner to scan some images from books and journals into a composition, but as always, only if you are sure your use is within fair use guidelines. (*See Chapter 20: Plagiarism, Copyright, and Intellectual Property, pp. 313–14.*) Credit the source of the image as well as the publication in which you found it.

18 Evaluating Sources

Digital technologies may grant fast access to a tremendous variety of sources, but it is up to you to evaluate each potential source to determine whether it is both *relevant* and *reliable*. A source is relevant if it pertains to your research topic. A source is reliable if it provides trustworthy information.

Evaluating sources requires you to think critically and make judgments about which sources will be useful for answering your research question. This process helps you manage your research and focus your time on those sources that deserve close scrutiny.

18a Question print sources.

Just because something is in print does not make it relevant or true. How can you determine whether a print source is likely to be both reliable and useful? Before assessing a source's reliability, make sure it is relevant to your topic. The box on the following pages provides some questions to ask about any source you are considering.

Relevance can be a tricky matter. Your sociology instructor will expect you to give special preference to sociological sources in a project on the organization of the workplace. Your business management

For MULTILINGUAL WRITERS

Questioning Sources

Although some cultures emphasize respect for established authors, the intellectual tradition of U.S. universities values careful questioning. Consider the pertinence and reliability of all sources.

CHECKLIST

Relevance and Reliabilty of Sources

1. Judging relevance

- ☐ **Do the source's title and subtitle indicate that it addresses your specific research question?** Is the level and degree of detail appropriate?
- ☐ **What is the publication date?** Is the material up-to-date, classic, or historic? The concept of "up to date" depends on discipline and topic. Ask your instructor how recent your sources need to be.
- ☐ **Does the table of contents of a book indicate that it contains useful information?**
- ☐ **If the source is a book, does it have an index?** Scan the index for keywords related to your topic.
- ☐ **Does the abstract at the beginning or summary at the end of an article suggest it will be useful?** An abstract or a summary presents the main points made in an article.
- ☐ **Does the work contain subheadings?** Skim the headings to see whether they indicate that the source covers useful information.

2. Judging reliability

- ☐ **What information can you find about the writer's credentials?** Consult biographical information about the writer in the source itself, in a biographical dictionary, or with an Internet search of the writer's name. Is the writer affiliated with a research institution? Is the writer an expert on the topic? Is the writer cited frequently in other sources about the topic?
- ☐ **Who is the publisher?** University presses and academic publishers are considered more scholarly than the popular press. Ask your instructor which publishers are most prominent in a specific discipline.

- ☐ **Does the work include a bibliography of works consulted or cited?** Trustworthy writers cite a variety of sources and document their citations properly. Does this source do so? Does the source include a variety of citations?

- ☐ **Does the work argue reasonably for its position and treat other views fairly?** What kind of tone does the author use? Is the work objective or subjective? Are the writer's arguments clear and logical? What is the author's point of view? Does he or she present opposing views fairly? (*For more on evaluating arguments, see Chapter 10: Arguments, pp. 184–93.*)

instructor will expect you to use material from that field in a project on the same topic. Be prepared to find that some promising sources turn out to be less relevant than you first thought.

 18b Question Internet sources.

www.mhhe.com/mhhb2

For an interactive tutorial on using the CARS checklist, go to

Research > CARS Source Evaluation Tutor

Although the questions in the Checklist box on pages 290–91 should be applied to online sources, Web resources also require additional methods of assuring the credibility of information presented. Most of the material in the library has been evaluated to some extent for credibility. Editors and publishers have reviewed the content of books, magazines, journals, and newspapers. Some presses and publications are more reputable than others. Subscription databases generally compile articles that originally appeared in print, and librarians try to purchase the most reliable databases. While you should still

SOURCE SMART

Evaluating Citations

When you look for sources using a database or library catalog, save yourself time by eliminating inappropriate search results. Based on the citation alone, you can judge:

- The author's level of expertise (with a simple Web, catalog, or database search).
- The title's relevance to your research question.
- The source's currency.
- The publisher's or publication's reputation.

evaluate all sources, you can have some confidence that most of the material you find in the library is credible.

In contrast, anyone can create a Web site that looks attractive but contains nonsense. Similarly, the people who post to blogs, discussion lists, and news groups may not be experts or even marginally well informed. So even though information on the Web may be valuable and timely, you must assess its credibility carefully. Consult the CARS (Credibility, Accuracy, Reasonableness, Support) Checklist box on pages 297–98 and consider the following questions when determining whether online information is reliable:

1. Who is hosting the site? Is the site hosted by a university or by a government agency (like the National Science Foundation or the National Endowment for the Humanities)? In general, sites hosted by institutions devoted to advancing knowledge are more likely to be trustworthy. However, they remain open to critical inquiry (as demonstrated by the NEA graph on p. 285).
2. Who is speaking on the site? A nationally recognized biologist is likely to be more credible on biological topics than a graduate student in biology. If you cannot identify the author, who is the editor or compiler? If you cannot identify an author, editor, or compiler, it is prudent not to use the source.
3. What links does the site provide? If it is networked to sites with obviously unreasonable or inaccurate content, you must question the credibility of the original site.
4. Is the information on the site supported with documentation from scholarly or otherwise reliable sources? Reliable sources of information could include government reports, for example. Do other sources cite this one?

Consider the following factors as well.

1. Assessing authority and credibility

Are the author (or editor) and sponsor of the Web site identifiable? Is the author's biographical information included? What does a Web search of the author's name reveal? Is there any indication that the author has relevant expertise on the subject? The following extensions in the Web address, or uniform resource locator (URL), can help you determine the type of site (which often tells you something about its purpose):

.com	commercial (business)	**.edu**	educational	**.mil**	military
.org	nonprofit organization	**.gov**	U.S. government	**.net**	network

TEXTCONNEX

Evaluating Sources

"Evaluating Web Pages: Techniques to Apply & Questions to Ask" <http://www.lib.berkeley.edu/TeachingLib/Guides/Internet/Evaluate.html>: This site from the UC Berkeley Library provides a step-by-step guide to evaluating online sources.

"Evaluating Sources of Information" <http://owl.english.purdue.edu/handouts/research/r_evalsource.html>: From the Purdue Online Writing Lab, this page provides guidelines for evaluating print and online sources.

A tilde (~) followed by a name in a URL usually means the site is a personal home page not affiliated with any organization.

2. Evaluating audience and purpose

How does the appearance of the site work with the tone of any written material to suggest an audience? (For example, a commercial site such as *Nike.com* uses music, graphics, and streaming technology to appeal to a certain kind of consumer.)

As Figures 18.1, 18.2, and 18.3 on the following pages suggest, a site's purpose influences the way it presents information and the reliability of that information. Is the site's main purpose to advocate a cause, raise money, advertise a product or service, provide factual information, present research results, provide news, share personal information, or offer entertainment? Sites focused on scholarship, with well-documented evidence, will be most useful to you.

Always try to view a site's home page so that you can best evaluate its audience and purpose. To find the home page, you may need to delete everything after the first slash in the URL.

3. Judging objectivity and bias

Look carefully at the purpose and tone of the text. Is there evidence of obvious bias? Nearly all sources express a point of view or bias either explicitly or implicitly. You should consult sources that represent a range of opinions on your topic. However, unreasonable sources have no place in academic debate. Clues that indicate a lack of reasonableness include an intemperate tone, broad claims, exaggerated statements of significance, conflicts of interest, no recognition of opposing views, and strident attacks on opposing views. (*For more on evaluating arguments, see Chapter 10: Arguments, pp. 184–93.*)

4. Weighing relevance and timeliness

In what ways does the information from the online source specifically address your topic or thesis? Are the site's intended audience and purpose similar to yours? Does the site indicate how recently it was updated, and are most of its links still working?

5. Context

How does the source fit with other information you have found or already know about the subject? If the source is a blog or a post on a discussion list, do others' comments or posts make the writer appear more credible?

Consider a student writing a paper on the reintroduction of gray wolves in the western United States following their near extinction. Many environmentalists have favored this program, while farmers and ranchers have worried about its impact on livestock. Recent debate has centered on whether wolf populations have recovered sufficiently to no longer need protection.

The student conducts a keyword search using an online search engine and finds the site in Figure 18.1, from the U.S. Fish and Wildlife Service. This site focuses on the gray wolf population in

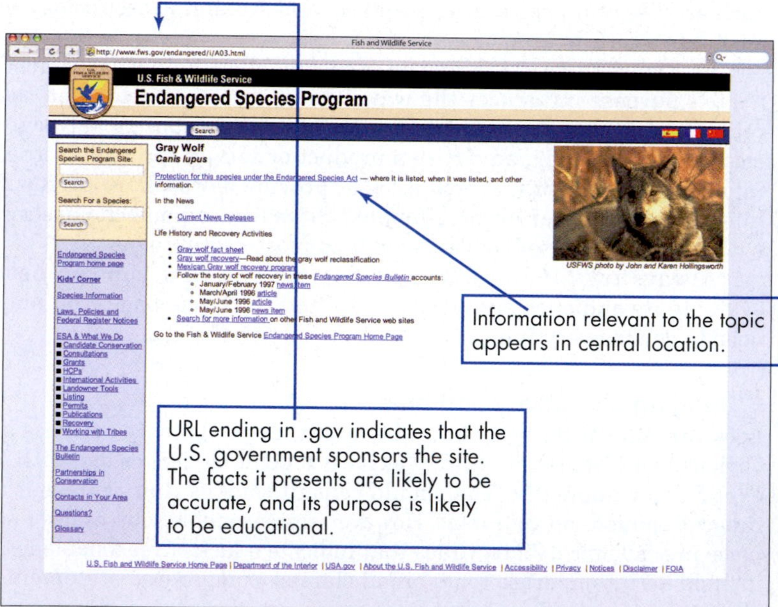

FIGURE 18.1 U.S. Fish & Wildlife Service Endangered Species Program site on the gray wolf. This government site provides information on the efforts to preserve and rebuild the gray wolf population in the United States.

America and its status under the Endangered Species Act. The site has a reasonable, somewhat objective stance. As the site of a U.S. government agency, its data is likely to be accurate, although such sites are not immune from politics or bias. For example, the U.S. Fish & Wildlife Service conducted the wolf reintroduction program and probably approves of it (whether or not it endorses continued protection for wolves). Information on the site appears in a simple, easy-to-follow format, indicating an educational purpose. It links to other government sites, such as the Department of the Interior site. Scrolling down, the student sees the site has been updated recently. This site's apparent authority, credibility, and purpose make it a good source for facts about the wolf reintroduction program.

Next the student finds the site in Figure 18.2. Following the link that says "About us," the student learns that the site is sponsored by the WWF (originally World Wildlife Fund), a nonprofit organization that advocates for environmental conservation. The site's purpose appears to be educational and persuasive: it includes information about wolves and a call to action on their behalf. It includes policy papers with clearly documented sources for the data, suggesting the

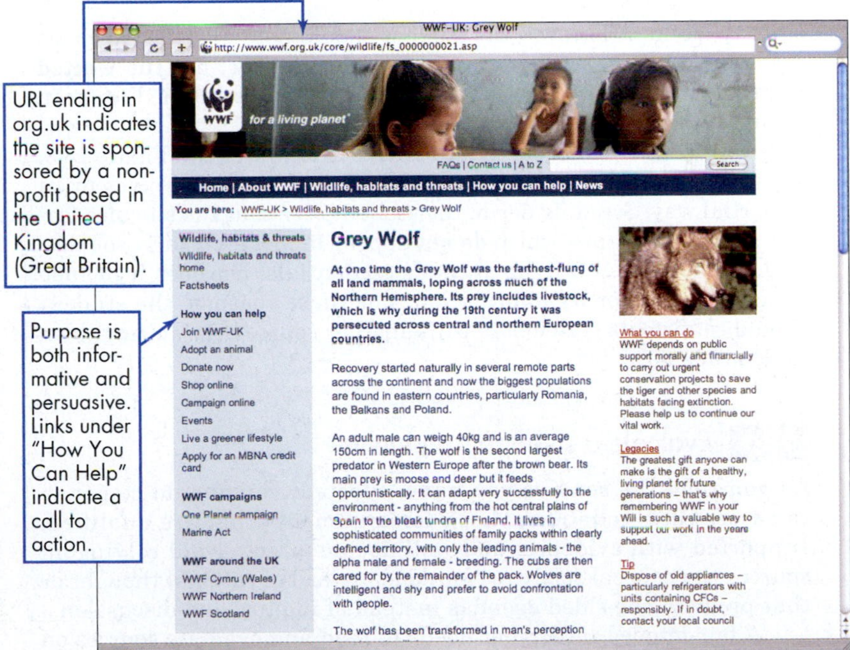

FIGURE 18.2 WWF (formerly World Wildlife Fund) page about Europe's grey wolf. This advocacy site describes efforts to preserve a wolf population in Europe.

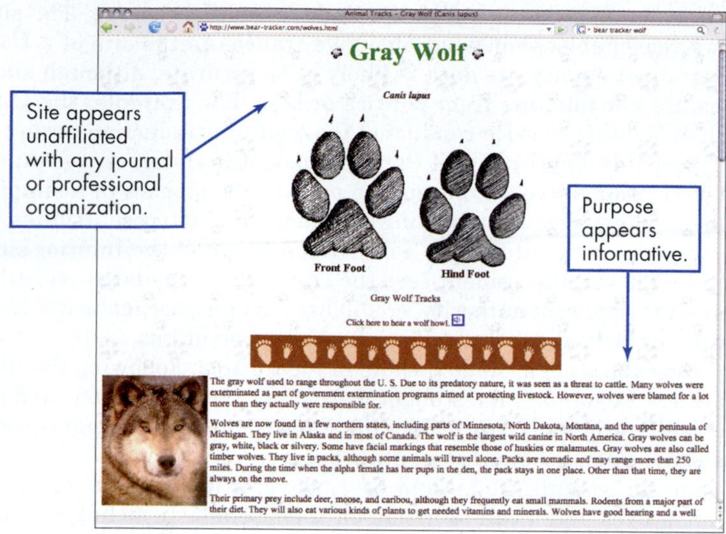

FIGURE 18.3 **This site's information appears to be accurate, but it does not document its sources or present its author's credentials.**

site's reliability. However, the student should note that the site deals only with the reintroduction of wolves in Europe, not the United States. It would be a relevant source if the student used the European reintroduction program as an example.

After further research, the student reaches the site in Figure 18.3. This site gives apparently accurate information about wolves in an impartial way. Scrolling down, the student sees that the site also features advertisements, which do not appear in most scholarly sources. The site does not state the author's credentials, nor does it include documentation for its information. For these reasons, the student should confirm its statements with another source before using them in an academic paper.

18c Evaluate a source's arguments.

As you read the sources you have selected, you should continue to assess their reliability. Look for arguments that are qualified, supported with evidence, and well documented. Avoid relying on sources that appeal solely to emotions instead of rational thought or that promote one-sided agendas instead of inquiry and discussion.

A fair-minded researcher needs to read and evaluate sources on many sides of an issue. Doing so includes consulting relevant primary sources if they exist.

CHECKLIST

Using the CARS Checklist to Evaluate Web Sites

A Web site that is **c**redible, **a**ccurate, **r**easonable, and **s**upported (CARS) should meet the following criteria.

Credibility

- ☐ The source is trustworthy; you would consider a print version to be authoritative (for example, an online edition of a respected newspaper or major news magazine).
- ☐ The argument and use of evidence are clear and logical.
- ☐ The author's or sponsor's credentials are available (visit the home page and look for a link that says "About Us").
- ☐ Quality control is evident (spelling and grammar are correct; links are functional).
- ☐ The source is a known or respected authority; it has organizational support (such as a university, a research institution, or a major news publication).

Accuracy

- ☐ The site is updated frequently, if not daily (and includes "last-updated" information).
- ☐ The site is factual, not speculative, and provides evidence for its assertions.
- ☐ The site is detailed; text appears in full paragraphs.
- ☐ The site is comprehensive, including archives, links, and additional resources. A search feature and table of contents or tabs allow users to quickly find the information they need.
- ☐ The site's purpose includes completeness and accuracy.

Reasonableness

- ☐ The site is fair, balanced, and objective. (Look at comments on a blog or related messages on a news group.)

(continued)

- ☐ The site makes its purpose clear (is it selling something? prompting site visitors to sign a petition? promoting a new film?).
- ☐ The site contains no conflicts of interest.
- ☐ The site content does not include fallacies or a slanted tone (*for more on fallacies, see Chapter 10: Arguments, pp. 188–91*).

Support

- ☐ The site lists sources for its information, providing links where appropriate.
- ☐ The site clarifies which content it is responsible for and which links are created by unrelated authors or sponsors.
- ☐ The site provides contact information for its authors and/or sponsors.
- ☐ If the site is an academic resource, it follows the conventions of a specific citation style (for example, MLA, APA).

Exercise 18.1 Web site evaluation

Working alone or in groups, choose one of the following topics:

1. The cost of prescription drugs in the United States
2. Alternative energy sources
3. Immigration
4. Global warming
5. The role of private and charter schools in a democracy

For your topic, find at least three Web sites and analyze them according to the CARS checklist. Describe and rate each site's credibility, accuracy, reasonablenes, and support. Be prepared to share example Web pages with your class (either print them out, or use a projection screen) and to point out how they demonstrate the characteristics you have identified.

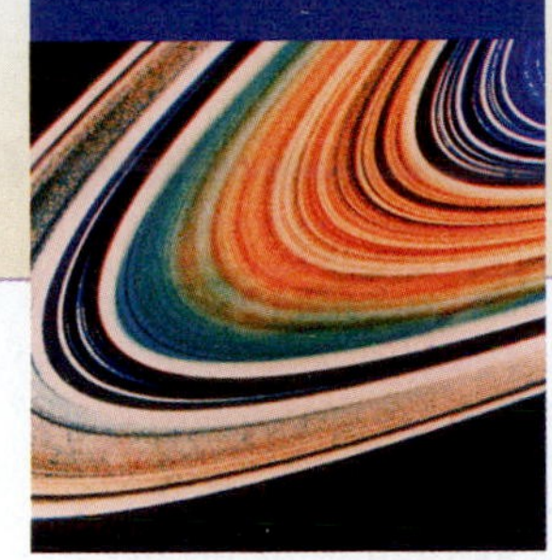

19 Doing Research in the Archive, Field, and Lab

Research involves more than finding answers to questions in books, journal articles, and other print and online resources (**secondary research**). (*See Chapter 15: Understanding Research, pp. 250–59.*) When you conduct **primary research**—looking up old maps, consulting census records, polling community members, interviewing participants in a campus protest, observing the natural world—you participate in the discovery of knowledge.

The three kinds of primary research discussed in this chapter are archival research, field research, and laboratory research:

- **Archival research:** An **archive** is a cataloged collection of documents, manuscripts, or other materials, possibly including receipts, wills, photographs, sound recordings, or other kinds of media. Usually, an archive is organized around one key person, movement, circumstance, or phenomenon.
- **Field research:** Field research takes you out into the world to gather and record information.
- **Laboratory research:** Most science courses you take will include a laboratory component. In the laboratory, you work individually or on a team to record each step of an experiment. Eventually, you will create your own experiments.

19a Adhere to ethical principles when doing primary research.

In the archive, field, or lab, you work directly with something precious and immediate: an original record, a group of people, or special

CHARTING the TERRITORY

Research in the Disciplines

Different forms of primary research are characteristic of different disciplines. Here are some examples:

- **Archival research:** Languages and literature; education; music and the performing arts; visual arts; media and popular culture; social sciences
- **Field research:** Social sciences; marketing and advertising; media and communication
- **Laboratory research:** Life sciences; physical sciences; computer science; engineering

materials. An ethical researcher shows respect for materials, experimental subjects, fellow researchers, and readers. Here are some guidelines for ethical research:

- Handle original documents and materials with great care, always leaving sources and data available for other researchers.
- Report your sources and results accurately.
- Follow proper procedures when working with human participants.

Research with human participants should also adhere to the following basic principles:

- **Confidentiality:** People who fill out surveys, participate in focus groups, or respond to interviews should be assured that their names will not be used without their permission.
- **Informed consent:** Before participating in an experiment, all participants must sign a statement affirming that they understand the general purpose of the research.
- **Minimal risk:** Participants in experiments should not incur any risks greater than they do in everyday life.
- **Protection of vulnerable groups:** Researchers must be held strictly accountable for research done with the physically disabled, prisoners, those who are mentally incompetent, minors, the elderly, and pregnant women.

Be fair when you refute the primary research or the views of others. Even if your purpose is to prove fellow researchers wrong, review their work and state their viewpoints in words that they themselves would recognize as accurate.

19b Prepare yourself for archival research.

Archives are found in libraries, museums, other institutions, private collections, and on video- and audiotape. Some archival collections are accessible through the Internet. Your own attic may contain family archives—letters, diaries, and photograph collections that could have value to a researcher. The more you know ahead of time about your area of study, the more likely you will be to see the significance of an item in an archival collection.

Archives generally require that you telephone or e-mail to arrange a time for your visit. Some archives may be restricted; call or e-mail well in advance to find out whether you will need references, a letter of introduction, or other qualifying papers.

Archives also generally require you to present a photo identification, and to leave personal items at a locker or coat check. They will also have strict policies about reproducing materials and rarely if ever allow anything to leave the premises. The more you know about the archive's policies and procedures before you visit, the more productive your visit will be.

19c Plan your field research carefully.

Field research involves recording observations, conducting interviews, and administering surveys. If your research plans include visiting a place of business, a house of worship, a school or hospital, or nearly any other building, call first and obtain permission. Explain the nature of your project, the date and time you would like to visit, how much time you think you will need, and exactly what it is you will be doing (observing? interviewing people? taking photographs?). Ask for a confirming letter or e-mail. If you need to cancel or reschedule your visit, be sure to give ample notice. Always write a thank-you note after you have concluded your research.

If you are denied permission to do your field research at a particular place, do not take it personally. Do *not* attempt to conduct your research without first obtaining permission. To do so is unethical and may constitute illegal trespassing.

1. Observing and writing field notes

When you use direct observation, keep careful records in order to retain the information you gather (*see Figure 19.1 on p. 303*). Here are some guidelines to follow:

- Be systematic in your observations, but be alert to unexpected behavior.
- Record what you see and hear as objectively as possible.
- Take more notes than you think you will need.
- When appropriate, categorize the types of behavior you are looking for, and devise a system for counting instances of each type.
- When you have recorded data over a significant period of time, group your observations into categories for more careful study.

(*For advice on conducting direct observations for a case study, see Chapter 9: Interpretive Analyses, pp. 175–78.*)

2. Conducting interviews

Interviews may be conducted in person, by phone, or online. To be useful as research tools, they require systematic preparation and implementation.

TEXTCONNEX

Online Information about Archives

Here are some Internet sites that will help you find and understand a wide range of archival sources:

- ***American Memory*** <http://memory.loc.gov/ammem>: This site offers access to more than 9 million digital items from over 100 collections of material on U.S. history and culture.
- ***ArchivesUSA*** <http://archives.chadwyck.com>: This subscription service is available through ProQuest. It provides information about 150,000 collections of primary source material and more than 5,000 other manuscript repositories.
- ***Radio Program Archive*** <http://umdrive.memphis.edu/mbensman/public>: This site lists radio archives available from the University of Memphis and explains how to obtain audio cassettes of significant radio programs.
- ***Repositories of Primary Sources*** <www.uidaho.edu/special-collections/OtherRepositories.html>: This site lists more than 5,000 Web sites internationally, including holdings of manuscripts, rare books, historical photographs, and other archival materials.
- ***Television News Archive*** <http://tvnews.vanderbilt.edu>: This site provides summaries of television news broadcasts and information on how to order videocassettes.
- ***U.S. National Archives and Records Administration*** (NARA) <http://www.nara.gov>: Learn how to use the National Archives in this site's research room, and then search the site for the documents you want.
- ***Virtual Library Museums Page*** <http://www.icom.org/vlmp>: This site lists online museums throughout the world.
- ***Women Writers Project*** <http://www.wwp.brown.edu/texts/wwoentry.html>: This site lists archived texts—by pre-Victorian women writers—that are available through the project.

- Identify appropriate people for your interviews based on your purpose.
- Do background research, and plan a list of open-ended questions.
- Take careful notes, and if possible make a recording of the interview (but only if you have obtained your subject's permission beforehand). Verify quotations.
- Follow up on vague responses with questions that ask for specific information. Do not rush your interviewees.

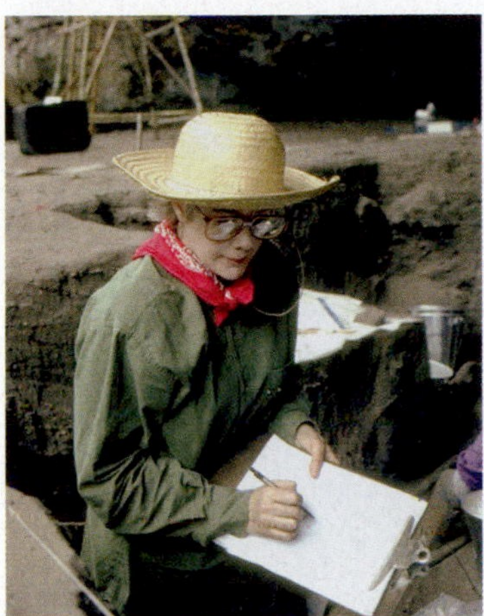

FIGURE 19.1 Observing and taking notes. Systematic, purposeful observation and careful note taking are crucial to the success of all field work. Archeologist Anna Roosevelt takes notes during the excavation of a site in the Amazon region of South America.

- Politely probe inconsistencies and contradictions.
- Write thank-you notes to interviewees, and later send them copies of your report.

You might identify appropriate subjects on your campus through a relevant academic department. For example, if your research paper is on the effects of globalization on manufacturing jobs in the United States, you might visit the home pages of your campus business and political science departments to see whether anyone on the faculty is studying that issue.

Group interviews, called *focus groups,* serve in a number of fields, including marketing, education, and psychology. To find subjects for

SOURCE SMART

Quoting from Interviews

Before an interview, obtain permission to quote the interviewee. If the interview is not being recorded (or captured on a transcript if online), use oversized quotation marks to enclose direct quotations in your notes. Record the interviewee's name and the location and date of the interview in your research notebook. Afterward, verify quotations with your interviewee.

a focus group, consider posting flyers around campus or advertising in your campus newspaper.

3. Taking surveys

Conducted either orally or in writing, **surveys** are made up of structured questions. Written surveys are called **questionnaires.**

The surveys and polls used by political campaigns and the news media are designed with the help of statisticians and tabulated according to complex mathematical equations. For many college research projects, an informal survey (one not designed to be statistically accurate) may be adequate. Try to approximate a random sampling of a large group.

LEARNING in COLLEGE

Conducting a Survey

Student Lara Delforest wanted to know if students would support a plan to provide more shuttle-bus service from existing parking garages.

She asked these questions to qualify a potential respondent:

1. Are you a student on this campus?
2. Do you currently drive to campus?
3. If you do drive, where do you park?
4. If you don't drive, how do you get to campus?

Lara thanked but did not ask further questions of respondents who were not regularly on campus or who did not drive or take public transportation. She asked these additional questions of the rest:

5. Is the availability of parking on or near campus a factor in your decision to drive or not to drive?
6. If you drive to campus, are you aware of other options? If so, what are those options?
7. For each of the options you just mentioned, explain what would make you consider or reject each one.
8. Are you in favor of creating more parking spaces on campus? Why or why not?
9. Would you be in favor of adding additional campus shuttle buses from existing off-campus parking? Why or why not?

Lara asked the respondents their full names (but accepted just first names) so that she could accurately identify them. To keep her notes organized, Lara turned to a new page of her notebook for each respondent.

The following suggestions will help you prepare informal surveys:

- **Define your purpose and your target population.** Are you trying to gauge attitudes, learn about typical behaviors, or both?
- **Write clear directions and questions.** For example, if you are asking multiple-choice questions, make sure that you cover all possible options and that your options do not overlap.
- **Use neutral language.** Make sure your questions do not suggest a preference for one answer over another.
- **Make the survey brief and easy to complete.** Most informal surveys should be no longer than one page (front and back).

Many colleges have offices that must review and approve student surveys. Check to see what guidelines your school may have.

19d Keep a notebook when doing lab research.

To provide a complete and accurate account of your laboratory work, keep careful records in a notebook. The following guidelines will help you take accurate notes on your research:

1. **Record immediate, on-the-spot, accurate notes on what happens in the lab.** Write down as much detail as possible. Measure precisely; do not estimate. Identify major pieces of apparatus, unusual chemicals, and laboratory animals in enough detail that a reader can determine, for example, the size or type of equipment you used. Use drawings, when appropriate, to illustrate complicated equipment setups. Include tables, when useful, to present results.
2. **Follow a basic format.** Present your results in a format that allows you to communicate all the major features of an experiment. The five basic sections you need are title, purpose, materials and methods, results, and conclusions. (*See Chapter 8: Informative Reports, pp. 147–54.*)
3. **Write in complete sentences.** Resist the temptation to use shorthand to record your notes. Later, the complete sentences will provide a clear record of your procedures and results. Highlight connections within and between sentences by using the following transitions: *then, next, consequently, because,* and *therefore.* Cause-effect relationships should be clear.

4. **Revise and correct your laboratory notebook in visible ways when necessary.** If you make mistakes in recording laboratory results, correct them as clearly as possible, either by erasing or by crossing out and rewriting on the original sheet. If you make an uncorrectable mistake in your lab notebook, simply fold the sheet lengthwise and mark "omit" on the face side.

   Unanticipated results often occur in the lab, and you may find yourself jotting down notes on a convenient piece of scrap paper. Attach these notes to your notebook.

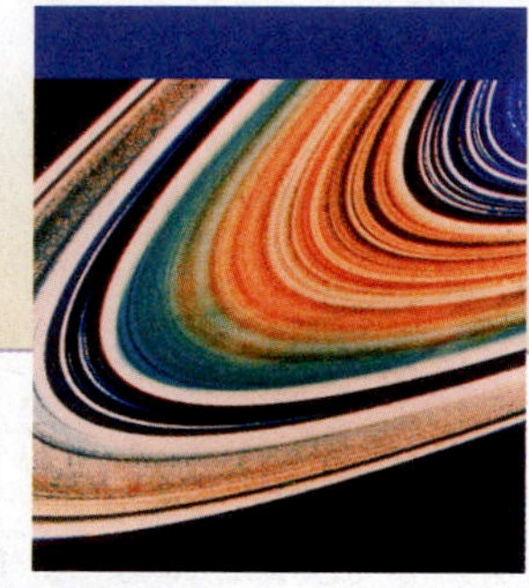

20 Plagiarism, Copyright, and Intellectual Property

www.mhhe.com/mhhb2
For more information, go to
Research > Avoiding Plagiarism > What Is Plagiarism?

Integrity and honesty require us to acknowledge others, especially when we use their words or ideas. Researchers who fail to acknowledge their sources—either intentionally or unintentionally—commit plagiarism. Buying a term paper from an online paper mill or "borrowing" a friend's completed assignment are obvious forms of plagiarism. But plagiarism also involves paraphrasing or summarizing others' material without properly citing the source of the idea or information. (*See Chapter 21: Working with Sources and Avoiding Plagiarism, pp. 322–32, for more on paraphrasing and summarizing.*)

Journalists who are caught plagiarizing are publicly exposed and often fired by the publications they write for. Scholars who fail to acknowledge the words and ideas of others lose their professional credibility, and often their jobs. Students who plagiarize may receive a failing grade for the assignment or course and face other disciplinary action—including expulsion. Your campus probably has a written policy regarding plagiarism and its consequences.

The Internet has made many types of sources available, and it can be unclear what, when, and how to cite. For example, bloggers and other Web authors often reproduce material from other sites, while some musicians make their music available for free download. Although the line between "original" and "borrowed" appears to be blurring, there are guidelines to help you credit sources appropriately.

20a Understand how plagiarism relates to copyright and intellectual property.

Related to plagiarism are copyright and intellectual property, which apply to *published* use of someone else's work. **Copyright** is the legal right to control the reproduction of any original work—a piece of writing, a musical composition, a play, a movie, a computer program, a photograph, a work of art. A copyrighted work is the **intellectual property** of the copyright holder, whether that entity is a publisher, a record company, an entertainment conglomerate, or the individual creator of the work. This section provides additional information on these important legal concepts.

1. Copyright

A copyrighted text—such as a novel, a short story in a magazine, or an article in an academic journal—cannot be reproduced (in print or online) without the written permission of the copyright holder. The copyright protects the right of authors and publishers to make money from their productions. The legal efforts of some musicians and recording companies to stop the free downloading of music from the Internet are based on copyright law. The musicians and companies claim—and the

SOURCE SMART

Determining What Is "Common Knowledge"

Information that an audience could be expected to know from many sources is considered common knowledge. You do not need to cite common knowledge if you use your own wording and sentence structure. Common knowledge can take various forms, including at least these four:

- Folktales with no particular author (for example, Johnny Appleseed spread apple trees across the United States)
- Common sense (for example, property values in an area will fall if crime rises)
- Historical facts and dates (for example, the United States entered World War II in 1941)
- Information found in many general reference works (for example, the heart drives the body's circulation system)

Maps, charts, graphs, and other visual displays of information are not considered common knowledge. Even though everyone knows that Paris is the capital of France, if you reproduce a map of France in your paper, you must credit the map's creator.

courts have so far agreed—that downloaders are stealing their intellectual property. Even when artists like Prince and Radiohead make their songs available online for free, they still control copyright. You could not sample one of these songs in a new work that you plan to sell without the artist's consent.

www.mhhe.com/ **mhhb2**

For information on material that does not need citing, go to

Research > Avoiding Plagiarism > Common Knowledge

2. Fair use

Most academic uses of copyrighted sources are protected under the **fair use** provision of copyright law. Under this provision, you can legally quote a brief passage from a copyrighted text in a paper without infringing on the copyright. Of course, to avoid plagiarism, you must identify the passage as a quotation and cite it properly. (*For details, see pp. 313–14 and 328–31.*)

3. Intellectual property

In addition to works protected by copyright, intellectual property includes patented inventions, trademarks, industrial designs, and similar intellectual creations that are protected by other laws.

SOURCE SMART

What Must Be Acknowledged?

You **do not** have to acknowledge:

- Common knowledge expressed in your words and sentence structure (*see the box on p. 307*)
- Your independent thinking
- Your original field observations, surveys, or experimental results

You **must** acknowledge:

- Any concepts you learned from a source, whether or not you copy the source's language
- Interviews other than surveys
- Abstracts
- Visuals
- Statistics, including those you use to create your own visuals (*see Chapter 17, pp. 281–83*)
- Your own work for another assignment (use *only* with your instructor's permission)

Acknowledge the source each time you cite from the material, regardless of the length of the selection. If you use multiple sources in a paragraph, make clear which sentences are from which sources.

20b Avoid plagiarism.

Under pressure, we tend to make poor choices. Inadvertent plagiarism occurs when busy students take notes carelessly, forgetting to jot down the source of a paraphrase or accidentally inserting material downloaded from a Web site into a paper. Deliberate plagiarism occurs when students wait until the last minute and then "borrow" a paper from a friend or copy and paste large portions of an online article into their own work. No matter how tired or pressured you may be, nothing can justify plagiarism.

To avoid plagiarism, adhere to these guidelines:

- When you receive your research assignment, write down your thoughts and questions before you begin looking at sources. Use this record to keep track of changes in your ideas.
- As you proceed with your research, distinguish your additional ideas from those of others by using a different color or font.
- Do not rely too much on one source, or you may easily slip into using that person's thoughts as your own.
- Keep accurate records while doing research and taking notes. If you do not know where you got an idea or a piece of information, do not use it in your paper until you find out.
- When you take notes, be sure to put quotation marks around words, phrases, or sentences taken verbatim from a source, and note the page number. If you use any of those words, phrases, or sentences when summarizing or paraphrasing the source, make sure to put them in quotation marks. Changing a word here and there while keeping a source's sentence structure or phrasing constitutes plagiarism, even if you credit the source for the ideas. (*For more on paraphrase, summary, and quotation, see Chapter 21: Working with Sources and Avoiding Plagiarism, pp. 322–28.*)
- Cite the sources of all ideas, opinions, facts, and statistics that are not common knowledge. (*See the box on p. 307.*)
- Choose an appropriate documentation style, and use it consistently and properly. (*See Part 4: Documenting across the Curriculum.*)

When working with electronic sources, keep in mind the following guidelines:

- Print out or save to your computer any online source you consult. Note the date on which you viewed the source. Keep the complete URL in case you need to view the source again. Some documentation styles require you to include the URL in your citation. (*See Chapter 21: Working*

TEXTCONNEX

Learning More about Plagiarism, Copyright and Fair Use, and Intellectual Property

Plagiarism

- For more information about plagiarism, see the Council of Writing Program Administrators' "Defining and Avoiding Plagiarism: The WPA Statement on Best Practices" <www.wpacouncil.org/positions/plagiarism.html>.
- Educators at Indiana University offer tips on avoiding plagiarism at <www.Indiana.edu/~frick/plagiarism.html>.
- Georgetown University's Honor Council offers an example of a campus honor code pertaining to plagiarism and academic ethics at <gervaseprograms.georgetown.edu/hc/plagiarism.html>.

Copyright and Fair Use

- For information on and a discussion of fair use, see *Copyright and Fair Use* at <fairuse.stanford.edu>, and the U.S. Copyright Office at <www.copyright.gov>.
- The University of Texas posts guidelines for fair use and multimedia projects at <www.utsystem.edu/OGC/IntellectualProperty/mmfruse.htm>.

Intellectual Property

- For information about what constitutes intellectual property and related issues, see the World Intellectual Property Organization Web site at <www.wipo.int>.
- For a legal perspective, the American Intellectual Property Law Association offers information and overviews of recent cases at <www.aipla.org>.

with Sources and Avoiding Plagiarism, pp. 315–16 for other information to note about your sources.)

- If you copy and paste a passage from a Web site into a word-processing file, use a different font to identify that material as well as the URL and your access date.
- Acknowledge all sites you use as sources, including those you access via links on another site.
- As a courtesy, request permission before quoting from blogs, news group postings, or e-mails.
- Acknowledge any audio, video, or illustrated material that has informed your research.

CHECKLIST

Avoiding Plagiarism

Sources

- ☐ Is my thesis my own idea, not something I found in one of my sources?
- ☐ Have I used a variety of sources, not just one or two?
- ☐ Have I identified each source clearly?
- ☐ Do I fully understand and explain all words, phrases, and ideas in my paper?
- ☐ Have I acknowledged all ideas that are neither based on my original thinking nor common knowledge?

Quotations

- ☐ Have I enclosed in quotation marks any uncommon terms, distinctive phrases, or direct quotations from a source?
- ☐ Have I checked all quotations against the original source?
- ☐ Do I include ellipsis marks and brackets where I have altered the original wording and capitalization of quotations?

Paraphrases

- ☐ Have I used my own words and sentence structure for all paraphrases?
- ☐ Have I maintained the original meaning?

Summaries

- ☐ Do all my summaries include my own wording and sentence structure? Are they shorter than the original text?
- ☐ Do they accurately represent the content of the original?

Documentation

- ☐ Have I indicated my source for all quotations, paraphrases, summaries, statistics, and visuals either within the text or in a parenthetical citation?
- ☐ Have I included citations for all visuals from other sources (or visuals based on data from other sources)?
- ☐ Have I included page numbers as required for all quotations, paraphrases, and summaries?
- ☐ Does every in-text citation have a corresponding entry in the list of works cited or references?

Permission

- ☐ If I am composing a public online text, have I received all needed permissions?

For MULTILINGUAL STUDENTS

Cultural Assumptions and Misunderstandings about Plagiarism

Respect for ownership of ideas is a core value in the United States. Your culture may consider the knowledge in classic texts a national heritage and, therefore, common property. As a result, you may have been encouraged to incorporate words and information from those texts into your writing without citing their source. In the United States, academic culture requires you to identify any use you make of someone else's original work and to cite the work properly in an appropriate documentation style (*see Part 4: Documenting across the Curriculum, which begins on p. 341*). You must similarly credit the source of ideas that are not considered common knowledge. You should accept these rules as nonnegotiable and apply them conscientiously to avoid plagiarism and its serious consequences. When in doubt about citation rules, ask your instructor.

TEXTCONNEX

Plagiarism and Online Sources

When you use material from a Web site, you might inadvertently be quoting material that has itself been plagiarized from another source. How can you be certain that material in an online source is being used fairly? Follow the guidelines in Chapter 18: Evaluating Sources to evaluate a Web site's reliability. You can also choose a sentence from the suspect material and enter it into a search engine. If you get a hit, investigate further to see if one site is copying from the other—or both are copying from some other source. Ask your instructor for further advice.

Although it is easy to copy and paste material from the Internet without acknowledgment, it is ill-advised to do so. Instructors can just as easily detect such plagiarism by taking the copied text and using a search engine to locate the original.

Posting material on a publicly accessible Web site is usually considered the legal equivalent of publishing it in print format. (Password-protected sites generally are exempt.) When writing a composition to be posted online and accessible to the general public, seek copyright permission from all your sources. (*See the guidelines for fair use below and the box on p. 310.*)

20c Use copyrighted materials fairly.

www.mhhe.com/mhhb2

For more information and interactive exercises, go to

Research > Avoiding Plagiarism > Using Copyrighted Materials

All original works, including student papers, graphics, videos, and e-mail, are covered by copyright, even if they do not bear an official copyright symbol. A copyright grants its owner—often the creator—exclusive rights to the use of a protected work, including reproducing, distributing, and displaying the work. The popularity of the Web as a venue of publication has led to increased concerns about the fair use of copyrighted material. Before you publish your paper on the Web or produce a multimedia presentation that includes audio, video, and graphic elements copied from a Web site, make sure that you have used copyrighted material fairly by considering these four questions:

- **What is the purpose of the use?** Educational, nonprofit, and personal uses are more likely to be considered fair than commercial use.

- **What is the nature of the work being used?** In most cases, imaginative and unpublished materials can be used only if you have the permission of the copyright holder.
- **What effect would this use have on the market for the original?** The use of a work is usually considered unfair if it would hurt sales of the original.
- **How much of the copyrighted work is being used?** The use of a small portion of a text is more likely to be considered fair than copying a whole work.

While no clear legal definition of "a small portion of text" exists, one conservative guideline is that you can quote up to fifty words from an article (print or online) and three hundred words from a book. It is safest to ask permission to republish an entire work or a substantial portion of a text (be cautious with poems, plays, and songs). Images and multimedia clips are considered entire works. Also, you may need permission to link your Web site to another.

When in doubt, always ask permission.

21 Working with Sources and Avoiding Plagiarism

Once you have a research question to answer, an idea about what the library and Internet have to offer, and some reliable, appropriate materials in hand, you are ready to begin working with your sources. Attention to detail and keeping careful records at this stage will help you stay organized, save time, and avoid plagiarism later.

21a Maintain a working bibliography.

As you research, compile a **working bibliography**—a list of those books, articles, pamphlets, Web sites, and other sources that seem most likely to help you answer your research question. Maintain an accurate and complete record of all sources you consult, so that you will be able to find any source again and cite all your sources accurately.

Although the exact bibliographic information you will need depends on your documentation style, the following list includes the major elements of most systems. (*See Part 4: Documenting across the Curriculum, pp. 341–450, for the requirements of specific documentation styles.*)

Book:

- Call number (so you can find the source again; not required for documentation)
- All authors, editors, and translators
- Title of chapter
- Title and subtitle of book
- Edition (if not the first), volume number (if applicable)
- Publication information (city, publisher, date)
- Medium (print)

Periodical article:

- Authors
- Title and subtitle of article
- Title and subtitle of periodical
- Date, edition or volume number, issue number
- Page numbers
- Medium (print)

Article from database (in addition to the above):

- Name of database
- Date you retrieved source
- URL of database's home page (if online)
- Page numbers (if any, as with a PDF)
- Medium (Web, CD-ROM, or DVD-ROM)

Internet source (including visual, audio, video):

- All authors, editors, or creators
- Title and subtitle of source
- Title of site, project, or database
- Version or edition, if any
- Publication information, if available, including any about a version in another medium (such as print, radio, or film)
- Date of electronic publication or latest update, if available
- Sponsor of site
- Date you accessed site
- URL of site
- Any other identifying numbers, such as a Digital Object Identifier (DOI)

Other sources:

- Author or creator
- Title
- Format (for example, photograph or lecture)
- Title of publication, if any

(*continued on p. 316*)

Other sources (*continued*)

- Publisher, sponsor, or institution housing the source
- Date of creation or publication
- Any identifying numbers

(*See the foldouts at the beginning of Chapters 23 and 24 for examples of these elements.*)

You can record bibliographic information on note cards or in a word-processing file; you can print out or e-mail to yourself bibliographic information from the results of online searches in databases and library catalogs; or you can record bibliographic information directly on photocopies or printouts of source material. You can also save most Web pages and other online sources to your computer.

1. Using note cards or a word processor

Before computers became widely available, most researchers used 3-by-5-inch or 4-by-6-inch note cards to compile the working bibliography, with each potential source getting a separate card as in Figure 21.1. This method is still useful. Besides not requiring a computer, it allows you to rearrange information when you are deciding how to organize your paper. You can use the cards to include all information necessary for documentation, to record brief quotations, and to note your own comments (carefully marked as yours).

Instead of handwriting on cards, you can record bibliographic information in a word-processor file. You can also combine the two methods, recording bibliographic information in a word-processing file, then printing it, cutting it out, and taping it on a note card.

SOURCE SMART

The Uses and Limits of Bibliographic Software

Programs like *Microsoft Word 2007* allow you to store source data, automatically insert citations in common documentation styles, and generate a list of references. These programs often do not incorporate the most recent updates to documentation styles. Nor do they accommodate all types of sources. Talk to your instructor before using bibliographic software, and check your citations carefully against the models in *Part 4: Documenting across the Curriculum* (*pp. 341–450*). Also double-check references that a database creates for you.

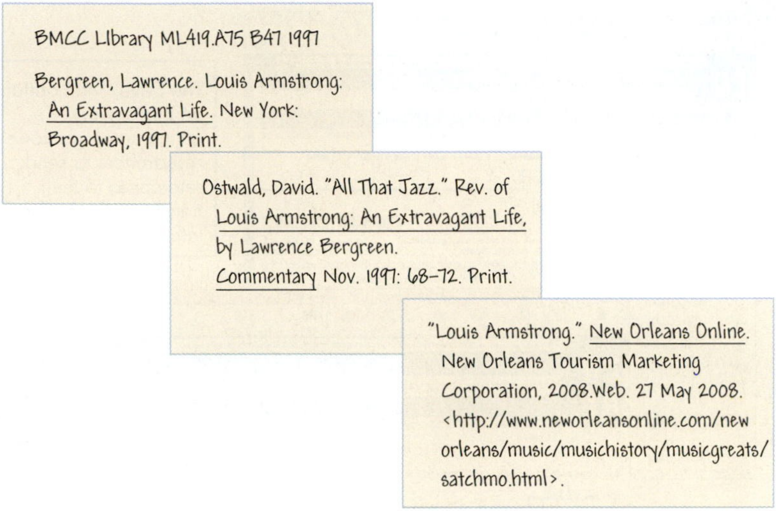

BMCC Library ML419.A75 B47 1997

Bergreen, Lawrence. Louis Armstrong: An Extravagant Life. New York: Broadway, 1997. Print.

Ostwald, David. "All That Jazz." Rev. of Louis Armstrong: An Extravagant Life, by Lawrence Bergreen. Commentary Nov. 1997: 68–72. Print.

"Louis Armstrong." New Orleans Online. New Orleans Tourism Marketing Corporation, 2008.Web. 27 May 2008. <http://www.neworleansonline.com/neworleans/music/musichistory/musicgreats/satchmo.html>.

FIGURE 21.1 Three sample bibliography note cards (in MLA style)—one for a book (*top*), one for a journal article (*middle*), and one for a Web site (*bottom*). (If typed, titles would be italicized instead of underlined. MLA style does not require call numbers or (usually) URLs, but it is useful to note this information while doing research.)

2. Printing the results of online searches in databases and library catalogs

Search results in online indexes and databases usually include complete bibliographic information about the sources they list. (*See Figure 16.3, p. 269, as well as the foldouts preceding Chapters 23 and 24 for illustrations showing where to find this information.*) You can print these results directly from your browser or, in some cases, save them on disk and transfer them to a word-processing file. Be sure to record also the name and URL of the database and the date of your search. (If you download the full text of an article from a database and refer to it in your paper, your citation must include information about the database if your documentation style requires it, as well as bibliographic information about the article itself.) If you rely on search-result printouts to compile your working bibliography, you may want to use a highlighter to indicate those sources you plan to consult.

You can similarly print out or save bibliographic information from the results of searches of online library catalogs. Some college libraries make it possible to compile a list of sources and e-mail it to yourself as in Figure 21.2 on the next page.

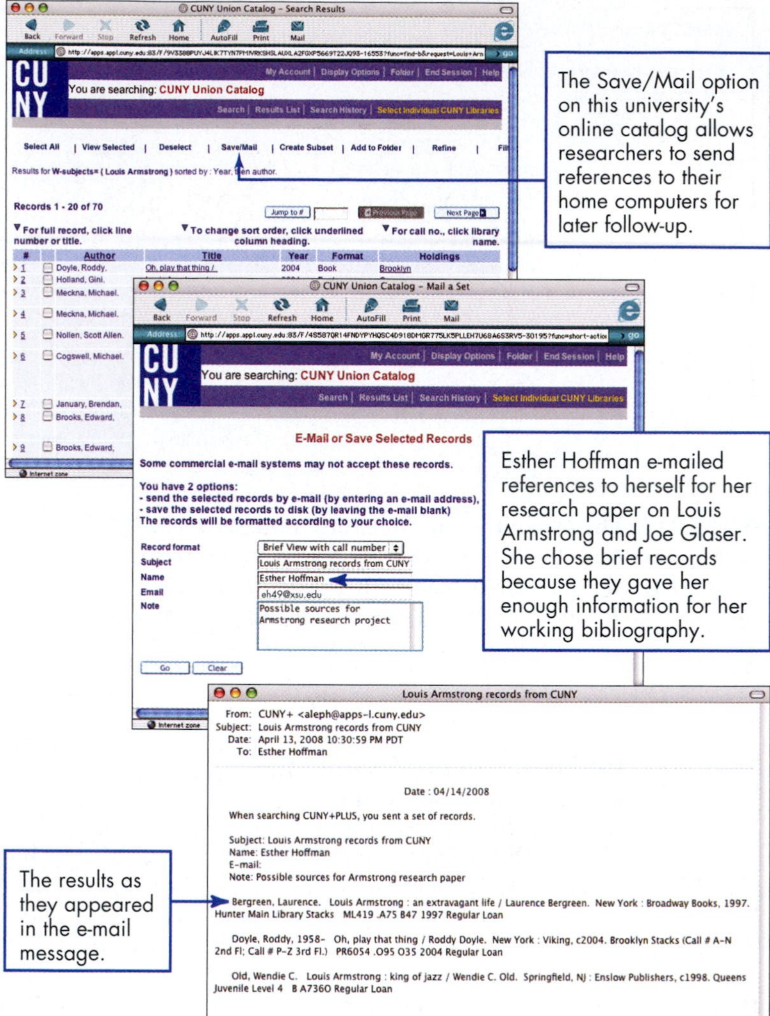

FIGURE 21.2 E-mailing the results of an online library catalog search.

3. Using photocopies and printouts from Web sites

If you photocopy articles, essays, or pages of reference works from a print or microfilm source, take time to note the bibliographic information on the photocopy. Spending a few extra minutes to do so can save you lots of time later. Similarly, if you print out a source you find on a Web site or copy it to your computer, be sure to note the site's author, sponsor, date of publication or last update, complete URL, and the date you visited it.

Bergreen, Laurence. *Louis Armstrong: An Extravagant Life.* New York: Broadway, 1997. Print.
Aimed at a popular audience, Bergreen's book provides a detailed history of Armstrong's life as well as its social context. Bergreen also presents Armstrong's relationship with manager Glaser throughout the years and Glaser's own colorful background. Essentially the partnership provided benefits to both performer and manager. (Ostwald notes a few errors.)

Collier, James Lincoln. *Louis Armstrong: An American Genius.* New York: Oxford UP, 1983. Print.
This scholarly study of Armstrong's life and work presents his formative influence on American music. Collier includes numerous telling details that support my ideas about Armstrong and Glaser's relationship, such as the fact that Glaser paid Armstrong's personal expenses while acting as his manager.

FIGURE 21.3 Sample annotated bibliography. A section of Esther Hoffman's annotated bibliography.

21b Create an annotated bibliography.

An annotated bibliography can be very useful to you in your research. The bibliography includes full citation details, correctly formatted, which you will need for your paper. The annotation provides a summary of major points for each source, including your own reactions and ideas about where this material might fit in your paper (*see Figure 21.3*). Also record your evaluation of the source's relevance and reliability (*see Chapter 18: Evaluating Sources, pp. 289–98*). As you conduct research, you will find that an annotated bibliography helps you remember what you have found in your search, as well as helping you organize your findings.

21c Take notes on your sources.

Taking notes helps you think through your research question. Having a research question in mind helps you read more systematically. Use a source heading or table of contents to look for the most relevant sections. As you work, you can take notes on the information you find in sources by annotating photocopies of the source material or by noting useful ideas and quotations on paper, on cards, or in a computer file. See if categories emerge that can help you organize your paper.

www.mhhe.com/mhhb2

For more information and interactive exercises, go to

Research > Research Techniques

1. Annotating

One way to take notes is to annotate photocopied articles and print-outs from online information services or Web sites, as in Figure 21.4

(*on p. 321*). (You also can do this for sources you save to your computer by using the Comments feature in your word processor (*see Chapter 5, pp. 80–81*).) As you read, write the following notes directly on the page or in the electronic file:

- On the first page, write down complete bibliographic information for the source.
- As you read, record your questions, reactions, and ideas. Note any potential new directions for your research.
- Comment on ideas that agree with or differ from those you have already thought about.
- Put important and difficult passages into your own words by paraphrasing or summarizing them. (*For help with paraphrasing and summarizing, see pp. 322–27.*)
- Highlight statements that you may want to quote because they are key to your readers' understanding of the issue or are especially well expressed.

2. Taking notes in a research journal or log

A **research journal** or **research log** is a tool for keeping track of your research. It can be a spiral or loose-leaf notebook, a box of note cards, a word-processing document on a laptop computer, or a blog—whatever you are most comfortable with. Use the journal to write down leads for sources to consult and to record ideas and observations about your topic as they occur to you. If you use a blog, you can link to potential sources.

When you have finished annotating a photocopy, printout, or electronic version of an article, use your research journal to explore some of the comments, connections, and questions you recorded. If you do not have a copy of the material to annotate, take notes directly in your journal. Writing down each idea on a separate card, notebook page, word-processing page, or blog entry (with appropriate tags) will make it easier to organize the material later. Whatever method you use, be sure to record the source's bibliographic information as well as the specific page number for each idea.

Enclose in quotation marks any exact words from a source. If you think you may forget that the phrasing, as well as the idea, came from someone else, label the passage a quotation and note the page number, as Esther Hoffman did in the following excerpt from her research journal:

Notes on Dan Morgenstern. "Louis Armstrong and the Development and Diffusion of Jazz." Louis Armstrong: A Cultural Legacy. Ed. Marc H. Miller. Seattle: U of Washington P and Queens Museum of Art, 1994. 94–145. Print.

- *Armstrong having trouble with managers. Fires Johnny Collins in London, 1933. Collins blocks Armstrong from playing with Chick Webb's band (pp. 124–25).*

Louis Armstrong / Satchmo http://www.neworleansonline.com/neworleans/music/musichistory/musicgreats/satchmo.html

www.NewOrleansOnline.com

NEW ORLEANS ONLINE.COM

Search

HOME | THINGS TO SEE AND DO | TRAVEL TOOLS | ACCOMMODATIONS | CALENDAR | ONLINE NEWSROOM

PLAN YOUR VISIT

New Orleans Tourism Marketing Corporation, 2008. Web. 7 May. 2008. <http://www.neworleansonline.com/neworleans/music/music history/musicgreats/satchmo.html>.

FEATURED STORY

Louis Armstrong

"Satchmo" — as he was affectionately called by his legions of friends — never boasted like his fellow New Orleanian, jazzman Jelly Roll Morton, that he invented jazz, or for that matter that he was one of its better players. But everyone who heard him play or hears his inimitable style today can only agree that Daniel Louis "Satchmo" Armstrong was perhaps the best there has ever been.

The worldwide popularity of jazz can be directly attributed to the infectious style of performance that "Satchmo" gave and the unselfishness that characterized his persona.

'Satchmo' worked at various unskilled jobs much of his youth. He sold coal and had a youthful propensity for mischief. On a dare from a friend, he fired a pistol on South Rampart Street. For firing a weapon in a public place, he received an 18-month sentence at the Colored Waif's Home where he eventually came under the influence of "Captain" Peter Davis. Sensing that young Armstrong possessed a burning desire to learn, Davis provided the basic musical training on the cornet to young Louis. With that kindly gesture the history of popular music was undoubtedly rewritten.

By 1922, young Satchmo was ready to join his idol, Joe "King" Oliver's Creole Jazz Band in Chicago. By the time of his arrival in the Windy City he had become an accomplished musician. Part of the influence that Armstrong brought to Chicago had been an incredible street training in the back alleys and clubs of Black Storyville, the area surrounding Liberty and Perdido Streets, the current site of New Orleans city government.

Armstrong wrote in his autobiography, "Satchmo," "There were all kinds of thrills for me in Storyville. On every corner I could hear music. And such good music...And that man Joe Oliver! My, my, that man kept me spellbound with that horn of his."

In the early '30s, Armstrong's popularity had reached such epic proportions that he and his band toured Europe, a major milestone for a performer, and especially a young black performer.

As the years passed, Armstrong's persona and star appeal continued to grow. Satchmo's popularity never waned during his entire life. He played for presidents, European royalty, the kings and queens of his beloved Africa. He frequently toured internationally as a special envoy for the U.S. State Department and represented his country and New O...

THINGS TO SEE & DO

History & Heritage
Restaurants & Cuisine
Music
Festivals
Museums & The Arts
Tours
Attractions
Shopping
Nightlife & Harrah's
Architecture
Sports and Recreation
French Quarter
Mardi Gras
Holiday Happenin's
Romantic New Orleans
Family
Multicultural
Gay & Lesbian Travel
Voluntourism

Early influence follow up?

Check my e-mail for this link!

Annotate, highlight, and underline on a Web page printout just as you would any other print resource.

If you are working at a library computer, see if you can e-mail a Web page to yourself so you can save it on your own computer. That way, you'll have both a print and an electronic record of the source.

FIGURE 21.4 An annotated Web page printout.

- *Armstrong turned to Glaser, an old Chicago acquaintance. Quote: "Joe Glaser ... proved to be the right man at the right time" (p. 128).*

Unless you think you might use a quotation in your paper, it is usually better to express the author's ideas in your own words in your notes. To do this you need to understand paraphrasing and summarizing.

SOURCE SMART

Deciding to Quote, Paraphrase, or Summarize

Point is eloquently, memorably, or uniquely stated	→	Quote
Details important but not uniquely or eloquently expressed	→	Paraphrase
Long section of material (with many points), main ideas important, details not important	→	Summarize
Part of longer passage is uniquely stated	→	Use quotation inside paraphrased or summarized passage

3. Paraphrasing

Paraphrase when a passage's details are important to your topic but its exact words are not memorable. When you paraphrase, you put someone else's statements into your words and sentence structures. A paraphrase should be about the same length and level of detail as the original. Paraphrase when you need to reorder a source's ideas or clarify complicated information. Cite the original writer and put quotation marks around any exact phrasing from the source. See the Source Smart box on page 323 for advice on approaching the task.

LEARNING in COLLEGE

Using Sources to Establish Your Credibility

As noted in Chapter 10, effective writers appeal to their audience by demonstrating that they are *reasonable, ethical,* and *empathetic* (*see pp. 197–98*). When you present relevant evidence from reliable sources, you demonstrate that you are reasonable. When you take care to put other writers' ideas into your own words and indicate the sources of all ideas and quotations that are not your own and that are not common knowledge, you demonstrate that you are ethical, and therefore trustworthy. When you carefully follow the citation formats required by the discipline that you are writing in, you demonstrate your consideration, or empathy, for your readers by making it easier for them to consult your sources if they wish to.

SOURCE SMART

Guidelines for Writing a Paraphrase

- **Read the passage carefully.** Focus on the sequence of ideas and important details.
- **Be sure you understand the material.** Look up any unfamiliar words.
- **Imagine addressing an audience that has not read the material.**
- **Without looking at the original passage, write down its main ideas and key details.**
- **Use clear, direct language.** Express complicated ideas as a series of simple ones.
- **Check your paraphrase against the original.** Make sure your text conveys the source's ideas accurately without copying its words or sentence structures. Add quotes around any phrases from the source or rewrite them.
- **Note the citation information.** List author and page number after every important point.

In the first unacceptable paraphrase that follows, the writer has done a word-for-word translation, using synonyms for some terms but retaining the phrases from the original (highlighted) and failing to enclose them in quotation marks ("nonsense syllables," "free invention of rhythm, melody, and syllables"). Notice also how close the sentence structures in the first faulty paraphrase are to the original.

SOURCE

Scat singing. A technique of jazz singing in which onomatopoeic or nonsense syllables are sung to improvised melodies. Some writers have traced scat singing back to the practice, common in West African musics, of translating percussion patterns into vocal lines by assigning syllables to characteristic rhythms. However, since this allows little scope for melodic improvisation and the earliest recorded examples of jazz scat singing involved the free invention of rhythm, melody, and syllables, it is more likely that the technique began in the USA as singers imitated the sounds of jazz instrumentalists.

—J. Bradford Robinson, *The New Grove Dictionary of Jazz* "Scat Singing" from *New Grove Dictionary of Jazz* 2e (OUP 2002), edited by Kernfield, B. Reproduced by permission of Oxford University Press, Inc.

UNACCEPTABLE PARAPHRASE: PLAGIARISM

> Scat is a way of singing that uses nonsense syllables and extemporaneous melodies. Some people think that scat goes back to the custom in West African music of turning drum rhythms into vocal lines. But that does not explain the free invention of rhythm, melody, and syllables of the first recorded instances of scat singing. It is more likely that scat was started in the U.S. by singers imitating the way instrumental jazz sounded (Robinson 425).

In the second example of a faulty paraphrase (below), the writer has merely substituted synonyms (such as "meaningless vocalization" instead of "nonsense syllables") for the original author's words and kept the source's sentence structure. Because it relies on the sentence structure of the original source, the paraphrase constitutes plagiarism.

UNACCEPTABLE PARAPHRASE (SENTENCE STRUCTURE OF SOURCE): PLAGIARISM

> Scat is a way of singing that uses meaningless vocalization and extemporaneous melodies. One theory is that scat originated from the West African custom of turning drum rhythms into singing. But that doesn't explain the loose improvisation of pulse, pitch, and sound of the first recorded instances of scat singing. Scat more probably was started in the United States by singers imitating the way instrumental jazz sounded (Robinson 425).

The third unacceptable paraphrase (below) alters the sentence structure of the source but plagiarizes by using some of the original wording (highlighted below) without quotation marks.

UNACCEPTABLE PARAPHRASE (WORDING FROM SOURCE): PLAGIARISM

> Scat, a highly inventive type of jazz singing, combines onomatopoeic or nonsense syllables with improvised melodies (Robinson 425).

By contrast, the acceptable paraphrase expresses all ideas from the original using different wording and phrasing. Although it quotes a few words from the source, the writer has used quotation marks and expressed the definition in a new way. The author's name indicates where the paraphrase begins.

ACCEPTABLE PARAPHRASE

> According to Robinson, scat is a highly inventive type of jazz singing that combines "nonsense syllables [with] improvised melodies." Although syllabic singing of drum rhythms occurs in West Africa, scat probably owes more to the early attempts of American singers to mimic both the sound and the inventive musical style of instrumental jazz (Robinson 425).

Note that an acceptable paraphrase that does not include a direct quotation still requires a citation.

In the following two paraphrases of a podcast, note that the unacceptable paraphrase copies words and phrasing from the source.

SOURCE

> Two of the greatest all-time performers in the history of popular music are coupled on this exciting and entertaining album. The Groa and Satchmo team up for a great bash that has been arranged for and constructed by the talented Billy May.
>
> — Fresh Sounds, "Bing Crosby Meets Louis Armstrong." *Jazzarific: Jazz Vinyl Podcast.*

UNACCEPTABLE PARAPHRASE: PLAGIARISM

> The Groa and Satchmo collaborate on this exciting album that the talented Billy May has arranged.

ACCEPTABLE PARAPHRASE

> The Fresh Sounds podcast describes this thrilling album that brings together two consummate performers, Bing Crosby and Louis Armstrong, with arrangements by Billy May (Fresh Sounds).

Exercise 21.1 Paraphrase

Read the following passage, annotating as necessary. Write a paraphrase of the passage, and then compare your paraphrase with those of your classmates. What are the similarities and differences among your paraphrases? How can you tell if a paraphrase is acceptable or unacceptable?

SOURCE

> The origins of jazz, an urban music, stemmed from the countryside of the South as well as the streets of America's cities. It resulted from two distinct musical traditions, those of West Africa and Europe. West Africa gave jazz its incessant rhythmic drive, the need to move and the emotional urgency that has served the music so well. The European ingredients had more to do with classical qualities pertaining to harmony and melody.
>
> The blending of these two traditions resulted in a music that played around with meter and reinterpreted the use of notes in new combinations, creating blue notes that expressed feelings both sad and joyous. The field hollers of Southern sharecropping slaves combined with the more urban, stylized sounds of musicians from New Orleans, creating a new music.

Gospel music from the church melded with what became known in the 20th century as the blues offered a vocal ingredient that translated well to instruments.

—JOHN EPHLAND, "Down Beat's Jazz 101: The Very Beginning" (from downbeat.com)

www.mhhe.com/mhhb2
For more information and interactive exercises, go to
Research > Avoiding Plagiarism > Summarize/Paraphrase

4. Summarizing

When you **summarize,** you state the main point of a piece, condensing paragraphs into sentences, pages into paragraphs, or a book into a few pages. As you work with sources, you will summarize more frequently than you quote or paraphrase. Summarizing works best

SOURCE SMART

Guidelines for Writing a Summary

- **Read the material carefully.** Determine which parts are relevant to your paper.
- **Be sure you understand the material.** Look up unfamiliar words.
- **Imagine addressing an audience that has not read the material.**
- **Identify the main point of the source, in your words.** Compose a sentence that names the text, the writer, what the writer does (reports, analyzes, argues), and the most important point.
- **Note any other points that relate to your topic.** State each one (in your words) in one sentence or less. Simplify complex language.
- **If the text is longer than a few paragraphs, divide it into sections, and in one or two sentences sum up each section.** Writers move between subtopics or from the statement of an idea to the supporting evidence. Compose a topic sentence for each of these sections. If possible, annotate the text to mark the different portions and highlight key sentences in each.
- **Combine your sentence stating the writer's main point with your sentences about secondary points or those summarizing the text's sections.**
- **Check your summary against the original** to see if it makes sense, expresses the source's meaning, and does not copy any wording or sentence structure.
- **Note all the citation information for the source.**

for very long passages or when the central idea of a passage is important but the details are not. See the Source Smart box on the previous page for advice on approaching the task.

Here are two summaries of the passage by John Ephland in Exercise 21.1. The unacceptable summary is simply a restatement of Ephland's thesis using much of his phrasing (highlighted).

UNACCEPTABLE SUMMARY: PLAGIARISM

> The origins of jazz are two distinct musical traditions, those of West Africa and Europe. New meters and new note combinations capable of expressing both sad and joyous feelings resulted from the blending of these two traditions.

The acceptable summary states Ephland's main point in the writer's own words. Note that the acceptable summary still requires a citation.

ACCEPTABLE SUMMARY

> According to Ephland, jazz has its roots in the musical traditions of both West Africa and Europe. It combines rhythmic, harmonic, and melodic features of both traditions in new and emotionally expressive ways (Ephland).

(For a summary of a longer passage, see Chapter 7: Reading, Thinking, Writing: The Critical Connection, p. 133.)

Exercise 21.2 Summary

Read the following passage and write a summary of it. Compare your summary with those of your classmates. What are the similarities and differences among your summaries? How does writing a paraphrase compare with writing a summary? Which task was more difficult, and why?

SOURCE

> Male musicians dominated the jazz scene when the music first surfaced, making it difficult for women to enter their ranks. The fraternity of jazzmen also frowned upon women wind instrumentalists. However, some African American women, in the late 19th century, played the instruments that were barred from the "opposite sex". . . . Many of their names have been lost in history, but, a few have survived. For example, Mattie Simpson, a cornetist, performed 'on principal and prominent streets of each city' (10) in Indianapolis, in 1895; Nettie Goff, a trombonist, was a member of The Mahara Minstrels, and Mrs. Laurie Johnson, a trumpeter, had a career that spanned 30 years. They all broke instrumental taboos.
>
> —Mario A. Charles, "The Age of a Jazzwoman: Valaida Snow, 1900–1956"

www.mhhe.com/mhhb2
For more information and interactive exercises, go to
Research > Avoiding Plagiarism > Using Quotations

5. Quoting directly

Sometimes the writer of a source will say something so eloquently and perceptively that you will want to include that writer's words as a **direct quotation** in your paper.

In general, quote:

- Primary sources (for example, in a paper about Louis Armstrong, a direct quotation from Armstrong or an associate)
- Literary sources, when you analyze the wording
- Sources containing very technical language that cannot be paraphrased
- An authority in the field whose words support your thesis
- Debaters explaining their different positions on an issue

To avoid inadvertent plagiarism, be careful to indicate that the content is a direct quotation when you copy it into your note cards or your research notebook. Place quotation marks around the direct quotation. You might also use a special color to indicate direct quotations or deliberately make quotation marks oversized.

When referring to most secondary sources, paraphrase or summarize instead of quoting. Your readers will have difficulty following a paper with too many quotations, and they may think you lack original ideas. Try to keep quotations short.

In some instances you may use paraphrase, summary, and quotation together. You might summarize a long passage, paraphrase an important section of it, and directly quote a short part of that section.

> ***Note:*** If you have used more than one quotation or substantial paraphrase every paragraph or two, revise your work to include more of your own reflections on the topic.

21d Synthesize: Take stock of what you have learned.

When you take stock, you assess the research you have done. You also synthesize what you have learned from the sources you have consulted. Think about how the sources you have read relate to one another. Ask yourself when, how, and why your sources agree or disagree, and consider where you stand on the issues they raise. Did anything you read surprise or disturb you? Writing down your responses to such questions can help you clarify what you have learned from working with sources.

In college writing, the credibility of your work depends on the relevance and reliability of your sources as well as the scope and depth of your reading and observation. College research projects usually require multiple viewpoints. A paper on Louis Armstrong, for example, is unlikely to be credible if it relies on only one source of information. A paper about an issue in the social sciences will not be taken seriously if it cites research on only one side of the debate.

As the context and kind of writing change, so too do the requirements for types and numbers of sources. As a general rule, however, you should consult more than two sources and use only sources that are both reliable and respected by people working in the field. To determine whether you have located appropriate and sufficient sources, ask yourself the following questions:

- Are your sources trustworthy? (*See Chapter 18: Evaluating Sources.*)
- If you have started to develop a tentative answer to your research question, have your sources provided you with a sufficient number of facts, examples, and ideas to support that answer?
- Have you used sources that examine the issue from several different perspectives?

21e Integrate quotations, paraphrases, and summaries properly and effectively.

For more information and interactive exercises, go to **Research > Avoiding Plagiarism > Using Sources Accurately**

Ultimately you will use some of the paraphrases, summaries, and quotations you have collected during the course of your research to support and develop the ideas you present in your research paper. Here are some guidelines for integrating them properly and effectively. (Examples in this section represent MLA style for in-text and block quotations.)

1. Integrating quotations

Short quotations should be enclosed in quotation marks and well integrated into your sentence structure. Set off longer quotations in blocks (*see p. 331*). The following example from Esther Hoffman's paper on Louis Armstrong and Joe Glaser shows the use of a short quotation:

> In his dedication to the unpublished manuscript "Louis Armstrong and the Jewish Family in New Orleans, the Year of 1907," Armstrong calls Glaser "the best friend that I ever had," while in a letter to Max Jones, he writes, "I did not get really happy until I got with my man—my dearest friend—Joe Glaser" (qtd. in Jones and Chilton 16).

The following poorly integrated quotation uses the wrong verb tense and distorts the meaning of the original: "Armstrong writes that he 'get really happy until I got with my man—my dearest friend—Joe Glaser.'" Always make sure a quotation works grammatically and logically in your writing.

When you are integrating someone else's words into your writing, use a **signal phrase** that indicates whom you are quoting. The signal phrases "Armstrong calls Glaser," and "he writes" identify Armstrong as the source of the two quotations in the passage on page 329.

A signal phrase indicates where your words end and the source's words begin. The first time you quote a source, include the author's full name. Often you will want to add the author's credentials (or authority to describe a topic): for example, "literary scholar Jacob Miller" or "Armstrong's wife, Lucille." You may also include the title of the work for context: "In *Louis Armstrong: An Extravagant Life,* biographer Laurence Bergreen argues . . . ."

Instead of introducing a quotation, the signal phrase can follow or interrupt it:

FOLLOWS "I did not get really happy until I got with my man—my dearest friend—Joe Glaser," writes Armstrong.

INTERRUPTS "I did not get really happy," writes Armstrong, "until I got with my man—my dearest friend— Joe Glaser."

The verb you use in a signal phrase should show the reader how you are using the quotation in your paper. If your source provides an example that strengthens your argument, you could say, "Mann *supports* this line of reasoning." (*See the box on p. 331.*)

MLA style places signal phrase verbs in the present or present perfect tenses (*Johnson writes; Gonzalez has written*); APA style uses the past and past perfect tenses (*Johnson wrote; Gonzalez has found*). (*See Chapter 22, pp. 337–38 for more on these documentation styles.*) When a quotation, paraphrase, or summary in MLA or APA style begins with a signal phrase, the ending citation includes the page number (unless the work lacks page numbers). You can quote without a signal phrase if you give the author's name in the parenthetical citation.

Brackets within quotations Sentences that include quotations must make sense grammatically. Sometimes you may have to adjust a quotation to make it fit properly into your sentence. Use brackets to indicate any minor adjustments you have made in wording, capitalization, or verb tense (*see 55i, pp. 772–73*). For example, *my* has been changed to *his* to make the quotation fit in the following sentence:

> Armstrong confided to a friend that Glaser's death "broke [his] heart" (Bergreen 490).

Ellipses within quotations Use ellipses to indicate that words have been omitted from the body of a quotation, but be sure that what you omit does not significantly alter the source's meaning. (*For more on using ellipses, see Chapter 54: Quotation Marks and 55j, pp. 774–77.*)

> As Morgenstern puts it, "Joe Glaser . . . proved to be the right man at the right time" (128).

Quotations in block format Quotations longer than four lines should be used rarely, because they tend to break up your text and make readers impatient. Research papers should consist primarily of your own analysis of sources. Always tell your readers why you want them to read a long quotation, and afterward, comment on it.

If you use a verse quotation longer than three lines or a prose quotation longer than four typed lines, set the quotation off on a new line and indent each line one inch (ten spaces) from the left margin. Indent the first line of each new paragraph in the quotation by another quarter inch. (*This is MLA style; for APA style, see Chapter 54, p. 758.*) Double-space above and below the quotation. If the quotation is more than one paragraph, indent the first line of each new paragraph a quarter inch. Do not use quotation marks with a block quotation. Writers often introduce a block quotation with a sentence ending in a colon. (*For examples of block quotations, see Chapter 54: Quotation Marks, p. 759.*)

Tips LEARNING in COLLEGE

Varying Signal Phrases

To keep your work interesting, to show the original writer's purpose (*Martinez describes* or *Lin argues*), and to connect the quotation to your reasoning (*Johnson refutes . . .*), use appropriate signal phrases such as following:

acknowledges	concedes	holds	refutes
adds	concludes	implies	rejects
admits	considers	insists	remarks
argues	contends	interprets	reports
asks	denies	maintains	responds
asserts	describes	notes	shows
charges	emphasizes	observes	speculates
claims	explains	points out	states
comments	expresses	proposes	suggests
complains	finds	proves	warns

Some single phrases, such as *considers*, make a claim more defensible. It is more difficult to support a more absolute claim about a source, such as *proves*. In general you should avoid ascribing emotion or tone to a written source unless that emotion is very clear. Avoid verbs like *smirks, huffs, retorts,* and *cries,* as well as adverbs such as *angrily, knowingly,* and *coyly*.

2. Integrating paraphrases and summaries

The principles for integrating paraphrases and summaries into your text are similar to those for including direct quotations. You want a smooth transition between a source's point and your own voice, and you want to accurately attribute the information to its source. Although you do not need to use ellipses or the block format for paraphrases and summaries (because they are in your own words), you will want to use signal phrases and citations.

Besides crediting others for their work, signal phrases can make ideas more interesting by giving them a human face. Here are some examples:

> *As biographer Laurence Bergreen points out,* Armstrong easily reached difficult high notes, the F's and G's that stymied other trumpeters (248).

In this passage, Esther Hoffman uses the signal phrase *As biographer Louis Bergreen points out* to identify Bergreen as the source of the paraphrased information about Louis Armstrong's extraordinary technical abilities.

> According to Howard Mandel in his blog entry "International Jazz at IAJE," young people today listen not only to pop music but also to jazz, especially its current eclectic styles.

This passage in a paper by Roger Hart uses the signal phrase *According to Howard Mandel* to lead into a summary of Mandel's blog entry. No citation is needed because the signal phrase names the author and the source lacks page numbers.

> A 1960 letter from Glaser to Lucille Armstrong corroborates Gold's account; it shows that Glaser assumed responsibility for buying the musician and his wife a new car as well as for filing the paperwork needed to retain the old license plate number.

In this passage, Esther Hoffman uses the word *corroborates* to signal her paraphrase of an original letter she found in the Louis Armstrong archives. She directly names the source (the author of the letter), so she does not need additional parenthetical documentation.

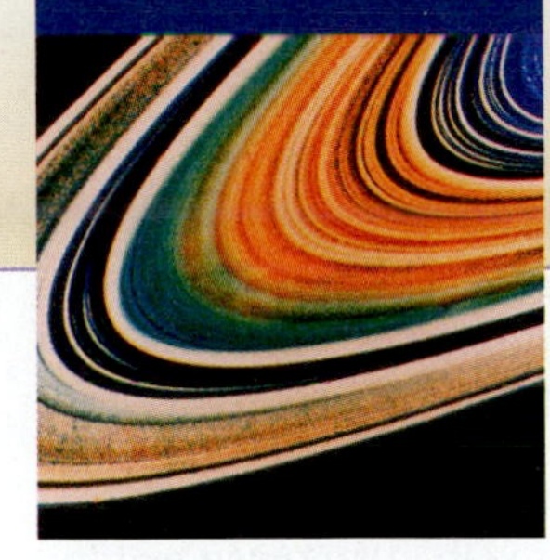

22 Writing the Paper

You have chosen a challenging research question and have located, read, and evaluated a variety of sources. Now you need a thesis that will allow you to share what you have learned as well as your perspective on the issue.

22a Plan and draft your paper.

Begin planning by recalling the context and purpose of your paper. If you have an assignment sheet, review it to see if the paper is supposed to be primarily informative, interpretive, or argumentative. Consider how much your audience is likely to know about your topic. Keep your purpose, audience, and context in mind as you decide on a thesis to support and develop.

1. Deciding on a thesis

Consider the question that guided your research as well as others provoked by what you have learned during your research. Revise the wording of these questions and summarize them in a central question that is interesting and relevant to your audience (*see Chapter 15: Understanding Research, pp. 254–57*). After you write down this question, compose an answer that you can use as your working thesis, as Esther Hoffman does in the following example:

> www.mhhe.com/mhhb2
> For help with developing a thesis, go to
> **Writing > Paragraph/Essay Development > Thesis/Central Idea**

HOFFMAN'S FOCAL QUESTION

> What kind of relationship did Louis Armstrong and Joe Glaser have?

HOFFMAN'S WORKING THESIS

> Armstrong and Glaser enjoyed not only a successful business partnership but also a complex friendship based on mutual respect and caring.

(*For more on devising a thesis, see Chapter 3: Planning and Shaping the Whole Essay, pp. 42–46.*)

2. Outlining a plan for supporting and developing your thesis

Guided by your tentative thesis, outline a plan that uses your sources in a purposeful way. Decide on the organization you will use to support your thesis—chronological, problem-solution, or thematic—and develop your support by choosing facts, examples, and ideas drawn from a variety of sources. A chronological organization presents examples from earliest to most recent, and a problem-solution structure introduces an issue and a means of addressing it. A thematic

> www.mhhe.com/mhhb2
> For interactive help with outlines, go to
> **Writing > Outlining Tutor**

organization orders examples from simple to complex, specific to general, or in another logical way. (*See Chapter 3: Planning and Shaping the Whole Essay, p. 46, for more on these organizational structures.*)

For her interpretive paper on Armstrong and Glaser, Hoffman decided on a thematic organization, an approach structured around raising and answering a central question:

- State the question: What kind of relationship did Louis Armstrong have with his longtime manager, Joe Glaser? Did Glaser dominate Armstrong?
- State the thesis: Armstrong and Glaser enjoyed a mutual business and personal relationship.
- Offer background information on the Jazz Age.
- Introduce Armstrong as a great musician who was once a poor waif.
- Introduce Glaser, Armstrong's manager for thirty-four years.
- Discuss Glaser as Armstrong's business manager and support for the idea that Glaser made Armstrong a star.
- Discuss Armstrong's resistance to being controlled by Glaser.
- Conclude: Armstrong and Glaser worked well together as friends who respected and cared for each other.

To develop this outline, Hoffman would need to list supporting facts, examples, or ideas for each point as well as indicate the sources of this information. Each section should center on her original thinking, backed by her analysis of sources. (*For more on developing an outline, see Chapter 3: Planning and Shaping the Whole Essay, pp. 47–51.*)

3. Organizing and evaluating your information

Your note-taking strategies will determine how you collect and organize your information. If you have taken notes on index cards, group them according to topic and subtopic, using your paper's formal or informal outline as a guide. For example, Esther Hoffman could have used the following categories to organize her notes:

Biography – Armstrong
Biography – Glaser
Glaser as manager
Conflict – A & G
Armstrong – media image
Jazz – general info

Sorting index cards into stacks corresponding to topics and subtopics allows you to see what you have gathered. A small stack of cards for a particular topic might mean that the topic is not as important to your thesis as you had originally thought—or that you may need to do additional research on that specific subtopic.

If your notes are primarily on your computer, you can create a new folder or page for each topic and subtopic, and then copy and paste to move information to the appropriate category.

As with all writing, the process of planning a research paper usually does not unfold in distinct steps. While outlining, you may revise your thesis. As you look for support for your outline in your research and notes, you may decide to adjust the outline or the thesis.

4. Writing a draft that you can revise, share, and edit

When you have a tentative thesis and a plan, you are ready to write a draft. Many writers find that they can present their thesis or focal question at the end of an introductory paragraph or two. The introduction should interest readers.

As you write beyond the introduction, be prepared to reexamine and refine your thesis and outline. When you draw on ideas from your sources, be sure to quote and paraphrase effectively and properly. Take care to integrate quotations, paraphrases, and summaries accurately (*see Chapter 21, pp. 329–32*). Include source citations in all your drafts. (*For advice on quoting and paraphrasing, see Chapter 21: Working with Sources and Avoiding Plagiarism, pp. 322–28, and section 22c of this chapter.*)

www.mhhe.com/mhhb2
For more information and interactive excercises, go to **Writing > Paragraph/Essay Development > Drafting and Revising**

Make your conclusion as memorable as possible. You may need to review the paper as a whole before writing the conclusion. In the final version of Hoffman's paper, on pages 378–90, note how she uses a visual and a play on words—"more than meets the eye"—to end her paper. In doing so, she enhances her concluding point—that Armstrong and Glaser were different, yet complementary, and that their relationship was complex. Hoffman did not come up with the last line of her paper until she revised and edited her first draft. It is not uncommon for writers to come up with fresh ideas for their introduction, body paragraphs, or conclusion at this stage—one reason why it is important to spend time revising and editing your paper. (*For more on revising, see Chapter 5: Revising and Editing, pp. 76–103.*)

5. Integrating visuals

Well-chosen visuals like photographs, drawings, charts, graphs, and maps can sometimes help illustrate your argument. In some cases, a visual might itself be a subject of your analysis. Esther Hoffman found two pictures in her archival research about Louis Armstrong. She describes both of them in her paper and was able to include a reproduction of one in her work.

There are two additional components to consider when integrating visuals into your paper: figure numbers and captions.

CHECKLIST

Revising and Editing a Research Paper

Consider these questions as you read your draft and gather feedback from your instructor and peers (*see also the Checklist box, "Avoiding Plagiarism," Chapter 20, pp. 311–12*):

Thesis and structure

- ☐ How does my paper address the topic and purpose given in the assignment?
- ☐ How does my thesis fit my evidence and reasoning?
- ☐ Is the central idea of each section based on my own thinking and backed with evidence from my sources?
- ☐ What strategies have I used to deal with the most likely critiques of my thesis? How might I address any that remain?
- ☐ Are the order of sections and the transitions between sections logical?
- ☐ What evidence do I have to support each point? Is it sufficient?

Editing: Use of sources

- ☐ Do my paraphrases and summaries alter the wording and sentence structure, but not the meaning, of the original text?
- ☐ Have I checked all quotations for accuracy and used ellipses or brackets where necessary?
- ☐ Do signal phrases set off and establish context for quotations, paraphrases, and summaries?
- ☐ Have I provided adequate in-text citation for each source? Do my in-text citations match my Works-Cited or References page?
- ☐ Do all of my illustrations have complete and accurate captions?

(*See also the Checklists "Revising Your Draft for Content and Organization," p. 82, "Revising Visuals," p. 93, "Editing Sentences and Words," pp. 94–95, and "Proofreading," p. 99.*)

- **Figure numbers:** Both MLA and APA styles require writers to number each image in a research paper. In MLA style, the word *figure* is abbreviated to *Fig*. In APA style, the full word *Figure* is written out.
- **Captions:** Each visual that you include in your paper must be followed by a caption that includes the title of the visual (if it has one; otherwise, a brief description will do) and its source. In MLA style, each caption begins with the figure number and a period after the number (Fig. 1.); in APA style, use italics for the figure number (*Figure 1*) and no period.

22b Revise your draft.

After you have completed a draft of your research paper, you may be asked to share it with other members of your class for peer review and feedback. If not, you still can use the checklist on page 336 to review your own work.

You may prefer to revise a hard copy of your draft by hand, or you might find it easier to use the Track Changes feature in your word-processing program. Either way, be sure to keep previous versions of your essay drafts. Even if your instructor does not require you to hand in preliminary drafts, it is useful to have a record of how your paper evolved—especially if you need to track down a particular source or want to reincorporate something that you had removed earlier in the process.

22c Document your sources.

www.mhhe.com/mhhb2
For help with documenting sources, go to Research > Avoiding Plagiarism > Citing Sources

Whenever you use information, ideas, or words from someone else's work, you must acknowledge that person. As noted in the box on page 307, the only exception to this principle is when you use information that is common knowledge, such as the chemical composition of water or the names of the thirteen original states. When you tell readers what sources you have consulted, they can more readily understand your paper as well as the conversation you are participating in by writing it.

How sources are documented varies by field and discipline. Choose a documentation style that is appropriate for the particular course you are taking, and use it properly and consistently.

Specific documentation styles meet the needs of different disciplines. Literature, foreign languages, and some other humanities disciplines use MLA style. Researchers in these disciplines use many historic texts including multiple editions of certain sources. The author's name and the page number, but not the year, appear in the in-text citation. The edition of the source appears in the Works-Cited list. The author's full

CHARTING the TERRITORY

Documentation Styles Explained in This Text

TYPE OF COURSE	DOCUMENTATION STYLE MOST COMMONLY USED	WHERE TO FIND THIS STYLE IN THE HANDBOOK
Humanities (English, religion, music, art, philosophy, history)	MLA (Modern Language Association) or Chicago (*Chicago Manual of Style*)	MLA: *pp. 342–90* Chicago: *pp. 423–41*
Social sciences (anthropology, psychology, sociology, education, and business)	APA (American Psychological Association)	APA: *pp. 391–422*
Sciences (mathematics, natural sciences, engineering, physical therapy, computer science)	CSE (Council of Science Editors)	CSE: *pp. 442–50*

name appears at the first mention of the work, and sources are referred to in present tense (because writing exists in the present).

APA style, used by practitioners of the social sciences, places the date of a work in the in-text citation because the currency of sources matters to these disciplines. References to past research appear in the past tense, and researchers are referred to only by last name in the text.

Chicago, or CMS, style, used by other humanities disciplines, has two forms. The first minimizes the in-text references to sources by using footnotes or endnotes indicated by superscript numerals. Disciplines that draw on it, such as history, tend to use many sources. An alternative form of Chicago style resembles APA style.

CSE style, used by the sciences, also has different forms. Name-year style shares important features with APA style, whereas citation-sequence and citation-name styles use endnotes with a number assigned to each source. The prevalence of abbreviations in CSE style indicates that researchers are expected to know the major texts in their fields.

If you are not sure which of the styles covered in this handbook to use, ask your instructor. If you are required to use an alternative, discipline-specific documentation style, consult the list of manuals on page 339.

CHARTING the TERRITORY

Style Manuals for Specific Disciplines

SPECIFIC DISCIPLINE	POSSIBLE STYLE MANUAL
Chemistry	Coghill, Anne M., and Lorrin R. Garson, eds. *The ACS Style Guide: A Manual for Authors and Editors*. 3rd ed. Washington: American Chemical Society, 2006.
Geology	Bates, Robert L., Rex Buchanan, and Marla Adkins-Heljeson, eds. *Geowriting: A Guide to Writing, Editing, and Printing in Earth Science.* 5th ed. Alexandria: American Geological Institute, 1995.
Government and Law	Garner, Diane L., and Diane H. Smith, eds. *The Complete Guide to Citing Government Information Resources: A Manual for Writers and Librarians.* Rev. ed. Bethesda: Congressional Information Service, 1993.
	Harvard Law Review et al. *The Bluebook: A Uniform System of Citation*. 18th ed. Cambridge: Harvard Law Review Assn., 2005.
Journalism	Goldstein, Norm, ed. *Associated Press Stylebook 2008.* New York: Associated Press, 2008.
Linguistics	Linguistic Society of America. "LSA Style Sheet." *LSA Bulletin*. Published annually in the December issue.
Mathematics	American Mathematical Society. *AMS Author Handbook: General Instructions for Preparing Manuscripts*. Providence: AMS, 2007.
Medicine	Iverson, Cheryl, ed. *American Medical Association Manual of Style: A Guide for Authors and Editors*. 10th ed. New York: Oxford University Press, 2007.
Political Science	American Political Science Association. *Style Manual for Political Science*. Rev. ed. Washington: APSA, 2001.

For her paper on Louis Armstrong and Joe Glaser, Esther Hoffman used the MLA documentation style. (*The final draft of the paper appears at the end of Chapter 23: MLA Documentation Style, on pp. 378–90.*)

22d Present and publish your work.

There are many ways to share the results of your research. New technologies make it possible to create sophisticated audio and video presentations and Web sites. In both your academic and your professional career, you will likely be called upon to present your ideas, information, and research using presentation software such as PowerPoint or through visual tools such as iDVD. You might use desktop publishing software to prepare a research manuscript for interoffice or interdepartmental publication, or for publication in a newspaper or journal. Make the presentation of your research suit your audience and your purpose.

(*For more information on oral presentations, see Chapter 13: Oral Presentations, pp. 221–26. To learn more about presentation software and other multimedia tools, see Chapter 14: Multimedia Writing, pp. 226–47. For a discussion of document design, see Chapter 6: Designing Academic Papers and Preparing Portfolios, pp. 104–17.*)

The Library of Congress houses the largest collection of books and documents in the world, and all U.S. libraries use its cataloging systems. The Library's architectural design suggests the Italian Renaissance; its interior features work by American artists.

PART 4

Nothing gives an author so much pleasure as to find his works respectfully quoted by other learned authors.

—Benjamin Franklin

Documenting across the Curriculum

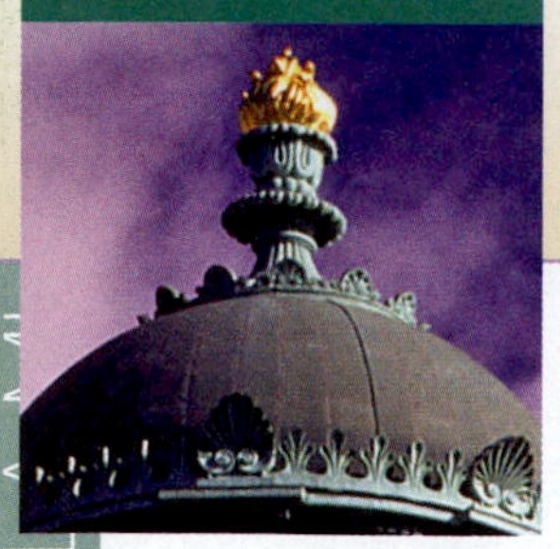

23 MLA Documentation Style

The documentation style developed by the Modern Language Association (MLA) is used by many researchers in the arts and humanities, especially by those who write about language and literature. The guidelines presented here are based on the seventh edition of the *MLA Handbook for Writers of Research Papers* (New York: MLA, 2009).

www.mhhe.com/mhhb2

For links to Web sites for documentation styles used in various disciplines, go to

Research > Links to Documentation Sites

23a The elements of MLA documentation style

College papers include information, ideas, and quotations from sources that must be accurately documented. Documentation allows others to see the path you have taken in researching and writing your paper. (*For more on what to document, see Chapter 22: Writing the Paper, pp. 333–40.*)

MLA style requires writers to list their sources in a works-cited list at the end of a paper. Answering the questions in the foldout charts that follow will help you find the appropriate model works-cited entry for your source. The reverse side of the foldout indicates where to find the information you need for a citation. (*See also the directory on pages 351–53.*)

WRITING OUTCOMES

Part 4: Documenting across the Curriculum

This section will help you answer questions such as:

Rhetorical Knowledge

- Which disciplines use MLA, APA, Chicago, and CSE styles? **(23–26)**

Critical Thinking, Reading, and Writing

- Why do I need to document my sources? **(23a, 24b–c, 25a, 26)**

Processes

- How should I label visuals in MLA **(23e)** and APA **(24d)** styles?

Knowledge of Conventions

- How do I cite sources in the text of my paper or in notes? (MLA: **23b**, APA: **24b**, Chicago: **25a**, CSE: **26a**)
- How and when do I create a listing of sources at the end of my paper in MLA **(23c)**, APA **(24c)**, and CSE **(26c)** styles?

Self-Assessment: *Take an online quiz at www.mhhe.com/mhhb2 to test your familiarity with the topics covered in Chapters 23–24. Pay special attention to the sections in these chapters that correspond to any questions you answer incorrectly.*

The MLA documentation style has three parts:

- In-text citations
- List of works cited
- Explanatory notes and acknowledgments

In-text citations and a list of works cited are mandatory; explanatory notes are optional.

23b MLA style: In-text citations

In-text citations let readers know that they can find full bibliographical information about your sources in the list of works cited at the end of your paper.

1. Author named in sentence In your first reference, give the author's full name as the source presents it. Afterward, use the last name only, unless two or more of your sources have the same last name (*see no. 6*) or unless two or more works by the same author appear in your works-cited list (*no. 3*).

signal phrase

As Thomas J. Hennessey explains, record deals were usually negotiated by "white middlemen" (127).

The parenthetical page citation comes after the closing quotation mark but before the period.

2. Author named in parentheses If you do not name the source's author in your sentence, then you must provide the name in the parentheses. (Give the full name if the author of another source has the same last name.)

Armstrong easily reached difficult high notes, the F's and G's that stymied other trumpeters (Bergreen 248).

no comma after author's name

There is no comma between the author's name and the page number. If you cite two or more distinct pages, however, separate the numbers with a comma: (Bergreen 450, 457).

3. Two or more works by the same author If you use two or more works by the same author, you must identify which work you are citing, either in your sentence or in an abbreviated form in parentheses: (Collier, *Louis Armstrong* 330).

book title is italicized

In *Louis Armstrong: An American Genius*, James Lincoln Collier reports that Glaser paid Armstrong's mortgage, taxes, and basic living expenses (330).

MLA IN-TEXT CITATIONS: DIRECTORY to SAMPLE TYPES

(See pp. 350–76 for works-cited examples.)

4. Two or three authors of the same work If a source has up to three authors, you should name them all either in your text, as the next example shows, or in parentheses: (Jones and Chilton 160, 220).

> According to Max Jones and John Chilton, Glaser's responsibilities included booking appearances, making travel arrangements, and paying the band members' salaries (160, 220).

5. More than three authors If a source has more than three authors, either list all the authors or give the first author's last name followed by "et al.," meaning "and others." Do the same in your works-cited list.

> Changes in social regulations are bound to produce new forms of subjectivity (Henriques et al. 275).

MLA IN-TEXT CITATIONS

- Name the author, either in a signal phrase such as "Laurence Bergreen maintains" or in a parenthetical citation.
- Include a page reference in parentheses. No "p." precedes the page number, and if the author is named in the parentheses, there is no punctuation between the author's name and the page number.
- Place the citation as close to the material being cited as possible and before any punctuation marks that divide or end the sentence except in a block quotation, where the citation comes one space after the period or final punctuation mark. See no. 12 for quotations ending with a question mark or an exclamation point.
- Italicize the titles of books, magazines, and plays. Place quotation marks around the titles of articles and short poems.
- For Internet sources, follow the same general guidelines as for print sources. Keep the parenthetical citation simple, providing enough information for your reader to find the full citation in your works-cited list. Cite either the author's name or the title of the site or article. Begin the parenthetical citation with the first word of the corresponding works-cited list entry.
- For works without page or paragraph numbers, give the author or title only. Often it is best to mention them in your sentence, in which case no parenthetical citation is needed.

6. Authors with the same last name If the authors of two or more of your sources have the same last name, include the first initial of the author you are citing (R. Campbell 63); if the first initial is also shared, use the full first name, as shown below.

> In the late nineteenth century, the sale of sheet music spread rapidly in a Manhattan area along Broadway known as Tin Pan Alley (Richard Campbell 63).

7. Organization as author Treat the organization as the author. If the name is long, put it in a signal phrase.

> The Centre for Contemporary Cultural Studies claims that "there is nothing inherently concrete about historiography" (10).

8. Unknown author When no author is given, cite a work by its title, using either the full title in a signal phrase or an abbreviated version in the parentheses. When abbreviating the title, begin with the word by which it is alphabetized in your works-cited list.

title of article
"Squaresville, USA vs. Beatsville" makes the Midwestern small-town home seem boring compared with the West Coast artist's "pad" (31).

The Midwestern small-town home seems boring compared with the West Coast artist's "pad" ("Squaresville" 31).

9. Entire work Acknowledge an entire work in your text, not in a parenthetical citation. Include the work in your list of works cited and include in the text the word by which the entry is alphabetized.

Sidney J. Furie's film *Lady Sings the Blues* presents Billie Holiday as a beautiful woman in pain rather than as the great jazz artist she was.

10. Paraphrased or summarized source If you include the author's name in your paraphrase or summary, include only the page number or numbers in your parenthetical citation. Signal phrases clarify that you are paraphrasing or summarizing.

signal phrase
Bergreen recounts how in Southern states, where blacks were prohibited from entering many stores, Glaser sometimes had to shop for the band's food and other supplies (378, 381).

11. Source of a long quotation For a quotation of more than four typed lines of prose or three of poetry, do not use quotation marks. Instead, indent the material you are quoting by one inch. Following the final punctuation mark of the quotation, allow one space before the parenthetical information.

Glaser managed the Sunset Café, a club where Armstrong often performed:

> There was a pronounced gangster element at the Sunset, but Louis, accustomed to being employed and protected by mobsters, didn't think twice about that. Mr. Capone's men ensured the flow of alcohol, and their presence reassured many whites. (Bergreen 279)

12. Source of a short quotation Close the quotation before the parenthetical citation. If the quotation concludes with an exclamation point or a question mark, place the closing quotation mark after that punctuation mark and place the sentence period after the parenthetical citation.

His innovative singing style also featured "scat," a technique that combines

brackets enclose a word that substitutes for omitted text

"nonsense syllables [with] improvised melodies" (Robinson 515).

Shakespeare's Sonnet XVIII asks, "Shall I compare thee to a summer's day?" (line 1).

13. One-page source You need not include a page number in the parenthetical citation for a one-page printed source.

14. Government publication To avoid an overly long parenthetical citation, name within your text the government agency that published the source.

According to a report issued by the Bureau of National Affairs, many employers in 1964 needed guidance to apply new workplace rules that ensured fairness and complied with the Civil Rights Act of 1964 (32).

15. Photograph, map, graph, chart, or other visual

VISUAL APPEARS IN YOUR PAPER

An aerial photograph of Manhattan (Fig. 3), taken by the United States Geographical Survey, demonstrates how creative city planning can introduce parks and green spaces within even the most densely populated urban areas.

If the caption you write for the image includes all the information found in a works-cited list entry, you need not include it in your list. (*See p. 386 for an example.*)

VISUAL DOES NOT APPEAR IN YOUR PAPER

An aerial photograph of Manhattan taken by the United States Geographical Survey demonstrates how creative city planning can introduce parks and green spaces within even the most densely populated urban areas (TerraServer-USA).

Provide a parenthetical citation that directs your reader to information about the source of the image in your works-cited list.

16. Web site or other online electronic source If you cannot find the author of an online source, then identify the source by title, either in your text or in a parenthetical citation. Because most online sources do not have set page, section, or paragraph numbers, they must usually be cited as entire works.

"Peter Davis gave [Armstrong] "basic musical training on the cornet" ("Louis Armstrong").

17. Work with numbered paragraphs or sections instead of pages Give the paragraph or section number(s) after the author's name and a comma. To distinguish them from page numbers, use the abbreviation *par(s).* or the type of division such as *section(s).*

> Rothstein suggests that many German Romantic musical techniques may have originated in Italian opera (par. 9).

18. Work with no page or paragraph numbers When citing an online or print source without page, paragraph, or other reference numbers, try to include the author's name in your text instead of in a parenthetical citation.

> author's name
> Crouch argues that Armstrong remains a driving force in present-day music, from country and western music to the chanted doggerel of rap.

19. Multivolume work When citing more than one volume of a multivolume work in your paper, include with each citation the volume number, followed by a colon, a space, and the page number.

> Schuller argues that even though jazz's traditional framework appears European, its musical essence is African (1: 62).

If you consult only one volume of a multivolume work, then specify that volume in the works-cited list (*see p. 390*), but not in the parenthetical citation.

20. Literary work

Novels and literary nonfiction books Include the relevant page number, followed by a semicolon, a space, and the chapter number.

> Louis Armstrong figures throughout Ellison's *Invisible Man*, including in the narrator's penultimate decision to become a "yes" man who "undermine[s] them with grins" (384; ch. 23).

If the author is not named in your sentence, add the name in front of the page number: (Ellison 384; ch. 23).

Poems Use line numbers, not page numbers.

> In "Trumpet Player," Hughes says that the music "Is honey / Mixed with liquid fire" (lines 19-20). This image returns at the end of the poem, when Hughes concludes that "Trouble / Mellows to a golden note" (43-44).

Note that the word *lines* (not italicized), rather than *l.* or *ll.*, is used in the first citation to establish what the numbers in parentheses refer to; subsequent citations need not use the word *lines* (again, not italicized).

Plays and long, multisection poems Use division (act, scene, canto, book, part) and lines, not page numbers. In the following example, notice that arabic numerals are used for act and scene divisions as well as for line numbers: (*Ham.* 2.3.22-27). The same is true for canto, verse, and lines in the following citation of Byron's *Don Juan:* (*DJ* 1.37.4-8). (The *MLA Handbook* lists abbreviations for titles of certain literary works.)

21. Religious text Cite material in the Bible, Upanishads, or Koran by book, chapter, and verse, using an appropriate abbreviation when the name of the book is in the parentheses rather than in your sentence. Name the edition from which you are citing.

> As the Bible says, "The wise man knows there will be a time of judgment" (*Holy Bible, Rev. Stand. Vers.*, Eccles. 8.5).

Note that titles of biblical books are not italicized.

22. Historical document For familiar documents such as the Constitution and the Declaration of Independence, provide the document's name and the numbers of the parts you are citing.

> Judges are allowed to remain in office "during good behavior," a vague standard that has had various interpretations (US Const., art. 3, sec. 1).

23. Indirect source When you quote or paraphrase a quotation you found in someone else's work, put *qtd. in* (not italicized, meaning "quoted in") before the name of your source.

> Armstrong confided to a friend that Glaser's death "broke [his] heart" (qtd. in Bergreen 490).

In your list of works cited, list only the work you consulted, in this case the indirect source by Bergreen.

24. Two or more sources in one citation When you credit two or more sources, use a semicolon to separate the citations.

> Giving up his other business ventures, Glaser now became Armstrong's exclusive agent (Bergreen 376-78; Collier 273-76; Morgenstern 124-28).

25. Two or more sources in one sentence Include a parenthetical reference after each idea or quotation you have borrowed.

> Ironically, Americans lavish more money each year on their pets than they spend on children's toys (Merkins 21), but the feral cat population—consisting of abandoned pets and their offspring—is at an estimated 70 million and growing (Mott).

26. Work in an anthology When citing a work in a collection, give the name of the specific work's author, not the name of the editor of the whole collection.

> When Dexter Gordon threatened to quit, Armstrong offered him a raise—without consulting with Glaser (Morgenstern 132).

Here, Morgenstern is cited as the source even though his work appears in a collection edited by Marc Miller. Note that the list of works cited must include an entry for Morgenstern (*see p. 390*).

27. E-mail, letter, or personal interview Cite by name the person you communicated with, using either a signal phrase or parentheses.

> Much to Glaser's surprise, both "Hello, Dolly" and "What a Wonderful World" became big hits after the rights had been sold (Jacobs).

In the works-cited list, after giving the person's last name you will need to identify the kind of communication and its date (*see pp. 362, 372, and 375*).

23c MLA style: List of works cited

MLA documentation style requires a works-cited page with full bibliographic information about your sources. The list of works cited should appear at the end of your paper, beginning on a new page entitled "Works Cited." Include only those sources you cite in your paper, unless your instructor tells you to prepare a "Works Consulted" list.

Books

1. Book with one author Italicize the book's title. Generally only the city, not the state, is included in the publication data. Conclude with the medium (print). Notice that in the example the publisher's name, *Wayne State University Press,* is abbreviated to *Wayne State UP.*

> Hennessey, Thomas J. *From Jazz to Swing: African-Americans and Their Music 1890-1935*. Detroit: Wayne State UP, 1984. Print.

MLA WORKS-CITED ENTRIES: DIRECTORY to SAMPLE TYPES

(*See pp. 343–50 for examples of in-text citations.*)

MLA WORKS-CITED ENTRIES *(continued)*

MLA WORKS-CITED ENTRIES *(continued)*

2. Two or more works by the same author(s) Give the author's name in the first entry only. For subsequent works authored by that person, replace the name with three hyphens and a period. Alphabetize by title.

Collier, James Lincoln. *Jazz: The American Theme Song*. New York: Oxford UP, 1993. Print.

---. *Louis Armstrong: An American Genius*. New York: Oxford UP, 1983. Print.

3. Book with two or three authors Name the two or three authors in the order in which they appear on the title page, putting the last name first for the first author only.

Davis, Miles, and Quincy Troupe. *Miles: The Autobiography*. New York: Simon, 1989. Print.

4. Book with four or more authors When a work has more than three authors, you may list them all or use the abbreviation *et al.* (meaning "and others") to replace the names of all authors except the first.

Henriques, Julian, et al. *Changing the Subject: Psychology, Social Regulation, and Subjectivity*. New York: Methuen, 1984. Print.

5. Organization as author Consider as an organization any group, commission, association, or corporation whose members are not identified on the title page.

Centre for Contemporary Cultural Studies. *Making Histories: Studies in History Writing and Politics*. London: Hutchinson, 1982. Print.

6. Book by an editor or editors If the title page lists an editor instead of an author, begin with the editor's name followed by the abbreviation *ed.* (not italicized). Use *eds.* when more than one editor is listed. Only the first editor's name should appear in reverse order.

Miller, Paul Eduard, ed. *Esquire's Jazz Book*. New York: Smith, 1944. Print.

7. Book with an author and an editor Put the author and title first, followed by the abbreviation *Ed.* (not italicized, for "edited by") and the name of the editor. However, if you cited something written by the editor see no. 15.

editor's name not in reverse order

Armstrong, Louis. *Louis Armstrong: A Self-Portrait*. Ed. Richard Meryman. New York: Eakins, 1971. Print.

8. Work in an anthology or chapter in an edited book List the author and title of the selection, followed by the title of the anthology, *Ed.* and the editor's name, publication data, page numbers of the selection, and medium.

Smith, Hale. "Here I Stand." *Readings in Black American Music*. Ed. Eileen Southern. New York: Norton, 1971. 286-89. Print.

9. Two or more items from one anthology Include a complete entry for the anthology beginning with the name of the editor(s). Each selection should have its own entry in the alphabetical list that includes only the author, title of the selection, editor, and page numbers.

entry for a selection from the anthology

Johnson, Hall. "Notes on the Negro Spiritual." Southern 268-75.

entry for the anthology

Southern, Eileen, ed. *Readings in Black American Music*. New York: Norton, 1971. Print.

entry for a selection from the anthology

Still, William Grant. "The Structure of Music." Southern 276-79.

10. Signed article in an encyclopedia or another reference work Cite the author's name, title of the entry (in quotation marks), title of the reference work (italicized), editor, publication information, and medium. Omit page numbers if entries appear in alphabetical order.

MLA LIST of WORKS CITED

- Begin on a new page with the centered title "Works Cited."
- Include an entry for every source cited in your text.
- Include author, title, publication data, and medium (such as print, Web, radio) for each entry, if available. Use a period to set off each of these elements from the others. Leave one space after the periods.
- Do not number the entries.
- Put entries in alphabetical order by author's or editor's last name. If the work has more than one author, see nos. 3 and 4 (*p. 353*). (If the author is unknown, use the first word of the title, excluding the articles *a, an*, or *the*).
- Italicize titles of books, periodicals, long poems, and plays. Put quotation marks around titles of articles, short stories, and short poems.
- Capitalize the first and last and all important words in all titles and subtitles. Do not capitalize articles, prepositions, coordinating conjunctions, and the *to* in infinitives unless they appear first or last in the title. Place a colon between title and subtitle unless the title ends in a question mark or an exclamation point.
- In the publication data, abbreviate months and publishers' names (Dec. rather than December; Oxford UP instead of Oxford University Press), and include the name of the city in which the publisher is located but not the state (unless the city is obscure or ambiguous): Ithaca: Cornell UP. Use n.p. in place of publisher or location information if none is available. If the date of publication is not given, provide the approximate date, enclosed in brackets: [c. 1975]. If you cannot approximate the date, write n.d. for "no date."
- Do not use p., pp., or page(s). Use n. pag. if the source lacks page or paragraph numbers or other divisions. When page spans over 100 have the same first digit, do not repeat it for the second number: 243–47.
- Abbreviate all months except May, June, and July.
- For articles and other print sources that skip pages, provide the page number for the beginning of the article followed by a plus (+) sign.
- Use a hanging indent: Start the first line of each entry at the left margin, and indent all subsequent lines of the entry five spaces (or one-half inch on the computer).
- Double-space within entries and between them.

Robinson, J. Bradford. "Scat Singing." *The New Grove Dictionary of Jazz*. Ed. Barry Kernfeld. Vol. 3. London: Macmillan, 2002. Print.

11. Unsigned entry in an encyclopedia or another reference work Start the entry with the title. For well-known reference works, omit the place and publisher.

"Scat." *Merriam-Webster's Collegiate Dictionary*. 11th ed. 2003. Print.

12. Article from a collection of reprinted articles

Haney-Peritz, Janice. "Monumental Feminism and Literature's Ancestral House: Another Look at 'The Yellow Wallpaper.'" *Women's Studies* 12.2 (1986): 113-28.
abbreviation for "reprinted"
Rpt. in *The Captive Imagination: A Casebook on "The Yellow Wallpaper."* Ed. Catherine Golden. New York: Feminist, 1992. 261-76. Print.

13. Anthology

Eggers, Dave, ed. *The Best American Nonrequired Reading 2007*. Boston: Houghton, 2007. Print.

14. Publisher's imprint For books published by a division within a publishing company, known as an "imprint," put a hyphen between the imprint and publisher.

title in title, see no. 22
Wells, Ken, ed. *Floating Off the Page: The Best Stories from* The Wall Street Journal's *"Middle Column."* New York: Wall Street Journal-Simon, 2002. Print.

15. Preface, foreword, introduction, or afterword When the writer of the part is different from the author of the book, use the word *By* after the book's title and cite the author's full name. If the book's sole author wrote the part and the book has an editor, use only the author's last name after *By*. If there is no editor and the author wrote the part, cite the complete book.

name of part of book
Crawford, Richard. Foreword. *The Jazz Tradition*. By Martin Williams. New York: Oxford UP, 1993. v-xiii. Print.

16. Translation The translator's name goes after the title, with the abbreviation *Trans.*

Goffin, Robert. *Horn of Plenty: The Story of Louis Armstrong*. Trans. James F. Bezov. New York: Da Capo, 1977. Print.

17. Edition other than the first Include the number of the edition: *2nd ed., 3rd ed.* (not italicized) and so on. Place the number after the title, or if there is an editor, after that person's name.

Panassie, Hugues. *Louis Armstrong*. 2nd ed. New York: Da Capo, 1980. Print.

18. Religious text Give the version, italicized; the editor's or translator's name (if any); and the publication information including medium.

New American Standard Bible. La Habra: Lockman Foundation, 1995. Print.

The Upanishads. Trans. Eknath Easwaran. Tomales, CA: Nilgiri, 1987. Print.

19. Multivolume work The first example indicates that the researcher used more than one volume of the work; the second shows that only the second volume was used.

Lissauer, Robert. *Lissauer's Encyclopedia of Popular Music in America*. 3 vols. New York: Facts on File, 1996. Print.

Lissauer, Robert. *Lissauer's Encyclopedia of Popular Music in America*. Vol. 2. New York: Facts on File, 1996. Print.

20. Book in a series After the medium, put the name of the series and, if available on the title page, the number of the work.

Floyd, Samuel A., Jr., ed. *Black Music in the Harlem Renaissance*. New York: Greenwood,

Name of series not italicized

1990. Print. Contributions in Afro-American and African Studies 128.

21. Republished book Put the original date of publication, followed by a period, before the current publication data.

original publication date

Cuney-Hare, Maud. *Negro Musicians and Their Music*. 1936. New York: Da Capo, 1974. Print.

22. Title in a title When a book's title contains the title of another book, do not italicize the second title. For the novel *Invisible Man*:

O'Meally, Robert, ed. *New Essays on* Invisible Man. Cambridge: Cambridge UP, 1988. Print.

23. Unknown author The citation begins with the title. In the list of works cited, alphabetize the citation by the first important word, excluding the articles *A, An,* and *The.*

Webster's College Dictionary. New York: Random; New York: McGraw, 1991. Print.

Note that this entry includes both of the publishers listed on the dictionary's title page; they are separated by a semicolon.

24. Book with illustrator List the illustrator after the title with the abbreviation *illus.* (not italicized). If you refer primarily to the illustrator, put that name before the title instead of the author's.

Carroll, Lewis. *Alice's Adventures in Wonderland and through the Looking-Glass.* Illus. John Tenniel. New York: Modern Library-Random, 2002. Print.

Tenniel, John, illus. *Alice's Adventures in Wonderland and through the Looking-Glass.* By Lewis Carroll. New York: Modern Library-Random, 2002. Print.

25. Graphic novel or comic book Cite graphic narratives created by one person as you would any other book or multivolume work. For collaborations, begin with the person whose work you refer to most and list others in the order in which they appear on the title page. Indicate each person's contribution. (*For part of a series, see no. 20.*)

Satrapi, Marjane. *Persepolis*. 2 vols. New York: Pantheon-Random, 2004-05. Print.

Moore, Alan, writer. *Watchmen*. Illus. David Gibbons. Color by John Higgins. New York: DC Comics, 1995. Print.

Periodicals

Periodicals are published at set intervals, usually four times a year for scholarly journals, monthly or weekly for magazines, and daily or weekly for newspapers. Between the author and the publication data are two titles: the title of the article, in quotation marks, and the title of the periodical, italicized. (*For online versions of print periodicals and periodicals published only online, see pp. 364–65 and 370–71.*)

26. Article in a journal with volume numbers Most journals have a volume number corresponding to the year and an issue number for each publication that year. The issue may be indicated by a month or season. Put the volume number after the title. Follow it with a period and the issue number. Give the year of publication in parentheses, followed by a colon, a space, and the page numbers of the article. End with the medium.

Tirro, Frank. "Constructive Elements in Jazz Improvisation." *Journal of the American Musicological Society* 27.2 (1974): 285-305. Print.

27. Article in a journal with issue numbers only Give only the issue number.

Lousley, Cheryl. "Knowledge, Power and Place." *Canadian Literature* 195 (2007): 11-30. Print.

28. Article in a monthly magazine Provide the month and year, abbreviating all months except May, June, and July.

Walker, Malcolm. "Discography: Bill Evans." *Jazz Monthly* June 1965: 20-22. Print.

29. Article in a weekly magazine Include the complete date of publication: day, month, and year.

Taylor, J. R. "Jazz History: The Incompleted Past." *Village Voice* 3 July 1978: 65-67. Print.

30. Article in a newspaper Provide the day, month, and year. If an edition is named on the top of the first page, specify the edition—*natl. ed.* or *late ed.* (without italics), for example—after the date. If the section letter is part of the page number, see the first example. Give the title of an unnumbered section with *sec* (not italicized). If the article appears on nonconsecutive pages, put a plus (+) sign after the first page number.

Blumenthal, Ralph. "Satchmo with His Tape Recorder Running." *New York Times* 3 Aug. 1999, natl. ed.: E1+. Print.

Just, Julie. "Children's Bookshelf." *New York Times* 15 Mar. 2009, natl. ed., Book Review sec.:13. Print.

31. Unsigned article The citation begins with the title and is alphabetized by the first word, excluding articles such as *A, An,* or *The.*

"Squaresville, USA vs. Beatsville." *Life* 21 Sept. 1959: 31. Print.

32. Review Begin with the name of the reviewer and, if there is one, the title of the review. Add *Rev. of* (without italics, meaning "review of") and the title plus the author or performer of the work being reviewed.

Ostwald, David. "All That Jazz." Rev. of *Louis Armstrong: An Extravagant Life*, by Laurence Bergreen. *Commentary* Nov. 1997: 68-72. Print.

33. Editorial Treat editorials as articles, but add the word *Editorial* (not italicized) after the title. If the editorial is unsigned, begin with the title.

Shaw, Theodore M. "The Debate over Race Needs Minority Students' Voices." Editorial. *Chronicle of Higher Education* 25 Feb. 2000: A72. Print.

34. Abstract of a journal article Collections of abstracts from journals can be found in the library's reference section. Include the publication information for the original article, followed by the title of the publication that provides the abstract, the volume, the year in parentheses, and the item or page number.

Theiler, Anne M., and Louise G. Lippman. "Effects of Mental Practice and Modeling on Guitar and Vocal Performance." *Journal of General Psychology* 122.4 (1995): 329-43. *Psychological Abstracts* 83.1 (1996): item 30039. Print.

35. Letter to the editor

Tyler, Steve. Letter. *National Geographic Adventure* Apr. 2004: 11. Print.

Other Print Sources

36. Government document Either the name of the government and agency or the name of the document's author comes first. If the government and agency name come first, follow the title of the document with the word *By* for a writer, *Ed.* for an editor, or *Comp.* for a compiler (if any), and give the name. Publication information and medium come last.

United States. Bureau of Natl. Affairs. *The Civil Rights Act of 1964: Text, Analysis, Legislative History; What It Means to Employers, Businessmen, Unions, Employees, Minority Groups.* Washington: BNA, 1964. Print.

For the format to use when citing the *Congressional Record,* see no. 75.

37. Pamphlet or brochure Treat as a book. If the pamphlet or brochure has an author, list his or her name first; otherwise, begin with the title.

All Music Guide to Jazz. 2nd ed. San Francisco: Miller Freeman, 1996. Print.

38. Conference proceedings Cite as you would a book, but include information about the conference if it is not in the title.

Mendel, Arthur, Gustave Reese, and Gilbert Chase, eds. *Papers Read at the International Congress of Musicology Held at New York September 11th to 16th, 1939*. New York: Music Educators' Natl. Conf. for the American Musicological Soc., 1944. Print.

39. Published dissertation Cite as you would a book. After the title, add *Diss.* (not italicized) for "dissertation," the name of the institution, the year the dissertation was written, and the medium.

Fraser, Wilmot Alfred. *Jazzology: A Study of the Tradition in Which Jazz Musicians Learn to Improvise*. Diss. U of Pennsylvania, 1983. Ann Arbor: UMI, 1987. Print.

40. Unpublished dissertation Begin with the author's name, followed by the title in quotation marks, the abbreviation *Diss.* (not italicized), the name of the institution, the year the dissertation was written, and the medium.

Reyes-Schramm, Adelaida. "The Role of Music in the Interaction of Black Americans and Hispanos in New York City's East Harlem." Diss. Columbia U, 1975. Print.

41. Abstract of a dissertation Use the format for an unpublished dissertation. After the dissertation date, give the abbreviation *DA* or *DAI* (for *Dissertation Abstracts* or *Dissertation Abstracts International*), then the volume number, the issue number, the date of publication, the page number, and the medium.

Quinn, Richard Allen. "Playing Together: Improvisation in Postwar American Literature and Culture." Diss. U of Iowa, 2000. *DAI* 61.6 (2001): 2305A. Print.

42. Published interview Name the person interviewed and give the title of the interview or the descriptive term *Interview* (not italicized), the name of the interviewer (if known and relevant), the publication information, and the medium.

Armstrong, Louis. Interview by Richard Meryman. "Authentic American Genius." *Life* 15 Apr. 1966: 92-102. Print.

43. Map or chart Cite as you would a book with an unknown author. Italicize the title of the map or chart, and add the word *Map* or *Chart* (not italicized) following the title.

Let's Go Map Guide to New Orleans. Map. New York: St. Martin's, 1997. Print.

44. Cartoon Include the cartoonist's name, the title of the cartoon (if any) in quotation marks, the word *Cartoon* (not italicized), the publication information, and the medium.

Myller, Jorgen. "Louis Armstrong's First Lesson." Cartoon. *Melody Maker* Mar. 1931: 12. Print.

45. Reproduction of artwork Treat a photograph of a work of art in another source like a work in an anthology (*no. 8*). Italicize the titles of both the artwork and the source, and include the institution or collection and city where the work can be found prior to information about the source in which it appears.

Da Vinci, Leonardo. *Mona Lisa*. N.d. Louvre, Paris. *Gardner's Art Through the Ages: A Concise History of Western Art*. By Fred S. Kleiner and Christin J. Mamiya. Belmont, CA: Thomson, 2008. 253. Print.

46. Advertisement Name the item or organization being advertised, include the word *Advertisement* (not italicized), and indicate where the ad appeared.

Hartwick College Summer Music Festival and Institute. Advertisement. *New York Times Magazine* 3 Jan. 1999: 54. Print.

47. Published letter Treat like a work in an anthology, but include the date. Include the number, if one was assigned by the editor. If you use more than one letter from a published collection, follow the instructions for cross-referencing in no. 9.

Hughes, Langston. "To Arna Bontemps." 17 Jan. 1938. *Arna Bontemps—Langston Hughes Letters 1925-1967*. Ed. Charles H. Nichols. New York: Dodd, 1980. 27-28. Print.

48. Personal letter To cite a letter you received, start with the writer's name, followed by the descriptive phrase *Letter to the author* (not italicized), the date, and MS (manuscript).

Cogswell, Michael. Letter to the author. 15 Mar. 2008. MS.

To cite someone else's unpublished personal letter, see no. 49.

49. Manuscripts, typescripts, and material in archives Give the author, a title or description (*Letter, Notebook*), the form (*MS.* if handwritten, *TS.* if typed), any identifying number, and the name and location of the institution housing the material. (Do not italicize any part of the citation.)

Glaser, Joe. Letter to Lucille Armstrong. 28 Sept. 1960. MS. Box 3. Louis Armstrong Archives. Queens College City U of New York, Flushing.

Pollack, Bracha. "A Man ahead of His Time." 1997. TS.

50. Legal source (print or online) To cite a specific act, give its name, Public Law number, its Statutes at Large number, page range, the date it was enacted, and the medium.

Energy Policy Act of 2005. Pub. L. 109-58. 119 Stat. 594-1143. 8 Aug. 2005. Print.

To cite a law case, provide the name of the plaintiff and defendant, the case number, the court that decided the case, the date of the decision, and the medium.

PRINT

Ashcroft v. the Free Speech Coalition. 535 US 234-73. Supreme Court of the US. 2002. Print.

WEB

Ashcroft v. the Free Speech Coalition. 535 US 234-73. Supreme Court of the US. 2002. *Supreme Court Collection*. Legal Information Inst., Cornell U Law School, n.d. Web. 20 May 2008.

For more information about citing legal documents or from case law, MLA recommends consulting *The Bluebook: A Uniform System of Citation,* published by the Harvard Law Review Association.

Online Sources

The examples that follow are based on guidelines for the citation of electronic sources in the seventh edition of the *MLA Handbook for Writers of Research Papers* (2009).

For scholarly journals published online, see no. 88. For periodical articles from an online database, see no. 92. Cite most other Web sources according to nos. 51–52. For works that also exist in another medium (e.g. print), the MLA recommends including information about the other version in your citation. See nos. 76–87.

Basic Web sources

51. Web site or independent online work Begin with the author, editor (*ed.*), compiler (*comp.*), director (*dir.*), performer (*perf.*), or translator (*trans.*), if any. Give the title (italicized), the version or edition (if any), the publisher or sponsor (or *n.p.*), publication date (or last update, or *n.d.*), medium, and your access date. (Use italics for the title only.) Citations 51–74 follow this format.

Raeburn, Bruce Boyd, ed. *William Ransom Hogan Archive of New Orleans Jazz*. Tulane U, 13 Apr. 2006. Web. 11 May 2008.

52. Part of a Web site or larger online work Give the title of the part in quotation marks.

Oliver, Rachel. "All About: Forests and Carbon Trading." *CNN.com*. Cable News Network, 11 Feb. 2008. Web. 14 Mar. 2008.

53. Personal Web site If no title is available, use a descriptive term such as "Home page."

no publisher

Henson, Keith. *The Keith Henson Jazzpage*. N.p., 1996. Web. 11 May 2008.

54. Home page for a course After the instructor's name, list the site title, then the department and school names.

Web site title

Hea, Kimme. *Spatial and Visual Rhetorics*. Dept. of English, U of Arizona, 4 Jan. 2003. Web. 11 May 2008.

55. Home page for an academic department

Department of English. U of Arizona, 14 May 2008. Web. 19 May 2008.

56. Personal page on a social networking site

Xiu Xiu. "Xiu Xiu." *MySpace.com*. MySpace, 26 Apr. 2008. Web. 11 May 2008.

57. Entire blog

McLennan, Doug. *Diacritical*. ArtsJournal, 20 Feb. 2008. Web. 11 May 2008.

58. Blog entry

McLennan, Doug. "The Rise of Arts Culture." *Diacritical*. ArtsJournal, 21 Nov. 2007. Web. 11 May 2008.

59. Article in an online magazine

Borushko, Matthew. "The Reinvention of Jazz." *The Atlantic.com*. Atlantic Monthly Group, 18 Apr. 2007. Web. 13 May 2008.

TEXTCONNEX

Web Addresses in MLA Citations

Only include the URL (Web address) of an online source in a citation if your reader would be unable to find the source without it (via a search engine). For example, basic citation information might not sufficiently identify your source if multiple versions of a document exist online without version numbers. Place a URL at the end of your citation in angle brackets and end with a period.

Raeburn, Bruce Boyd, ed. *William Ransom Hogan Archive of New Orleans Jazz.* Tulane U, 13 Apr. 2006. Web. 11 May 2008. <http://www.tulane .edu/~lmiller/JazzHome.html>.

If you need to divide a URL between lines, do so after a slash and do not insert a hyphen. If the URL is long (more than one line of your text), give the URL of the site's search page. Do not make the URL a hyperlink.

60. Article in an online newspaper

sponsor

Howard, Hilary. "A Cruise for Jazz Fans with a Soft Side." *New York Times*. New York Times, 11 May 2008. Web. 11 May 2008.

61. Editorial in an online newspaper Include the word *Editorial* (not italicized) after the published title of the editorial.

sponsor

"Schwarzenegger's Bad-News Budget." Editorial. *SFGate*. San Francisco Chronicle, 14 Jan. 2008. Web. 12 May 2008.

62. Letter to the editor in an online newspaper Include the name of the letter writer, as well as the word *Letter* (not italicized).

sponsor

Dow, Roger. Letter. *SFGate*. San Francisco Chronicle, 10 Jan. 2008. Web. 12 May 2008.

63. Online review

Kot, Greg. "The Roots Fuel Their Rage into 'Rising Down.'" Rev. of *Rising Down*, by the Roots. *chicagotribune.com*. Chicago Tribune, 11 May 2008. Web. 12 May 2008.

sponsor

64. Online interview See no. 42 for a print interview.

CITING ELECTRONIC SOURCES in MLA STYLE

- Begin with the name of the writer, editor, compiler, translator, director, or performer.
- Put the title of a short work in quotation marks.
- If there is no title, use a descriptive term such as *editorial* or *comment* (not italicized).
- Italicize the name of the publication or Web site. The online versions of some print magazines and newspapers have different titles than the print versions.
- Cite the date of publication or last update.
- For an online magazine or newspaper article or a Web original source, give the source (in quotation marks), the site title (italicized), version (if any), publisher or sponsor, date of publication, medium (*Web*), and access date. (*See p. 364.*)
- You may cite online sources that also appear in another medium with information about the other version (*see pp. 368–70*). (Do not cite online versions of print newspapers and magazines in this way.)
- For a journal article, include the article title (in quotation marks), periodical title (italicized), volume and issue numbers, and inclusive page numbers or *n. pag*. (not italicized). Conclude with the medium (Web) and access date. (*See pp. 370–71.*)
- To cite a periodical article from an online database, provide the print publication information, the database title (italicized), the medium, and your access date.
- If the source is not divided into sections or pages, include *n. pag*. (not italicized) for "no pagination." Give the medium (Web).
- Include your most recent date of access to the specific source (not the general site).
- Conclude the citation with a URL only if readers may have difficulty finding the source without it (*see the box on p. 365*).

Haddon, Mark. Interview by Dave Weich. *Powells.com*. Powell's Books, 24 June 2003. Web. 15 May 2008.

65. Article in an online encyclopedia or another reference work Begin with the author's name if any is given.

"Louis Armstrong." *Encyclopaedia Britannica Online*. Encyclopaedia Britannica, 2008. Web. 12 May 2008.

66. Entry in a wiki List the title of the entry, the wiki name, the sponsor, the date of latest update, the medium, and your access date. Check with your instructor before using a wiki as a source.

"Symphony." *Citizendium*. Citizendium Foundation, 1 Nov. 2007. Web. 12 May 2008.

67. Online map (Web only) Include the descriptive word *Map*.

"Denver, Colorado." Map. *Google Maps*. Google, 12 May 2008. Web. 12 May 2008.

68. Audio podcast

no publisher

Fresh Sounds. "Jazzarific: Bing Crosby Meets Louis Armstrong." *JazzVinyl.com*. N.p., 26 Dec. 2007. Web. 12 May 2008.

69. Video podcast

Mahr, Krista. "Saving China's Grasslands." *Time.com*. Time, Inc., 10 Oct. 2007. Web. 12 May 2008.

70. Online video (Web original) For material posted online from a film, TV series, or other non-Web source, see nos. 83 and 85.

Wesch, Michael. "The Machine Is Us/ing Us." *Digital Ethnography*. Kansas State U, 31 Jan. 2007. Web. 12 May 2008.

71. Posting to a news group or an electronic forum Treat an archived posting as a Web source. Use the subject line as the title of the posting and give the name of the Web site. If there is no subject, substitute *Online posting* (not italicized).

Pomeroy, Leslie K., Jr. "Racing with the Moon." *rec.music.bluenote*. N.p., 4 May 2008. Web. 12 May 2008.

72. Posting to an e-mail discussion list Include the author and use the subject line as the title.

Harbin, David. "Furtwangler's Beethoven 9 Bayreuth." *Opera-L Archives*. City U of New York, 3 Jan. 2008. Web. 12 May 2008.

73. Synchronous (real-time) communication Cite the online transcript of a synchronous communication as you would a Web site. Include a description, the title of the forum, the date of the event, the medium, and the date of access. If relevant, the speaker's name can begin the citation.

Curran, Stuart, and Harry Rusche. "Discussion: Plenary Log 6. Third Annual Graduate Student Conference in Romanticism." *Prometheus Unplugged: Emory MOO*. Emory U, 20 Apr. 1996. Web. 4 Jan. 1999.

74. Online government publication except the *Congressional Record* Begin with the name of the country, followed by the name of the sponsoring department, the title of the document, and the names (if listed) of the authors.

United States. National Commission on Terrorist Attacks upon the United States. *The 9/11 Commission Report*. By Thomas H. Kean, et al. 5 Aug. 2004. Web. 12 May. 2008.

75. *Congressional Record* (online or print) The *Congressional Record* has its own citation format, which is the same for print and online (apart from the medium). Abbreviate the title and include the date and page numbers. Give the medium (print or Web).

Cong. Rec. 28 Apr. 2005: D419-D428. Web. 12 May 2008.

Web sources also available in another medium

If an online work also appears in another medium (e.g., print), the MLA recommends (but does not require) that your citation include information about the other version of the work. (Information about the editor or sponsor of the Web site or database is optional in this model.) If the facts about the other version of the source are not available, cite as a basic Web source (*see nos. 51–52*). (Articles on the Web sites of newspapers and magazines are never cited with print publication information. *For academic journals, see nos. 88–91.*)

76. Online book Cite as a print book (*no. 1*). Instead of ending with *Print* (not italicized), give the Web site or database, the medium (Web), and your access date. Optional information about the site's sponsor, publisher, or editor follows the site name.

Arter, Jared Maurice. *Echoes from a Pioneer Life*. Atlanta: Caldwell, 1922. *Documenting the American South*. U of North Carolina, Chapel Hill. Web. 21 May 2008.

optional name and location of Web publisher

77. Selection from an online book Add the title of the selection after the author. If the online version of the work lacks page numbers, use *n. pag.* instead. (Capitalize the *n* in *n. pag.* when it follows a period.)

Sandburg, Carl. "Chicago." *Chicago Poems*. New York, Holt, 1916. N. pag. *Bartleby.com*. Web. 12 May 2008.

78. Online dissertation Give the Web site or database, the medium (Web), and your access date. Or cite as a basic Web source (*see nos. 51–52*).

Kosiba, Sara A. "A Successful Revolt? The Redefinition of Midwestern Literary Culture in the 1920s and 1930s." Diss. Kent State U, 2007. *OhioLINK*. Web. 12 May 2008.

79. Online pamphlet or brochure (also in print) Cite as a book. Give the title of the Web site or database, the medium (Web), and your access date. Or cite as a basic Web source (*see no. 51*).

United States. Securities and Exchange Commission. Division of Corporate Finance. *International Investing: Get the Facts*. Washington: GPO, 1999. *US Securities and Exchange Commission*. Web. 12 May 2008.

80. Online map or chart (also in print) See no. 43 for a print map. Remove the medium; add the title of the database or Web site, the medium (Web), and your access date. (See no. 67 for a Web-only map.) Or cite as a basic Web source (*see nos. 51–52*).

MTA New York City Subway. New York: Metropolitan Transit Authority, 2008. *MTA New York City Transit*. Web. 12 May 2008.

81. Online cartoon (also in print) See no. 44 for a cartoon. Remove the medium; add the database or site, the medium (Web), and your access date. Or cite as a basic Web source (*see nos. 51–52*).

Ziegler, Jack. "A Viking Funeral for My Goldfish." *New Yorker* 19 May 2008: 65. *Cartoonbank.com*. Web. 20 May 2008.

82. Online rendering of visual artwork Cite as you would the original (*no. 115*). Remove the medium; add the database or Web site, the medium (Web), and your access date. Or cite as a basic Web source (*see nos. 51–52*).

Seurat, Georges-Pierre. *Evening, Honfleur*. 1886. Museum of Mod. Art, New York. *MoMA.org*. Web. 8 May 2008.

83. Online video/film (also on film, DVD, or videocassette) See nos. 107–08 for a film or video. Remove the medium; add the database or site, the medium (Web), and your access date. Or cite as a basic Web source (*see nos. 51–52*).

Night of the Living Dead. Dir. George A. Romero. Image Ten, 1968. *Internet Archive*. Web. 12 May 2008.

84. Online radio program See no. 110 for a radio program. Remove the medium; add the database or site, the medium (Web), and your access date. Or cite as a basic Web source (*see nos. 51–52*).

"Bill Evans: 'Piano Impressionism.'" *Jazz Profiles*. Narr. Nancy Wilson. Natl. Public Radio. WGBH, Boston, 27 Feb. 2008. *NPR.org*. Web. 16 Mar. 2008

85. Online TV program See no. 111 for a TV program. Remove the medium; add the database or site, the medium (Web), and your access date. Or cite as a basic Web source (*see nos. 51–52*).

episode / director of episode (not series) / series / performer in series

"Local Ad." Dir. Jason Reitman. *The Office*. Perf. Steve Carrell. NBC. WNBC, New York, 12 Dec. 2007. *NBC.com*. Web. 12 May 2008.

86. Online broadcast interview See no. 112 for a broadcast interview. Remove the medium; add the database or site and the medium (Web), and give your access date. Or cite as a basic Web source (*see nos. 51–52*).

Jones, Sharon. Interview by Terry Gross. *Fresh Air*. Natl. Public Radio. WNYC, New York, 28 Nov. 2007. *NPR.org*. Web. 12 May 2008.

87. Online archival material Provide the information for the original. Add the Web site or database, the medium (Web), and your access date. Otherwise, cite as a basic Web source (*see nos. 51–52*).

date uncertain

Whitman, Walt. "After the Argument." [c. 1890]. The Charles E. Feinberg Collection of the Papers of Walt Whitman, Lib. of Cong. *The Walt Whitman Archive*. Web. 13 May 2008.

Works in online scholarly journals

Use the same format for all online journals, including those with print editions.

88. Article in an online journal Give the author, the article title (in quotation marks) or a term such as *Editorial* (not italicized), the journal title (italicized), the volume number, issue number, date, and the inclusive page range (or *n. pag.*—not italicized—if the source lacks page numbers). Conclude with the medium (Web) and your access date.

Parla, Jale. "The Wounded Tongue: Turkey's Language Reform and the Canonicity of the Novel." *PMLA* 123.1 (2008): 27-40. Web. 7 May 2008.

89. Review in an online journal

Friedman, Edward H. Rev. of *Transnational Cervantes*, by William Childers. *Cervantes: Bulletin of the Cervantes Society of America* 27.2 (2007): 41-43. Web. 13 May 2008.

90. Editorial in an online journal

Heitmeyer, Wilhelm, et al. "Letter from the Editors." Editorial. *International Journal of Conflict and Violence* 1.1 (2007): n. pag. Web. 14 May 2008.

91. Letter to the editor in an online journal

Destaillats, Frédéric, Julie Moulin, and Jean-Baptiste Bezelgues. Letter. *Nutrition & Metabolism* 4.10 (2007): n. pag. Web. 14 May 2008.

Works from online databases

In addition to information about the print version of the source, provide the title of the database (in italics), the medium (Web), and your access date.

92. Newspaper article from an online database

Blumenfeld, Larry. "House of Blues." *New York Times* 11 Nov. 2007: A33. *Academic Universe*. Web. 31 Dec. 2007.

93. Magazine article from an online database

Farley, Christopher John. "Music Goes Global." *Time* 15 Sept. 2001: 4+. *General OneFile*. Web. 31 Dec. 2007.

94. Journal article from an online database

Nielson, Aldon Lynn. "A Hard Rain." *Callaloo* 25.1 (2002): 135-45. *Academic Search Premier*. Web. 17 Mar. 2008.

95. Journal abstract from an online database

Dempsey, Nicholas P. "Hook-Ups and Train Wrecks: Contextual Parameters and the Coordination of Jazz Interactions." *Symbolic Interaction* 31.1 (2008): 57-75. Abstract. *Academic Search Premier*. Web. 17 Mar. 2008.

96. Work from a subscription service Cite the database but not the library subscription service (e.g., EBSCO, InfoTrac) or the subscribing library. Follow the format of nos. 92–95.

In the past, America Online offered personal database subscriptions. However, it has stopped doing so, and most subscription databases can be accessed at the library.

97. E-mail Include the author, the subject line (if any) in quotation marks, the descriptive term *Message to* (not italicized), and the name of the recipient, the date of the message, and the medium.

Hoffman, Esther. "Re: My Louis Armstrong Paper." Message to J. Peritz. 14 Apr. 2008. E-mail.

Other Electronic (Non-Web) Sources

98. A text file stored on your computer Cite local word-processor documents as manuscripts (*see no. 49*) and note the date last modified if you wish to cite a specific version. Record the file format as the medium.

McNutt, Lea. "The Origination of Avian Flight." 2008. *Microsoft Word* file.

Hoffman, Esther. "Louis Armstrong and Joe Glaser: More Than Meets the Eye." File last modified on 9 May 2008. *Microsoft Word* file.

99. A PDF file Treat local PDF files as published and follow the closest print model.

United States. US Copyright Office. *Report on Orphan Works*. Washington: US Copyright Office, 2006. PDF file.

100. An audio file Use the format for a sound recording (*see no. 113*). Record the file format as the medium.

Holiday, Billie. "God Bless the Child." *God Bless the Child*. Columbia, 1936. MP3 file.

101. A visual file Cite local image files as works of visual art (*see no. 115*). Record the file format as the medium.

Gursky, Andreas. *Times Square, New York*. 1997. Museum of Mod. Art, New York. JPEG file.

102. Other digital files Record the file format as the medium (for example, *XML file*). If the format is unclear, use the designation *Digital* *file*. Do not italicize the medium. Use the citation format of the most closely related print or nonprint source.

103. CD-ROM or DVD-ROM published periodically If a CD-ROM or DVD-ROM is revised on a regular basis, include in its citation the author, title of the work, any print publication information, medium, title of the CD-ROM or DVD-ROM (if different from the original title), vendor, and date of electronic publication.

Ross, Alex. "Separate Worlds, Linked Electronically." *New York Times* 29 Apr. 1996, late ed.: A22. CD-ROM. *New York Times Ondisc*. UMI-ProQuest. Dec. 1996.

104. CD-ROM or DVD-ROM not published periodically Works on CD-ROM or DVD-ROM are usually cited like books or parts of books if they are not revised periodically. The medium and the name of the vendor (if different from the publisher) appear after the publication data. For a work that also exists in print, give the print publication information (as in the example) followed by the medium, electronic publisher, and date of electronic publication.

print publisher omitted for pre-1900 work

Jones, Owen. *The Grammar of Ornament*. London, 1856. CD-ROM. Octavo, 1998.

105. CD-ROM or DVD-ROM with multiple discs List the total number of discs at the end of the entry, or give the number of the disc you reviewed if you used only one.

American Educational Research Association. *AERA Journals Collection*. Washington: AERA, 2007. CD-ROM. 10 discs.

106. Computer software Include the title, version, publisher, and date in your text or in an explanatory note. Do not include an entry in your works-cited list.

Audiovisual and Other Nonprint Sources

107. Film Begin with the title (italicized) (unless you want to highlight a particular contributor). For a film, cite the director and the featured performer(s) or narrator (*Perf.* or *Narr.*, neither italicized), followed by the distributor and year. Conclude with the medium.

Artists and Models. Dir. Raoul Walsh. Perf. Jack Benny, Ida Lupino, and Alan Townsend. Paramount, 1937. Film.

108. DVD or videotape See no. 107. Include the original film's release date if relevant. Conclude with the medium (*DVD* or *Videocassette*). Do not italicize the medium.

Casablanca. Dir. Michael Curtiz. Perf. Humphrey Bogart and Ingrid Bergman. 1942. Warner Home Video, 2000. DVD.

109. Personal/archival video or audio recording Give the date recorded and the location of the recording.

Adderley, Nat. Interview by Jimmy Owens. Rec. 2 Apr. 1993. Videocassette. Schomburg Center for Research in Black Culture, New York Public Lib.

110. Radio program Give the episode title (in quotation marks), the program title (italicized), the name of the series (if any), the network (call letters), the city, the broadcast date, and the medium. Name individuals if relevant.

"Legends Play 'Jazz in our Time.'" *Jazz Set*. Narr. Dee Dee Bridgewater. WBGO-FM, New York, 17 Jan. 2008. Radio.

111. TV program Cite as you would a radio program (*see no. 110*), but give *Television* as the medium.

episode director of episode series performer in series

"Local Ad." Dir. Jason Reitman. *The Office*. Perf. Steve Carrell. NBC. WNBC, New York, 12 Dec. 2007. Television.

112. Broadcast interview Give the name of the person interviewed, followed by the word *Interview* (not italicized) and the name of the interviewer if you know it. End with information about the broadcast and the medium.

Knox, Shelby. Interview by David Brancaccio. *NOW*. PBS. WNET, New York, 17 June 2005. Television.

113. Sound recording Start with the composer, conductor, or performer, depending on your focus. Include the following information: the work's title (italicized); the artist(s), if not already mentioned; the manufacturer; the date of release; and the medium.

Armstrong, Louis. *Town Hall Concert Plus*. RCA Victor, 1957. LP.

114. Musical composition Include only the composer and title, unless you are referring to a published score. Published scores are treated like books except that the date of composition appears after the title. Titles of instrumental pieces are not italicized when known only by form and number, unless the reference is to a published score.

Ellington, Duke. *Satin Doll.*

Haydn, Franz Josef. Symphony No. 94 in G Major.

reference to a published score

Haydn, Franz Josef. *Symphony No. 94 in G Major*. 1791. Ed. H. C. Robbins Landon. Salzburg: Haydn-Mozart, 1965. Print.

115. Artwork Provide the artist's name, the title of the artwork (italicized), the date (if unknown, write *n.d.*), the medium, and the institution or private collection and city (or *n.p.*) in which the artwork can be found. For anonymous collectors, write *Private collection* and omit city (do not write *n.p.*).

Leonard, Herman. *Louis Armstrong: Birdland 1949.* 1949. Photograph. Barbara Gillman Gallery, Miami.

116. Personal, telephone, or e-mail interview Begin with the person interviewed, followed by *Personal interview, Telephone interview,* or *E-mail interview* (not italicized) and the date of the interview. (*See no. 42 for a published interview.*)

Jacobs, Phoebe. Personal interview. 5 May 2008.

117. Lecture or speech Give the speaker, the title (in quotation marks), the name of the forum or sponsor, the location, and the date. Conclude with *Address* or *Lecture* (not italicized).

Taylor, Billy. "What Is Jazz?" John F. Kennedy Center for the Performing Arts, Washington. 14 Feb. 1995. Lecture.

118. Live performance To cite a play, opera, dance performance, or concert, begin with the title; followed by the authors (*By*); information such as the director (*Dir.*) and major performers; the site; the city; the performance date; and the word *Performance* (not italicized).

Ragtime. By Terrence McNally, Lynn Athrens, and Stephen Flaherty. Dir. Frank Galati. Ford Performing Arts Center, New York. 11 Nov. 1998. Performance.

119. Microfiche/microform/microfilm Cite as you would the print version. Include the medium, followed by the name of the microform and any identifying numbers.

Johnson, Charles S. "A Southern Negro's View of the South." *Journal of Negro Education* 26.1 (1957): 4-9. Microform. *The Schomburg Collection of the New York Public Library* 167 (1970): 101405.

120. Publication in more than one medium If you are citing a publication that consists of several different media, list alphabetically all of the media you consulted. Follow the citation format of the medium you used primarily (which is print in the example).

Sadker, David M., and Karen Zittleman. *Teachers, Schools, and Society: A Brief Introduction to Education*. New York: McGraw, 2007. CD-ROM, print, Web.

23d MLA style: Explanatory notes and acknowledgments

Explanatory notes are used to cite multiple sources for borrowed material or to give readers supplemental information. You can also use explanatory notes to acknowledge people who helped you with research and writing. Acknowledgments are a courteous gesture. If you acknowledge someone's assistance in your explanatory notes, be sure to send that person a copy of your paper.

TEXT

One answer to these questions is suggested by a large (24-by-36-inch) painting discovered in Armstrong's house.[2]

NOTE

[2]I want to thank George Arevalo of the Louis Armstrong Archives for his help on this project. George showed me the two pictures I describe in this paper. Seeing those pictures helped me figure out what I wanted to say—and why I wanted to say it. For introducing me to archival research and to the art of Louis Armstrong,

TEXTCONNEX

Electronic Submission of Papers

Some instructors may request that you submit your paper electronically. Keep these tips in mind:

- Confirm the appropriate procedure for submission.
- Find out in advance the preferred format for the submission of documents. *Always ask permission before sending an attached document to anyone.*
- If you are asked to send a document as an attachment, save your document as a "rich text format" (.rtf) file or in PDF format.
- As a courtesy, run a virus scan on your file before sending it electronically or submitting it on a disk or CD-ROM.

I also want to thank the head of the Louis Armstrong Archives, Michael Cogswell, and my English teacher, Professor Amy Tucker.

23e MLA style: Paper format

The following guidelines will help you prepare your research paper in the format recommended by the seventh edition of the *MLA Handbook for Writers of Research Papers*. For an example of a research paper that has been prepared using MLA style, see pages 379–90.

Materials Back up your final draft on a flash drive, CD, or DVD. Use a high-quality printer and high-quality, white 8½-by-11-inch paper. Put the printed pages together with a paper clip.

Heading and title Include a separate title page if your instructor requires one (see Figure 23.1). In the upper left-hand corner of the first page of the paper, one inch from the top and side, type on separate, double-spaced lines your name, your instructor's name, the

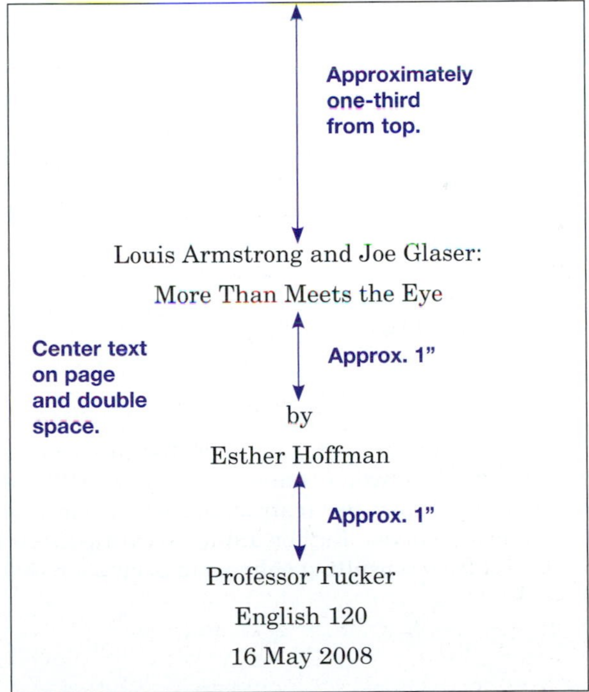

Approximately one-third from top.
Louis Armstrong and Joe Glaser:
More Than Meets the Eye
Center text on page and double space.
Approx. 1"
by
Esther Hoffman
Approx. 1"
Professor Tucker
English 120
16 May 2008

FIGURE 23.1 **A sample title page for a paper.**

course number, and the date. Double-space between the date and the paper's title and between the title and the first line of text, as well as throughout your paper. The title should be centered and properly capitalized (*see p. 379*). Do not italicize the title or put it in quotation marks or bold type.

If your instructor requires a title page, prepare it according to his or her instructions or like the example in Figure 23.1 on page 377. If your instructor requires a final outline, place it between the title page and the first page of the paper.

Margins and spacing Use one-inch margins all around, except for the top right-hand corner, where the page number goes. Your right margin should be ragged (not "justified," or even).

Double-space lines throughout the paper, including in quotations, notes, and the works-cited list. Indent the first word of each paragraph one-half inch (or five spaces) from the left margin. For block quotations, indent one inch (or ten spaces) from the left.

Page numbers Put your last name and the page number in the upper right-hand corner of the page, one-half inch from the top and flush with the right margin.

Visuals Place visuals (tables, charts, graphs, and images) close to the place in your text where you refer to them. Label and number tables consecutively (*Table 1, Table 2*) and give each one an explanatory caption; put this information above the table. The term *Figure* (abbreviated *Fig.*) is used to label all other kinds of visuals, except for musical illustrations, which are labeled *Example* (abbreviated *Ex.*). Place figure or example captions below the visual. Below all visuals, cite the source of the material and provide explanatory notes as needed. *(For more on using visuals effectively, see Part 1: Writing and Designing Texts.)*

23f Student paper in MLA style

As a first-year college student, Esther Hoffman wrote the following paper for her composition course. She knew little about Louis Armstrong and jazz before her instructor took the class to visit the Louis Armstrong Archives. Esther did archival research based on what she learned from consulting online and print sources.

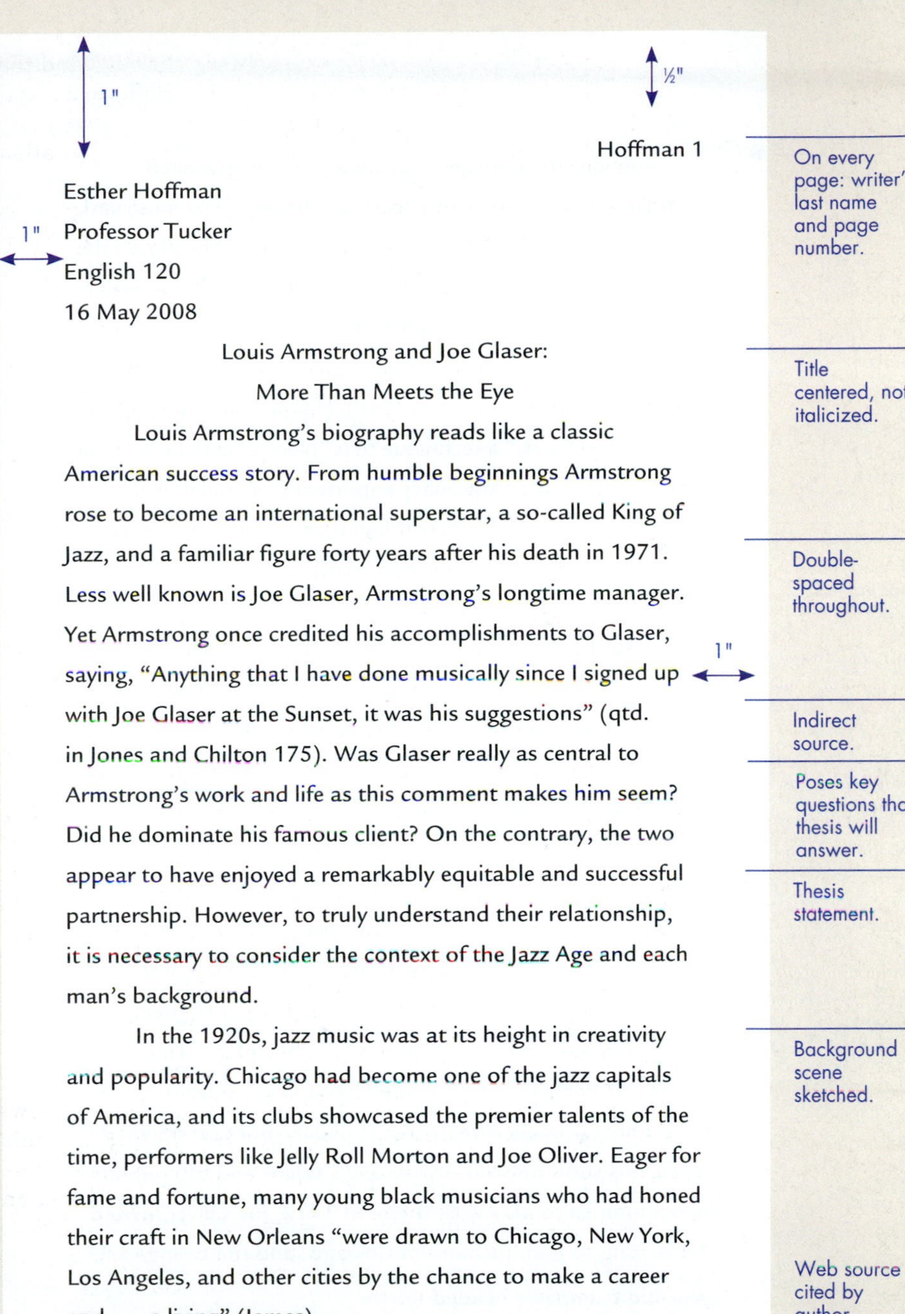

Hoffman 1

Esther Hoffman

Professor Tucker

English 120

16 May 2008

Louis Armstrong and Joe Glaser:
More Than Meets the Eye

Louis Armstrong's biography reads like a classic American success story. From humble beginnings Armstrong rose to become an international superstar, a so-called King of Jazz, and a familiar figure forty years after his death in 1971. Less well known is Joe Glaser, Armstrong's longtime manager. Yet Armstrong once credited his accomplishments to Glaser, saying, "Anything that I have done musically since I signed up with Joe Glaser at the Sunset, it was his suggestions" (qtd. in Jones and Chilton 175). Was Glaser really as central to Armstrong's work and life as this comment makes him seem? Did he dominate his famous client? On the contrary, the two appear to have enjoyed a remarkably equitable and successful partnership. However, to truly understand their relationship, it is necessary to consider the context of the Jazz Age and each man's background.

In the 1920s, jazz music was at its height in creativity and popularity. Chicago had become one of the jazz capitals of America, and its clubs showcased the premier talents of the time, performers like Jelly Roll Morton and Joe Oliver. Eager for fame and fortune, many young black musicians who had honed their craft in New Orleans "were drawn to Chicago, New York, Los Angeles, and other cities by the chance to make a career and . . . a living" (James).

Hoffman 2

Paragraph indent 5 spaces or ½".

Topic introduced.

MLA in-text citation: author (Bergreen) named in signal phrase.

MLA in-text citation: author named in parentheses.

Development by narration (*see p. 63*).

Web source cited by title.

Among these émigrés was Louis Armstrong, a gifted musician who developed into "perhaps the best [jazz musician] that has ever been" ("Louis Armstrong"). Armstrong played the trumpet and sang with unusual improvisational ability as well as technical mastery. As biographer Laurence Bergreen points out, Armstrong easily reached difficult high notes, the F's and G's that stymied other trumpeters (248). His innovative singing style also featured "scat," a technique that "place[s] emphasis on the human voice as an additionally important component in jazz music" (Anderson 329). According to one popular anecdote, Armstrong invented scat during a recording session; mid-song, he dropped his lyrics sheet and--not wanting to disrupt a great take--began to improvise (Edwards 619). Eventually Armstrong's innovations became the standard, as more and more jazz musicians took their cue from his style.

Armstrong's beginnings give no hint of the greatness that he would achieve. In New Orleans, he was born into poverty and received little formal education. As a youngster, Armstrong had to take odd jobs like delivering coal and selling newspapers so that he could earn money to help his family. At the age of twelve, Armstrong was placed in the Colored Waifs' Home to serve an eighteen-month sentence for firing a gun in a public place. There "Captain" Peter Davis gave him "basic musical training on the cornet" ("Louis Armstrong"). Older, more established musicians soon noticed Armstrong's talent and offered him opportunities to play with them. In 1922, Joe Oliver invited Armstrong to join his band in Chicago, and the twenty-one-year-old trumpeter headed north.

Hoffman 3

It was in Chicago that Armstrong met Joe Glaser. According to Bergreen, Glaser had a reputation for being a tough but trustworthy guy who could handle any situation. He was raised in a middle-class home by parents who were Jewish immigrants from Russia. As a young man, Glaser got caught up in the Chicago underworld and soon had a rap sheet that included indictments for running a brothel as well as for statutory rape.[1] Glaser's mob connections also led to his involvement in Chicago's club scene, a business almost completely controlled by gangsters like Al Capone. During the era of Prohibition, Glaser managed the Sunset Cafe, a club where Armstrong often performed:

> There was a pronounced gangster element at the Sunset, but Louis, accustomed to being employed and protected by mobsters, didn't think twice about that. Mr. Capone's men ensured the flow of alcohol, and their presence reassured many whites. (Bergreen 279)

By the early thirties, Armstrong had become one of the most popular musicians in the world. He attracted thousands of fans during his 1930 European tour, and his "Hot Five" and "Hot Seven" recordings were considered some of the best jazz ever played. Financially, Armstrong should have been doing very well, but instead he was having business difficulties. He owed money to Johnny Collins, his former manager, and Lil' Hardin, his ex-wife, was suing him for a share of the royalties on the song "Struttin' with Some Barbecue." At this point, Armstrong asked Glaser to be his business manager. Glaser quickly paid off Collins and settled with Lil' Hardin. Giving up his other business ventures, Glaser now became Armstrong's exclusive agent (Morgenstern 124-28; Collier 273-76; Bergreen 376-78). For

Focus introduced.

Superscript number indicating an explanatory note.

Block quotation indented 10 spaces or 1".

Summary of material from a number of sources.

Citation of multiple sources.

Hoffman 4

the next thirty-four years, his responsibilities included booking appearances, organizing the bands, making travel arrangements, and paying the band members' salaries (Jones and Chilton 160, 220).

Use of information from two separate pages in one source.

Some might posit that Glaser controlled all aspects of Armstrong's work and life. This view is suggested by a large (24-by-36-inch) oil painting discovered in Armstrong's house.[2] Joe Glaser is pictured in the middle of the canvas. Four black-and-white quadrants surround the central image of Glaser. One quadrant depicts a city scene, the scene in which Glaser thrived. The bottom two quadrants picture dogs, a reminder that Glaser raised show dogs. The remaining quadrant presents an image of Louis Armstrong. By placing Glaser in the center and Armstrong off in a corner, the unknown artist seems to suggest that even though Armstrong was the star, it was Glaser who made him one.

Development by description (*see p. 64*).

In fact, Glaser did advance Armstrong's career in numerous important ways. In 1935, he negotiated the lucrative record contract with Decca that led to the production of hits like "I'm in the Mood for Love" and "You Are My Lucky Star" (Bergreen 380). Glaser also decided when to sell the rights to Armstrong's songs. Determined to make as much money as possible, he sometimes sold the rights to a song as soon as it was released, especially when he thought the song might not turn out to be a big hit. However, in at least two instances, this money-making strategy backfired: much to Glaser's surprise, both "Hello, Dolly" and "What a Wonderful World" became big hits after the rights had been sold (Jacobs).

Presents a claim plus supporting evidence.

To expand Armstrong's popularity, Glaser increased his exposure to white audiences in the United States. In 1935, articles on Armstrong appeared in *Vanity Fair* and *Esquire*, two

Development by illustration (*see p.62*).

Hoffman 5

magazines with a predominantly white readership (Bergreen 385). Glaser also promoted Armstrong's movie career. At a time when only a handful of black performers were accepted in Hollywood, Armstrong had roles in a number of films, including *Pennies from Heaven* (1936) with Bing Crosby. Moreover, "Jeepers Creepers," a song Armstrong sang in *Going Places* (1938), received an Academy Award nomination (Bogle 149, 157). Of course, more exposure sometimes meant more discomfort, if not danger, especially when Armstrong and his band members were touring in the South. Bergreen recounts how in Southern states, where blacks were prohibited from entering many stores, Glaser sometimes had to shop for the band's food and other supplies (378, 381).

Note use of transitional expressions (*see pp. 88–89*).

As Armstrong's manager, Glaser also exerted some control over the musician's personal finances and habits. According to Dave Gold, an accountant who worked for Associated Booking, it was Glaser who paid Armstrong's mortgage, taxes, and basic living expenses (Collier 330). A 1960 letter from Glaser to Lucille Armstrong corroborates Gold's account; it shows that Glaser assumed responsibility for buying the musician and his wife a new car as well as for filing the paperwork needed to retain the old license plate number. More personal were Glaser's attempts to control Armstrong's habitual use of marijuana. In 1931, Armstrong received a suspended sentence after his arrest for marijuana possession. He continued to use the drug, however, especially during performances, and told Glaser that he wanted to write a book about marijuana's positive effects. Glaser flatly rejected the book idea and, fearful of a scandal, also forbade Armstrong's smoking any marijuana while on tour in Europe (Pollack).

Support by expert opinion (*see p. 187*).

Support by key fact (*see p. 187*).

Support by anecdote (*see p. 187*).

Hoffman 6

Restatement of thesis.

Clearly, Glaser was in a position to affect powerfully Armstrong's career and his life. However, Armstrong seemed to recognize that he gave Glaser whatever power over him the manager enjoyed. When he wanted to, Armstrong could and did resist Glaser's control, and that may be one reason why he liked and trusted Glaser as much as he did.

After Glaser became his manager, Armstrong no longer had to worry about the behind-the-scenes details of his career. He was free to concentrate on creating music and making the most of the opportunities his manager worked out for him. Glaser booked Armstrong into engagements with legendary performers like Benny Goodman, Ella Fitzgerald, and Duke Ellington. He also worked with the record companies to ensure that Armstrong would make the best and most profitable recordings possible (Bergreen 457). During the thirty-four years they worked together, both Armstrong and Glaser made lots of money. More important, their relationship freed Armstrong to make extraordinary music.

If Armstrong acquiesced to most of Glaser's business decisions, it may have been because he had no reason to resist them. However, when he deemed it necessary, Armstrong acted on his own. For example, in 1944 a talented band member named Dexter Gordon threatened to quit, so Armstrong offered him a raise--without consulting first with Glaser (Morgenstern 132). In 1957, when Armstrong wanted to put a stop to backstage crowding, he not only directed Glaser to make a sign prohibiting guests from going backstage but also told him exactly what to say on the sign (Armstrong, "Backstage Instructions"). As these incidents suggest, when Armstrong was displeased with the way his career was being handled, he acted to amend the situation.

Source cited: archival material.

Hoffman 7

Armstrong also knew how to resist Glaser's attempts to control the more personal aspects of his life. In a recent interview, Phoebe Jacobs, formerly one of Glaser's employees, sheds new light on the relationship between the manager and the musician. Armstrong's legendary generosity was tough on his pocketbook. It was well known that if someone needed money, Armstrong would readily hand over some bills. At one point, Glaser asked Jacobs to give Armstrong smaller denominations so that he would not give away so much money. The trumpeter soon figured out what was going on and admonished Jacobs for following Glaser's orders about money that belonged to him, not Glaser. On another occasion, Armstrong declined an invitation to join Glaser for dinner at a Chinese restaurant, saying, "I want to eat what I want to eat" (qtd. by Jacobs).

Even though he sometimes pushed Glaser away, Armstrong obviously loved and trusted his manager. In all the years of their association, the two men signed only one contract and, in the musician's words, "after that we didn't bother" (qtd. in Jones and Chilton 240). A picture of Joe Glaser in one of Armstrong's scrapbooks bears the following label in the star's handwriting: "the greatest." In his dedication to the unpublished manuscript "Louis Armstrong and the Jewish Family in New Orleans, the Year of 1907," Armstrong calls Glaser "the best friend that I ever had," while in a letter to Max Jones, he writes, "I did not get really happy until I got with my man--my dearest friend--Joe Glaser" (qtd. in Jones and Chilton 16). In 1969, Joe Glaser died. Referring to him again as "the greatest," Armstrong confided to a friend that Glaser's death "broke [his] heart" (qtd. in Bergreen 490).

Source cited: personal interview.

Authoritative quotation (*see p. 196*).

Memorable quotation (*see pp. 329–31*).

Wording of quotation adjusted (*see p. 330*).

Hoffman 8

Effective visual.

FIG. 1. An anonymous watercolor caricature of Armstrong with his manager, Joe Glaser, c. 1950. Louis Armstrong Archives, Queens College, City U of New York, Flushing.

Concludes with qualified version of thesis.

Memorable illustration.

Although there are hints of a struggle for the upper hand, the relationship between Louis Armstrong and Joe Glaser seems to have been genuinely friendly and trusting. Armstrong gave Glaser a good deal of authority over his career, and Glaser used that authority to make Armstrong a musical and monetary success. Armstrong was happy to take the opportunities that Glaser provided for him, but he was not submissive. This equitable and friendly relationship is depicted by another picture found in Armstrong's house. Although the 25-by-21-inch picture, shown in fig. 1., is a caricature that may seen jarring to contemporary viewers, when understood in its historical context it implies a mutual relationship between Armstrong and Glaser. The pair stand side by side, and Glaser has his hand on Armstrong's shoulder. Armstrong, who is dressed for a performance, looks and smiles at us as if he were facing an audience. But Glaser looks only at

Hoffman 9

Armstrong, the musician who was his main concern from 1935 to the day he died. In appearance alone, the men are clearly different. But seen in their longstanding partnership, the two make up a whole--one picture that offers us more than meets the eye.

Hoffman 10

New page, title centered.

Notes

Gives supplemental information about key source.

[1]Bergreen 372-76. Even though Ostwald points out a few mistakes in Bergreen's *Louis Armstrong: An Extravagant Life*, I think the book's new information about Glaser is useful and trustworthy.

Indent first line 5 spaces or ½".

[2]I want to thank George Arevalo of the Louis Armstrong Archives for his help on this project. George showed me the two pictures I describe in this paper. Seeing those pictures helped me figure out what I wanted to say--and why I wanted to say it. For introducing me to archival research and to the art of Louis Armstrong, I also want to thank the head of the Louis Armstrong Archives, Michael Cogswell, and my English teacher, Professor Amy Tucker.

Acknowledges others who helped.

Hoffman 11

Works Cited

New page, title centered.

Anderson, T. J. "Body and Soul: Bob Kaufman's *Golden Sardine*." *African American Review* 34.2 (2000): 329-46. *Academic Search Complete*. Web. 11 Apr. 2008.

Armstrong, Louis. "Backstage Instructions to Glaser." Apr. 1957. MS. Accessions 1997-26. Louis Armstrong Archives. Queens College City U of New York, Flushing.

---. "Louis Armstrong and the Jewish Family in New Orleans, the Year of 1907" 31 Mar. 1969. MS. Box 1. Louis Armstrong Archives. Queens College City U of New York, Flushing.

Bergreen, Laurence. *Louis Armstrong: An Extravagant Life*. New York: Broadway, 1997. Print.

Bogle, Donald. "Louis Armstrong: The Films." Miller 147-79.

Collier, James Lincoln. *Louis Armstrong: An American Genius*. New York: Oxford UP, 1983. Print.

Edwards, Brent Hayes. "Louis Armstrong and the Syntax of Scat." *Critical Inquiry* 28.3 (2002): 618-49. Print.

Glaser, Joe. Letter to Lucille Armstrong. 28 Sept. 1960. MS. Box 3. Louis Armstrong Archives. Queens College City U of New York, Flushing.

Jacobs, Phoebe. Personal interview. 5 May 2008.

James, Gregory N. *The Southern Diaspora: How the Great Migrations of Black and White Southerners Transformed America*. Chapel Hill: U of North Carolina P, 2007. N. pag. *Blues, Jazz, and the Great Migration*. Web. 7 May 2008.

Jones, Max, and John Chilton. *Louis: The Louis Armstrong Story, 1900-1971*. Boston: Little, 1971. Print.

"Louis Armstrong." *New Orleans Online*. New Orleans Tourism Marketing Corporation, 2008. Web. 7 May 2008.

Source: journal article in online database

Source: archival material.

3 hyphens used instead of repeating author's name.

Source: whole book.

Source: journal.

Source: personal interview.

Entries in alphabetical order.

Hoffman 12

Miller, Marc, ed. *Louis Armstrong: A Cultural Legacy*. Seattle: U of Washington P and Queens Museum of Art, 1994. Print.

Morgenstern, Dan. "Louis Armstrong and the Development and Diffusion of Jazz." Miller 95-145.

Ostwald, David. "All That Jazz." Rev. of *Louis Armstrong: An Extravagant Life*, by Laurence Bergreen. *Commentary* Nov. 1997: 68-72. Print.

Pollack, Bracha. "A Man ahead of His Time." 1997. TS.

Robinson, J. Bradford. "Scat Singing." *The New Grove Dictionary of Jazz*. Ed. Barry Kernfeld. Vol. 3. London: Macmillan, 2002. 515-16. Print.

Source: work in edited book cross-referenced to Miller

Source: review in a monthly magazine.

Hanging indent 5 spaces or ½".

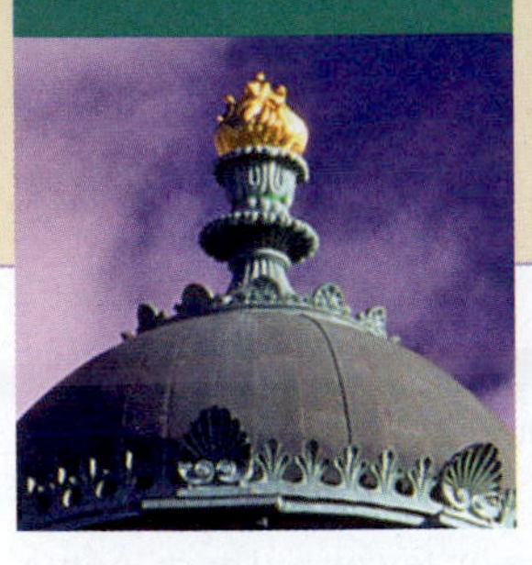

24 APA Documentation Style

Many researchers in behavioral and social sciences like psychology, sociology, and political science as well as in communications, education, and business use the documentation style developed by the American Psychological Association (APA). The guidelines presented here are based on the fifth edition of its *Publication Manual* (Washington: APA, 2001) and the *APA Style Guide to Electronic References* (Washington: APA, 2007). For updates to the APA documentation system, check the APA-sponsored Web site at <http://www.apastyle.org>.

24a The elements of APA documentation style

APA documentation style emphasizes the author and year of publication, making it easy for readers to tell if the sources cited are current. It has two mandatory parts:

- In-text citations
- List of references

APA style requires writers to list their sources in a list of references at the end of a paper. Answering the questions in the foldout charts that follow will help you find the appropriate model reference entry for your source. The reverse side of the foldout indicates where to find the information you need for a citation. (*See also the directory on pages 397–98.*)

www.mhhe.com/mhhb2

For links to Web sites for documentation styles used in various disciplines, go to

Research > Links to Documentation Sites

24b APA style: In-text citations

In-text citations let readers know that they can find full information about an idea you have paraphrased or summarized or the source of a quotation in the list of references at the end of your paper.

1. Author named in sentence Follow the author's name with the year of publication (in parentheses).

signal phrase

According to Brookfield (2001), nearly 12 percent of the Amazonian rain forest in Brazil has been shaped or influenced by thousands of years of indigenous human culture.

2. Author named in parentheses If you do not name the source's author in your sentence, then you must include the name in the parentheses, followed by the date and, if you are giving a quotation or a specific piece of information, the page number. Separate the name, date, and page number with commas.

The Organization of Indigenous Peoples of the Colombian Amazon attempted in 2001 to take legal action to ban such fumigation over indigenous lands. Their efforts were not supported by the Colombian government (Lloyd & Soltani, 2001, p. 5).

ampersand used within parentheses

3. Two to five authors If a source has five or fewer authors, name all of them the first time you cite the source.

As Kaimowitz, Mertens, Wunder, and Pacheco (2004) report in "Hamburger Connection Fuels Amazon Destruction," there are three key factors behind the burgeoning demand for Brazilian beef and the resulting burning of the Amazon rain forest for pasture.

If you put the names of the authors in parentheses, use an ampersand (&) instead of *and.*

There are three key factors behind the burgeoning demand for Brazilian beef and the resulting burning of the Amazon rain forest for pastureland (Kaimowitz, Mertens, Wunder, & Pacheco, 2004, p. 3).

After the first time you cite a work by three or more authors, use the first author's name plus *et al.* Always use both names when citing a work by two authors.

Another key factor is concern over livestock diseases in other countries (Kaimowitz et al., 2004, p. 4).

APA IN-TEXT CITATIONS: DIRECTORY to SAMPLE TYPES

(*See pp. 396–410. for examples of references entries.*)

APA IN-TEXT CITATIONS

- Identify the author(s) of the source, either in the sentence or in a parenthetical citation.
- Indicate the year of publication of the source following the author's name, either in parentheses if the author's name is part of the sentence or, if the author is not named in the sentence, after the author's name and a comma in the parenthetical citation.
- Include a page reference for a quotation or specific piece of information. Put "p." before the page number. If the author is named in the text, the page number appears in the parenthetical citation following the borrowed material. Page numbers are not necessary when you are summarizing the source as a whole or paraphrasing an idea found throughout a work. (*For more on summary, paraphrase, and quotation, see Chapter 21: Working with Sources and Avoiding Plagiarism, pp. 322–32.*)
- If the source does not have page numbers (as with many online sources), do your best to direct readers toward the specific part of the text you are citing. If the source has no page or paragraph numbering or easily identifiable headings, just use the name and date.

4. Six or more authors For in-text citations of a work by six or more authors, always give the first author's name plus *et al.* In the reference list, however, list the first six authors' names, followed by *et al.*

> As Barbre et al. (1989) have argued, using personal narratives enables researchers to connect the individual and the social.

5. Organization as author Treat the organization as the author, and spell out its name the first time the source is cited. If the organization is well known, you may use an abbreviation thereafter.

> According to a report issued by the Inter-American Association for Environmental Defense (2004), a significant proportion of Colombia's indigenous peoples live within these protected parklands.

> Public service announcements were used to inform parents of these findings (National Institute of Mental Health [NIMH], 1991).

In subsequent citations, only the abbreviation and the date need to be given: (*NIMH, 1991*).

6. Unknown author Give the first one or two important words of the title. Use quotation marks for titles of articles or chapters and italics for titles of books or reports.

> The transformation of women's lives has been hailed as "the single most important change of the past 1,000 years" ("Reflections," 1999, p. 77).

7. Two or more authors with the same last name If the authors of two or more sources have the same last name, always include their first initial, even if the year of publication differs.

> M. Smith (1988) showed how globalization has restructured both cities and states.

8. Two or more works by the same author in the same year Alphabetize the works by their titles in your reference list and assign a letter in alphabetical order (for example, *2006a*, *2006b*). Use that same year-letter designation in your in-text citation.

> J. P. Agarwal described the relationship between trade and foreign direct investment (FDI)(1996b).

9. Two or more sources cited at one time Cite the authors in the order in which they appear in the list of references, separated by a semicolon.

> Other years see greater destruction from large-scale economic and industrial initiatives, such as logging (Geographical, 2000; Kaimowitz et al., 2004, p. 2).

10. E-mail, letters, conversations To cite information received from unpublished forms of personal communication—such as conversations, letters, notes, and e-mail messages—give the source's initials and last name, and provide as precise a date as possible. Because readers do not have access to them, do not include personal communications in your reference list.

> According to ethnobotanist G. Freid (personal communication, May 4, 2008), the work of research scientists in the Brazilian Amazon has been greatly impeded within the past 10 years because of the destruction of potentially unrecorded plant species.

11. Specific part of a source Include the chapter (*chap.*), page (*p.*), figure, or table number.

> Despite the new law, the state saw no drop in car fatalities involving drivers ages 16–21 (Johnson, 2006, chap. 4).

12. Indirect source When referring to a source that you know only from reading another source, use the phrase *as cited in,* followed by the author of the source you actually read and its year of publication.

> According to the Center for International Forestry Research, an Indonesia-based NGO (as cited in Prugh, 2004), an area of land the size of Uruguay was deforested in the years 2002 and 2003 alone.

The work by Prugh would be included in the references list, but the work by the Center for International Forestry Research would not.

13. Electronic source Cite the author's last name and the publication date. If the document is a PDF (portable document format) file with stable page numbers, cite the page number. If the source has paragraph numbers instead of page numbers, use *para.* or ¶ instead of *p.* (*see no. 14*).

> Applications of herbicides have caused widespread damage to biodiversity, livestock, and crops and have caused "thousands" of peasants and indigenous peoples to flee these lands (Amazon Alliance, 2004).

Note: If the specific part lacks page or paragraph numbering, cite the heading and the number of the paragraph under that heading where the information can be found. If you cannot determine the date, use the abbreviation "n.d." in its place: (*Wilson, n.d.*).

14. Two or more sources in one sentence Include a parenthetical reference after each fact, idea, or quotation you have borrowed.

> By one estimate, nearly 12 percent of the Amazonian rain forest in Brazil has been shaped or influenced by thousands of years of indigenous human culture (Brookfield, 2001); the evidence is as basic as the *terra preta do Indio*, or "Indian Black Earth," for which the Brazilian region of Santarem is known (Glick, 2007, para. 4).

15. Sacred or classical text Cite within your text only, and include the version you consulted as well as any standard book, part, or section numbers.

> The famous song sets forth a series of opposites, culminating in "a time to love, and a time to hate; a time of war, and a time of peace" (Eccles. 3:8, King James Bible).

24c APA style: References

APA documentation style requires a list of references where readers can find complete bibliographical information about the sources referred to in your paper. The list should appear at the end of your paper, beginning on a new page titled "References."

Books

1. Book with one author

Brookfield, H. (2001). *Exploring agrodiversity*. New York: Columbia University Press.

2. Book with two or more authors

Goulding, M., Mahar, D., & Smith, N. (1996). *Floods of fortune: Ecology and economy along the Amazon*. New York: Columbia University Press.

3. Organization as author When the publisher is the author, use *Author* instead of repeating the organization's name as the publisher.

Deutsche Bank, Economics Department. (1991). *Rebuilding Eastern Europe*. Frankfurt, Germany: Author.

4. Two or more works by the same author List the works in publication order, with the earliest one first.

Wilson, S. (Ed.). (1997). *The indigenous people of the Caribbean*. Gainesville: University Press of Florida.

Wilson, S. (1999). *The emperor's giraffe and other stories of cultures in contact*. Boulder, CO: Westview Press.

If the works were published in the same year, put them in alphabetical order by title and add a letter (*a, b, c*) to the year to distinguish each entry in your in-text citations *(see no. 18)*.

5. Book with editor(s) Add *(Ed.)* or *(Eds.)* after the name. If a book lists an author and an editor, treat the editor like a translator (*see no. 8*).

Lifton, K. (Ed.). (1998). *The greening of sovereignty in world politics*. Cambridge, MA: MIT Press.

6. Selection in an edited book or anthology The selection's author, year of publication, and title come first, followed by the word

APA REFERENCE ENTRIES: DIRECTORY to SAMPLE TYPES

(*See pp. 391–95 for examples of in-text citations.*)

APA REFERENCE ENTRIES *(continued)*

In and information about the edited book. The page numbers of the selection go in parentheses after the book's title.

Wilmer, F. (1998). Taking indigenous critiques seriously: The enemy 'r' us. In K. Lifton (Ed.), *The greening of sovereignty in world politics* (pp. 55–60). Cambridge, MA: MIT Press.

7. Introduction, preface, foreword, or afterword List the author and the section cited. If the book has a different author, next write *In*, followed by the book's author and the title.

Bellow, S. (1987). Foreword. In A. Bloom, *The closing of the American mind: How higher education has failed democracy and impoverished the souls of today's students*. New York: Simon & Schuster.

8. Translation After the title of the translation, put the name(s) of the translator(s) in parentheses, followed by the abbreviation *Trans.*

Jarausch, K. H., & Gransow, V. (1994). *Uniting Germany: Documents and debates, 1944–1993* (A. Brown & B. Cooper, Trans.). Providence, RI: Berg.

9. Article in an encyclopedia or another reference work Begin with the author of the selection, if given. If no author is given, begin with the selection's title.

title of the selection

Arawak. (2000). In *The Columbia encyclopedia* (p. 2533). New York: Columbia University Press.

10. Entire dictionary or reference work Unless an author is indicated on the title page, list dictionaries by title, with the edition number in parentheses. (The in-text citation should include the title or a portion of the title.) (*See no. 9 on citing an article in a reference book and no. 11 on alphabetizing a work listed by title.*)

The American Heritage dictionary of the English language (4th ed.). (2000). Boston: Houghton Mifflin.

Hinson, M. (2004). *The pianist's dictionary*. Bloomington: Indiana University Press.

11. Unknown author or editor Start with the title. When alphabetizing, use the first important word of the title (excluding articles such as *The, A,* or *An*).

Give me liberty. (1969). New York: World.

APA LIST of REFERENCES

- Begin on a new page.
- Begin with the centered title "References."
- Include a reference for every in-text citation except personal communications (*see in-text citations no. 10 on p. 394*).
- Put references in alphabetical order by author's last name.
- Give the last name and first or both initials for each author. If the work has more than one author, see no. 2 (*p. 396*).
- Put the publication year in parentheses following the author or authors' names.
- Capitalize only the first word and proper nouns in titles. Also capitalize the first word following the colon in a subtitle.
- Use italics for titles of books but not articles. Do not enclose titles of articles in quotation marks.
- Include the city and publisher for books. If the city is not well known, include the state, using its two-letter postal abbreviation.
- Include the periodical name and volume number (both in italics) as well as the page numbers for a periodical article.
- Separate the author's or authors' name(s), date (in parentheses), title, and publication information with periods.
- Use a hanging indent: Begin the first line of each entry at the left margin, and indent all subsequent lines of an entry one-half inch (five spaces).
- Double-space within and between entries.

12. Edition other than the first

Smyser, W. R. (1993). *The German economy: Colossus at crossroads* (2nd ed.). New York: St. Martin's Press.

13. One volume of a multivolume work If the volume has its own title, put it before the title of the whole work. No period separates the title and parenthetical volume number.

Handl, G. (1990). The Mesoamerican biodiversity legal project. In *Yearbook of international environmental law* (Vol. 4). London: Graham & Trotman.

14. Republished book In-text citations should give both years: "As Le Bon (1895/1960) pointed out. . . ."

Le Bon, G. (1960). *The crowd: A study of the popular mind*. New York: Viking. (Original work published 1895)

Periodicals

15. Article in a journal paginated by volume Do not use *pp.* before the page numbers. Italicize the title of the periodical and the volume number.

da Cunha, M. C., & de Almeida, M. (2000). Indigenous people, traditional people and conservation in the Amazon. *Daedalus, 129*, 315.

16. Article in a journal paginated by issue Include the issue number (in parentheses after the volume number). The issue number is not italicized.

Epstein, J. (2002). A voice in the wilderness. *Latin Trade, 10*(12), 26.

17. Abstract For an abstract that appears in the original source, add the word *Abstract* in brackets after the title. If the abstract appears in a printed source that is different from the original publication, first give the original publication information for the article, followed by the publication information for the source of the abstract. If the dates of the publications differ, cite them both, with a slash between them, in the in-text citation: *Murphy (2003/2004)*.

Burnby, J. G. L. (1985, June). Pharmaceutical connections: The Maw's family [Abstract]. *Pharmaceutical Historian, 15*(2), 9–11.

Murphy, M. (2003). Getting carbon out of thin air. *Chemistry & Industry, 6*, 14–16. Abstract obtained from *Fuel & Energy Abstracts*, 2004, *45*(6), 389.

18. Two or more works in one year by the same author Alphabetize by title, and attach a letter to each entry's year of publication, beginning with *a*. In-text citations must use the letter as well as the year.

Agarwal, J. P. (1996a). *Does foreign direct investment contribute to unemployment in home countries?—An empirical survey* (Discussion Paper No. 765). Kiel, Germany: Institute of World Economics.

Agarwal, J. P. (1996b). Impact of Europe agreements on FDI in developing countries. *International Journal of Social Economics, 23*(10/11), 150–163.

19. Article in a magazine After the year, add the month for magazines published monthly or the month and day for magazines published weekly. Note that the volume number is also included.

Gross, P. (2001, February). Exorcising sociobiology. *New Criterion, 19,* 24.

20. Article in a newspaper Use *p.* or *pp.* with the section and page number. List all page numbers, separated by commas, if the article appears on discontinuous pages: *pp. C1, C4, C6.* If there is no identified author, begin with the title of the article.

Smith, T. (2003, October 8). Grass is green for Amazon farmers. *The New York Times,* p. W1.

21. Editorial or letter to the editor

Krugman, P. (2000, July 16). Who's acquiring whom? [Editorial]. *The New York Times,* Sec. 4, p. 15.

Deren, C. (2005, May 5). The last days of LI potatoes? [Letter to the editor]. *Newsday,* p. A49.

22. Unsigned article Begin the entry with the title, and alphabetize it by the first important word (excluding articles such as *The, A,* or *An*).

Reflection on a thousand years: Introduction. (1999, April 18). *The New York Times Magazine,* p. 77.

23. Review If the review is untitled, use the bracketed description in place of a title.

Kaimowitz, D. (2002). Amazon deforestation revisited [Review of the book *Brazil, forests in the balance: Challenges of conservation with development*]. *Latin American Research Review, 37,* 221–236.

Scott, A. O. (2002, May 10). Kicking up cosmic dust [Review of the motion picture *Star wars: Episode II—Attack of the clones*]. *The New York Times*, p. B1.

Other Print and Audiovisual Sources

24. Government document When no author is listed, use the government agency as the author.

U.S. Bureau of the Census. (1976). *Historical statistics of the United States: Colonial times to 1970*. Washington, DC: U.S. Government Printing Office.

For an enacted resolution or piece of legislation, see no. 57.

25. Report or working paper If the issuing agency numbered the report, include that number in parentheses after the title. For reports from a deposit service like the Educational Resources Information Center (ERIC), put the document number in parentheses at the end of the entry.

Agarwal, J. P. (1996a). *Does foreign direct investment contribute to unemployment in home countries?—An empirical survey* (Discussion Paper No. 765). Kiel, Germany: Institute of World Economics.

26. Conference presentation Treat published conference presentations as a selection in a book (*no. 6*), as a periodical article (*no. 15* or *no. 16*), or as a report (*no. 25*), whichever applies. For unpublished conference presentations, provide the author, the year and month of the conference, the title of the presentation, and the presentation's form, forum, and place.

Markusen, J. (1998, June). *The role of multinationals in global economic analysis*. Paper presented at the First Annual Conference in Global Economic Analysis, West Lafayette, IN.

Desantis, R. (1998, June). *Optimal export taxes, welfare, industry concentration and firm size: A general equilibrium analysis*. Poster session presented at the First Annual Conference in Global Economic Analysis, West Lafayette, IN.

27. Unpublished dissertation or dissertation abstract

Weinbaum, A. E. (1998). Genealogies of "race" and reproduction in transatlantic modern thought (Doctoral dissertation, Columbia University, 1998). *Dissertation Abstracts International, 58*, 229.

If you used the abstract but not the actual dissertation, treat the entry like a periodical article.

Weinbaum, A. E. (1998). Genealogies of "race" and reproduction in transatlantic modern thought. *Dissertation Abstracts International, 58*, 229.

28. Brochure, pamphlet, fact sheet, press release If there is no date of publication, put *n.d.* in place of the date. If the publisher is an organization, list it first, and name the publisher as *Author*.

United States Postal Service. (1995, January). *A consumer's guide to postal services and products* [Brochure]. Washington, DC: Author.

Union College. (n.d.). *The Nott Memorial: A national historic landmark at Union College* [Pamphlet]. Schenectady, NY: Author.

29. Film, DVD, videotape Begin with the cited person's name and, if appropriate, a parenthetical notation of his or her role. After the title, identify the medium as [*Motion picture*], followed by the country and name of the distributor. (*For online video, see no. 68.*)

Rowling, J. K., Goldenberg, M. (Writers), Yates, D. (Director), & Barron, D. (Producer). (2007). *Harry Potter and the order of the phoenix* [Motion picture]. United States: Warner Brothers Pictures.

For films and videotapes that might be hard to find, add the name and address of the distributor in parentheses after the bracketed medium information.

30. CD, audio recording See no. 65 for an MP3 or no. 66 for an audio podcast.

title of piece — title of album

Corigliano, J. (2007). Red violin concerto [Recorded by J. Bell]. On *Red violin concerto* [CD]. New York: Sony Classics.

31. Radio broadcast See no. 66 for an audio podcast.

Adamski, G., & Conti, K. (Hosts). (2007, January 16). *Legally speaking* [Radio broadcast]. Chicago: WGN Radio.

32. TV series For an entire TV series or specific news broadcast, treat the producer as author.

Simon, D., & Noble, N. K. (Producers). (2002). *The wire* [Television series]. New York: HBO.

33. Episode from a TV series Treat the writer as the author and the producer as the editor of the series. See no. 67 for a podcast TV series episode.

Burns, E., Simon, D. (Writers), & Johnson, C. (Director). (2002). The target [Television series episode]. In D. Simon & N. K. Noble (Producers), *The wire*. New York: HBO.

34. Advertisement

Geek Squad. (2007, December 10). [Advertisement]. Minneapolis/St. Paul: WCCO-TV.

35. Image, photograph, work of art If you have reproduced a visual, give the source information with the caption. See no. 51 for online visuals.

Smith, W. E. (1950). *Guardia civil, Spain* [Photograph]. Minneapolis: Minneapolis Institute of Arts.

36. Map or chart If you have reproduced a visual, give the source information with the caption (*for an example, see p. 415*). See no. 51 for online visuals.

Colonial Virginia. (1960). [Map]. Chapel Hill, VA: Virginia Historical Society.

37. Live performance

Ibsen, H. (Author), Bly, R. (Translator), & Carroll, T. (Director). (2008, January 12). *Peer Gynt* [Theatrical performance]. Guthrie Theater, Minneapolis, MN.

38. Musical composition

Rachmaninoff, S. (1900). *Piano concerto no. 2, opus 18* [Musical composition].

39. Lecture, speech, address List the speaker; the year, month, and date (if available); and the title of the presentation (in italics). Include location information when available. (For online versions, add "Retrieved from" and the URL.)

Cicerone, R. (2007, September 22). *Climate change in the U.S.* George S. Benton Lecture given at Johns Hopkins University. Baltimore, MD.

40. Personal interview Like other unpublished personal communications, personal interviews are not included in the reference list. See in-text citation entry no. 10 (*p. 394*).

A

APA ELECTRONIC REFERENCES (From *APA Style Guide to Electronic References* (2007))

Cite online works as you would the same works in another medium, apart from these concerns:

- Many online journal articles have a Digital Object Identifier (DOI), a unique alphanumeric string. Citations of online documents with DOIs do not require the URL or retrieval date.
- Include a retrieval date only for items that lack a publication date, items that probably will change (such as an in-press article), and reference sources (such as an encyclopedia article).
- Do not include information about a database or library subscription service in the citation unless the work is in only a few databases or difficult to find in print.
- For online journal articles, always include the issue number.
- Include the URL of the home page for items that require a subscription, appear in reference works, or appear in frames.
- Include the full URL for all other items, except those with a DOI.

Electronic Sources

41. Online journal article with a Digital Object Identifier (DOI) If your source has a DOI, include it at the end of the entry; URL and access date are not needed. Always include the issue number.

Ray, R., Wilhelm, F., & Gross, J. (2008). All in the mind's eye? Anger rumination and reappraisal. *Journal of Personality and Social Psychology, 94*(1), 133–145. doi:10.1037/0022-3514.94.1.133

42. Online journal article without a DOI Include the complete URL unless the source appears in a frame or is available only via subscription or search. In that case, include the home page URL. If your source is not likely to change (such as the final version of an article), no access date is needed. Always include the issue number. Place page numbers (if available) after the issue number.

Chan, L. (2004, November 3). Supporting and enhancing scholarship in the digital age: The role of open access institutional repository. *Canadian Journal of Communication, 29*(3), 277–300. Retrieved from http://www.cjc-online.ca/viewarticle.php?id=850

43. Journal article from an online, subscription, or library database Include database information only if the article is rare or found in just a few databases. If you include the database name, omit the URL.

Epstein, J. (2002). A voice in the wilderness. *Latin Trade, 10*(12), 26.

Gore, W. C. (1916). Memory, concept, judgment, logic (theory). *Psychological Bulletin, 13*(9), 355–358. Retrieved from PsycARTICLES database.

44. Abstract as original source

Welsh, W. (2003). *Evaluation of prison-based therapeutic community drug treatment programs in Pennsylvania* (NCJ No. 221276) [Abstract]. Retrieved from National Criminal Justice Reference Service abstracts database.

45. Published dissertation from a database Include the dissertation file number (AAT) at the end of the entry, if available.

Gorski, A. (2007). *The environmental aesthetic appreciation of cultural landscapes*. Retrieved from ProQuest Digital Dissertations. (AAT 1443335)

46. Newspaper or magazine article from a database Include database information only if the article is rare or found in just a few databases. Omit the URL.

Culnan, J. (1927, November 20). Madison to celebrate arrival of first air mail plane. *Wisconsin State Journal*, p. A1. Retrieved from Wisconsin Historical Society database.

47. Article in an online newspaper

Rohter, L. (2004, December 12). South America seeks to fill the world's table. *The New York Times*. Retrieved from http://www.nytimes.com

48. Article in an online magazine Include the volume number after the title if available (not shown below).

Biello, D. (2007, December 5). Thunder, hail, fire: What does climate change mean for the U.S.? *Scientific American*. Retrieved from http://www.sciam.com

49. Online exclusive magazine content

Francis, A. (2006, March 24). Fighting for the rainforest [Online exclusive]. *Newsweek International*. Retrieved from http://www.newsweek.com/id/47178

50. Article in an online newsletter

Use volume, issue, and page numbers if available. Often they are not, as below.

Gray, L. (2008, February). Corn gluten meal. *Shenandoah Chapter Newsletter, Virginia Native Plant Society*. Retrieved from http://www.vnps.org/chapters /shenandoah/Feb2008.pdf

51. Document or visual on a Web site

If the document is an entire article or report, include the basic information for an online document. If you have used a graph, chart, map, or image, give the source information following the figure caption (*for an example, see p. 415*).

Seattle. (2008). [Map]. Retrieved from http://www.mapquest.com

52. Article or report from a secondary source's Web site

Include information about the host organization's Web site in the retrieval statement.

World Health Organization. (1992). *ICD-10 criteria for borderline personality disorder*. Retrieved from BPD Sanctuary Web site: http://www.mhsanctuary.com /borderline/icd10.htm

53. Document on a university's Web site

Include relevant information about the university and department after the retrieval date.

Tugal, C. (2002, February). Islamism in Turkey: Beyond instrument and meaning. *Economy and Society*, *31*(1), 85–111. Retrieved November 7, 2008, from University of California–Berkeley, Department of Sociology Web site: http:// sociology.berkeley.edu/public_sociology_pdf/tugal.pps05.pdf

54. Section of an Internet document

United States Bureau of Oceans and International Environmental and Scientific Affairs. (2007, July 27). Projected greenhouse gas emissions. In *Fourth United*

States climate action report (chap. 4). Retrieved from http://www.state.gov/g/oes/rls/rpts/car/90312.htm

55. Online book Give information about the online source if the book exists only in electronic format or is difficult to locate in print.

Münsterberg, H. (1913). *Psychology and industrial efficiency*. Retrieved from http://www.gutenberg.org/etext/15154

56. Online government document except the *Congressional Record*

National Commission on Terrorist Attacks upon the United States. (2004, August 5). *The 9/11 Commission report*. Retrieved from http://www.gpoaccess.gov/911/index.html

57. *Congressional Record* (online or in print) For enacted resolutions or legislation, give the number of the congress after the number of the resolution or legislation, the *Congressional Record* volume number, the page number(s), and year, followed by (*enacted*).

H. Res. 2408, 108th Cong., 150 Cong. Rec. 1331–1332 (2004)(enacted).

Give the full name of the resolution or legislation when citing it within your sentence, but abbreviate the name when it appears in a parenthetical in-text citation: *(H. Res. 2408, 2004)*.

58. Online document lacking either a date or an author Place the title before the date if no author is given. Use the abbreviation *n.d.* (no date) for any undated document and give the retrieval date.

Center for Science in the Public Interest. (n.d.). *Food additives to avoid*. Retrieved March 4, 2008, from http://www.mindfully.org/Food/Food-Additives-Avoid.htm

59. Article in an online reference work Begin with the author's name, if given, followed by the publication date. If no author is given, place the title before the date. Include the date you accessed the article and the home page URL.

Special Olympics. (2008). In *Encyclopaedia Britannica online*. Retrieved February 15, 2008, from http://www.britannica.com

60. Wiki article Wikis are collaboratively written Web sites. Most are updated regularly, so include the access date in your citation. Check with your instructor before using a wiki article as a source.

Demographic transition. (2007, October 8). Retrieved March 3, 2008, from Citizendium: http://en.citizendium.org/wiki/Demographic_transition

61. Blog posting

Ben. (2008, February 18). Re: Opening the government's books at fedspending.org. Message posted to http://www.iq.harvard.edu/blog/sss/

62. Post to a newsgroup or discussion forum Provide the message's author, its date, and its subject line as the title. Give identifying information in brackets. After the phrase *Message posted to*, give the name of the newsgroup or forum, followed by the address of the archived message.

Jones, D. (2001, February 3). California solar power [Msg. 1]. Message posted to sci .space.policy, archived at http://yarchive.net/space/politics/california_power.html

63. Post to an electronic mailing list Provide the message's author, its date, and its subject line as the title. After the phrase *Message posted to*, give the name of the mailing list, followed by the address of the archived message.

Glick, D. (2007, February 10). Bio-char sequestration in terrestrial ecosystems—a review. Message posted to Terrapreta electronic mailing list, archived at http://bioenergylists.org/pipermail/terrapreta_bioenergylists.org /2007-February/000023.html

64. E-mail or instant message (IM) E-mail, instant messages, or other nonarchived personal communication should be cited in the body of your paper but not given in the references list (*see in-text citation entry no. 10, on p. 394*).

65. MP3

Hansard, G., & Irglova, M. (2006). Falling slowly. On *The swell season* [MP3]. Chicago: Overcoat Recordings.

66. Audio podcast

Glass, I. (Host). (2008, June 30). Social engineering [Show 358]. *This American Life.* Podcast retrieved from http://www.thisamericanlife.org

67. Podcast TV series episode

Reitman, J. (Director), & Novak, B. J. (Writer). (2007, December 12). Local ad [Television series episode]. In S. Carrell, M. Kaling, L. Eisenberg, & G. Stupnitsky (Producers), *The office.* Podcast retrieved from NBC: http://www.nbc.com/the_office/video/episodes.shtml

68. Online video

For an online speech, see no. 39.

Wesch, M. (2007). The machine is us/ing us [Video file]. Video posted to http://mediatedcultures.net/ksudigg/?p=84

69. Computer software

Cite only specialized software.

Buscemi, S. (2003). AllWrite! 2.1 with Online Handbook [Software]. New York: McGraw-Hill.

24d APA style: Paper format

The following guidelines are recommended by the *Publication Manual of the American Psychological Association,* fifth edition. For an example of a research paper that has been prepared using APA style, see pages 412–22.

Materials. Before printing your paper, make sure that you have backed up your final draft. Use a high-quality printer and high-quality white 8½-by-11-inch paper. Do not justify your text or hyphenate words at the right margin; it should be ragged.

Title page. The first page of your paper should be a title page. Center the title between the left and right margins in the upper half of the page, and put your name a few lines below the title. Most instructors will also want you to include the course number and title, the instructor's name, and the date. (*See p. 412 for an example.*)

Margins and spacing. Use one-inch margins all around, except for the upper right-hand corner, where the page number goes.

Double-space lines throughout the paper, including in the abstract, within any notes, and in the list of references. Indent the first word of each paragraph one-half inch (or five spaces).

For quotations of more than forty words, use block format and indent five spaces from the left margin. Double-space the quoted lines.

Page numbers and abbreviated titles. All pages, including the title page, should have a number preceded by a short (one- or two-word) version of your title. Put this information in the upper right-hand corner of each page, about one-half inch from the top.

Abstract. Instructors sometimes require an abstract—a 75- to 120-word summary of your paper's thesis, major points or lines of development, and conclusions. The abstract appears on its own numbered page, entitled "Abstract," and is placed right after the title page.

Headings. Primary headings should be centered, and all key words in the heading should be capitalized.

Secondary headings should be italicized and appear flush against the left-hand margin. Do not use a heading for your introduction, however. (*For more on headings, see Chapter 6: Designing Academic Papers and Preparing Portfolios, pp. 110–11.*)

Visuals. Place visuals (tables, charts, graphs, and images) close to the place in your text where you refer to them. Label each visual as a table or a figure, and number each kind consecutively (Table 1, Table 2). Provide an informative caption for each visual. Cite the source of the material, preceded by the word *Note* (italicized) and a period, and provide explanatory notes as needed. (*For more on using visuals effectively, see Chapter 4: Drafting Paragraphs and Visuals, pp. 62–72.*)

24e Student paper in APA style

Audrey Galeano researched and wrote a report on the indigenous peoples of the Amazon for her anthropology course, Indigenous Peoples and Globalization. Her sources included books, journal articles, and Web sites.

www.mhhe.com/mhhb2
For another sample of a paper in APA style, go to
Research > Sample Research Papers > APA Style

On every page: short title and page number.

Saving the Amazon 1

Title appears in full and centered on separate page with student's name, course information, and date.

Saving the Amazon:

Globalization and Deforestation

Audrey Galeano

Anthropology 314: Indigenous Peoples and Globalization

Professor Mura

May 3, 2008

Saving the Amazon 2

Abstract

The impact of globalization on fragile ecosystems is a complex problem. In the Amazon River basin, globalization has led to massive deforestation as multinational corporations exploit the rain forest's natural resources. In particular, large-scale industrial agriculture has caused significant damage to the local environment. In an effort to resist the loss of this ecosystem, indigenous peoples in the Amazon basin are reaching out to each other, to nongovernmental organizations (NGOs), and to other interest groups to combat industrial agriculture and promote sustainable regional agriculture. Although these efforts have had mixed success, it is hoped that the native peoples of this region can continue to live on their homelands without feeling intense pressure to acquiesce to industrialization or to relocate.

Abstract appears on a new page after the title page. First line is not indented.

Essay concisely and objectively summarized—key points included, but not details or statistics.

Paragraph should be no longer than 120 words.

1"

½"

Full title repeated on first page only.

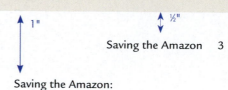

Saving the Amazon:
Globalization and Deforestation

For thousands of years, the indigenous peoples of the Amazon River basin have practiced forms of sustainable agriculture. These peoples developed ways of farming and hunting that enabled them to provide food and trade goods for their communities with minimal impact on the environment. These methods have endured despite colonization and industrialization. Today, the greatest threat to indigenous peoples in the Amazon River basin is posed by the massive deforestation caused by industrial-scale farming and ranching, as revealed in satellite images taken since 1988 by Brazil's National Institute of Space Research. (See graph in Figure 1.) Because of the injury to ecosystems and native ways of life, indigenous peoples and antiglobalization activists have joined forces to promote sustainable agriculture and the rights of native peoples throughout the Amazon River basin.

1"

Figure introduced and commented on.

Thesis statement.

Primary heading, centered, subtly reveals writer's stance.

Sustainable Lifeways, Endangered Lives

Recent work in historical ecology has altered our understanding of how humans have shaped what is romantically called "virgin forest." As anthropologist Anna Roosevelt (as cited in Society for California Archaeology, 2000) observes, "People adapt to environments but they also change them. There are no virgin environments on earth in areas where people lived." By one estimate, nearly 12 percent of the Amazonian rain forest in Brazil has been shaped or influenced by thousands of years of indigenous human culture (Brookfield, 2001); the evidence is as basic as the *terra preta do Indio,* or "Indian Black Earth," for which the Brazilian region of Santarem is known (Glick, 2007, para. 4).

Parenthetical citation of source with organization as author.

Information from two sources combined in one sentence.

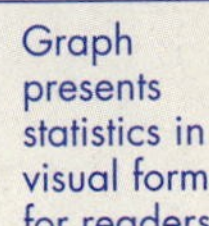

Graph presents statistics in visual form for readers.

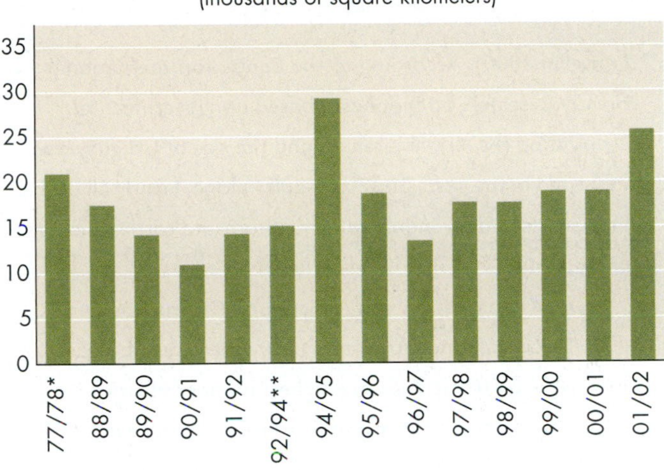

Figure 1. Annual deforestation rates in the Brazilian Amazon, 1988–2002 (square kilometers). *Note.* From National Institute of Space Research. (2002). In D. Kaimowitz, B. Mertens, S. Wunder, & P. Pacheco, *Hamburger connection fuels Amazon destruction: Cattle ranching and deforestation in Brazil's Amazon.* Retrieved April 16, 2008, from http://www.cifor.cgiar.org/publications/pdf_files/media/Amazon.pdf

Informative caption and source note appear below the figure.

The previous thousands of years of human influence on the Amazon is slight, however, compared with the modern-day destruction of rain forests around the globe, and in the Amazon River basin in particular. The sources of this destruction vary from country to country and year to year, with certain years affected more by climate change and other years seeing greater destruction from human initiatives, such as logging (Walker, Moran,

Support by key facts (*see p. 187*).

Paragraph expands on introductory paragraph.

& Anselin, 2000). According to the Center for International Forestry Research, an Indonesia-based nongovernmental organization (NGO), an area of land the size of Uruguay was deforested in the years 2002 and 2003 alone. Nearly all of this land was cleared for industrial agriculture and cattle ranching (Prugh, 2004).

Globalization and Agricultural Destruction

Large-scale industrial agriculture seeks out the least expensive ways to produce the highest number of crops. Perhaps the largest cash crop of the late 20th and early 21st centuries is soy, which has numerous uses and is among the least expensive crops to produce. According to Roberto Smeraldi, director of the environmental action group Friends of the Earth, "soybeans are the single biggest driver for deforestation" in the Brazilian Amazon; in the 12 months ending in August 2003, 9,169 square miles of rain forest had been cleared by soy farmers, ranchers, and loggers in Brazil (as cited in Stewart, 2004, paras. 4–5). Although Brazilian officials have attempted to regulate depredations of the rain forest by multinational soy producers, Stewart notes that, in 2003, soybean production brought nearly $8 billion to the Brazilian economy, forcing indigenous and small-scale farmers off their lands and damaging local climate.

Details introduced and linked to broader issue of globalization.

An Associated Press (AP) report reprinted on the Organic Consumer's Association Web site describes the impact of soy production on Brazil's Xingu National Park, a protected rain forest reserve that is home to 14 indigenous tribes. "The soy is arriving very fast. Every time I leave the reservation I don't recognize anything anymore because the forest keeps

Abbreviation given at first mention of organization.

First main cause of deforestation discussed.

disappearing," a director of the Xingu Indian Land Association is quoted as observing (AP, 2003, para. 11). Although the industrial soy farms have not crossed the borders of the Xingu National Park, they surround the protected lands and have raised fears that chemical pesticides and deforestation will dry up rivers and kill fish. "Our Xingu is not just what's here. It's a very long thread, and when it rains the soy brings venom down the same river that passes by our door," says Capivara chief Jywapan Kayabi (para. 24).

Abbreviation for organization used in parenthetical citation.

Cattle ranching has also led to the deforestation of the Amazon. The cattle population of the Amazon nations increased from 26 million in 1990 to 57 million in 2002 (Prugh, 2004). Attention to the destruction caused by industrial cattle-ranching began in the late 1980s. Barrett (2001) points out that ranchers were using lands already depleted of fertility and biodiversity by logging, road building, and colonization of the Brazilian Amazon in the 1960s and 1970s. Ranching, Barrett observes, "doesn't require nutrient-rich soil" and therefore "took the place vacated by other activities, along with the blame for soil erosion and loss of biodiversity" (p. 1).

Second main cause of deforestation discussed.

Page number given for quotation.

Indigenous Peoples and Regional Activism

Depopulation of these lands as a result of colonization meant that traditional agricultural practices were no longer sustained. In recent years, antiglobalization NGOs, the international movement for indigenous peoples' rights, and increased understanding of the consequences of deforestation are helping native peoples reclaim lands and reestablish traditional agricultural practices. However, some kinds of alliances and interventions are not as productive as others.

A contributing factor in the problem of deforestation shows the complexity of the situation.

Anthropologists da Cunha and de Almeida ask a provocative question: "Can traditional peoples be described as 'cultural conservationists'?" (2000, p. 315). Although as many as 50 indigenous groups in Amazonia still have no contact with the outside world, other indigenous peoples have secured their land rights through international efforts over the past 20 years. Some of these efforts, da Cunha and de Almeida argue, are influenced by romantic ideas about "noble savages" and fail to acknowledge the ways in which indigenous peoples in contemporary Brazil make a living from rain forest resources.

Local culture, history, and economics shown to be linked to global systems.

Barham and Coomes (1997) also note that a better understanding of how indigenous peoples live is necessary if the efforts of international groups such as Amazon Alliance are to succeed. Indigenous peoples need to see some material benefit from conservationist practices. After all, as da Cunha and de Almeida write, "Traditional peoples are neither outside the central economy nor any longer simply in the periphery of the world system" (2000).

Franke Wilmer (1998) suggests that "human action and its impact in the world are directed by a view that is dangerously out of touch with natural laws which, according to indigenous peoples, govern all life on this planet" (p. 57). For instance, although the Kayapo people of south-central Amazonia have been devastated by colonization, they still "used their knowledge to manipulate ecosystems in remarkable ways . . . to maximize biological diversity" (Brookfield, 2001, p. 141). Among the Kayapo's sustainable practices are crop rotation, the use of ash to fertilize fields, and the transition of older fields back to secondary forest (Brookfield, 2001).

Ellipses indicate omission in quotation.

Saving the Amazon 8

Some socially conscious global corporations have attempted to help indigenous Amazonian farmers develop sustainable, profitable crops. Two of the best-known efforts, described in a 2003 *New York Times* article by Tony Smith, provide a cautionary tale. In the 1990s, the British multinational "green" cosmetics company The Body Shop and American ice cream manufacturer Ben and Jerry's both developed "eco-friendly" products from the Amazon. Ben and Jerry's Rainforest Crunch ice cream used Brazil nuts that were harvested in a sustainable fashion by an Amazonian cooperative, and The Body Shop used the oils from Brazil nuts in some of its cosmetics. But Rainforest Crunch proved so popular that the cooperative could not meet the demand, and Ben and Jerry's had to turn to other suppliers, "some notorious for their antilabor practices" (Smith, 2003, p. W1). The Body Shop wound up being sued by a chief of the Kayapo tribe, whose image was used in Body Shop advertising without permission (Smith).

Problems caused by one of the solutions discussed.

The best solution might be for Brazilian businesses, developers, government officials, and indigenous peoples to work together. One new initiative described in the *Times* article is the cultivation of the sweet-scented native Amazon grass called priprioca, on which the Sao Paulo cosmetics company Natura is basing a new fragrance. Farmer Jose Mateus, who has grown watermelons and manioc on his small farm near the Amazon city of Belem, has agreed to grow priprioca instead–and he expects to get twice the price for the grass that he would for his usual crop (Smith, 2003). Eduardo Luppi, director of innovation for Natura, comments,

Solutions described, backed up with experts' quotations, which come from a secondary source.

"We do have the advantage that we are Brazilian and we are in Brazil. If you are in England or America and want to manage something like this in the Amazon by remote control, you can forget it" (as cited in Smith, 2003, p. W1).

Although indigenous peoples face extraordinary obstacles in their quest for environmental justice, some political officials support their struggles. In the Acre state of Brazil, Governor Jorge Viana was inspired by the example of martyred environmental activist Chico Mendes to secure financing from Brazil's federal development bank for sustainable development in his impoverished Amazonian state (Epstein, 2002). Viana, who holds a degree in forest engineering, told the journal *Latin Trade* that "we want to bring local populations into the policy of forest management. . . . We have to show them how to exploit without destroying" (as cited in Epstein, p. 26).

Essay concludes on a concerned yet optimistic note, balancing writer's and sources' concerns.

Conclusion

The social, economic, climate-related, and political pressures on the Amazonian ecosystem may prove insurmountable; report after report describes the enormous annual loss of rain forest habitat. The best hope for saving the rain forest is public pressure on multinational agricultural corporations to practice accountable, safe, and sustainable methods. In addition, it is important to encourage indigenous peoples to practice their age-old sustainable agriculture and land-management strategies while guaranteeing their rights and safety. Much in the Amazon has been ruined, but cooperative efforts like those discussed in this paper can nurture and sustain what remains for future generations.

Saving the Amazon 10

References

New page, heading centered.

Entries in alphabetical order and double-spaced.

Associated Press. (2003, December 18). *Soybeans: The new threat to Brazilian rainforest*. Retrieved April 8, 2008, from http://www.organicconsumers.org/corp/soy121903.cfm

Barham, B. L., & Coomes, O. T. (1997). Rain forest extraction and conservation in Amazonia. *The Geographical Journal, 163*(2), 180.

Barrett, J. R. (2001). Livestock farming: Eating up the environment? *Environmental Health Perspectives, 109*(7), A312.

Brookfield, H. (2001). *Exploring agrodiversity*. New York: Columbia University Press.

da Cunha, M. C., & de Almeida, M. (2000). Indigenous people, traditional people and conservation in the Amazon. *Daedalus, 129*(2), 315.

Epstein, J. (2002). A voice in the wilderness. *Latin Trade, 10*(12), 26.

Glick, D. (2007, February 10). Bio-char sequestration in terrestrial ecosystems--a review. Message posted to Terrapreta electronic mailing list, archived at http://bioenergylists.org /newsgroup-archive/terrapreta_bioenergylists.org/2007 -February/000023.html

Prugh, T. (2004). Ranching accelerates Amazon deforestation. *World Watch, 17*(4), 8.

Smith, T. (2003, October 8). Grass is green for Amazon farmers. *The New York Times,* p. W1.

Hanging indent 5 spaces or $\frac{1}{2}$".

Society for California Archaeology. (2000). *Interview with Dr. Anna Roosevelt*. Retrieved April 20, 2008, from http://www.scahome.org/about_california_archaeology /2000_Roosevelt.htm

Stewart, A. (2004, July 14). Brazil's soy success brings environmental challenges. *Dow Jones*. Retrieved from http://www.amazonia.org.br/English/noticias/noticia .cfm?id=116059

Walker, R., Moran, E., & Anselin, L. (2000). Deforestation and cattle ranching in the Brazilian Amazon: External capital and household processes. *World Development, 28*(4), 683–699.

Wilmer, F. (1998). Taking indigenous critiques seriously: The enemy 'r' us. In K. Lifton (Ed.), *The greening of sovereignty in world politics* (pp. 55–60). Cambridge, MA: MIT Press.

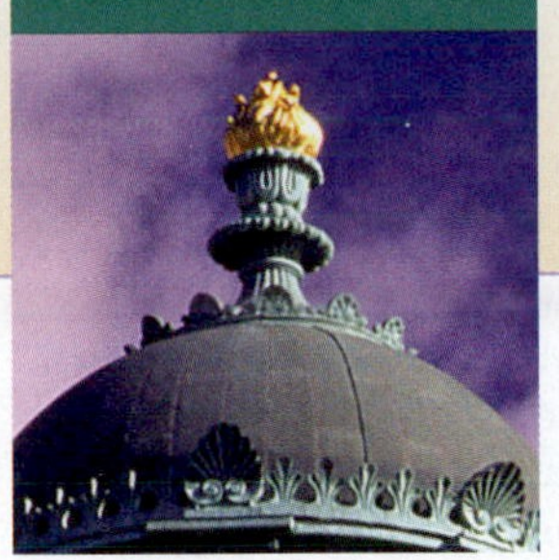

25 Chicago Documentation Style

There are many documentation styles besides those developed by the Modern Language Association (*see Chapter 23*) and the American Psychological Association (*see Chapter 24*). In this chapter, we cover the *Chicago Manual* style. To learn about other style types, consult the list of style manuals on page 338. If you are not sure which style to use, ask your instructor.

The note and bibliography style presented in the fifteenth edition of *The Chicago Manual of Style* (Chicago: University of Chicago Press, 2003) is used in many disciplines, including history, art, philosophy, business, and communications. This style has three parts:

- Numbered in-text citations
- Numbered footnotes or endnotes
- A bibliography of works consulted

www.mhhe.com/mhhb2

For links to Web sites for documentation styles in various disciplines, go to

Research > Links to Documentation Sites

The first two parts are necessary; the third is optional, unless your instructor requires it. (Chicago also has an alternative author-date system that is similar to APA style.) For more information on this style, consult the *Chicago Manual of Style*. For updates and answers to frequently asked questions about this style, go to the *Chicago Manual*'s Web site at <http://www.press.uchicago.edu> and click on "*Chicago Manual of Style* Web site."

25a Chicago style: In-text citations and notes.

Whenever you use information or ideas from a source, you need to indicate what you have borrowed by putting a superscript number in the text ([1]) at the end of the borrowed material. These superscript numbers are placed after all punctuation marks except for the dash.

> As biographer Laurence Bergreen points out, Armstrong easily reached difficult high notes, the F's and G's that stymied other trumpeters.[3]

If a quotation is fairly long, you can set it off as a block quotation. Indent it five spaces or one-half inch from the left margin, and double-space the quotation, leaving an extra space above and below it. Place the superscript number after the period that ends the quotation. (*See p. 439 for an example.*)

Each in-text superscript number must have a corresponding note either at the foot of the page or at the end of the text. Indent the first line of each footnote like a paragraph. Footnotes begin with the number and are single-spaced, with a double space between notes.

If you are using endnotes instead of footnotes, they should begin after the last page of your text on a new numbered page titled "Notes." Single-space within and double-space between endnotes.

The first time you cite a source in either a footnote or an endnote, you should include a full citation. Subsequent citations require less information.

FIRST REFERENCE TO SOURCE

3. Laurence Bergreen, *Louis Armstrong: An Extravagant Life* (New York: Broadway Books, 1997), 248.

ENTRY FOR SOURCE ALREADY CITED

6. Bergreen, 370.

If several pages pass between references to the same title, include a brief version of the title to clarify the reference.

ENTRY FOR SOURCE ALREADY CITED IN LONGER PAPER

7. Bergreen, *Louis Armstrong*, 370.

If you quote from the same work immediately after providing a full footnote, use the abbreviation *Ibid.* (Latin for "in the same place"), followed by the page number.

8. Ibid., 370.

25b Chicago style: Bibliography.

Some instructors require a separate list of works cited or of works consulted. If you are asked to provide a works-cited list, do so on a separate, numbered page titled "Works Cited." If the list should include all works you consulted, title it "Bibliography." Here is a sample entry:

Bergreen, Laurence. *Louis Armstrong: An Extravagant Life.* New York: Broadway Books, 1997.

25c Sample Chicago-style notes and bibliography entries.

CHICAGO STYLE: DIRECTORY to SAMPLE TYPES

Books

Books

1. Book with one author

NOTE

1. James Lincoln Collier, *Louis Armstrong: An American Genius* (New York: Oxford University Press, 1983), 82.

BIBLIOGRAPHY ENTRY

Collier, James Lincoln. *Louis Armstrong: An American Genius*. New York: Oxford University Press, 1983.

2. Multiple works by the same author After providing complete information in the first footnote, include only a shortened version of the title with the author's last name and the page number in any subsequent footnotes. In the bibliography, list entries either in

BIBLIOGRAPHY or WORKS-CITED LIST in CHICAGO STYLE

- Begin on a new page.
- Begin with the centered title "Works Cited" if you are including only works referred to in your paper. Use the title "Bibliography" if you are including every work you consulted.
- List sources alphabetically by author's (or editor's) last name.
- Capitalize the first and last words in titles as well as all important words and words that follow colons.
- Indent all lines except the first of each entry five spaces, using your word processor's hanging indent feature.
- Use periods between author and title as well as between title and publication data.
- Single-space each entry; double-space between entries.

alphabetical order by title or from earliest to most recent. After the first listing, replace the author's name with a "3-em" dash (type three hyphens in a row).

NOTES

7. Collier, *Jazz,* 154.

12. Collier, *Louis Armstrong,* 32.

BIBLIOGRAPHY ENTRIES

Collier, James Lincoln. *Jazz: The American Theme Song.* New York: Oxford University Press, 1993.

———. *Louis Armstrong: An American Genius.* New York: Oxford University Press, 1983.

3. Book with two or more authors In notes, you can name up to three authors. When there are three authors, put a comma after the first name and a comma plus *and* after the second.

NOTE

2. Miles Davis and Quincy Troupe, *Miles: The Autobiography* (New York: Simon & Schuster, 1989), 15.

BIBLIOGRAPHY ENTRY

Davis, Miles, and Quincy Troupe. *Miles: The Autobiography.* New York: Simon & Schuster, 1989.

When more than three authors are listed on the title page, use *and others* or *et al.* after the first author's name in the note.

NOTE

3. Julian Henriques and others, *Changing the Subject: Psychology, Social Regulation and Subjectivity* (New York: Methuen, 1984), 275.

BIBLIOGRAPHY ENTRY

Henriques, Julian, Wendy Holloway, Cathy Urwin, Couze Venn, and Valerie Walkerdine. *Changing the Subject: Psychology, Social Regulation and Subjectivity.* New York: Methuen, 1984.

Give all author names in bibliography entries.

4. Book with an author and an editor or a translator Put the author's name first and add the editor's (*ed.*) or translator's (*trans.*) name after the title. Spell out *Edited* or *Translated* in the bibliography entry.

NOTE

4. Louis Armstrong, *Louis Armstrong: A Self-Portrait,* ed. Richard Meryman (New York: Eakins Press, 1971), 54.

BIBLIOGRAPHY ENTRIES

Armstrong, Louis. *Louis Armstrong: A Self-Portrait.* Edited by Richard Meryman. New York: Eakins Press, 1971.

Goffin, Robert. *Horn of Plenty: The Story of Louis Armstrong.* Translated by James F. Bezov. New York: Da Capo Press, 1977.

5. Book with editor(s)

NOTE

5. Paul Eduard Miller, ed., *Esquire's Jazz Book* (New York: Smith & Durrell, 1944), 31.

BIBLIOGRAPHY ENTRY

Miller, Paul Eduard, ed. *Esquire's Jazz Book.* New York: Smith & Durrell, 1944.

6. Organization as author

NOTE

6. Centre for Contemporary Cultural Studies, *Making Histories: Studies in History Writing and Politics* (London: Hutchinson, 1982), 10.

BIBLIOGRAPHY ENTRY

Centre for Contemporary Cultural Studies. *Making Histories: Studies in History Writing and Politics.* London: Hutchinson, 1982.

7. Work in an anthology or part of an edited book Begin with the author and title of the specific work or part.

NOTES

7. Hale Smith, "Here I Stand," in *Readings in Black American Music,* ed. Eileen Southern (New York: Norton, 1971), 287.

8. Richard Crawford, foreword to *The Jazz Tradition,* by Martin Williams (New York: Oxford University Press, 1993).

BIBLIOGRAPHY ENTRIES

Smith, Hale. "Here I Stand." In *Readings in Black American Music*, edited by Eileen Southern, 286–89. New York: Norton, 1971.

Crawford, Richard. Foreword to *The Jazz Tradition,* by Martin Williams. New York: Oxford University Press, 1993.

In notes, descriptive terms such as *foreword* are not capitalized. In bibliography entries, these descriptive terms are capitalized.

8. Article in an encyclopedia or a dictionary For well-known reference works, publication data can be omitted from a note, but the edition or copyright date should be included. There is no need to include page numbers for entries in reference works that are arranged alphabetically; the abbreviation *s.v.* (meaning "under the word") plus the entry's title can be used instead.

NOTES

9. J. Bradford Robinson, "Scat Singing," in *The New Grove Dictionary of Jazz* (2002).

10. *Encyclopaedia Britannica,* 15th ed., s.v. "Jazz."

Reference works are not listed in the bibliography unless they are unusual or crucial to your paper.

BIBLIOGRAPHY ENTRY

Robinson, J. Bradford. "Scat Singing." In *The New Grove Dictionary of Jazz.* Edited by Barry Kernfeld. Vol. 3. London: Macmillan, 2002.

9. The Bible Abbreviate the name of the book, and use arabic numerals for chapter and verse, separated by a colon. Name the version of the Bible cited, and do not include the Bible in your bibliography.

NOTE

11. Eccles. 8:5 (Jerusalem Bible).

10. Edition other than the first Include the number of the edition after the title or, if there is an editor, after that person's name.

NOTE

12. Hugues Panassie, *Louis Armstrong,* 2d ed. (New York: Da Capo Press, 1980), 12.

BIBLIOGRAPHY ENTRY

Panassie, Hugues. *Louis Armstrong.* 2d ed. New York: Da Capo Press, 1980.

11. Multivolume work Put the volume number in arabic numerals followed by a colon, before the page number.

NOTE

13. Robert Lissauer, *Lissauer's Encyclopedia of Popular Music in America* (New York: Facts on File, 1996), 2:33–34.

BIBLIOGRAPHY ENTRY

Lissauer, Robert. *Lissauer's Encyclopedia of Popular Music in America.* Vol. 2. New York: Facts on File, 1996.

12. Work in a series Include the name of the series as well as the book's series number. The series name should not be italicized or underlined.

NOTE

14. Samuel A. Floyd, ed., *Black Music in the Harlem Renaissance,* Contributions in Afro-American and African Studies, no. 128 (New York: Greenwood Press, 1990), 2.

BIBLIOGRAPHY ENTRY

Floyd, Samuel A., ed. *Black Music in the Harlem Renaissance.* Contributions in Afro-American and African Studies, no. 128. New York: Greenwood Press, 1990.

13. Unknown author Cite anonymous works by title, and alphabetize them by the first word, ignoring *A*, *An*, or *The*.

NOTE

15. *The British Album* (London: John Bell, 1790), 2:43–47.

BIBLIOGRAPHY ENTRY

The British Album. Vol. 2. London: John Bell, 1790.

14. Source quoted in another source Quote a source within a source only if you are unable to find the original source. List both sources in the entry.

NOTE

16. Peter Gay, *Modernism: The Lure of Heresy* (New York: Norton, 2007), 262, quoted in Terry Teachout, "The Cult of the Difficult," *Commentary* 124, no. 5 (2007): 66–69.

BIBLIOGRAPHY ENTRY

Gay, Peter. *Modernism: The Lure of Heresy*. New York: Norton, 2007. Quoted in Terry Teachout. "The Cult of the Difficult." *Commentary* 124, no. 5 (2007): 66–69.

Periodicals

15. Article in a journal paginated by volume When journals are paginated by yearly volume, your citation should include the following: author, title of article in quotation marks, title of journal, volume number and year, and page number(s).

NOTE

17. Frank Tirro, "Constructive Elements in Jazz Improvisation," *Journal of the American Musicological Society* 27 (1974): 300.

BIBLIOGRAPHY ENTRY

Tirro, Frank. "Constructive Elements in Jazz Improvisation." *Journal of the American Musicological Society* 27 (1974): 285–305.

16. Article in a journal paginated by issue If the periodical is paginated by issue rather than by volume, add the issue number, preceded by the abbreviation *no*.

NOTE

18. Sarah Appleton Aguiar, "'Everywhere and Nowhere': Beloved's 'Wild' Legacy in Toni Morrison's *Jazz*," *Notes on Contemporary Literature* 25, no. 4 (1995): 11.

BIBLIOGRAPHY ENTRY

Aguiar, Sarah Appleton. "'Everywhere and Nowhere': Beloved's 'Wild' Legacy in Toni Morrison's *Jazz*." *Notes on Contemporary Literature* 25, no. 4 (1995): 11–12.

17. Article in a magazine Identify magazines by week (if available) and month of publication. In the note, give only the specific page cited; in the bibliography, give the full range of pages.

NOTE

19. Malcolm Walker, "Discography: Bill Evans," *Jazz Monthly,* June 1965, 22.

BIBLIOGRAPHY ENTRY

Walker, Malcolm. "Discography: Bill Evans." *Jazz Monthly,* June 1965, 20–22.

If the article cited does not appear on consecutive pages, do not put any page numbers in the bibliography entry. You can, however, give specific pages in the note. In Chicago style, the month precedes the date, and months are not abbreviated.

NOTE

20. J. R. Taylor, "Jazz History: The Incompleted Past," *Village Voice,* July 3, 1978, 65.

BIBLIOGRAPHY ENTRY

Taylor, J. R. "Jazz History: The Incompleted Past." *Village Voice,* July 3, 1978.

18. Article in a newspaper Provide the author's name (if known), the title of the article, the name of the newspaper, and the date of publication. Do not give a page number. Instead, give the section number or title if it is indicated. If applicable, indicate the edition (for example, *national edition*) before the section number.

NOTE

21. Ralph Blumenthal, "Satchmo with His Tape Recorder Running." *New York Times,* August 3, 1999, sec. E.

Newspaper articles cited in the text of your paper do not need to be included in a bibliography or reference list. However, if you are asked to include newspaper articles in the bibliography or reference list, or if you did not provide full citation information in the essay or the note, format the entry as follows.

BIBLIOGRAPHY ENTRY

Blumenthal, Ralph. "Satchmo with His Tape Recorder Running." *New York Times,* August 3, 1999, sec. E.

19. Unsigned article or editorial in a newspaper Begin the note and the bibliography or reference list entry with the name of the newspaper.

NOTE

22. *New York Times,* "A Promising Cloning Proposal," October 15, 2004.

BIBLIOGRAPHY ENTRY

New York Times, "A Promising Cloning Proposal," October 15, 2004.

Other Sources

20. Review If the review is untitled, start with the author's name (if any) and *review of* for a note or *Review of* for a bibliography entry.

NOTE

23. David Ostwald, "All That Jazz," review of *Louis Armstrong: An Extravagant Life,* by Laurence Bergreen, *Commentary,* November 1997, 72.

BIBLIOGRAPHY ENTRY

Ostwald, David. "All That Jazz." Review of *Louis Armstrong: An Extravagant Life,* by Laurence Bergreen. *Commentary,* November 1997, 68–72.

21. Interview Start with the name of the person interviewed. If a record of an unpublished interview exists, note the medium and where it may be found. Only interviews accessible to your readers are listed in the bibliography. Treat published interviews like articles.

NOTES

24. Louis Armstrong, "Authentic American Genius," interview by Richard Meryman, *Life,* April 15, 1966, 92.

25. Michael Cogswell, interview by author, May 3, 2008, tape recording, Louis Armstrong Archives, Queens College CUNY, Flushing, NY.

BIBLIOGRAPHY ENTRY

Armstrong, Louis. "Authentic American Genius." Interview by Richard Meryman. *Life,* April 15, 1966, 92–102.

22. Personal letter or e-mail Do not list in your bibliography.

NOTES

26. Jorge Ramados, letter to author, November 30, 2007.

27. Goerge Hermanson, e-mail message to author, November 15, 2007.

23. Government document If it is not already obvious in your text, name the country first.

NOTE

28. Bureau of National Affairs, *The Civil Rights Act of 1964: Text, Analysis, Legislative History; What It Means to Employers, Businessmen, Unions, Employees, Minority Groups* (Washington, DC: BNA, 1964), 22–23.

BIBLIOGRAPHY ENTRY

U.S. Bureau of National Affairs. *The Civil Rights Act of 1964: Text, Analysis, Legislative History; What It Means to Employers, Businessmen, Unions, Employees, Minority Groups.* Washington, DC: BNA, 1964.

24. Unpublished dissertation or document Include a description of the document as well as information about where it is available. If more than one item from an archive is cited, include only one entry for the archive in your bibliography (*see p. 441*).

NOTES

29. Adelaida Reyes-Schramm, "The Role of Music in the Interaction of Black Americans and Hispanos in New York City's East Harlem" (Ph.D. diss., Columbia University, 1975), 34–37.

30. Joe Glaser to Lucille Armstrong, September 28, 1960, Louis Armstrong Archives, Rosenthal Library, Queens College CUNY, Flushing, NY.

BIBLIOGRAPHY ENTRIES

Reyes-Schramm, Adelaida. "The Role of Music in the Interaction of Black Americans and Hispanos in New York City's East Harlem." Ph.D. diss., Columbia University, 1975.

Glaser, Joe. Letter to Lucille Armstrong. Louis Armstrong Archives. Rosenthal Library, Queens College CUNY, Flushing, NY.

25. DVD or videocassette Include the original release date before the publication information if it differs from the release date for the DVD or videocassette.

NOTE

31. *Wit,* DVD, directed by Mike Nichols (New York: HBO Home Video, 2001).

BIBLIOGRAPHY

Wit. DVD. Directed by Mike Nichols. New York: HBO Home Video, 2001.

26. Sound recording Begin with the composer or other person responsible for the content.

NOTE

32. Louis Armstrong, *Town Hall Concert Plus,* RCA INTS 5070.

BIBLIOGRAPHY ENTRY

Armstrong, Louis. *Town Hall Concert Plus.* RCA INTS 5070.

27. Artwork Begin with the artist's name, and include both the name and the location of the institution holding the work. Works of art are usually not included in the bibliography.

NOTE

33. Herman Leonard, *Louis Armstrong: Birdland 1949,* black-and-white photograph, 1949, Barbara Gillman Gallery, Miami.

28. CD-ROM or other electronic non-Internet source Indicate the format after the publication information.

NOTE

34. *Microsoft Encarta Multimedia Encyclopedia,* s.v. "Armstrong, (Daniel) Louis 'Satchmo'" (Redmond, WA: Microsoft, 1994), CD-ROM.

BIBLIOGRAPHY ENTRY

Microsoft Encarta Multimedia Encyclopedia. "Armstrong, (Daniel) Louis 'Satchmo.'" Redmond, WA: Microsoft, 1994. CD-ROM.

Online Sources

The fifteenth edition of *The Chicago Manual of Style* specifically addresses the documentation of electronic and online sources. In general, citations for electronic sources include all of the information required for print sources, in addition to a URL and, in some cases, the date of access. There are three key differences between Chicago- and MLA-style online citations:

- Chicago requires URLs for all online sources. They should not be enclosed in angle brackets.
- Months are not abbreviated, and the date is usually given in the following order: month, day, year (September 13, 2008).
- Dates of access are necessary only for sites that are frequently updated (such as news media sites or blogs) and for books.

29. Online book Include the date of access in parentheses.

NOTE

35. Carl Sandburg, *Chicago Poems* (New York: Henry Holt, 1916), http://www.bartleby.com/165/index.html (accessed March 18, 2008).

BIBLIOGRAPHY ENTRY

Sandburg, Carl. *Chicago Poems.* New York: Henry Holt, 1916. http://www.bartleby.com/165/index.html (accessed March 18, 2008).

30. Partial or entire Web site Identify as many of the following as you can: author (if any), title of short work or page (if applicable), title or sponsor of site, and URL.

NOTES

36. Bruce Boyd Raeburn, "An Introduction to New Orleans Jazz," *William Ransom Hogan Archive of New Orleans Jazz*, http://www.tulane.edu/~lmiller/BeginnersIntro.html.

37. Tulane University, *William Ransom Hogan Archive of New Orleans Jazz*, http://www.tulane.edu/~lmiller/JazzHome.html.

BIBLIOGRAPHY ENTRIES

Raeburn, Bruce Boyd. "An Introduction to New Orleans Jazz." *William Ransom Hogan Archive of New Orleans Jazz*. http://www.tulane.edu/~lmiller/BeginnersIntro.html.

Tulane University. *William Ransom Hogan Archive of New Orleans Jazz*. http://www.tulane.edu/~lmiller/JazzHome.html.

31. Article from an online journal, magazine, or newspaper Include the date of access if required or if the material is time sensitive.

NOTES

38. Janet Schmalfeldt, "On Keeping the Score," *Music Theory Online* 4, no. 2 (1998), http://www.societymusictheory.org/mto/issues/mto.98.4.2/mto.98.4.2.schmalfeldt_frames.html.

39. Michael E. Ross, "The New Sultans of Swing," *Salon,* April 18, 1996, http://www.salon.com/weekly/music1.html.

40. Don Heckman, "Jazz, Pop in Spirited Harmony," *Los Angeles Times,* August 10, 2005, http://articles.latimes.com/2005/08/10/calendar/et-hancock10 (accessed August 12, 2008).

BIBLIOGRAPHY ENTRIES

Schmalfeldt, Janet. "On Keeping the Score." *Music Theory Online* 4, no. 2 (1998). http://www.societymusictheory.org/mto/issues/mto.98.4.2/mto.98.4.2.schmalfeldt_frames.html.

Ross, Michael E. "The New Sultans of Swing." *Salon,* April 18, 1996. http://www.salon.com/weekly/music1.html.

Heckman, Don. "Jazz, Pop in Spirited Harmony." *Los Angeles Times,* August 10, 2005. http://articles.latimes.com/2005/08/10/calendar/et-hancock10 (accessed August 12, 2008).

32. Journal, magazine, or newspaper article from a library subscription database Give the home page URL. Access date is optional.

41. T. J. Anderson, "Body and Soul: Bob Kaufman's *Golden Sardine," African American Review* 34, no. 2 (Summer 2000): 329–46, http://www.ebsco.com (accessed April 11, 2008).

BIBLIOGRAPHY ENTRY

Anderson, T. J. "Body and Soul: Bob Kaufman's *Golden Sardine." African American Review* 34, no. 2 (Summer 2000): 329–46. http://www.ebsco.com (accessed April 11, 2008).

33. Blog posting

NOTE

42. Rich Copley, "Major Universities Can Have a Major Impact on Local Arts," *Flyover*, March 15, 2008, http://www.artsjournal.com/flyover/2008/03/major_universities_can_have_a.html (accessed March 18, 2008).

BIBLIOGRAPHY ENTRY

Copley, Rich. "Major Universities Can Have a Major Impact on Local Arts." *Flyover.* March 15, 2008. http://www.artsjournal.com/flyover/2008/03/major_universities_can_have_a.html (accessed March 18, 2008).

34. E-mail to discussion list

Give the URL if the posting is archived. Do not create a bibliography entry.

NOTE

43. Roland Kayser, e-mail to Opera-L mailing list, January 3, 2008, http://listserv.bccls.org/cgi-bin/wa?A2=ind0801A&L=OPERA-L&D=0&P=57634.

35. Podcast

NOTE

44. Fresh Sounds [pseud.], "Bing Crosby Meets Louis Armstrong," *Jazzarific: Jazz Vinyl Podcast*, http://jazzvinyl.podomatic.com/entry/2006-12-26T10_29_06-08_00.

BIBLIOGRAPHY ENTRY

Fresh Sounds [pseud.]. "Bing Crosby Meets Louis Armstrong." *Jazzarific: Jazz Vinyl Podcast.* http://jazzvinyl.podomatic.com/entry/2006-12-26T10_29_06-08_00.

25d Sample from a student paper in Chicago style.

The following excerpt from Esther Hoffman's paper on Louis Armstrong has been adapted and put into Chicago style so that you can see how citation numbers, endnotes, and bibliography work together. (*Hoffman's entire paper, in MLA style, can be found on pages 379–90.*)

Chicago style allows you the option of including a title page. If you do provide a title page, count it as page 1, but do not include the number on the page. Put page numbers in the upper right-hand corner of the remaining pages, except for the pages with the titles "Notes" and "Bibliography" or "Works Cited"; on these pages, the number should be centered at the bottom of the page.

www.mhhe.com/mhhb2
For a complete sample paper in Chicago style, go to
Research > sample Research papers > CMS Style

Louis Armstrong's life seems like a classic American success story. From humble beginnings Armstrong rose to become an international superstar, a so-called King of Jazz, and a familiar figure forty years after his death in 1971. Less well known is Joe Glaser, Armstrong's longtime manager. Yet Armstrong once credited his accomplishments to Glaser, saying, "Anything that I have done musically since I signed up with Joe Glaser at the Sunset, it was his suggestions."[1] Was Glaser really as central to Armstrong's work and life as this comment makes him seem? Did he dominate his famous client? Considered in the context of the Jazz Age and each man's background, the relationship between Armstrong and Glaser actually appears to have been a remarkably equitable and successful partnership.

In the 1920s, jazz music was at its height in creativity and popularity. Chicago had become one of the jazz capitals of America, and its clubs showcased the premier talents of the time, performers like Jelly Roll Morton and Joe Oliver. Eager for fame and fortune, many young black musicians who had honed their craft in New Orleans "were drawn to Chicago, New York, Los Angeles, and other cities by the chance to make a career and . . . a living."[2]

Among these émigrés was Louis Armstrong, a gifted musician who developed into "perhaps the best [jazz musician] that has ever been."[3] Armstrong played the trumpet and sang with unusual improvisational ability as well as technical mastery. As biographer Laurence Bergreen points out, Armstrong easily reached difficult high notes, the F's and G's that stymied other trumpeters.[4] His innovative singing style featured "scat," a technique that "place[s] emphasis on the human voice as an additionally important component in jazz music."[5] Eventually, Armstrong's innovations became the standard, as more and more jazz musicians took their cue from his style.

3

Armstrong's beginnings give no hint of the greatness that he would achieve. In New Orleans, he was born into poverty and received little formal education. As a youngster, Armstrong had to take odd jobs like delivering coal and selling newspapers so that he could earn money to help his family. At the age of twelve, Armstrong was placed in the Colored Waifs' Home to serve an eighteen-month sentence for firing a gun in a public place. There "Captain" Peter Davis gave him "basic musical training on the cornet."[6] Older, more established musicians soon noticed Armstrong's talent and offered him opportunities to play with them. In 1922, Joe Oliver invited Armstrong to join his band in Chicago, and the twenty-one-year-old trumpeter headed north.

It was in Chicago that Armstrong met Joe Glaser. According to Bergreen, Glaser had a reputation for being a tough but trustworthy guy who could handle any situation. He was raised in a middle-class home by parents who were Jewish immigrants from Russia. As a young man, Glaser got caught up in the Chicago underworld and soon had a rap sheet that included indictments for running a brothel as well as for statutory rape.[7] Glaser's mob connections also led to his involvement in Chicago's club scene, a business almost completely controlled by gangsters like Al Capone. During the era of Prohibition, Glaser managed the Sunset Café, a club where Armstrong often performed:

> There was a pronounced gangster element at the Sunset, but Louis, accustomed to being employed and protected by mobsters, didn't think twice about that. Mr. Capone's men ensured the flow of alcohol, and their presence reassured many whites.[8]

Notes

1. Max Jones and John Chilton, *Louis: The Louis Armstrong Story, 1900–1971* (Boston: Little, Brown, 1971), 175.

2. James N. Gregory, *The Southern Diaspora: How the Great Migrations of Black and White Southerners Transformed America* (Chapel Hill: University of North Carolina Press, 2007), 139.

3. New Orleans Tourism Marketing Corporation, "Louis Armstrong," *New Orleans Online,* http://www.neworleansonline.com/neworleans/music/musichistory/musicgreats/satchmo.html.

4. Laurence Bergreen, *Louis Armstrong: An Extravagant Life* (New York: Broadway Books, 1997), 248.

5. T. J. Anderson, "Body and Soul: Bob Kaufman's *Golden Sardine*,"*African American Review* 34, no. 2 (2000): 329–46, http://www.ebsco.com (accessed April 11, 2008).

6. New Orleans Tourism Marketing Corporation, "Louis Armstrong."

7. Bergreen, 372–76.

8. Ibid., 279.

Bibliography

Anderson, T. J. "Body and Soul: Bob Kaufman's *Golden Sardine*." *African American Review* 34, no. 2 (2000): 329–46. http://www.ebsco.com (accessed April 11, 2008).

Armstrong, Louis. "Authentic American Genius." Interview by Richard Meryman. *Life,* April 15, 1966, 92–102.

———. Louis Armstrong Archives. Rosenthal Library, Queens College CUNY, Flushing, NY.

———. *Town Hall Concert Plus.* RCA INTS 5070.

Bergreen, Laurence. *Louis Armstrong: An Extravagant Life.* New York: Broadway Books, 1997.

Bogle, Donald. "Louis Armstrong: The Films." In *Louis Armstrong: A Cultural Legacy,* edited by Marc H. Miller, 147–79. Seattle: University of Washington Press and Queens Museum of Art, 1994.

Collier, James Lincoln. *Jazz: The American Theme Song.* New York: Oxford University Press, 1993.

———. *Louis Armstrong: An American Genius.* New York: Oxford University Press, 1983.

Crawford, Richard. Foreword to *The Jazz Tradition,* by Martin Williams. New York: Oxford University Press, 1993.

Davis, Miles, and Quincy Troupe. *Miles: The Autobiography.* New York: Simon & Schuster, 1989.

Gregory, James, N. *The Southern Diaspora: How the Great Migrations of Black and White Southerners Transformed America.* Chapel Hill: University of North Carolina Press, 2007.

Jones, Max, and John Chilton. *Louis: The Louis Armstrong Story, 1900–1971.* Boston: Little, Brown, 1971.

Morgenstern, Dan. "Louis Armstrong and the Development and Diffusion of Jazz." In *Louis Armstrong: A Cultural Legacy,* edited by Marc H. Miller, 95–145. Seattle: University of Washington Press and Queens Museum of Art, 1994.

Writer includes *all* sources she consulted, not just those she cited in the body of her paper.

12

26 CSE Documentation Style

The Council of Science Editors (CSE) endorses three documentation styles in the seventh edition of *Scientific Style and Format: The CSE Manual for Authors, Editors, and Publishers* (Reston, VA: CSE, 2006):

- The **name-year style** includes the last name of the author and year of publication in the text. In the list of references, sources are in alphabetical order and unnumbered.
- The **citation-sequence style** includes a superscript number or a number in parentheses in the text. In the list of references, sources are numbered and appear in order of citation.
- The **citation-name style** also uses a superscript number or a number in parentheses in the text. In the list of references, however, sources are numbered and arranged in alphabetical order.

Learn your instructor's preferred style and use it consistently within a paper. Also ask your instructor about line spacing, headings, and other design elements, which the CSE manual does not specify.

www.mhhe.com/ mhhb2

For links to Web sites for documentation styles used in various disciplines, go to

Research > Links to Documentation Sites

26a CSE style: In-text citations

Name-year style Include the author's last name and the year of publication.

> According to Gleeson (1993), a woman loses 35% of cortical bone and 50% of trabecular bone during her lifetime.

> In epidemiologic studies, small increases in BMD and decreases in fracture risk have been reported in individuals using NSAIDS (Raisz 2001; Carbone et al. 2003).

Citation-sequence or citation-name style Insert a superscript number immediately after the relevant name, word, or phrase, and before any punctuation. Put a space before and after the superscript unless a punctuation mark follows.

> As a group, American women over 45 years of age sustain approximately 1 million fractures each year, 70% of which are due to osteoporosis [1].

That number now belongs to that source, and you should use it if you refer to that source again in your paper.

> According to Gleeson [6], a woman loses 35% of cortical bone and 50% of trabecular bone over her lifetime.

Credit more than one source at a time by referring to each source's number. Separate the numbers with a comma.

> According to studies by Yomo [2], Paleg [3], and others [1,4], barley seed embryos produce a substance that stimulates the release of hydrolytic enzymes.

If more than two numbers are in sequence, however, separate them with a hyphen.

> As several others [1-4] have documented, GA has an RNA-enhancing effect.

26b CSE style: List of references

Every source cited in your paper must correspond to an entry in your list of references, which should be prepared according to the guidelines in the box on page 444.

CSE STYLE: DIRECTORY to SAMPLE TYPES

CSE LIST of REFERENCES

- Begin on a new page after your text but before any appendices, tables, and figures.
- Use the centered title "References."
- Include only references that are cited in your paper.
- Start each entry with the author's last name, followed by initials for first and middle names. Add no spaces or periods between initials.
- Abbreviate periodical titles as shown in the CSE manual, and capitalize major words.
- Use complete book and article titles; capitalize the first word and any proper nouns or proper adjectives.
- Do not use italics, underlining, or quotation marks to set off any kind of title.
- List the extent of a source (number of pages or screens) at the end of the entry if your instructor requires it.

Name-Year Style

- Always put the date after the author's name.
- List the references in alphabetical order, but do not number them.

Citation-Sequence Style

- Put the date after the name of the book publisher or periodical.
- List and number the references in the order they first appear in the text.

Citation-Name Style

- Put the date after the name of the book publisher or periodical.
- List and number the references in alphabetical order. Make the numbering of your in-text citations match.

Books, Reports, and Papers

In *name-year style*, include the author(s), last name first; publication year; title; place; and publisher. In *citation-sequence* or *citation-name style,* include the same information, but put the year after the publisher.

1. Book with one author

NAME-YEAR

Bailey C. 1991. The new fit or fat. Boston (MA): Houghton Mifflin.

CITATION-SEQUENCE OR CITATION-NAME

1. Bailey C. The new fit or fat. Boston (MA): Houghton Mifflin; 1991.

2. Book with two or more authors List up to ten authors; if there are more than ten, use the first ten names with the phrase *and others* or *et al.* (not italicized).

NAME-YEAR

Begon M, Harper JL, Townsend CR. 1990. Ecology: individuals, populations, and communities. 2nd ed. Boston (MA): Blackwell.

CITATION-SEQUENCE OR CITATION-NAME

2. Begon M, Harper JL, Townsend CR. Ecology: individuals, populations, and communities. 2nd ed. Boston (MA): Blackwell; 1990.

3. Book with organization as author In *name-year style*, start the entry with the organization's abbreviation, but alphabetize by the full name.

NAME-YEAR

[NIH] National Institutes of Health (US). 1993. Clinical trials supported by the National Eye Institute (US): celebrating vision research. Bethesda (MD): US Dept. of Health and Human Services.

CITATION-SEQUENCE OR CITATION-NAME

3. National Institutes of Health (US). Clinical trials supported by the National Eye Institute (US): celebrating vision research. Bethesda (MD): US Dept. of Health and Human Services; 1993.

4. Chapter in a book

NAME-YEAR

O'Connell C. 2007. The elephant's secret sense: the hidden life of the wild herds of Africa. New York: Free Press. Chapter 9, Cracking elephant Morse code; p. 119-126.

CITATION-SEQUENCE OR CITATION-NAME

4. O'Connell C. The elephant's secret sense: the hidden life of the wild herds of Africa. New York: Free Press; 2007. Chapter 9, Cracking elephant Morse code; p. 119-126.

5. Book with editor(s)

NAME-YEAR

Wilder E, editor. 1988. Obstetric and gynecologic physical therapy. New York: Churchill Livingstone.

CITATION-SEQUENCE OR CITATION-NAME

5. Wilder E, editor. Obstetric and gynecologic physical therapy. New York: Churchill Livingstone; 1988.

6. Selection in an edited book

NAME-YEAR

Bohus B, Koolhaas JM. 1993. Psychoimmunology of social factors in rodents and other subprimate vertebrates. In: Ader R, Felten DL, Cohen N, editors. Psychoneuroimmunology. San Diego (CA): Academic Press. p. 807-830.

CITATION-SEQUENCE OR CITATION-NAME

6. Bohus B, Koolhaas JM. Psychoimmunology of social factors in rodents and other subprimate vertebrates. In: Ader R, Felten DL, Cohen N, editors. Psychoneuroimmunology. San Diego (CA): Academic Press; 1993. p. 807-830.

7. Technical report or government document Include the name of the sponsoring organization or agency as well as any report or contract number.

NAME-YEAR

Bolen S, Wilson L, Vassy J, Feldman L, Yeh J, Marinopoulos S, Wilson R, Cheng D, Wiley C, Selvin E, et al. (Johns Hopkins University Evidence-based Practice Center, Baltimore, MD). 2007. Comparative effectiveness and safety of oral diabetes medications for adults with type 2 diabetes. Comparative effectiveness review No. 8. Rockville (MD): Agency for Healthcare Research and Quality (US). Contract No.: 290-02-0018. Available from: AHRQ, Rockville, MD; AHRQ Pub. No. 07-EHC010-1.

CITATION-SEQUENCE OR CITATION-NAME

7. Bolen S, Wilson L, Vassy J, Feldman L, Yeh J, Marinopoulos S, Wilson R, Cheng D, Wiley C, Selvin E, et al. (Johns Hopkins University Evidence-based Practice Center, Baltimore, MD). Comparative effectiveness and safety of oral diabetes medications for adults with type 2 diabetes. Comparative effectiveness review No. 8. Rockville (MD): Agency for Healthcare Research and Quality (US); 2007. Contract No.: 290-02-0018. Available from: AHRQ, Rockville, MD; AHRQ Pub. No. 07-EHC010-1.

8. Paper in conference proceedings

NAME-YEAR

De Jong E, Franke L, Siebes A. c2007. On the measurement of genetic interactions. In: Berthold MR, Glen RC, Feelders AJ, editors. Proceedings of the AIP 940. 3rd International Symposium on Computational Life Science; 2007 Oct 4-5; Utrecht (Netherlands). Melville (NY): American Institute of Physics. p. 16-25.

CITATION-SEQUENCE OR CITATION-NAME

8. De Jong E, Franke L, Siebes A. On the measurement of genetic interactions. In: Berthold MR, Glen RC, Feelders AJ, editors. Proceedings of the AIP 940. 3rd International Symposium on Computational Life Science; 2007 Oct 4-5; Utrecht (Netherlands). Melville (NY): American Institute of Physics; c2007. p. 16-25.

9. Dissertation

NAME-YEAR

Bertrand KN. 2007. Fishes and floods: stream ecosystem drivers in the Great Plains [dissertation]. [Manhattan (KS)]: Kansas State University.

CITATION-SEQUENCE OR CITATION-NAME

9. Bertrand KN. Fishes and floods: stream ecosystem drivers in the Great Plains [dissertation]. [Manhattan (KS)]: Kansas State University; 2007.

Periodicals

When listing most periodical articles, include the author(s); year; title of article; title of journal (abbreviated); number of the volume; number of the issue, if available (in parentheses); and page numbers. In *name-year style*, put the year after the author(s). In *citation-sequence* or *citation-name style*, put the year after the journal title.

Up to ten authors can be listed by name. If you cannot determine the article's author, begin with the title.

10. Article in a journal that uses only volume numbers

NAME-YEAR

Devine A, Prince RL, Bell R. 1996. Nutritional effect of calcium supplementation by skim milk powder or calcium tablets on total nutrient intake in postmenopausal women. Am J Clin Nutr. 64:731-737.

CITATION-SEQUENCE OR CITATION-NAME

10. Devine A, Prince RL, Bell R. Nutritional effect of calcium supplementation by skim milk powder or calcium tablets on total nutrient intake in postmenopausal women. Am J Clin Nutr. 1996;64:731-737.

11. Article in a journal that uses volume and issue numbers

NAME-YEAR

Hummel-Berry K. 1990. Obstetric low back pain, a comprehensive review, part 2: evaluation and treatment. J Ob Gyn PT. 14(2):9-11.

CITATION-SEQUENCE OR CITATION-NAME

11. Hummel-Berry K. Obstetric low back pain, a comprehensive review, part 2: evaluation and treatment. J Ob Gyn PT. 1990;14(2):9-11.

12. Article in a magazine Indicate the year, month, and day (if available) of publication.

NAME-YEAR

Sternfeld B. 1997 Jan 1. Physical activity and pregnancy outcome. Review and recommendations. Sports Med. 33-47.

CITATION-SEQUENCE OR CITATION-NAME

12. Sternfeld B. Physical activity and pregnancy outcome. Review and recommendations. Sports Med. 1997 Jan 1:33-47.

Online Sources

Include information on author, title, and so forth, as with print works. Follow these special guidelines:

- Indicate the medium in brackets: [*Internet*] (not italicized).
- Include in brackets the date of the most recent update (if any) and the date you viewed the source.
- List the publisher or the sponsor, or use the bracketed phrase [*publisher unknown*] (not italicized).
- To include length of a document without page numbers, use designations such as [*16 paragraphs*] or [*4 screens*] (neither italicized).
- List the URL at the end of the reference, preceded by the phrase *Available from* (not italicized). Do not put a period after a URL unless it ends with a slash.

The following examples are in the citation-sequence or citation-name style. For name-year style, list the publication date after the author's name and do not number your references.

13. Article in an online journal

13. Krieger D, Onodipe S, Charles PJ, Sclabassi RJ. Real time signal processing in the clinical setting. Ann Biomed Engn [Internet]. 1998 [cited 2007 Oct 19]; 26(3): 462-472. Available from: http://www.springerlink.com/content/n31828q461h54282

14. Online book (monograph)

14. Kohn LT, Corrigan JM, Donaldson MS, editors. To err is human: building a safer health system [Internet]. Washington (DC): National Academy Press; c2000 [cited 2007 Oct 19]. Available from: http://www.nap.edu/books/0309068371/html

15. Material from a Web site

15. Hutchinson JR. Vertebrate flight [Internet]. Berkeley (CA): University of California; c1994-2008 [modified 2005 Sep 29; cited 2008 Jan 15]. Available from: http://www.ucmp.berkeley.edu/vertebrates/flight/flightintro.html

16. Material from a library subscription database

CSE does not specify a format. Give the information for a print article with database title and publication information.

16. Baccarelli A, Zanobetti A, Martinelli I, Grillo P, Lifang H, Lanzani G, Mannucci PM, Bertazzi PA, Schwartz, J. Air pollution, smoking, and plasma homocysteine. Environ Health Perspect [Internet]. 2007 Feb [cited 2007 Oct 23];115(2):176-181. Health Source: Nursing/Academic Edition. Birmingham (AL): EBSCO. Available from: http://www.ebsco.com

26c Sample references list: CSE name-year style

www.mhhe.com/mhhb2

For the complete sample paper that includes these, go to Research > Sample Research Papers > CSE Style

References

Anderson A. 1991. Early bird threatens archaeopteryx's perch. Science. 253(5015):35.

Geist N, Feduccia A. 2000. Gravity-defying behaviors: identifying models for protoaves. Am Zoologist. 40(4):664-675.

Goslow GE, Dial KP, Jenkins FA. 1990. Bird flight: insights and complications. Bioscience. 40(2):108-116.

Hinchliffe R. 1997. Evolution: the forward march of the bird-dinosaurs halted? Science. 278(5338):597-599.

Hutchinson JR. Vertebrate flight [Internet]. c1994-2008. Berkeley (CA): University of California; [modified 2005 Sep 29; cited 2008 Jan 15]. Available from: http://www.ucmp.berkeley.edu/vertebrates/flight/flightintro.html

Liem K, Bernis W, Walker W, Grande L. 2001. Functional anatomy of the vertebrates: an evolutionary perspective. New York: Harcourt College Publishers.

Padian K. 2001. Cross testing adaptive hypothesis: phylogenetic analysis and the origin of bird flight. Am Zoologist. 41(30):598-607.

(Read the complete student paper on *www.mhhe.com/mhhb2*.)

www.mhhe.com/mhhb2
For the complete sample paper that include these, go to
Research > Sample Research Papers > CSE Style

26d Sample references list: CSE citation-name style

Here are the same references as in 26c but in citation-name style, listed and numbered in alphabetical order. Citation-sequence style would look the same, but entries would be in the order in which they were cited in the paper.

References

1. Anderson A. Early bird threatens archaeopteryx's perch. Science. 1991;253(5015):35.

2. Geist N, Feduccia A. Gravity-defying behaviors: identifying models for protoaves. Am Zoologist. 2000;40(4):664-675.

3. Goslow GE, Dial KP, Jenkins FA. Bird flight: insights and complications. Bioscience. 1990;40(2):108-116.

4. Hinchliffe R. Evolution: the forward march of the bird-dinosaurs halted? Science. 1997;278(5338):597-599.

5. Hutchinson JR. Vertebrate flight [Internet]. Berkeley (CA): University of California; c1994-2008 [modified 2005 Sep 29; cited 2008 Jan 15]. Available from: http://www.ucmp.berkeley.edu/vertebrates/flight/flightintro.html

6. Liem K, Bernis W, Walker W, Grande L. Functional anatomy of the vertebrates: an evolutionary perspective. New York: Harcourt College Publishers; 2001.

7. Padian K. Cross testing adaptive hypothesis: phylogenetic analysis and the origin of bird flight. Am Zoologist. 2001; 41(30):598-607.

The content and design of this page from one of the National Audubon Society's annual reports shows donors how their money helps this environmental organization—and why its cause matters.

PART 5

> The aim of education must be the training of independently acting and thinking individuals, who, however, see in the service of the community their highest life problem.
>
> —Albert Einstein

Writing beyond College

27 Service Learning and Community-Service Writing

s road, writing is a way of connecting classroom, work-
nmunity.

27a Address the community on behalf of your organization.

Your ability to research and write can be of great value to organizations that serve the community. Courses at every level of the university, as well as extracurricular activities, offer opportunities to work with organizations such as homeless shelters, tutoring centers, and environmental groups. If you are writing a newsletter, press release, or funding proposal for a community group, ask yourself these questions:

- What do community members talk about?
- How do they talk about these issues, and why?
- Who is an outsider (member of the community), and who is an insider (member of the organization)?
- How can I best write from the inside to the outside?

Your answers will help you shape your writing so that it reaches its intended audience and moves the members of that audience to action.

WRITING OUTCOMES

Part 5: Writing beyond College

This section will help you answer questions such as:

Rhetorical Knowledge

- What is community-service writing? **(27a)**
- What should I consider when writing professional e-mail? **(29e)**

Critical Thinking, Reading, and Writing

- What kind of writing can help me address an issue in my community? **(28a)**
- How can I write an effective letter of complaint? **(28b)**

Processes

- How do I apply for a job? **(29b, c, d)**
- What are some online resources for job-hunting? **(29e)**

Knowledge of Conventions

- What should go on my résumé? **(29b)**
- How should I format my résumé and cover letter? **(29b, c)**

WRITING beyond COLLEGE

A Writer at Work

When Laura Amabisca entered Glendale Community College, she volunteered to be a tutor in the writing center. Upon transferring to Arizona State University West, she joined the Writing Tutors' Club. She also became a mentor for other Glendale Community College students who were trying to build the confidence to transfer to the university.

In a course in advanced expository writing, she drew on these experiences for an essay on the special needs of community-college transfer students. She also wrote a letter on the same theme to the student newspaper.

The sense of involvement Amabisca felt about her on-campus service motivated her to visit the ASU West Volunteer Office. She then became a volunteer for America Reads, a national literacy project. The Phoenix office of America Reads asked Amabisca to help design a public relations campaign. Amabisca volunteered to draft a brochure to convince other college students to join the project. In this way, she moved from involvement on her own campus to service in the wider community.

Writing on behalf of a community organization almost always involves negotiation and collaboration. A community organization may revise your draft to fit its needs. In these situations, having a cooperative attitude is as important as having strong writing skills.

Even if you are not writing on behalf of a group, you can still do community-service writing. You can write in your own name to raise an issue of concern to the community in a public forum; for example, you might write a newspaper editorial or a letter to a public official (*see Chapter 28: Letters to Raise Awareness and Share Concern*).

27b Design brochures, newsletters, and posters with an eye to purpose and audience.

www.mhhe.com/mhhb2
For interactive help with document design, go to
Writing > Visual Rhetoric > Document Design

If you are participating in a service learning program or an internship, you may have opportunities to design brochures and newsletters for wide distribution and posters to create awareness and promote events. To create an effective brochure, newsletter, or poster, you will need to integrate your skills in document design with what you have learned about purpose and audience.

Here are a few tips:

1. Consider how your reader will access the pages of the brochure or newsletter. Will it be distributed by mail? By hand? Electronically? What are the implications for the overall design?

2. It may be a good idea to sketch the design in pencil so that you have a plan before you start using the high-tech capabilities of the computer.
3. In making decisions about photographs, illustrations, type faces, and the design in general, think about the overall image you want to convey about the sponsoring organization.
4. If the organization has a logo, include it; if not, suggest designing one. A logo is a small visual symbol, like the Nike "swoosh" or the distinctive font used for Coca-Cola.
5. Set up a template for a brochure or newsletter so that you can create future editions easily. In word-processing and document-design programs, a template is a blank document that includes all of the formatting and codes a specific document requires. When you use a template, you just "plug in" new content and visuals—the format and design are already done.

For example, notice how the brochure for the PSFS Building in Philadelphia, Pennsylvania, shown in Figure 27.1, purposefully connects the history and importance of an architectural landmark with the prestige of Loews Hotel, into which "the world's first Modernist skyscraper" has been renovated. The brochure has an informative and also a subtly persuasive purpose. Its intent is to make readers feel that by staying at the Loews Philadelphia Hotel, they will be participating in a great tradition. The front cover is divided in half, with a striking photo of the building on the left side and an account of its history on the right. The name of the hotel appears in white letters near the bottom of the page. The interior page places a vintage photo of the revered banking establishment next to an image of hotel comfort. On both pages, quotations running vertically beside the photographs reinforce the building's architectural significance.

The Harvard Medical School newsletter entitled "Women's Health Watch," shown in Figure 27.2 on page 456, has a simple, clear design. The designer keeps in mind the newsletter's purpose and audience, which are explicitly stated in the title and the headline below it. The shaded area on the right lists the topics that are covered on the interior pages so that readers can get to the information they need quickly and easily. The Web address is prominently displayed in blue so that readers can find more information. The lead article, "Does Excess Vitamin A Cause Hip Fracture?" is designed simply in two columns, with the headline in bold type, subheadings in blue, a readable typeface, and a graphic strategically placed to break up the text and add visual interest. In all these ways, the design supports the Harvard Medical School's purpose of informing the general public about advances in medical research. (*For more information on document design, see Chapter 6, Designing Academic Papers and Preparing Portfolios, pp. 104–17.*)

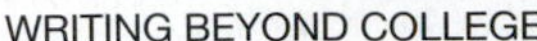

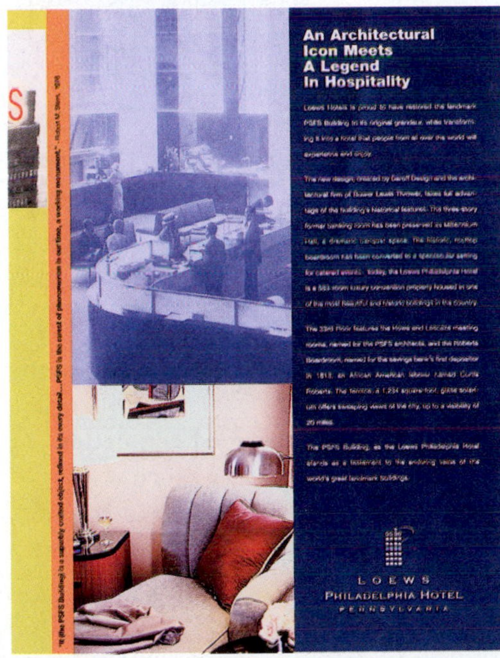

FIGURE 27.1 Example of a brochure.

H A R V A R D
Women's Health Watch
INFORMATION FOR ENLIGHTENED CHOICES FROM HARVARD MEDICAL SCHOOL

Does Excess Vitamin A Cause Hip Fracture?

Hip fracture is one of the most dreaded risks of aging. More than 350,000 hip fractures occur annually in the United States, mostly in women over 65. Half of these women never regain the ability to live independently. About 20% die within a year. Many others suffer chronic pain, anxiety, and depression. The consequences are so grim that many older women contacted in surveys on this subject say they'd rather die than suffer a hip fracture that would send them to a nursing home.

Current recommendations on reducing fracture risk advise women to exercise, make sure they get enough calcium and vitamin D, and, if necessary, take medications that help preserve bone strength. Some women also learn strategies for preventing falls or take classes such as tai chi to improve their balance. Now, a new study suggests that we should also pay attention to vitamin A. At high levels, this essential nutrient may actually increase our risk for hip fracture.

15% of women age 50 will suffer a hip fracture before age 80.

NEW STUDY FINDS LINK

Researchers at Harvard Medical School reported in the Jan. 2, 2002, *Journal of the American Medical Association* on the relationship between postmenopausal hip fracture and vitamin A intake. The data came from 72,337 women enrolled in the Nurses' Health Study. The women were divided into five groups according to their average daily consumption, over an 18-year period, of vitamin A from food and supplements.

Researchers then correlated vitamin A intake with hip fracture incidence. They found that women with the highest intake—3,000 micrograms (mcg) or more per day—had a 48% greater risk for hip fractures, compared to women with the lowest intake (1,250 mcg or less per day). The increased risk was mainly due to *retinol*, a particular form of vitamin A. In fact, women consuming 2,000 mcg of retinol or more daily had a hip fracture risk almost *double* that of women whose daily intake was under 500 mcg. In contrast, consuming high levels of *beta-carotene*, also a source of vitamin A, had a negligible impact on hip fracture risk. Participants taking hormone replacement therapy (HRT) were somewhat protected from the effects of too much retinol.

ABOUT VITAMIN A

Vitamin A is important for vision, the immune system, and the growth of bone, hair, and skin cells. Retinol, also called "preformed vitamin A," is the active form of the vitamin. It occurs naturally in animal products such as eggs, whole milk, cheese, and liver. Other food sources of vitamin A are *carotenoids*, which are found in green leafy vegetables and in dark yellow or orange fruits and vegetables. The body can convert these plant compounds to retinol. Beta-carotene is the most plentiful carotenoid and it converts most efficiently. Even so, you need about 12 times as much beta-carotene as retinol to get the same amount of vitamin A.

Because vitamin A is lost in the process of removing fat, many fat-free dairy products are fortified with retinol. So are some margarines and ready-to-eat cereals. The vitamin A in supplements and multivitamins may come from retinol, beta-carotene, or both. Beta-carotene is preferable because it's also an antioxidant.

Although vitamin A deficiency is a leading cause of blindness in developing countries, it's not a major problem in the United States. The main concern here is excess vitamin A, which can produce birth defects, liver damage, and reduced bone mineral density (BMD). →

Volume IX Number 7
March 2002

www.health.harvard.edu

FIGURE 27.2 **Example of a well-designed newsletter.**

28 Letters to Raise Awareness and Share Concern

Your ability to write and your willingness to share your opinions and insight can influence community events and affect the way businesses treat you. A letter to a local politician regarding a current issue or to a corporation regarding customer service can accomplish much if clearly argued, concisely phrased, and appropriately directed.

28a Write about a public issue.

Your task in writing to a newspaper, community organization, or public figure is to present yourself as a polite, engaged, and reasonable person who is invested in a particular issue and who can offer a compelling case for a particular course of action.

Most publications, corporations, and nonprofit organizations include forms, links, or e-mail addresses on their Web sites for submitting letters or comments. Whenever possible, use online options instead of writing a print letter. Here are some guidelines:

- Address the appropriate person or department by name. Consult the organization's Web site for this information.
- Concisely state your area of concern in the subject line.
- Include your message in the body of your e-mail, not as an attachment: an organization's server may screen out your message as spam.
- Keep it brief. Many organizations and corporations receive millions of e-mails each week. Most publications post specific word-count limits for letters to the editor or comments.
- Follow the conventions of professional e-mail (*see pp. 471–73*). Use standard capitalization and punctuation.
- Keep your tone polite and professional (neither combative nor overly chatty).

If you send a print letter, use the following guidelines:

- Address the appropriate person(s). If you are writing to a newspaper or magazine's editorial pages, see how published letters are addressed ("To the editors," for example), and whether guidelines are available. If you are writing to an organization, consult its Web site or call the main number to find out the preferred means of address and submission. It is always best to address your letter to a specific person or department.
- Use the format for a business letter. (*See the business letter in block format on pp. 459–60.*)

- Write no more than three or four paragraphs. (E-mails should be shorter.)

Regardless of medium, follow this format:

- In the first paragraph, clearly and briefly state the matter you wish to address and why it is important to you. For example, if you are writing to your local school board, you should state that you are the parent of a child at the local school.
- In the second paragraph, provide clear and compelling evidence for your concern. If relevant, propose a solution.
- In your conclusion, thank the reader for considering your thoughts. Repeat any request for specific action, such as having an item added to the agenda of the next school board meeting. If you want a specific response, politely request an e-mail or telephone call. If you intend to follow up on your letter, note that you will be calling or writing again within a week (or however long is appropriate).

Below and on pages 459–60 are letters by two different writers addressing the same community issue. One e-mailed his local newspaper; the other wrote to the principal of her local school. Note how they tailor their letters for their specific audiences, purposes, and mediums.

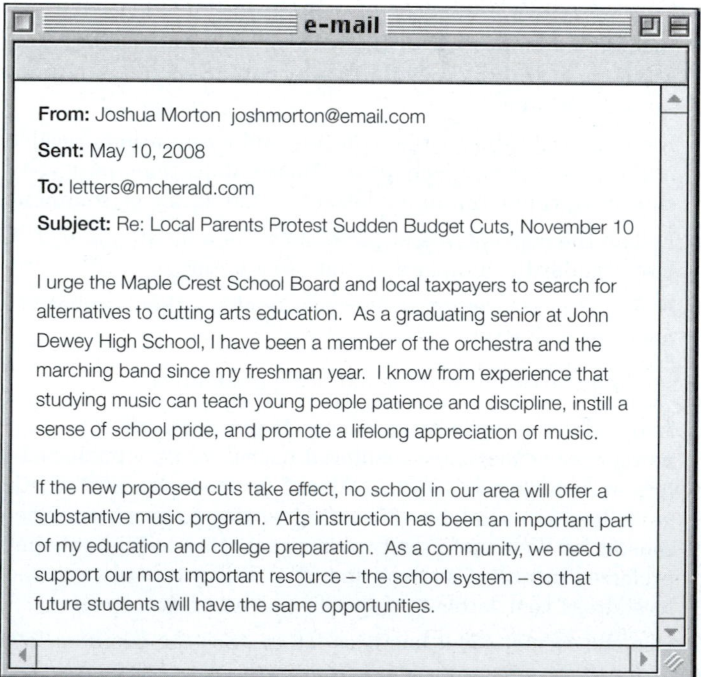

e-mail

From: Joshua Morton joshmorton@email.com

Sent: May 10, 2008

To: letters@mcherald.com

Subject: Re: Local Parents Protest Sudden Budget Cuts, November 10

I urge the Maple Crest School Board and local taxpayers to search for alternatives to cutting arts education. As a graduating senior at John Dewey High School, I have been a member of the orchestra and the marching band since my freshman year. I know from experience that studying music can teach young people patience and discipline, instill a sense of school pride, and promote a lifelong appreciation of music.

If the new proposed cuts take effect, no school in our area will offer a substantive music program. Arts instruction has been an important part of my education and college preparation. As a community, we need to support our most important resource – the school system – so that future students will have the same opportunities.

1324 Owen Drive
Maple Crest, NJ 07405
May 3, 2008

Return address and date.

Double space.

Dr. Joann Malvern
Principal
Middle Park Elementary School
47 Valley Street
Maple Crest, NJ 07405

Inside address.

Double space.

Dear Dr. Malvern:

Salutation.

Double space.

1"

I am a parent of two children who attend Middle Park Elementary School. My son is in the third grade, and my daughter is in the sixth grade. We have lived in Maple Crest for ten years, and my children have always attended local schools. We have been delighted with the attention and opportunities that both children have received in their classrooms. However, the School Board's proposed new budget cuts would, I believe, significantly reduce both that attention and the opportunities all children currently enjoy.

Body—paragraphs single-spaced, double space between paragraphs.

In a letter to all Middle Park parents that was sent home with children during the last week of April, you outlined changes for the upcoming school year. The area of greatest concern to me is the termination of three classroom assistant positions and the reduction of the music teacher's position from full- to part-time. You stated that the reason for these reductions was a call from the Board of Education to cut operating costs for the next school year.

The presence of classroom assistants has helped teachers to maintain discipline in the classroom as well as offer additional attention to every child in the classroom. The school's music teacher, Mr. Jack Delvarez, has inspired both of my children to take up musical instruments, and all parents look forward to the Fall and Spring concerts.

I know from my conversations with other Middle Park parents that we would appreciate the opportunity to suggest alternative ways to save money and preserve the high quality of education that Middle Park currently offers. I would like to request that a special Parent-Teacher Association meeting be held within the next two weeks in order to discuss the sudden nature of these staffing changes as well as other options.

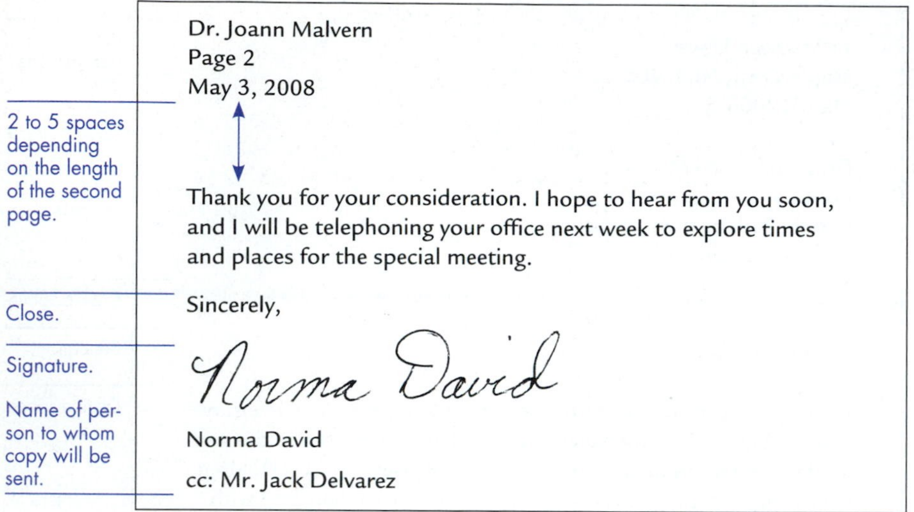
Dr. Joann Malvern
Page 2
May 3, 2008

Thank you for your consideration. I hope to hear from you soon, and I will be telephoning your office next week to explore times and places for the special meeting.

Sincerely,

Norma David

Norma David

cc: Mr. Jack Delvarez

28b Write as a consumer.

Your ability to write can influence how you are treated as a client or a customer by large and seemingly faceless organizations. A carefully constructed message can convey a legitimate grievance or express pleasure.

1. Writing a letter of complaint

Suppose you had ordered a product from an online store as a gift, only to find your purchase delayed in transit so that it arrived too late. Following the Customer Service link on the Web site, you compose an e-mail letter of complaint like the one on page 461. In writing such a letter, present yourself as a reasonable person who has experienced unfair treatment. (If you are writing on behalf of your company or as a representative of your company, your letter should state the complaint calmly and propose a resolution.)

Here are some guidelines for writing a letter of complaint.

- If possible, send the complaint via e-mail unless you must submit supporting documentation (such as receipts).
- If you are sending a print letter, use the business format on pp. 459–60.
- Follow any procedures for submitting a complaint specified on the company's Web site.
- Address the letter to the person in charge by name. (If you do not know the correct name and title to use, consult the corporate Web site or call the company.)
- Propose reasonable recompense and enclose receipts, if appropriate. Keep the original receipts and documents,

enclosing photocopies with your letter. Do *not* send scans of receipts as e-mail attachments.

- In the first paragraph, concisely state the problem and the action you request.
- In the following paragraphs, narrate clearly and objectively what happened. Refer to details such as the date and time of the incident so that the person you are writing to can follow up.
- Recognize those who tried to help you as well as those who did not.
- Mention previous positive experiences with the organization, if you can. Your protest will have more credibility if you come across as a person who does not usually complain.
- Conclude by thanking the person you are writing to for his or her time and expressing the hope that you will be able to continue as a customer.
- Send copies to the people whom you mention.
- Keep copies of all correspondence for your records.

Consider, for example, the e-mail below written by Edward Kim.

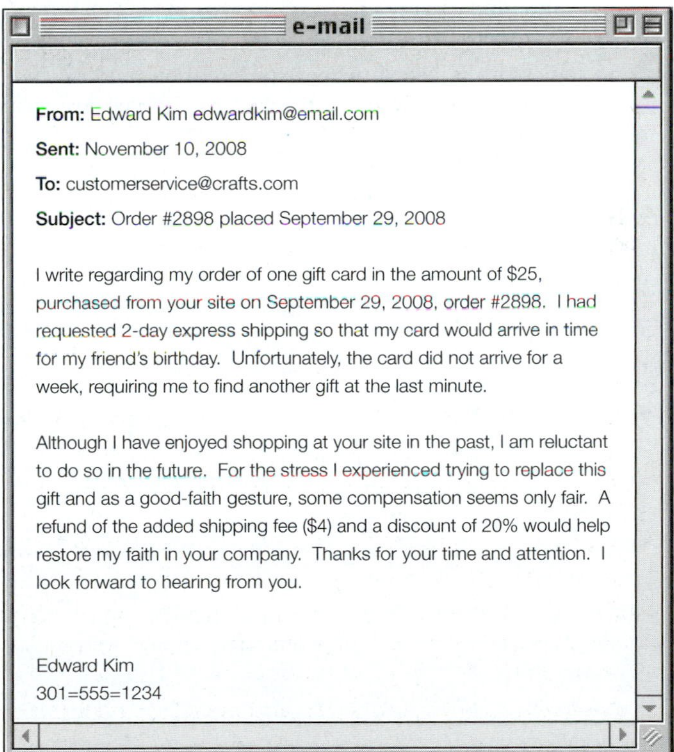

e-mail

From: Edward Kim edwardkim@email.com

Sent: November 10, 2008

To: customerservice@crafts.com

Subject: Order #2898 placed September 29, 2008

I write regarding my order of one gift card in the amount of $25, purchased from your site on September 29, 2008, order #2898. I had requested 2-day express shipping so that my card would arrive in time for my friend's birthday. Unfortunately, the card did not arrive for a week, requiring me to find another gift at the last minute.

Although I have enjoyed shopping at your site in the past, I am reluctant to do so in the future. For the stress I experienced trying to replace this gift and as a good-faith gesture, some compensation seems only fair. A refund of the added shipping fee ($4) and a discount of 20% would help restore my faith in your company. Thanks for your time and attention. I look forward to hearing from you.

Edward Kim
301=555=1234

2. Writing a letter of praise

On the other hand, suppose that you wish to thank an airline employee who has been exceptionally helpful. In the workplace, you might write a letter of praise to a colleague who worked long hours to complete a project, or to congratulate a team for bringing in new clients. The writing techniques are similar for both praise and protest letters.

- Address the letter to the person in charge by name. (If you do not know the correct name and title to use, call the corporate headquarters.)
- If you are sending a print letter, use the format for a business letter.
- In the first paragraph, concisely state the situation and the help that was provided.
- In the following paragraphs, narrate what happened, referring to details such as the date and time of the incident so that the person you are writing to can follow up with the person who helped you.
- Conclude by thanking the person you are writing to for his or her time and expressing your intention to continue doing business with the company.
- Send copies to the people whom you mention (and to the supervisor or human resources department if you are writing to a coworker).

29 Writing to Get and Keep a Job

Like many students, you may already have a job on or off campus, or you may be doing an internship or volunteering for a community-based organization. Strong writing skills will also help you find a good job once you leave college and advance in your chosen career.

29a Explore internship possibilities, and keep a portfolio of career-related writing.

www.mhhe.com/mhhb2
For more information on professional writing, go to
Learning > College to Career

An internship, in which you do actual work in your chosen field, is a vital connection between the classroom and the workplace. You gain academic credit for what you learn from the job. Writing and learning go together. During your internship, keep a journal to record and analyze your experiences, as well as a file of any writing you do on the job. Your final project for the internship credit may require you to analyze the file of writing that you have produced.

Files of writing from internships, clippings of articles and editorials you have written for the student newspaper, writing you have done for a community organization—these and other documents demonstrate your ability to apply intellectual concepts to real-world demands. Organized into a portfolio, this material displays your marketable skills. Your campus career resource center may offer assistance in compiling a portfolio. The center may also keep your portfolio on file for you and send it to future employers or graduate schools.

To begin your search for a suitable internship, visit your campus career counseling center. Many local nonprofit organizations, television and radio stations, newspapers, and both small and large companies offer internship opportunities through campus career centers.

Although your internship might pay only a modest amount (or nothing at all), your employer will nonetheless have high expectations of you. If this is your first time working in an office or a professional environment, be sure that you understand not only what is expected of you in terms of work, but also how to fit in with the workplace culture.

- **Always be on time.** Your employer is making an investment in you. Even if you are not being paid, you are learning about a possible career field and picking up invaluable business skills.
- **Dress appropriately.** If, as is likely, you meet with a representative of your employer's human resources

division when you begin work, ask about any dress codes. Even if you are interning in an organization that permits informal or creative attire, it is probably best to dress conservatively.

- **Understand what is expected.** The first few weeks of an internship might involve nothing more than filing and word processing. Once you have demonstrated your responsibility and efficiency, you might be assigned to work on more complex and interesting projects. Remember, at the end of your internship you want to have a strong reference for future positions.
- **Ask questions.** If you want to pursue a career in the field in which you are interning, be sure to ask lots of questions of your coworkers. Find out, for example, what additional coursework you should take to prepare. What is an entry-level position like in this field? How do people rise to greater levels of responsibility? What are the field's key issues and challenges?
- **Request a recommendation.** Ask—politely, and with plenty of advance notice—if your employer would provide you with a letter of recommendation to show potential employers in the future. (Your campus career center will probably keep such letters on file for you and will assist you with your job search after graduation.) Also ask if you may list your supervisor as a reference for future job applications.

29b Keep your résumé up-to-date and available on a computer disk.

A **résumé** is a brief summary of your education and work experience that you send to prospective employers. It is never finished. As you continue to learn, work, and write, you should be rethinking and reorganizing your résumé. You will want to emphasize different accomplishments and talents for different employers. Saving your résumé as a computer file allows you to tailor it to the needs and requirements of its readers.

Your résumé should be designed for quick reading. Expect the person reviewing it to give it no more than sixty seconds at first glance. Make that first impression count. Design a document that is easy to read, attractively formatted, and flawlessly edited.

Guidelines for writing a résumé

Always include the following *necessary* categories in a résumé:

- Heading (name, address, telephone number, e-mail address)
- Education (in reverse chronological order; do not include high school)
- Work experience (in reverse chronological order)
- References (often placed on a separate sheet; for many situations, you can add the line "References available on request" instead)

Include the following *optional* categories as appropriate:

- Objective
- Honors and awards
- Internships
- Activities and service
- Special skills

Sometimes career counselors recommend that you list a career objective right under the heading of your résumé. If you do so, be sure you know what the prospective employer is looking for and tailor your résumé accordingly.

Laura Amabisca has organized the information in her résumé (*p. 466*) by time and by categories. Within each category, she has listed items from the most to least recent. This reverse chronological order gives appropriate emphasis to what she is doing now and has just done. Because she is applying for jobs in public relations, she has highlighted her internship in that field by placing it at the top of her experience section.

The résumé on page 466 reflects appropriate formatting for print. Note the use of a line rule, alignment of text, bullet points, and bold and italic type. These elements organize the information visually, directing the reader's eye appropriately.

Amabisca's scannable résumé (*p. 467*) contains no italics, bold, or other formatting so it may be submitted electronically or entered into an employer's database (*see the box on p. 468*).

Amabisca's entire résumé is just one page. A brief, well-organized résumé is more attractive to potential employers than a rambling, multipage one.

The résumé features active verbs such as *supervised.*

LAURA AMABISCA
20650 North 58th Avenue, Apt. 15A
Glendale, AZ 85308
623-555-7310
lamabisca@peoplelink.com

Objective

To obtain a position as public relations assistant at a not-for-profit organization

Education

Arizona State University West, Phoenix

- Bachelor of Arts, History, Minor in Global Management (May 2008)
- Senior Thesis: Picturing the Hopi, 1920–1940: A Historical Analysis

Glendale Community College, Glendale, AZ (2004–2006)

Experience

Public Relations Office, Arizona State University West
Intern (Summer 2007)

- Researched and reported on university external publications.
- Created original content for print and Web.
- Assisted in planning fundraising campaign and events.

Sears, Bell Road, Phoenix, AZ
Assistant Manager, Sporting Goods Department (2006–present)

- Assist sales manager in day-to-day operations.
- Supervise team of sales associates.
- Ensure quality customer service.

Sales Associate, Sporting Goods Department (2003–2006)

- Recommended products to meet customer needs.
- Processed sales and returns.

Stock Clerk, Sporting Goods Department (2000–2003)

- Received, sorted, and tracked incoming merchandise.
- Stocked shelves to ensure appropriate supply on sales floor.

Special Skills

Language: Bilingual: Spanish/English
Computer: Windows, Mac OS, MS Office, HTML

Activities

America Reads
Tutor, Public Relations Consultant (2007)

- Taught reading to first-grade students.
- Created brochure to recruit tutors.

Multicultural Festival, Arizona State University West
Student Coordinator (2007)
Organized festival of international performances, crafts, and community organizations.

Writing Center, Glendale Community College
Tutor (2004–2006)
Met with peers to help them with writing assignments.

References

Available upon request to Career Services, Arizona State University West

LAURA AMABISCA
20650 North 58th Avenue, Apt. 15A
Glendale, AZ 85308
623-555-7310
lamabisca@peoplelink.com

OBJECTIVE
To obtain a position as public relations assistant at a not-for-profit organization

EDUCATION
Arizona State University West, Phoenix
* Bachelor of Arts, History, Minor in Global Management (May 2008)
* Senior Thesis: Picturing the Hopi, 1920-1940: A Historical Analysis

Glendale Community College, Glendale, AZ (2004–2006)

EXPERIENCE
Public Relations Office, Arizona State University West (Summer 2007)
Intern
* Researched and reported on university external publications.
* Created original content for print and Web.
* Assisted in planning fundraising campaign and events.

Sears, Bell Road, Phoenix, AZ
Assistant Manager, Sporting Goods Department (2006–present)
* Supervise team of sales associates.
* Ensure quality customer service.

Sales Associate, Sporting Goods Department (2003–2006)
* Recommended products to meet customer needs.
* Processed sales and returns.

Stock Clerk, Sporting Goods Department (2000–2003)
* Received, sorted, and tracked incoming merchandise.
* Stocked shelves to ensure appropriate supply on sales floor.

SPECIAL SKILLS
Language: Bilingual: Spanish/English
Computer: Windows, Mac OS, MS Office, HTML

ACTIVITIES
America Reads (2007)
Tutor, Public Relations Consultant
* Taught reading to first-grade students.
* Created brochure to recruit tutors.

Multicultural Festival, Arizona State University West (2007)
Student Coordinator
Organized festival of international performances, crafts, and community organizations.

Writing Center, Glendale Community College (2004–2006)
Tutor
Met with peers to help them with writing assignments.

REFERENCES
Available upon request to Career Services, Arizona State University West

Amabisca uses a simple font and no bold or italic type, ensuring that the résumé will be scannable.

Amabisca includes keywords (highlighted) to catch the eye of a potential employer or match desired positions in a database. Amabisca knows that a position in public relations requires computer skills, communication skills, and experience working with diverse groups of people. Keywords such as *sales*, *bilingual*, *HTML*, and *public relations* are critical to her résumé.

29c Write a tailored application letter.

A clear and concise **application letter** should always accompany a résumé. Before drafting your letter, do some research about the organization you are writing to. For example, even though Laura Amabisca was already familiar with the Heard Museum, she found out the name of the director of public relations. (*Amabisca's application letter appears on p. 470.*) Call the organization, or look on its Web site, and find out the name of the person responsible for your area of interest. If you are unable to identify an appropriate name, it is better to direct the letter to "Dear Director of Public Relations" than to "Dear Sir or Madam."

Here are additional guidelines for composing a letter of application:

- **Tailor your letter.** A form letter accompanied by a generic résumé is not an effective way of getting a job interview. Before writing an application letter or preparing a résumé, you should try to find out exactly what the employer is looking for. You can then tailor your documents to those precise requirements.
- **Use business style.** Use the block form shown on pages 459–60. Type your address flush at the top of the page, starting each line at the left margin. Place the date at the

TEXTCONNEX

Electronic and Scannable Résumés

Many employers now request résumés by e-mail and electronically scan print résumés. Others ask you to type your résumé into a form on the company's Web site. Here are some tips for using electronic technology to submit your résumé.

- Contact the human resources department of a potential employer and ask whether your résumé should be scannable.
- Do not include any unusual symbols or characters. Use minimal formatting and no colors, unusual fonts, or decorative flourishes.
- Include specific keywords that allow employers to locate your electronic résumé in a database. See the résumé section of *Monster.com* at http://resume.monster.com for industry-specific advice on appropriate keywords and other step-by-step advice.
- If the employer expects the résumé as an e-mail attachment, save it in a widely readable form such as rich text format (RTF) or PDF. Use a clear, common typeface in an easy-to-read size.
- Configure your e-mail program to send you an automated reply when your résumé has been successfully received.

left margin two lines above the recipient's name and address. Use a colon (:) after the greeting. Double-space between single-spaced paragraphs. Use a traditional closing (*Sincerely, Sincerely yours, Yours truly*). Make sure that the inside address and the address on the envelope match exactly.

- **Be professional.** Your letter should be crisp and to the point. Avoid personal details. Be direct and objective in presenting your educational background (starting with college, not high school) and work-related experience. Maintain a courteous and dignified tone toward the prospective employer.
- **Limit your letter to three or four paragraphs.** Focus clearly and concisely on what the employer needs to know. In the first paragraph, identify the position you are applying for, mention how you heard about it, and briefly state that you are qualified. In the following one or two paragraphs, explain your qualifications, elaborating on the most pertinent items in your résumé. Because Amabisca was applying for a public relations job at a museum of Native American culture, she chose to highlight her internship and her thesis. In an application letter for a management position at American Express, she emphasized her work experience at Sears, including the fact that she had moved up in the organization through positions of increasing responsibility.
- **State your expectation for future contact.** Conclude with a one- or two-sentence paragraph informing the reader that you are anticipating a follow-up to your letter.
- **Use *Enc.* if you are enclosing additional materials.** Decide whether it is appropriate to enclose supporting materials other than your résumé, such as samples of your writing. Amabisca decided to do so because she was applying for her ideal job and had highly relevant materials to send. If you have been instructed to send a cover letter and résumé by e-mail as attachments, include the word *Attachments* after your e-mail "signature."

For MULTILINGUAL STUDENTS

Applying for a Job

Before applying for an internship or a job in the United States, be sure that you have the appropriate visa or work permit. American employers are required by law to confirm such documentation before they hire anyone. (American citizens must prove their citizenship as well.) For more information, visit your campus international student center as well as the campus career resource center.

Amabisca writes to a specific person and uses the correct salutation (*Mr., Ms., Dr.,* etc.). Never use someone's first name in an application letter, even if you are already acquainted.

Amabisca briefly sums up her work experience. This information is also available on her résumé, but she makes evident in her cover letter why she is applying for the job. Without this explanation, a potential employer might not even look at her résumé.

Amabisca demonstrates her familiarity with the museum to which she is applying. This shows her genuine interest in joining the organization.

20650 North 58th Avenue, Apt. 15A
Glendale, AZ 85308
August 17, 2008

Ms. Jaclyn Abel
Director of Public Relations
Heard Museum
2301 North Central Avenue
Phoenix, AZ 85004

Dear Ms. Abel:

I am writing to apply for the position of Public Relations Assistant that you recently advertised in the *Arizona Republic*. I believe that my experience and qualifications fit well with your needs at the Heard, a museum that I have visited and loved all my life.

As the enclosed résumé indicates, I have experience in the public relations field. While at Arizona State University West, I worked as an intern in the Public Relations Office, where I was responsible for analyzing and reporting on the image projected by the university's external publications. I also had a hand in creating the brochure for the University-College Center and participated in planning ASU West's "Dream Big" campaign. In addition I assisted in organizing an opening convocation attended by 800 people. This work in the not-for-profit sector has prepared me well for employment at the Heard.

Additionally, my undergraduate major in U.S. history has helped me understand the rich heritage of Native Americans. In my senior thesis, which received the Westmarc Writing Award, I studied the history of the relationship between the Hopis and the Anglo population as reflected in photographs taken from 1920 to 1940. Although my thesis focuses on a specific tribe, I have been interested for many years in Native-American culture and have often made use of resources in the Heard. I think that I would do a superior job of presenting the Heard as the premier museum of Native American culture.

Confidential reference letters are available from ASU West Career Services. I sincerely hope that we will have an opportunity to talk further about the Heard Museum and its outstanding cultural contributions to the Phoenix metropolitan area. Please contact me at 623-555-7310.

Sincerely,

Laura Amabisca

Enc.

29d Prepare in advance for the job interview.

An interview with a potential employer is like an oral presentation. You should prepare in advance, rehearse before an audience, and be prepared to answer unexpected questions. Many campus career resource centers offer free seminars on interviewing skills and can also arrange for you to role-play an interview with a career guidance counselor.

- Call to confirm your interview the day before it is scheduled. Determine how much time you will need to get there. A late appearance at an interview can count heavily against you.
- Dress modestly and professionally.
- Bring an extra copy of your résumé and cover letter.
- Expect to speak with several people—perhaps someone from human resources as well as the person for whom you would work and other people in his or her department.
- *Always* send a personalized thank-you note or e-mail to everyone who took the time to meet you. In each, mention an interesting point from the interview conversation and reiterate your enthusiasm for the job. Send these notes within twenty-four hours of your interview.

29e Apply what you learn in college to your on-the-job writing.

Once you get a job, writing is a way to establish and maintain lines of communication with your colleagues and other contacts. When you write in the workplace, you should imagine a reader who is pressed for time and wants you to get to the point immediately.

1. Writing e-mail and memos in the workplace

In the workplace, you will do much of your writing online, in the form of e-mail. *(For more on e-mail, see Chapter 1, Learning across the curriculum, pp. 11–12.)* Most e-mail programs set up messages in memo format, with "To," "From," "Date," and "Subject" lines, as in Figure 29.1 on page 472.

E-mail in the workplace requires a more formal style than the e-mail you send to family and friends. In an e-mail for a business occasion—communication with colleagues, a request for information, or a thank-you note after an interview—you should observe the same care with organization, spelling, and tone that you would in a business letter. More specifically:

- Use a concise subject line to cue the reader as to the intent of the e-mail. When replying to messages, replace subject lines that do not clearly reflect the topic.

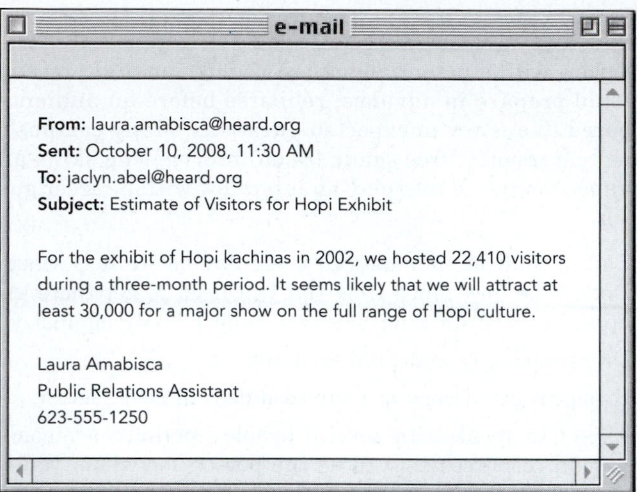

e-mail
From: laura.amabisca@heard.org
Sent: October 10, 2008, 11:30 AM
To: jaclyn.abel@heard.org
Subject: Estimate of Visitors for Hopi Exhibit
For the exhibit of Hopi kachinas in 2002, we hosted 22,410 visitors during a three-month period. It seems likely that we will attract at least 30,000 for a major show on the full range of Hopi culture.
Laura Amabisca
Public Relations Assistant
623-555-1250

FIGURE 29.1 Sample workplace e-mail.

- Maintain a courteous tone. Use joking, informality, and sarcasm cautiously, as they can cause the recipient to misunderstand your intent.
- Make sentences short and to the point. Use short paragraphs.
- Use special formatting such as italics sparingly, as not all readers will be able to view it.
- Use standard punctuation and capitalization.
- Close with your name and contact information. (*See the example above.*)
- Particularly when you do not know the recipient, use the conventions of letter-writing such as opening with "Dear" and ending with "Sincerely."

Business memos are used for communication with others within an organization. Like business e-mails, they are concise and formal. Memos may establish meetings, summarize information, or make announcements. (*See the example on p. 474.*) They generally contain the following elements and characteristics:

- A header at the top that identifies author, recipient, date, and subject
- Block paragraphs that are single-spaced within the paragraph and double-spaced between paragraphs
- Bulleted lists and other design elements (such as headers) to set off sections of longer memos

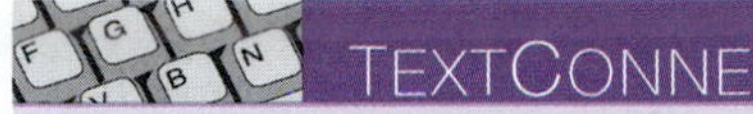

TEXTCONNEX

E-mail in the Workplace

Anything you write using a company's or an organization's computers is considered company property. If you want to gossip with a coworker, do so over lunch. If you want to e-mail your best friend about your personal life, do so from your home computer. The following guidelines will help you use e-mail wisely:

- When you are replying to an e-mail that has been sent to several people (the term *cc* means "carbon copy") determine whether your response should go to all of the original recipients or just to the original sender. Avoid cluttering other people's in-boxes.
- Open attachments from known senders only.
- File your e-mail as carefully as you would paper documents. Create separate folders in your e-mail program for each client, project, or coworker. Save any particularly important e-mails as separate files.
- Although it may be acceptable for you to browse news and shopping sites during your breaks and lunchtime, do not visit any sites while in the workplace that would embarrass you if a colleague or your supervisor suddenly looked over your shoulder.

- A section at the bottom that indicates other members of the organization who have received copies of the memo
- A professional tone

Whether you are writing an e-mail message or a conventional memo, consider both the content and the appearance of the document. For example, presenting your information as a numbered or bulleted list surrounded by white space aids readability and allows you to highlight important points and to emphasize crucial ideas. (*For more help with document design, see Chapter 6, pp. 104–17.*)

2. Writing other business genres

Readers have built-in expectations for conventional forms of business communication and know what to look for when they read them. Besides the memo, there are a number of common business genres:

- **Business letters:** Use business letters to communicate formally with people outside an organization. Typically, letters in business format have single-spaced block paragraphs with double spacing between the paragraphs. (*See the example on pp. 459–60 in Chapter 28.*)

- **Business reports and proposals:** Like college research papers, business reports and proposals can be used to

Heading: Addressees' names, sender's name and initials, date, and subject

To: Sonia Gonzalez, Grace Kim, Jonathan Jones
From: Jennifer Richer, Design Team Manager *JR*
Date: March 3, 2008
Re: Meeting on Monday

Please plan to attend a meeting on Monday at 9:00 a.m. in Room 401. At that time, we'll review our progress on the library project as well as outline future activities to ensure the following:

- Client satisfaction
- Maintenance of the current schedule
- Operation within budget constraints

In addition, we will discuss assignments related to other upcoming projects, such as the renovation of the gymnasium and science lab.

Please bring design ideas and be prepared to brainstorm. Thanks.

Person receiving copy

Copy: Michael Garcia, Director, Worldwide Design

inform, analyze, and interpret. An abstract, sometimes called an *executive summary,* is almost always required, as are tables and graphs. (*For more on these visual elements, see Chapter 3: Planning and Shaping the Whole Essay, pp. 51–54.*)

- **Evaluations and recommendations:** You might need to evaluate a person, or you might be called on to evaluate a product or a procedure and recommend whether the company should buy or use it. Like the reviews and critiques that col-

TEXTCONNEX

Writing Connections

Monster Career Advice <http://career-advice.monster.com/resume-tips/home.aspx>: This site provides sample résumés and cover letters in addition to career advice.

Job Central <http://jobstar.org/tools/resume/samples.cfm>: This site provides samples of résumés for many different situations, as well as sample cover letters.

lege writers compose, workplace evaluations are supposed to be reasonable as well as convincing. It is important to be fair, so you should always support your account of both strengths and weaknesses with specific illustrations or examples.

- **Presentations**: In many professions, information is presented in ways both formal and informal to groups of people. You might suddenly be asked to offer an opinion in a group meeting; or you might be given a week to prepare a formal presentation, with visuals, on an ongoing project. (*For more information on oral presentations, see Chapter 13, pp. 221–26. To learn more about PowerPoint and other presentation tools, see Chapter 14, pp. 232–37.*)

www.mhhe.com/mhhb2

For more information on PowerPoint, go to

Writing > PowerPoint Tutorial

Like DNA, which provides a chemical blueprint for the construction of living organisms, grammar and syntax provide a blueprint for transforming words into intelligible sentences.

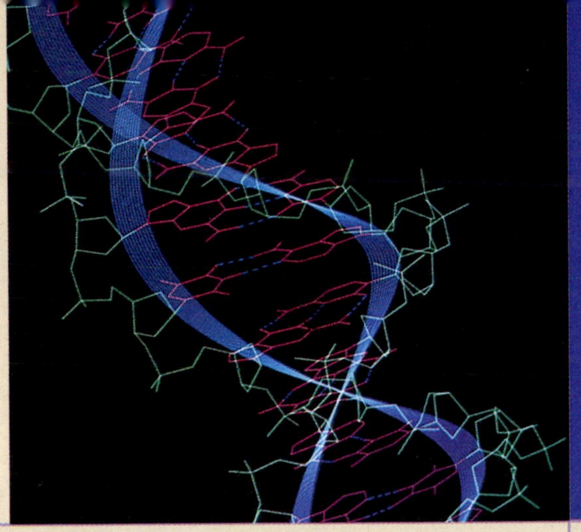

PART 6

Grammar and rhetoric are complementary. . . . Grammar maps out the possible; rhetoric narrows the possible down to the desirable or effective.

—Francis Christensen

Grammar Basics

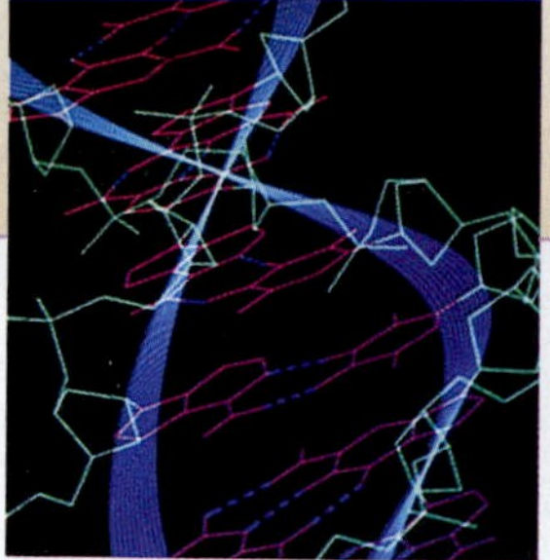

30 Parts of Speech

Written language, although based on the grammar of spoken language, has a logic and rules of its own. This chapter and the next (*Chapter 31: Sentence Basics*) explain the basic rules of standard written English.

Grammar gives us a way of talking about how sentences are put together to make sense. Take, for example, this group of words, adapted from Lewis Carroll's poem "Jabberwocky":

> The toves gimbled in the wabe.

Most of these are nonsense words: Carroll made them up. What makes a sentence meaningful, however, is not just its individual words. Because of the form of the words in this sentence and the way they relate to each other, we can answer questions about them:

www.mhhe.com/ **mhhb2**

For information and exercises on parts of speech, go to

Editing > Parts of Speech

> What gimbled in the wabe? *The toves did.*
>
> What did the toves do in the wabe? *They gimbled.*
>
> Where did the toves gimble? *They gimbled in the wabe.*

We can answer these questions because we can tell from the form and relationship of the words what grammatical role each one plays in the sentence.

WRITING OUTCOMES

Part 6: Grammar Basics

This section will help you answer questions such as:

Rhetorical Knowledge

- When are interjections used in academic writing? **(30h)**
- How does English word order differ from that of other languages? **(31c)**

Critical Thinking, Reading, and Writing

- How do I find the subject and predicate of a sentence? **(31b, c)**
- How can I find out whether a verb is transitive or intransitive? **(31c)**

Processes

- During editing, should I add a comma after an *–ing* verb phrase that begins a sentence? **(31f)**

Knowledge of Conventions

- What are the parts of speech? **(30)**
- What are the five common sentence patterns in English? **(31c)**

Self-Assessment: *Take an online quiz at www.mhhe.com/mhhb2 to test your familiarity with the topics covered in Chapters 30–31. Pay special attention to the sections in these chapters that correspond to any questions you answer incorrectly.*

CHARTING the TERRITORY

Grammar, Human Thought, and the Origins of Language

The study of grammar—or, more broadly, **syntax,** the rules for forming grammatical sentences in a language—is not confined to English or other language departments. Psychologists, linguists, and philosophers study grammar and syntax for clues to the nature of the human mind. Anthropologists and psychologists study the limited language abilities of chimpanzees and other primates for evidence of syntax and clues to the origin of language. Similarly, paleontologists, archeologists, and art historians study the first appearance of another form of symbolic communication—art—for clues to the emergence of our capacity for syntax and language.

English has eight primary grammatical categories, or **parts of speech:** *verbs, nouns, pronouns, adjectives, adverbs, prepositions, conjunctions,* and *interjections.* All English words belong to one or more of these categories. Particular words can belong in different categories,

The Eight Parts of Speech in English

- **Verbs** report action (*run, write*), condition (*bloom, sit*), or state of being (*be, seem*).
- **Nouns** name people (*Shakespeare, actors, Englishman*), places (*Manhattan, city, island*), things (*Kleenex, handkerchief, sneeze, cats*), and ideas (*Marxism, justice, democracy, clarity*).
- **Pronouns** (*she, her, herself, who, that, all*) take the place of nouns.
- **Adjectives** (*green, smaller, perfect*) modify nouns and pronouns by answering questions like *Which one? What kind? How many? What size? What condition?*
- **Adverbs** (*quietly, better, never*) modify verbs, other adverbs, adjectives, and whole clauses. They usually answer such questions as *When? Where? How? How often? How much? To what degree?* and *Why?*
- **Prepositions** (*on, in, at, by, as well as*) usually appear as part of a **prepositional phrase.** Their main function is to allow the noun or pronoun in the phrase to modify another word in the sentence.
- **Conjunctions** (*and, but, both . . . and, neither . . . nor, after*) join words, phrases, or clauses and indicate their relation to each other.
- **Interjections** (*alas, oh no*) are forceful expressions, usually written with an exclamation point.

depending on the role they play in a sentence. For example, the word *button* can be a noun:

► **The *button* is on the coat.**

or a verb:

► **He will *button* his jacket now.**

www.mhhe.com/mhhb2
For information and exercises on verbs, go to
Editing > Verbs and Verbals

30a Verbs

Verbs carry a lot of information. They report action (*run, write*), condition (*bloom, sit*), or state of being (*be, seem*). Verbs also change form to indicate person, number, tense, voice, and mood (*see Chapters 34: Subject-Verb Agreement, and 35: Problems with Verbs*). To do all this, a **main verb** is sometimes accompanied by one or more **helping verbs,** thereby becoming a **verb phrase.** Helping verbs precede the main verb in a verb phrase.

► **The play *begins* (mv) at eight.**

► **I *may* (hv) *change* (mv) seats after the play *has* (hv) *begun* (mv).**

1. Main verbs

Main verbs change form to indicate when something occurs (**tense**) and to whom it occurs (**person** and **number**). If a word does not indicate tense, it is not a main verb. All main verbs have five forms, except for *be,* which has eight.

BASE FORM	(*talk, sing*)
PAST TENSE	Yesterday I (*talked, sang*).
PAST PARTICIPLE	In the past, I have (*talked, sung*).
PRESENT PARTICIPLE	Right now I am (*talking, singing*).
-S FORM (PRESENT TENSE THIRD-PERSON SINGULAR)	Usually he/she/it (*talks, sings*).

Whether or not English is your first language, verb forms—especially irregular verb forms—can be troublesome. (*For more on subject-verb agreement and verb tense, see Chapter 34: Subject-Verb Agreement, pp. 536–51, Chapter 35: Problems with Verbs, pp. 551–75, and the list of common irregular verbs on pp. 554–55.*)

2. Helping verbs that show time

Some helping verbs—mostly forms of *be, have,* and *do*—function to signify time (*will have been playing, has played*) or emphasis (*does play*).

Forms of *do* are also used to ask questions (*Do you play?*). Here is a more comprehensive list of such helping (or **auxiliary**) verbs:

be, am, is	being, been	do, does, did
are, was, were	have, has, had	

3. Modals: Helping verbs that show manner

Other helping verbs, called **modals,** signify the manner, or mode, of an action. Modals fall into two categories:

- one-word
- phrasal

One-word modals Unlike the auxiliaries *be, have,* and *do,* one-word modals such as *may, must,* and *will* are rarely used alone as main verbs, nor do they change form to show person or number. One-word modals do not add *-s* endings, two of them are never used together (such as *might could*), and each is followed by the base form of the verb without *to* (*He could be nicer*).

► **Contrary to press reports, she *will*[hv] not *run*[mv] for political office.**

Note that a negative word such as *not* may come between the helping and the main verb.

The one-word modals are as follows:

can	might	shall
could	will	should
may	would	must

Phrasal modals Phrasal modals do change form to show time, person, and number.

► **Yesterday, I *was going to*[hv] *study*[mv] for three hours.**

► **Next week, I *am going to*[hv] *study*[mv] three hours a day.**

Here are some phrasal modals:

have to	be supposed to	be able to
have got to	be going to	
used to	be allowed to	

For MULTILINGUAL STUDENTS

For more on the form and meaning of modal verbs, see Chapter 64: English Basics (*pp. 847–50*).

Exercise 30.1 Identifying verbs

Underline the main verb in each sentence. If there is a helping verb or verbs, circle them.

EXAMPLE Government of the people, by the people, for the people shall not perish from the earth.

1. An increasing number of Americans, both men and women, undergo cosmetic surgery for aesthetic rather than medical reasons.
2. Not long ago, the average American believed that only Hollywood celebrities underwent facelifts and tummy tucks.
3. Do you think that you need to improve your physical appearance?
4. Men, often in their mid-forties, are choosing a variety of surgical procedures, including hair replacement and chin augmentation.
5. For a lean, flat abdomen, a cosmetic surgeon may suggest both abdominoplasty and liposuction.
6. People are now able to achieve their ideal body image, not through exercise and diet, but through elective cosmetic surgery.

30b Nouns

Nouns name people (*Shakespeare, actors, Englishman*), places (*Manhattan, city, island*), things (*Kleenex, handkerchief, sneeze, cats*), and ideas (*Marxism, justice, democracy, clarity*). Often they are preceded by **articles** such as *a* or *the*. Nouns function as subjects, objects, and complements.

► *Shakespeare* lived in *England* and wrote *plays* about the human *condition*.

1. Proper nouns and common nouns

Proper nouns name specific people, places, and things and are always capitalized: *Aretha Franklin, Hinduism, Albany, Microsoft.* All other nouns are **common nouns:** *singer, religion, capital, corporation.*

2. Count nouns and noncount nouns

A common noun that refers to something specific that can be counted is a **count noun.** Count nouns can be singular or plural, like *cup* or *suggestion* (*four cups, several suggestions*). **Noncount nouns** are nonspecific; these common nouns refer to categories of people, places, or things and cannot be counted. They do not have a plural form. (*The pottery is beautiful. His advice was useful.*)

SOME COUNT and NONCOUNT NOUNS

Count Nouns	*Noncount Nouns*
cars	transportation
computers	Internet
facts	information
clouds	rain
stars	sunshine
tools	equipment
machines	machinery
suggestions	advice
earrings	jewelry
tables	furniture
smiles	happiness

For MULTILINGUAL STUDENTS

For help using quantifiers with count and noncount nouns, see Chapter 64: English Basics (*pp. 841–43*).

3. Concrete nouns and abstract nouns

Nouns that name things that can be perceived by the senses are called **concrete nouns:** *boy, wind, book, song.* **Abstract nouns** name qualities and concepts that do not have physical properties: *charity, patience, beauty, hope.* (*For more on using concrete and abstract nouns, see Chapter 49: Exact Language, pp. 700–1.*)

4. Singular nouns and plural nouns

Most nouns name things that can be counted and are **singular** or **plural.** Singular nouns typically become plural by adding *s* or *es: boy/boys, ocean/oceans, church/churches, agency/agencies.* Some count nouns have irregular plurals, such as *man/men, child/children,* and *tooth/teeth.* Noncount nouns like *intelligence* and *electricity* do not form plurals.

5. Collective nouns

Nouns such as *team, family, herd,* and *orchestra*—called **collective nouns**—are treated as singular. They are not noncount nouns, however, because collective nouns can be counted and can be made plural: *teams, families.* (*Also see Chapter 34: Subject-Verb Agreement, pp. 544–46, and Chapter 36: Problems with Pronouns, p. 589.*)

6. Possessive nouns

Nouns change their form to indicate possession, or ownership. To form a singular **possessive noun,** add apostrophe plus *s* (*'s*); for plural nouns ending in *s*, just add an apostrophe ('). (*Also see Chapter 61: Apostrophes, pp. 813–19.*)

SINGULAR	insect	insect's sting
PLURAL	neighbors	neighbors' car

www.mhhe.com/ mhhb2

For information and exercises on pronouns, go to

Editing > Pronouns

30c Pronouns

A pronoun takes the place of a noun. The noun that the pronoun replaces is called its **antecedent.** (*For more on pronoun-antecedent agreement, see Chapter 36: Problems with Pronouns, pp. 586–91.*)

► **The *snow* fell all day long, and by nightfall *it* was three feet deep.**

The box on page 486 summarizes the various kinds of pronouns. Each type is explained below.

1. Personal pronouns

The **personal pronouns** *I, me, you, he, his, she, her, it, we, us, they,* and *them* refer to specific people or things and vary in form to indicate person, number, gender, and case. (*For more on pronoun referents and case, such as distinguishing between* I *and* me, *see Chapter 36: Problems with Pronouns, pp. 575–97.*)

► ***You* told *us* that *he* gave Jane a lock of *his* hair.**

2. Possessive pronouns

Like possessive nouns, **possessive pronouns** indicate ownership. However, unlike possessive nouns, possessive pronouns do not add apostrophes: *my/mine, your/yours, her/hers, his, its, our/ours, their/theirs.*

► **Brunch is at *her* place this Saturday.**

► ***Hers* was the best performance of the evening.**

3. Reflexive pronouns and intensive pronouns

Pronouns ending in *-self* or *-selves* are either reflexive or intensive. **Reflexive pronouns** refer back to the subject and are necessary for sentence sense.

► **Many of the women blamed *themselves* for the problem.**

Intensive pronouns add emphasis to the nouns or pronouns they follow and are grammatically optional.

► **President Harding *himself* drank whiskey during Prohibition.**

4. Relative pronouns

Who, whom, whose, that, and *which* are relative pronouns. A **relative pronoun** relates a dependent clause—a word group containing a subject and verb and a subordinating word—to an antecedent noun or pronoun in the sentence.

dependent clause

► In Kipling's story, Dravot is the man *who* would be king.

The form of a relative pronoun varies according to its **case**—the grammatical role it plays in the sentence. (*For more on pronoun case, particularly distinguishing between* who *and* whom, *see Chapter 36: Problems with Pronouns, pp. 584–86.*)

The relative pronouns *whatever, whichever, whoever, whomever,* and *what* introduce noun clauses and do not have antecedents.

5. Demonstrative pronouns

The **demonstrative pronouns** *this, that, these,* and *those* point out nouns and pronouns that come later.

► *This* is the book literary critics have been waiting for.

Sometimes these pronouns function as adjectives: *This book won the Pulitzer.* Sometimes they are noun equivalents: *This is my book.*

6. Interrogative pronouns

Interrogative pronouns such as *who, whatever,* and *whom* are used to ask questions.

► *Whatever* happened to you?

The form of the interrogative pronouns *who, whom, whoever,* and *whomever* indicates the grammatical role they play in a sentence. (*See Chapter 36: Problems with Pronouns, page 576.*)

7. Indefinite pronouns

Indefinite pronouns such as *someone, anybody, nothing,* and *few* refer to a nonspecific person or thing and do not change form to indicate person, number, or gender.

► *Anybody* who cares enough to come and help may take some home.

Most indefinite pronouns are always singular (*anybody, everyone*). Some are always plural *(many, few)*. A handful can be singular or plural (*any, most*). (*See Chapter 34: Subject-Verb Agreement, pp. 547–48.*)

8. Reciprocal pronouns

Reciprocal pronouns such as *each other* and *one another* refer to the separate parts of their plural antecedent.

► My sister and I are close because we live near *each other.*

PRONOUNS

Personal (Including Possessive)

SINGULAR	PLURAL
I, me, my, mine	we, us, our, ours
you, your, yours	you, your, yours
he, him, his	they, them, their, theirs
she, her, hers	
it, its	

Reflexive and Intensive

SINGULAR	PLURAL
myself	ourselves
yourself	yourselves
himself, herself, itself	themselves
oneself	

Relative

who	whoever	what	whatever	that
whom	whomever	whose	whichever	which

Demonstrative

this, that, these, those

Interrogative

who	what	which
whoever	whatever	whichever
whom	whomever	whose

Indefinite

SINGULAR		PLURAL	SINGULAR/PLURAL
anybody	nobody	both	all
anyone	no one	few	any
anything	none	many	either
each	nothing	several	more
everybody	one		most
everyone	somebody		some
everything	someone		
much	something		
neither			

Reciprocal

each other	any other

Exercise 30.2 Identifying nouns and pronouns

Underline the nouns and circle the pronouns in each sentence.

EXAMPLE **We have nothing to fear but fear itself.**

1. Following World War I, the nation witnessed an unprecedented explosion of African-American fiction, poetry, drama, music, art, social commentary, and political activism.
2. Many African-American intellectuals, artists, cultural critics, and political leaders during the 1920s and 1930s were drawn to Harlem, a vibrant section of upper Manhattan in New York City.
3. Sociologist and intellectual Alain Locke, author of *The New Negro,* is best known as the New Negro Movement's founder.
4. W. E. B. DuBois was the author of *The Souls of Black Folk,* and he was also a cofounder of the National Association for the Advancement of Colored People (NAACP), a preeminent civil rights organization.
5. These intellectuals of the Harlem Renaissance profoundly influenced each other.
6. They spoke about the effect of marginality and alienation on themselves and on the shaping of their consciousness as African Americans.
7. Zora Neal Hurston was herself a cultural anthropologist who studied the folklore of the rural South, which is reflected in her novel *Their Eyes Were Watching God.*
8. Nella Larson, author of *Quicksand* and *Passing,* was awarded a Guggenheim fellowship in 1929 for her creative writing.
9. Who among the visual artists during the Harlem Renaissance did not use Africa as a source of inspiration?

Exercise 30.3 Identifying types of nouns and pronouns

On a separate sheet of paper, list each noun and pronoun that you identified in Exercise 30.2. For each noun, label it proper or common, count or noncount, concrete or abstract, and singular or plural. Also identify the one collective noun and the one possessive noun. For each pronoun, label it personal, possessive, reflexive, intensive, relative, demonstrative, interrogative, indefinite, or reciprocal. Note whether the pronoun is singular or plural.

www.mhhe.com/mhhb2
For information and exercises on adjectives, go to
Editing > Adjectives and Adverbs

30d Adjectives

Adjectives modify nouns and pronouns by answering questions like *Which one? What kind? How many? What size? What color? What condition?* and *Whose?* Adjectives can:

- describe (*red* car, *dangerous* mission)
- enumerate (*tenth* floor, *seventy-six* trombones)
- identify (*British* parliament, *American* constitution)
- define (*democratic* constitution, *capitalist* economy)
- limit (*one* person, *that* person).

Determiners are a type of adjective that precedes and labels a noun. They include **articles** (*a, an, the*), **quantifiers** (*one, some, any, more, less*), and possessives (*my, your, their*).

For MULTILINGUAL STUDENTS

For help with using articles appropriately, see Chapter 64: English Basics (*pp. 838–45*).

Some proper nouns have an adjective form. Like the nouns from which they derive, these **proper adjectives** are capitalized: *Britain / British.* Pronouns and nouns can also function as adjectives (*his green car, the car door*), and adjectives often have forms that allow you to make comparisons (*great, greater, greatest*).

► **The *decisive* and *diligent* king regularly attended meetings of the council.** [What kind of king?]

► ***These four artistic* qualities affect how an advertisement is received.** [Which, how many, what kind of qualities?]

► ***My little blue* Volkswagen died *one icy winter* morning.** [Whose, what size, what color car? Which, what kind of morning?]

► **Lincoln was one of the country's *greatest* presidents.** [The adjective compares Lincoln with other presidents.]

Most often, adjectives appear before the noun they modify. However, **descriptive adjectives**—adjectives that designate qualities or attributes—may come before or after the noun or pronoun they modify, depending on the stylistic effect a writer wishes to achieve. Adjectives that describe the subject and follow linking verbs (*be, am, is, are, was, being, been, appear, become, feel, grow, look, make, prove, smell, sound, seem, taste*) are called **subject complements.**

BEFORE THE SUBJECT

The *sick* and *destitute* poet no longer believed that love would save him.

AFTER THE SUBJECT

The poet, *sick* and *destitute,* no longer believed that love would save him.

AFTER A LINKING VERB

No longer believing that love would save him, the poet was *sick* and *destitute.*

For MULTILINGUAL STUDENTS

For information on the order of adjectives in English, see Chapter 64: English Basics (*pp. 844–45*).

30e Adverbs

www.mhhe.com/mhhb2
For information and exercises on adverbs, go to
Editing > Adjectives and Adverbs

Adverbs modify verbs, other adverbs, and adjectives, answering such questions as *When? Where? How? How often? How much? To what degree?* and *Why?* They often end in *-ly* (*beautifully, gracefully, quietly*).

► **The authenticity of the document is *hotly* contested.** [How is it contested?]

Like adjectives, adverbs can be used to compare (*less, lesser, least*). In addition to modifying individual words, they can be used to modify whole clauses. Adverbs can be placed at the beginning or end of a sentence or before the verb they modify, but they should not be placed between the verb and its direct object.

► **The water was *brilliant* blue and *icy* cold.** [The adverbs intensify the adjectives *blue* and *cold.*]

► **Dickens mixed humor and pathos *better* than any other English writer after Shakespeare.** [The adverb compares Dickens with other writers.]

► ***Consequently,* he is still read by millions.**

Consequently is a **conjunctive adverb** that modifies the independent clause that follows it and shows how the sentence is related to the preceding sentence.

Conjunctive adverbs indicate the relation between one clause and another, but unlike conjunctions (*and, but*), they are not grammatically strong enough on their own to hold the two clauses together. A period or semicolon is also needed.

► **Swimming is an excellent exercise for the heart and for the muscles; *however*, swimming is not as effective a weight control measure as jogging is.**

See also section 30g on conjunctions.

COMMON CONJUNCTIVE ADVERBS

Addition	***Comparison/Contrast***	***Emphasis***
also	however	certainly
besides	instead	indeed
furthermore	likewise	still
moreover	nevertheless	
	nonetheless	
	otherwise	
	similarly	

Result	***Time***
accordingly	finally
consequently	meanwhile
hence	next
then	now
therefore	subsequently
thus	suddenly
	then

The negators *no*, *not*, and *never* are among the most common adverbs.

SAY *NO* ONLY ONCE

In English, it takes only one negator (*no* / *not* / *never*) to change the meaning of a sentence from positive to negative. When two negatives are used together, they may seem to cancel each other out.

► **They don't have ~~no~~ any reason to go there.**

Words like *why* and *where* are relative adverbs and introduce adjective clauses.

Exercise 30.4 Identifying adjectives and adverbs

Underline the adjectives and circle the adverbs in each sentence.

EXAMPLE **Peter Piper (patiently) picked a peck of pickled peppers.**

1. A growing number of Americans are overweight or clinically obese.
2. Obesity increases a person's risk for type 2 diabetes, heart disease, high blood pressure, stroke, liver damage, cancer, and premature death.
3. Fad diets promise Americans rapid but temporary weight loss, not weight management.
4. Robert C. Atkins, M.D., author of *Dr. Atkins' New Diet Revolution,* best explains a low-carbohydrate, high-protein diet.
5. Other fad diets, such as the Sugar Busters diet, work on the premise that high glycemic carbohydrates are primarily responsible for weight gain.
6. In the best seller *Eat Right for Your Type,* naturopath Peter J. D'Adamo argues that certain foods should be avoided based on a person's blood type.
7. Many other fad diets, such as the grapefruit diet and the cabbage diet, promise quick weight loss.
8. Many fad diets inevitably drive dieters to carbohydrate cravings and binge eating.
9. Few fad diets emphasize the need for dieters to increase their metabolic rate significantly with regular aerobic exercise.

30f Prepositions

Prepositions (*on, in, at, by*) usually appear as part of a **prepositional phrase.** Their main function is to allow the noun or pronoun in the phrase to modify another word in the sentence. Prepositional phrases always begin with a preposition and end with a noun, pronoun, or other word group that functions as the **object of the preposition** (in *time,* on the *table*).

A preposition can be one word (*about, despite, on*) or a word group (*according to, as well as, in spite of*). Place prepositional phrases as close as possible to the words they modify. Adjectival prepositional phrases usually appear immediately after the noun or pronoun they modify and answer questions like *Which one?* and *What kind of?* Adverbial phrases can appear anywhere in a sentence; they answer questions like *When? Where? How?* and *Why?*

AS ADJECTIVE Many species *of birds* nest there.

AS ADVERB The younger children stared *out the window.*

COMMON PREPOSITIONS

about	by	near
above	by means of	of
according to	by way of	on
across	down	on account of
after	during	over
against	except	since
along	except for	through
along with	excluding	to
among	following	toward
apart from	from	under
as	in	underneath
as to	in addition to	until
as well as	in case of	up
at	in front of	up to
because of	in place of	upon
before	in regard to	via
behind	including	with
below	inside	with reference to
beside	instead of	with respect to
between	into	within
beyond	like	without

For MULTILINGUAL STUDENTS

For more on using prepositions, see Chapter 66: Identifying and Editing Common Errors (*pp. 865–66*). For a list of common idioms including prepositions, see Chapter 49; Exact Language (*pp. 702–3*).

30g Conjunctions

Conjunctions join words, phrases, or clauses and indicate their relation to each other. Conjunctive adverbs serve a similar function (30e).

1. Coordinating conjunctions

The common **coordinating conjunctions** (or **coordinators**) are *and, but, or, for, nor, yet,* and *so. For* and *so* always join independent clauses (*for more on clauses see Chapter 31: Sentence Basics, p. 503*). Coordinating conjunctions join elements of equal weight or function.

- ► She was strong and *healthy.*
- ► The war was short *but* devastating.
- ► They must have been tired, *for* they had been climbing all day long.

2. Correlative conjunctions

The **correlative conjunctions** also link sentence elements of equal value, but they always come in pairs: *both . . . and, either . . . or, neither . . . nor,* and *not only . . . but also.*

► *Neither* the doctor *nor* the social worker believes his story.

3. Subordinating conjunctions

Common **subordinating conjunctions** (or **subordinators**) link sentence elements that are not of equal importance. Because subordinating conjunctions join unequal sentence parts, they are used to introduce dependent, or subordinate, clauses in a sentence.

► The software will not run properly *if* the computer lacks sufficient memory.

(*For help in punctuating sentences with conjunctions, see Chapter 51: Commas, pp. 718–21 and 741–42.*)

COMMON SUBORDINATING CONJUNCTIONS

Subordinating Words

after	once	until
although	since	when
as	that	whenever
because	though	where
before	till	wherever
if	unless	while

Subordinating Phrases

as if	even though	in that
as soon as	even when	rather than
as though	for as much as	so that
even after	in order that	sooner than
even if	in order to	

For MULTILINGUAL STUDENTS

For information on using coordination and subordination appropriately, see Chapter 65, English Sentence Structure (*pp. 860–61*).

30h Interjections

Interjections are forceful expressions, usually written with an exclamation point. They are not often used in academic writing except in quotations of dialogue.

► *"Wow!"* Davis said. "Are you telling me that there's a former presidential adviser who hasn't written a book?"

► Tell-all books are, *alas,* the biggest sellers.

Exercise 30.5 Chapter review: Parts of speech

In the following sentences, label each word according to its part of speech: verb (v), noun (n), pronoun (pn), adjective (adj), adverb (adv), preposition (prep), conjunction (conj), or interjection (interj).

EXAMPLE Tell-all (adj) books (n) are (v), alas (interj), the (adj) biggest (adj) sellers (n).

1. Cancer begins when your body's cells divide abnormally and form a malignant growth or tumor.
2. Many types of cancer can, alas, attack parts of your body imperceptibly, including your body's skin, organs, and blood.
3. One of the most commonly diagnosed types of cancer in the United States, however, is skin cancer.
4. People who are fair-skinned and freckled are more prone to develop skin cancer if they are exposed often to ultraviolet radiation.
5. Many people are relieved to discover that most skin cancers can usually be treated successfully if detected early.

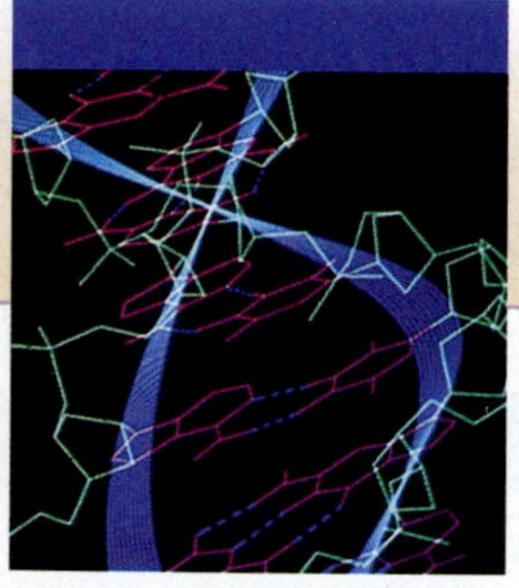

31 Sentence Basics

Every complete **sentence** contains at least one **subject** (a noun and its modifiers) and one **predicate** (a verb and its objects, complements, and modifiers) that fit together to make a statement, ask a question, give a command, or express an emotion.

► [The *children*]subject [*solved* the puzzle.]predicate

► [*Whatever she decides*]subject [*is* fine with me.]predicate

31a Sentence purpose

When you write, your purpose helps you decide which sentence type—declarative, interrogative, imperative, or exclamatory—to use.

Sentence Types and Their Purposes

1. **Declarative sentences** provide information (*declare*) something about their subjects.

   ► He watches *Sex and the City* reruns.

2. **Interrogative sentences** pose questions about their subjects.

   ► Does he watch *Sex and the City* reruns?

3. **Imperative sentences** demand something of their subjects.

   ► Do not watch reruns of *Sex and the City*.

4. **Exclamatory sentences** emphasize a point or express strong emotion.

   ► I'm really looking forward to watching *Sex and the City* reruns with you!

31b Subjects

1. Simple subjects and complete subjects

The **simple subject** of a sentence is the noun or pronoun that names the topic of the sentence. The **complete subject** is the simple subject plus its modifiers. To find the complete subject, ask who or what the sentence is about. Then, to find the simple subject, identify the noun or pronoun within the complete subject. (If the simple subject has no modifiers, then it is also the complete subject.)

complete subject

simple subject

► *Three six-year-old children* solved the puzzle in less than five minutes.

The subject answers the question "Who solved the puzzle?"

To identify the subject of a question, it sometimes helps to rephrase the question as a declarative sentence.

► Did Claudius murder Hamlet's father? [Question]

simp subj

► Claudius murdered Hamlet's father. [Question rephrased]

The subject answers the question "Who murdered Hamlet's father?"

It is useful to know how to isolate the simple subject of a sentence when you have a question about subject-verb agreement. (*See Chapter 34, pp. 536–51.*)

2. Compound subjects

A **compound subject** contains two or more simple subjects connected with a conjunction such as *and, but, or,* or *neither . . . nor.*

compound
simple simple

► Original *thinking* and bold *design* are characteristics of her work.

3. Implied subjects

In **imperative sentences,** which give directions or commands, the **subject** *you* is usually **implied,** not stated. A helping verb is needed to transform an imperative sentence into a question.

impl
subj

► [*You*] Keep this advice in mind.

hv

► *Would* you keep this advice in mind?

4. Subject position

In English declarative sentences, the subject usually precedes the verb. In sentences beginning with *there* or *here* followed by some form of *be,* the subject comes after the verb.

simple subject

► Here are the *remnants* of an infamous empire.

31c Predicates: Verbs and their objects or complements

1. Simple predicates and complete predicates

In a sentence, the **predicate** says something about the subject. The verb (including any helping verbs) constitutes the **simple predicate.** The verb and any **modifiers, objects,** or **complements** make up the **complete predicate.**

complete predicate
simple pred

► The Fugitive Slave Act of 1850 *dismayed many Northerners.*

2. Compound predicates

A **compound predicate** contains two or more predicates connected with a conjunction such as *and, but, or,* or *neither . . . nor.*

compound predicate

► The Fugitive Slave Act of 1850 *dismayed many Northerners* and *contributed to the outbreak of the Civil War ten years later.*

Exercise 31.1 Identifying the subject and predicate

Place one line under the complete subject and two lines under the complete predicate in each sentence. Circle the simple subject and simple predicate. If the subject is implied, write "implied subject" instead.

EXAMPLE Little Jack Horner sat in a corner.

1. Did Gene Roddenberry, the creator and producer of *Star Trek,* anticipate that his science fiction television series would be watched by people of all ages for more than thirty years?
2. Both Captain James T. Kirk from *Star Trek: The Original Series* and Captain Jean-Luc Picard from *Star Trek: The Next Generation* command a ship called the *Enterprise.*
3. Do not forget that the captain in *Star Trek: Voyager* is a woman, Kathryn Janeway.
4. There are six *Star Trek* series: *The Original Series, The Next Generation, Deep Space Nine, Voyager, Enterprise,* and *The Animated Adventures.*
5. Captain Benjamin Sisko commanded Starfleet's Deep Space Nine station and served as the emissary for the Bajoran people.

3. Verb types and sentence patterns

Verbs fall into one of three categories—*linking, transitive,* or *intransitive*—depending on how they function in a sentence. The kind of verb determines what elements the complete predicate must include. Most meaningful English sentences follow one of the five basic patterns summarized in the box on page 499 and discussed below.

1. Linking verbs and subject complements A **linking verb** joins a subject to more information about it that is located on the other side of the verb. That information is called the **subject complement.** The subject complement may be a noun (predicate nominative), an adjective (predicate adjective), or a pronoun.

	subject	predicate: linking verb	predicate: subject complement
NOUN	Ann Yearsley	was	*a milkmaid.*
ADJECTIVE	Hamlet	is	*indecisive.*
PRONOUN	His enemy	was	*himself.*

For MULTILINGUAL STUDENTS

English Word Order: A Brief Overview

English has a fairly fixed word order compared with many other languages. As a result, multilingual writers often make mistakes when they transfer word order patterns from their native languages into English.

The basic word order of an English sentence is subject (S), verb (V), object (O). French, Spanish, and Cantonese Chinese share this word order:

S V O

► **The child threw the ball.** [correct English word order]

Other languages, such as Japanese, Korean, Turkish, and Farsi, follow an S-O-V pattern:

S O V

► **The child the ball threw.** [unacceptable in English]

Still other languages, such as Hebrew and Arabic, follow a V-S-O pattern:

V S O

► **Threw the child the ball.** [unacceptable in English]

Unlike Spanish, English requires that a subject appear in all but imperative sentences. Unlike Arabic, it does not allow verb omission.

Language differences in word order at the level of the phrase may also cause problems for multilingual writers. For example, in English, auxiliary verbs normally precede main verbs and prepositions precede their objects.When constructing a sentence, also keep in mind that English does not allow double negation; the negative meaning is conveyed either by the form of the verb or by another word in the sentence. Thus, *I don't have no homework during vacation* needs to be corrected to either *I don't have any homework during vacation* or *I have no homework during vacation.*

(*For more on word order in English, see Chapter 65: English Sentence Structure, pp. 855–60.*)

The most frequently used linking verb is the *be* verb (*am, is, are, was, were*). Verbs such as *seem, look, appear, feel, become, smell, sound,* and *taste* can also function as links between a sentence's subject and its complement.

► **That new hairstyle *looks* beautiful.**

► **The music *sounds* chaotic.**

2. Transitive verbs and direct objects A **transitive verb** identifies an action that the subject performs or does to somebody or something else—the receiver of the action, or **direct object.** To complete its meaning, a transitive verb needs a direct object in the predicate. Direct objects are usually nouns, pronouns, or word groups that act like nouns or pronouns.

	subject	predicate: trans verb	predicate: direct object
NOUN	Lincoln	delivered	*the address.*
PRONOUN	He	delivered	*it.*
WORD GROUP	He	said	*no more than was needed.*

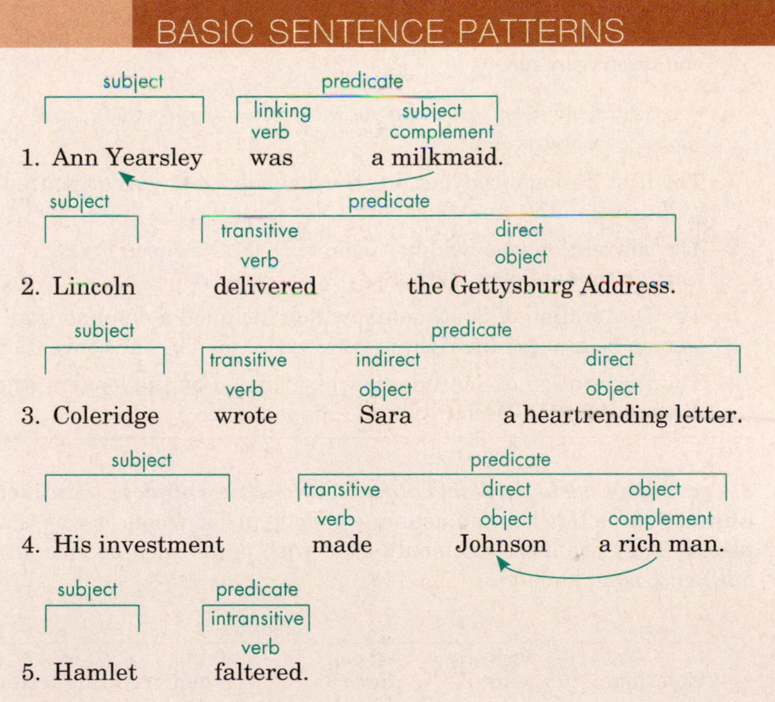

Transitive verbs, unlike linking verbs or intransitive verbs, have two voices: active and passive. In a sentence with a transitive verb in the **active voice,** the subject is doing the action and the direct object is being acted upon.

	subj	trans verb	dir obj
ACTIVE	Parents	sometimes consider	their *children* unreasonable.

When this sentence is rewritten in the **passive voice,** the direct object (*children*) becomes the subject, and the original subject (*parents*) becomes part of a phrase introduced with the preposition *by*.

PASSIVE Children are sometimes considered unreasonable by their parents.

(*For more on voice in verbs, see Chapter 35: Problems with Verbs, pp. 572–74.*)

Exercise 31.2 Using active and passive voice

Rewrite each sentence, changing the verb from the passive to the active voice.

EXAMPLE

A new nation was brought forth on this continent by our fathers four score and seven years ago.

Four score and seven years ago our fathers brought forth on this continent a new nation.

1. The first national convention on women's rights was organized by Lucretia Mott and Elizabeth Cady Stanton.
2. The convention was held by them in 1848 at Seneca Falls, a town in upstate New York.
3. The Declaration of Sentiments, which included a demand that women be granted the right to vote, was issued by the convention.
4. The Declaration of Sentiments was modeled by the leaders who drafted it on the Declaration of Independence.

3. Transitive verbs, indirect objects, and direct objects **Indirect objects** name to whom an action was done or for whom it was completed. They are most commonly used with verbs such as *give, ask, tell, send, sing,* and *write.*

subject	predicate		
	trans verb	ind obj	dir obj
Coleridge	wrote	*Sara*	a heartrending letter.
The general	gave	*the army*	new orders.

For MULTILINGUAL STUDENTS

Word Order of Direct and Indirect Objects

In a typical English predicate both the direct and indirect objects follow the verb. Unless the indirect object (IO) is preceded by a preposition (such as *to, for, of*), the IO is placed before the direct object (DO):

► **The student wrote his teacher a note.** (IO: his teacher; DO: a note)

► **The student wrote a note to his teacher.** (IO: to his teacher; DO: a note)

but not:

► **The student wrote to his teacher a note.** [unacceptable in English] (IO: to his teacher; DO: a note)

Note, however, that in standard English, the indirect object cannot follow the verb if the direct object is a pronoun (a frequent source of errors among multilingual writers):

► **The student wrote his teacher it.** [unacceptable in English] (IO: his teacher; DO: it)

Indirect objects usually appear after the verb but before the direct object. However, verbs that imply action done to or for a person (such as *announce, demonstrate*, and *say*) require the indirect object to begin with *to* or *for* and follow the direct object.

subj	trans verb	dir obj	ind obj
The general	**announced**	**the new orders**	**to *the army*.**

4. Transitive verbs, direct objects, and object complements In addition to a direct object and an indirect object, a transitive verb can take another element in its predicate: an **object complement.** An object complement describes or renames the direct object it follows.

subject	predicate		
	trans verb	dir obj	object complement
His investment	made	Johnson	*a rich man.*
The judge	declared	the plaintiff	*the winner.*
The decision	left	the company	*bankrupt.*

For MULTILINGUAL STUDENTS

Including Only One Direct Object

In English, a sentence with a transitive verb must include an explicit direct object. For example, *Take it* is a complete sentence, but *Take!* is not, even if *it* is clearly implied. Be careful not to repeat the object, especially if the object includes a relative adverb (*where, when, how*) or a relative pronoun (*which, who, what*), even if the relative pronoun does not appear in the sentence but is only implied.

► **Our dog guards the house *where* we live ~~there~~.**

5. Intransitive verbs An **intransitive verb** describes an action by a subject, but it is not an action that is done directly to anything or anyone else. Therefore, an intransitive verb cannot take an object or a complement.

subject	predicate intrans verb
Hamlet	*faltered.*
The empire	*collapsed.*
The runners	*tired.*

However, adverbs and adverb phrases often appear in predicates built around intransitive verbs. In the sentence that follows, the complete predicate is in italics and the intransitive verb is underlined.

► **Hamlet *<u>faltered</u> in his resolve to avenge his father's murder.***

Some verbs, such as *cooperate, assent, disappear,* and *insist,* are always intransitive. Others, such as *increase, grow, roll,* and *work,* can be either transitive or intransitive.

LEARNING in COLLEGE

Using the Dictionary to Select Prepositions, and to Identify Transitive and Intransitive Verbs

Your dictionary tells you whether a verb is *v.i.* (intransitive), *v.t.* (transitive), or both. It also tells you—or shows by example—the appropriate preposition to use when you are modifying an intransitive verb with an adverbial phrase. For example, we may *accede to* a rule, but if and when we *comply,* it has to be *with* something or someone.

TRANSITIVE	trans verb I *grow* carrots and celery in my victory garden.
INTRANSITIVE	intrans verb My son *grows* taller every week.

Exercise 31.3 Identifying objects and complements of verbs

Underline the verb in each sentence, and label it transitive (trans), intransitive (intrans), or linking (link). If the verb is transitive, circle and label the direct object (DO) and label any indirect object (IO) or object complement (OC). If the verb is linking, circle and label the subject complement (SC).

EXAMPLE trans DO
The ancient Mayas deserve a place in the history of mathematics.

1. Hybrid cars produce low tailpipe emissions.
2. Automakers promise consumers affordable gasoline-electric cars.
3. Hybrid cars are desirable alternatives to gasoline-powered vehicles.
4. Their two sources of power make hybrid cars fuel efficient.
5. Consumers agree that automakers should design and manufacture more hybrid models.

31d Phrases and clauses

A **phrase** is a group of related words that lacks a subject, a predicate, or both. Phrases function within sentences but not on their own. A **clause** is a group of related words that includes a subject and a predicate. Some clauses are independent; others are dependent, or subordinate. **Independent clauses** can stand on their own as complete sentences. **Dependent,** or **subordinate, clauses** cannot stand alone; they function in sentences as adjectives, adverbs, or nouns.

www.mhhe.com/mhhb2
For information and exercises on phrases and clauses, go to
Editing > Phrases and Clauses

31e Noun phrases and verb phrases

A **noun phrase** consists of a noun or noun substitute plus all of its modifiers. Noun phrases can function as a sentence's subject, object, or subject complement.

SUBJECT	*The old, dark, ramshackle house* collapsed.
OBJECT	Greg cooked *an authentic, delicious haggis* for the Robert Burns dinner.

SUBJECT COMPLEMENT	Tom became *an accomplished and well-known cook.*

A **verb phrase** is a verb plus its helping verbs.

► Mary should have *photographed* me.

www.mhhe.com/mhhb2
For information and exercises on verbs and verbals, go to **Editing > Verbs and Verbals**

31f Verbals and verbal phrases

Verbals are words derived from verbs. They function as nouns, adjectives, or adverbs, not as verbs.

VERBAL AS NOUN	*Crawling* comes before walking.
VERBAL AS ADJECTIVE	Chris tripped over the *crawling* child.
VERBAL AS ADVERB	The child went *crawling* across the floor.

Verbals may take modifiers, objects, and complements to form three kinds of **verbal phrases:** participial, gerund, and infinitive.

1. Participial phrases

A **participial phrase** begins with either a present **participle** (the *-ing* form of a verb) or a past participle (the *-ed* or *-en* form of a verb). Participial phrases always function as adjectives. A comma often follows a participial phrase that begins a sentence.

► *Working in groups,* the children solved the problem.

► *Insulted by his remark,* Elizabeth refused to dance.

► His pitching arm, *broken in two places by the fall,* would never be the same again.

2. Gerund phrases

A **gerund** is the *-ing* form of a verb used as a noun. A **gerund phrase** uses the *-ing* form of the verb, just as some participial phrases do, but gerund phrases always function as nouns, not adjectives. A comma never follows a gerund phrase that begins a sentence.

subj
► *Walking one hour a day* will keep you fit.

dir obj
► The instructor praised *my acting in both scenes.*

3. Infinitive phrases

An **infinitive phrase** is formed using the **infinitive,** or *to* form, of a verb: *to be, to do, to live.* It can function as an adverb, an adjective, or a noun and can be the subject, subject or object complement, or direct object in a sentence. In constructions with *make*, *let*, or *have*, the *to* is omitted.

noun/subj
► ***To finish his novel*** **was his greatest ambition.**

adj/obj comp
► **He made many efforts *to finish his novel* for his publisher.**

adv/dir obj
► **He needed *to finish his novel.***

adv/dir obj
► **His publisher made him *finish his novel.***

31g Appositive phrases

Appositives rename nouns or pronouns and appear right after the word they rename.

noun — appositive
► **One researcher, *the widely respected R. S. Smith,* has shown that a child's performance on such tests can be very inconsistent.**

Sometimes appositives rename other parts of speech.

vb appositive
► **Computers can rip, or copy, audio files from CDs.**

31h Absolute phrases

Absolute phrases modify an entire sentence. They include a noun or pronoun; a participle; and their related modifiers, objects, or complements. They provide details or causes.

► **The sheriff strode into the bar, *his hands hovering over his pistols.***

► **The actors took their bows, *their spirits lifted by the applause.***

Exercise 31.4 Identifying phrases

For the underlined words in the sentences below, identify the kind of phrase each is and how it functions in the sentence.

EXAMPLE **Raking leaves is a seasonal chore for many American teenagers.** [*verbal phrase, gerund, functioning as the subject of the sentence*]

1. The earliest of the little-known ancient civilizations of the Andes emerged more than four thousand years ago.

2. The Chavin culture, the earliest Andean culture with widespread influence, dates to between 800 and 200 BCE.
3. The distinctive art style of the Chavin culture probably reflects a compelling and influential religious movement.
4. The Paracas and Nazca cultures appear to have been the regional successors to the Chavin culture on Peru's south coast.
5. The Moche culture, encompassing most of Peru's north coast, flourished from about CE 200 to 700.
6. The primary function of Moche warfare was probably to secure captives for sacrifice.
7. Interpreting the silent remnants of past cultures is the archaeologist's challenge.

31i Dependent clauses

Although **dependent clauses** (also known as **subordinate clauses**) have a subject and a predicate, they cannot stand alone as complete sentences. They are introduced by subordinators—either by a subordinating conjunction such as *after, in order to, since* (*for a more complete listing, see the box on p. 493*), or by a relative pronoun such as *who, which,* or *that* (*for more, see the box on p. 486*). Dependent clauses function in sentences as adjectives, adverbs, or nouns.

1. Adjective clauses

An **adjective clause** (also called a **relative clause**) modifies a noun or pronoun. Relative pronouns (*who, whom, whose, which,* or *that*) or relative adverbs (*where, when*) are used to connect adjective clauses to the nouns or pronouns they modify. The relative pronoun usually follows the word that is being modified and also serves to point back to the noun or pronoun. (*For help with punctuating restrictive and nonrestrictive clauses, see Chapter 51: Commas, pp. 727–33.*)

► **Odysseus's journey, *which can be traced on modern maps,* has inspired many works of literature.**

In adjective clauses, the direct object sometimes comes before rather than after the verb.

dir obj subj verb

► **The contestant *whom he most admired* was his father.**

2. Adverb clauses

An **adverb clause** modifies a verb, an adjective, or an adverb and answers the questions adverbs answer: *When? Where? What? Why?* and

How? Adverb clauses are often introduced by subordinators (*after, when, before, because, although, if, though, whenever, where, wherever*).

► *After we had talked for an hour,* he began to get nervous.

► He reacted *as if he already knew.*

3. Noun clauses

A **noun clause** is a dependent clause that functions as a noun. It may serve as the subject, object, or complement of a sentence. A noun clause is usually introduced by a relative pronoun (*who, which, that*) or a relative adverb (*how, what, where, when, why*).

SUBJECT	*What he saw* shocked him.
OBJECT	The instructor found out *who had skipped class.*
COMPLEMENT	The book was *where I had left it.*

As in an adjective clause, in a noun clause the direct object or subject complement can come first, violating the typical sentence order.

dir obj subj verb

► The doctor wondered *whom he* should bill for the consultation.

4. Elliptical clauses

In an **elliptical clause** one or more grammatically necessary words are omitted because their meaning and function are clear from the surrounding context.

► This is the house [that] Jack built.

► After Antietam, Lincoln decided [that] it was time to issue the Emancipation Proclamation.

► Two are better than one [is].

Exercise 31.5 Identifying dependent clauses

Underline any dependent clauses in the sentences below. Identify each one as an adjective, adverb, or noun clause.

EXAMPLE Because they were among the first to develop the concept of zero, the ancient Mayas deserve a prominent place in the history of mathematics. [*adverb clause*]

1. During the 1970s and 1980s, Asian-American writers, who often drew upon their immigrant experiences, gained a wide readership.
2. Because these writers wrote about their struggles and the struggles of their ancestors, readers were able to learn about the Chinese Exclusion Act of 1892 and the internment of Japanese Americans during World War II.
3. Many readers know Amy Tan as the Chinese-American novelist who wrote *The Joy Luck Club,* which was adapted into a feature film, but are unfamiliar with most of her other novels, such as *The Kitchen God's Wife, The Hundred Secret Senses,* and *The Bonesetter's Daughter.*

31j Sentence structures

Sentences can be classified into four types by the number of clauses they contain and how those clauses are joined: simple, compound, complex, and compound-complex.

1. Simple sentences

A **simple sentence** is composed of only one independent clause. Although a simple sentence does not include any dependent clauses, it may have several embedded phrases, a compound subject, and a compound predicate.

INDEPENDENT CLAUSE

The bloodhound is the oldest known breed of dog.

INDEPENDENT CLAUSE: COMPOUND SUBJ + COMPOUND PRED

Historians, novelists, short-story writers, and playwrights write about characters, design plots, and usually seek the dramatic resolution of a problem.

2. Compound sentences

A **compound sentence** contains two or more coordinated independent clauses but no dependent clause. The independent clauses may be joined by a comma and a coordinating conjunction or by a semicolon with or without a conjunctive adverb.

► **The police arrested him for drunk driving, so he lost his car.**

► **The sun blasted the earth; *therefore,* the plants withered and died.**

3. Complex sentences

A **complex sentence** contains one independent clause and one or more dependent clauses.

independent clause / dependent clause

► He consulted the dictionary *because he did not know how to pronounce the word.*

4. Compound-complex sentences

A **compound-complex sentence** contains two or more coordinated independent clauses and at least one dependent clause (italicized in the example).

► She discovered a new world of international finance, but she worked so hard investing other people's money *that she had no time to invest any of her own.*

Exercise 31.6 Classifying sentences

Identify each sentence as simple, compound, complex, or compound-complex.

EXAMPLE Biotechnology promises great benefits for humanity, but it also raises many difficult ethical issues. [compound]

1. Rock and roll originated in the 1950s.
2. Chuck Berry, Jerry Lee Lewis, and Elvis Presley were early rock-and-roll greats.
3. Teenagers loved the new music, but it disturbed many parents.
4. As much as the music itself, it was the sexually suggestive body language of the performers that worried the older generation.
5. The social turmoil that marked the 1960s influenced many performers, and some began to use their music as a vehicle for protest.

Exercise 31.7 Chapter review: Sentence basics

Circle the simple subjects and verbs in the following passage. Place one line under each independent clause and two lines under each dependent clause. (Recall that an independent clause can stand on its own as a complete sentence.)

Many argue that the blues and jazz are the first truly American musical forms. With its origins in slave narratives, the blues took root during the 1920s and 1930s as African-American composers, musicians, and singers performed in the cabarets and clubs of Harlem. Jazz, however, has its origins in New Orleans. Today, we can still appreciate the music of Bessie Smith, Duke Ellington, and B. B. King.

Rock and roll is also a distinctively American form of music. Our country's first "rock star" was without a doubt Elvis Presley, who emerged on the nation's airwaves in the mid-1950s with such hits as *Heartbreak Hotel, Don't Be Cruel,* and *All Shook Up.* A decade later, Americans were expressing themselves musically through rhythm and blues, pop, folk rock, and protest music. Today, thanks to recording technology, we have easy access to our country's rich musical history.

This detail from a first century CE wall painting in the ancient Roman city of Pompeii shows a woman writing on a wax-covered tablet. Working on tablets like this, Roman writers could smooth over words and make corrections with ease.

PART 7

There is a core simplicity to the English language and its American variant, but it's a slippery core.

—STEPHEN KING

Editing for Grammar Conventions

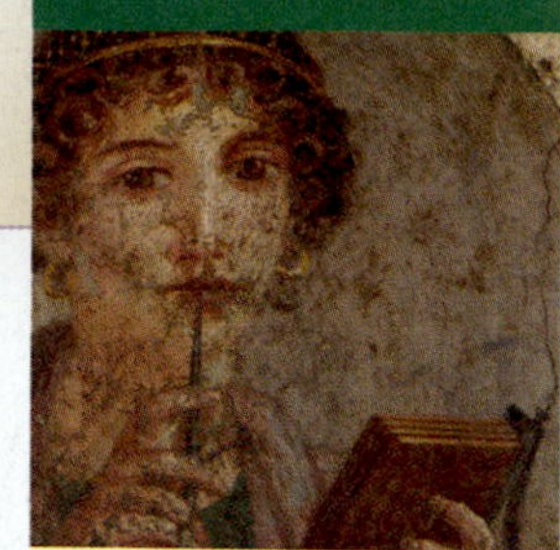

32 Sentence Fragments

A **sentence fragment** is an incomplete sentence treated as if it were complete. It may begin with a capital letter and end with a period, question mark, or exclamation point, but it lacks one or more of the following:

- a complete verb
- a subject
- an independent clause

Although writers sometimes use them intentionally (*see the box "Charting the Territory: Intentional Fragments" on p. 517*), fragments are rarely appropriate in college assignments.

✓ 32a Learn how to identify sentence fragments.

You can identify fragments in your work by asking yourself three questions as you edit:

WRITING OUTCOMES

Part 7: Editing for Grammar Conventions

This section will help you answer questions such as:

Rhetorical Knowledge

- Are sentence fragments ever acceptable? **(32b)**
- When should I use the passive voice? **(35l)**

Critical Thinking, Reading, and Writing

- What is wrong with the sentence *A student should enjoy their college experience?* How can I fix it without introducing sexism? **(36m)**

Processes

- Can my word processor's grammar checker help me edit for grammar conventions? **(32–34, 36–37)**

Knowledge of Conventions

- Should I use *lie* or *lay*? **(35c)**
- Should I use *who* or *whom*? **(36j)**
- Is it correct to say *He feels badly*? **(37f)**

Self-Assessment: *Take an online quiz at www.mhhe.com/mhhb2 to test your familiarity with the topics covered in Chapters 32–37. Pay special attention to the sections in these chapters that correspond to any questions you answer incorrectly.*

Three Questions for Identifying Fragments

1. Do you see a complete verb?
2. Do you see a subject?
3. Do you see *only* a dependent clause?

www.mhhe.com/mhhb2

For more information on and practice avoiding sentence fragments, go to

Editing > Sentence Fragments

1. Do you see a complete verb?

A **complete verb** consists of a main verb and any helping verbs needed to indicate tense, person, and number (*see Chapter 35: Problems with Verbs, p. 561*). A group of related words without a complete verb is a phrase fragment, not a sentence.

FRAGMENT The ancient Mayas were among the first to develop many mathematical concepts. *For example, the concept of zero.* [no verb]

SENTENCE The ancient Mayas were among the first to develop many mathematical concepts. *For example, they developed the concept of zero.*

Caution: **Don't be fooled by verbals. Verbals** are verb forms that function as nouns, adjectives, or adverbs, but not as verbs. The present participle and gerund take the *-ing* form of a verb (as in *working*), the participle takes the *-ed* form (as in *worked*), and the infinitive takes the *to* form (as in *to work*). All may function as verbals (*see Chapter 31: Sentence Basics, pp. 504–05*).

FRAGMENT Pool hustlers deceive their opponents in many ways. *For example, deliberately putting so much spin on the ball that it jumps out of the intended pocket.* [*Putting* is a verbal, not a verb.]

SENTENCE Pool hustlers deceive their opponents in many ways. *For example, they will deliberately put so much spin on the ball that it jumps out of the intended pocket.*

2. Do you see a subject?

A subject is the *who* or *what* that a sentence is about (*see Chapter 31: Sentence Basics, pp. 495–96*). A group of related words without a subject or a complete verb is a phrase fragment, not a sentence.

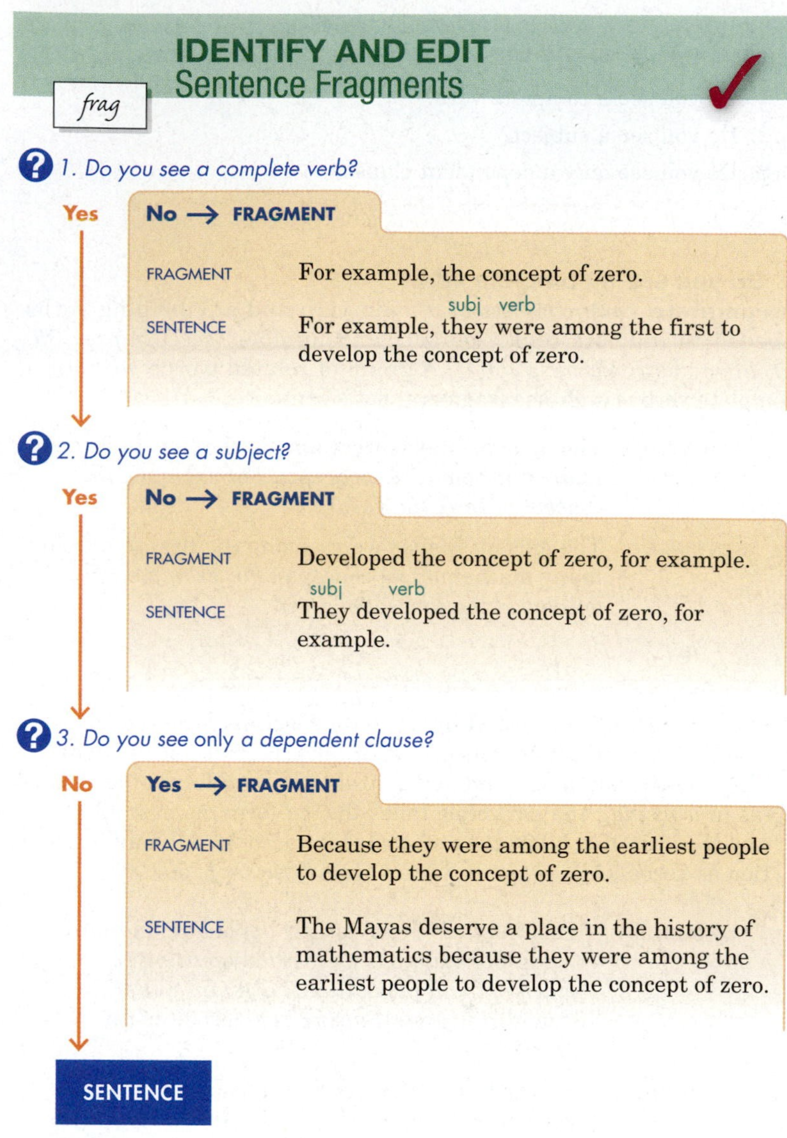
IDENTIFY AND EDIT
Sentence Fragments
frag
1. Do you see a complete verb?
Yes
No → FRAGMENT
FRAGMENT For example, the concept of zero.
SENTENCE For example, they were among the first to develop the concept of zero.
subj verb
2. Do you see a subject?
Yes
No → FRAGMENT
FRAGMENT Developed the concept of zero, for example.
SENTENCE They developed the concept of zero, for example.
subj verb
3. Do you see only a dependent clause?
No
Yes → FRAGMENT
FRAGMENT Because they were among the earliest people to develop the concept of zero.
SENTENCE The Mayas deserve a place in the history of mathematics because they were among the earliest people to develop the concept of zero.
SENTENCE

FRAGMENT The students had a lot of work to do after class. *Study for the midterm, for example.* [no subject]

SENTENCE The students had a lot of work to do after class. *They had to study for the midterm, for example.*

3. Do you see *only* a dependent clause?

An independent clause has a subject and a complete verb and can stand on its own as a sentence. A **dependent,** or subordinate, **clause** also has a subject and a complete verb, but it begins with a subordinating word such as *although, because, since, that, unless, which,* or *while.* Dependent clauses function within sentences as modifiers or nouns, but they cannot stand as sentences on their own (*see Chapter 31: Sentence Basics, pp. 506–08*).

FRAGMENT The ancient Mayas deserve a place in the history of mathematics. *Because they were among the earliest people to develop the concept of zero.*

SENTENCE The ancient Mayas deserve a place in the history of mathematics *because they were among the earliest people to develop the concept of zero.*

Exercise 32.1 Identifying fragments

Underline the fragments in the following passage, and identify each as either a phrase (without a subject or verb) or a dependent clause.

EXAMPLE I am headed to the library tonight.

dependent clause
Because I have a paper due.

Pool hustlers deceive their opponents in many ways. Sometimes appearing unfamiliar with the rules of the game. They may try acting as if they are drunk. Or pretend to be inept. For example, they will put so much spin on the ball that it jumps out of the intended pocket. So their opponents will be tricked into betting. Some other ways to cheat. When their opponents are not looking, pool hustlers may remove their own balls from the table. Then change the position of the balls on the table. Because today's pool balls have metallic cores. Hustlers can use electromagnets to affect the path of the balls. Be aware of these tricks!

Fragments and Grammar Checkers

Grammar checkers identify some fragments, but they will not tell you what a fragment is missing or how to edit it. Grammar checkers can also miss fragments without subjects that could be interpreted as commands. In commands, the subject—*you*—is implied. *Develop the concept of zero, for example* is a complete sentence as a command to the reader, but clearly it is not intended as such (*see Chapter 31: Sentence Basics, p. 496*).

32b Edit sentence fragments.

You can repair sentence fragments by editing them in one of two ways:

1. Transform them into sentences.

► **Pool hustlers deceive their opponents in many ways. For example, *they* deliberately ~~putting~~ so much spin on the ball that it jumps out of the intended pocket.**

► **Many people feel threatened by globalization. ~~Because they~~ *They* think it will undermine their cultural traditions.**

2. Attach them to a nearby independent clause.

► **Pool hustlers deceive their opponents in many ways~~.~~*,* ~~For example,~~ *for example, by* deliberately putting so much spin on the ball that it jumps out of the intended pocket.**

► **Many people feel threatened by globalization~~.~~ ~~Because~~ *because* they think it will undermine their cultural traditions.**

Two Ways to Correct Sentence Fragments

1. Transform them into sentences.
2. Attach them to a nearby independent clause.

The approach to take in any particular case is a stylistic decision. Sometimes one approach may produce better results than the other, and in other instances the results may seem equally effective.

You may, for example, choose to rewrite a fragment as a sentence for emphasis.

► **The ambulance crew gave us tips on handling emergencies. ~~Stressing~~ *They stressed* the importance of staying calm.**

CHARTING the TERRITORY

Intentional Fragments

Advertisers often use attention-getting fragments: "Hot deal. Big savings." "Nothing but net." "Because you're worth it." In everyday life we often speak in fragments, like this, for example:

"Feeling okay?"
"Fine."

As a result, people who write fiction and drama use fragments to create realistic dialogue. Writers also sometimes use fragments deliberately in other contexts for stylistic effect. Keep in mind, however, that advertising, literary writing, and college writing have different contexts and purposes. In formal writing, use intentional sentence fragments sparingly, if at all.

Rewriting long fragments as separate sentences can help keep your writing direct and concise.

► Students with good time management habits start studying right away in the evening. ~~Whereas others,~~ *Others*^ the procrastinators, may go running first, or make phone calls, or clean their rooms, or surf the Internet, or watch television—anything to avoid getting to work.

Attaching a fragment to a related sentence, on the other hand, can highlight the relationship between ideas.

► The Mayas built great cities/~~Even~~ *even*^ though they lacked metal tools.

32c Connect a phrase fragment to another sentence, or add the missing elements.

1. Watching for verbals

Phrase fragments frequently begin with verbals. Here is an example of a phrase fragment that begins with an *-ing* verbal.

FRAGMENT That summer, we had the time of our lives. *Fishing in the early morning hours, splashing in the lake after lunch, exploring the woods before dinner, and playing Scrabble until it was time for bed.*

One way to fix this fragment is to transform it into an independent clause with its own subject and verb:

► **That summer, we had the time of our lives. ~~Fishing~~ *We fished* in the early morning hours, ~~splashing~~ *splashed* in the lake after lunch, ~~exploring~~ *explored* the woods before dinner, and ~~playing~~ *played* Scrabble until it was time for bed.**

Notice that all of the *-ing* verbals in the fragment need to be changed to keep the phrases in the new sentence parallel. (*For more on parallelism, see Chapter 42: Faulty Parallelism, pp. 637–45.*)

For MULTILINGUAL STUDENTS

Avoiding Fragments

A fragment is a group of words punctuated as a sentence but missing some components of a sentence. Fragments are almost never acceptable in formal writing in standard American English. Many languages other than English, however, permit constructions that, translated literally into English, would be fragments.

Missing verb: Some languages—Russian and Chinese, for example—permit omission of the auxiliary or linking verb *be.* Transferred directly into English, this pattern can result in fragments like *He very happy with the news,* instead of the correct *He is very happy with the news.*

Missing subject: Spanish and Portuguese permit the dropping of a subject when it is a pronoun that is otherwise indicated by a verb ending. Transferred into English, this pattern can result in fragments like *Always takes pleasure in reading,* instead of the correct *He* [or *she*] *always takes pleasure in reading.*

Subordinate clause used on its own: Some languages permit a dependent clause to stand alone when it follows a main clause. Transfer of the Japanese *because* clause, for example, can result in fragments like *Because he had problems with sentence structure.* To be correct in English, a subordinate clause must be attached to an independent clause, as in *He had to work with a tutor because he had problems with sentence structure.*

Another way to fix the problem is to attach the fragment to the part of the previous sentence that it modifies (in this case, *the time of our lives*):

► **That summer, we had the time of our lives/, ~~Fishing~~ *fishing* in the early morning hours, splashing in the lake after lunch, exploring the woods before dinner, and playing Scrabble until it was time for bed.**

Not all verbal phrase fragments begin with the verbal. *His hands hovering over his pistols* is a fragment. (*See Chapter 31, Sentence Basics, pp. 503–06 for more on phrases.*)

2. Watching for prepositional fragments

Phrase fragments can also begin with one-word prepositions such as *as, at, by, for, from, in, of, on,* or *to.* To correct these types of fragments, it is usually easiest to attach them to a nearby sentence.

► **Impressionist painters often depicted their subjects in everyday situations/, ~~At~~ *at* a restaurant, perhaps, or by the seashore.**

3. Watching for transitional phrases

Some fragments start with two- or three-word prepositions that function as transitions. Such transitional phrases include *as well as, as compared with, except for, in addition to, in contrast with, in spite of,* and *instead of.*

► **For the past sixty-five years, the growth in consumer spending has been both steep and steady/ ~~As~~ *as* compared with the growth in gross domestic product (GDP), which fluctuated significantly between 1929 and 1950.**

4. Watching for words and phrases that introduce examples

Check word groups beginning with expressions that introduce examples—such as *for example, like, specifically,* or *such as*—to make sure they are complete sentences. If they are fragments, edit to make them into sentences or attach them to an independent clause.

► **Elizabeth I of England faced many dangers as a princess. For example, ~~falling~~ *she fell* out of favor with her sister, Queen Mary, and ~~being~~ *was* imprisoned in the Tower of London.**

► **The experiment did not account for other variables/ ~~Such~~ *such* as light, water, and air temperature.**

5. Watching for appositives

An **appositive** is a noun or noun phrase that renames a noun or pronoun.

► **In 1965, Lyndon Johnson increased the number of troops in Vietnam/, ~~A~~ *a* former French colony in Southeast Asia.**

6. Watching for fragments that consist of lists

Usually, you can connect a list to the preceding sentence using a colon. If you want to emphasize the list, consider using a dash instead.

► **In the 1930s, three great band leaders helped popularize jazz/: Louis Armstrong, Benny Goodman, and Duke Ellington.**

7. Watching for fragments that are parts of compound predicates

A **compound predicate** is made up of at least two verbs as well as their objects and modifiers, connected by a coordinating conjunction such as *and, but,* or *or.* The parts of a compound predicate have the same subject and should be together in one sentence.

► **The group gathered at dawn at the base of the mountain/ ~~And~~ *and* assembled their gear in preparation for the morning's climb.**

Exercise 32.2 Editing to repair phrase fragments

Repair the phrase fragments in the items that follow by attaching them to a sentence or adding words to turn them into sentences.

EXAMPLE

Film music can create a mood ~~.~~, ~~Such~~ such as romantic, lighthearted, or mysterious.

1. The ominous music prepares us for a shocking scene. And confuses us when the shock does not come.
2. Filmmakers may try to evoke nostalgic feelings. By choosing songs from a particular era.
3. The musical producer used a mix of traditional songs and new compositions. In the Civil War drama *Cold Mountain.*
4. Usually filmmakers edit the images first and add music later. To be sure that the music supports the visual elements.
5. Music can provide transitions between scenes. Marking the passage of time, signaling a change of place, or foreshadowing a shift in mood.
6. Exactly matching the rhythms of the music to the movement on screen is known as "Mickey Mousing." After the animated classic.
7. To create atmosphere, filmmakers sometimes use sounds from nature. Such as crashing waves, bird calls, and moaning winds.
8. Do not underestimate the effect of a short "dead track," the complete absence of sound. Forcing us to look intently at the image.

32d Connect a dependent-clause fragment to another sentence, or make it into a sentence by eliminating or changing the subordinating word.

Dependent-clause fragments begin with a subordinating word. Subordinating words include subordinating conjunctions such as *because, although, since,* or *while* (*see Chapter 30: Parts of Speech, pp. 492–93*) and relative pronouns such as *who* or *which* (*see Chapter 30, p. 485*). A fragment that begins with a subordinating word can usually be attached to a nearby independent clause.

► **On the questionnaire, none of the thirty-three subjects indicated concern about the amount or kind of fruit the institution served ~~.~~, ~~Even~~ even though all identified diet as an important issue for those with diabetes.**

► **Hubble discovered that the universe is expanding~~.~~, ~~Which~~ which means it must have originated in what astronomers call the Big Bang.**

Punctuation tip: A comma follows an adverbial dependent clause that begins a sentence. If the clause appears at the end of a sentence, it is usually not preceded by a comma unless it is a contrasting thought.

As the next example shows, however, it is sometimes better to transform such a fragment into a complete sentence by deleting the subordinating word.

► **The solidarity of our group was undermined in two ways. ~~When participants~~ Participants either disagreed about priorities or advocated significantly different political strategies.**

For MULTILINGUAL STUDENTS

Adding a Subject Pronoun to a Dependent Clause

In English, a dependent clause needs a subject, even if it repeats the subject of the main clause. *The tire lost air because was punctured* should be changed to *The tire lost air because it was punctured* (*it* = subject). In a dependent clause that begins with a relative pronoun, however, the pronoun is the subject. For example, *that* is the subject of the dependent clause in this sentence: *We replaced the tire that was punctured.*

Exercise 32.3 Editing to repair dependent-clause fragments

Correct the dependent-clause fragments in the following items by attaching them to a sentence or by eliminating or replacing the subordinating word.

EXAMPLE

The most commonly traded stone in Mesopotamia was obsidian~~.~~, ~~Which~~ which is black, volcanic, and glasslike.

1. Ancient people traded salt. Which is an important nutrient.
2. Some groups resorted to war and conquest. Because they wanted to gain control over valuable goods and resources.
3. When they could, people transported large stones by river. Since doing so required less effort than other means of moving them.
4. Obsidian is hard and makes a sharp edge. Even though it is brittle.
5. After a while, a type of currency developed. When traders began exchanging silver bars or rings.
6. The earliest writing appeared in Mesopotamia. After people there began living in cities.
7. Agriculture thrived in Egypt. Because the Nile flooded regularly.
8. Although the Egyptians had abundant crops and large supplies of limestone. They imported many goods.
9. Egypt added gold objects to its lengthy list of exports. After its artisans began to work the precious metal in about 4000 BCE.
10. Egypt's first king was Menes. Who united the country by conquest in about 3150 BCE.

Exercise 32.4 Chapter review: Sentence fragments

Return to Exercise 32.1 (*p. 515*), and edit the passage to repair sentence fragments using what you have learned in this chapter.

Exercise 32.5 Chapter review: Sentence fragments

Edit the following passage to repair fragments.

> According to the United States Constitution, which was ratified in 1788, the president and vice president of the United States were not to be elected directly by the people in a popular election. But elected indirectly by an "electoral college," made up of "electors." Who were at first often chosen by the state legislatures. In the early nineteenth century, the population of the United States grew rapidly and electors were increasingly chosen by statewide popular vote. Gradually making the electoral college system more democratic. Nonetheless, in the elections of 1824, 1876, 1888, and 2000, the elected candidate won the vote in the electoral college. But not a majority of the popular vote.

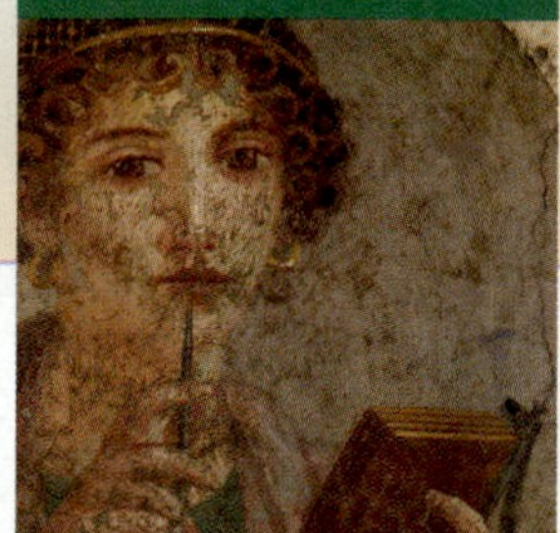

33 Comma Splices and Run-on Sentences

Comma splices and run-on sentences are sentences with improperly joined independent clauses. An **independent clause** is a clause that can stand on its own as a sentence (*see Chapter 31: Sentence Basics, p. 503*). Comma splices and run-ons confuse readers, leaving them unsure how one clause relates to the other or where one ends and the next begins.

comma not strong enough to hold together

33a Learn how to identify comma splices and run-on sentences.

www.mhhe.com/mhhb2
For information and exercises on comma splices, go to
Editing > Comma Splices

A **comma splice** is a sentence containing two independent clauses joined only by a comma.

COMMA SPLICE [Dogs that compete in the annual Westminster Dog Show are already champions]*independent clause*, [they have each won at least one show before arriving at Madison Square Garden.]*independent clause*

www.mhhe.com/mhhb2
For information and exercises on run-on sentences, go to
Editing > Fused Sentences

A **run-on sentence,** sometimes called a **fused sentence,** does not even have a comma between the independent clauses.

RUN-ON [From time to time, new breeds enter the ring]*independent clause* [the Border collie is a recent addition to the show.]*independent clause*

1. Recognizing situations in which comma splices and run-ons often occur

Writers may mistakenly join independent clauses in a comma splice or a run-on sentence in three situations:

Situations in Which Writers May Mistakenly Join Two Independent Clauses in a Comma Splice or Run-on

1. When a transitional expression or conjunctive adverb links the second clause to the first
2. When the second clause specifies or explains the first
3. When the second clause begins with a pronoun

1. Comma splices and run-ons often occur when clauses are linked with a transitional expression or a conjunctive adverb. Transitional expressions are phrases such as *as a result, for example, in addition, in other words,* and *on the contrary*. **Conjunctive adverbs** are words such as *however, consequently, moreover,* and *nevertheless*. (*See p. 532 for a list of familiar conjunctive adverbs and transitional expressions.*)

independent clause / independent clause

COMMA SPLICE Rare books can be extremely valuable, for example, an original edition of Audubon's *Birds of America* is worth thousands of dollars.

For example is a transitional expression.

independent clause / independent clause

RUN-ON Most students complied with the new policy however a few refused to do so.

However is a conjunctive adverb.

(*For help punctuating a sentence in which a transitional expression or conjunctive adverb links the clauses, see Chapter 52: Semicolons, p. 746.*)

2. Comma splices and run-ons may also occur when the second clause of a sentence either specifies or explains the first clause.

independent clause / independent clause

RUN-ON The economy changed in 1991 corporate bankruptcies increased by 40 percent.

3. Comma splices and run-ons may also occur when one independent clause is followed by another that begins with a pronoun.

independent clause / independent clause

COMMA SPLICE President Garfield was assassinated, he served only six months in office.

2. Finding comma splices and run-ons

To find comma splices and run-ons, begin by checking those sentences that include transitional expressions or conjunctive adverbs. If a comma precedes one of these words or phrases, you may have found a comma splice. If no punctuation precedes one of them, you may have found a run-on sentence. Check the word groups that precede and follow the conjunctive adverb or transitional expression. Can they both stand alone as sentences? If so, you have found a comma splice or a run-on sentence.

A second method for locating comma splices is to check sentences that contain commas. Can the word groups that appear on both sides of the comma stand alone as sentences? If so, you have found a comma splice. Similarly, if you see two word groups that can stand alone as sentences with *no* punctuation between them, you have found a run-on.

Exercise 33.1 Identifying comma splices and run-on sentences

Bracket the comma splices and run-on sentences in the following passage. For each error, note if it is a comma splice (CS) or a run-on sentence (RO).

EXAMPLE [**The Gutenberg Bible is one of the first printed books, copies are extremely rare.**] CS

Rare books can be extremely valuable. Most books have to be in good shape to fetch high prices nevertheless some remain valuable no matter what. A first edition of Audubon's *Birds of America* can be worth more than a million dollars however it must be in good condition. On the other hand, even without a cover, an early edition of Cotton Mather's *An Ecclesiastical History of New England* will be worth at least three thousand dollars. Generally speaking, the newer a book is the more important its condition, even a book from the 1940s will have to be in excellent condition to be worth three figures. There are other factors that determine a book's value, certainly whether the author has signed it is important. Even students can collect books for instance they can search for bargains and great "finds" at yard and garage sales. In addition, used-book and author sites on the Internet offer opportunities for beginning collectors.

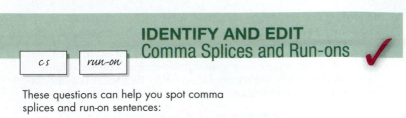

IDENTIFY AND EDIT
Comma Splices and Run-ons

These questions can help you spot comma splices and run-on sentences:

1. Does the sentence contain only one independent clause?

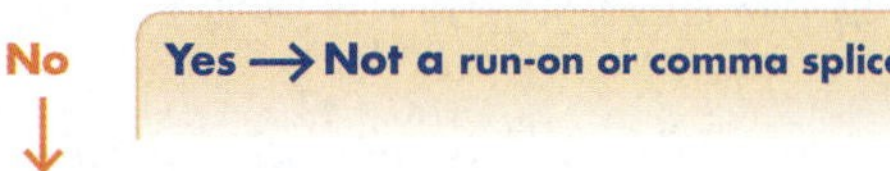

2. Does it contain two independent clauses joined by a comma and a coordinating conjunction such as and, but, or, nor, for, so, or yet?

3. Does it contain two independent clauses joined by a semicolon or a semicolon and a transitional expression?

No ↓ **Yes → Not a run-on or comma splice**

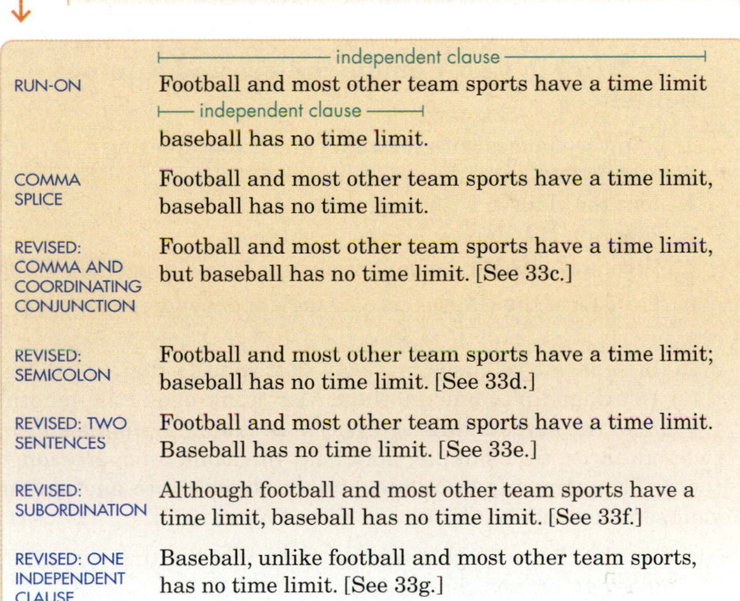

RUN-ON	Football and most other team sports have a time limit [independent clause] baseball has no time limit. [independent clause]
COMMA SPLICE	Football and most other team sports have a time limit, baseball has no time limit.
REVISED: COMMA AND COORDINATING CONJUNCTION	Football and most other team sports have a time limit, but baseball has no time limit. [See 33c.]
REVISED: SEMICOLON	Football and most other team sports have a time limit; baseball has no time limit. [See 33d.]
REVISED: TWO SENTENCES	Football and most other team sports have a time limit. Baseball has no time limit. [See 33e.]
REVISED: SUBORDINATION	Although football and most other team sports have a time limit, baseball has no time limit. [See 33f.]
REVISED: ONE INDEPENDENT CLAUSE	Baseball, unlike football and most other team sports, has no time limit. [See 33g.]

Comma Splices, Run-on Sentences, and Grammar Checkers

Computer grammar checkers are unreliable at distinguishing properly from improperly joined independent clauses. One grammar checker, for example, correctly flagged this sentence for incorrect comma usage:

Many history textbooks are clear, some are hard to follow.

It failed, however, to flag this longer alternative (also a comma splice):

Many history textbooks are clear and easy to read, some are dense and hard to follow.

It also failed to flag this run-on:

The best history books are clear they are also compelling.

33b Edit comma splices and run-on sentences in one of five ways.

Comma splices and run-ons can be edited in five ways:

Five Ways to Edit Comma Splices and Run-on Sentences

1. Join the clauses with a comma and a coordinating conjunction.
2. Join the clauses with a semicolon.
3. Separate the clauses into two sentences.
4. Turn one of the independent clauses into a dependent clause.
5. Transform the clauses into a single independent clause.

Join (or separate) clauses in a way that reflects their meaning and their relationship to one another. Also think about the length and rhythm of the surrounding sentences. Breaking a comma splice into two sentences, for example, may help you avoid an overly long sentence. Transforming two independent clauses into one may make your sentence more concise.

1. Join the clauses with a comma and a coordinating conjunction (*and, but, or, nor, for, so, yet*).

   ► **Many history textbooks are dense and hard to follow,**
   but
   the good ones are clear and easy to read.
   ^

2. Join the clauses with a semicolon if they are closely related.

► **From time to time, new breeds enter the ring; the Border collie is a recent addition to the show.**

You can also add an appropriate conjunctive adverb or transitional expression, followed by a comma.

► **From time to time, new breeds enter the ring** *; for instance,* **the Border collie is a recent addition to the show.**

3. Separate the clauses into two sentences.

► **Salt air corrodes metal easily** *. Therefore,* **~~therefore~~ automobiles in coastal regions require frequent washing.**

4. Turn one of the independent clauses into a dependent clause.

► **Treasure hunters shopping at garage sales should be realistic/** *because* **valuable finds are extremely rare.**

5. Transform the two clauses into a single independent clause.

► **The best history books are clear/** *and* **~~they also~~ tell a compelling story.**

Tips LEARNING in COLLEGE

When (If Ever) Is a Comma Splice Not a Comma Splice?

Many writers believe that it is acceptable, and stylistically effective, to combine short independent clauses with a comma. They often make this choice when one of the clauses is negative and the other is positive.

Don't worry, be happy.

Float like a butterfly, sting like a bee.

Many readers, however, including many college professors, consider these to be comma splices in need of correction. In college writing it is best to replace the comma in sentences like these with a semicolon.

33c Join the two clauses with a comma and a coordinating conjunction such as *and, but, or, nor, for, so,* or *yet.*

If you decide to correct a comma splice or a run-on by joining the two clauses, be sure to choose the coordinating conjunction that most clearly expresses the logical relationship between the clauses.

► **John is a very stubborn person,** *so* **I had a hard time convincing him to let me take the wheel.**

33d Join the two clauses with a semicolon.

Like a coordinating conjunction, a semicolon tells your reader that two clauses are logically connected. However, a semicolon alone does not spell out the logic of the connection.

► **Most students complied with the new policy**~~,~~*;* **a few refused to do so.**

To make the logic of the connection clear, you can add an appropriate conjunctive adverb or transitional expression (*see the box on p. 532*).

► **Most students complied with the new policy**~~,~~ *; however,* **a few refused to do so.**

Exercise 33.2 Editing to repair comma splices and run-on sentences

Some of the sentences below contain comma splices, and some are run-ons. Circle the number of each sentence that is correct. Edit those that are not correct using either (1) a semicolon and, if appropriate, a conjunctive adverb or transitional expression or (2) a comma with a coordinating conjunction.

EXAMPLE **Slavery has always been an oppressive institution,** *but* **its severity has varied from society to society throughout history.**

1. The earliest large societies probably did not depend on slave labor, but that does not mean the people in them were free to work where and how they pleased.
2. All early civilizations were autocratic in a sense all people in them were slaves.
3. No one knows when slavery began, it was common in many ancient agricultural civilizations.

4. The ancient Egyptians enslaved thousands of people from Nubia and other parts of Africa, some of these people were then sent to Mesopotamia.
5. Egypt's kings also used slaves to build some of the country's most famous monuments, for example, the pyramids were almost entirely the work of slaves.
6. Some stones in the Great Pyramid of Giza weigh nearly one hundred tons they could never have been set in place without the effort of thousands of workers.
7. In ancient Mesopotamia slavery was not necessarily a lifelong condition, in fact slaves could sometimes work their way to freedom.
8. In both Egypt and Mesopotamia, slaves could sometimes own property.

Punctuation tip: A conjunctive adverb or transitional expression is usually followed by a comma when it appears at the beginning of the second clause of a sentence. It can also appear in the middle of a clause, set off by two commas, or at the end, preceded by a comma.

► **Most students complied with the new policy** *; however,* **a few refused to do so.**

► **Most students complied with the new policy** *;* **a few** *, however,* **refused to do so.**

► **Most students complied with the new policy** *;* **a few refused to do so** *, however.*

Often the first independent clause introduces the second one. In this situation, you can add a colon instead of a semicolon. A colon is also appropriate if the second clause expands on the first one in some way. (*See Chapter 53: Colons, p. 753.*)

► **Professor Johnson then revealed his most important point: the paper would count for half of my grade.**

33e Separate the clauses into two sentences.

The simplest way to correct comma splices and run-on sentences is to turn the clauses into separate sentences. The simplest solution is not always the best solution, however, especially if the result is one short,

FAMILIAR CONJUNCTIVE ADVERBS and TRANSITIONAL EXPRESSIONS

Conjunctive Adverbs		***Transitional Expressions***
also	nevertheless	as a result
besides	next	for example
certainly	nonetheless	for instance
consequently	now	in addition
finally	otherwise	in the meantime
furthermore	similarly	in fact
however	still	in other words
incidentally	then	of course
indeed	therefore	on the contrary
instead	thus	
likewise	undoubtedly	
meanwhile		
moreover		

simple sentence followed by another. The simplest solution works well in this example because the second sentence is a compound sentence.

► **I realized that it was time to choose~~,~~ [. Either] ~~either~~ I had to learn how to drive, or I had to move back to the city.**

When the two independent clauses are part of a quoted passage, with a phrase such as *he said* or *she noted* between them, each clause should be a separate sentence.

► **"Physical force is wrongly considered to be used to protect the weak," Gandhi said~~,~~[.] "~~it~~ [It] makes them dependent upon their so-called defenders or protectors."**

33f Turn one of the independent clauses into a dependent clause.

Turning one of the clauses in a comma splice or a run-on sentence into a dependent (subordinate) clause can clarify the relationship between the clauses by indicating which carries the main point and which conveys a subordinate idea. In editing the following sentence, for example, the writer chose to make the clause about *a few* her main point. Readers will expect subsequent sentences to tell them more about those few students who refused to comply.

Although most
► ~~Most~~ students complied with the new policy, ~~however~~ a few refused to do so.

33g Transform the two clauses into one independent clause.

It is sometimes possible to transform the two clauses into one clear and correct independent clause, particularly when both clauses have the same subject. This kind of transformation, although often challenging, can reward you with a clearer, more concise sentence than the other solutions might produce.

► I realized that it was time ~~to choose~~, either ~~I had~~ to learn to drive or ~~I had~~ to move back to the city.

Often you can change one of the clauses to a phrase and place it next to the word it modifies.

, first printed in the nineteenth century,
► Baseball cards are an obsession among some collectors~~, the cards were first printed in the nineteenth century~~.

Exercise 33.3 Editing to repair comma splices and run-on sentences

Some of the following sentences contain comma splices, and some are run-ons. Circle the number of each sentence that is correct. Edit those that are not correct by (1) separating the clauses into two sentences, (2) changing one clause into a dependent clause introduced by a subordinating word, or (3) combining the clauses into one independent clause.

EXAMPLE The human population of the world, ~~was~~ no more than about 10 million at the beginning of the agricultural revolution 10,000 years ago, it had increased to about 800 million by the beginning of the Industrial Revolution in the eighteenth century.

1. Globally, population has increased steadily particular regions have suffered sometimes drastic declines.
2. For example, Europe lost about one-third of its population when the bubonic plague struck for the first time in the fourteenth century.
3. The plague was not the only catastrophe to strike Europe in the fourteenth century, a devastating famine also slowed population growth at the beginning of the century.
4. Images of death and destruction pervade the art of the time these images reflect the demoralizing effect of the plague.
5. The native population of Mexico collapsed in the wake of European conquest and colonization in the sixteenth century, it dropped from perhaps as many as 25 million in 1500 to little more than 1 million by 1600.
6. Hernando Cortés used diplomacy and superior military technology—horses and cannons—to conquer the Aztecs, whose forces vastly outnumbered his.
7. These were not the only reasons for Spanish success, however, at least as important was the impact of a smallpox epidemic on Aztec population and morale.
8. The population decline had many causes, these included the conquerors' efforts to destroy native culture and exploit native labor as well as the devastating effect of disease.

FIGURE 33.1 The plague in art. This painting from a fifteenth-century manuscript shows the plague, in the form of an army of death, advancing on a city.

Exercise 33.4 Chapter review: Comma splices and run-ons

Turn back to Exercise 33.1 (*p. 526*). Edit the paragraph to eliminate comma splices and run-ons using the methods described in this chapter.

Exercise 33.5 Chapter review: Comma splices and run-ons

Edit the passage that follows to eliminate comma splices and run-on sentences.

The economy of the United States has always been turbulent. Many people think that the Great Depression of the 1930s was the only economic cataclysm this country has suffered the United States has had a long history of financial panics and upheavals. The early years of the nation were no exception.

Before the revolution, the American economy was closely linked with Britain's, during the war and for many years after it Britain barred the import of American goods. Americans, however, continued to import British goods with the loss of British markets the new country's trade deficit ballooned. Eventually this deficit triggered a severe depression social unrest followed. The economy began to recover at the end of the 1780s with the establishment of a stable government, the opening of new markets to American shipping, and the adoption of new forms of industry. Exports grew steadily throughout the 1790s, indeed the United States soon found itself in direct competition with both England and France.

The American economy suffered a new setback beginning in 1803 England declared war on France. France and England each threatened to impound any American ships engaged in trade with the other. President Thomas Jefferson sought to change the policies of France and England with the Embargo Act of 1807, it prohibited all trade between the United States and the warring countries. Jefferson hoped to bring France and England to the negotiating table, the ploy failed. The economies of France and England suffered little from the loss of trade with the United States, meanwhile the United States' shipping industry came almost to a halt.

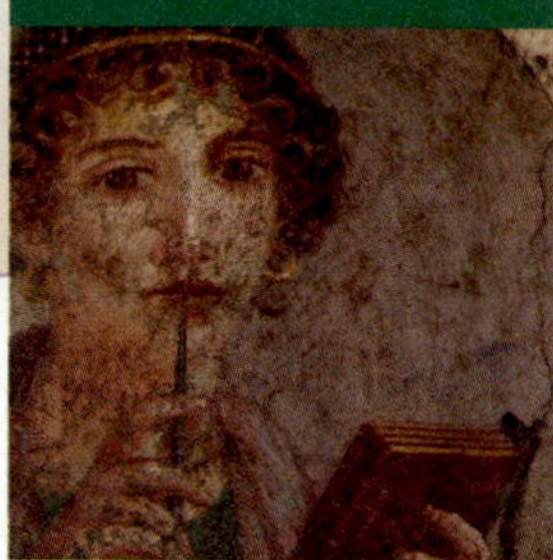

34 Subject-Verb Agreement

The relationship between the subject of a sentence (or clause) and the form of its corresponding verb is termed **subject-verb agreement.** In English, subjects vary in two ways: number and person.

- **Number** refers to whether a subject is singular (only one) or plural (more than one).
- **Person** refers to the identity of the subject:

Identity of Subject

First person	The speaker or writer of the sentence	The pronouns *I* (singular) and *we* (plural)
Second person	The person or people the sentence addresses	The pronoun *you* (singular and plural)
Third person	The people or things the sentence is about	Can include all nouns and noun phrases as well as the pronouns *he*, *she*, and *it* (singular) and *they* (plural)

Verbs have different forms depending on the number and person of the subject. The subject and verb agree when the form of the verb corresponds with the subject in number and person.

► **A *bear lives* in the woods near my home.**

Bear is a third-person singular noun, and *lives* is the third-person singular form of the verb.

► **Many North American *mammals hibernate* in the winter.**

Mammals is a third-person plural noun, and *hibernate* is the third-person plural form of the verb.

► ***We hold* these truths to be self-evident.**

We is the subject form (or subjective case, *see p. 576*) of the first-person plural personal pronoun, and *hold* is the first-person plural form of the verb.

► ***You have* studied harder than your roommate.**

You is the subject form of the second-person personal pronoun (singular in this sentence), and *have* is the second-person singular form of the helping verb. (When a sentence contains a helping verb, the helping verb rather than the main verb agrees with the subject.)

✓ 34a Identify problems with subject-verb agreement.

www.mhhe.com/mhhb2

For information and exercises on subject-verb agreement, go to **Editing > Subject-Verb Agreement**

1. Knowing the standard subject-verb combinations

To form the present tense third-person singular in regular verbs, add the ending *-s* or *-es*. The other forms have no ending.

Present Tense Forms of the Regular Verb *Read*

	SINGULAR	PLURAL
First person	I *read.*	We *read.*
Second person	You *read.*	You *read.*
Third person	He, she, it *reads.*	They *read.*

Several important verbs, however, have irregular forms in both the present and the past tense. These include the verbs *be, have,* and *do* (*see the next page*).

Tips LEARNING in COLLEGE

Subject-Verb Agreement

Mistakes in subject-verb agreement often involve the use of the *-s* (or *-es*) ending with nouns and verbs.

- Adding *-s* to most nouns makes them *plural.*
- Adding *-s* (or *-es*) to regular present tense verbs makes them *singular.*

In other words, for proper agreement in the present tense, if a noun that is the subject of a sentence ends with an *s*, the verb should not; if the noun does not end with an *s*, the verb should.

SINGULAR	PLURAL
The team play**s** five games.	The team**s** play five games.
The school teach***es*** good behavior.	The school**s** teach good behavior.

Present Tense and Past Tense Forms of the Irregular Verb *Be*

	SINGULAR	PLURAL
First person	I *am/was* here.	We *are/were* here.
Second person	You *are/were* here.	You *are/were* here.
Third person	He, she, it *is/was* here.	They *are/were* here.

Present Tense Forms of the Verb *Have*

	SINGULAR	PLURAL
First person	I *have.*	We *have.*
Second person	You *have.*	You *have.*
Third person	He, she, it *has.*	They *have.*

Present Tense Forms of the Verb *Do* and Its Negative *Don't*

	SINGULAR	PLURAL
First person	I *do/don't.*	We *do/don't.*
Second person	You *do/don't.*	You *do/don't.*
Third person	He, she, it *does/doesn't.*	They *do/don't.*

2. Recognizing situations in which problems with subject-verb agreement often occur

Several situations can lead to subject-verb agreement errors:

1. Avoid mistaking a word that comes between the subject and the verb for the subject:

► **The candidate's position on foreign policy issues**

troubles
~~trouble~~ some voters. (The subject is *position,* not *issues.*)

Situations in Which Writers May Make Errors in Subject-Verb Agreement

1. When words come between the subject and the verb
2. When the subject is compound, collective, or indefinite
3. When the subject follows the verb
4. When there is a subject complement as well as a subject
5. When a relative pronoun is the subject of a dependent clause
6. When the subject is a gerund phrase (a phrase beginning with an *-ing* verb treated as a noun)

2. Avoid being confused by compound, collective, or indefinite subjects:

► **The chorus ~~are~~ [is] singing Beethoven's Ninth Symphony in Carnegie Hall.**

Chorus is a collective noun, a unit made up of many persons or things but treated as a single entity.

3. Avoid being confused when the subject follows the verb:

► **Often in the wake of a natural catastrophe ~~follows~~ [follow] financial disasters.**

The subject is the plural noun *disasters.*

4. Avoid confusing the subject complement for the subject:

► **The goal of the new law ~~are~~ [is] improvements in air and water quality.**

The subject is the singular noun *goal;* the subject complement is *improvements.*

5. Avoid being confused when a relative pronoun is the subject of a dependent clause:

► ***Anorexia nervosa* is among the eating disorders that ~~afflicts~~ [afflict] teenagers.**

The relative pronoun *that* refers to the plural noun *disorders,* so it takes the plural form of the verb.

6. Avoid being confused when the subject is a gerund phrase (a phrase beginning with an *-ing* verb treated as a noun):

► **Reducing emissions of greenhouse gases ~~are~~ [is] a goal of the Kyoto Treaty.**

The subject is the gerund phrase *reducing emissions of greenhouse gases.*

Exercise 34.1 Identifying subject-verb agreement

In each sentence, underline the subject, and circle the verb that goes with it.

EXAMPLE **Graphic design studios (require/requires) their designers to be trained in the use of design software.**

1. Nowadays computers (gives/give) graphic designers a great deal of freedom.
2. Before computers, a design (was/were) produced mostly by hand.
3. Alternative designs (is/are) produced much faster on the computer than by hand.
4. With computers, a designer (is/are) able to reduce or enlarge text in seconds.
5. Page layout programs (takes/take) some of the drudgery out of combining images with text.
6. Designers (has/have) the option of removing blemishes and other imperfections from photographs.
7. They (doesn't/don't) have to make special prints to show their work to others.
8. Designs (is/are) e-mailed as attachments all the time.
9. Still, the design professional (doesn't/don't) feel that the computer is anything more than just another tool.
10. Nonetheless, to be a graphic designer today you (needs/need) to be ready to spend a lot of time staring at a screen.

Subject-Verb Agreement and Grammar Checkers

Computer grammar checkers are unreliable guides to subject-verb agreement. One grammar checker, for example, failed to flag this sentence for correction:

The candidate's position on foreign policy issues trouble some voters.

The subject is the singular noun *position,* and the verb should be *troubles.* Apparently, however, the grammar checker interpreted a word that follows the subject—the plural noun *issues*—as the subject and let the sentence pass with the incorrect verb form.

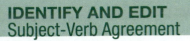

IDENTIFY AND EDIT Subject-Verb Agreement

1. *Find the verb.*

PROBLEM SENTENCE Hamlet and Claudius *brings* [verb] down the Danish royal family.

Verbs are words that specify action, condition, or state of being.

2. *Ask the who or what question to identify the subject.*

PROBLEM SENTENCE *Hamlet and Claudius* [subject] *brings* [verb] down the Danish royal family.

The answer to the question "Who brings" is *Hamlet and Claudius.*

3. *Determine the person (first, second, or third) and number (singular or plural) of the subject.*

PROBLEM SENTENCE *Hamlet and Claudius* [subject] brings down the Danish royal family.

The subject of the sentence—*Hamlet and Claudius*—is a compound joined by *and,* and is third-person plural.

4. *If necessary, change the verb to agree with the subject.*

EDITED PROBLEM SENTENCE Hamlet and Claudius ~~brings~~ *bring* down the Danish royal family.

Bring is the third-person plural form of the verb.

34b Learn to edit errors in subject-verb agreement.

When you are checking for subject-verb agreement, begin by finding the subject. To locate the subject, find the verb (for example, *is*), and then ask the *who* or *what* question about it ("Who is?" "What is?"). Does that subject match the verb in person and number? If it does not, then you have to bring subject and verb into agreement. Changing the verb to agree with the subject usually solves the problem.

► **Hamlet and Claudius ~~brings~~ *bring* down the Danish royal family.**

Sometimes, however, you may want to reword your sentence to avoid awkwardness or confusion even after you have corrected for subject-verb agreement.

CORRECT BUT AWKWARD	Either three French hens, two turtledoves, or a partridge in a pear tree is what I want.
REVISED	I want either three French hens, two turtledoves, or a partridge in a pear tree.

34c Do not lose sight of the subject when other words separate it from the verb.

It is easy to lose sight of the subject when other words intervene between it and the verb. If you are confused, remember to ask the *who* or *what* question about the verb.

► **The leaders of the trade union ~~opposes~~ *oppose* the new law.**

The answer to the question "Who opposes?" is *leaders,* a plural noun, so the verb should be in the plural form: *oppose.*

> ***Note:*** If a word group beginning with *as well as, along with,* or *in addition to* follows a singular subject, the subject does not become plural.

► **My teacher, as well as other faculty members, ~~oppose~~ *opposes* the new school policy.**

34d Distinguish plural from singular compound subjects.

Compound subjects are made up of two or more parts. The two parts are joined by either a coordinating conjunction (*and, or, nor*) or a correlative conjunction (*both . . . and, either . . . or, neither . . . nor*).

1. Treating most compound subjects joined by *and* as plural

Most subjects that are joined by *and* should be treated as plural.

PLURAL *The king and his advisers were* shocked by this turn of events.

PLURAL This poem's *first line and last word have* a powerful effect on the reader.

2. Treating some compound subjects joined by and as singular

There are exceptions to the rule that subjects joined by *and* are plural. Compound subjects should be treated as singular in the following circumstances:

1. When they refer to the same entity:

► *My best girlfriend and most dependable adviser is* my mother.

2. When they are considered a single unit:

► In some ways, *forty acres and a mule continues* to be what is needed.

3. When they are preceded by the word *each* or *every:*

► *Each* man, woman, and child *deserves* respect.

3. Treating subjects joined by *or, nor, either . . . or,* or *neither . . . nor* as either plural or singular depending on context

Compound subjects connected by *or, nor, either . . . or,* or *neither . . . nor* can take either a singular or a plural verb, depending on the subject that is closer to the verb. (It often sounds better to place the plural subject closer to the verb.)

SINGULAR Either the children or *their mother is* to blame.

PLURAL Neither the experimenter nor *her subjects were* aware of the takeover.

The verb also agrees in person with the closer subject. Rephrase awkward sentences.

CORRECT Either you or *I am* going to leave.

BETTER *One of us is* going to leave.

34e Treat most collective nouns—nouns like *audience, family,* and *committee*—as singular subjects.

A **collective noun** names a unit made up of many people or things, treating it as an entity. Some familiar examples are *audience, family, group,* and *committee.*

1. Treating most collective nouns as singular

When a collective noun is the subject of a sentence, it is usually singular.

► The *audience fills* the theater.

Units of measurement—amounts, fractions, and percentages—take a singular verb when they are used collectively.

► *One-fourth* of the liquid *was* poured into the test tube.

► *One hundred thirty feet is* the maximum safe depth for recreational scuba diving.

► *Three hundred dollars is* a high price to pay.

The collective noun *number* is always treated as singular when it is preceded by *the.*

► The *number* of casualties *was* underreported.

2. Using a singular verb with nouns that are plural in form but singular in meaning

Some nouns are plural in form—that is, they end in *s*—but singular in meaning. Examples include the names of fields of study like *physics, mathematics,* and *statistics* and the word *news.*

► That *news leaves* me speechless.

► *Statistics is* important in most social sciences.

Note, however, that a word like *statistics* takes a plural verb when it designates specific results rather than a subject of study.

► The *statistics confirm* that smoking is dangerous.

3. Treating the titles of works; the names of companies, institutions, or countries; and words as words as singular

► *The Misfits features* Monroe and Gable in their last film.

► *Simon and Schuster* no longer *publishes* college textbooks.

► The *United States was* a charter member of the United Nations.

► *Mice is* an example of an irregular plural noun in English.

4. Recognizing when some collective nouns should be considered plural

When the members of a group are acting as individuals, the collective subject can be considered plural.

► The *committee were discussing* the issue among themselves.

You may want to revise the subject of such a sentence with a clarifying plural noun to avoid awkwardness.

► The *members of the committee were discussing* the issue among themselves.

Units of measurement take a plural verb when they refer to a collection of individual people or things.

► ***One-fourth* of the students in the class *are* failing the course.**

► ***Seventy-five percent* of the applicants *are* unemployed.**

The collective noun *number* takes a plural verb when preceded by *a*.

► **A *number* of cases *do* not fit the predicted pattern.**

Exercise 34.2 Editing for subject-verb agreement

Underline the simple subjects and verbs in each of the following sentences, and then check for subject-verb agreement. Circle the number of each correct sentence. Repair the other sentences by changing the verb form.

EXAMPLE **The audience for new productions of Shakespeare's plays** *appears* **~~appear~~ to be growing.**

1. Designers since the invention of printing has sought to create attractive, readable type.
2. A layout shows the general design of a book or magazine.
3. Half of all ad pages contains lots of white space.
4. The size of the page, width of the margins, and style of type is some of the things that concern a designer.
5. China and Japan were centers for the development of the art of calligraphy.
6. Neither a standard style of lettering nor a uniform alphabet were prevalent in the early days of the printing press.
7. A pioneering type designer and graphic artist were Albrecht Dürer.
8. A number of contemporary typefaces show the influence of Dürer's designs.
9. A design committee approve any changes to the look of a publication.
10. Each letter and punctuation mark are designed for maximum readability.

34f Treat most indefinite subjects—subjects like *everybody, no one, each,* and *none*—as singular.

Indefinite pronouns such as *everybody* and *no one* do not refer to a specific person or item.

1. Recognizing that most indefinite pronouns are singular

The following indefinite pronouns are always singular:

anybody	everybody	nothing
anyone	everyone	one
anything	everything	somebody
each	no one	someone
either	nobody	something

► ***Everyone*** **in my hiking club** ***is*** **an experienced climber.**

None and *neither* are singular when they appear by themselves.

► ***Neither sees*** **a way out of this predicament.**

2. Recognizing that some indefinite pronouns are always plural

A handful of indefinite pronouns (*both, few, many, several*) are always plural because they mean "more than one" by definition. *Both,* for example, always indicates two.

► ***Both*** **of us** ***want*** **to go to the rally for the environment.**

► ***Several*** **of my friends** ***were*** **very happy about the outcome of the election.**

3. Recognizing that some indefinite pronouns can be either plural or singular

Some indefinite pronouns (*some, any, all, most*) may be either plural or singular. To decide, consider the context of the sentence, especially noting any noun or pronoun that the indefinite pronoun refers to.

► ***Some*** **of the** ***book is*** **missing, but** ***all*** **of the** ***papers are*** **here.**

Tips

LEARNING in COLLEGE

Are* None *and* Neither *Ever Plural?

If a prepositional phrase that includes a plural noun or pronoun follows *none* or *neither,* the indefinite pronoun seems to have a plural meaning. Although some writers treat *none* or *neither* as plural in such situations, other authorities on language maintain that these two pronouns are always singular. It is a safe bet to consider them singular.

SINGULAR **In the movie, five men set out on an expedition, but *none* of them *returns.***

SINGULAR ***Neither* of the hikers *sees* a way out of this predicament.**

34g Make sure that the subject and verb agree when the subject comes after the verb.

In most English sentences, the verb comes after the subject. Sometimes, however, a writer may invert the order for emphasis. To check for agreement, first locate the verb, and then ask the *who* or *what* question to find the subject.

► **In the courtyard *stand a leafless tree and a rusted arbor.***

What *stand in the courtyard?* The compound subject—*tree* and *arbor*—requires the plural verb *stand.*

In sentences that begin with *there is* or *there are,* the subject always follows the verb.

► **There *is* a worn wooden *bench* in the shade of the two trees.**

34h Make sure that the verb agrees with its subject, not the subject complement.

A **subject complement** renames and specifies the sentence's subject. It follows a **linking verb**—a verb, often a form of *be,* that joins the subject to its description or definition: *Children are innocent.* In the sentence that follows, the singular noun *gift* is the subject. *Books* is the subject complement. Therefore, *are* has been changed to *is* to agree in number with *gift.*

► **One gift that gives her pleasure ~~are~~ *is* books.**

34i *Who, which,* and *that* (relative pronouns) take verbs that agree with the subject they replace.

When a relative pronoun such as *who, which,* or *that* is the subject of a dependent clause, the pronoun is taking the place of a noun that appears earlier in the sentence—its **antecedent.** Therefore, the verb that goes with *who, which,* or *that* needs to agree with this antecedent. In the following sentence, the relative pronoun *that* is the subject of the dependent clause *that has dangerous side effects. Disease,* a singular noun, is the antecedent of *that;* therefore, the verb in the dependent clause is singular.

► **Measles is a childhood *disease that has* dangerous side effects.**

When *one of the* or *only one of the* precedes the antecedent in a sentence, writers can become confused about which form of the verb to use. The phrase *one of the* implies "more than one" and is, therefore, plural. *Only one of the* implies "just one," however, and is singular. Generally, use the plural form of the verb when the phrase *one of the* comes before the antecedent. Use the singular form of the verb when *only one of the* comes before the antecedent.

PLURAL **Tuberculosis is *one of the* diseases *that have* long, tragic histories in many parts of the world.**

SINGULAR **Barbara is the *only one of the* managers *who has* a degree in physics.**

34j Gerund phrases (phrases beginning with an *-ing* verb treated as a noun) take the singular form of the verb when they are subjects.

A **gerund phrase** is an *-ing* verb form followed by objects, complements, or modifiers. When a gerund phrase is the subject in a sentence, it is singular.

► ***Experimenting with drugs is* a dangerous rave practice.**

Exercise 34.3 Editing for subject-verb agreement problems

Circle the number of each sentence in which subject and verb agree. In the others, change verbs as needed for agreement.

EXAMPLE **The best part of the play ~~are~~ *is* her soliloquies.**

1. The Guerilla Girls are a group of women who acts on behalf of female artists.
2. One of their main concerns are to combat the underrepresentation of women artists in museum shows.
3. No one knows how many Guerilla Girls there are, and none of them have ever revealed her true identity.
4. The Guerilla Girls maintain their anonymity by appearing only in gorilla masks.
5. Some people claim that a few famous artists is members of the Guerilla Girls.
6. Their story begin in 1985, when the Museum of Modern Art in New York exhibited a major survey of contemporary art.
7. Fewer than ten percent of the artists represented was women.
8. Not everyone is amused by the protests of the Guerilla Girls.
9. They often shows up in costume at exhibits dominated by the work of male artists.
10. Several of the Guerilla Girls have coauthored a book.

Exercise 34.4 Chapter review: Subject-verb agreement

Edit the passage to correct subject-verb agreement errors.

The end of the nineteenth century saw the rise of a new kind of architecture. Originating in response to the development of new building materials, this so-called modern architecture characterizes most of the buildings we sees around us today.

Iron and reinforced concrete makes the modern building possible. Previously, the structural characteristics of wood and stone limited the dimensions of a building. Wood-frame structures becomes unstable above a certain height. Stone can bear great weight, but architects building in stone confronts severe limits on the height of a structure in relation to the width of its base. The principal advantage of iron and steel are that they reduce those limits, permitting much greater height than stone.

At first the new materials was used for decoration. However, architects like Hermann Muthesius and Walter Gropius began to use iron and steel as structural elements within their buildings. The designs of Frank Lloyd Wright also shows how the development of iron and steel technology revolutionized building interiors. When every wall do not have to bear weight from the floors above, open floor plans is possible.

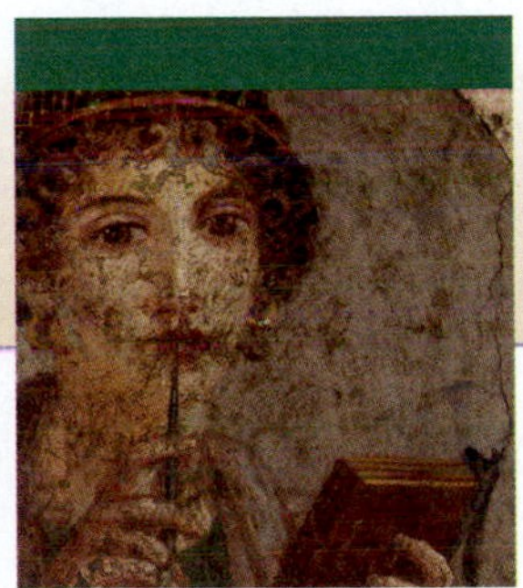

35 Problems with Verbs

Verbs provide a great deal of information. They report action (*run, write*) and show time (*going, gone*). They change form to indicate person (first, second, or third—*I, we; you; he, she, it, they*) and number (singular or plural). They also change to indicate mood and voice.

VERB FORMS

35a Learn the principal forms of regular and irregular verbs.

All English verbs except the verb *be* have five principal forms:

www.mhhe.com/mhhb2
For information and exercises on verbs, go to
Editing > Verbs and Verbals

The FIVE PRINCIPAL VERB FORMS

BASE FORM	■ The form you find if you look up the verb in a dictionary. (For irregular verbs, dictionaries give other forms as well.) ■ Used to indicate an action occurring at the moment or habitually (**present tense**) when the subject is *I* or *you* (first- and second-person singular) or a plural noun or pronoun (first-, second-, and third-person plural). (*See Chapter 34: Subject-Verb Agreement, pp. 536–42.*)
-*S* FORM (PRESENT TENSE, THIRD-PERSON SINGULAR)	■ Used to indicate an action occurring at the moment or habitually (present tense) when the subject is a singular noun, a singular pronoun like *anyone,* or the personal pronouns *he, she,* and *it.* (*See Chapter 34: Subject-Verb Agreement, pp. 536–42.*)
PAST TENSE FORM	■ Used to indicate an action completed at a specific time in the past.
PAST PARTICIPLE	■ Used with *have, has,* or *had* to form the perfect tenses. (*See 35g, pp. 562–65.*) ■ Used with a form of the verb *be* to form the passive voice. (*See 35l, pp. 573–75.*) ■ Used sometimes as an adjective (the *polished* silver).
PRESENT PARTICIPLE	■ Used with a form of the verb *be* to form the progressive tenses. (*See 35g, pp. 562–65.*) ■ Used sometimes as a noun (the *writing* is finished) or an adjective (the *smiling* man).

- base form
- *-s* form (present tense, third-person singular)
- past tense form
- past participle
- present participle

Regular verbs all form the past tense and the past participle in the same way, by adding *-d* or *-ed* to the base form. Here are the five principal forms of the regular verb *walk* with an example of each in a sentence:

BASE	*walk*	The students *walk* to school.
PRESENT TENSE THIRD-PERSON SINGULAR (-S)	*walks*	The student *walks* to school.
PAST TENSE	*walked*	The student *walked* to school.
PAST PARTICIPLE	*walked*	The student had *walked* to school.
PRESENT PARTICIPLE	*walking*	The student is *walking* to school.

Irregular verbs, in contrast, do not form the past tense or past participle in a consistent way. Here are the five principal forms of the irregular verb *begin* with an example of each in a sentence:

BASE	*begin*	The concerts *begin* at nine.
-S	*begins*	The concert *begins* at nine.
PAST TENSE	*began*	The concert *began* at nine.
PAST PARTICIPLE	*begun*	The concert had *begun* at nine.
PRESENT PARTICIPLE	*beginning*	The concert is *beginning* at nine.

The irregular verb *be,* unlike any other English verb, has eight principal forms:

BASE	*be*
THREE PRESENT TENSE FORMS	I *am.* He, she, it *is.* We, you, they *are.*
TWO PAST TENSE FORMS	I, he, she, it *was.* We, you, they *were.*
PAST PARTICIPLE	*been*
PRESENT PARTICIPLE	*being*

35b Identify and edit problems with common irregular verbs.

If you are not sure which form of an irregular verb is called for in a sentence, consult the list of common irregular verbs on the next two pages. You can also find the past tense and past participle forms of irregular verbs by looking up the base form in a standard dictionary.

► **In *A Midsummer Night's Dream,* Shakespeare ~~weaved~~ *wove* together two complementary plots.**

FORMS of COMMON IRREGULAR VERBS

BASE	PAST TENSE	PAST PARTICIPLE
arise	arose	arisen
awake	awoke	awoke/awakened
be	was/were	been
beat	beat	beaten
become	became	become
begin	began	begun
blow	blew	blown
break	broke	broken
bring	brought	brought
buy	bought	bought
catch	caught	caught
choose	chose	chosen
cling	clung	clung
come	came	come
do	did	done
draw	drew	drawn
drink	drank	drunk
drive	drove	driven
eat	ate	eaten
fall	fell	fallen
fight	fought	fought
flee	fled	fled
fly	flew	flown
forget	forgot	forgotten/forgot
forgive	forgave	forgiven
freeze	froze	frozen
get	got	gotten/got
give	gave	given
go	went	gone
grow	grew	grown
hang	hung	hung (for things)
hang	hanged	hanged (for people)
have	had	had
hear	heard	heard
hit	hit	hit
know	knew	known
lose	lost	lost
pay	paid	paid
raise	raised	raised

IRREGULAR VERBS (continued)

BASE	PAST TENSE	PAST PARTICIPLE
ride	rode	ridden
ring	rang	rung
rise	rose	risen
say	said	said
see	saw	seen
set	set	set
shake	shook	shaken
sit	sat	sat
spend	spent	spent
spin	spun	spun
steal	stole	stolen
strive	strove/strived	striven/strived
swear	swore	sworn
swim	swam	swum
swing	swung	swung
take	took	taken
tear	tore	torn
tread	trod	trod/trodden
wear	wore	worn
weave	wove	woven
wring	wrung	wrung
write	wrote	written

LEARNING in COLLEGE

Finding a Verb's Principal Forms

If you are unsure of a verb's principal forms, check a dictionary. If the verb is regular, the dictionary will list only the base form, and you will know that you should form the verb's past tense and past participle by adding *-ed* or *-d*. If the verb is irregular, the dictionary will give its principal forms.

Dictionary entry for an irregular verb:

Preferred past tense form given first

sing (sing) v., sang or, often, sung; sung; singing

part of speech (v., verb) past participle present participle

1. Using the correct forms of irregular verbs such as *ride* (*rode / ridden*)

The forms of irregular verbs with past tenses that end in *-e* and past participles that end in *-n* or *-en,* such as *ate / eaten, rode / ridden, wore / worn, stole / stolen,* and *swore / sworn,* are sometimes confused.

► He had ~~ate~~ *eaten* the apple.

► They had ~~rode~~ *ridden* the whole way on the bus.

► I could have ~~swore~~ *sworn* the necklace was here.

2. Using the correct forms of *went* and *gone, saw* and *seen*

Went and *saw* are the past tense forms of the irregular verbs *go* and *see. Gone* and *seen* are the past participle forms. These verb forms are commonly confused. Check carefully to make sure that you are using the correct form as you edit your writing.

► I had ~~went~~ *gone* there yesterday.

► We ~~seen~~ *saw* the rabid dog and called for help.

3. Using the correct forms of irregular verbs such as *drink* (*drank/drunk*)

For a few irregular verbs, such as *swim* (*swam / swum*), *drink* (*drank / drunk*), and *ring* (*rang / rung*), the difference between the past tense form and the past participle is only one letter. Be careful not to mix up these forms in your writing.

► I had ~~drank~~ *drunk* more than eight bottles of water that day.

► On August 6, Gertrude Caroline Ederle ~~swum~~ *swam* the English Channel, becoming the first woman to do so.

Exercise 35.1 Using irregular verb forms

Use the past participle or past tense form of the verb in parentheses, whichever is apropriate, to fill in the blanks in the following sentences.

EXAMPLE Today, a woman's right to vote is *taken* for granted. (take)

For MULTILINGUAL STUDENTS

Nonstandard Irregular Verb Forms

In many dialects of English, the forms of some irregular verbs vary from those of standard English. In academic writing, however, always use the standard forms. When in doubt, consult the list of irregular verbs on pages 554–55.

► **The neighborhood gardeners ~~growed~~ *grew* their own vegetables in the empty lot.**

► **The Sistine Chapel frescoes ~~be~~ *were* cleaned over a twenty-year period.**

► **Achilles ~~drug~~ *dragged* Hector's body three times around the walls of Troy.**

1. Elizabeth Cady Stanton and Lucretia Mott _____ two of the founders of the women's rights movement in the United States. (be)
2. The movement had _____ out of the abolitionist movement. (grow)
3. Stanton and Mott hoped to address the inequalities between men and women that they _____ in American society. (see)
4. In 1848, hundreds of people, both men and women, _____ to Seneca Falls in upstate New York for the first convention on women's rights. (go)
5. Many of the words in the convention's Declaration of Sentiments were _____ directly from the Declaration of Independence. (draw)
6. With the Declaration of Sentiments' demand for a woman's right to vote, the women's suffrage movement had _____ . (begin)

35c Distinguish between *lie* and *lay*, *sit* and *set*, and *rise* and *raise*.

Even the most experienced writers commonly confuse the verbs *lie* and *lay, sit* and *set,* and *rise* and *raise.* The correct forms are given on the following page.

Often-Confused Verbs and Their Principal Forms

BASE	PAST TENSE	PAST PARTICIPLE	PRESENT PARTICIPLE
lie (to recline)	lay	lain	lying
lay (to place)	laid	laid	laying
lie (to speak an untruth)	lied	lied	lying
sit (to be seated)	sat	sat	sitting
set (to put on a surface)	set	set	setting
rise (to go/get up)	rose	risen	rising
raise (to lift up)	raised	raised	raising

One verb in each of these groups (*lay, set, raise*) is **transitive,** which means that an object receives the action of the verb. The other verbs (*lie, sit, rise*) are **intransitive** and cannot take an object. You should use a form of *lay, set,* or *raise* if you can replace the verb with *place* or *put*. (*See Chapter 31: Sentence Basics, pp. 497–503, for more on transitive and intransitive verbs.*)

- ► **The dog *lies* down on the floor and closes his eyes.**
- ► **The dog *lays a bone* at your feet.** (dir obj: *a bone*)
- ► **The technician *sits* down at the table.**
- ► **She *sets the samples* in front of her.** (dir obj: *the samples*)
- ► **The flames *rise* from the fire.**
- ► **The heat *raises the temperature* of the room.** (dir obj: *the temperature*)

LEARNING in COLLEGE

Using Lie *and* Lay *Correctly*

Lie (to recline) and *lay* (to place) are also confusing because the past tense of the irregular verb *lie* is *lay* (*lie, lay, lain*). To avoid using the wrong form, always double-check the verb *lay* when it appears in your writing.

► **He washed the dishes carefully, and then ~~lay~~ *laid* them on a clean towel.**

Exercise 35.2 Distinguishing commonly confused verbs

Some of the sentences that follow have the wrong choice of verb. Edit the incorrect sentences, and circle the number next to each sentence that is already correct.

EXAMPLE She was ~~laying~~ *lying* down after nearly fainting.

1. Humans, like many other animals, usually lay down to sleep.
2. We found the manuscript lying on the desk where he left it.
3. The restless students had been setting at their desks all morning.
4. The actor sat the prop on the wrong table.
5. The archaeologists rose the lid of the tomb.
6. The Wright brothers' contraption rose above the sands of Kitty Hawk.

35d Do not forget to add an -*s* or -*es* ending to the verb when it is necessary.

In the present tense, almost all verbs add an -*s* or -*es* ending if the subject is third-person singular. (*See Chapter 34: Subject-Verb Agreement, pp. 537–41, for more on standard subject-verb combinations.*) Third-person singular subjects can be nouns (*woman, Benjamin, desk*), pronouns (*he, she, it*), or indefinite pronouns (*everyone*).

► The stock market ~~rise~~ *rises* when the economic news is good.

If the subject is in the first person (*I* or *we*), the second person (*you*), or the third-person plural (*people, they*), the verb does *not* add an -*s* or -*es* ending.

► You invest~~s~~ your money wisely.

► People need~~s~~ to learn about a company before buying its stock.

35e Do not forget to add a -*d* or an -*ed* ending to the verb when it is necessary.

When they are speaking, people sometimes leave the -*d* or -*ed* ending off certain verbs such as *asked, fixed, mixed, supposed to,* and *used to.* In writing, however, the endings should be included on all regular verbs in the past tense and all past participles of regular verbs.

► **The driving instructor ~~ask~~ *asked* the student driver to pull over to the curb.**

► **After we had ~~mix~~ *mixed* the formula, we let it cool.**

Also check for missing *-d* or *-ed* endings on past participles used as adjectives.

► **The ~~concern~~ *concerned* parents met with the school board.**

Exercise 35.3 Editing for verb form

Underline the verbs in each sentence. Then check to ensure that the correct verb forms are used according to the advice in sections 35a–e. Circle the number of each correct sentence. Edit the remaining sentences.

EXAMPLE **The dentist has ~~forgave~~ *forgiven* Maya for biting his finger.**

1. Humans are tremendously adaptable creatures.
2. Desert peoples have learn that loose, light garments protects them from the heat.
3. They have long drank from deep wells that they digged for water.
4. Arctic peoples have developed cultural practices that keeps them alive in a region where the temperature rarely rise above zero for months at a time.
5. Many people in mountainous areas have long builded terraces on steep slopes to create more land for farming.
6. Anthropologists and archaeologists have argued about whether all cultural practices have an adaptive purpose.
7. Some practices may have went from adaptive to destructive.
8. For example, in ancient times irrigation canals increased food production in arid areas.
9. After many centuries passed, however, the canals had deposit so much salt on the irrigated fields that the fields had became unfarmable.

35f Make sure your verbs are complete.

With only a few exceptions, all English sentences must contain complete verbs. A **complete verb** consists of the main verb along with any helping verbs that are needed to express the tense (*see pp. 562–70*) or voice (*see pp. 572–74*). **Helping verbs** include forms of *be, have,* and *do.* (*Be* and *have* indicate tense, whereas *do* is used for questions, negation, and emphasis.) Other helping verbs include the modal verbs *can, could, may, might, shall, should,* and *will.*

	helping verb	main verb	
► **The economy**	***was***	**growing**	**at a fast rate.**
► **The author**	***has***	**written**	**a first-rate thriller.**
► **They**	***should***	**reach**	**their destination soon.**
► **The campaign**	***might***	**begin**	**early this year.**

Helping verbs can be part of contractions (*He's running, we'd better go*), but they cannot be left out of the sentence entirely.

► **They** ^*will* **be going on a field trip next week.**

When a modal verb combines with *have,* we sometimes in colloquial speech (but rarely in writing) use a contraction such as *would've.* Do not use *would of.*

For MULTILINGUAL STUDENTS

For more on modals and other helping verbs, see Chapter 64: English Basics (*pp. 846–48*).

Linking verbs are another type of verb that writers sometimes accidentally omit. A **linking verb,** often a form of *be,* connects the subject to a description or definition of it.

► **Mountains *are* beautiful.**

Like helping verbs, linking verbs can be part of contractions (*She's a student*), but they should not be left out entirely.

► **Montreal** ^*is* **a major Canadian city.**

VERB TENSE

35g Use verb tenses accurately.

Tenses show the time of a verb's action. English has three basic time frames: present, past, and future. Each tense has simple, perfect, and progressive verb forms to indicate the time span of the actions that are taking place. The verbs in the clauses and phrases of a sentence must follow a **sequence of tenses** that logically reflects the relationships in time among the actions each expresses. (*For the present tense forms of a typical verb and of the verbs* be, have, *and* do, *see 34a, pp. 537–38;* *for the principal forms of regular and irregular verbs, which are used to form tenses,* *see 35a and 35b, pp. 551–57.*)

1. The simple present and past tenses use only the verb itself (the base form or the *-s* form), without a helping verb or verbs.

The **simple present tense** is used for actions occurring at the moment, habitually, or at a set future time. The **simple past tense** is used for actions completed at a specific time in the past.

SIMPLE PRESENT

Every May, she *plans* next year's marketing strategy.

The marketing meeting *starts* at 9:00.

SIMPLE PAST

In the early morning hours before the office opened, she *planned* her marketing strategy.

2. The simple future tense takes *will* plus the verb.

The **simple future tense** is used for actions that have not yet begun.

SIMPLE FUTURE

In May, I *will plan* next year's marketing strategy.

3. Perfect tenses take a form of *have* (*has*, *had*) plus the past participle.

The **perfect tenses** are used to indicate actions that were or will be completed by the time of another action or a specific time.

PRESENT PERFECT

She *has* already *planned* next year's marketing strategy.

PAST PERFECT

By the time she resigned, Mary *had* already *planned* next year's marketing strategy.

FUTURE PERFECT

By the end of May, she *will have planned* next year's marketing strategy.

When the verb in the past perfect is irregular, be sure to use the proper form of the past participle.

► By the time the week was over, both plants had ~~grew~~ grown five inches.

4. Progressive tenses take a form of *be* (*am, are, were*) plus the present participle.

The **progressive forms** of the simple and perfect tenses are used to indicate ongoing action.

PRESENT PROGRESSIVE

She *is planning* next year's marketing strategy now.

PAST PROGRESSIVE

She *was planning* next year's marketing strategy when she started to look for another job.

References to planned events that did not happen take *was/were going to:* She *was going to* plan the marketing strategy, but she left the company first.

FUTURE PROGRESSIVE

During the month of May, she *will be planning* next year's marketing strategy.

For MULTILINGUAL STUDENTS

When Not to Use the Progressive Tenses

Some verbs are not used in the progressive tenses, even when they describe a continuous state or action. Typically, these verbs relate to thoughts, preferences, and ownership.

► I ~~was understanding~~ understood the lecture until the last ten minutes.

► The manager ~~is wanting~~ wants the report by the end of the day.

► They ~~are owning~~ own the house they are renovating.

A SUMMARY of ENGLISH TENSES

Present Tenses

Simple present	base form/*-s* form	They *study* in the library. She *studies* in the library.
Present perfect	*has/have* + past participle	She *has studied* all day. They *have studied* all day.
Present progressive	*am/is/are* + present participle	I *am studying* for an exam. Juan *is studying* for an exam. We *are studying* for an exam.
Present perfect progressive	*have/has been* + present participle	They *have been studying* since noon. She *has been studying* since noon.

Past Tenses

Simple past	past tense	The students *visited* Peru last summer.
Past perfect	*had* + past participle	They *had planned* a trip to Peru the summer before.
Past progressive	*was/were* + present participle	They *were planning* a trip to Peru to see the Andes Mountains.
Past perfect progressive	*had been* + present participle	They *had been planning* a trip to Peru for many years.

Future Tenses

Simple future	*will* + base form	We *will study* the Incas before we return next summer.
Future perfect	*will have* + past participle	They *will have studied* the Incas by the time they return.
Future progressive	*will be* + present participle	They *will be studying* the Incas to prepare for their return.
Future perfect progressive	*will have been* + present participle	They *will have been studying* the Incas for a full year by the time they return.

5. Perfect progressive tenses take *have* plus *be* plus the verb.

Perfect progressive tenses indicate an action that takes place over a specific period of time. The **present perfect progressive tense** is used for actions that start in the past and continue to the present; the **past** and **future perfect progressive tenses** are used for actions that ended or will end at a specified time or before another action.

PRESENT PERFECT PROGRESSIVE

She *has been planning* next year's marketing strategy since the beginning of May.

PAST PERFECT PROGRESSIVE

She *had been planning* next year's marketing strategy when she was offered another job.

FUTURE PERFECT PROGRESSIVE

By May 18, she *will have been planning* next year's marketing strategy for more than two weeks.

The tense of the verb in an independent clause determines which verb tenses can be used in any related dependent clause.

INDEPENDENT CLAUSE (IC) TENSE	DEPENDENT CLAUSE (DC) TENSE	EXAMPLE
Present	Present	The students *take notes* [IC] as the teacher *lectures* [DC]. **IC and DC actions simultaneous**
	Past	I *am* glad [IC] that the movie finally *ended* [DC]. **DC action in past; IC action in present**
	Present perfect	He *says* [IC] that he *has played* piano for years [DC]. **DC action in past extending to present**
Past	Past	Maria *liked* the biology class [IC] that she *took* last semester [DC]. **Two completed actions, potentially simultaneous**
	Past perfect	We *reached* the airport [IC] after the flight *had left* [DC]. **IC follows another past event**
	Present	Eric *realized* [IC] that China *is* a very big country [DC]. **IC action in past; DC states an enduring fact**
Present perfect or past perfect	Past tense	I *have wanted* to study physics [IC] since I *was* ten [DC]. **DC action at fixed point in past; IC action extends to present**
Future	Present	Manuel *will celebrate* [IC] when he *finishes* his paper [DC]. **IC and DC actions simultaneous**
	Past	Akbar *will pass* the test [IC] if he *guessed* correctly on question 12 [DC]. **IC action in future; DC action in past**
	Present perfect	I *will go* to Spain in the spring [IC] if I *have saved* enough money [DC]. **Both actions in future; DC action will happen first**

35h Use the past perfect tense to indicate an action completed at a specific time or before another event.

When a past event was ongoing but ended before a particular time or another past event, use the past perfect rather than the simple past to describe it.

► **Before the Johnstown Flood occurred in 1889, people in the area** *had* **expressed their concern about the safety of the dam on the Conemaugh River.**

People expressed their concern before the flood occurred.

If two past events happened simultaneously, however, use the simple past, not the past perfect, to describe them.

► **When the Conemaugh flooded, many people in the area ~~had~~ lost their lives.**

35i Use the present tense for literary events, scientific facts, and introductions to quotations.

If the conventions of a discipline require you to state what your paper does, do so in the present, not the future, tense.

► **In this paper, I *describe* the effects of increasing NaCl concentrations on the germination of radish seeds.**

Here are some other special uses of the present tense:

- By convention, events in a novel, short story, poem, or other literary work are described in the present tense.

  ► **Even though Huck's journey down the river ~~was~~** *is* **an escape from society, his relationship with Jim ~~was~~** *is* **a form of community.**

- Artworks and musical compositions are also conventionally described in the present tense.

  ► **Breughel's paintings ~~captured~~** *capture* **the social conditions of his time.**

- Like events in a literary work, scientific facts are considered to be perpetually present, even though they were discovered in the past.

  ► **Mendel discovered that genes ~~had~~ *have* different forms, or alleles.**

- The present tense is also used to introduce a quotation, paraphrase, or summary of someone else's writing.

  ► **William Julius Wilson ~~wrote~~ *writes* that "the disappearance of work has become a characteristic feature of the inner-city ghetto" (31).**

CHARTING the TERRITORY

Reporting Research Findings

Although a written work can be seen as always present, research findings are thought of as having been collected at one time in the past. Use the past or present perfect tense to report the results of research:

► **Three of the compounds (nos. 2, 3, and 6) ~~respond~~ *responded* positively by turning purple.**

► **Clegg (1990) ~~reviews~~ *has reviewed* studies of workplace organization focused on struggles for control of the labor process.**

Exercise 35.4 Using verb tenses

Underline the verb that best fits the sentence.

EXAMPLE **Marlowe (<u>encounters</u>/encountered) Kurtz in the climax of Conrad's *Heart of Darkness*.**

1. Newton showed that planetary motion (followed/follows) mathematical laws.
2. In *Principia Mathematica*, Newton (states/stated), "To every action there is always opposed an equal reaction."
3. Newton (publishes/published) the *Principia* in 1675.

4. With the *Principia,* Newton (had changed/changed) the course of science.
5. By the time of his death, Newton (had become/became) internationally famous.
6. Scientists and philosophers (were absorbing/absorbed) the implications of Newton's discoveries long after his death.

Exercise 35.5 Editing for verb tense

Edit the following passage, replacing or deleting verb parts so that the tenses reflect the context of the passage.

EXAMPLE **Returning to the area, the survivors ~~had~~ found massive destruction.**

For some time, anthropologists are being puzzled by the lack of a written language among the ancient Incas of South America. The Incas, who had conquered most of Andean South America by about 1500, had sophisticated architecture, advanced knowledge of engineering and astronomy, and sophisticated social and political structures. Why aren't they having a written language as well?

Ancient Egypt, Iraq, and China, as well as early Mexican civilizations such as the Aztec and Maya, had all been having written language. It is seeming strange that only the Incas will have lacked a written language.

Anthropologists now think that the Incas have possessed a kind of written language after all. Scholars will believe that the Incas used knots in multicolored strings as the medium for their "writing." The Incas called these strings *khipu.*

35j Make sure infinitives and participles fit with the tense of the main verb.

Infinitives and participles are **verbals,** words formed from verbs that have various functions within a sentence. Because they are derived from verbs and can express time, verbals need to fit with the main verb in a sentence. Verbals can also form phrases by taking objects, modifiers, or complements.

1. Using the correct tense for infinitives

An **infinitive** is *to* plus the base verb (*to breathe, to sing, to dance*). The perfect form of the infinitive is *to have* plus the past participle (*to have breathed, to have sung, to have danced*).

The tense of an infinitive needs to fit with the tense of the main verb. If the action of the infinitive happens at the same time as or after the action of the main verb, use the present tense (*to* plus the base form).

► **I hope *to sing and dance* on Broadway next summer.**

The infinitive expresses an action (*to sing and dance*) that will occur later than the action of the sentence (*hope*), so the infinitive needs to be in the present tense.

If the action of the infinitive happened before the action of the main verb, use the perfect form.

► **My talented mother would like *to have sung and danced* on Broadway as a young woman, but she never had the chance.**

The action of the main verb (*would like*) is in the present, but the missed opportunity is in the past, so the infinitive needs to be in the perfect tense.

2. Using the correct tense for participles that are part of phrases

Participial phrases can begin with the present participle (*breathing, dancing, singing*), the present perfect participle (*having breathed, having danced, having sung*), or the past participle (*breathed, danced, sung*). If the action of the participle happens simultaneously with the action of the sentence's verb, use the present participle.

► ***Singing one hour a day together,* the chorus developed perfect harmony.**

The chorus developed harmony as they sang together, so the present participle (*singing*) is appropriate.

If the action of the participle happened before the action of the main verb, use the present perfect or past participle form.

► ***Having breathed* the air of New York, I exulted in the possibilities for my life in the city.**

The breathing took place before the exulting, so the present perfect (*having breathed*) is appropriate.

► ***Tinted* with a strange green light, the western sky looked threatening.**

The green light had to appear before the sky started to look threatening, so the past participle (*tinted*) is the right choice.

Exercise 35.6 Choosing tense sequence

Underline the form of the infinitive or participle that fits the main verb in each sentence.

EXAMPLE **We hope (to complete/ to have completed) the project by next week.**

1. Magellan's expedition was the first (to circle/to have circled) the globe.
2. They expected the tide (to free/to have freed) the ship from the sandbar.
3. They expected the tide (to free/to have freed) the ship by the time the storm arrived.
4. (To grasp/Grasping) the tiller, the sailor turned the ship into the wind.
5. (Completing/Having completed) the voyage, the crew returned to port.
6. (Covered/Having covered) with phosphorus, Ahab's harpoon glowed eerily.

MOOD

The **mood** of a verb indicates the writer's attitude. English verbs have three moods: indicative, imperative, and subjunctive.

- Use the **indicative mood** to state or question facts, acts, and opinions. *Our collection is on display. Did you see it?*
- Use the **imperative mood** for commands, directions, and entreaties. The subject of an imperative sentence is always *you,* but the *you* is usually understood, not written out. *Shut the door!*
- Use the **subjunctive mood** to express a wish or a demand or to make a statement contrary to fact. *I wish I were a millionaire.*

35k Use the subjunctive mood for wishes, requests, and conjecture.

The mood that writers have the most trouble with is the subjunctive.

Verbs in the subjunctive mood may be in the present tense, the past tense, or the perfect tense. The form of the present tense subjunctive is the same as the base form of the verb, but with no change to signal person or number: *accompany* or *be,* not *accompanies* or *am, are, is.* Also, the verb *be* has only one past tense form in the subjunctive mood: *were.*

1. Using the subjunctive mood to express a wish

WISHES

If only I *were* more prepared for this test.

We wish we *were* on vacation.

The candidates wish the election *were* over.

> ***Note:*** In everyday conversation, many speakers use the indicative rather than the subjunctive when expressing wishes (*If only I was more prepared for this test*).

2. Using the subjunctive mood for requests, recommendations, and demands

Because requests, recommendations, and demands have not yet happened, they—like wishes—are expressed in the subjunctive mood. Words such as *ask, insist, recommend, request,* and *suggest* indicate the subjunctive mood; the verb in the *that* clause that follows should be in the subjunctive.

DEMANDS AND RECOMMENDATIONS

I insist that all applicants *find* their seats by 8:00 AM.

They suggest that we *be* [not *are*] on our way early to avoid traffic.

The doctor recommended that he *stop* [not *stops*] smoking.

3. Using the subjunctive in statements that are contrary to fact

Often, speculative or contrary-to-fact statements contain a subordinate clause that begins with *if.* The verb in the *if* clause should be in the subjunctive mood.

SPECULATIVE OR CONTRARY-TO-FACT STATEMENTS

He would not be so irresponsible if his father *were* [not *was*] still alive.

If Hamlet *were* more decisive, the play would be less interesting.

Contrary-to-fact statements describing past events take this form:

I *would have baked* a cake if I *had known* [not *would have known*] you were coming.

Note: Some common expressions of conjecture are in the subjunctive mood, including *as it were, come rain or shine, far be it from me,* and *be that as it may*.

Exercise 35.7 Using the subjunctive

Fill in each blank with the correct form of the base verb in parentheses. Some of the sentences are in the subjunctive; others are in the indicative or imperative mood.

EXAMPLE **We ask that everyone *bring* pencils to the exam. (bring)**

1. The stockholders wish the company ______ run more profitably. (be)
2. The board demanded that the CEO ______. (resign)
3. "If I ______ you," said the board chairperson, "I would take a long vacation." (be)
4. Judging from the stock's recent rise, the management change ________ investors. (please)
5. ________ share value or face the consequences! (increase)

VOICE

The term **voice** in verbs refers to the relation of the subject of a sentence to the action of the verb. A verb is in the **active voice** when the subject of the sentence does the acting; it is in the **passive voice** when the subject is acted upon by an agent that is implied or by one that is expressed in a prepositional phrase. Only transitive verbs—verbs that take objects—can be passive.

To make a verb passive, use the appropriate form of the *be* verb plus the past participle. To transform a sentence from active to passive, make the direct object the subject, and make the subject part of a phrase introduced by the preposition *by*.

	original subject	active verb	direct object
ACTIVE	Professor Jones	*solved*	the problem.
	old dir obj/ new subject	passive verb	old subject
PASSIVE	The problem	*was solved*	by Professor Jones.

In a passive sentence, you can also leave the doer of the action—the subject of the active sentence—unidentified.

PASSIVE The problem *was solved.*

To change a passive sentence to an active sentence, make the subject the direct object and make the actor the subject.

35l Choose the active voice unless a special situation calls for the passive.

The passive voice emphasizes the recipient rather than the doer of the action. In general, you should use it only when the doer of the action is not known or is less important than the recipient of the action.

PASSIVE My car *was stolen* last night. [The identity of the thief is unknown.]

ACTIVE Alexander Graham Bell invented the telephone in 1876. [The emphasis is on the inventor.]

PASSIVE The telephone was invented in 1876, about thirty years after the telegraph. [The emphasis is on the invention, not the inventor.]

CHARTING the TERRITORY

Passive Voice in Scientific Writing

To keep the focus on objects and actions, scientists writing about the results of their research regularly use the passive voice in their laboratory reports.

PASSIVE A sample of 20 radish seeds *was germinated* on filter paper soaked in a 10% sodium chloride solution.

Exercise 35.8 Changing active to passive and passive to active

Rewrite each active-voice sentence in the passive voice and each passive-voice sentence in the active voice. If a passive-voice sentence has no identified agent, you may need to supply one.

EXAMPLES **Roberto handled the request.**
The request was handled by Roberto.

My car was stolen last night.
Someone [Somebody, A thief] stole my car last night.

1. Fourscore and seven years ago, our fathers brought forth on this continent a new nation.
2. Humpty Dumpty could not be put together again.
3. The impressive sales of the new product raised the company's stock price.
4. The Great Depression was caused by many factors.
5. The economy is sustained by consumer spending.
6. Economic developments affect the outcome of many presidential elections.

Exercise 35.9 Chapter review: Problems with verbs

Underline the correct verb or verb phrase within the parentheses.

1. Anthropologists are forced (to have confronted/to confront) certain ethical issues in the course of their work.
2. In the field, they (be careful/must be careful) that their work (not harms, does not harm) the people they are studying by (having introduced/introducing) diseases or disruptive goods and customs.
3. Anthropologists (should aware/should be aware) that their mere presence (changes/has changed) the behavior of their subjects.
4. Although anthropologists may wish (to be/to have been) invisible, they cannot help (to affect/affecting) their surroundings.
5. When anthropologists (write/will write), they face other ethical considerations.
6. As Michael F. Brown (asks/asked), "Who owns native culture?"
7. In other words, what can anthropologists (do/have done) with the information they gather?
8. Many insist that a researcher (get/gets) permission to reveal details of religious ceremonies.

Exercise 35.10 Chapter review: Problems with verbs

Edit the following passage, adding, deleting, and changing verbs and verb phrases as needed to reflect the tense, mood, and voice suggested by the sentence and the overall passage.

The *American Heritage Dictionary* defined a state as "the supreme public power within a sovereign political entity." We typically thought of "the state" as the apparatus of government: the elected officials, appointed bureaucrats, and their employees, as well as the rules, traditions, buildings, weapons, and tools that the state controls. How the phenomenon of the state arise?

Anthropologists not agreed on the answer to this question. Many will be surmising a correlation between the development of the state and the rise of large-scale agriculture. One group of researchers believes that states tend to develop where trade routes intersected. Another group of researchers believed that several factors, such as population density, war, and environmental limitations, interacted to produce states.

In the 1950s, anthropologists believe that the need to administering large-scale irrigation systems gave rise to the first states. The first function of the state was to be controlling water. Researchers later founded that some states developed without irrigation systems, whereas other areas with hydraulic systems never will develop into states.

36 Problems with Pronouns

Pronouns are words that take the place of nouns. (*For a complete list of pronouns, see Chapter 30: Parts of Speech, p. 486*)

- Editing for **pronoun case** involves making sure that a pronoun's form correctly reflects its function—as subject, as object, or to indicate possession.
- Editing for **pronoun-antecedent agreement** involves making sure a pronoun agrees grammatically with the word or words it replaces.
- Editing for **pronoun reference** involves making sure the relationship between a pronoun and the word or words it replaces is clear and unambiguous.

www.mhhe.com/mhhb2
For information and exercises on pronouns, go to
Editing > Pronouns

PRONOUN CASE

The term **case** refers to the function of a noun or pronoun in a sentence. There are three main cases in English:

- subjective (subjects and subject complements)
- objective (objects of verbs and prepositions)
- possessive

Nouns and indefinite pronouns (such as *everybody, somebody,* and *everything*) have the same form in the subjective and objective case. They form the possessive case with an apostrophe or an apostrophe and an *-s*. (*For more on using apostrophes to indicate possession, see Chapter 61: Apostrophes, pp. 816–18*)

Most personal pronouns and some relative and interrogative pronouns, however, have different forms for each case.

		SUBJECTIVE	OBJECTIVE	POSSESSIVE
Personal pronouns	**Singular**	I	me	my, mine
		you	you	yours
		he/she/it	him/her/it	his, hers, its
	Plural	we	us	ours
		you	you	yours
		they	them	their, theirs
Case-sensitive relative and interrogative pronouns		who, whoever	whom, whomever	whose

subjective		possessive	objective
The community	supports	the mayor's	program.
The program	benefits	the town's	children.
The children	deserve	everyone's	support.
Everyone	contributes		time and money.
We	support	his	program.
It	benefits		us.
They	deserve	our	support.

✓ 36a Identify problems with pronoun case.

When a pronoun's case does not match its function in a sentence, readers feel that something is wrong. Case errors are usually easy to spot in simple sentences in which a pronoun stands alone as subject or object.

► ~~Me~~ *I* hit the ball.

► The ball hit ~~I~~ *me*.

Problems arise in more complicated situations that obscure a pronoun's function. These include the following:

Situations That Lead to Pronoun Case Errors

1. Pronouns in compound structures
2. Pronouns in subject complements
3. Pronouns in appositives
4. *We* or *us* before a noun
5. Pronouns in comparisons with *than* or *as*
6. Pronouns are subjects or objects of infinitives
7. Pronouns preceding a gerund
8. Use of *who/whom* and *whoever/whomever* in dependent clauses and questions

36b Learn to edit for pronoun case.

Editing for case always involves identifying the function of a pronoun—is it part of a subject, a subject complement, a direct object, or the object of a preposition?—and matching the pronoun's form to its function. Often, stripping away words to isolate the pronoun reveals errors clearly.

► [The author and] me share many interests.

Isolating *me* shows that it is clearly wrong and should be replaced with *I*. (*See section 36c on the correct use of pronouns in compound structures.*)

When formal and informal usage conflict, you may need to consult the rules in sections 36c–36g. In everyday speech, for example, when you knock on a door and someone asks "Who's there?" you are probably more likely to answer "It's me" than the formally correct "It is I." *(See section 36d below for more on the correct use of pronouns in subject complements.)*

36c Use the correct pronoun in compound structures.

Compound structures (words or phrases joined by *and, or,* or *nor*) can appear as subjects or objects. If you are not sure which form of a pronoun to use in a compound structure, treat the pronoun as the only subject or object, and note how the sentence sounds.

SUBJECT Angela and ~~me~~ I were cleaning up the kitchen.

If you treat the pronoun as the only subject, the sentence is clearly wrong: *Me [was] cleaning up the kitchen.* The correct form is the subjective pronoun *I*.

OBJECT My parents waited for an explanation from John and ~~I~~ me.

If you treat the pronoun as the only object, the sentence is clearly wrong: *My parents waited for an explanation from I.* The correct form is the objective pronoun *me.*

Pronouns in a prepositional phrase starting with *between* always take the objective case: *between you and me*, not *you and I*.

Pronoun Case and Grammar Checkers

Some computer grammar checkers reliably flag many, but by no means all, errors in pronoun case. One grammar checker, for example, missed the case error in the following sentence:

> Ford's son Edsel, *who* the auto magnate treated cruelly, was a brilliant automobile designer. [should be *whom*]

(*See section 36j, pp. 584–86, for a discussion of* who *and* whom.)

36d Use the correct pronoun in subject complements.

A **subject complement** renames and specifies the sentence's subject. It follows a **linking verb,** which is a verb, often a form of *be,* that links the subject to its description or definition: *Alaska is beautiful.*

SUBJECT COMPLEMENT Mark's best friends are Jane and ~~me~~ I.

If you think editing like this results in sentences that sound too awkward or formal, try switching the order to turn the pronoun into the subject.

SUBJECT **Jane and I are Mark's best friends.**

Exercise 36.1 Choosing pronoun case

Underline the pronoun in parentheses that is appropriate to the sentence.

EXAMPLE **Michael and (I/me) grew up in Philadelphia.**

1. The first person to receive a diploma was (I/me). Matt and Lara followed behind me.
2. Throughout the ceremony I joked with Lara and (he/him), enjoying my last official college event with them.
3. Lara joked that the people least likely to succeed after college were Matt and (her/she).
4. That outcome is highly unlikely, however, because Lara and (he/him) were tied for valedictorian.
5. Graduation was a bittersweet day for my friends and (I/me).

36e Use the correct pronoun in appositives.

Appositives are nouns or noun phrases that rename nouns or pronouns. They appear right after the word or words they rename and have the same function in the sentence as the renamed word or words do.

► **The two weary travelers, Ramon and ~~me~~ I, found shelter in an old cabin.**

The appositive renames the subject, *two weary travelers,* so the pronoun should be in the subjective case: *I.*

► **The police arrested two protesters, Jane and ~~I~~ me.**

The appositive renames the direct object, *protesters,* so the pronoun should be in the objective case: *me.*

IDENTIFY AND EDIT
Pronoun Case

case

Follow these steps to decide on the proper form of pronouns in compound structures:

1. Identify the compound structure (a pronoun and a noun or other pronoun joined by and, but, or, *or* nor*) in the problem sentence.*

compound structure

PROBLEM SENTENCE [Her or her roommate] should call the campus technical support office and sign up for broadband Internet service.

compound structure

PROBLEM SENTENCE The director gave the leading roles to [my brother and I].

2. Isolate the pronoun that you are unsure about; then read the sentence to yourself without the rest of the compound structure. If the result sounds wrong, change the case of the pronoun (subjective to objective, or vice versa), and read the sentence again.

PROBLEM SENTENCE [Her ~~or her roommate~~] should call the campus technical support office and sign up for broadband Internet service.

Her should call the campus technical support office sounds wrong. The pronoun should be in the subjective case: *she*.

PROBLEM SENTENCE The director gave the leading roles to [~~my brother and~~ I]

The director gave the leading roles to I sounds wrong. The pronoun should be in the objective case: *me*.

3. If necessary, correct the original sentence.

- ~~Her~~ *She* or her roommate should call the campus technical support office and sign up for broadband Internet service.
- The director gave the leading roles to my brother and ~~I~~ *me*.

36f Use either *we* or *us* before a noun, depending on the noun's function.

When *we* or *us* comes before a noun, it has the same function in the sentence as the noun it precedes.

► ~~Us~~ *We* students never get to decide such things.

We renames the subject: *students.*

► Things were looking desperate for ~~we~~ *us* campers.

Us renames the object of the preposition *for: campers.*

Exercise 36.2 Choosing pronoun case with appositives

Underline the pronoun in parentheses that is appropriate to the sentence.

EXAMPLE (We/Us) players are ready to hit the field.

1. (We/Us) Americans live in a cultural melting pot.
2. My parents, for example, have passed on Finnish and Spanish cultural traditions to their children, my two brothers and (I/me).
3. Our grandparents have told fascinating stories about our ancestors to (we/us) grandchildren.
4. On New Year's Eve, the younger family members, my brothers and (I/me), tell fortunes according to a Finnish custom, and then, following a Spanish tradition, the whole family eats grapes.
5. My grandmother gave her oldest grandchild, (I/me), a journal with her observations of our family's varied cultural traditions—our own melting pot.

36g Use the correct pronoun in comparisons with *than* or *as*.

In comparisons, words are often left out of a sentence because the reader knows what they would be. When a pronoun follows *than* or *as,* make sure you are using the correct form by mentally adding the missing word or words.

► **The tuition hikes affect them as much as [the hikes affect] *us*.**

► **Meg is quicker than *she* [is].**

If a sentence with a comparison sounds too awkward or formal, add the missing words: *Meg is quicker than she is.*

Note also that some sentences can be correct with either a subjective or an objective pronoun—depending on the sense of the omitted words—but with a very different meaning in each case.

► **My brother likes our dog more than *I* [do].**

► **My brother likes our dog more than [he likes] *me*.**

36h Use the correct form when the pronoun is the subject or the object of an infinitive.

An **infinitive** is *to* plus the base verb (*to breathe, to sing, to dance*). Whether a pronoun functions as the subject or the object of an infinitive, it should be in the objective case.

► **We wanted our lawyer and her to defend us against this unfair charge.** (subject: her; object: us)

Both the subject of the infinitive (*her*) and its object (*us*) are in the objective case.

36i Use the possessive case in front of a gerund.

When a noun or pronoun appears before a **gerund** (an *-ing* verb form functioning as a noun), it should usually be treated as a possessive. Possessive nouns are formed by adding *'s* to singular nouns (*the teacher's desk*) or an apostrophe only (') to plural nouns (*three teachers' rooms*). (*See Chapter 61: Apostrophes, pp. 814–15.*)

► **The ~~animals~~ *animals'* fighting disturbed the entire neighborhood.**

► **Because of ~~them~~ *their* screeching, no one could get any sleep.**

When the *-ing* word is functioning as a modifier, not a noun, use the subjective or objective case for the pronoun that precedes it. Compare these two sentences, for example.

► **The teacher punished *their* cheating.**

► **The teacher saw *them* cheating.**

In the first sentence, *cheating* is the object of the sentence, modified by the possessive pronoun *their*. In the second, the pronoun *them* is the object of the sentence, modified by *cheating*.

Exercise 36.3 Choosing pronoun case with comparisons, infinitives, and gerunds

Underline the pronoun in parentheses that is appropriate to the sentence.

EXAMPLE **Troy is a better driver than (<u>she</u>/her).**

FIGURE 36.1 Elizabeth Barrett Browning.

1. Robert Browning, an admirer of Elizabeth Barrett, started to court (she/her) in 1844, thus beginning one of the most famous romances in history.
2. Elizabeth Barrett's parents did not want Robert Browning and (she/her) to marry, but the couple wed secretly in 1846.
3. (Their/Them) moving to Italy from England helped Elizabeth improve her poor health.
4. Even though Robert Browning also had great talent, Elizabeth was recognized as a poet earlier than (he/him).
5. Today, however, he is considered as prominent a poet as (she/her).

Exercise 36.4 Editing for pronoun case

Edit the following passage, substituting the correct form of the pronoun for any pronoun in the wrong case.

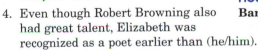

EXAMPLE **The winning points were scored by Hatcher and ~~I~~** *me* **.**

Sociolinguists investigate the relationship between linguistic variations and culture. They spend a lot of time in the field to gather data for analysis. For instance, them might compare the speech patterns of people who live in a city with those of people who reside in the suburbs. Sociolinguists might discover differences in pronunciation or word choice. Their researching helps us understand both language and culture.

Us laypeople might confuse sociolinguistics with sociology. Sociolinguists do a more specialized type of research than do most sociologists, who study broad patterns within societies. Being concerned with such particulars as the pronunciation of a single vowel, sociolinguists work at a finer level of detail than them.

36j Distinguish between *who* and *whom.*

The relative pronouns *who, whom, whoever,* and *whomever* are used to introduce dependent clauses and in questions. Their case depends on their function in the dependent clause or question.

SUBJECTIVE who, whoever

Who wrote Hamlet?

Shakespeare is the playwright *who* wrote Hamlet.

Whoever wrote Hamlet had remarkable insight into human nature.

OBJECTIVE whom, whomever

The playwright *whom* audiences most admire is Shakespeare.

Of *whom* was Shakespeare thinking when he invented such a complex character?

Whomever Shakespeare imagines, he imagines in rich psychological detail.

Although the distinction between the subjective and objective forms is fading from informal speech, readers expect to see it maintained in formal writing. Here are some suggestions for deciding which form to use.

1. **Determine how the pronoun functions in a dependent clause.** If the pronoun is functioning as a subject and is performing an action, use *who* or *whoever.* If the pronoun is the object of a verb or preposition, use *whom* or *whomever.*

   ► **Henry Ford was the industrialist *who* introduced assembly-line techniques to automobile manufacture.**

   Who refers to Henry Ford, the person performing the action in a dependent clause—introducing assembly-line techniques.

► **It is he *whom* we should credit with making automobiles widely affordable.**

Whom refers to Ford and is the object of the verb *credit.* You can check the pronoun for case by rephrasing the clause and substituting an appropriate personal pronoun: *We should credit whom [him] for making automobiles widely affordable.*

► **Ford's son Edsel, *whom* the auto magnate treated cruelly, was a brilliant automobile designer.**

Whom, which refers to *Edsel,* is the object of the verb *treated.* Again, you can check the pronoun for case by rephrasing the clause: *The auto magnate treated whom [him] cruelly.*

Be on the lookout for expressions like *they say* or *people think,* which can obscure the function of a relative pronoun when they come between it and a verb.

► **It was Ford *who* [not *whom*] historians think revolutionized the American workplace.**

The pronoun is the subject of *revolutionized,* not the object of *think.*

2. **Determine how the pronoun functions in a question.** To choose the correct form for the pronoun, answer the question with a personal pronoun.

► ***Who* founded the General Motors Corporation?**

The answer could be *He founded it. He* is in the subjective case, so *who* is correct.

► ***Whom* did the Chrysler Corporation turn to for leadership in the 1980s?**

The answer could be *It turned to him. Him* is in the objective case, so *whom* is correct.

Exercise 36.5 Choosing between *who* and *whom*

Underline the pronoun that is appropriate to the sentence.

EXAMPLE **Arlia is the one (who/whom) people say will have the top sales results.**

1. (Who/Whom) invented the light bulb? Thomas Edison did.
2. He was a scientist and inventor (who/whom) also invented the phonograph and improved the telegraph, telephone, and motion picture technology.
3. Edison, (who/whom) patented 1,093 inventions in his lifetime, was nicknamed the "Wizard of Menlo Park."
4. The hardworking Edison, (who/whom) everyone greatly admired, believed that "genius is one percent inspiration and ninety-nine percent perspiration."
5. (Who/Whom) should we remember the next time we switch on the light? Thomas Edison.

PRONOUN-ANTECEDENT AGREEMENT

www.mhhe.com/mhhb2
For information and exercises on pronoun-antecedent agreement, go to
Editing > Pronoun-Antecedent Agreement

A pronoun's **antecedent** is the word or words—nouns or other pronouns—to which the pronoun refers. A pronoun must match its antecedent in person (first, second, or third), number (plural or singular), and gender (masculine: *he / him / his;* feminine: *she / her / hers;* or neuter: *it / its*).

antecedent

► **The *snow* fell all day long, and by nightfall *it* was three feet deep.**

The antecedent, *snow,* is neuter third-person singular.

antecedent

► ***Margo and I* discussed *our* relationship over dinner.**

The antecedent, *Margo and I,* is first-person plural.

antecedent

► ***Jake* and I discussed *his* problems with Margo.**

The antecedent, *Jake,* is masculine third-person singular.

For MULTILINGUAL STUDENTS

In English, most nouns are neuter in gender. The exceptions are nouns that specifically name females or males, such as *woman, girl, sister, mother, man, boy, brother, father,* and names like *Louis* and *Anna.*

The gender of a pronoun should match its antecedent, not the word it modifies.

► **Penelope waited twenty years for *her* [not *his*] husband Odysseus to return from Troy.**

✓ 36k Identify and edit problems with pronoun-antecedent agreement.

Problems with pronoun-antecedent agreement tend to occur:

- When a pronoun's antecedent is an indefinite pronoun, a collective noun, or a compound noun.
- When writers are trying to avoid the generic use of *he.*

In both cases, editing requires clearly identifying the person, number, and gender of the antecedent and making sure the pronoun agrees with it.

The use of a singular masculine pronoun to refer generically to both male and female individuals is now considered sexist and unacceptable. Editing to avoid this usage often requires rewording a sentence—changing a singular antecedent to a plural one, for example—to avoid awkwardness.

36l Choose the right pronoun to agree with an indefinite-pronoun antecedent.

Indefinite pronouns, such as *someone, anybody,* and *nothing,* refer to nonspecific people or things. They sometimes function as antecedents for other pronouns.

Most indefinite pronouns are singular (*anybody, anyone, anything, each, either, everybody, everyone, everything, much, neither, no one, nobody, none, nothing, one, somebody, someone, something*).

ALWAYS SINGULAR Did *either* of the boys lose *his* bicycle?

A few indefinite pronouns—*both, few, many,* and *several*—are plural.

ALWAYS PLURAL *Both* of the boys lost *their* bicycles.

The indefinite pronouns *all, any, more, most,* and *some* can be either singular or plural depending on the noun to which the pronoun refers.

PLURAL The students debated, *some* arguing that *their* assumptions about the issue were more credible than the teacher's.

SINGULAR The bread is on the counter, but *some* of *it* has already been eaten.

36m Avoid gender bias with indefinite-pronoun and generic-noun antecedents.

Writers often mismatch the plural pronouns *they* and *their* with singular indefinite pronoun antecedents.

singular antecedent — plural pronoun

INCORRECT ***Everybody* took *their* turn.**

In the sentence above, changing *their* to *his* would correct the pronoun-antecedent problem. Presumably, however, *everybody* includes both men and women, so using *his* is unacceptable.

Notice how the writer edited the following sentence to avoid gender bias while remedying the agreement problem.

> ► **~~None~~ *All* of the great Romantic writers believed that their achievements ~~equaled~~ *fell short of* their aspirations.**

Replacing *their* in the original sentence with *his* would have made the sentence probably untrue and certainly biased: many women were writing and publishing during the Romantic Age. The writer could have changed *their* to *his or her* to avoid bias but thought *his or her* sounded awkward. To solve the problem the writer chose an indefinite pronoun that can have a plural meaning (*all*) and revised the sentence. An alternative would be to eliminate the indefinite pronoun altogether:

> ► **The great Romantic writers believed that their achievements fell short of their aspirations.**

Generic nouns present a similar challenge. A **generic noun** represents anyone and everyone in a group—a typical doctor, the average voter. Do not use a singular generic noun as the antecedent for a plural pronoun.

INCORRECT

The responsible citizen decides their vote based on issues, not personality.

However, because most groups consist of both males and females, to correct such a sentence by changing *their* to the generic *his* would usually be sexist. Strategies for avoiding gender bias with generic nouns are the same as those just described for indefinite pronouns and are summarized in the Identify and Edit box on the next page.

> ***Note:*** The use of *their* to avoid gender bias when referring to a singular antecedent or generic noun is becoming increasingly common in everyday speech, and some writers consider it acceptable. In academic writing, however, this usage is rarely acceptable.

> **Pronoun-Antecedent Agreement and Grammar Checkers**
>
> Do not rely on computer grammar checkers to alert you to problems in pronoun-antecedent agreement. Computer grammar checkers are not yet fully capable of detecting these problems.

36n Treat most collective nouns as singular.

Collective nouns such as *team, family, jury, committee,* and *crowd* are treated as singular unless the people in the group are acting as individuals.

► **All together, the crowd surged through the palace gates, trampling over everything in ~~their~~ *its* path.**

The phrase *all together* indicates that this writer does not see—and does not want readers to see—the crowd as a collection of distinct individuals. Therefore, the plural *their* has been changed to the singular *its.*

► **The committee left the conference room and returned to ~~its~~ *their* offices.**

In this case, the writer sees—and wants readers to see—the members of the committee as individuals returning to separate offices.

If you are using a collective noun that has a plural meaning, consider adding a plural noun to clarify the meaning.

► **The *committee members* left the conference room and returned to *their* offices.**

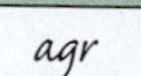

IDENTIFY AND EDIT
Pronoun-Antecedent Agreement and Gender Bias

Try these three strategies for avoiding gender bias when an indefinite pronoun or generic noun is the antecedent in a sentence:

1. *If possible, change the antecedent to a plural indefinite pronoun or a plural noun.*

   - ~~Each~~ *All* of us should decide ~~their~~ *our* vote on issues, not personality.
   - ~~The responsible citizen decides~~ *Responsible citizens decide* their vote on issues, not personality.

2. *Reword the sentence to eliminate the pronoun.*

   - Each of us should ~~decide their~~ vote on issues, not personality.
   - The responsible citizen ~~decides their vote~~ *votes* on issues, not personality.

3. *Substitute* he or she *or* his or her *(but never* his/her*) for the singular pronoun to maintain pronoun-antecedent agreement.*

   - Each of us should decide ~~their~~ *his or her* vote on issues, not personality.
   - The responsible citizen decides ~~their~~ *his or her* vote on issues, not personality.

   Caution: Use this strategy sparingly. Using *he or she* or *his and her* several times in quick succession makes for tedious reading.

36o Choose the right pronoun for a compound antecedent.

Compound antecedents joined by *and* are almost always plural.

► **To remove all traces of the crime, James put the book and the magnifying glass back in ~~its~~ *their* place.**

When a compound antecedent is joined by *or* or *nor,* the pronoun should agree with the closest part of the compound antecedent. If one part is singular and the other is plural, the sentence will be smoother and more effective if the plural antecedent is closest to the pronoun.

PLURAL Neither *the child nor the parents* shared *their* food.

When the two parts of the compound antecedent refer to the same person, or when the word *each* or *every* precedes the compound antecedent, use a singular pronoun.

SINGULAR Being *a teacher and a mother* keeps *her* busy.

SINGULAR *Every* poem and letter by Keats has *its* own special power.

Exercise 36.6 Editing for pronoun-antecedent agreement

Some of the sentences that follow contain errors in pronoun-antecedent agreement. Circle the number of each correct sentence, and edit the others so that the pronouns agree with their antecedents. Rewrite sentences as necessary to avoid gender bias; you may eliminate pronouns or change words. There will be several possible answers for rewritten sentences.

EXAMPLE Neither the dog nor the cats ate ~~its~~ *their* chow.

1. Everybody at the displaced-persons camp had to submit his medical records before boarding the ships to the United States.
2. Many were forbidden to board because they had histories of tuberculosis and other illnesses.
3. This was always devastating news because no one wanted to be separated from their family.
4. Some immigrants resorted to forging his medical records.
5. After all, a mother could not be separated from their children, and the family had to get to America.
6. Immigrants had heard that a doctor in America takes good care of their patients and felt they had a chance for a better life there.

www.mhhe.com/mhhb2
For information and exercises on pronoun reference, go to
Editing > Pronoun Reference

PRONOUN REFERENCE

A pronoun must refer clearly to a specific antecedent if its meaning or the meaning of the sentence it appears in is to be clear. Consider this sentence:

► **Near the end of Homer's *Odyssey*, Odysseus and Telemachus take their revenge on the suitors harassing his wife, Penelope.**

To whose wife does the pronoun *his* refer? We can not tell from the sentence whether the antecedent is Odysseus, Telemachus, or even Homer. The **pronoun reference** is vague.

✓ 36p Identify and edit problems with pronoun reference.

Problems with pronoun reference take three common forms:

- **Ambiguous reference:** The pronoun has two or more equally plausible antecedents.
- **Implied reference:** The antecedent is implied but not explicitly stated.
- **Pronoun too far from antecedent:** A single antecedent is stated, but the reader may have trouble finding it because too much material comes between the antecedent and pronoun.

Editing for pronoun reference requires writers to be alert to potential vagueness and ambiguity and, especially, to think of their readers. Whose wife are the suitors harassing? The writer of the sentence above knows, but readers are left wondering. One solution is to replace the pronoun with the correct name.

► **Near the end of Homer's *Odyssey*, Odysseus and Telemachus take their revenge on the suitors harassing ~~his~~ *Odysseus's* wife, Penelope.**

36q Avoid ambiguous pronoun references.

If a pronoun can refer to more than one noun in a sentence, the reference is ambiguous. In the following unedited sentence, who is the antecedent of *him* and *his*—Hamlet or Horatio?

VAGUE The friendly banter between Hamlet and Horatio eventually provokes him to declare that his world view has changed.

BETTER The friendly banter between Hamlet and Horatio eventually provokes Hamlet to declare that his world view has changed.

The reader now knows that Hamlet is doing the declaring but may still be uncertain whose world view, Hamlet's or Horatio's, Hamlet thinks has changed. Eliminating this additional ambiguity without awkwardly repeating Hamlet's name a third time requires rewriting.

CLEAR The friendly banter between Hamlet and Horatio eventually provokes Hamlet to admit to a changed view of the world.

Here is another example in which rewriting clarifies an ambiguous reference.

VAGUE Jane Austen and Cassandra corresponded regularly when she was in London.

CLEAR When Jane Austen was in London, she corresponded regularly with Cassandra.

Place clauses beginning with *who, that*, and *which* directly after the words they modify to avoid the risk of ambiguous reference.

VAGUE I bought the book from the store down the street that my friend had recommended.

CLEAR I bought the book that my friend had recommended from the store down the street.

Change indirect quotes to direct quotes to promote clarity.

VAGUE Sammy told Joe he had a lot of work to do.

CLEAR Sammy told Joe, "You have a lot of work to do." *or* Sammy told Joe, "I have a lot of work to do."

36r Watch out for implied pronoun references.

A pronoun must refer to an explicitly stated noun or pronoun antecedent.

► **Every weekday afternoon, my brothers cycle home from school, and then they leave ~~them~~ *their bikes* in the driveway.**

In the original sentence, the writer relied confusingly on the verb *cycle* to imply the antecedent—*their bikes*—of the pronoun *them.*

► **In ~~Wilson's~~ *his* essay "When Work Disappears," ~~he~~ *Wilson* proposes a four-point plan for the revitalization of blighted inner-city communities.**

In the original sentence, the antecedent for *he* is unclear but implied by the possessive noun *Wilson's*. In the edited sentence, which clarifies who is proposing the plan, the antecedent of *his* is the explicitly stated noun *Wilson*.

1. Using clear references for *this*, *that*, and *which*

Writers often use the pronouns *this, that,* and *which* to refer loosely—and vaguely—to ideas expressed in preceding sentences. To make sentences containing one of these pronouns clearer, either change the pronoun to a specific noun or add a specific antecedent or clarifying noun.

VAGUE As government funding for higher education decreases, tuition increases. Are we students supposed to accept *this* without protest?

CLEAR As government funding for higher education decreases, tuition increases. Are we students supposed to accept *these higher costs* without protest?

CLEAR As government funding for higher education decreases, tuition increases. Are we students supposed to accept *this situation* without protest?

2. Using clear references for *they* and *it*

The pronouns *they* and *it* should refer to definite, explicitly stated antecedents. If the antecedent is unclear, replace the pronoun with a noun, or rewrite the sentence to eliminate the pronoun.

► **In some countries such as Canada, ~~they pay~~ [the government pays] for such medical procedures.**

► **~~In the~~ [The] textbook/ ~~it~~ states that borrowing to fund the purchase of financial assets results in a double-counting of debt.**

It can be a personal pronoun (I like *it*), part of an idiomatic expression (*It's* a nice day), or the beginning of a sentence in which the subject is delayed (*It* is clear you don't understand). Do not use it in more than one of these senses in the same sentence.

INAPPROPRIATE I like *it* when *it* is a nice day.

REVISED I like *it* when the weather is nice.

3. Reserving *you* for directly addressing the reader

In formal writing, you should reserve the pronoun *you* (as this sentence itself illustrates) for directly addressing the reader—that is, you should use it to mean "you, the reader." Avoid using *you* as a synonym for words that refer to individual people, like *one* or *a person*.

INAPPROPRIATE	You could be executed for heresy during the Spanish Inquisition.
REVISED	One could be executed for heresy during the Spanish Inquisition.
REVISED	Accused heretics faced execution during the Spanish Inquisition.

36s Keep track of pronoun reference in paragraphs.

When the same noun is the antecedent for pronouns in a sequence of related sentences, as in a paragraph, a pronoun's antecedent does not have to be stated in every sentence as long as it is stated at the beginning. To maintain clarity and variety, alternate between pronouns and the antecedent noun.

► **Berlioz's unconventional music irritated the opera and concert establishment. To get a hearing for his works, he had to arrange concerts at his own expense. Although he had a following of about twelve hundred who faithfully bought tickets to his concerts, ~~he~~** *Berlioz* **needed supplementary income from journalism to finance the performances.**

If long phrases, clauses, or sentences separate a pronoun and its antecedent, readers may lose track of the antecedent.

► **In her writing, Toni Morrison explores dimensions of the African American experience. Novels like *Beloved, The Bluest Eye,* and *Jazz* comment powerfully on the circumstances of African Americans. ~~She~~** *Morrison* **also wrote *Playing in the Dark,* a work of literary criticism.**

36t Use *who, whom,* and *whose,* not *that* or *which,* to refer to people.

In everyday speech, people often use *that* and *which* interchangeably with *who, whom,* and *whose* to refer to people. In formal writing, however, only *who, whom,* or *whose* should be used to refer to people. *That* and *which* refer to animals or things. (Occasionally *that* may refer to collective, anonymous groups of people.)

► **FDR was the president ~~that~~ *who* led the country during World War II.**

► **Animal shelters take in dogs ~~who~~ *that* have been abandoned.**

Who and *whom* may, however, be used to refer to animals with names.

► **Ferdinand is the bull ~~that~~ *who* wanted only to sit and smell the flowers, not to snort and romp about like the other bulls.**

Exercise 36.7 Editing to clarify pronoun reference

Rewrite each sentence to eliminate unclear pronoun references. Some sentences have several possible correct answers.

EXAMPLE **You are not allowed to drive without a license.**

People without licenses are not allowed to drive.

1. The tight race between presidential candidates John Kerry and George W. Bush in 2004 compelled him to campaign intensively in many states.
2. The candidates debated three times, answering them thoughtfully.
3. During one debate, Kerry told Bush that he had an inadequate plan of action.
4. After Bush's election, he promised to return money to some taxpayers.
5. When Kerry challenged the numbers behind Bush's proposed tax cuts, Bush accused Kerry of being "wishy-washy." This stuck throughout the campaign.
6. With Kerry as president, they would work on strengthening the economy with more jobs and higher incomes.

7. Even after all the campaigning, debating, and polling, you were still left wondering who would win the election on Tuesday, November 2, 2004.

Exercise 36.8 Chapter review: Problems with pronouns

Edit the passage below so that all pronouns have clear antecedents, agree with their antecedents, and are in the appropriate case.

Margaret Mead was probably the best-known anthropologist of the twentieth century. It was she whom wrote *Coming of Age in Samoa,* a book well known in the 1930s and still in print today. It was her who gave us the idea that Melanesian natives grow up free of the strictures and repressions that can characterize adolescence in our society. Her writings found an audience just as the work of Sigmund Freud was becoming widely known in the United States.

In his work, he argued for "an incomparably freer sexual life," saying that rigid attitudes toward sexuality contributed to mental illness among we Westerners. Her accessible and gracefully written account of life among the Samoans showed them to be both relatively free of pathology and relaxed about sexual matters. Their work both provoked and contributed to a debate over theories about the best way to raise children.

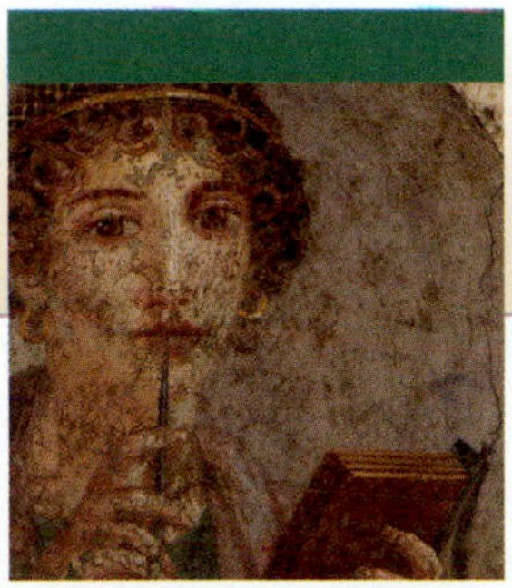

37 Problems with Adjectives and Adverbs

Adjectives and **adverbs** are words that describe. Because they qualify the meanings of other words—for example, telling which, how many, what kind, where, or how—we say that they *modify* them. Adjectives modify nouns and pronouns. Adverbs modify verbs, adjectives, and other adverbs. Adverbs can also modify entire phrases and clauses.

www.mhhe.com/mhhb2
For information and exercises on adjectives and adverbs, go to
Editing > Adjectives and Adverbs

What Adjectives and Adverbs Do

Adjectives modify:

NOUNS	The stock price took a **sudden** (adjective) *plunge* (noun).
PRONOUNS	*It* (pron) was **low** (adj).

Adverbs modify:

VERBS	The price *plunged* (verb) **suddenly** (adverb).
ADJECTIVES	The **abnormally** (adverb) *low* (adj) price attracted bargain hunters.
ADVERBS	The price recovered **unusually** (adverb) *quickly* (adverb).
PHRASES	It fell **nearly** (adverb) *to its twelve-month low* (phrase).
CLAUSES	It ended the day **almost** (adverb) *where it began* (clause).

37a Identify and edit problems with adjectives and adverbs.

When they are used with care, adjectives and adverbs add flavor and precision to writing. The problems writers have with adjectives and adverbs fall mostly into two categories:

Common Problems with Adjectives and Adverbs

1. Improperly using an adverb as an adjective
2. Using incorrectly formed comparative and superlative adjectives and adverbs

To identify and correct errors of the first type, writers need first to identify the kind of word or words being modified. If they are nouns or pronouns, the modifier should be an adjective; if not, it should probably be an adverb.

► The price plunged ~~sudden~~ *suddenly*.

The adverb *suddenly* replaces the adjective *sudden* in this sentence because it modifies the verb *plunged,* not the noun *price.*

To identify and edit problems with comparatives and superlatives, consult the rules and guidelines in section 37g (*pp. 604–06*).

Adjectives, Adverbs, and Grammar Checkers

Computer grammar checkers are sensitive to some problems with adjectives and adverbs, but they miss far more than they catch. A grammar checker failed to flag the error in each of the following sentences (and, indeed, in most of the problem sentences throughout this chapter):

The price took a *suddenly* plunge. [should be *sudden*]

The price plunged *sudden.* [should be *suddenly*]

37b Use adjectives to modify nouns or pronouns.

Adjectives modify nouns and pronouns; they do not modify any other kind of word. Adjectives tell what kind or how many and may come before or after the noun or pronoun they modify.

► ***Ominous gray*** **clouds loomed over the lake.**

► **The *looming* clouds, *ominous* and *gray,* frightened the children.**

► **The dealer stocks more *white* cars than *red* ones.**

Some proper nouns have adjective forms. Proper adjectives, like the proper nouns they are derived from, are capitalized: *Victoria/Victorian, Britain/British, America/American, Shakespeare/Shakespearean.*

Occasionally, descriptive adjectives function as nouns:

► **The *unemployed* should not be equated with the *lazy.***

► **F. Scott Fitzgerald wrote that the *rich* "are different from you and me."**

Present and past participles can be adjectives.

► **The *limiting* factor was our lack of resources.**

► **The *limited* resources prevented us from acting.**

(For more on the use of participles as adjectives, see Chapter 64: English Basics, pp. 850–52.)

For MULTILINGUAL STUDENTS

Using Adjectives

Unlike some languages such as Russian and Spanish, in English, adjectives do not change form to agree with plural nouns or pronouns.

► **The recipe calls for one green pepper and two ~~reds~~ *red* peppers.**

For more about adjectives in English, including rules for ordering adjectives when several act together to modify the same word, see Chapter 64: English Basics, pages 844–45.

37c Use nouns as adjectives sparingly.

In some cases, a noun is used as an adjective without a change in form:

► ***Cigarette* smoking harms the lungs and is banned in offices.**

Long strings of noun modifiers, however, are confusing and tedious to read. Consider revising sentences with more than one or two noun modifiers in a row.

CONFUSING The customer service improvement plan manager explained the new procedures.

BETTER The manager responsible for planning improvements in customer service explained the new procedures.

37d Use adverbs to modify verbs, adjectives, and other adverbs.

Adverbs modify verbs, adjectives, other adverbs, and even whole phrases and clauses. They tell where, when, why, how, how often, how much, or to what degree.

► **Dickens mixed humor and pathos *better* than any other English writer after Shakespeare.**

The adverb *better* modifies the verb *mixed.*

► **The *notoriously* quick-tempered batter *hotly* contested the umpire's call.**

The adverb *notoriously* modifies the adjective *quick-tempered* (which, in turn, modifies the noun *batter*); the adverb *hotly* modifies the verb *contested.*

► **The jurors came to a verdict *ominously swiftly.***

The adverb *ominously* modifies the adverb *swiftly,* which modifies the verb *came.*

► ***Afterward,* the defendants thanked their lawyers.**

The adverb *afterward* modifies the entire independent clause that follows it.

37e Do not use an adjective when an adverb is needed.

In conversation, we sometimes treat adjectives as adverbs. In writing, this informal usage should be avoided.

NONSTANDARD	The crowd yelled *loud* after the game-winning home run.
REVISED	The crowd yelled *loudly* after the game-winning home run.

The adjective *loud* tries to do the work of its adverb counterpart, *loudly,* to modify the verb *yelled.*

Tips LEARNING in COLLEGE

Recognizing Adverbs and Adjectives

Many adverbs in English end in *-ly,* but not all words that end in *-ly* are adverbs. Some, like *lovely,* are adjectives (*the lovely painting*). Other adverbs—*almost, now, often,* for example—do not end in *-ly.*

Adjectives, likewise, have no single form. Common endings for adjectives include *-al (comical), -an (vegetarian), -ful (wonderful), -ish (fiendish),* and *-ous (famous),* but some adjectives—*bad, large, red, short, small, tall,* for example—have no ending.

Finally, some words—including *fast, only, hard,* and *straight*—are both adjectives and adverbs. Their function depends on the context in which they appear.

When you are in doubt, consult a dictionary.

NONSTANDARD She *sure* made me work hard for my grade.

REVISED She *certainly* made me work hard for my grade.

The adjective *sure* tries to do the work of an adverb modifying the verb *made.*

After a direct object, use an adjective to modify the object and an adverb to modify the verb of the sentence.

ADJECTIVE The test made me *nervous.*

ADVERB I took the test *nervously.*

37f Use adjectives after linking verbs to describe the subject.

A **linking verb** connects the subject of a sentence to its description. The most common linking verb is *be.* A descriptive adjective that modifies a sentence's subject but appears after a linking verb is called a **subject complement.**

► During the winter, both Emily and Anne *were sick.*

► The road *is long, winding,* and *dangerous.*

Other linking verbs are related to states of being and the five senses: *appear, become, feel, grow, look, smell, sound,* and *taste.* Verbs related to the senses can be either linking or action verbs, depending on the meaning of the sentence.

► The actor's *gesture looks awkward.*

Here *look* is a linking verb and *awkward* is a subject complement modifying *gesture.*

► The actor *looks awkwardly* over his shoulder.

Here *looks* is an action verb modified by the adverb *awkwardly.*

Pay particular attention to the distinction between *bad* and *badly* or *good* and *well* when these words follow verbs of this kind.

► The crop grows *badly* in wet regions.

▶ **The weather grew *bad* as the hurricane approached.**

▶ **The crop looks *good* compared with last year's.**

Otherwise identical sentences can have very different meanings depending on whether a writer chooses the adjective or adverb.

ADJECTIVE The dog smelled *bad.*

The dog smelled *good.*

In both sentences, the adjectives modify the noun *dog,* which is connected to the adjectives by the linking verb *smelled.* The first sentence indicates that the dog needed a bath; the second, that the dog had probably recently had one.

ADVERB The dog smelled *well.*

The dog smelled *badly.*

The adverbs modify the verb *smelled,* an action verb in these sentences. The dog in the first sentence might be good at tracking; the dog in the second probably would not be.

Note, however, that *well* can function as an adjective and subject complement with a linking verb to describe a person's health.

▶ **After the treatment, the patient felt *well* again.**

Good and *bad* appear after *feel* to describe emotional states.

▶ **I feel *bad* [not *badly*] for her because she does not feel *well.***

Exercise 37.1 Identifying adjectives and adverbs

In the sentences that follow, underline and label all adjectives (adj), nouns used as adjectives (n), and adverbs (adv). Then draw an arrow from each modifier to the word or words it modifies.

EXAMPLE **The water was chillingly cold.** (chillingly: adv; cold: adj)

1. The spread of destructive viruses to computers around the world is a serious problem with potentially deadly consequences.
2. Carried by infected e-mails, the viruses spread fast, moving from computer to computer at the click of a mouse.

3. Viruses have hit businesses badly in the past, disrupting railroads, delaying flights, and closing stores and offices.
4. Because viruses are so harmful, computer users should install antivirus software and update it regularly.
5. Other precautions include maintaining a good firewall and screening e-mail well to avoid opening suspicious messages.

Exercise 37.2 Editing adjectives and adverbs

Edit the sentences that follow so that adjectives are not used where adverbs belong and adverbs are not used where adjectives belong. Circle the number of any sentence that is already correct.

EXAMPLE **She hid the money so ~~good~~ *well* that she could not find it when she needed it.**

1. Sociology, the scholarly study of human society, is well and thriving today.
2. The discipline's intellectual roots reach real far back, to the eighteenth century.
3. Auguste Comte (1798–1857) invented the word *sociology,* and mostly sociologists would probable agree that he founded the discipline.
4. According to Comte, scientific laws control human social behavior as sure as they control the motion of planets around the sun.
5. Comte believed his scientific approach was good because it would further human progress.
6. Emile Durkheim (1858–1917) helped place modern sociology on a well foundation.
7. Durkheim argued that societies can be good understood only if analyzed on their own terms, apart from the individuals who constitute them.

37g Use positive, comparative, and superlative adjectives and adverbs correctly.

Most adjectives and adverbs have three forms, or **degrees,** that indicate comparison:

- the positive degree
- the comparative degree
- the superlative degree

The **positive degree** is the simple form of the adjective or adverb, the one found in the dictionary. It applies to the modified word or words alone.

POSITIVE ADJECTIVE

Pennsylvania is a *large* state.

We are tackling a *difficult* problem.

They drive an *expensive* car.

POSITIVE ADVERB

The first batter hit the ball *far*.

The company performs the play *confidently*.

The **comparative degree** of an adjective or adverb compares two things.

COMPARATIVE ADJECTIVE

New York is *larger* than Pennsylvania.

This problem is *more difficult* than the last one.

You drive a *less expensive* car than theirs.

COMPARATIVE ADVERB

The second batter hit the ball *farther* than the first.

The company performs *more confidently* now than last season but *less confidently* than the season before.

The **superlative degree** of an adjective or adverb compares three or more things, indicating which is the greatest or least.

SUPERLATIVE ADJECTIVE

Texas is the *largest* state in the Southwest.

This problem is the *most difficult* we have encountered so far.

We drive the *least expensive* car we can find.

SUPERLATIVE ADVERB

The third batter hit the ball *farthest* of all.

The company performs *most confidently* on Friday nights and *least confidently* on Tuesday nights.

1. Forming comparatives and superlatives

For most one-syllable adjectives, add *-er* to form the comparative and *-est* to form the superlative.

► **Mercury is the ~~most near~~ nearest planet to the sun.**

For one- or two-syllable adjectives ending in the letter *y*, change the *y* to *i* and then add the *er* or *est* ending.

> ► **The ~~most lovely~~ *loveliest* sunsets come after volcanic eruptions.**

For most other adjectives of two or more syllables, use *more* and *most*.

A few short adverbs take *-er* and *-est* endings to form the comparative and superlative (*harder/hardest*). Most adverbs, however, including all adverbs that end in *-ly*, form the comparative with *more* and *most* (*more loudly/most loudly*).

> ► **She sings *more loudly* than we expected.**

Several common adjectives and adverbs—*good* and *well*, for example—have irregular comparative and superlative forms.

> ► **He felt ~~gooder~~ *better* as his fever broke.**

Some of these irregular adjectives and adverbs are listed in the box on page 607. When in doubt, consult a dictionary.

Note: For all adjectives and adverbs, form negative comparisons and superlatives with *less* and *least*.

> ► **The grass may seem *greener* on the other side of the fence, but you may find it *less green* when you get there.**

2. Watching out for double comparatives and superlatives

Use either an *-er* or an *-est* ending or *more/most* to form the comparative or superlative, as appropriate. Do not use both.

> ► **Since World War II, Britain has been the ~~most~~ closest ally of the United States.**

3. Being aware of concepts that cannot be compared

Do not use comparative or superlative forms with adjectives such as *unique, infinite, impossible, perfect, round, square,* and *destroyed.* These concepts are *absolutes.* If something is unique, for example, it is the only one of its kind, making comparison impossible.

> ► **You will never find ~~a more unique~~ *another* restaurant ~~than~~ *like* this one.**

COMPARISON in ADJECTIVES and ADVERBS: EXAMPLES of REGULAR and IRREGULAR FORMS

Regular Adjectives

	POSITIVE	COMPARATIVE	SUPERLATIVE
One-syllable adjectives	red	redder less red	reddest least red
Two-syllable adjectives ending in *y*	lonely	lonelier less lonely	loneliest least lonely
Other adjectives of two or more syllables	famous	more/less famous	most/least famous

Regular Adverbs

	POSITIVE	COMPARATIVE	SUPERLATIVE
One-syllable adverbs	hard	harder less hard	hardest least hard
Most other adverbs	truthfully	more/less truthfully	most/least truthfully

Irregular Adjectives

POSITIVE	COMPARATIVE	SUPERLATIVE
good	better	best
bad	worse	worst
little	less, littler	least, littlest
many	more	most
much	more	most
some	more	most

Irregular Adverbs

POSITIVE	COMPARATIVE	SUPERLATIVE
badly	worse	worst
well	better	best

37h Avoid double negatives.

The words *no, not,* and *never* can modify the meaning of nouns and pronouns as well as other sentence elements.

NOUN	You are *no* friend of mine.
ADJECTIVE	The red house was *not* large.
VERB	He *never* ran in a marathon.

However, it takes only one negative word to change the meaning of a sentence from positive to negative. When two negatives are used together, they cancel each other out, resulting in a positive meaning. Unless you want your sentence to have a positive meaning (*I am not unaware of your feelings in this matter*), edit by changing or eliminating one of the negative words.

► **They do not have ~~no~~ *any* reason to go there.**

► **He ~~cannot~~ *can* hardly do that assignment.**

Note that *hardly* has a negative meaning and cannot be used with *no, not,* or *never.*

Exercise 37.3 Editing comparisons

Edit the sentences that follow so that adjectives and adverbs are used correctly in comparisons. Some of the sentences are already correct; circle their numbers.

EXAMPLE **He felt ~~badder~~ *worse* as his illness progressed.**

1. Biotechnology, perhaps the controversialest application of science in recent decades, is the basis of genetic engineering, cloning, and gene therapy.
2. Some of these fields are more popular than others.
3. Ethicists find it more easy to defend the genetic engineering of plants than the cloning of animals.
4. Gene therapy is often a last resort for people suffering from the worser types of cancer.
5. Gene therapy, one of the more newer forms of biotechnology, involves introducing cells containing specialized genetic material into the patient's body.
6. Cloning, a way of creating an exact duplicate of an organism, is probably more hard to justify than any other biotechnological procedure.

7. A female lamb cloned in Scotland in 1997 seemed no different from others of her breed.
8. Despite the successes that have been achieved with animal cloning, most people do not want no humans to be cloned.

Exercise 37.4 Chapter review: Problems with adjectives and adverbs

Edit the following passage to correct any problems with adjectives and adverbs.

Although there are many approaches to sociology, the two most commonest ones are functionalism and conflict theory. The functionalist view, usual associated with Harvard sociologist Talcott Parsons, sees society as a whole that tries to maintain equilibrium, or stasis. No ancestor of conflict theory is most famous than Karl Marx, who invented the concept of class warfare. Promoted here in the United States by the African-American sociologist W. E. B. Dubois, conflict theory sees society as made up of groups that cannot hardly avoid being in conflict or competition with one another.

For a functionalist like Parsons, societies are best understood according to how good they maintain stability. On the other hand, for a conflict theorist like Dubois, a society is more better analyzed in terms of how its parts compete for power.

CHECKLIST

Editing for Grammar Conventions

How can you tell if one of your sentences has a grammatical problem? Ask yourself the following questions:

- ☐ Is each sentence grammatically complete, or is some necessary part missing? Does each sentence include a subject, a complete verb, and an independent clause? (*See Chapter 32: Sentence Fragments, pp. 512–23.*)
- ☐ Does any sentence seem like two or more sentences jammed together without a break? If a sentence has more than one independent clause, are those clauses joined in an acceptable way? (*See Chapter 33: Comma Splices and Run-on Sentences, pp. 524–35.*)
- ☐ Do the key parts of each sentence fit together well, or are the subjects and verbs mismatched in person and number? (*See Chapter 34: Subject-Verb Agreement, pp. 536–51.*)
- ☐ Is the time frame of events represented accurately, conventionally, and consistently, or are there problems with verb form, tense, and sequence? (*See Chapter 35: Problems with Verbs, pp. 551–75.*)
- ☐ Do the pronouns in every sentence clearly refer to a specific noun or pronoun and agree with the nouns or pronouns they replace? (*See Chapter 36: Problems with Pronouns, pp. 576–97.*)
- ☐ Does the form of each modifier match its function in the sentence? (*See Chapter 37: Problems with Adjectives and Adverbs, pp. 597–609.*)

Frank Lloyd Wright's Robie House features 174 stained-glass windows. Sunlight brings out the clarity of each window's design; in turn, the designs—a variety of geometric, colorful patterns—transform the light.

PART 8

I . . . believe that words *can* help us move or keep us paralyzed, and that our choices of language and verbal tone have something—a great deal—to do with how we live our lives and whom we end up speaking with and hearing.

—ADRIENNE RICH

Editing for Clarity

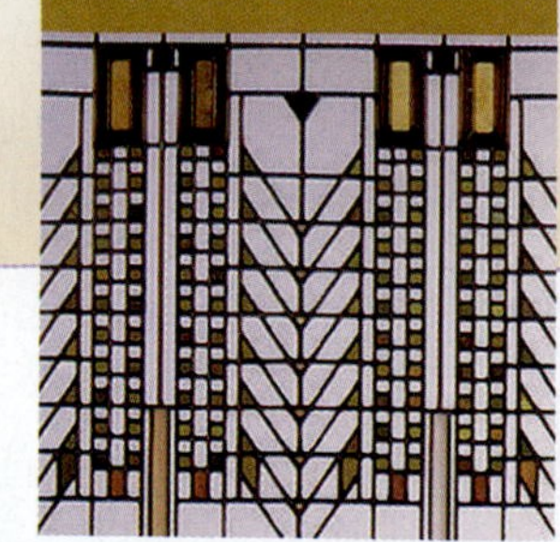

38 Wordy Sentences

Writers are **concise** when they use as few words as needed to be clear and engaging. A sentence does not have to be short and simple to be concise. Instead, every word in it must count.

www.mhhe.com/mhhb2
For information on and practice avoiding wordiness, go to
Editing > Wordiness

38a Identify and edit wordiness.

Be on the lookout for wordiness as you revise your work and hone your ideas. To make your writing concise, be aware of the sources of wordiness described in this chapter and know how to counter them.

How to Make Your Writing More Concise

1. Recognize and eliminate wordy phrases and empty words.
2. Recognize and eliminate unnecessary repetition.
3. Recognize and revise constructions built around weak verbs and nouns derived from verbs.
4. Recognize opportunities to reduce clauses to phrases and phrases to single words.
5. Recognize opportunities to combine several repetitive sentences into one more concise sentence.

WRITING OUTCOMES

Part 8: Editing for Clarity

This section will help you answer questions such as:

Rhetorical Knowledge

- What is parallelism, and how can I use it to emphasize important ideas? **(42)**
- How can I use subordination to clarify relationships between ideas? **(44d)**

Critical Thinking, Reading, and Writing

- What is wrong with phrases like *past history* and *in close proximity to*? **(38c)**
- How do direct and indirect quotations differ? **(41e)**

Processes

- Can my word processor's grammar checker help me edit for clarity? **(38–46)**

Knowledge of Conventions

- What is wrong with the comparison *I like manga more than Rafael?* **(39d)**
- What is the problem with *the reason . . . is because?* **(40b)**

Self-Assessment: *Take an online quiz at www.mhhe.com/mhhb2 to test your familiarity with the topics covered in Chapters 38–46. Pay special attention to the sections in these chapters that correspond to any questions you answer incorrectly.*

Wordiness and Grammar Checkers

Most computer grammar and style checkers inconsistently recognize wordy structures. One style checker, for example, flagged most passive verbs and some *it is* and *there are* (expletive) constructions, but not others. It also flagged the redundant expression *true fact* but missed the equally redundant *round circle* and the empty phrase *it is a fact that.*

IDENTIFY AND EDIT
Wordy Sentences

W

To make your writing concise, ask yourself these questions as you edit your writing:

1. *Do any sentences contain wordy or empty phrases such as* at this point in time? *Do any of them contain redundancies or other unnecessary repetitions?*

- ~~The fact is that at this point in time more~~ More women than men now attend college.
- Total college enrollments have increased steadily ~~upward~~ since the 1940s, but since the 1970s women have enrolled in greater numbers than men ~~have~~.

  compound structure

2. *Can any clauses be reduced to phrases, or phrases to single words? Can any sentences be combined to reduce repetitive information?*

- ~~Reports that come from college~~ College officials ~~indicate~~ report that applications from women exceed those from men/ ~~This pattern indicates~~, indicating that women will continue to outnumber men in college for some time to come.

3. *Do any sentences include* there is, *or* there are, *or* it is *expressions; weak verbs; or nouns derived from verbs?*

- In 1970, ~~there were~~ men outnumbered women in college by more than 1.5 million. ~~more men in college than women.~~
- This trend ~~is a reflection of~~ reflects broad changes in gender roles throughout American society.

38b Eliminate wordy phrases and empty words.

1. Spotting wordy phrases

Make your sentences more concise by replacing common wordy phrases with appropriate one-word alternatives.

WORDY Due to the fact that I have at this point in time driven my car more than three thousand miles, I should in the not-too-distant future schedule an appointment for the purpose of changing the oil.

CONCISE Because I have now driven my car more than three thousand miles, I should schedule an oil change soon.

The following table lists some common wordy phrases and their concise alternatives.

WORDY PHRASES	CONCISE ALTERNATIVES
at this point in time	now
in this day and age	nowadays, today
at that point in time	then
in the not-too-distant future	soon
at all times	always
until such time as	until
in close proximity to	near
is necessary that	must
is able to	can
has the ability to	can
has the capacity to	can
due to the fact that	because
for the reason that	because
in spite of the fact that	although
in the event that	if
in order to	to
for the purpose(s) of	to
by means of	by

2. Recognizing empty words and phrases

Some phrases are empty, or meaningless, in that they provide little or no information. Cutting **empty phrases** strengthens your writing.

► We had just begun ~~the process of~~ setting up our tent when the storm hit.

► ~~The fact is,~~ Geraldine Ferraro was the first woman to be nominated for vice president by a major party.

► **The Nile is ~~to all intents and purposes~~ the longest river in the world.**

You can often rephrase sentences to eliminate words like *manner, nature, character, way, type,* or *kind.*

decisively.

► **The mayor reacted ~~in a decisive manner.~~**

honesty and candor.

► **The job ~~is the kind that~~ requires ~~a person with an honest character who can communicate in a candid way.~~**

Be on the alert, too, for opportunities to replace long descriptive phrases with brief, more vivid synonyms.

waffled

► **The candidate ~~did not give a straight answer~~ when asked about Medicare.**

of homicide.

► **The detectives saw no evidence ~~to suggest the death was not from natural causes.~~**

38c Eliminate unnecessary repetition.

www.mhhe.com/mhhb2

For information on and practice avoiding redundancy, go to

Editing > Eliminating Redundancies

1. Spotting redundancy

Words are **redundant** when they needlessly repeat information.

► **She is writing a ~~fictional~~ historical novel ~~set in the past~~ about Anne Hutchinson and the settling of Rhode Island.**

A historical novel *is* a work of fiction set in the past.

Be on the lookout for such commonplace redundancies as the following:

biography of the life	join together
blue in color	mix together
close proximity	past history
cooperate together	refer back
few in number	repeat again
final result	small in size
first and foremost	square (round, triangular) in shape
full and complete	underlying foundation

For MULTILINGUAL STUDENTS

Redundancy and the Implied Meaning of English Words

Because sentences with redundancies may be perfectly grammatical, you may find it hard to spot them. In English, for example, the concept of *together* is implicit in the word *cooperate*—that is, cooperating is always something two or more parties do together. As a result, the phrase *cooperate together* is redundant.

► **The United States pledged to cooperate ~~together~~ with its major trading partners.**

Ask your teachers and peers for help in pointing out redundancies in your writing, and look up unfamiliar words in a dictionary.

Sometimes, modifiers such as *very, rather,* and *really* and intensifiers such as *absolutely, definitely,* and *incredibly* do not add meaning to a sentence but are simply redundant. Delete them.

► **The ending ~~definitely~~ shocked us very much.**

2. Reducing wordiness with elliptical constructions

Elliptical constructions allow you to omit otherwise grammatically necessary words from a sentence when their meaning and function are clear from the surrounding context.

► **The children enjoyed watching television more than ~~they enjoyed~~ reading books.**

► **In ancient times, many astronomers knew ~~that~~ the earth was round but did not know ~~that~~ it revolved around the sun.**

Commas sometimes indicate the omission.

► **He wanted to go to Rome, his wife, to Paris.**

Note: Sometimes writers deliberately repeat words for emphasis. (*See Chapter 45: Sentence Variety and Emphasis, pp. 669–70.*)

Exercise 38.1 Identifying and editing wordy or empty phrases and unnecessary repetition

Eliminate wordy or empty phrases and unnecessary repetition to make the following sentences concise.

EXAMPLE

The ~~The truth is that the time of the~~ rainy season in Hawaii is from ~~the month of~~ November to ~~the month of~~ March.

1. Charlotte Perkins Gilman was first and foremost known as a woman who was a champion of women's rights.
2. She was born on the date July 3, 1860, in the city of Hartford, which is in the state of Connecticut.
3. Gilman's "The Yellow Wallpaper," a novella about the holy matrimony of marriage and a state of madness, still speaks to contemporary readers in this present day and age.
4. The leading female heroine in Gilman's story is diagnosed by her physician husband as having an illness that is mental in origin.
5. Gilman wrote and published her book *Women and Economics* in the year 1898 and then published her book *Concerning Children* in the year 1900.

38d Make your sentences straightforward.

Concise sentences are straightforward; they get to the point quickly. Roundabout sentences often result from expletive constructions and expressions built around static verbs like *to be* and *to have.*

1. Avoiding expletive constructions

An **expletive construction** starts with the word *it* or *there* followed by a form of the verb *be* and takes the place of a subject that appears later in the sentence. These constructions can sometimes be effective, especially to introduce or emphasize a subject. Consider, for example, this famous line from Shakespeare's *Hamlet:* "There are more things in heaven and earth, Horatio, than are dreamt of in your philosophy." In most cases, however, eliminating expletive constructions will make your sentences more concise.

ROUNDABOUT	There were millions of people who donated generously to help victims of the earthquake.
CONCISE	Millions of people donated generously to help victims of the earthquake.

2. Using strong verbs

As you edit your writing, look for roundabout expressions that combine a noun with a form of *be* or *have.* If the noun derives from a verb, replace the roundabout expression with the verb.

ROUNDABOUT The stylistic similarities between "This Lime-Tree Bower" and "Tintern Abbey" are an indication that Coleridge had an influence on Wordsworth.

CONCISE The stylistic similarities between "This Lime-Tree Bower" and "Tintern Abbey" indicate that Coleridge influenced Wordsworth.

The passive voice also lends itself to roundabout construction. Changing verbs from the passive to the active voice often results in stronger, more concise sentences.

ROUNDABOUT The valley was surveyed by the archaeologists for the purpose of locating sites that had been occupied by the Incas.

CONCISE The archaeologists surveyed the valley for Inca sites.

(*For more on strong verbs, see Chapter 46: Active Verbs, pp. 671–74.*)

38e Shorten clauses and phrases.

For conciseness and clarity, look for opportunities to simplify sentences by turning modifying clauses into phrases.

► **The film *Dirty Pretty Things,* ~~which was~~ directed by Stephen Frears, portrays the struggles of illegal immigrants in London.**

Also look for opportunities to reduce phrases to single words.

► **Stephen Frears's film *Dirty Pretty Things* portrays the struggles of illegal immigrants in London.**

38f Combine sentences.

Sometimes you can combine several short, repetitive sentences into a single more concise sentence.

WORDY Little Red Riding Hood crossed the river. After that, she walked through the woods. Finally, she arrived at Grandmother's house.

CONCISE Little Red Riding Hood went over the river and through the woods to Grandmother's house.

WORDY Hurricane Floyd had a devastating effect on our town. The destruction resulted from torrential rains. Flooding submerged Main Street under eight feet of water. The rain also triggered mudslides that destroyed two houses.

CONCISE Hurricane Floyd's torrential rains devastated our town, submerging Main Street under eight feet of water and triggering mudslides that destroyed two houses.

(*For more on combining sentences and clauses, see Chapter 42: Faulty Parallelism, pp. 637–42, and Chapter 44: Coordination and Subordination, pp. 653–62.*)

Exercise 38.2 Writing straightforward sentences

Use the techniques described in sections 38d–f to make each of the following passages into a single concise sentence.

EXAMPLE: ORIGINAL

The play opened on October 1. There were many reviews in which critics gave it a pan. The public loathed it too, which is why it closed after a run of two weeks.

EXAMPLE: REVISED

The play opened on October 1, but critics panned it, the public loathed it, and it closed after a two-week run.

1. There are many concerns that environmentalists have about whether genetically modified food products are absolutely safe for the environment.
2. Soybeans that are genetically engineered are very resistant to certain artificially made herbicides. These beans are also very resistant to certain artificially made insecticides.
3. These soybeans, which are resistant, permit the use of larger quantities of herbicides by farmers than before.
4. The herbicides kill surrounding plants. They also kill insects that are not considered pests, such as the Monarch butterfly.
5. There are also concerns from consumers about the handling of genetically modified soy crops. One of these concerns is that the genetically modified soy crops are not segregated from soy crops that have not been genetically modified.

Exercise 38.3 Chapter review: Wordy sentences

Use the techniques described in this chapter to make the following passage concise.

In this day and age, people definitely should take preventive precautions to prevent identity theft from happening to them. Identity thieves have the ability to use someone else's personal information to commit fraud or theft, such as opening a fraudulent credit card account. Identity thieves also have the capacity to create counterfeit checks. This type of theft is often done in such a clever manner that often the victim of identity theft never realizes that his or her identity has been stolen. People whose identity has been stolen should first and foremost contact the Federal Trade Commission (FTC) for the purpose of disputing fraudulent charges. There is also the fact that people should learn how they can minimize the chance that they will face the risk of becoming a victim of this type of crime.

39 Missing Words

When editing, do not omit words that are necessary to your meaning.

✓ 39a Identify and edit problems with missing words.

www.mhhe.com/mhhb2
For information and exercises on missing words, go to
Editing > Word Choice

Writers sometimes omit from sentences words that are needed to make the sentences clear or grammatically complete. The desire to avoid repetition or the mistaken assumption that the rest of the sentence conveys the required information is usually at the root of these omissions. Writers should be particularly alert for missing words in compound structures, in dependent clauses beginning with *that,* and in comparisons.

Situations in Which Needed Words Often Go Missing

1. Compound structures
2. Dependent clauses beginning with *that*
3. Comparisons

Here is an example that combines all three of these situations:

► He claims [^that] *Watchmen* is better [^than *Iron Man*]; I [^claim] that *Iron Man* is [^better than *Watchmen*].

IDENTIFY AND EDIT
Missing Words

To avoid omissions that might confuse your readers, ask yourself these questions as you edit your writing:

1. Are any additional words needed to make a sentence idiomatic and grammatical?

- Commuting in carpools, ^by train, or ^by bus can help reduce the nation's consumption of oil.
- My neighbor takes the bus, and I ^take the train.

2. Is the word that *missing when it is needed for clarity?*

- Many companies suggest ^that their employees carpool or take mass transit to work.

3. Are all comparisons clear and complete?

- Carpooling is more energy-efficient ~~.~~ ^than driving alone.
- Driving alone is less energy-efficient than any ^other way of commuting to work.

Missing Words and Grammar Checkers

Computer grammar checkers are entirely unreliable at flagging most instances of the kinds of missing-word errors discussed in this chapter. In fact, one grammar checker failed to flag errors in any of the chapter's example sentences.

39b Add words that are needed to make compound structures complete and clear.

For conciseness, words can sometimes be omitted from compound structures (which are then called *elliptical structures*). In the following example, the second *is* can be omitted because the verb in the first

For MULTILINGUAL STUDENTS

Obligatory Words in English

In English the subject and the verb are obligatory components of a sentence.

- Every English clause must have an explicit subject—a noun, phrase, pronoun, or filler word like *there* or *it*—even if the rest of the sentence seems unambiguously to imply the subject. The only exceptions are imperative sentences—commands—in which the subject, *you,* is understood.
- Every clause must have a verb, even if it is a linking verb (like *be*). Also, the verb must be complete (a main verb along with any helping verbs that are needed to express tense or voice).

part of the compound structure is also *is: The defendant's anger is extreme and his behavior violent.*

Do not leave out part of a compound structure unless both parts of the compound are the same, however. If an idiom calls for different prepositions in each part of a compound structure, both prepositions should appear in the sentence.

► **The gang members neither cooperated ^*with* nor listened to the authorities.**

One cooperates *with* but listens *to,* so both prepositions are needed in this sentence.

► **The performers stood and sang for an hour without interruption.**

In this case, both verbs require the same preposition, *for,* so it needs to appear only once.

Similarly, when grammar requires different forms of a word in each part of a compound, both forms should appear in the sentence.

► **The boss flies first class; the rest of us ^*fly* economy class.**

► **The coach declared that our team has never ^*been* and will never be defeated.**

If a word functions differently in the halves of a compound, it must be repeated.

► **I am happy to help and ^*am* planning to work with you until we complete the project.**

Here, *am* is a linking verb in the first clause and a helping verb in the second.

Sometimes, to avoid ambiguity, you may need to repeat a word even when it serves the same function in both parts of a compound.

► **The author dedicated the book to her children and ^*her* teachers.**

The repetition makes it clear that the children and the teachers are not the same people.

39c Include *that* when it is needed for clarity.

The subordinator *that* should be omitted only when the clause it introduces is short and the sentence's meaning is clear: *Carrie Underwood sings the kinds of songs many women love.* Usually, *that* should be included.

► **The attorney argued ^*that* men and women should receive equal pay for equal work.**

39d Make comparisons clear.

To be clear, comparisons must be complete. If you have just said, "Peanut butter sandwiches are boring," you can say immediately afterward, "Curried chicken sandwiches are more interesting," but you cannot say in isolation, "Curried chicken sandwiches are more interesting." You need to name who or what they are more interesting than—in other words, you need to complete the comparison.

www.mhhe.com/mhhb2
For information on and practice avoiding faulty comparisons, go to
Editing > Faulty Comparisons

Check comparisons to make sure your meaning is clear. In the following example, does the writer mean that she loved her grandmother more than her sister did—or more than she loved her sister? To clarify, add the missing words.

► **I loved my grandmother more than my sister ^*did*.**

► **I loved my grandmother more than ^*I loved* my sister.**

When you use *as* to compare people or things, be sure to use it twice:

► **Napoleon's temper was ^*as* volatile as a volcano.**

Include the words *other* or *else* to clarify comparisons when the subject of the comparison belongs to the same category of people or things to which it is being compared.

► **High schools and colleges stage *The Laramie Project* more than**

other

any ^ play.

The sentence compares *The Laramie Project,* itself a play, with other plays.

else

► **Professor Koonig has written more books than anyone ^ in her department.**

The sentence compares Professor Koonig with other members of her own department.

► ***No Country for Old Men,* a modern-day Western, won more awards**

other

than any ^ movie in 2008.

Do not include *other* or *else,* however, when comparing people or things that belong to different categories.

► ***No Country for Old Men*, a modern-day Western, won more awards than any ~~other~~ science fiction movie in 2008.**

Use a possessive form when comparing attributes or possessions.

WEAK	Plato's philosophy is easier to read than *that of Aristotle.*
BETTER	Plato's philosophy is easier to read than *Aristotle's.*

Keep in mind that complex comparisons may require more than one addition to be completely clear.

than Jones's book

► **Smith's book is longer, ^ but his account of the war is more interesting**

Jones's account

than ^ ~~Jones's~~.

39e Add articles (*a, an, the*) where necessary.

In English, omitting an article usually makes an expression sound odd, unless the omission occurs in a series of nouns.

a

► **A dog that bites should be kept on ^ leash.**

the

► **He gave me ^ books he liked best.**

► **I have a fish tank, birdcage, and rabbit hutch.**

Note: If the articles in a series are not the same, each one must be included.

► I have an aquarium, ^a birdcage, and ^a rabbit hutch.

For MULTILINGUAL STUDENTS

For more information about the use of articles, consult Chapter 64: English Basics, pages 840–41.

39f Make intensifiers complete.

In college writing, do not use words such as *so, such,* and *too* without a follow-up clause or phrase. "Her book is *so* good" cannot stand on its own, but with a completing clause, it can: "Her book is *so* good *that I couldn't put it down.*"

Exercise 39.1 Chapter review: Editing for missing words

Read the following paragraphs carefully, and supply any missing words.

Most early scientists thought the speed of light was infinite. The Italian scientist Galileo never agreed nor listened to arguments of his contemporaries. He set up experiment to measure the speed of light between two hills that were a known distance apart. Although its results were ambiguous, Galileo's experiment was more influential than any experiment of his day.

Almost one hundred years later, the Danish astronomer Olaus Roemer devised a sophisticated experiment to measure speed of light. Roemer hypothesized the farther away planet Jupiter is from Earth, the longer its light will take. Knowing Jupiter's distance from Earth at various times of the year, Roemer calculated the speed of light at 141,000 miles per second. Roemer's result was closer than that of any earlier scientist to the actual speed of light, which is now known to be 186,281.7 miles per second in a vacuum.

According to Albert Einstein's theory of relativity, the speed of light has never and will never be exceeded. The speed of light is variable, however. For instance, it travels about twenty-five percent slower through water.

40 Mixed Constructions

When a sentence's parts do not fit together either grammatically or logically, the result is a **mixed construction.** Because they confuse readers, mixed constructions must be revised for clarity.

✓ 40a Identify and edit mixed constructions.

Mixed constructions occur when writers start a sentence one way and then, midway through, change grammatical direction. The writer of the following example begins the sentence with a prepositional phrase (a phrase introduced by a preposition such as *at, by, for, in,* or *of*) and then, midway through, tries to make that phrase into the subject. A prepositional phrase cannot be the subject of a sentence, however.

www.mhhe.com/mhhb2
For information on and practice avoiding mixed constructions, go to
Editing > Mixed Constructions

MIXED-UP SENTENCE For family members who enjoy one another's company often decide on a vacation spot together.

The mixed construction obscures the writer's meaning and must be revised. Different solutions will produce different effects. The most straightforward option, eliminating the preposition *for,* makes *family members* the subject of the verb *decide.* The result is a statement of fact about close families.

REVISED SENTENCE Family members who enjoy one another's company often decide on a vacation spot together.

Perhaps the writer instead intended to recommend joint vacation planning as something for close families to consider. In that case, an alternative is to leave the opening as a prepositional phrase, change *decide* from a verb to a gerund (*deciding*) that serves as the subject, add the linking verb *is,* and provide a subject complement (*rewarding*) for the prepositional phrase to modify. (A **subject complement** is a word or word group that specifies or describes the subject of a linking verb.)

REVISED SENTENCE For family members who enjoy one another's company, deciding together on a vacation spot is often rewarding.

In the following sentence, the dependent clause *when a* curandero *is consulted* cannot serve as the subject of the sentence.

MIXED-UP SENTENCE In Mexican culture, when a *curandero* is consulted can address spiritual or physical illness.

One revision transforms the dependent clause into an independent clause with a subject and a predicate (a complete verb) that make sense together.

REVISED SENTENCE In Mexican culture, a *curandero* can be consulted for spiritual or physical illness.

Here are two alternative revisions, each of which picks up on different words in the original, to slightly different effect in each case.

REVISED SENTENCE In Mexican culture, when people suffer from spiritual or physical illness, they consult a *curandero.*

REVISED SENTENCE In Mexican culture, the *curandero's* role is to address people's spiritual and physical illnesses.

Sometimes you may have to separate your ideas into more than one sentence to clarify the point you are trying to make. The writer of the following sentence is attempting to do two things at one time: contrast England and France in 1805 and define the difference between an oligarchy and a dictatorship.

MIXED-UP SENTENCE In an oligarchy like England was in 1805, a few people had the power rather than a dictatorship like France, which was ruled by Napoleon.

By using two sentences instead of one, the writer makes both ideas clear.

REVISED SENTENCE In 1805, England was an oligarchy, a state ruled by the few. In contrast, France under Napoleon was a dictatorship, a state ruled by one person.

Mixed Constructions and Grammar Checkers

As with missing words, computer grammar checkers are unreliable at detecting mixed constructions.

Note: The editing symbol for mixed constructions is *mix*.

40b Make sure predicates match their subjects.

A **predicate** is the complete verb along with any words that modify it, any objects or complements, and any words that modify them. A predicate must match a sentence's subject both logically and grammatically. When it does not, the result is **faulty predication.**

FAULTY PREDICATION The best kind of education for me would be a university with both a school of music and a school of government.

A university is an institution, not a type of education, so the sentence needs to be revised.

REVISED SENTENCE A university with both a school of music and a school of government would be best for me.

Avoid using the phrases *is where, is when,* and *the reason is . . . because.* These phrases may sound logical, but they usually result in faulty predication.

FAULTY PREDICATION Photosynthesis is where carbon dioxide, water, and chlorophyll interact in the presence of sunlight to form carbohydrates.

Photosynthesis is not a place, so *is where* is illogical. Also, to be grammatically correct, the linking verb *is* needs to be followed by a subject complement.

REVISED SENTENCE Photosynthesis is the production of carbohydrates from the interaction of carbon dioxide, water, and chlorophyll in the presence of sunlight.

Although *is because* may seem logical, it creates an adverb clause following the linking verb rather than the required subject complement.

FAULTY PREDICATION The reason the joint did not hold is because the coupling bolt broke.

To fix this kind of faulty predication, turn the adverb clause into a noun clause by changing *because* to *that,* or change the subject of the sentence.

► **The reason the joint did not hold is ~~because~~ *that* the coupling bolt broke.**

or

► **~~The reason the~~ *The* joint did not hold ~~is~~ because the coupling bolt broke.**

Exercise 40.1 Chapter review: Mixed constructions

Edit the following paragraph to eliminate mixed constructions. Some sentences may not need correction, and there may be several acceptable options for editing those that do need it.

Electrons spin around the nucleus of an atom according to definite rules. The single electron of a hydrogen atom occupies a kind of spherical shell around a single proton. According to the discoveries of quantum physics, states that we can never determine exactly where in this shell the electron is at a given time. The indeterminacy principle is a rule where we can only know the probability that the electron will be at a given point at a given moment. The set of places where the electron is most likely to be is called its orbital. By outlining a set of rules for the orbitals of electrons, the Austrian physicist Wolfgang Pauli developed the concept of the quantum state. Through using this concept permits scientists to describe the energy and behavior of any electron in a series of four numbers. The first of these, or principal quantum number, is where the average distance of the electron from the nucleus is specified. For the other quantum numbers describe the shape of the orbital and the "spin" of the electron. That no two electrons can ever be in exactly the same quantum state, according to Pauli's basic rule. The reason chemists use the four quantum numbers as a shorthand for each electron in an atom is because they can calculate the behavior of the atom as a whole.

41 Confusing Shifts

When you are editing, look for jarring shifts in point of view, tense, mood, or voice that may confuse your readers.

41a Identify and edit confusing shifts.

Confusing shifts can involve many of the problems discussed in other chapters of this handbook. Shifts in person and number, for example, may involve errors in pronoun-antecedent agreement (*see Chapter 36: Problems with Pronouns, pp. 586–91*). Often, however, confusing shifts occur in otherwise grammatically correct sentences.

In general, confusing shifts fall into four categories:

Four Categories of Confusing Shifts

1. Inappropriate shifts in person and number
2. Inappropriate shifts in verb tense
3. Inappropriate shifts in verb mood and voice
4. Inappropriate shifts from indirect to direct quotations and questions

Confusing Shifts and Grammar Checkers

Because confusing shifts can occur in otherwise grammatical sentences, computer grammar checkers rarely flag them. Consider this blatant example:

The teacher entered the room and then roll is called.

Although the sentence shifts confusingly from past to present tense and from active to passive voice, it passed muster on at least one grammar checker.

✓ 41b Make your point of view consistent in person and number.

A writer has three points of view to choose from. First person (*I* or *we*) emphasizes the writer and is used in personal writing. Second person (*you*) focuses attention on the readers and is used to give them orders, directions, or advice. Third person (*he, she, it, one,* or *they*) is topic oriented and therefore prevalent in academic writing. Once you choose a point of view, you should use it consistently.

1. Correcting shifts in person

Writers sometimes make jarring shifts in person when they compose generalizations. For example, the writer of the following sentence initially shifted from the third person (*students*) to the second person (*you*), a common kind of confusing shift.

► **According to the new rules, students will be allowed access to computers only if ~~you~~ *they* arrive before 9 p.m.**

Note: Do not use *you* unless you are addressing the reader directly. If you are writing *about* someone rather than *to* them, then use the third person.

2. Correcting shifts in number

Confusing shifts in number occur when writers switch from singular to plural or plural to singular for no apparent reason. To correct such shifts, you should usually choose the plural to avoid using *his or her* or introducing gender bias. (*See Chapter 36: Problems with Pronouns, pp. 588–90 and Chapter 48: Appropriate Language, pp. 693–95.*)

In the following sentence, the writer changed the singular noun *person* to the plural *people* to agree with the plural pronoun *they.*

People are
► ~~A person is~~ ^ often assumed to be dumb if they are attractive and smart if they are unattractive.

The alternative, changing the pronoun to the singular, would have resulted in gender bias or the awkward repetition of the phrase *he or she.*

Also be aware that confusing shifts in number can occur between nouns that are logically connected. As originally phrased, the following example sentence suggests that the students have only one pencil among them. There are two ways to clarify the confusion.

pencils
► **The students brought ~~a~~ soft lead ~~pencil~~ ^ to the exam.**

or

Each student
► **~~The students~~ ^ brought a soft lead pencil to the exam.**

Similarly, the following example sentence, as originally phrased, suggests that a group of job applicants might be sharing a single résumé. Again, two solutions are available.

résumés.
► **All of the applicants have ~~a~~ strong ~~résumé~~ ^.**

or

Every applicant has
► **~~All of the applicants have~~ ^ a strong résumé.**

Exercise 41.1 Making point of view consistent

Edit the following sentences so that they are consistent in person and number.

EXAMPLE

they
When people vote, ~~you~~ ^ participate in government.

or

you
When ~~people~~ ^ vote, you participate in government.

1. On November 30, 1974, archeologists discovered the 3.5 million-year-old skeleton of an early hominid (or human ancestor) you call Lucy.
2. If you consider how long ago Lucy lived, one might be surprised so many of her bones remained intact.

IDENTIFY AND EDIT
Confusing Shifts

shift

To avoid confusing shifts, ask yourself these questions as you edit your writing:

1. Does the sentence shift from one point of view to another? For example, does it shift from third person to second?

- Over the centuries, millions of laborers helped build and maintain the Great Wall of China, and *most of them* ~~if you were one, you probably~~ suffered great hardship as a result.

2. Are the verbs in your sentence consistent in the following ways:

In tense (past, present, or future)?

- Historians call the period before the unification of China the Warring States period. It *ended* ~~ends~~ when the ruler of the Ch'in state conquered the last of his independent neighbors.

In mood (statements vs. commands or hypothetical conditions)?

- If a similar wall *were* ~~is~~ built today, it would cost untold amounts of time and money.

In voice (active vs. passive)?

- The purpose of the wall was to protect against invasion, but *it also promoted* commerce. ~~was promoted by it also.~~

3. Are quotations and questions clearly phrased in either direct or indirect form?

- The visitor asked the guide*, "When* ~~when~~ did construction of the Great Wall begin?*"*
- The visitor asked the guide when ~~did~~ construction of the Great Wall *began.* ~~begin?~~

3. When an early hominid like Lucy reached full height, they were about three and a half feet tall.
4. When these early hominids were born, she could expect to live about thirty years.
5. Lucy and the other hominids who lived with her in what is today Ethiopia, Africa, all walked upright and could manipulate a tool with their dextrous hands.

✓ 41c Keep your verb tenses consistent.

Verb tenses show the time of an action in relation to other actions. Writers are expected to choose a time frame for their work—present, past, or future—and use it consistently, changing tense only when the meaning requires it. For example, the following sentence is about a *present* inquiry into *past* events and so requires a shift from present tense to past tense.

APPROPRIATE SHIFT IN TENSE Our inquiry begins with a look at how the Germanic invasions affected the identity of the late Roman world.

The following sentence, in contrast, refers only to past events, but it shifts confusingly from present tense to past tense.

CONFUSING SHIFT IN TENSE According to the traditional view, the medieval period begins when Rome fell.

REVISED According to the traditional view, the medieval period began when Rome fell.

You may find yourself shifting confusingly between past and present tense when narrating events that are still vivid in your mind.

► The wind was blowing a hundred miles an hour when suddenly there ~~is~~ *was* a big crash, and a tree ~~falls~~ *fell* into the living room.

You may also introduce inconsistencies when you are using the present perfect tense, perhaps because the past participle causes you to slip from present tense to past tense.

► She has admired many strange buildings at the university but ~~thought~~ *thinks* that the new Science Center ~~looked~~ *looks* completely out of place.

www.mhhe.com/mhhb2

For information and exercises on shifts in verb tense and voice, go to

Editing > Verb and Voice Shifts

41d Avoid unnecessary shifts in mood and voice.

Besides tense, verbs in a sentence also have a mood and a voice. There are three basic **moods:** the **indicative,** used to state or question facts, acts, and opinions; the **imperative,** used to give commands or advice; and the **subjunctive,** used to express wishes, conjectures, and hypothetical conditions. Unnecessary shifts in mood can confuse and distract your readers. Be on the lookout for shifts between the indicative and the subjunctive and between the indicative and the imperative.

- ► **If he ~~goes~~ *could go* to night school, he would take a course in accounting.**
- ► **The sign says that in case of emergency passengers should follow the instructions of the train crew and ~~don't~~ *should not* leave the train unless instructed to do so.**

Most verbs have two voices. In the **active voice** the subject does the acting; in the **passive voice** the subject is acted upon. Do not shift abruptly from one voice to the other, especially when the subject remains the same.

- ► **The Impressionist painters hated black. ~~Violet,~~ *They favored violet,* green, blue, pink, and red*.* ~~were favored by them.~~**

CHARTING the TERRITORY

Present Tense and Literary Works

By convention, the present tense is used to write about the content of literary works.

- ► **David Copperfield observes other people with a fine and sympathetic eye. He describes villains such as Mr. Murdstone and heroes such as Mr. Micawber in unforgettable detail. However, Copperfield ~~was~~ *is* not himself an especially interesting character.**

Exercise 41.2 Keeping verbs consistent in tense, mood, and voice

Edit the following sentences so that the verbs are consistent in tense, mood, and voice unless meaning requires a shift. If a sentence is correct as is, circle its number.

EXAMPLE

The Silk Road, the famous trade route that linked Asia and Europe, *followed* **~~follows~~ the Great Wall of China for much of its length.**

1. Many visitors who have looked with amazement at the Great Wall of China did not know that its origins reached back to the seventh century BCE.
2. In 221 BCE the ruler of the Ch'in state conquered the last of its independent neighbors and unifies China for the first time.

FIGURE 41.1 The Great Wall of China.

3. The Ch'in ruler ordered the walls the states had erected between themselves to be torn down, but the walls on the northern frontier were combined and reinforced.
4. Subsequent Chinese rulers extended and improved the wall until the seventeenth century CE, when it reached its present length of more than four thousand miles.
5. History shows that as a defense against invasion from the north, the wall was not always effective.
6. China was conquered by the Mongols in the thirteenth century, and the Manchus took control of the empire in the seventeenth century.
7. The wall, however, also served as a trade route and had helped open new regions to farming.
8. As a result, was it not for the wall, China's prosperity might have suffered.

41e Be alert to awkward shifts between direct and indirect quotations and questions.

Indirect quotations report what others wrote or said without repeating their words exactly. **Direct quotations** report the words of others exactly and should be enclosed in quotation marks. (*For more on punctuating quotations, see Chapter 54: Quotation Marks, pp. 755–60 and 763–65.*)

Shifts from one form of quotation to the other within a sentence can leave readers confused.

SHIFT: INDIRECT TO DIRECT QUOTATION	In his famous inaugural speech, President Kennedy called on Americans not to ask what their country could do for them but instead "ask what you can do for your country."
REVISED: INDIRECT	In his famous inaugural speech, President Kennedy called on Americans not to ask what their country could do for them but instead to ask what they could do for their country.
REVISED: DIRECT	In his famous inaugural speech, President Kennedy said, "My fellow Americans, ask not what your country can do for you; ask what you can do for your country."

Shifts from indirectly to directly posed questions are similarly confusing.

SHIFT: INDIRECT TO DIRECT QUESTION	The performance was so bad the audience wondered had the performers ever rehearsed.
REVISED: INDIRECT	The performance was so bad the audience wondered whether the performers had ever rehearsed.
REVISED: DIRECT	Had the performers ever rehearsed? The performance was so bad the audience was not sure.

Exercise 41.3 Chapter review: Confusing shifts

Edit the following passage, changing words as necessary to avoid confusing shifts.

From about the first to the eighth century CE the Moche civilization dominated the north coast of what is now Peru. The people of this remarkable civilization are sophisticated engineers and skilled artisans. They built enormous adobe pyramids and a vast system of irrigation canals was created and maintained. Moche smiths forged spectacular gold ornaments as well as copper tools and weapons. The Moche potter sculpted realistic-looking portraits and scenes of everyday life onto clay vessels; they also decorated vessels with intricate drawings of imposing and elaborately garbed figures involved in complex ceremonies. One such scene, which appeared on many Moche vessels, depicted a figure archaeologists call the Warrior Priest engaged in a ceremony that involves the ritual sacrifice of bound prisoners.

A question is what do these drawings represent. You wonder whether they depict Moche gods and mythological events, or do they represent actual figures from Moche society conducting actual Moche rituals? A dramatic discovery in 1987 provided an answer to these questions. In that year, archaeologists have uncovered a group of intact Moche tombs at a site called Sipán. In one of the tombs were the remains of a man who had been buried clothed in stunningly rich regalia. As this outfit was carefully removed by the archaeologists, they realized that it corresponded to the outfit worn by the Warrior Priest depicted on Moche pottery. If the warrior priest was just a mythological figure, then this tomb should not exist, but it did. In other words, the archaeologists realized, the man in the tomb was an actual Moche Warrior Priest.

42 Faulty Parallelism

Parallelism is the presentation of equal (or parallel) ideas in the same (or parallel) grammatical form: individual terms with individual terms, phrases with phrases, and clauses with clauses. It allows the concise expression of ideas and emphasizes connections among them.

► Little Red Riding Hood went

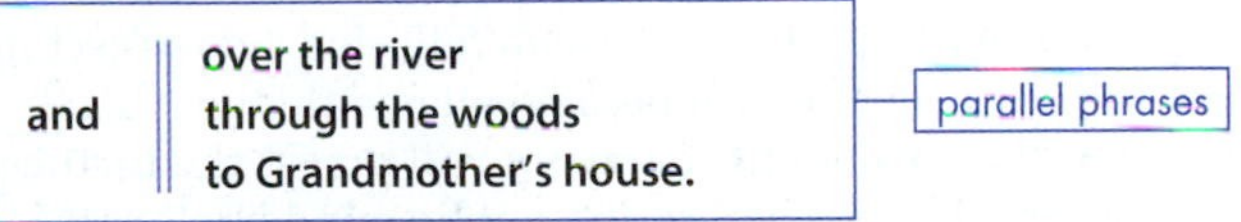

over the river
and through the woods
to Grandmother's house.
parallel phrases

► In the Declaration of Independence, Jefferson wrote, "We hold these truths to be self-evident:

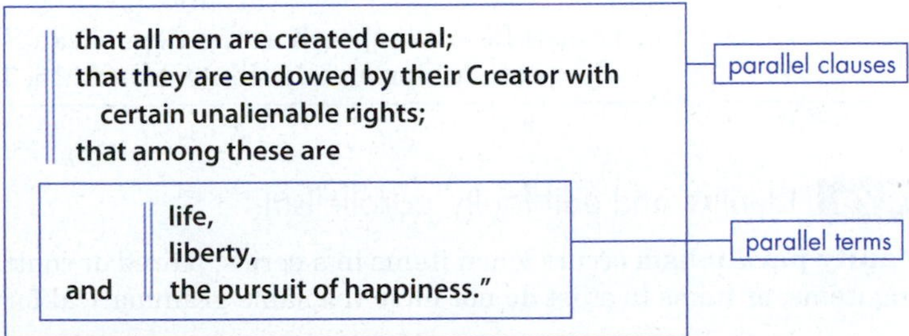

that all men are created equal;
that they are endowed by their Creator with certain unalienable rights;
that among these are
life,
liberty,
and the pursuit of happiness."
parallel clauses
parallel terms

A **balanced sentence** presents contrasting ideas using the same grammatical structure.

► **Horatio is not a major character or actor in the drama; he is a minor figure and foil to Hamlet.**

Parallel structure can unify the sentences in a paragraph. In his "I Have a Dream" speech, Martin Luther King Jr. states, "*Let freedom ring* from the snowcapped Rockies of Colorado! *Let freedom ring* from the curvaceous slopes of California! But not only that; *let freedom ring* from Stone Mountain of Georgia!

As you edit your writing, look for ways you can use parallelism to combine and give forceful expression to related ideas.

www.mhhe.com/mhhb2
For information and exercises on parallelism, go to
Editing > Parallelism

FIRST DRAFT

Claudius, Hamlet's uncle, strides confidently through the action of the play. His crown is ill-gotten, but he reaps its benefits. He smiles confidently. Those close to him are assured that he is indeed the rightful king.

REVISED

Claudius, Hamlet's uncle, strides confidently through the action of the play, *reaping* the benefits of his ill-gotten crown, *smiling* confidently, and *assuring* those close to him that he is indeed the rightful king.

Exercise 42.1 Identifying effective parallelism

Underline the parallel elements in the following passage.

> I believe this government cannot endure permanently half slave and half free. I do not expect the Union to be dissolved—I do not expect the house to fall—but I do expect it will cease to be divided. It will become all one thing, or all the other. Either the opponents of slavery will arrest the further spread of it, and place it where the public mind shall rest in the belief that it is in the course of ultimate extinction; or its advocates will push it forward till it shall become alike lawful in all the states, old as well as new, North as well as South.
>
> —ABRAHAM LINCOLN, speech at the Republican State Convention, Springfield, Illinois, June 16, 1858

✓ 42a Identify and edit faulty parallelism.

Faulty parallelism occurs when items in a series, paired or contrasting items, or items in a list do not have the same grammatical form.

Situations in Which Faulty Parallelism Occurs

1. In sentences that present equivalent items in a series
2. In sentences that pair equivalent items with a conjunction or contrast them with a comparative expression
3. In outlines and headings, and in numbered and bulleted lists

Faulty Parallelism and Grammar Checkers

Computer grammar checkers cannot recognize equivalent ideas that require parallel form.

42b Make items in a series parallel.

A list or series of equally important items should be parallel in grammatical structure. Phrases should balance phrases; clauses should balance clauses; and within phrases and clauses, equivalent elements should be of the same kind—nouns with nouns, for example, or verbs with verbs.

In the following sentence, the writer deleted *constructing* to make the last item in the series consistent with the rest of the items, which are all nouns or nouns modified by adjectives.

► **The development plan included apartment buildings, single-family houses, a park, and ~~constructing~~ two new schools.**

In the next sentence, the writer changed the last item in the series to give all three items the same form: action verb followed by direct object.

► **According to the Constitution, the president heads the executive branch of government, nominates the justices of the Supreme Court, and ~~is commander-in-chief of~~** *commands* **the nation's armed forces.**

In the next sentence, the writer changed a noun to an adjective. Notice that the writer also decided to repeat the word *too* to make the sentence more forceful and memorable.

► **My sister obviously thought that I was too young,** *too* **ignorant, and ~~a troublemaker.~~** *too troublesome.*

42c Make paired ideas parallel.

When you join ideas with a conjunction or distinguish between them with a comparative expression, state them in parallel form.

IDENTIFY AND EDIT Faulty Parallelism

//

To avoid faulty parallelism, ask yourself these questions as you edit your writing:

1. Are the items in a series in parallel form?

◆ The senator stepped to the podium, ~~an angry glance shooting toward~~ ^*glanced angrily at* her challenger, and began to refute his charges.

2. Are paired items in parallel form?

◆ Her challenger, she claimed, ~~had~~ not only ^*had* accused her falsely of accepting illegal campaign contributions, but ~~his contributions were from illegal sources also.~~ ^*also had accepted illegal contributions himself.*

3. Are the items in outlines and lists in parallel form?

FAULTY PARALLELISM

She listed four reasons for voters to send her back to Washington:

1. Ability to protect the state's interests
2. Her seniority on important committees
3. Works with members of both parties to get things done
4. Has a close working relationship with the president

REVISED

She listed four reasons for voters to send her back to Washington:

1. *Her ability* to protect the state's interests
2. *Her seniority* on important committees
3. *Her ability* to work with members of both parties to get things done
4. *Her* close working *relationship* with the president

1. Pairing ideas with coordinating conjunctions

Coordinating conjunctions—*and, but, or, nor, for, so,* and *yet*—join elements of equal weight or function.

FAULTY PARALLELISM	The job requires initiative and leading others.
REVISED	The job requires *initiative* and *leadership*.
FAULTY PARALLELISM	Climbing the mountain was hard, but to descend was not much easier.
REVISED	*Climbing* the mountain was hard, but *descending* was not much easier.

2. Pairing ideas with correlative conjunctions

Correlative conjunctions are paired words—*not only . . . but also; both . . . and; either . . . or; neither . . . nor*—that link sentence elements of equal value. To be parallel, the expressions that follow each element in the pair should have the same form.

FAULTY PARALLELISM	Successful teachers must both inspire students and also challenging them is important.
REVISED	Successful teachers must both *inspire* and *challenge* their students.
FAULTY PARALLELISM	The school board concluded not only that the district should enlarge the existing elementary school but also build another one.
REVISED	The school board concluded that the district should *not only enlarge* the existing elementary school *but also build* another one.

3. Comparing ideas with *than* or *as*

To be parallel, ideas compared with expressions involving *than* or *as* should have the same grammatical form.

FAULTY PARALLELISM	Many people find that having meaningful work is more important than high pay.
REVISED	Many people find that *having meaningful work* is more important than *earning high pay*.
REVISED	Many people find that *meaningful work* is more important than *high pay*.

42d Repeat function words as needed to keep parallels clear.

Function words indicate the function of or relationship among other words in a sentence. They include articles (*the, a, an*), prepositions (*to, for,* and *by,* for example), subordinating conjunctions (*because, although,* and *that,* for example), and the word *to* in infinitives (*to eat, to grow*). You can omit repeated function words from parallel structures whenever the structures are clear without them, but you should include them otherwise.

In the following sentence, the writer omitted the function word *to* from the second and third infinitives because the sentence is clear without the words.

► **Her goals for her retirement were to travel, ~~to~~ study art history, and ~~to~~ write a book about Michelangelo.**

The writer of the next sentence, however, repeated the infinitive *to* in order to make clear where one goal ends and the next begins.

► **The project has three goals: to survey the valley for Inca-period sites, ^to excavate a test trench at each site the survey locates, and ^to excavate one of those sites completely.**

Exercise 42.2 Correcting faulty parallelism

Revise the following sentences to eliminate any faulty parallelism.

EXAMPLE: ORIGINAL

Newlywed couples need to learn to communicate effectively and budget in a wise manner.

EXAMPLE: REVISED

Newlywed couples need to learn to communicate effectively and budget wisely.

1. *Impressionism* is a term that applies primarily to an art movement of the late nineteenth century, but the music of some composers of the era is also considered impressionist.
2. The early impressionists include Edouard Manet, Claude Monet, and Mary Cassatt, and also among them are Edgar Degas and Camille Pissarro.
3. Impressionist composers include Claude Debussy, and Maurice Ravel is considered an impressionist also.
4. Just as impressionism in art challenged accepted conventions of color and line, in music the challenge from impressionism was to accepted conventions of form and harmony.

FIGURE 42.1 ***At the Opera*, an impressionist painting by Mary Cassatt.**

5. Critics at first condemned both impressionist artists and impressionist music.
6. Women impressionist painters included Mary Cassatt from the United States and Berthe Morisot, who was French.
7. Among Monet's goals were to observe the changing effects of light and color on a landscape and record his observations quickly.
8. To accomplish these goals he would often create not just one but a series of paintings of a subject over the course of a day.

42e Make the items in outlines, headings, and lists parallel.

If you are writing a paper that includes headings or a formal outline of headings, make sure the items at each level of heading are consistent in emphasis and parallel in grammatical structure. (*See Chapter 3: Planning and Shaping the Whole Essay, pp. 47–50, for more on developing an outline and making headings parallel.*)

In the first-draft outline shown here, the writer mixed a phrase with a question in the first-level headings, and phrases with complete sentences in the second-level headings. In the revised outline, the writer opted for phrases throughout, with the phrases at each level of heading parallel in form with the others at the same level.

FIRST-DRAFT OUTLINE WITH FAULTY PARALLELISM

Germany's Path to Continuing Prosperity

- I. Economic realities
  - A. Large gap between eastern and western Germany's GDP
  - B. The public-sector deficit is ballooning.
  - C. Lower than expected FDI inflows
  - D. Steady increase in trade
- II. What are Germany's economic prospects?
  - A. Workforce and location attractive to investors
  - B. Negatives—labor costs, taxation rates, and regulations

REVISED OUTLINE

Germany's Path to Continuing Prosperity

- I. Economic realities
  - A. Large gap between eastern and western Germany's GDP
  - B. Ballooning public-sector deficits
  - C. Lower than expected FDI inflows
  - D. Steady increase in trade
- II. Economic prospects
  - A. Positives—workforce and location
  - B. Negatives—labor costs, taxation rates, and regulations

Items in a bulleted or numbered list should also be parallel.

NUMBERED LIST WITH FAULTY PARALLELISM

The plot can be reduced to seven main events:

1. Dorothy runs away from home but returns as a tornado strikes.
2. She is transported to Oz and gains the ruby slippers.
3. Befriends three fantastic creatures.
4. They met the Wizard, who sent them on a mission.
5. Dorothy confronts and destroys the Wicked Witch.
6. Dorothy and her friends learn that the Wizard is a fraud.
7. The return home.

REVISED LIST

The plot can be reduced to seven main events:

1. Dorothy runs away from home but returns as a tornado strikes.
2. She is transported to Oz and gains the ruby slippers.
3. She befriends three fantastic creatures.
4. They meet the Wizard, who sends them on a mission.
5. Dorothy confronts and destroys the Wicked Witch.
6. Dorothy and her friends learn that the Wizard is a fraud.
7. Dorothy returns home and is reunited with her family.

Exercise 42.3 Chapter review: Faulty parallelism

Edit the following passage so that parallel ideas are presented in parallel structures.

People can be classified as either Type A or Type B personalities depending on their competitiveness, how perfectionistic they are, and ability to relax. Type A people are often workaholics who not only drive themselves hard but also are driving others hard. In the workplace, employers often like Type A personalities because they tend to work quickly, punctually, and are efficient. However, because Type A people can characteristically also be impatient, verbally aggressive, or show hostility, they tend not to rise to top management positions as often as Type B people. Type A people also tend to be acutely aware of time, talking quickly, they interrupt when others are speaking, and try to complete other people's sentences. A Type B person in contrast takes the world in stride, walking and talking more slowly, and listens attentively. Type B people are better at dealing with stress and keep things in perspective, rather than being worried the way Type A people do.

People with traits that put them clearly on either end of the continuum between Type A and Type B should try to adopt characteristics of the opposite type. For example, to moderate some of their characteristic behaviors and reduce their risk of high blood pressure and heart disease, Type A people can use exercise, relaxation techniques, diet, and meditate. Understanding one's personality is half the battle, but implementing change takes time, discipline, and patience is needed.

43 Misplaced and Dangling Modifiers

When a modifying word, phrase, or clause is misplaced or dangling, readers get confused.

43a Identify and edit misplaced modifiers.

A **modifier** is misplaced when the reader cannot easily determine what it modifies or when it awkwardly disrupts the flow of a sentence. Be on the alert for **misplaced modifiers** as you revise your writing.

Misplaced Modifiers

1. Fall confusingly far from the expressions they modify
2. Ambiguously modify more than one expression
3. Awkwardly disrupt the relationships among the grammatical elements of a sentence

www.mhhe.com/mhhb2
For information and exercises on misplaced modifiers, go to
Editing > Misplaced Modifiers

43b Put modifiers close to the words they modify.

For clarity, modifiers should come immediately before or after the words they modify. In the next example, the clause *after the police arrested them* modifies *protesters,* not *destroying.* Putting the clause before the word it modifies makes it clear that if any property destruction occurred, it occurred before—not after—the arrest.

Misplaced Modifiers and Grammar Checkers

Some computer grammar checkers reliably flag split infinitives but only occasionally flag other types of misplaced modifiers. One grammar checker, for example, flagged the split infinitive in this sentence:

The sign asks people to not walk on the grass.

It also caught the misplaced modifier in this sentence:

SAT scores may in comparison to other measures of academic potential be overrated.

It missed, however, the misplaced modifier *with a loud crash* in this sentence:

The valuable vase with a loud crash fell to the floor and broke into hundreds of pieces.

After the police arrested them, the

► ~~The~~ protesters were charged with destroying college property. ~~after the police arrested them.~~

Like adverbial clauses, prepositional phrases used as adverbs are easy to misplace. The following sentence was revised to make it clear that the hikers were watching the storm from the porch.

From the cabin's porch, the

► ~~The~~ hikers watched the storm gathering force. ~~from the cabin's porch.~~

43c Clarify ambiguous modifiers.

Because adverbs can modify what precedes or what follows them, it is important that writers position adverbs carefully.

1. Moving squinting modifiers

A modifier that could describe either what precedes or what follows it is called a **squinting modifier** and should be repositioned for clarity. As originally written, the following sentence leaves unclear whether the historians in question are *objecting vehemently* or *arguing vehemently*. Changing the position of *vehemently* eliminates this ambiguity.

vehemently

► Historians who object to this account ~~vehemently~~ argue that the presidency was never endangered.

IDENTIFY AND EDIT
Misplaced Modifiers

mm

To avoid misplaced modifiers, ask yourself these questions as you edit your writing:

1. Are all the modifiers close to the expressions they modify?

At the beginning of the Great Depression, people
- ~~People~~ ^ panicked and all tried to get their money out of the banks at the same time, forcing many banks to close.^ ~~at the beginning of the Great Depression.~~

2. Are any modifiers placed in such a way that they modify more than one expression? Pay particular attention to limiting modifiers such as only, even, *and* just.

- President Roosevelt ^*quickly* declared a bank holiday, ^ ~~quickly~~ helping to restore confidence in the nation's financial system.
- Congress enacted many programs to combat the Depression ~~only~~ within ^*only* the first one hundred days of Roosevelt's presidency.

3. Do any modifiers disrupt the relationships among the grammatical elements of the sentence?

Given how entrenched segregation was at the time, the
- ~~The~~ ^ president's wife, Eleanor, was a surprisingly strong~~, given how entrenched segregation was at the time,~~ advocate for racial justice in Roosevelt's administration.

2. Repositioning limiting modifiers

Problems often occur with **limiting modifiers** such as *only, even, almost, nearly,* and *just.* When you edit, check every sentence that includes one of these modifiers. In the next example, does the writer mean that vegetarian dishes are the only dishes served at dinner or that dinner is the only time when vegetarian dishes are available? Editing clears up the ambiguity.

AMBIGUOUS The restaurant *only offers* vegetarian dishes for dinner.

REVISED The restaurant *offers only* vegetarian dishes for dinner.

REVISED The restaurant *offers* vegetarian dishes *only* at dinner.

43d Move disruptive modifiers.

When a lengthy modifying phrase or clause separates grammatical elements that belong together, the resulting sentence can be difficult to read.

It is often acceptable to separate a subject from its verb with a long adjectival phrase that modifies the subject, as in the following sentence.

► **Descartes and Hume, two of Europe's most prominent philosophers, deal with the issue of personal identity in different ways.**

In contrast, a long adverbial phrase between subject and verb is almost always awkward. In the following sentence, the adverbial phrase beginning with *despite* initially came between the subject and verb, disrupting the flow of the sentence. With the modifying phrase at the beginning of the sentence, the edited version restores the connection between subject and verb.

Despite their similar conceptions of the self,

► **^Descartes and Hume~~, despite their similar conceptions of the self,~~ deal with the issue of personal identity in different ways.**

An adverb or adverbial phrase that falls between a verb and its direct object is also likely to be disruptive.

bitterly

► **Newton^ contested ~~bitterly~~ Leibniz's claim to have invented calculus.**

, without any apparent hesitation,

► **The *Jeopardy* contestant^ answered ~~without any apparent hesitation~~ the question.**

43e Avoid splitting infinitives.

An **infinitive** couples the word *to* with the base form of a verb. In a **split infinitive,** one or more words intervene between *to* and the verb form. Avoid separating the parts of an infinitive with a modifier unless keeping them together results in an awkward or ambiguous construction.

In the following sentence, the word *not* awkwardly splits the infinitive *to disturb* and should be moved to precede it.

not

► **The librarian asks us to ~~not~~ disturb other patrons.**

In the next example, however, the modifier *successfully* should be moved, but the modifier *carefully* should probably stay where it is, even though it splits the infinitive *to assess. Carefully* needs to be close to the verb it modifies, but putting it between *have* and *to* would be awkward, and putting it after *assess* would cause ambiguity because readers might think it modifies *projected economic benefits.*

successfully,

► **To ~~successfully~~ complete this assignment students have to carefully assess projected economic benefits in relation to potential social problems.**

Exercise 43.1 Repositioning misplaced modifiers

Edit the following sentences to correct any misplaced modifiers. If a sentence is acceptable as written, circle its number.

EXAMPLE

Although

~~Global warming has received, although~~ long a cause for concern among

global warming has received

scientists and environmentalists, scant attention from some governments.

1. R. Buckminster Fuller developed during his career as an architect and engineer some of the most important design innovations of the twentieth century.
2. Fuller, a weak student, was expelled from Harvard.
3. Fuller resolved to dedicate his life to improving people's lives after suffering from a period of severe depression at the age of 32.
4. Fuller intended his efficient designs to not waste precious resources.
5. Those who doubted Fuller often were proved wrong.
6. Fuller is known as the inventor of the geodesic dome to most people today.
7. The geodesic dome is a spherical structure that is both lightweight and economical, which Fuller developed in the late 1940s.
8. Today there are more than 300,000 domes around the world based on Fuller's designs.

9. His contention that wind generators on high-voltage transmission towers could supply much of the electricity the United States needs, policy makers have largely ignored.
10. His twenty-eight books have sold more than a million copies, in which he wrote about a range of social, political, cultural, and economic issues.

✓ 43f Learn to identify and edit dangling modifiers.

A **dangling modifier** is a descriptive phrase that implies an actor different from the sentence's subject. When readers try to connect the

IDENTIFY AND EDIT Dangling Modifiers

dm

To avoid dangling modifiers, ask yourself these questions when you see a descriptive phrase at the beginning of a sentence:

1. What is the subject of the sentence?

- Snorkeling in Hawaii, ancient sea turtles were an amazing sight.

The subject of the sentence is *sea turtles*.

2. Could the phrase at the beginning of the sentence possibly describe this subject?

- Snorkeling in Hawaii, ancient sea turtles were an amazing sight. [? arrows linking "Snorkeling" and "turtles"]

No, sea turtles do not snorkel in Hawaii or anywhere else.

3. Who or what is the phrase really describing? Either make that person or thing the subject of the main clause, or add a subject to the modifier.

- Snorkeling in Hawaii, ^we saw^ ancient sea turtles, ~~were~~ an amazing sight.
- ~~Snorkeling~~ ^While we were snorkeling^ in Hawaii, ancient sea turtles ~~were an amazing sight.~~ ^amazed us.^

modifying phrase with the subject, the results may be humorous as well as confusing.

The following sentence, for example, describes a *crowded beach* as *swimming.*

DANGLING MODIFIER *Swimming toward the boat on the horizon,* the crowded beach felt as if it were miles away.

www.mhhe.com/mhhb2
For information and exercises on avoiding dangling modifiers, go to
Editing > Dangling Modifiers

Fixing a dangling modifier requires explicitly naming its implied actor, either as the subject of the sentence or in the modifier itself.

REVISED Swimming toward the boat on the horizon, *I* felt as if the crowded beach were miles away.

REVISED As *I swam* toward the boat on the horizon, the crowded beach seemed miles away.

Note that you usually can not correct a dangling modifier simply by moving it. In the following sentence, for example, no matter where the modifying phrase falls, the sentence retains its unintended meaning, that the town had been struggling in the wilderness for weeks. (The intended subject, *them*, appears in the sentence but not as the grammatical subject.)

DANGLING MODIFIER *After struggling for weeks in the wilderness,* the town pleased them mightily.

STILL DANGLING The town pleased them mightily *after struggling for weeks in the wilderness.*

To revise, make the actor implied in the modifying phrase explicit.

REVISED After struggling for weeks in the wilderness, *they* were mightily pleased to come upon the town.

Use of the passive voice can lead to dangling modifiers, particularly when the subject of the sentence is not named.

DANGLING MODIFIER To survive in the desert, adaptations are needed.

REVISED To survive in the desert, animals must develop adaptations.

Dangling Modifiers and Grammar Checkers

Computer grammar checkers cannot distinguish a descriptive phrase that properly modifies the subject of the sentence from one that implies a different actor. As a result, they do not flag dangling modifiers.

Exercise 43.2 Correcting dangling modifiers

Edit the following sentences to correct any dangling modifiers. If a sentence is acceptable as is, circle its number.

EXAMPLE

Passengers ^ *that was entering the station* ^

~~Entering the station, passengers~~ waited to board the train.

1. Admired by many women artists as a pioneer in the mostly male art world, Georgia O'Keeffe lived and worked without regard to social conventions or artistic trends.
2. One of the most admired American artists of the twentieth century, her color-saturated images of cactus flowers, bleached bones, and pale skies are widely reproduced.
3. Growing up in Wisconsin, art was always important to her.
4. Defending her gifted student to the principal, one of her teachers said, "When the spirit moves Georgia, she can do more in a day than you or I can do in a week."
5. Without informing her, some of O'Keeffe's drawings were exhibited by Alfred Steiglitz at his 291 Gallery.
6. Marrying in 1924, O'Keeffe and Steiglitz enjoyed one of the most fruitful collaborations of the modernist era.

Exercise 43.3 Chapter review: Misplaced and dangling modifiers

Edit the following passage to eliminate any misplaced or dangling modifiers.

Henri Matisse and Pablo Picasso are considered often to have been the formative artists of the twentieth century. Although rivals for most of their careers, a traveling exhibit called "Matisse Picasso" exhibited their work side by side in museums in London, Paris, and New York.

Picasso's work may in comparison to Matisse's be more disturbing, and some say it is, in addition, more daring and experimental. Yet Matisse too, with his use of vivid colors and distorted shapes, was a daring innovator.

Looking for similarities, the works of both artists suggest an underlying anxiety. Yet each in different ways responded to this anxiety. Matisse painted tranquil yet often emotionally charged domestic scenes, whereas Picasso fought his inner fears with often jarringly disquieting images, by contrast.

44 Coordination and Subordination

Coordination and subordination are tools for structuring sentences to clarify the relationships among the ideas you want to convey. Used effectively, these tools add grace and energy to your writing and help your readers follow your train of thought.

44a Identify coordination and subordination and use them effectively.

www.mhhe.com/mhhb2

For information and exercises on coordination and subordination, go to

Editing > Coordination and Subordination

Coordination gives two or more ideas equal weight.

equal ideas

► **The sky grew dark, and the wind began to howl.**

equal ideas

► **The newlyweds were poor but happy.**

Subordination makes one idea depend on another and is therefore used to combine ideas that are not of equal importance.

subordinate idea / main idea

► **Because the storm knocked the power out, we ate dinner by candlelight.**

Coordination, Subordination, and Grammar Checkers

Computer grammar and style checkers can flag some of the problems associated with coordination and subordination, like errors in punctuation, for example, or excessively long sentences. Only a human, however, can evaluate relationships among ideas and decide how best to use coordination and subordination to structure those ideas in sentences.

Note: The abbreviation used to flag faulty or excessive coordination is *coord*.

The abbreviation used to flag inappropriate or faulty subordination is *sub*.

44b Use coordination to combine ideas of equal importance.

Coordination should be used only when two or more ideas deserve equal emphasis. You can use coordination to join phrases and words within clauses or to join two or more independent clauses.

1. To coordinate words and phrases within a clause, join them with a coordinating conjunction (*and, but, or, for, nor, yet,* or *so*).

► **The auditorium was huge *and* acoustically imperfect.**

2. To coordinate two or more independent clauses, use a comma plus a coordinating conjunction, insert a semicolon by itself, or insert a semicolon and a conjunctive adverb such as *moreover, nevertheless, however, therefore,* or *subsequently.* (*For more on conjunctive adverbs, see Chapter 30: Parts of Speech, pp. 489–90.*)

► **The tenor bellowed loudly, *but* no one in the back could hear him.**

► **The days are getting shorter; winter is approaching.**

► **Jones did not agree with her position on health care; *nevertheless,* he supported her campaign for office.**

3. You can also coordinate words, phrases, and independent clauses with a correlative conjunction such as *not only . . . but also; both . . . and, either . . . or.*

► **The scholarship included *not only* full tuition *but also* money for living expenses.**

► ***Either* Frodo will destroy the ring of power *or* Sauron will destroy Middle Earth.**

44c Avoid faulty or excessive coordination.

1. Recognizing faulty coordination

When writers use coordination to join elements that are not logically equivalent or to join elements with an inappropriate coordinating word, the result is **faulty coordination.**

The following sentence, for example, is confusing because the writer has coordinated two ideas that are not equivalent.

FAULTY COORDINATION The tortoise beat the hare, but the hare is a faster runner than the tortoise.

What the writer wants to say is that the tortoise won *despite* the hare's ability to run faster than the tortoise. The idea of the hare's speed is subordinate, not equal to, the idea of the tortoise's victory.

REVISED The tortoise beat the hare even though the hare can run faster than the tortoise.

Be sure to use the coordinating conjunction that reflects the relationship between the elements you are coordinating. The conjunction *and,* for example, suggests equivalence, whereas *but* suggests contrast. *Or* suggests options, *for* implies cause, and *so* suggests a result.

FAULTY COORDINATION The hare was fast, *and* victory went to the sure and steady tortoise.

REVISED The hare was fast, *but* victory went to the sure and steady tortoise.

2. Avoiding excessive coordination

When writers use coordination to string together too many ideas at once, the result is **excessive coordination.**

EXCESSIVE COORDINATION

The speedy hare challenged the plodding tortoise to a race and immediately established a large early lead, but his initial burst of speed tired him and, feeling sure of himself, he decided to rest a bit before finishing the race, but he fell asleep, and the tortoise passed him and won, so the moral of the story is, "Sure and steady wins the race."

REVISED

The speedy hare challenged the plodding tortoise to a race. The hare established a large early lead, but his initial burst of speed tired him. Feeling sure of himself, he decided to rest a bit before finishing the race. He fell asleep, however, and the tortoise passed him and won. The moral of the story is, "Sure and steady wins the race."

44d Use subordination for ideas of unequal importance.

Subordination, not coordination, should be used to indicate that information is of secondary importance and to show its logical relation to the main idea.

When the
► ~~The~~ police arrived, ~~and~~ the burglars ran away.

► The fourth set of needs to be met, ~~are~~ esteem needs, ~~and they~~
includes
~~include~~ the need for success, self-respect, and prestige.

To show the relationship between ideas of unequal importance, express the main idea in an independent clause and secondary ideas in subordinate clauses or phrases.

> ***Note:*** Commas often set off subordinate ideas, especially when the subordinate clause or phrase opens the sentence. (*For more on using commas, see Chapter 51: Commas, pp. 718–45.*)

1. Put secondary ideas in subordinate clauses introduced by a relative pronoun (adjective clause) or a subordinating conjunction (adverb clause). The relative pronouns include *who, whom, that, which, whoever, whomever,* and *whose.*

   , which will be added to the beaker later,
   ► **The blue liquid ^ must be kept at room temperature. ~~It will be added to the beaker later.~~**

   , who penned the phrase "All men are created equal,"
   ► **Thomas Jefferson ^ was a slaveholder. ~~He penned the phrase "All men are created equal."~~**

Subordinating conjunctions include *after, although, because, if, since, when,* and *where.* (*For a fuller list of subordinating conjunctions, see Chapter 30: Parts of Speech, p. 493.*)

, although he
► **Christopher Columbus encountered the Americas in 1492/ ^ ~~He~~ never understood just what he had found.**

After he *, Wordsworth*
► **^ ~~Wordsworth~~ wrote the opening four sections/ ^ ~~He~~ put the work aside for two years.**

2. Put secondary ideas in appositive phrases (*see Chapter 31: Sentence Basics, p. 505*).

   , one of the founders of the women's rights movement in the United States,
   ► **Elizabeth Cady Stanton ^ helped organize the Seneca Falls Convention of 1848. ~~She was one of the founders of the women's rights movement in the United States.~~**

3. Put secondary ideas in other modifying phrases or words.

   Hoping for a better life, my
   ► **^ ~~My~~ grandparents immigrated to the United States in the late nineteenth century. ~~They were hoping for a better life.~~**

powerful *destructive, fast-moving*
► The ^ earthquake triggered a ^ tsunami. ~~The earthquake was powerful.~~ ~~The tsunami was destructive and fast-moving.~~

44e Avoid faulty or excessive subordination.

1. Making major ideas the focus

Major ideas belong in main clauses, not in subordinate clauses or phrases where readers are unlikely to give them the attention they deserve. The writer revised the following sentence because the subject of the paper was definitions of literacy, not who values literacy.

FAULTY SUBORDINATION	Literacy, which has been defined as the ability to talk intelligently about many topics, is highly valued by businesspeople as well as academics.
REVISION	Highly valued by businesspeople as well as academics, literacy has been defined as the ability to talk intelligently about many topics.

SUBORDINATING WORDS and THEIR MEANINGS

Subordinating words fall into a variety of meaning categories. These include

- **time**—*after, as, before, since, until, when, whenever, while*
  Before the race began, the hare was confident of victory.
- **place**—*where, wherever*
  The tortoise passed the spot *where* the hare lay sleeping.
- **identification**—*that, which, who, whose*
  The tortoise, *who* never stopped to rest, passed the hare.
- **cause or effect**—*as, because, since, so that*
  The hare lost *because* he fell asleep.
- **purpose**—*in order that, so that, that*
  The hare stopped *so that* he could rest and catch his breath.
- **condition**—*if, provided that, unless*
  If the hare hadn't stopped, he would have won.
- **contrast**—*although, as if, even though, though, whereas, while*
  The tortoise, *although* much the slower of the two contestants, won the race.

2. Choosing the right subordinating word

When you subordinate one idea to another, make sure to choose a subordinating word that properly and unambiguously expresses the logical relationship between the two ideas (*see the box "Subordinating Words and Their Meanings" on page 657*).

The subordinating word *since* in the following example is ambiguous. Does it refer to time or cause? Revision clears up the confusion.

FAULTY SUBORDINATION	Since she won reelection, the mayor has acted on her plan to increase salaries for town officials.
REVISION	Since winning reelection, the mayor has acted to increase salaries for town officials.
REVISION	Winning reelection has permitted the mayor to propose salary increases for town officials.

The writer of the next example has inappropriately used the relative pronoun *where,* which specifies location, to introduce a subordinate clause that refers to time.

FAULTY SUBORDINATION	Where time permits, students should take advantage of the city's museums.
REVISION	*When* time permits, students should take advantage of the city's museums.

Like is a preposition that can introduce examples: *I enjoy Asian foods like spring rolls and Pad Thai.* While *like* is sometimes used to join clauses in everyday speech, academic writing requires the conjunction *as*.

► **The movie was exciting ~~like~~ ^as a thriller should be.**

3. Avoiding excessive subordination

Excessive subordination results from stringing together too many subordinate expressions at once. Like excessive coordination, it can leave readers confused. When a sentence seems overloaded, try separating it into two or more sentences.

EXCESSIVE SUBORDINATION

Big-city mayors, who are supported by public funds, should be cautious about spending taxpayers' money for personal needs, such as home furnishings, especially when municipal budget shortfalls have caused extensive job layoffs, angering city workers and the general public.

REVISED

Big-city mayors should be cautious about spending taxpayers' money for personal needs, especially when municipal budget shortfalls have caused extensive job layoffs. They risk angering city workers and the general public by using public funds for home furnishings.

For MULTILINGUAL STUDENTS

Language-Specific Differences in Coordination and Subordination

The English rhetorical tradition prizes subordination. However, the rhetorical traditions associated with other languages—Arabic and Farsi, for example—stress coordination, favoring constructions that may strike English-speaking readers as awkward. Be aware of these cultural preferences as you write, and try to achieve a balance of structural patterns.

Exercise 44.1 Using coordination and subordination

Combine the following sets of sentences, using coordination, subordination, or both to clarify the relationships among ideas.

EXAMPLE

France was a major player in Europe's late-nineteenth-century imperial expansion. It began the conquest of Vietnam in 1858. By 1883 it controlled the entire country.

France, a major player in Europe's late-nineteenth-century imperial expansion, began its conquest of Vietnam in 1858 and controlled the entire country by 1883.

1. France divided Vietnam into three administrative regions. This was before World War II.
2. Most Vietnamese opposed French rule. Many groups formed to regain the country's independence.
3. Vietnam remained a French-administered colony during World War II. It was under Japanese control, however, from 1940 to 1945.
4. By the end of the war, a Communist group called the Viet Minh had emerged as Vietnam's dominant nationalist organization. Ho Chi Minh (1890–1969) was the leader of the Viet Minh.

5. In 1945 the Viet Minh declared independence. They took control of northern Vietnam. The French, however, regained control of the south. The British helped the French.
6. The French reached an agreement with Ho Chi Minh in 1946. The agreement would have made Vietnam an autonomous country tied to France.
7. The agreement broke down. War started. The French wanted to reassert colonial control over all of Vietnam. Ho Chi Minh wanted total independence.
8. The United States supported the French. Russia and China supported the Viet Minh.
9. The French suffered a major defeat at Dien Bien Phu in 1954. After that they realized they could not defeat the Viet Minh.
10. An agreement reached in Geneva left Vietnam divided into two regions. One region was the communist-controlled north. The other region was the noncommunist south.

Exercise 44.2 Avoiding inappropriate or excessive coordination and subordination

Rewrite the numbered passages that follow to eliminate inappropriate or excessive coordination or subordination. Do not hesitate to break up long strings of clauses into two or more sentences when it seems appropriate to do so.

EXAMPLE

The Industrial Revolution triggered economic and social upheavals, including changes in family structure, patterns of work, and the distribution of wealth, and in 1848, in the wake of these upheavals, the governments of France, Italy, and several central European countries were all threatened with revolution.

The Industrial Revolution triggered economic and social upheavals, including changes in family structure, patterns of work, and the distribution of wealth. In 1848, in the wake of these upheavals, the governments of France, Italy, and several central European countries were all threatened with revolution.

1. During the early years of the Industrial Revolution, the many thousands of people who had left the countryside to move to Europe's fast-growing cities in search of work encountered poverty, disease, lack of sanitation, and exhausting, dangerous factory jobs, making cities breeding grounds for insurrection, and this threat of unrest increased after an international financial crisis in 1848 and the epidemic of bankruptcies and unemployment that followed it.

2. France's King Louis-Phillipe, hopelessly unpopular, abdicated the throne in February and the country was thrown into a revolution in which citizens set up barricades in the narrow streets of Paris, restricting the movement of government troops.
3. Revolutionary fervor also took hold in Vienna, the capital of the Austrian Empire, and at the same time, nationalist forces gained strength in Hungary and other regions of the empire, prompting Hungarian nationalists to demand autonomy from Vienna and radicals in Prague to demand greater autonomy for the empire's Slavic peoples.
4. By the middle of 1848, however, events had begun to turn against the revolutionaries, and the rulers of the Austrian Empire used divisions among the revolutionaries to reassert their power, and the Empire provided supplies and encouragement to Romanian nationalists who feared persecution in an independent Hungary.

44f Use coordination and subordination to combine short, choppy sentences.

Short sentences are easy to read, but several of them in a row can become so monotonous that meaning gets lost.

CHOPPY My cousin Jim is not an accountant. Nevertheless he does my taxes every year. He suggests various deductions. These deductions reduce my tax bill considerably.

You can use subordination to combine a series of short, choppy sentences like these to form a longer, more meaningful sentence. Put the idea you want to emphasize in the main clause, and use subordinate clauses and phrases to include the other ideas. In the following revision, the main clause is italicized.

REVISED Even though he is not an accountant, *my cousin Jim does my taxes every year,* suggesting various deductions that reduce my tax bill considerably.

If a series of short sentences includes two major ideas of equal importance, use coordination for the two major ideas and subordinate the secondary information. The following revision shows that Smith's and Johnson's opinions are equally important. The information about bilingual education is of secondary interest.

CHOPPY Bilingual education is designed for children. The native language of these children is not English. Smith supports bilingual education. Johnson opposes bilingual education.

REVISED Smith supports bilingual education for children whose native language is not English; Johnson, however, opposes bilingual education.

Exercise 44.3 Chapter review: Coordination and subordination

Edit the following passage to correct faulty coordination and subordination, and to eliminate choppy sentences and excessive coordination and subordination.

Germany and Italy were not always unified nations. For centuries they were divided into many city-states. They were also divided into many kingdoms, dukedoms, fiefdoms, and principalities. These city-states, kingdoms, dukedoms, fiefdoms, and principalities had maintained their autonomy for centuries.

Largely responsible for the unifications of Italy and Germany were two men. These men were Camillo di Cavour and Otto von Bismarck. Cavour became prime minister of the republic of Piedmont in 1852. Bismarck became chancellor of Prussia in 1862. Cavour was a practitioner of *realpolitik,* and *realpolitik* is a political policy based on the ruthless advancement of national interests. Bismarck was also a practitioner of *realpolitik.*

Cavour hoped to govern Piedmont in a way that would inspire other Italian states to join it to form a unified nation. Increasing the power of parliament, modernizing agriculture and industry, and building a railroad that encouraged trade with the rest of Europe, he also modernized the port of Genoa, updated the court system and installed a king, Victor Emmanuel, all of which made hopes for nationhood center on Piedmont. With the help of Napoleon III, Cavour engaged in a crafty political maneuver. Napoleon III was the emperor of France. Cavour induced Austria to attack Piedmont and then with French help defeated the Austrian armies, thus inspiring Modena and Tuscany to join Piedmont.

Bismarck used similar tactics in pursuit of unification as he prearranged French neutrality, and then he attacked and destroyed the Austrian army at Sadowa, and he eliminated Austrian influence in Prussia, and he paved the way for Prussian control of a large north German federation by 1867. Both men continued to use these tactics until they succeeded with the unification of Germany in 1871 and of Italy in 1879.

45 Sentence Variety and Emphasis

Readers will tune out a writer whose sentences and paragraphs are uniform in length and structure. Monotonous writing, like the first of the two passages that follow, is a chore to read. Lively writing, like the second passage, keeps readers engaged and focused on the writer's arguments. The key to lively writing is variety.

MONOTONOUS

The Greek historian Herodotus called Egypt "the gift of the Nile." He might have called Harappan society "the gift of the Indus." He did not know about Harappan society, however. The Nile's waters come from rain and melting snow in towering mountains. The waters of the Indus come from rain and melting snow in the Hindu Kush and the Himalayas. The Himalayas have the world's highest peaks. The waters of both rivers charge downhill. They pick up enormous quantities of silt. They carry the silt for hundreds of kilometers. The waters lose force as they course through lowlands. As they do so, they deposit a burden of rich soil.

VARIED AND LIVELY

If the Greek historian Herodotus had known of Harappan society, he might have called it "the gift of the Indus." Like the Nile, the Indus draws its waters from rain and melting snow in towering mountains—in this case, the Hindu Kush and Himalayas, the world's highest peaks. As the waters charge downhill, they pick up enormous quantities of silt, which they carry for hundreds of kilometers. Like the Nile again, the Indus then deposits its burden of rich soil as it courses through lowlands and loses its force.

—from Bentley and Ziegler, *Traditions and Encounters,* second edition, p. 91

> ***Note:*** The abbreviation used to flag a passage that needs greater variety is *var*.

Variety, Emphasis, and Grammar Checkers

Monotony is not a grammatical error. A computer grammar checker might flag a very long sentence or a repeated word, but it can not decide whether the sentence is too long, whether the repetition is unwarranted, or whether ideas deserve emphasis.

www.mhhe.com/mhhb2
For information and exercises on sentence variety, go to
Editing > Sentence Variety

45a Vary your sentence openings.

In a simple English sentence, the subject usually comes first. When you begin all the sentences in a passage with the subject, however, you risk losing your readers' attention. To open some of your sentences in a different way, try moving a modifier to the beginning.

Adverbial modifiers are words, phrases, or clauses that modify verbs, adjectives, and other adverbs, as well as whole phrases and clauses. You can often position them in a variety of places in a sentence, including the beginning.

Eventually,
► ^Armstrong's innovations ~~eventually~~ became the standard.

In at least two instances, this
► ^~~This~~ money-making strategy backfired^. ~~in at least two instances.~~

Adjectival modifiers are words and phrases that modify nouns. They include participles and participial phrases, which you can often place at the beginning of a sentence for variety. *(For more on participles and participial phrases, see Chapter 31: Sentence Basics, p. 504.)*

Pushing the other children aside,
► ^Joseph~~, pushing the other children aside,~~ demanded that the teacher give him a cookie first.

Stunned by the stock market crash, many
► ^~~Many~~ brokers~~, stunned by the stock market crash,~~ committed suicide.

> ***Caution:*** If you decide to put a participial phrase at the beginning of a sentence, make sure that the phrase describes the explicit subject of the sentence or you will end up with a dangling modifier. *(See Chapter 43: Misplaced and Dangling Modifiers, pp. 650–51.)*

Clarify relationships between two sentences by starting the second with a transitional expression or coordinating conjunction.

However, today
► She usually walks in the park in the afternoon. ^~~Today~~ she stayed inside because it was raining.

But after
► I usually love dessert. ^~~After~~ that meal I couldn't eat another bite.

You also can place an infinitive phrase, appositive phrase, or absolute phrase at the beginning of a sentence. *(See Chapter 31: Sentence Basics, pp. 504–05.)*

For MULTILINGUAL STUDENTS

Adverbial Modifiers and Subject-Verb Order

In standard English word order, the subject of a sentence precedes the verb. When certain adverbs come at the beginning of a sentence, however, they force changes in this order, usually requiring the subject to fall between a helping verb and the main verb. Adverbs that have this effect include *never, not since, seldom, rarely, in no case,* and *not until.*

subj | help verb | main verb

FAULTY **Rarely Simon has tried harder at work than he did today.**

help verb | subj | main verb

REVISED **Rarely has Simon tried harder at work than he did today.**

subj | verb

FAULTY **Never we expected such a difficult assignment.**

help verb | subj | main verb

REVISED **Never did we expect such a difficult assignment.**

Exercise 45.1 Varying sentence openings

Rewrite each sentence so that it does not begin with the subject.

EXAMPLE **He would ask her to marry him in his own good time.**

In his own good time, he would ask her to marry him.

1. Germany entered World War II better prepared than the Allies, as it had in World War I.
2. The Germans, gambling on a quick victory, struck suddenly in both 1914 and 1939.
3. The United States entered World War II in 1942.
4. World War II, fought with highly mobile armies, never developed into the kind of prolonged stalemate that had characterized World War I.
5. The productive power of the United States, swinging into gear by the spring of 1943, contributed to the Allied victory.

45b Vary the length and structure of your sentences.

As you edit your work, check to see if you have overused one kind of sentence structure. Are all or most of the sentences in a passage short and simple? If so, use coordination and subordination to combine some of the short sentences into longer, compound or complex sentences. (*For more on types of sentences, see Chapter 31: Sentence Basics, pp. 508–09; for more on coordination and subordination, see Chapter 44, pp. 653–62.*)

If, on the other hand, all or most of your sentences are long and complex, put at least one of your main ideas into a short, simple sentence. Long passages of sentences that employ coordinating conjunctions can be monotonous as well. Your goal is to achieve a good mix in a way that highlights your central ideas. Note, for example, the way a writer revised this paragraph both to make it flow better and to clarify the discussion of sharks that closes it.

DRAFT

I dived quickly into the sea. I peered through my mask at the watery world. It turned darker. A school of fish went by. The distant light glittered on their bodies and I stopped swimming. I waited to see if the fish might be chased by a shark. I was satisfied that there was no shark and continued down.

REVISED

I dived quickly into the sea, peering through my mask at a watery world that turned darker as I descended. A school of fish went by, the distant light glittering on their bodies. Concerned that a shark might be chasing them, I stopped swimming and waited. No shark appeared. I continued down.

45c Include a few cumulative and periodic sentences.

Cumulative sentences accumulate information. They begin with a subject and verb and then add detail in a series of descriptive participial or absolute phrases. (*See Chapter 31: Sentence Basics, pp. 504–05 for more on participial and absolute phrases.*)

The following example, with the participial phrases italicized, illustrates the force a cumulative sentence can have.

► **The motorcycle spun out of control, *plunging down the ravine, crashing through a fence,* and *coming to rest at last on its side.***

Besides making your writing more forceful, cumulative sentences can also be used to add details, as the following example shows.

► **Wollstonecraft headed for France, *her soul determined to be free, her mind committed to reason, her heart longing for love.***

Periodic sentences provide another way to increase the force of your writing, while at the same time calling attention to key ideas. In a **periodic sentence,** the key word, phrase, or idea appears at the end, precisely where readers are most likely to remember it.

LACKLUSTER Young people fell in love with the jukebox in 1946 and 1947 and turned away from the horrors of World War II.

FORCEFUL In 1946 and 1947, young people turned away from the horrors of World War II and fell in love—with the jukebox.

LACKLUSTER The test of power for writers is their ability to imagine what is not the self, to familiarize the strange and mystify the familiar.

FORCEFUL The ability of writers to imagine what is not the self, to familiarize the strange and mystify the familiar, is the test of their power.

—TONI MORRISON

Exercise 45.2 Constructing cumulative sentences

Combine the sentences in each numbered item that follows to create cumulative sentences.

EXAMPLE

Europe suffered greatly in the fourteenth century. The Hundred Years War consumed France and England. Schism weakened Europe's strongest unifying institution, the Church. The Black Death swept away one third of the population.

Europe suffered greatly in the fourteenth century, with the Hundred Years War consuming France and England; schism weakening the Church, Europe's strongest unifying institution; and the Black Death sweeping away one third of the population.

1. The Black Death started in China around 1333. It spread to Europe over trade routes. It killed one third of the population in two years. It proved to be one of the worst natural disasters in history.
2. It was a horrible time. Dead bodies were abandoned on the streets. People were terrified of one another. Cattle and livestock were left to roam the countryside.
3. It was all for themselves. Friends deserted friends. Husbands left wives. Parents even abandoned children.

Exercise 45.3 Constructing periodic sentences

Rewrite the sentences that follow so that the keywords (underlined) appear at the end.

EXAMPLE

Prince Gautama achieved enlightenment while sitting in deep meditation under a Bo-tree after a long spiritual quest.

Sitting in deep meditation under a Bo-tree after a long spiritual quest, Prince Gautama achieved enlightenment.

1. The Indus River in Pakistan was home to one of the earliest civilizations in the world, as were the Nile River in Egypt, the Tigris and Euphrates rivers in Iraq, and the Yellow River in China.
2. In 1921, archeologists discovered the remains of Harappa, one of the two great cities of the Indus civilization, which until then was unknown to modern scholars.
3. The Indus civilization, which flourished from about 2500 to 1700 BCE, had two main centers, Harappa and another city, Mohenjo-Daro.

45d Try an occasional inversion, rhetorical question, or exclamation.

Most of the sentences you write will be declarative in purpose, designed to make statements. Most of the time, those statements will follow the normal sentence pattern of subject plus verb plus object. Occasionally, though, you might try using an inverted sentence pattern or another sentence type, such as a rhetorical question or an exclamation. (*For more on sentence types and their purposes, see Chapter 31: Sentence Basics, p. 495.*)

1. Using inversions

An **inversion** is a sentence in which the verb comes before the subject. In a passage on the qualities of various contemporary artists, the following inversion makes sense and adds interest.

► **Characteristic of Smith's work are bold design and original thinking.**

As the following example illustrates, poets often use inversion for dramatic effect.

► **Into the jaws of Death, / Into the mouth of Hell / Rode the six hundred.**

—from "The Charge of the Light Brigade"
by Alfred Lord Tennyson

Because many inversions sound odd, however, they should be used infrequently and carefully.

2. Using rhetorical questions

To get your readers to participate more actively in your work, you can ask them a question. Because you do not expect your audience to answer you, this kind of question is called a **rhetorical question.**

► **Players injured at an early age too often find themselves without a job, without a college degree, and without physical health. Is it any wonder that a few turn to drugs and alcohol, become homeless, or end up in a morgue long before their time?**

Rhetorical questions are attention-getting devices that work best in the middle or at the end of a long, complicated passage. Sometimes they can also help you make a transition from one topic to another. Avoid using them more than a few times in a paper, however, and do not begin an essay with a broad rhetorical question, such as "Why should we study *Huckleberry Finn*?"

3. Using exclamations

In academic writing, exclamations are rare. If you decide to use one for special effect, be sure that you want to express strong emotion about the idea and can do so without losing credibility with your readers.

► **Wordsworth completed the thirteen-book *Prelude* in 1805, after seven years of hard work. Instead of publishing his masterpiece, however, he devoted himself to revising it—for 35 years! The poem, in a fourteen-book version, was finally published in 1850, after he had died.**

45e Repeat keywords for emphasis.

By repeating keywords within a parallel construction you can provide rhythmic emphasis to key points.

► **The costumes *were red*; the lights *were red*; and the props *were red*.**

► **[W]e here highly resolve . . . that government of *the people*, by *the people*, for *the people* shall not perish from the earth.**

—from Abraham Lincoln's Gettysburg Address

Use this strategy sparingly, however, so that it retains its power. (*See Chapter 38: Wordy Sentences, pp. 615–16, and Chapter 42: Faulty Parallelism, pp. 637–42*).

When relevant, arrange a series of parallel elements in order of increasing importance.

► **The softball team won the local, regional, and national championships.**

Exercise 45.4 Chapter review: Sentence variety

Revise the following passage for variety and emphasis using the strategies presented in this chapter.

The United Nations was established in 1945. It was intended to prevent another world war. It began with twenty-one members. Nearly every nation in the world belongs to the United Nations today.

The United Nations has four purposes, according to its charter. One purpose is to maintain international peace and security. Another is to develop friendly relations among nations. Another is to promote cooperation among nations in solving international problems and in promoting respect for human rights. Last is to provide a forum for harmonizing the actions of nations.

All of the members of the United Nations have a seat in the General Assembly. The General Assembly considers numerous topics. These topics include globalization, AIDS, and pollution. Every member has a vote in the General Assembly.

A smaller group within the United Nations has the primary responsibility for maintaining international peace and security. This group is called the Security Council. The Security Council has five permanent members. They are China, France, the Russian Federation, the United Kingdom, and the United States. The Security Council also has ten elected members. The General Assembly elects the members of the Security Council. The elected members serve for two-year terms.

46 Active Verbs

Active verbs such as *run, shout, write,* and *think* are more direct and forceful than forms of the *be* verb (*am, are, is, was, were, been, being*) or passive-voice constructions. As you edit your work for clarity, pay attention to verb choice. The more active verbs you use, the stronger and clearer your writing will be.

www.mhhe.com/**mhhb2**
For information and exercises on active verbs, go to
Editing > Verbs and Verbals

Active Verbs and Grammar Checkers

Computer grammar checkers generally do not flag weak uses of the *be* verb because they cannot tell when a usage is appropriate and when it clutters a sentence.

Some grammar checkers do flag most passive-voice sentences, but their suggestions for revising them can sometimes make things worse. It requires a writer's judgment to determine how best—if at all—to revise a passive-voice sentence.

46a Consider alternatives to some *be* verbs.

Although it is not a strong verb, *be* does a lot of work in English. As a linking verb, a form of *be* can connect a subject with an informative adjective or a noun complement.

► **Germany *is* relatively poor in natural resources.**

► **Decent health care *is* a necessity, not a luxury.**

As a helping verb, a form of *be* can work with a present participle to indicate an ongoing action.

► **Macbeth *was* returning from battle when he met the three witches.**

Be verbs are so useful, in fact, that writers can easily overwork them. Watch for weak, roundabout sentences containing *be* verbs, and consider replacing those verbs with active verbs.

demonstrates
► **The mayor's refusal to meet with our representatives ~~is a demonstration of~~ his lack of respect for us, as well as for the environment.**

Exercise 46.1 Editing for overuse of be verbs

In the following sentences, replace *be* verbs with active verbs.

EXAMPLE

puzzled
The contradictory clues ~~were a puzzle to~~ the detective.

1. Historians are generally in agreement that the Egyptians were the inventors of sailing around 3000 BCE.
2. Many years passed before mariners were to understand that boats could sail upwind.
3. The invention of the keel was an improvement in sailboat navigation.
4. Steamships and transcontinental railroads were contributing factors in the disappearance of commercial sailing ships.
5. Today, either diesel or steam engines are the source of power for most ships.

46b Prefer the active voice.

Transitive verbs can be in the active or passive voice. In the **active voice,** the subject of the sentence acts; in the **passive voice,** the subject is acted upon.

ACTIVE The Senate finally passed the bill.

PASSIVE The bill was finally passed by the Senate.

The passive voice downplays the actors as well as the action, so much so that a passive-voice sentence may leave the actors entirely unspecified.

► **The bill was finally passed.**

Who or what passed the bill? The sentence does not tell us.

Unless you have a good reason to use the passive voice, prefer the active voice. It is more forceful, and it prevents the impression of evasiveness that results from leaving the actor in a sentence unidentified.

PASSIVE Polluting chemicals were dumped into the river.

ACTIVE Industrial Products Corporation dumped polluting chemicals into the river.

When the recipient of the action is more important than the doer of the action, however, the passive voice is the more appropriate choice.

► **After her heart attack, my mother was taken to the hospital.**

Mother and the fact that she was taken to the hospital are more important than who took her to the hospital.

Note: The symbol for flagging a passive voice construction that should be changed to the active voice is *pass*.

CHARTING the TERRITORY

Passive Voice

The passive voice is often used in scientific reports to keep the focus on the experiment and its results rather than on the experimenters.

► **After the bacteria were isolated, they were treated carefully with nicotine and were observed to stop reproducing.**

Business writers sometimes use—and overuse—the passive voice when they wish to communicate impersonally and objectively. However, memos, proposals, and other business genres usually benefit from the active voice.

Exercise 46.2 Editing to avoid the passive voice

Change the verbs in the following sentences from passive to active voice. In some cases you may have to give an identity to an otherwise unidentified actor. Circle the number of any sentence that is already in the active voice or that is better left in its passive-voice form.

EXAMPLE **The milk was spilled.**

Someone spilled the milk.

1. The remote islands of Oceania were settled by Polynesian sailors beginning in the early first millennium CE.
2. Around 500, Hawaii was reached.
3. By about 900, settlers had reached Easter Island, the most remote island in Polynesia.
4. New Zealand, the largest Polynesian island, was also the last to be settled.
5. These immensely long voyages were probably made by families of settlers in open, double-hulled sailing canoes.

Exercise 46.3 Chapter review: Active verbs

Minimize the use of the passive voice and the *be* verb in the following paragraph.

The idea of a lighter-than-air balloon was first conceived by inventors in the Middle Ages. Not until October 15, 1783, however, was Pilatre de Rosier successful in ascending in a hot air balloon. Five weeks later, he and a companion were makers of history again, accomplishing the world's first aerial journey with a five-mile trip across the city of Paris. For the next century, lighter-than-air balloons were considered the future of human flight. Balloonists were able to reach heights of up to three miles and made long, cross-country journeys. In 1859, for instance, a balloonist was carried from St. Louis to Henderson, New York. Balloonists were unable, however, to control the movement of their craft. To overcome this deficiency, efforts were made to use hand-cranked propellers and even giant oars. The invention of the internal-combustion engine was what finally made it possible to create controllable, self-propelled balloons, which are known as airships. Hot air was replaced by hydrogen in the earliest airships. Hydrogen gas catches fire easily, however, and this was the doom of the airship as a major means of travel. In 1937, the German airship *Hindenburg* exploded as it was landing in New Jersey, a tragedy that was described by a radio announcer in a live broadcast. As a result, helium has replaced hydrogen in today's airships.

CHECKLIST

Editing for Clarity

As you revise, check your writing for clarity by asking yourself these questions:

- ☐ Are all sentences concise and straightforward? Are any overloaded in ways that make them difficult to read and understand? (*See Chapter 38: Wordy Sentences, pp. 612–20.*)
- ☐ Are all sentences complete? Are any necessary words missing from compounds or comparisons? (*See Chapter 39: Missing Words, pp. 620–25.*)
- ☐ Do the parts of each sentence fit together in a way that makes sense, or is the sentence mixed up? (*See Chapter 40: Mixed Constructions, pp. 626–29.*)
- ☐ Do the key parts of each sentence fit together well, or are there disturbing mismatches in person, number, or grammatical structure? (*See Chapter 41: Confusing Shifts, pp. 629–37, and Chapter 42: Faulty Parallelism, pp. 637–45.*)
- ☐ Are the parts of each sentence clearly and closely connected, or are some modifiers separated from what they modify? (*See Chapter 43: Misplaced and Dangling Modifiers, pp. 645–52.*)
- ☐ Are the focus, flow, and voice of the sentences clear, or do some sentences have confusing shifts or ineffective coordination and subordination? (*See Chapter 41: Confusing Shifts, pp. 629–37, and Chapter 44: Coordination and Subordination, pp. 653–62.*)
- ☐ Do sentence patterns vary sufficiently? Is the mixture of long and short sentences enough to keep the reader alert and interested? (*See Chapter 45: Sentence Variety and Emphasis, pp. 663–70.*)
- ☐ Are all verbs strong and emphatic, or are the passive voice, the *be* verb, or other weak or too-common verbs overused? (*See Chapter 46: Active Verbs, pp. 671–74.*)

This detail of a Mayan vase shows a scribe at work. Scribes—who documented the deeds of rulers with carefully chosen words—were esteemed in the great Mayan cities that flourished on the Yucatan Peninsula from around 100 to 900 CE.

PART 9

> The difference between the right word and the almost right word is the difference between lightning and the lightning bug.
>
> —MARK TWAIN

Editing for Word Choice

47 Dictionaries and Vocabulary

The more words you know and can use correctly, the more precise, compelling, and evocative your writing will be.

Ways to Increase Your Vocabulary

1. Keep a dictionary and a thesaurus handy.
2. Read widely.
3. Use context to infer the meaning of unfamiliar words.
4. Learn the meaning of common prefixes and suffixes.
5. Keep a journal of new words.

47a Make using the dictionary a habit.

A standard desk dictionary—such as the *Random House Webster's College Dictionary,* the *Webster's New World Dictionary,* or the *American Heritage College Dictionary*—contains 140,000 to 180,000 entries. Along with words and their definitions, most dictionaries

WRITING OUTCOMES

Part 9: Editing for Word Choice

This section will help you answer questions such as:

Rhetorical Knowledge

- Is my writing too informal or formal for college assignments? **(48b)**
- Should I use *their, there,* or *they're*? **(50)**

Critical Thinking, Reading, and Writing

- How can I tell if a word is slang or nonstandard? **(47a)**
- How can I avoid biased language and stereotypes in my writing? **(48e)**

Processes

- Should I use my word processor's thesaurus? **(49b)**
- How can I revise to make my writing more precise? **(49c)**

Conventions

- How can I avoid misusing words? **(49a)**
- How can I learn common English idioms? **(49d)**

Self-Assessment: *Take an online quiz at www.mhhe.com/mhhb2 to test your familiarity with the topics covered in Chapters 47–50. Pay special attention to the sections in these chapters that correspond to any questions you answer incorrectly.*

provide additional information such as the correct spellings of important place names, the official names of countries with their areas and populations, and the names of capital cities. Biographical entries give birth and death years and enough information to explain each person's importance to society. Many dictionaries also include lists of abbreviations and symbols, names and locations of colleges and universities, titles and correct forms of address, and conversion tables for weights and measures.

Unabridged dictionaries, which you will find in the reference section of your college library, are more comprehensive than desk dictionaries and may consist of multiple volumes. They are especially valuable when you are analyzing literature or studying an English text from an earlier period. The most comprehensive unabridged dictionary is the *Oxford English Dictionary* (also known as the *OED*), a ten-volume work of 22,000 pages that contains more than 400,000 entries, including words no longer in use. Each entry begins with the earliest meaning and pronunciation of the word and charts changes and variations in usage over time.

All dictionaries include guides to their use, usually in the front. The guides explain the terms and abbreviations that appear in the entries as well as special notations such as *slang, nonstandard,* and *vulgar.*

Figure 47.1 shows a representative entry from the *Random House Webster's College Dictionary,* with each section of the entry

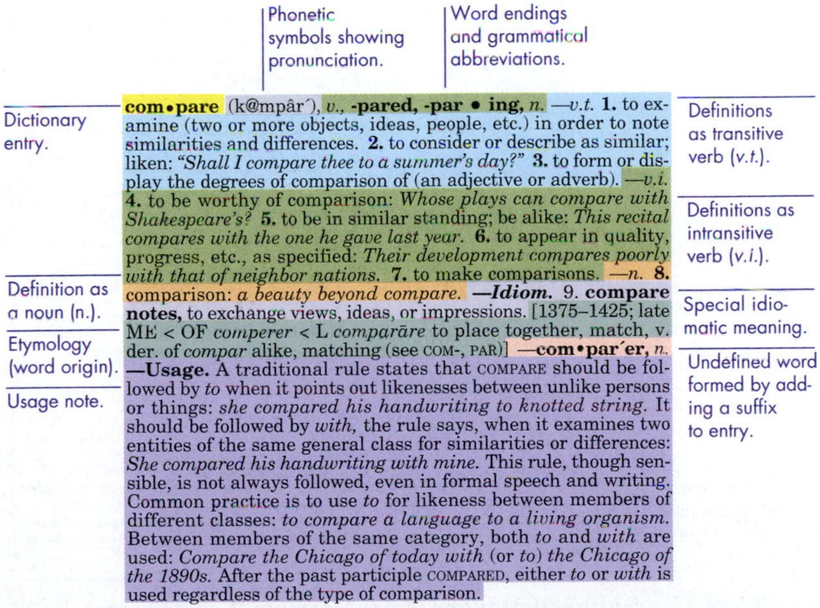

Phonetic symbols showing pronunciation.

Word endings and grammatical abbreviations.

Dictionary entry.

Definitions as transitive verb (*v.t.*).

Definitions as intransitive verb (*v.i.*).

Definition as a noun (n.).

Special idiomatic meaning.

Etymology (word origin).

Undefined word formed by adding a suffix to entry.

Usage note.

com•pare (k@mpâr´), *v.,* **-pared, -par • ing,** *n.* —*v.t.* **1.** to examine (two or more objects, ideas, people, etc.) in order to note similarities and differences. **2.** to consider or describe as similar; liken: *"Shall I compare thee to a summer's day?"* **3.** to form or display the degrees of comparison of (an adjective or adverb). —*v.i.* **4.** to be worthy of comparison: *Whose plays can compare with Shakespeare's?* **5.** to be in similar standing; be alike: *This recital compares with the one he gave last year.* **6.** to appear in quality, progress, etc., as specified: *Their development compares poorly with that of neighbor nations.* **7.** to make comparisons. —*n.* **8.** comparison: *a beauty beyond compare.* —***Idiom.*** 9. **compare notes,** to exchange views, ideas, or impressions. [1375–1425; late ME < OF *comperer* < L *comparāre* to place together, match, v. der. of *compar* alike, matching (see COM-, PAR)] —**com•par´er,** *n.* —**Usage.** A traditional rule states that COMPARE should be followed by *to* when it points out likenesses between unlike persons or things: *she compared his handwriting to knotted string.* It should be followed by *with,* the rule says, when it examines two entities of the same general class for similarities or differences: *She compared his handwriting with mine.* This rule, though sensible, is not always followed, even in formal speech and writing. Common practice is to use *to* for likeness between members of different classes: *to compare a language to a living organism.* Between members of the same category, both *to* and *with* are used: *Compare the Chicago of today with* (or *to*) *the Chicago of the 1890s.* After the past participle COMPARED, either *to* or *with* is used regardless of the type of comparison.

FIGURE 47.1 The entry for the word *compare* in the *Random House Webster's College Dictionary.*

highlighted and labeled. The labels refer to the kinds of information discussed on pages 680–82. Note that other dictionaries, although they all provide the same kind of information as in this example, may format or order that information differently.

Dictionaries also appear in most word-processing software packages and on Web sites (see Figure 47.2). They vary in size and level of detail.

1. Spelling, word division, and pronunciation

Entries in a dictionary are listed in alphabetical order according to their standard spelling. In the *Random House Webster's College Dictionary,* the verb *compare* is entered as **com•pare.** The dot separates the word into its two syllables. If you had to divide the word *compare* at the end of a line, you would place the hyphen where the dot appears.

Phonetic symbols in parentheses following the entry show its correct pronunciation; explanations of these symbols appear on the bottom of each right-hand page in some dictionaries. The second syllable of *compare* receives the greater stress; when you pronounce the word correctly, you say "comPARE." In the dictionary on page 679, an accent mark (´) appears after the syllable

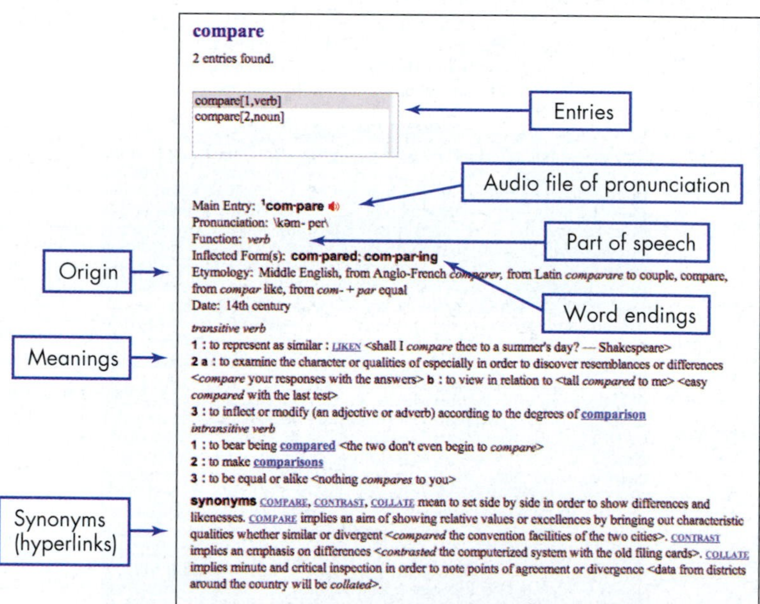
compare

2 entries found.

compare[1,verb]
compare[2,noun]

Main Entry: [1]**com·pare**
Pronunciation: \kəm- per\
Function: *verb*
Inflected Form(s): **com·pared; com·par·ing**
Etymology: Middle English, from Anglo-French *comparer,* from Latin *comparare* to couple, compare, from *compar* like, from *com-* + *par* equal
Date: 14th century

transitive verb
1 : to represent as similar : LIKEN <shall I *compare* thee to a summer's day? — Shakespeare>
2 a : to examine the character or qualities of especially in order to discover resemblances or differences <*compare* your responses with the answers> **b** : to view in relation to <tall *compared* to me> <easy *compared* with the last test>
3 : to inflect or modify (an adjective or adverb) according to the degrees of comparison
intransitive verb
1 : to bear being compared <the two don't even begin to *compare*>
2 : to make comparisons
3 : to be equal or alike <nothing *compares* to you>

synonyms COMPARE, CONTRAST, COLLATE mean to set side by side in order to show differences and likenesses. COMPARE implies an aim of showing relative values or excellences by bringing out characteristic qualities whether similar or divergent <*compared* the convention facilities of the two cities>. CONTRAST implies an emphasis on differences <*contrasted* the computerized system with the old filing cards>. COLLATE implies minute and critical inspection in order to note points of agreement or divergence <data from districts around the country will be *collated*>.

FIGURE 47.2 Online dictionary (from Merriam-Webster.com).

SOURCE: www.merriam-webster.com/dictionary

CHECKLIST

Using a Dictionary

- ☐ **Use the guide words.** Guide words at the top of each dictionary page tell you the first and last words on the page. Locate a word by looking for guide words that appear before and after your word in an alphabetical listing.
- ☐ **Try alternate spellings.**
- ☐ **Use the pronunciation key.** The letters and symbols that indicate each word's pronunciation are explained in a separate section at the front or back of a dictionary. In some dictionaries, they are also summarized at the bottom of each right-hand page of entries. Pronouncing new words aloud will help you learn them.
- ☐ **Pay attention to the parts of speech in a definition.** A word's meaning may depend on how it is used in a sentence—that is, its part of speech.
- ☐ **Always test the meaning you find.** Substitute the dictionary meaning for the word in your sentence and see if the sentence makes sense.

that receives the primary stress. Online dictionaries often include a recording of the pronunciation.

Dictionaries usually do not give the plurals of nouns if they are formed by adding an *s,* unless the word is foreign (*gondolas, dashikis*). Dictionaries do note irregular plurals—such as *children* for *child.*

Note: Some dictionaries list alternate spellings, always giving the preferred spelling first or placing the full entry under the preferred spelling only.

2. Word endings and grammatical labels

In Figure 47.1 on page 679, the abbreviation *v.* immediately after the pronunciation tells you that *compare* is most frequently used as a verb. The *-pared* shows the simple past and past participle form of the verb; the present participle form, *-paring,* follows, indicating that *compare* drops the final *e* when *-ing* is added. The next abbreviation, *n.,* indicates that *compare* can sometimes function as a noun, as in the phrase *beyond compare.*

Here is a list of common abbreviations for grammatical terms:

adj.	adjective	*prep.*	preposition
adv.	adverb	*pron.*	pronoun
conj.	conjunction	*sing.*	singular
interj.	interjection	*v.*	verb
n.	noun	*v.i.*	intransitive verb
pl.	plural	*v.t.*	transitive verb
poss.	possessive		

3. Definitions, word origins, and undefined run-on entries

In the sample entry for *compare* on page 679, the definitions begin after the abbreviation *v.t.,* which indicates that the first three meanings relate to *compare* as a transitive verb. A little farther down in the entry, *v.i.* introduces definitions of *compare* as an intransitive verb. Next, after *n.,* comes the definition of *compare* as a noun. Finally, the word *Idiom* signals a special meaning not included in the previous definitions. As an idiom, *compare notes* means "to exchange views, ideas, or impressions," not to examine how two sets of notes are alike and different.

Included in most dictionary entries is an etymology—a brief history of the word—set off in brackets. There we see the date of the first known use of the word in English together with the earlier words from which it is derived. *Compare* came into English between 1375 and 1425 and was derived from the Old French word *comperer,* which came from Latin. Etymological information can be useful to writers who need to define a word for their readers.

Most dictionaries also list, as undefined run-on entries, words formed by adding a suffix to the base word. The sample entry, for example, includes the noun *comparer* as a run-on entry.

4. Usage

A usage note concludes some main entries in the dictionary. In the sample entry for *compare* on page 679, the usage note discusses the differences between the expressions *compare to* and *compare with,* indicating in what circumstances each should be used.

Dictionary entries may also indicate whether a word or definition is nonstandard, slang, colloquial (informal), or archaic (old-fashioned). Avoid these usages in college writing. (*See Chapter 48: Appropriate Language, pp. 689–91.*)

CHARTING the TERRITORY

Specialized Dictionaries

In the library's reference section, you can usually find numerous specialized dictionaries such as biographical and geographical dictionaries; foreign language dictionaries; dictionaries of first lines of poems and of famous quotations; dictionaries of legal and medical terms; and dictionaries of philosophy, sociology, engineering, and other disciplines. These dictionaries can help you write an essay or simply expand your knowledge of various subjects. Ask the reference librarian to help you locate a useful specialized dictionary for your topic or field.

For MULTILINGUAL STUDENTS

Strategies for Dictionary and Thesaurus Use

Understanding a word requires knowing how and in what contexts to use it appropriately. As you develop fluency in English, you may find it useful to keep on hand a usage guide like Michael Swanson's *Practical English Usage,* as well as one of the following ESL dictionaries:

Random House Webster's Dictionary of American English, ESL/Learner's Edition
Longman Advanced American Dictionary
Oxford ESL Dictionary

As an advanced learner of English, however, you should move beyond specialized ESL dictionaries and consult standard dictionaries. To achieve both precise and nuanced expression, you should also supplement the dictionary with a thesaurus. As you encounter new words, pay close attention to the context in which they are used—both grammatically and in relation to the meaning of surrounding words.

47b Consult a thesaurus for words that have similar meanings.

The word *thesaurus* in Latin means "treasury" or "collection." A **thesaurus** is a dictionary of synonyms. Several kinds of thesauruses are available, many called *Roget's* after Peter Mark Roget (pronounced roZHAY), who published the first one in 1852. Thesauruses are included in most word-processing software packages, as well as online.

Use a thesaurus when you are looking for the word that most precisely conveys your intended meaning or when you are looking for an alternative to a word you have overused. When choosing a word from a thesaurus, consider both the word's **denotation,** or primary meaning, and its **connotations,** the feelings and images associated with it (*see Chapter 49: Exact Language, pp. 696–700*). Do not use an unfamiliar word from a thesaurus without first checking the word's meaning in a dictionary.

Exercise 47.1 Using a dictionary and a thesaurus

Look up the following words in a thesaurus, and find two synonyms for each. Then, in each case, use a dictionary to find the definition of the original word and the two synonyms. Finally, use all three words—the original and both synonyms—in one or more sentences.

1. idea
2. pretty
3. good
4. say
5. look

47c Read for pleasure.

Whether you find it in a best-selling novel by Scott Turow or in a sophisticated magazine like the *Atlantic,* a new word you come across in something you read for fun or personal interest will stay with you at least as well as one you encounter in a text assigned for class.

TEXTCONNEX

Online "Word-a-Day" Services and Books of Curious Words

A number of Web sites will send you a daily e-mail containing an interesting or unusual word, its definition, origin, and even a sound clip demonstrating its pronunciation.

- Perhaps the best known of these sites is AWAD, or A.Word.A.Day, run by Anu Garg <www.wordsmith.org/awad.html>.
- Merriam-Webster <www.m-w.com/cgi-bin/mwwod.pl> and the *Oxford English Dictionary* <www.oed.com/cgi/display/wotd> sponsor similar sites.

Anu Garg and Stuti Garg's book *A Word a Day* is a selection of words from the AWAD mailings. Other books such as William Espy's *Thou Improper, Thou Uncommon Noun* and Erin McKean's *Weird and Wonderful Words* can also be fun places to find new words.

Reading Scott Turow's *The Burden of Proof*, for example, you would encounter words such as *putrefaction* (the rot or decay of organic matter), *craven* (fearful, cowardly), and *Anglophile* (an admirer of English ways). A recent issue of *Travel and Leisure* magazine contained *ribald* (indecent or irreverent in speech) and *riposte* (a sharp reply in speech or action). Even catalogs and advertisements can contain interesting words, such as *peerless* (unequaled), *cordovan* (a type of leather originally from Córdoba, Spain), and *tumultuous* (noisy and disorderly).

Exercise 47.2 Learning new words

Scan a book, magazine, or Web site that interests you, and jot down ten words that are unfamiliar to you. Look up the words in a dictionary, and use each in a sentence.

47d Learn the meanings of new words by their context.

When reading for a class assignment, for work, or for pleasure, it is a good idea to have a dictionary nearby. Often, however, you may find you can deduce the meaning of an unfamiliar word—even without a dictionary—by examining the familiar words around it.

1. Embedded definitions

Textbooks and other academic materials often define specialized vocabulary or terms when they are first used in a sentence.

- ► **Fables are brief stories that have an explicitly stated moral.**
- ► **An entire week of rehearsal was spent on blocking—directing the actors' movements on the stage.**
- ► **Speaking in run-on sentences is a symptom of mania (a mental illness characterized by an exaggeratedly elevated mood, an inflated sense of self-importance, and profuse and rapidly changing ideas).**

2. Comparisons and other parallel constructions

Parallel constructions (*see Chapter 42: Faulty Parallelism, pp. 637–45*) often distinguish among or group together two or more terms or concepts, providing clues to the meaning of unfamiliar words. In the following sentence, for example, the word *although* sets up a contrast between *obedient and well-behaved* on the one hand and *recalcitrant* on the other, suggesting that *recalcitrant* is the opposite of *obedient and well-behaved.*

- ► **Although Jack was usually obedient and well-behaved, his brother was often recalcitrant.**

A list of examples can similarly suggest the meaning of new words. In the following sentence, the examples convey the sense of *cloying* as overly sentimental or excessively sweet.

► **Constant phone calls, daily offerings of roses and stuffed animals, and other cloying actions can repel the beloved.**

47e Learn new words by analyzing their parts.

You may be able to deduce the meaning of an unfamiliar word if you can recognize the meaning of its parts. Many words consist of a prefix or suffix (or both) attached to a root word, as in *preview* (*pre* + *view*) or *viewer* (*view* + *er*). Others may consist of two or more root words joined together as a compound word, as in viewpoint (*view* + *point*). Learning how prefixes and suffixes modify base words will help you decode unfamilar words.

1. Prefixes

A **prefix** is a syllable that attaches to the beginning of a root word, creating a new word with its own meaning. For example, the prefix *semi-,* meaning "half," joins with *circle* to produce *semicircle,* which means "half-circle." Similarly, the prefix *extra,* meaning "beyond," joins with *ordinary* to produce *extraordinary,* which means "beyond

COMMON PREFIXES

PREFIX	MEANING	EXAMPLES
a-	without	amoral, atonal
ab-	away from, off	abduct, abbreviate
ad-	toward, near	adverb, adjoin
anti-	against	antiwar, antidote
bi-	two	bisect, bicycle
co-, com-, con-	with, together	cosign, combine, condescend
contra-, counter-	against, opposite	contradict, counteract
de-	from, against	detach, demerit
deci-, deca	ten	decimal, decameter
dis-	remove from, negate	disappear, disavow
du-	two	duplicate, duplicity
ex-	from, beyond	exit, external
extra-	beyond	extraordinary, extrasensory
il-, im-, in-, ir-	not	illegal, impossible, incomplete, irrational
inter-	between, among	interaction, intersect
mal-	bad	malfunction, malcontent

COMMON PREFIXES (continued)

PREFIX	MEANING	EXAMPLES
mis-	wrong	mistake, misuse
mono-	one, same	monotone, monorail
multi-	many	multicultural, multimedia
non-	no, not	nonsense, noncombatant
pre-	before	preview, predate
post-	after	postgraduate, postscript
pro-	in front of, for	prologue, pro-business
quad-, quar-	four	quadrilateral, quarter
re-	again, back	restart, recline
semi-	half	semicircle, semiprecious
sub-	under	submarine, substandard
super-	above	superscript, supersonic
syn-, sym-	together	synchronize, symphony
trans-	across	transatlantic, translate
tri-	three	triangle, tricycle
un-	not	unhappy, undo
uni-	one	uniform

the ordinary." See the box on page 686 and above for a list of common prefixes and their meanings.

2. Suffixes

Suffixes are syllables that are attached to the ends of words. They usually modify the meaning of a word by changing it from one part of speech to another. With different suffixes, for example, the adjective *pure* becomes the adverb *purely* and the noun *purity*. Similarly, the noun *fear* becomes the adjective *fearless* and, with the addition of a second suffix, the noun *fearlessness*. See the box on the next page for a list of common suffixes and their meanings.

Exercise 47.3 Chapter review: Dictionaries and vocabulary

Look for compounds and use context and your knowledge of prefixes and suffixes to infer the meaning of the underlined words in the following passage. Write down your inferred definitions; then check them against a dictionary and write down the dictionary definition that most closely matches the meaning of the words as they are used in the passage.

> The Enlightenment ideals promoted by the American and French revolutions—freedom, equality, and popular sovereignty—appealed to peoples throughout Europe

COMMON SUFFIXES

SUFFIX	MEANING	EXAMPLES
-able	capable of, given to	miserable, laughable
-al	pertaining to	natural, seasonal
-ance, -ence	act, process, or quality of	continuance, difference
-ant	characterized by, one who	observant, assistant
-ary	pertaining to	legendary, monetary
-dom	quality or state	wisdom, freedom
-en	made of, make	wooden, tighten
-ful	full of	plentiful
-hood	quality, state, or sharing a quality or state	motherhood, neighborhood
-ion	act or process of	creation, motivation
-ish	related to	childish, selfish
-ism	principles of, practice of, quality of	Marxism, heroism
-ist	one concerned with	Marxist, lobbyist
-ity	quality or state of	abnormality, insanity
-ize	make or subject to	privatize, penalize
-ness	quality or state of	kindness, fondness
-less	without	friendless, fearless
-ly	in the manner or way of	ghostly, gladly
-ment	action or process	commitment, indictment

and the Americas. In the Caribbean and South America, they inspired revolutionary movements: slaves in the French colony of Saint-Domingue rose against their overlords and established the independent republic of Haiti, and Euro-American leaders mounted independence movements in Central America and South America. The ideals of the American and French revolutions also encouraged social reformers to organize broader programs of liberation. Whereas the American and French revolutions guaranteed political and legal rights to white men, social reformers sought to extend these rights to women and slaves of African ancestry. During the nineteenth century, all European and Euro-American states abolished slavery, but former slaves and their descendants remained an underprivileged and often oppressed class in most of the Atlantic world. The quest for women's rights also proceeded slowly during the nineteenth century.

—from Bentley and Ziegler, *Traditions and Encounters*

48 Appropriate Language

Language is appropriate when it fits your topic, purpose, and audience. Consider, for example, how differently you would describe an unpleasant work experience to a close friend as opposed to a potential employer during a job interview. A more formal choice of words would obviously be appropriate in the business setting. You may also have witnessed someone using language that subtly discriminates against a group of people, and you may have felt how inappropriate that language was.

In academic and professional writing, **standard English** is the form of English that can be understood by everyone and is considered clear and appropriate. In academic and professional situations, language that is overly formal and pretentious can be just as inappropriate as overly informal language.

www.mhhe.com/mhhb2
For information and exercises on appropriate language, go to
Editing > Word Choice

48a Avoid slang, regional expressions, and nonstandard English in college writing.

1. Avoiding slang

Slang is a very informal and playful type of language that is used within a social group or discourse community (*see Charting the Territory: Discourse Communities below*). There is, for example, surfer slang (*aggro, gremmies, landshark*), coffeehouse slang (*cap, skinny, whipless*), and even publishing slang (*comp, slush pile, dead matter*). Teen slang is the most extensive and short-lived (remember *phat*?), serving to bond a generation. In college papers, however, slang terms and the hip tone that goes with them should be avoided.

CHARTING the TERRITORY

Discourse Communities

People who share certain interests, knowledge, and customary ways of communicating constitute a **discourse community.** Members of the discourse community of baseball fans, for example, talk and write about *switch-hitters, batting averages,* and *earned-run averages*—terms that may be unfamiliar to people outside the community. Each of us belongs to several discourse communities. The more familiar you are with a discourse community, the more you will know about the language that is appropriate in that community.

SLANG In *Heart of Darkness,* we hear a lot about a *dude* named Kurtz, but we don't see the *guy* much.

REVISED In *Heart of Darkness,* Marlow, the narrator, talks almost continually about Kurtz, but we meet Kurtz himself only at the end.

2. Avoiding nonstandard dialects and regional expressions

American English consists of numerous **dialects** and varieties of the language that are distinguished from other varieties by differences in vocabulary, pronunciation, and grammar. A dialect is used by a particular geographic or ethnic group, such as Cajun English and New York English. In American colleges, professions, and businesses, the dominant dialect is standard English. If you speak a dialect that varies from standard English, be aware of the differences for those occasions when standard English is preferred. Common nonstandard words are labeled as such in the dictionary.

Dialects particular to a geographic area may contain **regionalisms,** or expressions unique to that region. Examples of regionalisms are *memberize* for "recall," *y'all* for "all of you," and *pockeybook* for "purse." Use regionalisms in writing only to report conversation or evoke a place. Usually, regionalisms are not appropriate for college papers.

48b Use an appropriate level of formality.

College writing assignments usually call for a style that avoids the extremes of the colloquial and the pretentious. Language that is appropriate to informal conversation but not precise enough for academic writing is known as **colloquial** language, and includes slang and regionalisms. It may be labeled "colloquial" or "informal" in the dictionary.

COLLOQUIAL Shakespeare's character Hamlet sure has a mixed bag of emotions.

REVISED Shakespeare's character Hamlet is racked by conflicting emotions.

Pretentious or **stilted language** is language that is overly formal, abstract, and wordy. It forces readers to work hard at decoding its meaning—and eventually readers lose interest. Choose a complex word only when it communicates your meaning more precisely than a simpler word.

PRETENTIOUS Romantic lovers are characterized by a preoccupation with a deliberately restricted set of qualities in the love object that are viewed as means to some ideal end.

REVISED People in love tend to idealize the beloved.

48c Avoid jargon.

The technical language of specialists is appropriate in many contexts and has a place in college writing. Without it, no one could write a lab report, an economic analysis, or a philosophical argument.

Jargon is technical language used in an inappropriate context. If you want to be understood, you should not use discourse that is appropriate for specialists when you are writing for a wider audience.

JARGON Pegasus Technologies, a leading B2C solutions provider, developed a Web-based PSP system to support standard off-line brands in meeting their loyalty-driven marketing objectives via the Internet space.

REVISED Pegasus Technologies developed a system for businesses that helps them create Web sites to run contests and other promotions for their customers.

If you need to use technical terms when writing for nonspecialists, be sure to define them.

► Armstrong's innovative singing style featured "scat," a technique that combines "nonsense syllables [with] improvised melodies" (Robinson 425).

48d Avoid most euphemisms and all doublespeak.

Euphemisms substitute nice-sounding words like *correctional facility* and *passing away* for such harsh realities as *prison* and *death*. On some occasions, a euphemism like *passing away* may serve a useful purpose; for example, you may wish to avoid upsetting a grieving person. Usually, however, words should not be used to evade or deceive.

Doublespeak is the deceitful use of language. Its purpose is not to prevent hurt feelings but to confuse or mislead readers. As the following example shows, doublespeak obscures facts.

► A revenue enhancement program will be implemented in response to last year's negative gains.

The writer tries to obscure bad news by using *revenue enhancement* instead of *tax* or *price hike* and *negative gains* instead of *deficit* or *loss*.

Exercise 48.1 Editing for informal language, pretentious language, jargon, and euphemisms

Edit the following sentences so that they are suitable for college writing.

1. With the invention of really cool steel engraving and mechanical printing presses in the nineteenth century, publishers could make tons of books like practically overnight.

2. France was the womb of nineteenth-century realism, a fecund literary land that gave birth to those behemoths of realism Stendhal, Balzac, and Flaubert.
3. Flaubert really hated the bourgeoisie because he thought they never thought about anything but cash, stuff, and looking good in front of others.
4. Flaubert's *Madame Bovary* is the story of this really bored provincial chick who dreams of being a fancy lady, cheats on her husband, and then does herself in.
5. Intense class antagonisms, combined with complex currents of historical determinism, extending back into the ancient traditions of serfdom and the czar, may precisely index the factors constitutive of the precipitant flowering of the Russian novel in the nineteenth century.
6. The present writer's former belief that nineteenth-century literature is incomprehensible is no longer operational.

48e Do not use biased or sexist language.

Be on the lookout for subtle stereotypes that demean, ignore, or patronize people on the basis of gender, race, religion, national origin, ethnicity, physical ability, sexual orientation, occupation, or any other human condition. Also, be careful in your use of *we* and *they*. Do not assume readers will share your background. Revise for inclusiveness.

1. Avoiding stereotypes

A **stereotype** is a society's simplified image or generalization about a racial, ethnic, or social group. Stereotypes are never completely true and can in fact be grossly misrepresentative. Even when positive, stereotypes lump individuals together and should be avoided.

► ~~Although the~~ *The* Browns are *an* Irish ~~Catholics, there are only~~ *Catholic family with* two children*.* ~~in the family.~~

► ~~Because Asian students are whizzes at math, we~~ *We* all wanted ~~them~~ *math whizzes* in our study group.

Refer to groups as they refer to themselves (*Asian,* not *Oriental*). Do not refer unnecessarily to someone's ethnicity, religion, age, or other circumstances.

2. Avoiding sexist language

Sexist clichés and stereotypes **Sexist language** demeans or stereotypes women and men, but women are usually the explicit targets. Consider the meaning of words or phrases like *the weaker sex, the fair sex, the little woman, my better half, working mother, lady lawyer, housewife, poetess,* and *coed.*

Avoiding bias also means avoiding subtle stereotypes. For example, not all heads of state are or have to be men.

BIASED Wives of heads of state typically have their own administrative staffs.

REVISED Spouses of heads of state typically have their own administrative staffs.

BIASED We advertised for a new secretary because we needed another girl in the office.

REVISED We advertised for a new secretary because we had too much work for the staff on hand.

Women and men should be referred to in parallel ways: ladies and gentlemen (not ladies and men), men and women, husband and wife. Names should also be given parallel treatment: Virginia Woolf and Lytton Strachey, or Woolf and Strachey, not Virginia and Strachey.

The generic he Traditionally, the pronoun *he* and other masculine pronouns—*he, him, his, himself*—have been used generically to refer to unspecified individuals of either gender. This convention is no longer acceptable. Whenever possible, replace the masculine pronouns *he, him, his,* and *himself* when they are being used generically to refer to both women and men. One satisfactory way to replace masculine pronouns is to use the plural.

BIASED Everybody had his way.

REVISED We all had our way.

Some writers alternate *he* and *she, him* and *her.* This strategy may be effective in some writing situations, but switching back and forth can also be distracting. The constructions *his or her* and *he or she* are acceptable, as long as they are not used excessively or more than once in a sentence.

AWKWARD

Each student in the psychology class was to choose a different book according to his or her interests, to read the book overnight, to do without his or her normal sleep, to write a short summary of what he or she had read, and then to see if he or she dreamed about the book the following night.

REVISED

Each student in the psychology class was to choose an interesting book, read it overnight without getting a normal night's rest, write a short summary of the book the next morning, and then see if he or she dreamed about the book the following night.

The construction *his/her* and the unpronounceable *s/he* are not acceptable in academic writing.

> ***Note:*** Using the neuter impersonal pronoun *one* can sometimes help you avoid masculine pronouns. *One* can make your writing sound stuffy, however, so it is usually better to try another option.
>
> **STUFFY** The American creed holds that if one works hard, one will succeed in life.
>
> **REVISED** The American creed holds that those who work hard will succeed in life.

(*For more on editing to avoid the generic use of* he, him, his, *or* himself, *see Chapter 36: Problems with Pronouns, pp. 588–90.*)

***The generic* man** Just as *he* and *him* have been used generically to represent both males and females, the syllable *man* as a word or suffix has been used generically to refer to all humanity. Today, however, the use of *man* to represent both men and women should be avoided. Also, choose substitutes for words that contain *man* but could apply to both men and women (*see the "Gender-Neutral Alternatives" box on the next page*).

BIASED The chairman of the department reviews grant applications.

REVISED The department chair reviews grant applications.

For MULTILINGUAL STUDENTS

Biased Language

English speakers are sensitive to language that may stereotype or offend groups of people. As an educated user of English, you should be aware of potential pitfalls in the forms and connotations of words. Regardless of the usage norms in your native language, you should generally avoid gender stereotyping in the names of jobs. Use plural forms of pronouns to make generalizations about human traits or activities (for example, by replacing the generic *mankind* with terms like *humanity* or *humankind*).

GENDER-NEUTRAL ALTERNATIVES to GENDER-SPECIFIC TERMS: SOME EXAMPLES

GENDER-SPECIFIC TERM	GENDER-NEUTRAL ALTERNATIVE
chairman	chair, chairperson
congressman	representative, member of Congress
fireman	firefighter
forefathers	ancestors
man, mankind	people, humans, humanity
man-made	artificial
policeman	police officer
postman	mail carrier
salesman	sales representative
spokesman	spokesperson
-ess (poetess, actress, stewardess, etc.)	poet, actor, flight attendant

Exercise 48.2 Editing to eliminate biased language

Identify the biased language in each of the following sentences, and rewrite each sentence using the suggestions in section 48e.

EXAMPLE

flight attendants

Because ~~stewardesses~~ travel so much, child care is an issue for them.

1. Man is fast approaching a population crisis.
2. Each of us must do his part to reduce the production of greenhouse gases.
3. Every housewife should encourage her children to make recycling a habit, and every corporate chief executive officer should encourage his employees to carpool or take mass transit whenever possible.
4. Congressmen should make conservation and environmental protection legislative priorities.
5. If he tried, the average motorist could help reduce our dependence on oil.

Exercise 48.3 Chapter review: Appropriate language

Edit the following passage to make the language appropriate for a college paper.

> The writer of novels Henry James had many illustrious forefathers. His grandfather William traversed the Atlantic in 1789 with little more than a Latin grammar book and a desire to see the battlefields of the Revolutionary War. When William James met his maker in 1832, he left an estate worth $3 million, or about $100 million in today's cash. This little something was to be divided among eleven children and his better half, Catherine Barber James. William's fourth kid, Henry, who is often referred to as the elder Henry James so's that he is not confused with the novelist, became a lecturer and writer on metaphysics. His big thing was the doctrines of the Swedish mystic Emanuel Swedenborg. Although some thought the elder Henry James a few plates short of a picnic, his work was very well known and influential during his lifetime.

49 Exact Language

As you revise, be on the lookout for problems with **diction,** or word choice. Do the words you have chosen reflect your intended meaning as precisely as they should?

> ***Note:*** The editing symbol for questionable word choice is ***ww***, which is an abbreviation for "wrong word."

www.mhhe.com/mhhb2

For information and exercises on exact language, go to

Editing > Word Choice

Selecting the right word involves two aspects of its meaning. A word has a primary (or explicit) meaning, called its **denotation,** and a secondary (or implicit) meaning, called its **connotation.**

✓ 49a Avoid misusing words.

A word's denotation is what you would find if you looked up the word in a dictionary. Be careful not to misuse words that have similar but distinct denotations, or words that sound alike but have different meanings.

affects *effect*

► **The medication ~~effects~~ concentration but has no ~~affect~~ on appetite.**

flouted

► **Murdock ~~flaunted~~ the no-smoking rule.**

Consult a dictionary or the Glossary of Usage in Chapter 50 for help with commonly misused terms. See also the list of Common Homonyms and Near Homonyms in Chapter 63: Spelling, pp. 829–31.

You can reduce mistakes in your use of new terms by consulting a dictionary whenever you include an unfamiliar word in your writing.

exhibited

► **The aristocracy ~~exuded~~ numerous vices, including greed**

licentiousness

and ~~license~~.

Also, check your course textbooks for glossaries that can help you use new terms properly.

Think critically about the suggestions made by your word-processing program's spell checker. (*For more on spell checkers, see Chapter 5: Revising and Editing, p. 96 and Chapter 63: Spelling, p. 825.*) Sometimes the spell checker will incorrectly guess the word you intended. Carefully review the list of options and look up any unfamiliar words. In the example, the writer mistyped the word *instate* as *enstate* and received the incorrect suggestion *estate*.

instate

► **We needed approval to ~~estate~~ the change.**

As you edit, read carefully to make sure that you have the right word in the right place.

Exercise 49.1 Avoiding the misuse of words

In the following sentences, replace any of the underlined words that are misused with a word with an appropriate denotation, and circle those that are properly used. For help, consult a dictionary or the Glossary of Usage in Chapter 50.

EXAMPLE

complement

► **Computer software and computer hardware ~~compliment~~**

each other.

~~one another.~~

1. The nineteenth-century Englishman Charles Babbage was probably the first person to conceive of a general-purpose computing machine, but the ability to build one alluded him.

FIGURE 49.1 The incredible shrinking computer. Almost any of today's laptop computers (right) has more computing power than the first general-purpose digital computer (left), the massive ENIAC (Electronic Numerical Integrator and Calculator).

2. Because she was able to imply the kinds of instructions that would work with Babbage's machine, some historians cite Ada Lovelace, daughter of the poet Byron, as the first computer programmer.
3. Incredulous as it may seem, the first general-purpose digital electronic computer was 100 feet long and 10 feet high but had less computing power than one of today's inexpensive laptop computers.
4. The U.S. government was the principle source of funding for some of the most important advances in computing after World War II.
5. Without the invention of the transistor, today's small, powerful computing devices would not have been plausible.

49b Choose words with suitable connotations.

To use words effectively, you need to know their connotations as well as their denotations. Connotations come from the feelings and images people associate with a word, so they influence what readers understand a writer to be saying.

Consider, for example, the following three statements:

Murdock *ignored* the no-smoking rule.
Murdock *disobeyed* the no-smoking rule.
Murdock *flouted* the no-smoking rule.

Even though the three sentences depict the same event, each sentence describes Murdock's action somewhat differently. If Murdock *ignored* the rule, it may simply have been because he did not know or care about it. If he *disobeyed* the rule, he must have known about it and consciously decided not to follow it, but what if he *flouted* the rule? Well, then there was probably a look of disdain on his face as he made sure that others would see him ostentatiously puffing away at a cigarette.

As you revise, consider replacing any word whose connotations do not exactly fit what you want to say.

► **The players' union should ~~request~~ *demand* that the NFL amend its pension plan.**

If you cannot think of a more suitable word, consult a print or an electronic thesaurus (*see Chapter 47*) for **synonyms,** words with similar meanings. Keep in mind, however, that most words have connotations that allow them to work in some contexts but not in others. To find out more about a synonym's connotations, look up the word in a dictionary.

Synonyms and Your Word Processor's Thesaurus

Many word-processing programs include a thesaurus that lets you replace a word with a synonym. Make sure that the connotations of the synonym you choose are appropriate to the context in which you are using it.

For MULTILINGUAL STUDENTS

Connotation and Usage Problems

Most students whose first language is not English consider vocabulary use a major challenge. Even though you may learn the meaning of a word, you may have trouble using it correctly. Certain types of word combinations are determined by conventional use rather than by their literal meaning (for example, you *do* homework, but you *make* a plan).

Conscious or unconscious translation from your native language will always be part of your learning, but you should try to study English words and phrases in context, with sensitivity to their connotations. It helps to keep a dictionary close by (*see Chapter 47: Dictionaries and Vocabulary, pp. 678–88*).

Exercise 49.2 Choosing words with suitable connotations

Use a dictionary or thesaurus to list as many synonyms as you can for each of the underlined words in the passages that follow. Discuss why you think the authors chose the underlined words.

1. Space and time capture the imagination like no other scientific subject. . . . They form the arena of reality, the very fabric of the cosmos. Our entire existence—everything we do, think, and experience—takes place in some region of space during some interval of time. Yet science is still struggling to understand what space and time actually are.

   —BRIAN GREENE, *The Fabric of the Cosmos*

2. On Waverly Street, everybody knew everybody else. It was only one short block, after all—a narrow strip of patched and repatched pavement, bracketed between a high stone cemetery wall at one end and the commercial clutter of Govans Road at the other. The trees were elderly maples with lumpy, bulbous trunks. The squat clapboard houses seemed mostly front porch.

   —ANNE TYLER, *Saint Maybe*

49c Include specific and concrete words.

In addition to general and abstract terms, clear writers use words that are specific and concrete. Such words can help your readers grasp your particular message.

General words name broad categories of things, such as *trees, books, politicians,* or *students.* **Specific words** name particular kinds of things or items, such as *pines, Victorian novels, Republicans,* or *college sophomores.*

Abstract words name qualities and ideas that do not have physical properties, such as *charity, beauty, hope,* or *radical.* Use them in general statements, and follow those statements with specific details. **Concrete words** name things we can sense by touch, taste, smell, hearing, and sight, such as *velvet, vinegar, smoke, screech,* or *sweater.*

By creating images that appeal to the senses, specific and concrete words can help make your writing more precise.

VAGUE The trees were affected by the bad weather.

PRECISE The small pines shook in the gale.

VAGUE Their generosity helped the library.

PRECISE Their $5 million gift paid for the library's new online catalog.

As you edit, make sure that you have developed your ideas with specific and concrete details. Also check for overused, vague terms—such as *factor, thing, good, nice,* and *interesting*—and replace them with more specific and concrete alternatives.

► The protesters were charged with ~~things~~ *crimes* they never ~~did~~ *committed*.

Exercise 49.3 Including specific and concrete words

Draw on your own knowledge, experience, and imagination to rewrite the following paragraph with invented details described in specific and concrete language.

EXAMPLE

Niagara Falls is an awe-inspiring sight.

The waters of the Niagara River flow over the edge of the half-mile-wide, crescent-shaped Horseshoe Falls and plunge with a roar to the bottom of the cataract two hundred feet below.

Last summer I worked as an intern at a company in a field that interests me. The work was hard and the hours were long, but I gained a lot of experience. At first I was assigned only routine office work. As I learned more about the business, however, my employers began to give me more interesting tasks. By the end of the summer I was helping out on several high-priority projects. My employers liked my work and offered me another internship for the following summer.

49d Use standard idioms.

An **idiom** is a customary expression whose meaning does not relate in a predictable way to the meaning of the words it is composed of. Often idioms involve expressions with prepositions. We are not capable *to* but capable *of;* we do not go *with* the car but *in* the car or simply *by* car; we do not abide *with* a rule but *by* a rule. We might meet someone *at* the train station or, a bit later, *on* the train. In some parts of the United States, people wait *in* line to go to a movie; in other parts, they wait *on* line.

Some verbs, called **phrasal verbs,** include a preposition to make their meaning complete. These verbs often have an idiomatic meaning that changes significantly when the attached preposition changes.

Henry *made up* with Gloria.
Henry *made off* with Gloria.
Henry *made out* with Gloria.

If you are not sure which preposition to use with a verb, consult the box on idiomatic expressons below or look up the main word in a dictionary.

For MULTILINGUAL STUDENTS

For more on phrasal verbs and idiomatic expressions, see Chapter 66: Identifying and Editing Common Errors, pages 865–69.

IDIOMATIC EXPRESSIONS

Common Adjective + Preposition Combinations

afraid of: fearing someone or something
anxious about: worried
ashamed of: embarrassed by someone or something
aware of: know about
content with: having no complaints about; happy about
fond of: having positive feelings for
full of: filled with
grateful to (*someone*) (*for something*): thankful; appreciative
interested in: curious; wanting to know more about
jealous of: feeling envy toward
proud of: pleased about
responsible to (*someone*) (*for something*): accountable; in charge
satisfied with: having no complaints about
suspicious of: distrustful of
tired of: had enough of; bored with

Common Verb + Preposition Combinations

apologize to: express regret for actions
arrive at (*an event at a specific location*): come to a building or a house (*I arrived at the Louvre at ten.*)
arrive in (*a place*): come to a city/country (*I arrived in Paris.*)
blame for: hold responsible; accuse
complain about: find fault; criticize
concentrate on: focus; pay attention
congratulate on: offer good wishes for success
consist of: contain; be made of
depend on: trust
explain to: make something clear to someone
insist on: be firm
laugh at: express amusement
look up: visit
rely on: trust

IDIOMATIC EXPRESSIONS (*continued*)

smile at: act friendly toward
take care of: look after; tend
thank for: express appreciation
throw at: toss an object toward someone or something without expecting that the object will be caught
throw to: toss something to someone to catch
throw (something) away: discard
throw (something) out: discard; present an idea for consideration
worry about: feel concern; fear for someone's safety or well-being

Common Particles (verb + preposition combinations that create *verb phrasals,* expressions with meanings that are different from the meaning of the verb itself)

break down: stop functioning
bring up: mention in conversation; raise a child
call off: cancel
call up: contact by telephone
catch up on: get up-to-date information on
catch up with: reach the same place as
drop in on: visit unexpectedly
drop off: deliver
fill out: complete
find out: discover
get away with: avoid discovery
get off (your chest): tell a long-concealed secret or problem
get off (the couch): stand up
get over: recover
give up: surrender; stop work on
leave out: omit
look down on: despise
look forward to: anticipate
look into: research
look up: check a fact
look up to: admire
put up with: endure
run across: meet unexpectedly
run out: use up
send off: say goodbye to
stand up for: defend
take after: resemble
take off: leave the airport (a plane); miss time from work
turn down: reject

49e Create suitable figures of speech.

Figurative language, or **figures of speech,** are imaginative expressions, usually comparisons, that modify the literal meaning of other words. Two of the most common figures of speech are similes and metaphors.

A **simile** is a comparison that contains the word *like* or *as*.

► **His smile was like the sun peeking through after a rainstorm.**

A **metaphor** is an implied comparison. It treats one thing or action, such as a critic's review, as if it were something else, in this case, an extreme method of clearing land.

► **The critic's slash-and-burn review devastated the cast.**

Because it is compressed, a metaphor is often more forceful than a simile.

Other common figures of speech include personification, hyperbole, and hyperbole's counterpart, understatement. **Personification** is a form of metaphor in which human qualities are attributed to objects, animals, or abstract ideas.

► **The stormy sea tossed the little boat cruelly about.**

Hyperbole is deliberate exaggeration.

► **The speech was endless.**

Understatement is exaggeratedly restrained comparison.

► **The speech was certainly more engaging than a recitation of the phone book.**

Figurative comparisons can make your prose more vivid, but only if they suit your subject and purpose. Be careful to avoid **mixed metaphors;** if you use two or more comparisons together, make sure they are compatible. Not only does the following sentence mix three incompatible figures (a mineral, running, and a ship), but two of the three are also unsuitable (running a race, boarding a ship).

MIXED His presentation of the plan was so *crystal clear* that in a *burst of speed* we decided *to come aboard.*

REVISED His clear presentation immediately convinced us to support the plan.

Exercise 49.4 Recognizing figures of speech

Identify and explain the figures of speech (simile, metaphor, personification, hyperbole, and understatement) in the following passages.

EXAMPLE

A miss is as good as a mile.

This expression is a simile suggesting that an error is an error, whether small ("a miss") or large ("a mile").

1. Her voice is full of money.

—F. Scott Fitzgerald, *The Great Gatsby*

2. She runs the gamut of emotions from A to B.

—Quip attributed to Dorothy Parker and said to be about the actress Katharine Hepburn

3. The farm was crouched on a bleak hillside, whence its fields, fanged with flints, dropped steeply to the village of Howling a mile away.

—Stella Gibbons, *Cold Comfort Farm*

4. America is woven of many strands; I would recognize them and let it so remain. . . . Our fate is to become one, and yet many.

—Ralph Ellison, *Invisible Man*

5. Our military forces are one team—in the game to win regardless of who carries the ball.

—Omar Bradley, *Testimony to the Committee on Armed Services, House of Representatives, October 19, 1949*

6. The hardest thing in the world to understand is the income tax.

—Albert Einstein

7. We are such stuff
As dreams are made on, and our little life
Is rounded with a sleep.

—Shakespeare, *The Tempest, IV, i, 149*

49f Avoid clichés.

A **cliché** is an overworked expression or figure of speech. The moment we read the first word or two of a cliché, we know how it will end. If someone says, "She hit the nail on the ____," we expect the next word to be *head*. We have heard this expression so often that it no longer creates a vivid picture in our imagination.

It is usually best to rephrase a cliché as simply as you can in plain language.

CLICHÉ When John turned his papers in three weeks late, he had to *face the music.*

BETTER When John turned his papers in three weeks late, he had to *accept the consequences.*

The list in the box on this page gives some common clichés to avoid.

SOME COMMON CLICHÉS

acid test
agony of suspense
beat a hasty retreat
beyond the shadow of a doubt
blind as a bat
blue as the sky
brave as a lion
brutal murder
bustling cities
calm, cool, and collected
cold, hard facts
cool as a cucumber
crazy as a loon
dead as a doornail
deep, dark secret
depths of despair
doomed to disappointment
every dog has his day
face the music
few and far between
flat as a pancake
gild the lily
give 110 percent
green with envy
heave a sigh of relief
hit the nail on the head
in this day and age
ladder of success
last but not least
live from hand to mouth
livid with rage
the other side of the coin
paint the town red
pale as a ghost
pass the buck
pick and choose
poor but honest
poor but proud
pretty as a picture
primrose path
proud possessor
quick as a flash
quiet as a church mouse
rise and shine
rise to the occasion
sadder but wiser
shoulder to the wheel
sink or swim
smart as a whip
sneaking suspicion
sober as a judge
straight and narrow
tempest in a teapot
tired but happy
tried and true
ugly as sin
untimely death
walking the line
wax eloquent
white as a ghost
white as a sheet
worth its weight in gold

Exercise 49.5 Chapter review: Exact language

Edit the following passage for misused words, clichés, and ineffective figures of speech. Also, when appropriate, replace abstract and general words with concrete and specific words.

During the boom times of the 1920s, making money in the stock market was like shooting fish in a barrel. Conjecture in stocks was so intense that the price of a share could double overnight.

Poorly regulated, the markets sometimes fell prey to foul play by unscrupulous businesses. Brokers would inflate the price of a stock by staging rumors about a company; they would then sell out their own shares of the stock for a profit before the public discovered that the rumors were fragrant lies.

The stock market crashed to the bottom of the barrel in 1929, pulling the rug out from under the prosperous Twenties. Many speculators who had procured stocks on credit went bankrupt, followed by the financial institutions that had provided the speculators with capitol.

The Great Depression came on fast and furious after the crash. The prolonged financial slump had climbed to new heights by 1932, when the country voted out Herbert Hoover. Franklin D. Roosevelt was elected as the champion of workers and the down-and-out. The new president instigated a legislative program known as the New Deal that sought to ease the affects of the Depression. It was not until World War II boasted production dramatically that the U.S. economy at long last regained its footing.

50 Glossary of Usage

www.mhhe.com/mhhb2

For an online glossary of usage with exercises, go to

Editing > Word Choice

The following words and expressions are often confused (such as *advice* and *advise*), misused (such as *etc.*), or considered nonstandard (such as *could of*). Consulting this list will help you use these words more precisely.

a, an Use *a* with a word that begins with a consonant sound: *a cat, a dog, a one-sided argument, a house.* Use *an* with a word that begins with a vowel sound: *an apple, an X-ray, an honor.*

accept, except *Accept* is a verb meaning "to receive willingly": *Please accept my apologies. Except* is a preposition meaning "but": *Everyone except Julie saw the film. Except* can be a verb meaning "exclude": *The university excepts students who pass an exam from the foreign-language requirement.*

adapt, adopt *Adapt* means "to adjust or become accustomed to": *They adapted to the customs of their new country. Adopt* means "to take as one's own": *We adopted a puppy.*

advice, advise *Advice* is a noun meaning "suggestion"; *advise* is a verb meaning "recommend": *I took his advice and deeply regretted it. I advise you to disregard it, too.*

affect, effect As a verb, *affect* means "to influence": *Inflation affects our sense of security.* As a noun, *affect* means "a feeling or an emotion": *To study affect, psychologists probe the unconscious.* As a noun, *effect* means "result": *Inflation is one of the many effects of war.* As a verb, *effect* means "to make or accomplish": *Inflation has effected many changes in the way we spend money.*

aggravate Colloquially, *aggravate* means "irritate," but in formal writing it means "intensify" or "worsen": *The need to refuel the plane aggravated the delay, which irritated the passengers.*

agree to, agree with *Agree to* means "consent to"; *agree with* means "be in accord with": *They will agree to a peace treaty, even though they do not agree with each other on all points.*

ain't A slang contraction for *is not, am not,* or *are not, ain't* should not be used in formal writing or speech.

all ready, already *All ready* means "fully prepared." *Already* means "previously." *We were all ready to go out when we discovered that Jack had already ordered a pizza.*

all right, alright The spelling *alright* is nonstandard. Use *all right: He told me it was all right to miss class tomorrow.*

all together, altogether *All together* expresses unity or common location. *Altogether* means "completely," often in a tone of ironic understatement. *At the NRA convention, it was altogether startling to see so many guns set out all together on one table.*

allude, elude, refer to *Allude* means "to refer indirectly": *He alluded to his miserable adolescence. Elude* means "to avoid" or "to escape from": *She eluded the police for nearly two days.* Do not use *allude* to mean "to refer directly": *The teacher referred* [not *alluded*] *to page 468 in the text.*

allusion, illusion An *allusion* is an indirect reference, and an *illusion* is a false appearance or impression: *The student's allusion to the first act of* Hamlet *created the illusion that he had read the play.*

almost, most *Almost* means "nearly." *Most* means "the greater part of." Do not use *most* when you mean *almost. He wrote to me about almost* [not *most*] *everything he did. He told his mother about most things he did.*

a lot *A lot* is always two words. Do not use *alot.*

A.M., AM, a.m. These abbreviations mean "before noon" when used with numbers: 6 A.M., 6 AM, 6 a.m. Be consistent in the form you choose, and do not use the abbreviations as a synonym for *morning: In the morning* [not *a.m.*], *the train is full.*

among, between Generally, use *among* with three or more nouns, *between* with two. *The distance between Boston and Knoxville is a thousand miles. The desire to quit smoking is common among those who have smoked for a long time.*

amongst American English prefers *among.* (*Amongst* is common in British English.)

amoral, immoral *Amoral* means "neither moral nor immoral" and "not caring about moral judgments." *Immoral* means "morally wrong." *Unlike such amoral natural disasters as earthquakes and hurricanes, war is intentionally violent and therefore immoral.*

amount, number Use *amount* for quantities that cannot be counted; use *number* for quantities that can be counted. *The amount of oil left underground in the United States is a matter of dispute, but the number of oil companies losing money is tiny.*

an *See* a, an.

and/or *And/or* means "one or the other or both." It appears in business writing but is considered awkward in academic writing. *We will meet with the managing director and/or the director of marketing. We will meet with the managing director, the director of marketing, or both.*

anxious, eager *Anxious* means "fearful": *I am anxious before a test. Eager* signals strong interest or desire: *I am eager to be done with that exam.*

anymore, any more *Anymore* means "no longer." *Any more* means "no more." Both are used in negative contexts. *I do* *not enjoy dancing anymore. I do not want any more peanut butter.*

anyone/any one, anybody/any body, everyone/every one, everybody/every body *Anyone, anybody, everyone,* and *everybody* are singular indefinite pronouns: *Anybody can make a mistake.* When the pronoun *one* or the noun *body* is modified by the adjective *any* or *every,* the words should be separated by a space: *A good mystery writer accounts for every body that turns up in the story.*

anyplace Use *anywhere* instead of the more informal *anyplace.*

anyways/anywheres Use *anyway* or *anywhere* instead.

as Do not use *as* as a synonym for *since, when,* or *because. I told him he should visit Alcatraz since* [not *as*] *he was going to San Francisco. When* [not *as*] *I complained about the meal, the cook said he did not like to eat there himself. Because* [not *as*] *we asked her nicely, our teacher decided to cancel the exam.*

as, like In formal writing, avoid the use of *like* as a conjunction: *He sneezed as if* [not *like*] *he had a cold. Like* is perfectly acceptable as a preposition that introduces a comparison: *She handled the reins like an expert.*

assure, ensure, insure *Assure* means "promise." *Ensure* and *insure* mean "make secure," but *insure* is used in specific business contexts: *He assured me the company would insure my home against flooding, ensuring my ability to recover from a major storm.*

at Avoid the use of *at* to complete the notion of *where:* not *Where is Michael at?* but *Where is Michael?*

awful, awfully Use *awful* and *awfully* to convey the emotion of terror or wonder (awe-full): *The vampire flew out the window with an awful shriek.* In writing, do not use *awful* to mean "bad" or *awfully* to mean "very" or "extremely."

awhile, a while *Awhile* is an adverb: *Stay awhile with me. A while* is an article and a noun. Always use *a while* after a preposition: *Many authors are unable to write anything else for a while after they publish their first novel.*

bad, badly *Bad* is an adjective used after a linking verb such as *feel. Badly* is an adverb. *She felt bad about playing the piano badly at the recital.*

being as, being that Do not use *being as* or *being that* as synonyms for *since* or *because. Because* [not *being as*] *the mountain was there, we had to climb it.*

belief, believe *Belief* is a noun meaning "conviction"; *believe* is a verb meaning "to have confidence in the truth of." *Her belief that lying was often justified made it hard for us to believe her story.*

beside, besides *Beside* is a preposition meaning "next to" or "apart from": *The ski slope was beside the lodge. She was beside herself with joy. Besides* is both a preposition and an adverb meaning "in addition to" or "except for": *Besides a bicycle, he will need a tent and a pack.*

better Avoid using *better* in expressions of quantity: *Crossing the continent by train took more than* [not *better than*] *four days.*

between, among *See* among, between.

bring, take Use *bring* when an object is being moved toward the speaker, *take* when it is being moved away: *Please bring me a new disk and take the old one home with you.*

but that, but what In expressions of doubt, avoid writing *but that* or *but what* when you mean *that: I have no doubt that* [not *but that*] *you can learn to write well.*

can, may *Can* refers to ability; *may* refers to possibility or permission. *I see that you can rollerblade without crashing into people, but nevertheless you may not rollerblade on the promenade.*

can't hardly This double negative is ungrammatical and self-contradictory. *I can* [not *can't*] *hardly understand algebra. I can't understand algebra.*

capital, capitol *Capital* can refer to wealth or resources, or to a city; *capitol* refers to a building where lawmakers meet. *Protesters traveled to the state capital to converge on the capitol steps.*

censor, censure *Censor* means "to remove or suppress material." *Censure* means "to reprimand formally." (Both can be nouns as well.) *The Chinese government has been censured by the U.S. Congress for censoring newspapers.*

cite, sight, site The verb *cite* means "to quote or mention": *Be sure to cite all your sources in your bibliography.* As a noun, the word *sight* means "view": *It was love at first sight. Site* is a noun meaning "a particular place" as well as "a location on the Internet."

compare to, compare with Use *compare to* to point out similarities between two things: *She compared his singing to the croaking of a wounded frog.* Use *compare with* to assess differences or likenesses: *Compare Shakespeare's* Antony and Cleopatra *with Dryden's* All for Love.

complement, compliment *Complement* (literally, "to complete") means "to go well with" (verb) or "something that goes well with something else" (noun): *That scarf complements her eyes. I consider sauerkraut the perfect complement to sausages. Compliment* means "praise" (verb or noun): *He complimented the chef after the delicious dinner. She received many compliments on her thesis.*

conscience, conscious The noun *conscience* means "a sense of right and wrong": *His conscience bothered him.* The adjective *conscious* means "awake" or "aware": *I was conscious of a presence in the room.*

continual(ly), continuous(ly) *Continual* means "repeated regularly and frequently": *She continually checked her computer for new e-mail. Continuous* means "extended or prolonged without interruption": *The car alarm made a continuous wail in the night.*

could care less *Could care less* is nonstandard; use *does not care at all* instead: *She does not care at all about her physics homework.*

could of, should of, would of Avoid these nonstandard forms of *could have, should have,* and *would have.*

criteria, criterion *Criteria* is the plural form of the Latin word *criterion,* meaning "standard of judgment." *The criteria are not very strict. The most important criterion is whether you can do the work.*

data *Data* is the plural form of the Latin word *datum,* meaning "fact." Although informally used as a singular noun, in writing, treat *data* as a plural noun: *The data indicate that recycling has gained popularity.*

differ from, differ with *Differ from* expresses a lack of similarity; *differ with* expresses disagreement. *The ancient Greeks differed greatly from the Persians. Aristotle differed with Plato on some important issues.*

different from, different than The correct idiom is *different from.* Avoid *different than. The east coast of Florida is very different from the west coast.*

discreet, discrete *Discreet* means "tactful" or "prudent." *Discrete* means "separate" or "distinct." *What is a discreet way of telling them that these are two discrete issues?*

disinterested, uninterested *Disinterested* means "impartial": *We expect members of a jury to be disinterested. Uninterested* means "indifferent" or "unconcerned": *Most people today are uninterested in alchemy.*

don't, doesn't *Don't* is the contraction for *do not* and is used with *I, you, we, they,* and plural nouns. *Doesn't* is the contraction for *does not* and is used with *he, she, it,* and singular nouns. *You don't know what you're talking about. He doesn't know what you're talking about either.*

due to, because of *Due to* is an overworked and often confusing expression when it is used for *because of.* Use *due to* only in expressions of time in infinitive constructions or in other contexts where the meaning is "scheduled." *The plane is due to arrive in one hour. He missed* *the train because of* [not *due to*] *a car accident.*

each and every Use one of these words or the other but not both. *Every cow came in at feeding time. Each one had to be watered.*

each other, one another Use *each other* in sentences involving two subjects and *one another* in sentences involving more than two. *Husbands and wives should help each other. Classmates should share ideas with one another.*

eager, anxious *See* anxious, eager.

effect, affect *See* affect, effect.

e.g., i.e. The abbreviation *e.g.* stands for the Latin words meaning "for example." The abbreviation *i.e.* stands for the Latin for "that is." *Come as soon as you can, i.e., today or tomorrow. Bring fruit with you, e.g., apples and peaches.* In formal writing, replace the abbreviations with the English words: *Keats wrote many different kinds of lyrics, for example, odes, sonnets, and songs.*

either, neither Both *either* and *neither* are singular: *Neither of the two boys has played the game. Either of the two girls is willing to show you the way home.* When used as an intensive, *either* is always negative: *She told him she would not go either.*

elicit, illicit The verb *elicit* means "to draw out." The adjective *illicit* means "unlawful." *The detective was unable to elicit any information about other illicit activity.*

elude, allude *See* allude, elude, refer to.

emigrate, immigrate *Emigrate from* means "to move away from one's country": *My grandfather emigrated from Greece in 1905. Immigrate to* means "to move to another country and settle there": *Grandpa immigrated to the United States.*

eminent, imminent, immanent *Eminent* means "celebrated" or "well known": *Many eminent Victorians were melancholy and disturbed. Imminent* means "about to happen" or "about to come": *In August 1939, many Europeans sensed that war was imminent. Immanent* refers to something invisible but dwelling throughout the world: *Medieval Christians believed that God's power was immanent through the universe.*

ensure, assure, insure *See* assure, ensure, insure.

enthused Use *enthusiastic* instead: *He was enthusiastic about the new movie.*

etc. The abbreviation *etc.* stands for the Latin *et cetera,* meaning "and others" or "and other things." Because *and* is included in the abbreviation, do not write *and etc.* In a series, a comma comes before *etc.,* just as it would before the coordinating conjunction that closes a series: *He brought string, wax, paper, etc.* In most college writing, it is better to end a series of examples with a final example or the words *and so on.*

everybody/every body, everyone/every one *See* anyone/any one. . . .

except, accept *See* accept, except.

expect, suppose *Expect* means "to hope" or "to anticipate": *I expect a good grade on my final paper. Suppose* means "to presume": *I suppose you did not win the lottery on Saturday.*

explicit, implicit *Explicit* means "stated outright." *Implicit* means "implied, unstated." *Her explicit instructions were to go to the party without her, but the implicit message she conveyed was disapproval.*

farther, further *Farther* describes geographical distances: *Ten miles farther on is a hotel. Further* means "in addition" when geography is not involved: *He said further that he did not like my attitude.*

fewer, less *Fewer* refers to items that can be counted individually; *less* refers to general amounts. *Fewer people signed up for indoor soccer this year than last. Your argument has less substance than you think.*

first, firstly *Firstly* is common in British English but not in the United States. *First, second, third* are the accepted forms.

flaunt, flout *Flaunt* means "to wave" or "to show publicly" with delight, pride, or arrogance: *He flaunted his wealth by wearing overalls lined with mink. Flout* means "to scorn" or "to defy," especially publicly without concern for the consequences: *She flouted the traffic laws by running through red lights.*

former, latter *Former* refers to the first and *latter* to the second of two things mentioned previously: *Mario and Alice are both good cooks; the former is fonder of Chinese cooking, the latter of Mexican.*

further, farther *See* farther, further.

get In formal writing, avoid colloquial uses of *get,* as in *get with it, get it all together, get-up-and-go, get it,* and *that gets me.*

good, well *Good* is an adjective and should not be used in place of the adverb *well. He felt good about doing well on the exam.*

half, a half, half a Write *half, a half,* or *half a* but not *half of, a half a,* or *a half of. Half the clerical staff went out on strike. I want a half-dozen eggs to throw at the actors. Half a loaf is better than none, unless you are on a diet.*

hanged, hung People are *hanged* by the neck until dead. Pictures and all other things that can be suspended are *hung.*

hardly Use *can hardly* instead of *can't hardly* to avoid a double negative: *I can hardly wait for spring break.*

hopefully *Hopefully* means "with hope." It is often misused to mean "it is hoped." *We waited hopefully for our ship to come in* [not *Hopefully, our ship will come in*].

i.e., e.g. *See* e.g., i.e.

if . . . then Avoid using these words in tandem. Redundant: *If I get my license, then I can drive a cab.* Better: *If I get my license, I can drive a cab. Once I get my license, I can drive a cab.*

if, whether Use *whether* instead of *if* when expressing alternatives: *If we go to the movies, we don't know whether we'll see a comedy or a drama.*

illicit, elicit *See* elicit, illicit.

illusion, allusion *See* allusion, illusion.

imminent, immanent *See* eminent, imminent, immanent.

immigrate, emigrate *See* emigrate, immigrate.

immoral, amoral *See* amoral, immoral.

implicit, explicit *See* explicit, implicit.

imply, infer *Imply* means "to suggest without stating directly": *By putting his fingers in his ears, he implied that she should stop singing. Infer* means "to draw a conclusion": *When she dozed off during his declaration of love, he inferred that she did not feel the same way about him.*

in, in to, into *In* refers to a location inside something: *Charles kept a snake in his room. In to* refers to motion with a purpose: *The resident manager came in to capture it. Into* refers to movement from outside to inside or from separation to contact: *The snake escaped by crawling into a drain. The manager ran into the wall, and Charles got into big trouble.*

incredible, incredulous *Incredible* stories and events cannot be believed; *incredulous* people do not believe. *Nancy told an incredible story of being abducted by a UFO over the weekend. We were all incredulous.*

inside of, outside of The "of" is unnecessary in these phrases: *He was outside the house.*

insure, assure, ensure *See* assure, ensure, insure.

ironically *Ironically* means "contrary to what was or might have been expected" in a sense that implies human foolishness or unintentional humor. *Ironically, the peace activists were planning a "War Against Hate" campaign.* It should not be confused with *surprising* ("unexpected") or with *coincidentally* ("occurring at the same time or place"). *Coincidentally, her wedding day was the only day it rained all summer.*

irregardless This construction is a double negative because both the prefix *ir-* and the suffix *-less* are negatives. Use *regardless* instead.

is when, is where Do not use these constructions when defining something: *Photosynthesis is the process by which* [not *is when* or *is where*] *plants produce energy from sunlight.*

it's, its *It's* is a contraction, usually for *it is* but sometimes for *it has: It's often been said that English is a difficult language to learn. Its* is a possessive pronoun: *The dog sat down and scratched its fleas.*

kind, kinds *Kind* is singular: *This kind of house is easy to build. Kinds* is plural and should be used only to indicate more than one kind: *These three kinds of toys are better than those two kinds.*

kind of, sort of These constructions should not be used to mean *somewhat* or *a little: I was somewhat tired after the party.*

lay, lie *Lay* means "to place." Its main forms are *lay, laid,* and *laid.* It generally has a direct object, specifying what has been placed: *She laid her book on the steps and left it there. Lie* means "to recline" and does not take a direct object. Its main forms are *lie, lay,* and *lain: She often lay awake at night.*

lead, led *Lead* is a noun referring to a metal. Take care not to confuse it with *led,* the past tense of the verb *lead: The captain led the basketball team to victory.*

leave, let *Leave* means "to go away." *Let* means "to allow": *I wish the teacher would let me leave class early.*

less, fewer *See* fewer, less.

like, as *See* as, like.

literally *Literally* means "actually" or "exactly as written": *Literally thousands gathered along the parade route.* Do not use *literally* as an intensive adverb when it can be misleading or even ridiculous, as here: *His blood literally boiled.*

loose, lose *Loose* is an adjective that means "not securely attached." *Lose* is a verb that means "to misplace." *Better tighten that loose screw before you lose the whole structure.*

lots, lots of Do not use these colloquial terms in academic writing. Instead, use *very, a great deal,* or *much.*

may, can *See* can, may.

may of, might of These nonstandard forms of *may have* and *might have* should not be used in academic writing.

maybe, may be *Maybe* is an adverb meaning "perhaps": *Maybe he can get a summer job as a lifeguard. May be* is a verb phrase meaning "is possible": *It may be that I can get a job as a lifeguard, too.*

moral, morale *Moral* means "lesson," especially a lesson about standards of behavior or the nature of life: *The moral of the story is do not drink and drive. Morale* means "attitude" or "mental condition": *Office morale dropped sharply after the dean was arrested.*

more important, more importantly Use *more important.*

most, almost *See* almost, most.

must of Avoid the use of *must of,* a nonstandard form of *must have.*

myself (himself, herself, etc.) Pronouns ending with *-self* refer to or intensify other words: *Jack hurt himself. Standing in the doorway was the man himself.* When you are unsure whether to use *I* or *me, she* or *her, he* or *him* in a compound subject or object, you may be tempted to substitute one of the *-self* pronouns. Don't do it. *The quarrel was between her and me* [not *myself*]. (*Also see Chapter 36: Problems with Pronouns on pp. 577–80.*)

neither, either *See* either, neither.

nohow, nowheres These words are nonstandard for *anyway, in no way, in any way, in any place,* and *in no place.* Do not use them in formal writing.

number, amount *See* amount, number.

off of Omit the *of: She took the painting off the wall.*

OK, O.K., okay Instead of using these informal terms in academic writing, choose a more specific word to express your intended meaning. *Her paper was* *acceptable* [not *okay*]. *This is a convenient* [not *okay*] *time for me to talk.*

one another, each other *See* each other, one another.

outside of, inside of *See* inside of, outside of.

passed, past *Passed* is the past tense of the verb *pass*: *We passed the gym on our way to the library. Past* means "of a former time" or "beyond": *She is the past president of the board. The library is just past the gym.*

percent (per cent), percentage *Percent* (also spelled *per cent*) appears after a specific numeral. The word is spelled out in nontechnical writing. *Percentage* appears alone or with an adjective: *The candidate received 40 percent* [not *40%, forty percent,* or *forty %*] *of the vote. She needed a larger percentage to win the election.*

plus Avoid using *plus* as a coordinating conjunction (use *and*) or a transitional expression (use *moreover*). *He had to walk the dog, empty the garbage, and* [not *plus*] *write a term paper.*

practicable, practical *Practicable* is an adjective applied to things that can be done: *A space program that would land human beings on Mars is now practicable. Practical* means "sensible": *Many people do not think such a journey is practical.*

precede, proceed *Precede* means "come before"; *proceed* means "go forward." *Despite the heavy snows that preceded us, we managed to proceed up the hiking trail.*

previous to, prior to Avoid these wordy and somewhat pompous substitutions for *before.*

principal, principle *Principal* is an adjective meaning "most important" or a noun meaning "the head of an organization" or "a sum of money": *Our principal objections to the school's principal are that he is a liar and a cheat. Principle* is a noun meaning "a basic standard or law": *We believe in the principles of honesty and fair play.*

proceed, precede *See* precede, proceed.

raise, rise *Raise* means "to lift or cause to move upward." It takes a direct object—someone raises something: *I raised the windows in the classroom. Rise* means "to go upward." It does not take a direct object—something rises by itself: *We watched the balloon rise to the ceiling.*

real, really Do not use the word *real* when you mean *very*: *The cake was very* [not *real*] *good.*

reason is because, reason why These are redundant expressions. Use either *the reason is that* or *because*: *The reason he fell on the ice is that he cannot skate. He fell on the ice because he cannot skate.*

refer to *See* allude, elude, refer to.

relation, relationship *Relation* describes a connection between things: *There is a relation between smoking and lung cancer. Relationship* describes a connection between people: *The brothers have always had a close relationship.*

respectfully, respectively *Respectfully* means "with respect": *Treat your partners respectfully. Respectively* means "in the given order": *The three Williams she referred to were Shakespeare, Wordsworth, and Yeats, respectively.*

rise, raise *See* raise, rise.

set, sit *Set* is usually a transitive verb meaning "to establish" or "to place." It takes a direct object, and its principal parts are *set, set,* and *set*: *DiMaggio set the standard of excellence in fielding. She set the box down in the corner. Sit* is usually intransitive, meaning "to place oneself in a sitting position." Its principal parts are *sit, sat,* and *sat*: *The dog sat on command.*

shall, will *Shall* was once the standard first-person future form of the verb *to be* when a simple statement of fact was intended: *I shall be twenty-one on my next birthday.* Today, most writers use *will* in the ordinary future tense for the first person: *I will celebrate my birthday by throwing a big party. Shall* is still used in questions. *Shall we dance?*

should of *See* could of, should of, would of.

site, sight, cite *See* cite, sight, site.

some Avoid using the adjective *some* in place of the adverb *somewhat: He felt somewhat* [not *some*] *better after a good night's sleep.*

somebody, some body; someone, some one *Somebody* and *someone* are indefinite pronouns meaning "some person." *Some body* is a noun (*body*) and an adjective (*some*). *Some one* is a pronoun or adjective (*one*) and an adjective (*some*). *Somebody on television recommended a shampoo that would give hair some body. Someone told me some one person was to blame for the problem. (Also see Chapter 36: Problems with Pronouns, p. 587.)*

some of *See* all/all of. . . .

someone, some one; somebody, some body *See* somebody, some body; someone, some one.

sometime, some time, sometimes *Sometime* is an adverb meaning "at an unspecified future time." *Some time* consists of the adjective *some* modifying the noun *time* and means "a period of time." *Sometimes* is an adverb meaning "occasionally." *Sometime next week we should go to the movies if you have some time. I like to see films sometimes.*

somewheres Use *somewhere* or *someplace* instead.

stationary, stationery *Stationary* means "standing still": *I worked out on my stationary bicycle. Stationery* is writing paper: *That stationery smells like a rose garden.*

suppose, expect *See* expect, suppose.

sure Avoid confusing the adjective *sure* with the adverb *surely: The dress she wore to the party was surely bizarre.*

sure and, sure to *Sure and* is often used colloquially. In formal writing, *sure to* is preferred: *Be sure to* [not *Be sure and*] *get to the wedding on time.*

take, bring *See* bring, take.

than, then *Than* is a conjunction used in comparisons: *I am taller than you. Then* is an adverb referring to a point in time: *We will sing and then dance.*

that, which Many writers use *that* for restrictive (i.e., essential) clauses and *which* for nonrestrictive (i.e., nonessential) clauses. *The bull that escaped from the ring ran through my china shop, which was located in the square. (Also see Chapter 51: Commas, pp. 727–32.)*

their, there, they're *Their* is a possessive pronoun: *They gave their lives. There* is an adverb of place: *She was standing there. They're* is a contraction of *they are: They're reading more poetry this semester.*

theirself, theirselves, themself Use *themselves.*

them Do not use *them* in place of *these* or *those*: *Those* [not *them*] *cupcakes were delicious.*

this here, these here, that there, them there When writing, avoid these nonstandard forms and use *this, these, that,* and *them.*

to, too, two *To* is a preposition; *too* is an adverb; *two* is a number. *The two of us got lost too many times on our way to his house.*

toward, towards *Toward* is preferred over *towards* in American English, but both are acceptable.

try and, try to *Try to* is the standard form: *Try to* [not *try and*] *understand.*

uninterested, disinterested *See* disinterested, uninterested.

unique *Unique* means "one of a kind." Do not use any qualifiers with it: *The idea is unique* [not *very unique*].

use, utilize These terms are interchangeable, but *use* is preferable because it is simpler: *We must learn how to use the computer's external hard drive.*

verbally, orally To say something *orally* is to say it aloud: *We agreed orally to share credit for the work, but when I asked her to confirm it in writing, she refused.* To say something *verbally* is to use words: *His eyes flashed anger, but he did not express his feelings verbally.*

wait for, wait on People *wait for* those who are late; they *wait on* tables.

weather, whether The noun *weather* refers to the atmosphere: *She worried that the weather would not clear up in time for the victory celebration. Whether* is a conjunction referring to a choice between alternatives: *I can not decide whether to go now or next week.*

well, good *See* good, well.

whether, weather *See* weather, whether.

which, who, whose *Which* is used for things, *who* and *whose* for people. *My fountain pen, which I had lost last week, was found by a child who had never seen one before, whose whole life had been spent with ballpoints.*

who, whom Use *who* with subjects and their complements. Use *whom* with objects of verbs: *The person who will fill the position is Jane, whom you met last week.* (*Also see Chapter 36: Problems with Pronouns, pp. 584–86.*)

who's, whose *Who's* is a contraction of *who is*: *Who's in charge here? Whose* is a possessive pronoun: *Whose car is blocking the driveway?*

will, shall *See* shall, will.

would of *See* could of, should of, would of.

your, you're *Your* is a possessive pronoun: *Is that your new car? You're* is a contraction of *you are: You're a lucky guy.*

CHECKLIST

Editing for Word Choice

Keep the following questions in mind to be sure that you understand words in your reading and use them effectively and appropriately in your writing:

- ☐ Do you have a dictionary at hand for unfamiliar words you encounter in your reading? Do you have a thesaurus at hand while you write to find the most appropriate word to convey your meaning? Can you infer the meaning of unfamiliar words from contextual clues? (*See Chapter 47: Dictionaries and Vocabulary, pp. 678–88.*)
- ☐ Is your language appropriate to the assignment? Does it include any euphemisms, misleading doublespeak, inappropriate slang expressions, regionalisms, or jargon? Have you used any stereotyping, biased, or sexist expressions? (*See Chapter 48: Appropriate Language, pp. 689–96.*)
- ☐ Have you chosen words with the appropriate connotations? Have you confused words that have similar denotations? (*See Chapter 49: Exact Language, pp. 696–701 and Chapter 50: Glossary of Usage, pp. 707–16.*)
- ☐ Have you enriched your language with specific and concrete words and suitable figures of speech? Have you avoided clichés? (*See Chapter 49: Exact Language, pp. 696–707.*)

Musical notation includes punctuation-like symbols that composers use to indicate stops or pauses as well as to cue changes in dynamics, key, and tempo.

PART 10

No steel can pierce the human heart so chillingly as a period at the right moment.

—Isaac Babel

Sentence Punctuation

51 Commas

In the first section of this chapter, we review when a comma is needed and when it is optional. The section beginning on page 740 covers common misuses of commas.

www.mhhe.com/mhhb2

For information and exercises on commas, go to

Editing > Commas

COMMON USES OF THE COMMA

Although it is tempting to think that commas indicate a pause for breath, reading a sentence aloud and adding commas in places where you pause is not a reliable way to punctuate your sentences.

✓ 51a Place a comma before a coordinating conjunction that joins two independent clauses.

An independent clause is a group of words that could stand alone as a sentence (*see 31d, p. 503*). When a coordinating conjunction (*and, but, for, nor, or, so, yet*) is used to join two independent clauses, put a

WRITING OUTCOMES

Part 10: Sentence Punctuation

This section will help you answer questions such as:

Rhetorical Knowledge

- In a journalism class, should I place a comma before *and* as part of a series? **(51b)**
- When should I use dashes in academic writing? **(55b–d)**

Critical Thinking, Reading, and Writing

- How should I set off words I have added to a quotation? **(55i)**
- How do I use ellipses to indicate omissions from quotations? **(55j)**

Processes

- Can my word processor's grammar checker help me edit for punctuation? **(51–56)**

Knowledge of Conventions

- What are common misuses of the comma? **(51k–q)**
- How do I place periods, question marks, and exclamation points with quotation marks? **(54h)**

Self-Assessment: *Take an online quiz at www.mhhe.com/mhhb2 to test your familiarity with the topics covered in Chapters 51–56. Pay special attention to the sections in these chapters that correspond to any questions you answer incorrectly.*

comma before the coordinating conjunction. Joining two independent clauses without a coordinating conjuction results in a comma splice (*see Chapter 33: Comma Splices and Run-ons, pp. 524–35*).

Editing to Add Commas Where Needed

- Use a comma to separate coordinated independent clauses. (*See 51a.*)

  independent clause, | coordinating conjunction | + independent clause

  ► Prices rose steadily, but profits still fell.

- Use commas to separate items in a series and coordinate adjectives. (*See 51b–c.*)

  item, item, item

  ► The gift should be unique, inexpensive, and returnable.

  adjective, adjective

  ► He described her as a beautiful, talented child.

- Use a comma to set off an introductory element from an independent clause. (*See 51d.*)

  introductory element, independent clause

  ► Mysteriously, the image reappeared.

- Use commas to set off nonessential elements that interrupt, interject, or modify. (*See 51e–g.*)

  beginning of sentence, nonessential phrase, end of sentence

  ► The flower garden, untended for years, produced only weeds.

- Use a comma to separate a direct quotation from the phrase that signals it. (*See 51h.*)

  signal phrase, direct quotation

  ► Mead said, "I am glad that I am alive."

- Use commas to separate parts of dates, addresses, titles, and numbers. (*See 51i.*)

  city, state, day, year

  ► They traveled to Orlando, Florida, on January 5, 2009.

- Use a comma to take the place of an omitted word or to prevent misreading. (*See 51j.*)

  omitted word: *had*

  ► The punch bowl had a crack and the crystal glass, a chip.

	and	
	but	
	for	
independent clause,	nor	independent clause
	or	
	so	
	yet	

► **He felt a pain in his knee, and he began to play cautiously.**

> ***Note:*** Do not place a comma between the coordinating conjunction and the second independent clause. (*See 51m, pp. 741–42.*)

If you are joining two long clauses that contain commas, using a semicolon instead of a comma and a coordinating conjunction between the two clauses can make your sentence clearer for readers.

► **After his knee surgery, he needed almost a year to recover~~, but~~ ; once his doctor gave her approval, *however,* he began to play with his old skill, enthusiasm, and nerve.**

If you are joining two short clauses, the comma is optional unless it is needed for clarity.

► **I ran and they cheered.**

Do not use a comma with a coordinating conjunction that joins word groups that cannot stand alone as sentences (*see 51l, p. 741*).

Commas and Grammar Checkers

Grammar checkers usually do not highlight missing commas following introductory elements or between independent clauses joined by a coordinating conjunction such as *and.* They also cannot judge whether a sentence element is essential or nonessential.

Exercise 51.1 Using commas with coordinating conjunctions

Edit the following sentences, adding commas as needed between independent clauses joined by a coordinating conjunction.

EXAMPLE **Organ transplants have saved many lives, so people should consider filling out a donor card.**

1. Surgeons began attempting organ transplants in the early twentieth century but the first successful transplant did not take place until 1954.
2. The transplant was from one identical twin to another and the twin who received the organ—a kidney—lived for eight years after the operation.
3. Recently, surgeons have transplanted hands and face transplants are on the horizon.
4. Face transplants raise ethical issues so this type of operation is controversial.
5. Some organs for transplant operations come from live donors but most organs come from cadavers.

Exercise 51.2 Combining sentences with commas and coordinating conjunctions

Use a comma and a coordinating conjunction to combine each set of sentences into one sentence. Vary your choice of conjunctions.

EXAMPLE **The experiment did not support our hypothesis~~. We~~**, *yet we* **considered it a success.**

1. Asperger's syndrome and autism are not the same. Asperger's syndrome is often confused with autism.
2. People with Asperger's syndrome have normal IQs. They have difficulty interacting with others in a social setting.
3. Children with this disorder often engage in solitary, repetitive routines. In school they may have difficulty working in groups.
4. People with Asperger's syndrome also have a difficult time with nonverbal communication. They may be unable to read other people's body language.
5. The public has only recently become aware of Asperger's syndrome. Drugs that can cure this neurobiological disorder have yet to be developed.

51b Use commas between items in a series.

A comma should appear between each of three or more items in a series.

► **Three industries that have been important to New England are** first item, second item, third item **shipbuilding, tourism, and commercial fishing.**

Occasionally, separating the items in a sentence with commas only—omitting *and, or,* or another coordinating conjunction before the last item—can help you add emphasis: *Her coat was thin, muddy, torn.*

Commas clarify which items are part of the series. In the following example, the third comma clarifies that the hikers are packing lunch *and* snacks, not chocolate and trail mix for lunch.

CONFUSING For the hiking trip, we needed to pack lunch, chocolate and trail mix.

CLEAR For the hiking trip, we needed to pack lunch, chocolate, and trail mix.

Items in a series can consist of words, phrases, or clauses. If the items in a series contain commas, separate the items with semicolons instead of commas (*see 52d, p. 747*).

► **During the play's three acts, the characters gather at a deserted, lonely house by the seashore; discover that one of their number, an obnoxious business executive, has been murdered; and call on the hero, an off-duty police officer, to help them solve the mystery.**

When three or more items within a sentence are preceded by numbers or letters, treat them as items within a series.

► **The hawks that have built their nest on a ledge of this building prey on (1) squirrels, (2) pigeons, and (3) other small birds.**

CHARTING the TERRITORY

Commas in Journalism

If you are writing for a journalism course, you may be required to leave out the final comma that precedes *and* in a series, just as magazines and newspapers usually do. Follow the convention that your instructor prefers.

51c Use commas between coordinate adjectives.

Two or more adjectives placed side by side before a noun or pronoun are either coordinate or cumulative. **Coordinate adjectives** act individually to modify a noun or pronoun; each adjective should be separated from the next one with a comma.

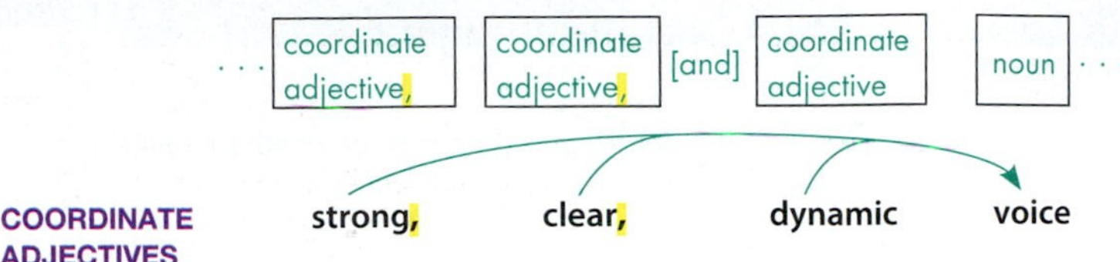

COORDINATE ADJECTIVES

Cumulative adjectives act as a set: the first cumulative adjective modifies the following adjective or adjectives as well as the noun or pronoun. Because they act as a set, cumulative adjectives are not separated by commas.

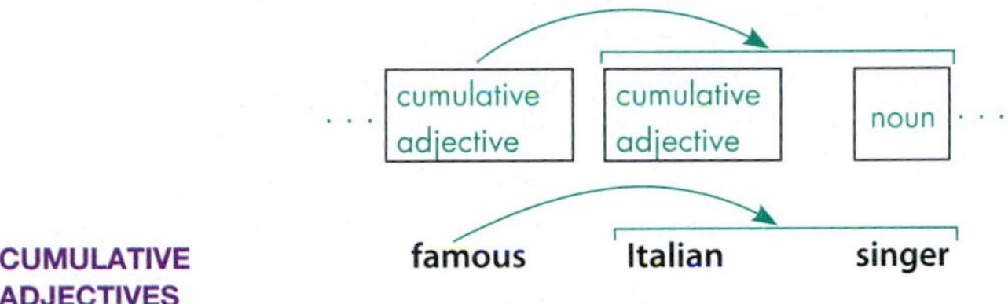

CUMULATIVE ADJECTIVES

If you are not sure whether a comma should separate two or more adjectives, try changing the order of the adjectives or putting the word *and* between them. If the sentence sounds wrong, then do not add a comma.

► Luciano Pavarotti was a famous (adj) Italian (adj) tenor (noun); he was known for his strong (adj), clear (adj), dynamic (adj) voice (noun).

In the example above, we could say that Pavarotti had a clear, strong, dynamic voice, but it would be awkward to say that he was an Italian famous tenor.

Note that the comma is placed between the coordinate adjectives, not between the adjective and the noun.

► I'm tired of that boring (adj), monotonous (adj)/ song (noun).

Also note that a comma is not used between two coordinate adjectives joined by *and* or between a number and an adjective.

► He addressed a crowd of loud (adj)/ and excited (adj) supporters.

► The scientist focused her attention on the two/ black bears under a tree.

IDENTIFY AND EDIT
Commas with Coordinate Adjectives

Follow these steps if you have trouble determining whether commas should separate two or more adjectives that precede a noun:

1. Identify the adjectives.

PROBLEM SENTENCE Ann is an [excellent art] teacher and a [caring generous] mentor.

Note that nouns such as *art* can also be used as adjectives.

2. Try changing the order of the adjectives or putting the word and *between them. Then read the adjectives and noun to yourself. How do they sound?*

PROBLEM SENTENCE Ann is an [art excellent] teacher and a [generous caring] mentor.

We could say that Ann is a generous caring mentor, but it would be awkward to say that she is an art excellent teacher.

PROBLEM SENTENCE Ann is an [excellent and art] teacher and a [caring and generous] mentor.

We could say that Ann is a caring and generous mentor, but it would be awkward to say that she is an excellent and art teacher.

3. If the phrase sounds wrong, the adjectives are cumulative and don't need a comma between them. If the phrase sounds right, the adjectives are coordinate and require a comma. If need be, correct the original sentence.

Ann is an excellent art teacher and a caring, generous mentor.

Exercise 51.3 Using commas with series of nouns and adjectives

Edit the following sentences, adding commas as needed to separate items in a series and coordinate adjectives. Some sentences may be correct; circle their numbers.

EXAMPLE **One part of the wall was covered with pictures of leaping, prancing animals.**

1. Scholars have studied prehistoric cave paintings for almost a century.
2. Paintings have been found in North America Europe Africa and Australia.
3. Paintings found in southeastern France contain images of animals birds and fish.
4. Some scholars believe that the cave painter may have been a rapturous entranced shaman.
5. We can picture the flickering dazzling torchlight that guided the painter's way through dank dark passageways.
6. Mixing colors with their saliva and blowing the paint onto the wall with their breath must have given the cave painters feelings of creative power supernatural control and expressive glory.

FIGURE 51.1 An image of a horse painted around 15,000 years ago on the wall of a cave in Lascaux, France.

✓ 51d Use a comma after an introductory word group that is not the subject of the sentence.

A comma both attaches an introductory word, phrase, or clause to and distinguishes it from the rest of the sentence.

[introductory word,] [rest of sentence]

► ***Finally,*** **the speeding car careened to the right.**

[introductory phrase,] [rest of sentence]

► ***Reflecting on her life experiences,*** **Washburn was satisfied.**

[introductory clause,] [rest of sentence]

► ***Until he noticed the handprint,*** **the detective had no clues.**

Do not add a comma after a word group that functions as the subject of the sentence, however. Be especially careful with word groups that begin with *-ing* words.

subject

► **Persuading Washington lawmakers is one of a lobbyist's main tasks.**

introductory word group — subject

► **Persuading Washington lawmakers, lobbyists pursue the interests of their clients.**

A comma is also not used following the opening phrase in an inverted sentence, where the subject follows the verb (*see 51o, p. 742*).

verb subject

► **In the bushes lurked a poisonous snake.**

When the introductory phrase contains fewer than five words and there is no danger of confusion without a comma, the comma is optional.

► ***For several hours* we rode on in silence.**

Exercise 51.4 Using commas with introductory word groups

Edit the following sentences, adding commas as needed after introductory word groups. Some sentences may be correct; circle their numbers.

EXAMPLE **During the early Middle Ages, Western Europeans remained fairly cut off from the East.**

1. After the year 1000 CE Europeans became less isolated.
2. To the Holy Lands traveled Western pilgrims and merchants in a steady stream.
3. Increasingly aware of the rich civilizations beyond their borders Europeans began to enter into business relationships with the cities and countries in the East.
4. Establishing contact with the principal ports of the eastern Mediterranean and Black seas allowed merchants to develop a vigorous trade.
5. As this trade expanded across the Mediterranean world Western Europeans were able to enjoy spices and other exotic products.
6. In the thirteenth and fourteenth centuries European missionaries and merchants traveled to China, India, and the Near East.

Exercise 51.5 Combining sentences with commas and introductory word groups

Combine the following sentences into one sentence using the suggestions in parentheses. Revise the wording of the sentences as necessary.

EXAMPLE **~~Some researchers are~~ To studying short-term memory~~. They~~ , some researchers conducted an experiment that tested the results of pressure on students' memory. (introductory phrase)**

1. The researchers are Dr. Sian Bellock of Miami University of Ohio and Dr. Thomas Carr of Michigan State. An article about their work appeared in the *New York Times.* (introductory phrase)
2. They administered two math tests to two groups of students. The experiment took place recently. (introductory word)
3. One test was a low-pressure situation. The other test was a high-pressure situation. (introductory clause)
4. Strong students performed well on the low-pressure test. They did not perform as well on the high-pressure test. (introductory clause)
5. Other students had lower scores on the first test. Their performance on the second test was about the same as on the first. (introductory phrase)
6. The results were a surprise. They suggest that high-pressure situations interfere with the short-term memories of the strongest students. (introductory word)

✓ 51e Use a comma or commas to set off nonessential (nonrestrictive) elements.

Nonessential, or **nonrestrictive,** elements add information to a sentence but are not required for its basic meaning to be understood. They are set off with commas. They can also be set off with dashes or parentheses. (*See 55c on pp. 768–69 and 55f on p. 770.*)

main part of sentence, | nonrestrictive element

► **Robert's essay won the contest, *which was sponsored by the local paper.***

The words *which was sponsored by the local paper* give more information about the contest, but they do not tell you more about Robert's essay, which is what the sentence is about.

first part of sentence, | nonrestrictive element, | rest of sentence

► **Robert's essay, *which was about charter schools,* won the contest.**

The words *which was about charter schools* tell you more about the essay but are not necessary to identify which essay won the contest.

Essential, or **restrictive,** elements identify who or what the writer is describing. Readers need these elements to understand the sentence's meaning so they are not set off with commas.

first part of sentence | restrictive element | rest of sentence

► **The essay *that was about charter schools* won the contest.**

The words *that was about charter schools* tell you which essay the sentence is about and are essential to conveying the sentence's meaning: that the essay on charter schools was the winner.

In the first two examples, the commas help you see that the words they set off are an aside—a piece of additional information. In the third example, the words are more than an aside. They identify the essay for the reader. Therefore, they are restrictive and are not set off with commas.

Sometimes the addition of a comma or commas can subtly change a sentence's meaning, as in the next pair of sentences.

► **The customers, demanding a refund, lined up by the register.**

The commas set off a phrase that gives us additional information about all of the customers in question: they are demanding a refund.

► **The customers demanding a refund lined up by the register.**

We can assume that out of all the customers in the store only the group named—those demanding a refund—lined up by the register.

In this case, the context would determine whether to enclose *demanding a refund* with commas. Notice how a preceding sentence can affect the meaning of the sentence in question and determine whether a comma is needed:

► **Two customers with angry looks on their faces approached the checkout counter. The customers, demanding a refund, lined up by the register.**

► **The store opened at the usual time. The customers demanding a refund lined up by the register.**

If you are unsure if an element is restrictive or nonrestrictive, imagine the sentence without it. Would the reader know which person, place, or thing you are describing? Would the basic meaning of the sentence remain unchanged? If so, the element is nonrestrictive and should be set off with commas.

1. Commas with nonrestrictive clauses

A **clause** is a group of words with a subject and a verb. **Adjective clauses,** which begin with *who, whom, whose, which, that, when, where,* or *why,* are dependent clauses that modify a noun or pronoun in an independent clause. **Adverb clauses,** which can begin with *when* or *where* or with a subordinating conjunction (*see 31i, pp. 506–8*), modify a verb in an independent clause. Adjective or adverb clauses can be nonrestrictive or restrictive.

An adjective clause is nonrestrictive and should be set off with commas when it does not identify the person, place, or thing that is being described, even if it supplies important information.

nonrestrictive

► **Odysseus, *who is constantly tested on his epic voyage,* returns home after a twenty-year absence.**

The phrase *who is constantly tested on his epic voyage* does not identify the noun it modifies, *Odysseus,* even though it does tell us something important about him.

An adjective clause is restrictive—not set off with commas—when it is essential to the meaning of the noun it modifies.

restrictive

► **I had read many studies on the subject, but the studies *that Johnson recommended* were the most helpful.**

Without the adjective clause, the sentence does not make sense: *I had read many studies on the subject, but the studies were the most helpful.* The adjective clause identifies the studies the writer thinks were helpful and is essential to the meaning of the sentence.

Note: Use *that* only with restrictive adjective clauses. *Which* can introduce either restrictive or nonrestrictive adjective clauses. Some writers prefer to use *which* only with nonrestrictive clauses.

that

► **I had read many studies on the subject, but the studies ~~which~~ ^ Johnson recommended were the most helpful.**

An adverb clause at the beginning of a sentence is considered an introductory word group and should be set off with a comma (*see 51d, pp. 725–27*). Adverb clauses that are within or at the end of sentences are usually essential to the meaning of the sentence and are not set off with commas.

restrictive

► **Ruiz refused the prize *because he objected to the judging process.***

The clause *because he objected to the judging process* tells why Ruiz did what he did and is therefore essential.

However, some adverb clauses are nonessential, or nonrestrictive. (See the top of page 731 for an example.)

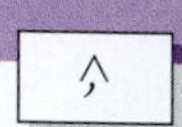

IDENTIFY AND EDIT
Commas with Nonrestrictive Words or Word Groups

Follow these steps if you have trouble deciding whether a word or word group should be set off with a comma or commas:

1. Identify the word or word group that may need to be set off with commas. Pay special attention to words that appear between the subject and verb.

PROBLEM SENTENCE — Dorothy Parker (subj) [a member of the famous Algonquin Round Table] wrote (verb) humorous verse as well as short stories.

PROBLEM SENTENCE — Her poem (subj) ["One Perfect Rose"] is (verb) a lament about a well-intentioned gift that falls short.

2. Read the sentence to yourself without the word or word group. Does the basic meaning stay the same, or does it change? Can you tell what person, place, or thing the sentence is about?

SENTENCE WITHOUT THE WORD GROUP — Dorothy Parker wrote humorous verse as well as short stories.

The subject of the sentence is identified by name, and the basic meaning of the sentence does not change.

SENTENCE WITHOUT THE WORD GROUP — Her poem is a lament about a well-intentioned gift that falls short.

Without the words "One Perfect Rose" we cannot tell what poem the sentence is describing.

3. If the meaning of the sentence stays the same without the word or word group, set it off with commas. If the meaning changes, the word or word group should not be set off with commas.

- Dorothy Parker, a member of the famous Algonquin Round Table, wrote humorous verse as well as short stories.
- Her poem "One Perfect Rose" is a lament about a well-intentioned gift that falls short.

The sentence is correct. Commas are not needed to enclose "One Perfect Rose."

nonrestrictive

► **Ruiz, *when asked why he refused the prize,* cited his objections to the judging process.**

The sentence's meaning would be the same without the nonrestrictive clause: *Ruiz cited his objections to the judging process.*

Adverb clauses beginning with *although, even though, though,* and *whereas* present a contrasting thought and are usually nonrestrictive.

nonrestrictive

► **Ruiz will not accept the prize, *even though it is a great honor.***

2. Commas with nonrestrictive phrases

Phrases that modify nouns and verbs can also be restrictive or nonrestrictive. An **adjective phrase** begins with a preposition (for example, *at, by, for, with*) or a verbal (a verb form with an *-ing, -ed,* or *-en* ending that can have various functions within a sentence). Nonrestrictive adjective phrases are set off with commas.

nonrestrictive adjective phrase

► **Some people, *by their faith in human nature or their general goodwill,* bring out the best in others.**

The sentence would have the same basic meaning without the nonrestrictive phrase (*Some people bring out the best in others*).

A restrictive adjective phrase identifies the noun it modifies and should not be set off with commas.

restrictive adjective phrase

► **People *fighting for their rights* can inspire others to join a cause.**

The adjective phrase tells readers which people the writer means.

3. Commas with nonrestrictive appositives

Appositives are nouns or noun phrases that rename nouns or pronouns and generally appear right after the word they rename. They can appear at the beginning, in the middle, or at the end of a sentence. Nonrestrictive appositives supply extra information about the noun or noun phrase, but they do not identify or limit it. Nonrestrictive appositives are set off with commas.

nonrestrictive

► **One researcher, *the widely respected R. S. Smith,* has shown that a child's performance on IQ tests is not reliable.**

The noun *researcher* is limited by the word *one,* and the appositive, *the widely respected R. S. Smith,* provides additional information about that one researcher, including his name.

Restrictive appositives indicate which person, place, or thing is being named. They are not set off with commas.

restrictive

► **The researcher *R. S. Smith* has shown that a child's performance on IQ tests is not reliable.**

The meaning of the noun *researcher* is restricted to the name *R. S. Smith.*

Exercise 51.6 Using commas with nonrestrictive elements

Edit the following sentences, adding commas as needed to set off nonrestrictive clauses, adjective phrases, and appositives. Some sentences may be correct; circle their numbers.

EXAMPLE **The brain, connected by nerves to all the other parts of the body, seems to be the seat of the mind, an abstract term for the workings of the brain.**

1. The mind-body problem under debate for centuries concerns the relationship between the mind and the body.
2. Prehistoric peoples must have observed that when a person died the body remained and the mind departed.
3. Since the time of the ancient Greeks the prevailing opinion has been that the mind and the body are separate entities.
4. Plato the Greek philosopher is often credited with originating the concept of mind-body dualism.
5. The French philosopher René Descartes described the mind and the body as independent.
6. Descartes's influential theories helped lay the foundation for scientific rationalism which views nature as a vast machine.

Exercise 51.7 Combining sentences with commas and nonrestrictive word groups

Combine the following sentences into one sentence using the suggestions in parentheses. Revise the wording of the sentences as necessary.

EXAMPLE **Brazil, ~~is~~ the largest country on the South American continent/, ~~Brazil~~ has an area of more than three million square miles. (nonessential appositive)**

1. The people in Brazil speak Portuguese. Brazil was formerly a colony of Portugal. (essential clause)
2. Peru is famous for its spectacular scenery. The Amazon River snakes through the northeastern part of the country and the Andes Mountains stretch along its coast. (nonessential phrase)
3. Argentina is in the southern part of South America. It exports beef to the United States and other countries. (nonessential clause)
4. The coast of Venezuela is on the Caribbean Sea. Venezuela is north of the equator. (nonessential phrase)
5. A number of islands dot the Caribbean Sea. They are north of Venezuela. (essential phrase)
6. Chile stretches from the central part of South America to its southern tip. Chile is the longest country in South America. (nonessential appositive)

51f Use a comma or commas with transitional expressions, parenthetical expressions, contrasting comments, and absolute phrases.

1. Transitional expressions

Transitional expressions show the relationship between ideas in two or more clauses or sentences and make the sentence in which they appear clearer. Conjunctive adverbs (*however, therefore, moreover*) and transitional phrases (*for example, on the other hand*) are usually set off by commas when used at the beginning, in the middle, or at the end of a sentence. You can also use a dash or dashes (*see 55c, on pp. 768–69*) or, in some cases, parentheses (*see 55f, on p. 770*) to set off transitional expressions. (*For a list of transitional expressions, see Chapter 33, p. 532.*)

► Brian Wilson, *for example,* was unable to cope with the pressures of touring with the Beach Boys.

► *As a matter of fact,* he had a nervous breakdown shortly after a tour.

► He is still considered one of the most important figures in rock and roll, *however.*

When a transitional expression connects two independent clauses, use a semicolon before and a comma after it.

► The Beatles were a phenomenon when they toured the United States in 1964; *subsequently,* they became the most successful rock band of all time.

Short expressions such as *also, at least, certainly, instead, of course, then, perhaps,* and *therefore* do not always need to be set off with commas.

► **I found my notes and *also* got my story in on time.**

2. Parenthetical expressions

Parenthetical expressions are like whispered asides or a shrug in a conversation. The information they provide is relatively insignificant and could easily be left out. Therefore, they are set off with a comma or commas.

► **Human cloning, *so they say,* will be possible within a decade.**

► **The experiments would take a couple of weeks, *more or less.***

3. Contrasting comments

Contrasting comments beginning with words such as *not, unlike,* or *in contrast to* should be set off with commas.

► **Will Ferrell is famous as a comedian, *not a tragedian.***

Exception: Contrasting comments that begin with *but* are often not set off with commas: *He was poor but honest.*

4. Absolute phrases

Absolute phrases usually include a noun (*sunlight*) followed by a participle (*shining*) and modify whole sentences. Set them off with commas.

► **The snake slithered through the tall grass, *the sunlight shining now and then on its green skin.***

51g Use a comma or commas to set off words of direct address, *yes* and *no*, mild interjections, and tag sentences.

Like nonrestrictive phrases and clauses, words that interrupt a sentence are set off by commas because they are not essential to the sentence's meaning.

direct address

► **We have finished this project, *Mr. Smith,* without any help from your foundation.**

► ***Yes,* I will meet you at noon.**

interjection

► **We must leave, *sadly,* this evening.**

A **tag sentence** is a normal sentence with a phrase or question attached (or "tagged") on the end. Use a comma to set off the tag. When the tag is a question, end the sentence with a question mark.

► **This is the right key, *I think*.** (tag)

► **This is the right door, *don't you think*?** (tag)

Exercise 51.8 Using commas to set off other nonessential sentence elements

Edit the following sentences, adding commas where they are needed to set off nonessential sentence elements.

EXAMPLE **Yes, I will go with you to dinner; however, I must leave by ten, not a minute later.**

1. Millions of viewers watch reality-based television shows. Cultural critics however argue that shows such as *The Amazing Race, Survivor,* and *The Bachelor* exploit human greed and the desire for fame.
2. These shows so the critics say take advantage of our insecurities.
3. The participants who appear on these shows are average, everyday people not actors.
4. *The Amazing Race* follows its subjects contestants hoping to beat out their competitors through travelling around the world and solving puzzles.
5. The message is always the same: You too can be rich and famous Average Jane or Joe.
6. Yes many of these shows hold the promise that anyone can win a million dollars and gain instant notoriety.
7. These shows of course are extremely enjoyable.
8. Their entertainment value is why we watch them don't you think?

51h Use a comma or commas to separate a direct quotation from the phrase that signals it.

Commas are used with quotation marks to set off a quotation from the words that identify its source, such as *she said* or *Robert Rubin maintains*. When the signal phrase introduces the quotation, the comma precedes the opening quotation mark. When the signal phrase follows the quotation, the comma goes inside the quotation marks. (*See Chapter 54: Quotation Marks, pp. 758–66, for more on punctuating quotations.*)

► **Irving Howe declares, "Whitman is quite realistic about the place of the self in an urban world" (261).**

► **"Whitman is quite realistic about the place of the self in an urban world," declares Irving Howe (261).**

Exception: If the words that introduce the quotation form a complete sentence, you can use a colon instead of a comma to introduce the quotation, especially if it is long.

► **Thomas Paine inspired the colonists with a famous rallying cry: "These are the times that try men's souls. The summer soldier and the sunshine patriot will, in this crisis, shrink from the service of their country; but he that stands it *now*, deserves the love and thanks of man and woman."**

If the quoted sentence is interrupted, use commas to set off the interrupting words.

► **"When we interpret a poem," DiYanni says, "we explain it to ourselves in order to understand it."**

If you are quoting more than one sentence and interrupting the quotation between sentences, the interrupting words should end with a period.

► **"But it is not possible to give to each department an equal power of self defence," James Madison writes in *The Federalist No. 51*. "In republican government the legislative authority, necessarily, predominates."**

A comma is not needed if the quotation ends with a question mark or an exclamation point.

► **"Where are my glasses?" she asked in a panic.**

► **"I don't know!" he replied angrily.**

Commas are not used to separate indirect quotations or paraphrases from the source of the quotation.

► **Irving Howe notes/ that Whitman realistically depicts the urban self as free to wander (261).**

Exercise 51.9 Using commas to set off direct quotations

Edit the following sentences to correct problems with the use of commas. Some sentences may be correct; circle their numbers.

EXAMPLE "Nothing I studied was on the test," she moaned to her friends.

1. Professor Bartman entered the room and proclaimed "Today we will examine Erikson's eight stages of human development."
2. "Who may I ask has read the assignment," he queried.
3. "Patricia" he hissed "please enlighten the rest of the class."
4. "What would you like to know?" she asked.
5. Now smiling, he replied "Begin by telling us what the eight stages are."
6. She explained that the first stage is when infants must learn to trust that their needs will be met.

51i Use commas with parts of dates and addresses, with people's titles, in numbers, and in parts of correspondence.

1. Dates

Use a comma or paired commas in dates when the month, day, and year are included or when the day of the week is followed by the date. Do not use commas when the day of the month is omitted or when the day appears before the month.

- On March 4, 1931, she traveled to New York.
- She traveled to New York on March 4, 1931.
- On Wednesday, March 4, she traveled to New York.
- In March 1931 she traveled to New York.
- On 4 March 1931 she traveled to New York.

When a season appears with a year, a comma is not needed: *spring 2009.*

2. Addresses

Use a comma or commas to set off the parts of an address or the name of a state, but do not use a comma preceding a zip code.

- He lived at 1400 Crabgrass Lane, Garrison, New York.
- At Cleveland, Ohio, the river changes direction.

► **Here is my address for the summer: 63 Oceanside Drive, Apt. 2A, Surf City, New Jersey 06106.**

3. People's titles or degrees

Put a comma between the person's name and the title or degree when it comes after the name. If the sentence continues, place another comma after the title or degree.

► **Luis Mendez, MD, gave her the green light to resume her exercise regimen.**

If an abbreviation such as *Jr.* or a roman numeral such as *II* follows a name, it usually is not necessary to set it off with a comma or commas. (Consult your discipline's style manual.)

► **The show was hosted by Milton Clark Jr.**

4. Numbers

When a number has more than four digits, use commas to mark off the numerals by hundreds—that is, by groups of three beginning at the right.

► **Andrew Jackson received 647,276 votes in the 1828 presidential election.**

If the number is four digits long, the comma is optional.

► **The survey had 1856 [or 1,856] respondents.**

Exceptions: Street numbers, zip codes, telephone numbers, page numbers (p. 2304), and years (1828) do not include commas.

Within text, you should use a comma to separate two numbers that appear together, whether the numbers are spelled out or given as numerals: *ten feet, six inches; page 15, paragraph 4; act 3, scene 1.*

For MULTILINGUAL STUDENTS

Long Numbers

In some other languages, periods, not commas, are used to mark off numerals by hundreds. In American English, however, periods indicate decimals only; commas are used in long numbers.

5. Parts of correspondence

Add a comma after the greeting in an informal letter and after the closing in any kind of letter.

► **Dear Aunt Di,**

► **Sincerely yours,**

► **With best wishes,**

A colon follows the greeting in a business letter.

► **Dear Professor Chodoff:**

51j Use a comma to take the place of an omitted word or phrase or to prevent misreading.

When a writer omits one or more words from a sentence to create an effect, a comma is often needed to make the meaning of the sentence clear for readers. In the following example, the second comma substitutes for the phrase *he found.*

► **Under the tree he found his puppy, and under the car, his cat.**

Commas are also used to keep readers from misunderstanding a writer's meaning when words are repeated or might be misread.

► **Many birds that sing, sing first thing in the morning.**

► **Any offbeat items that can be, are sold at online auction sites.**

It is often better, however, to revise the sentence and avoid the need for the clarifying comma.

► **Many songbirds sing first thing in the morning.**

► **A wide variety of offbeat items are sold at online auction sites.**

Exercise 51.10 Editing for conventional and stylistic uses of commas

Edit the following sentences, adding commas where they are needed.

EXAMPLE **Before work she visits her father, and after work, her mother.**

1. Families lured west by the Homestead Act of 1862 were promised "free land," and with this land the opportunity for a new life.
2. Any belongings that could be were piled into Conestoga wagons for the long journey west.
3. The journey from Missouri to Oregon, a 2000-mile trip, was made by some 150000 people during the mid-nineteenth century.
4. Born in Wisconsin on February 7 1867, children's book author Laura Ingalls Wilder traveled with her family throughout the West, settling in various places.

5. In October 1880 Wilder and her family were living in De Smet South Dakota; they experienced the first of a series of blizzards that lasted until May 1881.
6. Mary Anne Miller PhD wrote her dissertation on the pioneer experience.

COMMON MISUSES OF THE COMMA

Comma errors result when writers place commas between grammatical elements that belong together. (*See also Chapter 33: Comma Splices and Run-on Sentences, pp. 524–35.*)

51k Do not use commas to separate major elements in an independent clause.

Do not use a comma to separate a subject from its verb or a verb from its object.

► **Reflecting on one's life/ is necessary for emotional growth.**

The subject, *reflecting*, should not be separated from the verb, *is*.

Editing to Eliminate Unnecessary Commas

- Delete commas that separate a subject from a verb or a verb from an object. (*See 51k.*)

subject verb object
► **Kahn's homage to his father/ contains/ moments of humor.**

- Delete commas that separate compound word groups unless the word groups are independent clauses. (*See 51l.*)

subject subject verb verb
► **Evan/ and Sam were drinking tea/ and reading in my room.**

- Delete a comma that follows a preposition or a coordinating or subordinating conjunction. (*See 51m.*)

sub conj prep
► **Although/ he is a famous actor, he is in/ emotional limbo.**

- Delete commas that set off restrictive elements. (*See 51n.*)

restrictive clause
► **The knowledge/ that Pete had lied/ was hard for her to bear.**

- Delete a comma after an introductory phrase if the phrase begins an inverted sentence. (*See 51o.*)

► **In the heart of the forest/ lives Baba Yaga.**

- Delete a comma that falls before the first or after the last item in a series. In a series of adjectives, also delete a comma placed between the last adjective and the noun it modifies. (*See 51p.*)

  ► **The shelf held/ a kettle, a pot, and a dusty, greasy/ pan.**

- Delete commas that appear with other punctuation, with some exceptions. (*See 51q.*)

  ► **"Isn't my home cooking better than any restaurant's?/" asked her cousin.**

► **Washburn resolved/ that she would succeed.**

The verb, *resolved,* should not be separated from its direct object, the subordinate clause *that she would succeed.*

51l Do not use commas to separate compound word groups unless the word groups are independent clauses.

A comma should not be used between word groups joined with a coordinating conjunction (such as *and*) unless each word group could stand alone as a sentence.

► **Injuries were so frequent that he became worried/ and started to play more cautiously.**

Here, *and* joins two verbs (*became* and *started*), not two independent clauses.

► **He is worried that injuries are more frequent/ and that he will have to play more cautiously to avoid them.**

Here, *and* joins two subordinate clauses—both beginning with the word *that*—not two independent clauses.

51m Do not place commas after prepositions or conjunctions.

A comma should not be placed after a preposition or a conjunction unless you are inserting a parenthetical phrase. Avoid the common error of placing a comma after *although, such as, like,* and *than.*

► **The *duomo* in Siena was begun in the thirteenth century, and/ it was used as a model for other Italian cathedrals.**

► **Puppets were used in the stage version of *The Lion King* to represent many different animals, although/ human actors were still needed to operate them.**

51n Do not use commas to set off restrictive modifiers, restrictive appositives, or slightly parenthetical words or phrases.

Words that are necessary to identify the noun or pronoun they describe should not be set off with commas. (*For more on restrictive modifiers, see 51e, pp. 727–33.*)

restrictive clause

► **The applicants *who had studied for the admissions test* were restless and eager for the exam to begin.**

restrictive appositive

► **The director *Michael Curtiz* was responsible for many great films in the 1930s and 1940s, including *Casablanca*.**

Concluding adverb clauses that begin with *after, as soon as, before, because, if, since, unless,* and *when* are usually essential to a sentence's meaning and should not be set off with commas.

► **I am eager to test the children's IQ again *because significant variations in a child's test score indicate that the test itself may be flawed.***

If setting off a brief parenthetical remark would interrupt the flow of the sentence, the commas can be left out.

► **Science is *basically* the last frontier.**

> ***Note:*** An adverb clause that appears at the beginning of a sentence is an introductory element and is usually followed by a comma: *Until we meet, I am continuing my work on the budget.* (*See 51d, pp. 725–27, and 51e, pp. 727–33.*)

51o Do not use a comma after a phrase that begins an inverted sentence.

Although commas are used to set off introductory phrases (*see 51d, pp. 725–27*), do not use them after a phrase that appears at the beginning of an inverted sentence. A sentence is "inverted" when the verb precedes the subject.

verb subject

► **Deep in the jungle/ prowls a tiger.**

51p Do not place a comma before the first or after the last item in a series. Do not place a comma between an adjective and a noun, even in a series of coordinate adjectives.

Use commas to separate items in a series but never before the first item in the series. Do not place a comma after the final item in a series either, unless another comma rule calls for its use (for example, if the series falls at the end of an introductory word group or independent clause).

► **He wanted to record/ country music, blues, ballads, and gospel/ on the same album.**

► **He has long, ropy/ arms and/ small, close-set/ eyes.**

> ***Exception:*** If a nonrestrictive appositive consists of a series of items, you can set it off with commas.
>
> ► **He wanted to record four types of music, country music, blues, ballads, and gospel, on the same album.**
>
> Often, however, dashes are a better option in this situation (*see 55c, pp. 768–69*).

51q Do not use a comma to repeat the function of other punctuation.

A comma is never used before an opening parenthesis. It is used after a closing parenthesis only when another comma rule applies. In the following example, the comma following the closing parenthesis sets off the introductory clause.

► **When they occupy an office cubicle/ (a relatively recent invention), workers need to be especially considerate of their neighbors.**

When a question mark or an exclamation point ends a quotation, a comma is unnecessary.

► **"Why did Rome fall?/ " he asked the class.**

Commas are never placed next to dashes.

► **I saw her/—what a surprise—/ with my brother.**

Exercise 51.11 Editing for misused commas

Edit to eliminate unnecessary or disruptive commas in the following sentences. Some of the commas are correctly placed.

EXAMPLE **The Constitution, which was ratified in 1789, reflects the colonial and/ revolutionary experience of the thirty-nine men/ who signed it.**

1. The colonies revolted against British rule, but English tradition provided ideas about, government, power, and freedom, that were expressed in the Declaration of Independence and, later in the Constitution.
2. The Constitution was, in part, designed to confine power, and limit government.
3. To this end, the Framers, (the name given to the creators of the Constitution), confined government to certain expressly granted powers, and denied certain specific powers.
4. The Bill of Rights was added, to the Constitution to guarantee freedom of, speech, assembly, and other individual liberties.
5. However, the separation of powers, was the most significant provision, according to some political scientists.
6. Each of the three branches of government, acts as a check on the others, in an arrangement that, has, in fact, prevented abuses of power.
7. In *Marbury v. Madison,* the Supreme Court assumed authority to review legislation, and executive actions, and to declare them unconstitutional, and invalid.
8. The Framers respected self-government, but distrusted, popular majorities.
9. Presidential voting, direct election of senators, and primary elections, strengthen the majority's influence, and are rooted in ideas deeply held by Americans,—that the people must have substantial control.
10. In this balancing of interests, lie the genius, power, and strength of the Constitution.

Exercise 51.12 Chapter review: Commas

Edit the following passage, adding and deleting commas as needed.

Every society has families but the structure of the family varies from, society to society. Over time the function of the family, has changed so that in today's postindustrial society for instance the primary function of the family is to provide "emotional gratification" according to Professor Paula Stein noted sociologist of Stonehall University New Hampshire. In a recent interview Stein also said "Images of the family tend to be based on ideals not realities." To back up this claim Stein pointed to, a new as yet unpublished survey of more than 10000 married American couples, that she and her staff conducted. Expected to be released in the October 17 2008 edition of the *Weekly Sociologist,* the survey indicates that the biggest change has been the increase in the variety of family arrangements including singles single parents and childless, couples. Most Americans marry for love they say, but research portrays courtship as an analysis of costs benefits assets and liabilities, not unlike a business deal.

Virtually all children, are upset by divorce, but most recover in a few years while others suffer lasting serious, problems. Despite the high rate of divorce which reached its height in 1979, Americans still believe in the institution of marriage as indicated by the high rate of remarriages that form *blended families.* "Yes some see the breakup of the family as a social problem or the cause of other problems but, others see changes in the family as adaptations to changing social conditions as I do" concluded the professor.

52 Semicolons

Semicolons join statements that are closely related and grammatically equivalent. They also mark major breaks within some sentences that contain commas.

Semicolons and Grammar Checkers

Computer grammar checkers catch some comma splices that can be corrected by putting a semicolon between the two clauses, and they also catch some incorrect uses of the semicolon. They cannot tell you when a semicolon *could* be used for clarity, however, nor can they tell you if a semicolon is the best choice.

www.mhhe.com/mhhb2
For information and exercises on semicolons, go to
Editing > Semicolons

52a Use a semicolon to join independent clauses.

A semicolon is an effective way to link two clauses if readers are able to see the relationship between the two without the help of a coordinating conjunction. Each clause in this example has a subject and a verb and could stand alone as a sentence, but the writer chose a semicolon to mark the close relationship between the statements.

► **Tracy Kidder wanted to write about architecture; *House* is the result.**

Sometimes, the close relationship is a contrast.

► **Philip had completed the assignment; Lucy had not.**

Semicolons are useful when repairing comma splices and run-on sentences (*see Chapter 33, pp. 527–29*).

52b Use semicolons with transitional expressions that connect independent clauses.

Transitional expressions, including transitional phrases (*after all, even so, for example, in addition, on the contrary*) and conjunctive adverbs (*consequently, however, moreover, nevertheless, then, therefore*), indicate the way in which two clauses are related to each other. When a transitional expression appears between two clauses, it is preceded by a semicolon and usually followed by a comma.

► **Sheila had to wait until the plumber arrived; consequently, she was late for the exam.**

If the transitional expression is a short word such as *then,* the comma is often omitted. In academic writing, however, it is usually best to include it.

Note: The semicolon always appears between the two clauses, even when the transitional expression appears in another position within the second clause. Wherever it is placed, the transitional expression is usually set off with a comma or commas.

► **My friends are all taking golf lessons; my roommate and I, however, are more interested in tennis.**

► **My friends are all taking golf lessons; my roommate and I are more interested in tennis, however.**

Joining two independent clauses with a comma and a transitional expression results in a comma splice (*see Chapter 33, pp. 524–25*).

52c Use care when placing a semicolon before a conjunction.

A comma is the correct punctuation before a coordinating conjunction (*and, but, for, nor, or, so, yet*) that joins independent clauses.

► **Forsythia blooms in the early spring, *but* azaleas bloom later.**

However, if the independent clauses contain internal commas, a semicolon can help the reader identify where the clauses begin and end.

► **The closing scenes return to the English countryside, recalling the opening; *but* these scenes are bathed in a different, cooler light, suggesting that memories of her marriage still haunt her.**

If you are in doubt, it is always correct to use a comma before a coordinating conjunction.

52d Use semicolons to separate items in a series when the items contain commas.

Typically, commas are used to separate items in a series.

► **The committee included Curtis Youngblood, Roberta Collingwood, and Darcy Coolidge.**

Semicolons can take the place of commas when the items within the series contain other commas. The semicolons mark the breaks between the items, and the commas mark breaks within them.

► **The committee included Dr. Curtis Youngblood, the county medical examiner; Roberta Collingwood, the director of the bureau's criminal division; and Darcy Coolidge, the chief of police.**

> ***Exception:*** This rule is an exception to the general principle that there should be a full sentence (independent clause) on each side of a semicolon.

Exercise 52.1 Editing using semicolons

Use semicolons to correct any comma splices and run-on sentences in the following items. (*See Chapter 33 for a detailed discussion of comma splices and run-ons.*) Also add semicolons in place of commas in sentences that contain two independent clauses with internal commas joined by a coordinating conjunction or a series with internal commas (*see 52c and 52d*).

EXAMPLE **The witness took the stand/; the defendant, meanwhile, never looked up from her notepad.**

1. The Pop Art movement flourished in the United States and in Britain in the 1960s it was a reaction to the abstract art that had dominated the art scene during the 1950s.
2. Pop artists were inspired by popular culture and consumerism, for example, they painted advertisements, comic strips, supermarket products, and even dollar bills!
3. The artists' goal was to transform ordinary daily experiences into art, they also wanted to comment on the modern world of mass production.
4. Pop artist Andy Warhol used silkscreening techniques to create identical, mass-produced images on canvas, so the result was repeated images of Campbell's soup cans and Coca-Cola bottles, as well as famous people like Marilyn Monroe, Elvis Presley, and Jacqueline Kennedy.
5. Other pop artists include Roy Lichtenstein, who is best known for his depiction of cartoons, Richard Hamilton, who is famous for his collages of commercial art, and David Hockney, whose trademark theme is swimming pools.
6. These artists all attained great fame in the art world however, many people did not accept their work as real art.

Exercise 52.2 Combining sentences with semicolons

Use a semicolon to combine each set of sentences into one sentence. Add, remove, or change words as necessary. Use a semicolon and a transitional expression between clauses for at least two of your revised sentences. More than one answer is possible for each item.

EXAMPLE **A recent *New York Times* article discusses new discoveries/ ~~These discoveries are~~ about personality in animals/; *the* ~~Some~~ scientists ~~are~~ quoted in the article~~. The scientists~~ are studying personality traits in hyenas and wild birds.**

1. Some scientists are studying a European bird related to the chickadee. The scientists are at the Netherlands Institute of Ecology. They are conducting experiments with this bird.
2. Another scientist has studied hyena populations. His name is Dr. Samuel Gosling. Dr. Gosling asked handlers to rate the hyenas using a questionnaire. He adapted a version of a questionnaire used for humans.
3. These studies and others indicate that animals display personality traits. These traits include boldness and shyness. Bold birds quickly investigate new items in their environment. Shy birds take more time.
4. Bold birds have an advantage over shy birds in some situations. They do not have an advantage in other situations.
5. Some experts on human personality are skeptical. They doubt that animals have the same personality traits that humans do. Scientists who study personality in animals need to be careful to avoid anthropomorphism. That is the tendency to attribute human characteristics to animals.

52e Edit to correct common semicolon errors.

Writers sometimes use semicolons when commas or colons are needed. Avoid these common errors.

1. Do not use a semicolon to join independent clauses linked by a coordinating conjunction unless the clauses contain commas.

   coordinating conjunction

   ► **Women in the nineteenth century wore colorful clothes~~;~~, *but* their clothes look drab in black-and-white photographs.**

2. Do not use a semicolon to join an independent clause to a dependent clause.

   dependent clause

   ► ***Although cats seem tame*~~;~~, they can be fierce hunters.**

   Some instructors consider the dependent clause in the uncorrected version of this sentence to be a type of sentence fragment. (*For help with fragments, see Chapter 32, pp. 512–23.*)

3. Do not use a semicolon to join an independent clause to a phrase.

   phrase

   ► **He has always hated birthday parties~~;~~, *even as a child.***

► **Foremost among the German competition horses is the Hanoverian;, *a great show-jumping breed.*** (appositive)

4. Do not use a semicolon to introduce a list or a quotation. A colon should usually be used for this purpose. (*See Chapter 53, pp. 752–55, for more on using colons.*)

► **My day was planned;: *a morning walk, an afternoon in the library, and an evening with friends.*** (list)

► **Boyd warns of the difficulty in describing Bach;: *"Even his physical appearance largely eludes us."*** (quotation)

You can also use a dash to introduce a list. (*See Chapter 55, pp. 766–72, for more on dashes.*)

An occasional semicolon adds variety to your writing. Too many semicolons can make your writing seem monotonous, however. If you have used three or more semicolons in a paragraph, you should edit your sentences to eliminate most of them. (*For help with sentence variety, see Chapter 45, pp. 663–70.*)

Exercise 52.3 Chapter review: Semicolons

Edit the following passage, using semicolons as appropriate to join independent clauses or separate items in a list. Delete any incorrectly used semicolons, and supply the correct punctuation.

EXAMPLE **Professional writers need to devote time every day to their writing; because otherwise they can lose momentum. Some writers carve out a few hours in the morning; others wait for the stillness of night.**

DNA fingerprinting is a technique that can be used to identify a person accurately, it is also known as DNA profiling. DNA is present in cells and can be isolated from the following; blood, skin, hair, and sweat. DNA fingerprinting can be used to diagnose inherited disorders in fetuses and newborn babies; it can be used to study and research genetic disorders; it is also a key tool in determining paternity or maternity. Criminal identification and forensics rely on DNA fingerprinting to connect suspects to biological evidence; and it has proven a very precise method by which to convict suspects.

DNA fingerprinting may eventually become a means of personal identification, it would work as a kind of genetic bar code. Many people like Tim Smith express their discomfort with this idea; "It sounds like something out of a science fiction movie." Although it may seem like science fiction; the U.S. armed services has already started a program to collect DNA fingerprints to make it easy to identify casualties. This may appear to be a practical way to keep track of people, ensuring clear identification in an emergency situation; but it is a controversial issue, causing some people to rethink joining the military or even to leave the military because they do not want to have their DNA filed in a databank.

Information derived from DNA fingerprinting should be more private than other medical information for several reasons: it includes information about a person's future, such as possible genetic illnesses, the DNA code has not yet been fully broken, making it likely that further research will reveal even more information, and a person's DNA is connected to family, potentially revealing information about parents, siblings, and children. Luckily, it would be expensive and very time-consuming to isolate, analyze, and file the DNA information for all human beings; so picture IDs and Social Security numbers are here to stay for at least a while longer.

53 Colons

Colons function within sentences to introduce elements, and they also have other conventional uses.

Colons and Grammar Checkers

Computer grammar checkers may point out when you have used a colon incorrectly. However, because colons are usually optional, most of the time you will need to decide for yourself whether a colon is your best choice in a sentence.

www.mhhe.com/ mhhb2
For information and exercises on colons, go to
Editing > Colons

53a Use a colon after a complete sentence to introduce a list, an appositive, or a quotation.

Like an announcer on a television show, a colon draws the reader's attention to what it is introducing. It is used after a complete sentence (independent clause) to introduce lists, appositives (nouns or noun phrases that appear right after the word they rename), and quotations.

independent clause / list
- ► **Several majors interest me: biology, chemistry, and art.**

independent clause / appositive
- ► **She shared with me her favorite toys: a spatula and a pot lid.**

independent clause / quotation
- ► **He said the dreaded words: "Let's just be friends."**

Note: If you introduce a quotation with a signal phrase such as *he said* or *Morrison comments* instead of a complete sentence, you should use a comma, not a colon, before the quotation.

When you use a colon to introduce a sentence element, make sure that it is preceded by an independent clause (a clause with a subject and a verb that can stand alone as a sentence).

lacks a complete verb—not an independent clause

INCORRECT **Three kinds of futility dealt with in the novel: pervasive poverty, lost love, and inescapable aging.**

independent clause

CORRECT **Three kinds of futility are dealt with in the novel: pervasive poverty, lost love, and inescapable aging.**

The words *the following* or *as follows* often appear at the end of the introductory sentence.

► **The three ingredients are as follows: *graham crackers, marshmallows, and chocolate bars.***

53b Use a colon when a second closely related independent clause elaborates on the first one.

The colon can be used to link independent clauses when the second clause restates or elaborates on the first. Use a colon between two independent clauses of this sort when you want to emphasize the second clause.

► **I can predict tonight's sequence of events: my brother will arrive late, talk loudly, and eat too much.**

> ***Note:*** When a complete sentence follows a colon, the first word may begin with either a capital or a lowercase letter. Be consistent throughout your document.

53c Use colons to indicate ratios and times of day, for city and publisher citations in bibliographies, to separate titles and subtitles, and in business letters and memos.

► **The ratio of armed to unarmed members of the gang was 3:1.**

► **He woke up at 6:30 in the morning.**

► **New York: McGraw-Hill, 2009**

► ***Possible Lives: The Promise of Public Education in America***

► **Dear Mr. Worth:**

► **Date:** **September 25, 2008**
To: **Dean John Kim**
From: **Professor Christine Soros**
Re: **Department Meeting**

CHARTING the TERRITORY

Biblical Citations

Colons are often used to separate biblical chapters and verses (John 3:16), but the Modern Language Association (MLA) recommends using a period instead (John 3.16).

In some situations, such as in the military, time is expressed in four digits without a colon: *1500 hours* instead of *3:00*.

53d Edit to eliminate unnecessary colons.

Do not use a colon to separate sentence parts that belong together, such as a verb and its object or complement or a preposition and its object or objects.

verb complement

► **The elements in a good smoothie are: yogurt, fruit, and honey.**

preposition objects

► **Some feel cancer can be prevented by: diet, exercise, and screening.**

Do not use a colon after *such as, for example,* or *including,* even when you are introducing a list.

► **I am ready for a change, *such as:* a new job or a new apartment.**

Expressions like *that is* and *namely,* which often precede appositives, should follow the colon: *He had a next-to-impossible goal: namely, a career in the major leagues.*

Do not use a colon between an independent clause and a phrase or a dependent clause. Some instructors consider this error to be a sentence fragment. (*For help with fragments, see Chapter 32, pp. 512–23.*)

I had no

► **~~No~~ such luck: the doctor was not at home.**

we

► **Before the children go to lunch: , ~~We~~ will observe their interactions.**

Do not use more than one colon in the same sentence.

► **He was taken in by ~~a new con:~~ the Spanish lottery scam: the victim is told that he or she has won a big prize and is asked to send financial information to the officer of a fake Spanish company.**

Exercise 53.1 Chapter review: Colons

Edit the following passage by adding or deleting colons.

EXAMPLE **The director of the soup kitchen is considering ways to raise funds, for example: a bake sale, car wash, or readathon.**

Ciguatera is a form of food poisoning, humans are poisoned when they consume reef fish that contain toxic substances called ciguatoxins. These toxins accumulate at the end of the food chain: large carnivorous fish prey on smaller herbivorous fish. These smaller fish feed on ciguatoxins, which are produced by microorganisms that grow on the surface of marine algae. Ciguatoxins are found in certain marine fish, snapper, mackerel, barracuda, and grouper. People should avoid eating fish from reef waters, including: the tropical and subtropical waters of the Pacific and Indian oceans and the Caribbean sea.

Some people think that ciguatera can be destroyed by: cooking or freezing the fish. People who consume reef fish should avoid eating: the head, internal organs, or eggs. People who eat contaminated fish experience gastrointestinal and neurological problems: vomiting, diarrhea, numbness, and muscle pains. Most physicians offer the same advice, "Eat fish only from reputable restaurants and dealers."

54 Quotation Marks

As an academic writer, you are engaged in a dialogue with the work of other scholars, and you will often need to incorporate their words into your papers. Parts 3 and 4 discuss the process of researching and documenting sources. This chapter covers the use of quotation marks—as well as the punctuation marks that appear with them—to present other people's written and spoken words in your papers. It also explains other uses of quotation marks.

www.mhhe.com/mhhb2
For information and exercises on quotation marks, go to
Editing > Quotation Marks

As you proofread your papers, bear in mind that every opening quotation mark (") must be accompanied by a closing mark (") and vice versa. A missing closing quotation mark is all too easy to overlook.

> ***Note:*** You should credit the source of direct quotations using the documentation style appropriate to your audience. Most of the examples in this chapter are not fully documented because they are not meant to illustrate documentation styles; *that advice is given in detail in Part 4: Documenting across the Curriculum.*

54a Use quotation marks to indicate the exact words of a speaker or writer.

Direct quotations from written material may include whole sentences or only a few words or phrases.

► **In *Angela's Ashes*, Frank McCourt writes, "Worse than the ordinary miserable childhood is the miserable Irish childhood."**

► **Frank McCourt believes that being Irish worsens what is all too "ordinary"—a "miserable childhood."**

Note: Do not use quotation marks to set off an **indirect quotation**, which reports what a speaker said but does not use the exact words.

► **He said that "he didn't know what I was talking about."**

Quotation Marks and Grammar Checkers

Computer grammar checkers cannot determine where a quotation should begin and end. In addition, they miss many errors in the use of quotation marks with other marks of punctuation. A grammar checker did not highlight the error in the following sentence.

► **Barbara Ehrenreich observes, "There are no Palm Pilots, cable channels, or Web sites to advise the low-wage job seeker".** [The period should come before the closing mark.]

54b Use quotation marks to set off brief direct quotations and lines of dialogue.

Quotation marks are used to incorporate brief direct quotations within the main body of your text. Longer direct quotations are set off from the main text by indenting them (*see 54d*).

1. Using signal phrases to introduce quotations

If you introduce a quotation with a signal phrase such as *he said* or *she noted,* add a comma after the phrase and use a capital letter to begin the quotation.

► **Hamilton says, "That is the miracle of Greek mythology—a humanized world."**

If the phrase follows the quotation, add a comma at the end of the quotation, before the closing quotation mark. (If the quotation ends in a question mark or an exclamation point, however, do not add a comma.) Capitalize the first letter of the quotation even if the first word does not begin a sentence in the original source.

► **"The only white people who came to our house were welfare workers and bill collectors," James Baldwin wrote.**

If you interrupt a quoted sentence with a signal phrase, place quotation marks around both parts of the quoted sentence and set the signal phrase off with commas. Note that the first word of the second part of the quoted sentence is not capitalized.

► **"The first thing that strikes one about Plath's journals," writes Katha Pollitt in *The Atlantic*, "is what they leave out."**

To interrupt a quotation of two or more sentences with a signal phrase, attach the signal phrase to the first sentence with a comma and put a period after it. The next sentence begins with an opening quotation mark and a capital letter.

► **"There are at least four kinds of doublespeak," William Lutz observes. "The first is the euphemism, an inoffensive or positive word or phrase used to avoid a harsh, unpleasant, or distasteful reality."**

2. Using complete sentences to introduce quotations

When you are introducing a quotation with a complete sentence, use a colon.

► **Hamilton credits the Greeks with a shift in the portrayal of gods: "Until then, gods had no semblance of reality."**

3. Integrating quotations into your sentence

When a quotation is integrated into a sentence's structure, treat the quotation as you would any other sentence element, adding a comma or not as appropriate.

► **Saying that the moth "now knew death," Woolf contemplates its strangeness.**

► **Hoagland has described the essay as a work that "hangs somewhere on a line between two sturdy poles."**

4. Quoting dialogue

When you are quoting dialogue between two or more speakers, you should usually begin a new paragraph to indicate a change in speaker.

► **"I don't know what you're talking about," he said. "I did listen to everything you told me."**
"If you had been listening, you would know what I was talking about."

If a speaker continues for more than a paragraph, begin each subsequent paragraph with quotation marks, but do not insert a closing quotation mark until the end of the quotation.

54c Use single quotation marks, slashes, ellipses, and brackets with direct quotations as required.

Along with the quotation marks indicating that material comes from another source, you may also need to use single quotation marks, slashes, ellipses, and brackets when quoting. The box that follows indicates where you can find detailed coverage of these four marks in this text.

Punctuation Mark	**Use in Direct Quotation**	**Section (*Page No.*)**
Single quotation marks ' '	Enclose a quotation within a quotation	54e (*p. 760*)
Slash /	Mark line division within a poetry quotation	55k (*p. 777*)
Ellipses . . .	Mark missing words within a quotation	55j (*pp. 774–77*)
Brackets [ ]	Show changes, additions, or comments from an outside source within a quotation	55i (*pp. 772–73*)

54d Set off long quotations in indented blocks rather than using quotation marks.

If you are using a long quotation, set it off from the text as an **extract,** or a **block quotation.** If you are following MLA style, a quotation of five typed lines or more of prose or four or more lines of a poem should be treated as a block quotation. If you are following APA style, a quotation of forty words or more should be set off in this way. Always double-space the lines in a block quotation, as well as the lines above and below it. The lines of a block quotation should be indented one inch (ten spaces) in MLA style and one-half inch (five spaces) in APA style. (*For more information, on these styles, see Chapters 23 and 24.*)

Do not surround a block quotation with quotation marks. However, if the passage that you are quoting contains quotation marks, include them exactly as they appear in the passage. If your quotation is more than one paragraph long, indent the first line of each new paragraph an extra quarter inch (three spaces) if you are following MLA style and one-half inch (five spaces) if you are following APA style. The following examples are in MLA style.

PROSE EXTRACT

As Carl Schorske points out, the young Freud was passionately interested in classical archaeology:

> He cultivated a new friendship in the Viennese professional elite—especially rare in those days of withdrawal—with Emanuel Loewy, a professor of archaeology. "He keeps me up till three o'clock in the morning," Freud wrote appreciatively to Fleiss. "He tells me about Rome." (273)

Colon used to introduce quotation.

Quotation marks for quotation within passage.

POETRY EXTRACT

In the following lines from "Crossing Brooklyn Ferry," Walt Whitman celebrates the beauty of the Manhattan skyline and his love for the city:

> Ah what can ever be more stately and admirable
>   to me than mast-hemm'd Manhattan?
> River and sunset and scallop-edg'd waves of flood-tide?
> The sea-gulls oscillating their bodies, the hay-boat
>   in the twilight, and the belated lighter?
> What gods can exceed these that clasp me by
>   the hand, and with voices I love call me promptly
>   and loudly by my nighest name as I approach? (92–95)

Colon used to introduce quotation.

Indent turned lines an extra ¼ inch (3 spaces).

When quoting poetry, represent the formatting, spelling, capitalization, and punctuation of the original work.

Ferlinghetti's interpretation of Klimt's painting leads him to this conclusion:

> She
>   will not open
>   He
>   is not the One (59–62)

Formatting of poem follows the original.

Note: Writers often end a sentence introducing a block quotation with a colon. If your instructor allows, you may introduce the quotation with the beginning of a sentence that the quotation completes. If you do so, the quotation should not begin with a capital letter unless it starts with a proper noun.

54e Use single quotation marks to enclose a quotation within a quotation.

Unless you are using a block quotation, set off a quotation within a quotation with a pair of single quotation marks.

► **Kenneth Burke notes with displeasure that his "procedures have been characterized as 'intuitive' and 'idiosyncratic.' "**

Note: In the unlikely event that you need to include quotation marks within an already embedded quotation or title, use double quotation marks again: "*I agree with the article titled 'The "Animal Rights" War on Medicine.'*"

Exercise 54.1 Using double and single quotation marks

Below is a passage from the Seneca Falls Declaration (1848) by Elizabeth Cady Stanton, followed by a numbered series of quotations from this passage. Add, delete, or replace quotation marks to quote from the passage accurately. Some sentences may be correct; circle their numbers.

> The history of mankind is a history of repeated injuries and usurpations on the part of man toward woman, having in direct object the establishment of an absolute tyranny over her. To prove this, let facts be submitted to a candid world.
>
> WHEREAS, The great precept of nature is conceded to be that "man shall pursue his own true and substantial happiness." Blackstone in his *Commentaries* remarks that this law of Nature being coeval with mankind, and dictated by God himself, is of course superior in obligation to any other. It is binding over all the globe, in all countries and at all times; no human laws are of any validity if contrary to this, and such of them as are valid, derive all their force,

and all their validity, and all their authority, mediately and immediately, from this original; therefore,

RESOLVED, That such laws as conflict, in any way, with the true and substantial happiness of woman, are contrary to the great precept of nature and of no validity, for this is "superior in obligation to any other."

EXAMPLE **As Elizabeth Cady Stanton points out, "The great precept of nature is conceded to be that 'man shall pursue his own true and substantial happiness.'"**

1. "The history of mankind is a history of repeated injuries and usurpations on the part of man toward woman," Elizabeth Cady Stanton asserts, "having in direct object the establishment of an absolute tyranny over her."
2. To prove this, writes Stanton, let facts be submitted to a candid world.
3. Stanton argues that men have oppressed women throughout history.
4. Stanton contends "that all laws are subject to natural laws."
5. Stanton resolves "that such laws as conflict, in any way, with the true and substantial happiness of woman, are contrary to the great precept of nature and of no validity, for this is "superior in obligation to any other.""

54f Use quotation marks to enclose titles of short works such as articles, poems, and stories.

The titles of long works, such as books, are usually put in italics or underlined (*see Chapter 60, pp. 809–10*). The titles of book chapters, essays, most poems, and other short works are usually put in quotation marks.

For when to use quotation marks with titles in a works-cited or references list, see the chapter in Part 4: Documenting across the Curriculum that covers the documentation style you are using.

> ***Note:*** If quotation marks are needed within the title of a short work, use single quotation marks: "The 'Animal Rights' War on Medicine."

TITLES THAT SHOULD BE ENCLOSED in QUOTATION MARKS

- **Essays**
  "Once More to the Lake"
- **Songs**
  "Seven Nation Army"
- **Short poems**
  "Daffodils"
- **Short stories**
  "The Tell-Tale Heart"
- **Articles in periodicals**
  "Scotland Yard of the Wild" (from *American Way*)
- **Book chapters or sections**
  "The Girl in Conflict" (Chapter 11 of *Coming of Age in Samoa*)
- **Part of a Web site**
  "Explainer" (part of the *Slate* site)
- **Episodes of radio and television programs**
  "I Can't Remember" (on *48 Hours*)
- **Titles of unpublished works, including student papers, theses, and dissertations**
  "Louis Armstrong and Joe Glaser: More than Meets the Eye"

Do not, however, use quotation marks to enclose the title of your own paper on your title page.

54g Use quotation marks to indicate that a word or phrase is being used in a special way.

Occasionally, you can use quotation marks around a word or phrase that someone else uses, or has used, in a way that you or your readers may not agree with.

► **The "worker's paradise" of Stalinist Russia included slave-labor camps.**

Quotation marks used in this way function as raised eyebrows do in conversation and should be used sparingly. Do not use quotation marks to distance yourself from slang, clichés, or trite expressions. Avoid those expressions altogether.

Words cited as words and words that you are defining can also be put in quotation marks, although the more common practice is to italicize them. (You should be consistent throughout your paper.)

► **The words "compliment" and "complement" sound alike but have different meanings.**

► **"Chatter," the communications intercepted by an intelligence agency, needs to be interpreted to be useful.**

You should enclose a word you are defining in quotation marks only when you introduce and explain it, not afterward.

Use quotation marks to give the English translation of a word in another language.

► ***Merci* means "thank you."**

Finally, do not enclose well-known nicknames in quotation marks: *President Bill Clinton,* not *President "Bill" Clinton.*

54h Place punctuation marks within or outside quotation marks, as convention and your meaning require.

As you edit, check closing quotation marks and the punctuation that appears next to them to make sure that you have placed them in the correct order.

1. Periods and commas

Place the period or comma before the final quotation mark, even when the quotation is brief. When single and double quotation marks appear together, both should be placed after the period or comma (*see the example in 54e on p. 760*).

► **"Instead of sharing an experience the spectator must come to grips with things," Brecht writes in "The Epic Theatre and Its Difficulties."**

However, place the period or comma after a parenthetical citation.

► **Brecht wants the spectator to "come to grips with things" (23).**

2. Question marks and exclamation points

Place a question mark or an exclamation point after the final quotation mark if the quoted material is not itself a question or an exclamation.

► **How does epic theater make us "come to grips with things"?**

Place a question mark or an exclamation point before the final quotation mark when it is part of the quotation. No additional punctuation is needed after the closing quotation unless there is a parenthetical citation.

► **"Are we to see science in the theater?" Brecht was asked.**

► **Brecht was asked, "Are we to see science in the theater?"**

► **Brecht was asked, "Are we to see science in the theater?" (27).**

3. Colons and semicolons

Place colons and semicolons after the final quotation mark.

► **Dean Wilcox cited the items he called his "daily delights": a free parking space for his scooter at the faculty club, a special table in the club itself, and friends to laugh with after a day's work.**

4. Dashes

Place a dash outside either an opening or a closing quotation mark, or both, if it precedes or follows the quotation or if two dashes are used to set off the quotation.

► **One phrase—"time is running out"—haunted me.**

Place a dash inside either an opening or a closing quotation mark if it is part of the quotation.

► **"Where is the—" she called. "Oh, here it is. Never mind."**

Exercise 54.2 Using quotation marks with other punctuation

Edit the following sentences to correct problems with the use of quotation marks with other punctuation. Some sentences may be correct; circle their numbers.

EXAMPLE **In June 1776, Richard Henry Lee proposed that the Continental Congress adopt a resolution that "these united Colonies are, and of right ought to be, free and independent States."/**

1. "We hold these truths to be self-evident", wrote Thomas Jefferson in 1776.
2. Most Americans can recite their "unalienable rights:" "life, liberty, and the pursuit of happiness."
3. According to the Declaration of Independence, "whenever any form of government becomes destructive to these ends, it is the right of the people to alter or to abolish it."!
4. The signers of the Declaration of Independence contended that the "history of the present King of Great Britain is a history of repeated injuries and usurpations, all having in direct object the establishment of an absolute tyranny over these states."
5. What did the creators of this document mean by a "candid world?"
6. Feminists and civil rights advocates have challenged the Declaration's most famous phrase "—all men are created equal"—on grounds that these "unalienable rights" were originally extended only to white men who owned property.

54i Edit to correct common errors in using quotation marks.

Writers are sometimes overzealous in their use of quotation marks or unsure about how to use end punctuation with the closing mark. Watch out for the following errors in particular.

1. Do not use quotation marks to distance yourself from slang, clichés, or trite expressions. Avoid overused or slang expressions in college writing. If your writing situation permits slang, however, do not enclose it in quotation marks.

   ► **Californians are reputed to be very "laid back."**

   Revising the sentence is usually a better solution:

   ► **Californians have a reputation for being relaxed and carefree.**

2. Do not use quotation marks for indirect quotations.

   ► **He told his boss that "the company lost its largest account."**

   Another way to correct this sentence is to change it into a direct quotation.

   ► **He said to his boss, "We just lost our largest account."**

3. Do not add another question mark or exclamation point to the end of a sentence that concludes with a quotation ending in one of those marks.

   ► **What did Juliet mean when she cried, "O Romeo, Romeo! wherefore art thou Romeo?"?**

   If you quote a question within a sentence that makes a statement, place a question mark before the closing quotation mark and a period at the end of the sentence.

   ► **"What was Henry Ford's greatest contribution to the Industrial Revolution?" he asked.**

4. Do not use quotation marks to enclose the title of your own paper on the title page or above the first line of the text.

   ► **"Edgar Allan Poe and the Paradox of the Gothic"**

   If you use a quotation or the title of a short work in your title, though, put quotation marks around that quotation or title.

   ► **Edgar Allan Poe's "The Raven" and the Paradox of the Gothic**

Exercise 54.3 Chapter review: Quotation marks

Edit the following passage to correct problems with the use of quotation marks.

> On August 28, 1963, Dr. Martin Luther King Jr. delivered his famous 'I Have a Dream' speech at the nation's Lincoln Memorial. According to King, "When the architects of our republic wrote the magnificent words of the Constitution and the Declaration of Independence, they were signing a promissory note to which every American was to fall heir". King declared that "this note was a promise that all men, yes, black men as well as white men, would be guaranteed the unalienable rights of life, liberty, and the pursuit of happiness." This promissory note, however, came back "marked "insufficient funds."" King's speech, therefore, was designed to rally his supporters to "make justice a reality."
>
> Unlike the more militant civil rights leaders of the 1950s, King advocated nonviolence. This stance is why King said that the 'Negro community' should not drink "from the cup of bitterness and hatred" and that they should not use physical violence.
>
> King's dream was uniquely American: "I have a dream that one day this nation will rise up and live out the true meaning of its creed: 'We hold these truths to be self-evident: that all men are created equal.' " King challenged all Americans to fully embrace racial equality. Nearly fifty years later, we must ask ourselves if King's dream has in fact become a reality. Are "all of God's children, black men and white men, Jews and Gentiles, Protestants and Catholics . . . able to join hands and sing in the words of the old Negro spiritual, "Free at last! free at last! thank God Almighty, we are free at last!?" "

55 Dashes, Parentheses, and Other Punctuation Marks

Like commas, dashes and parentheses are used to set off information within a sentence. Dashes emphasize and parentheses deemphasize the set-off material.

► **Our neighbors have taken up bird-watching, an ideal pastime for nature-starved city dwellers.**

► **We were surprised that Jim—a man who never owned a pair of sneakers—spends hours in the park.**

► **Carrie (who now lives in Florida) introduced them to the hobby.**

Brackets are also used to set off information from an outside source within a quotation or to set off material within parentheses. Ellipses indicate that words have been deleted from a quotation, and slashes indicate line breaks in quotations from poetry, among other uses.

Other Punctuation Marks and Grammar Checkers

All of the punctuation marks covered in this chapter involve judgment calls on the writer's part. Computer grammar checkers will not tell you when you might use a pair of dashes or parentheses to set off material in a sentence, for example. They may catch some errors in the use of these marks, but in general you will need to proofread your work to make sure that you are using these marks correctly.

55a Use the dash provided by your word-processing program, or form it by typing two hyphens.

www.mhhe.com/mhhb2

For information and exercises on dashes, go to

Editing > Dashes

A typeset dash, sometimes called an em dash, is a single, unbroken line about as wide as a capital M (—). Most word-processing programs provide the em dash as a special character or will convert two hyphens to an em dash as an autoformat function. Otherwise, you can make a dash on the keyboard by typing two hyphens in a row (--) with no space between them. Do not put a space before or after the dash. A handwritten dash should be about as long as two hyphens.

55b Use a dash to highlight an explanation or a list that begins or ends a sentence.

A dash indicates a very strong pause and emphasizes what comes immediately before or after it.

► **I think the Comets will win the tournament—*their goalie has the best record in the league.***

► ***Coca-Cola, potato chips, and brevity*—these are the marks of a good study session in the dorm.**

Do not break up an independent clause with a dash.

► Haydn, Mozart, ~~,~~ and Beethoven~~—~~are the most famous composers of the classical period.

55c Use one or two dashes to highlight a nonessential phrase or an independent clause within a sentence.

Dashes are especially useful for inserting clarifying information such as a definition, an example, or an appositive (a word or phrase that renames a noun) into a sentence.

DEFINITION In addition to the trumpet, he played the cornet—*a wind instrument smaller than a trumpet, with three valves.*

EXAMPLE All finite creatures—*including humans*—are incomplete and contradictory.

APPOSITIVE Located in east London, Smithfield Market—*a huge meat market*—has a long history.

Make sure that the word or words set off with dashes appear next to the word they are clarifying.

► On a day hike we ~~found~~—my sisters and I—found a wounded owl.

A dash or pair of dashes can also be used to insert a contrast.

CONTRAST Watercolor paint is easy to buy—*but hard to master.*

Independent clauses can also be inserted into a sentence using dashes.

► The first rotary gasoline engine—*it was made by Mazda*—burned 15 percent more fuel than conventional engines.

If the clause you are adding is a question or an exclamation, the question mark or exclamation point should precede the second dash: *I never imagined—how could I?—that he would return.* When editing, make sure that your sentence is clear and complete without the material within brackets.

► Because we wanted the tickets so badly—it was the last performance of the season—~~so~~ we stood in line for hours.

The two parts of the original sentence (without the inserted material) do not fit together: *Because we wanted the tickets so badly so we stood in line for hours.* Removing *so* fixes the problem.

55d Use a dash or dashes to indicate a sudden break in tone, thought, or speech.

► **Breathing heavily, the archaeologist opened the old chest in wild anticipation and found—old socks and an empty soda can.**

► **His last words were "There's nothing here except—"**

This use is rare in academic writing.

> ***Note:*** Commas, semicolons, and periods should never appear beside dashes. An opening or a closing quotation mark sometimes appears next to a dash, as in the preceding example, but the two marks should never overlap.

55e Do not overuse dashes.

Used sparingly, dashes can be effective, but too many dashes make your writing disjointed.

CHOPPY After we found the puppy—shivering under the porch—we brought her into the house—into the entryway, actually—and wrapped her in an old towel—to warm her up.

SMOOTHER After we found the puppy shivering under the porch, we brought her into the house—into the entryway, actually—and wrapped her in an old towel to warm her up.

Exercise 55.1 Using dashes

Insert or correct dashes where needed in the following sentences.

EXAMPLE **Women ^—once shut out of electoral office altogether ^—have made great progress in recent decades.**

1. Patsy Mink, Geraldine Ferraro, Antonia Novello, and Madeleine Albright all are political pioneers in the history of the United States.

2. Patsy Mink the first Asian-American woman elected to the U.S. Congress served for twenty-four years in the U.S. House of Representatives.
3. Geraldine Ferraro she was a congresswoman from Queens, New York became the first female vice presidential candidate when she was nominated by the Democratic Party in 1984.
4. Antonia Novello—former U.S. Surgeon General—was the first woman—and the first Hispanic—to hold this position.
5. Madeleine Albright, the first female Secretary of State, has observed, "To understand Europe, you have to be a genius-or French."

FIGURE 55.1 Dr. Antonia Novello testifying during her confirmation hearing.

www.mhhe.com/mhhb2
For information and exercises on parentheses, go to Editing > Parentheses

55f Use parentheses to enclose supplementary information.

Parentheses are useful when you want to insert additional—but nonessential—information about a sentence element. Parentheses can enclose an explanation, an example, a brief but pertinent digression, or an abbreviation. Parentheses are always used in pairs (an opening and a closing parenthesis).

EXPLANATION The last four telephone bills (September to December) have each been more than fifty dollars.

EXAMPLE Every household is filled with items (buttons, for example) that people will never use but will not throw away.

DIGRESSION Envious of the freedoms adults enjoy, few children realize (I never did) how stressful adult life can be.

ABBREVIATION When quoting poetry in the style of the Modern Language Association (MLA), put the line numbers in parentheses following the quotation.

Caution: Enclose information in parentheses only occasionally in your writing. If you notice that you have used parentheses more than once or twice in a paper, ask yourself whether, in each case, the information they enclose could be deleted or incorporated into your sentence without the parentheses.

55g Use parentheses to enclose numbers or letters, according to convention.

Parentheses are used to enclose numbers or letters that label items in a list that is part of a sentence.

► **He wants the sales data to be updated in (1) the monthly report, (2) the quarterly forecast, and (3) the annual budget.**

Do not use parentheses to enclose the numbers or letters in a list set up so that each entry starts a new line.

Parentheses are also used to enclose page numbers and other reference information in the MLA, APA, Chicago, and CSE name-year documentation styles (*see Part 4 for details*). They are also used in business writing to enclose a numeral following a spelled-out number and, in some disciplines, to set off alternate forms of a measurement.

► **The contract will terminate in sixty (60) days.**

► **I added the compound to 2 liters (2.114 quarts) of water.**

55h Learn the conventions for capitalization and punctuation with parentheses.

1. The first word of a sentence that stands by itself within parentheses should begin with a capital letter, and the sentence should conclude with a period, a question mark, or an exclamation point.

   ► **Folktales and urban legends often reflect the concerns of a particular era. (The familiar tale of a cat accidentally caught in a microwave oven is an example.)**

2. The first word of a sentence in parentheses that appears within another sentence should not begin with a capital letter unless the word is a proper noun. The sentence should not end with a period, a comma, or a semicolon. However, it can end with a question mark or an exclamation point.

   ► **John Henry (he was the man with the forty-pound hammer) was a hero to miners fearing the loss of their jobs to machines.**

   ► **The most popular major in this school a decade ago was business administration (although wasn't psychology a close second?).**

   ► **Dirt absorbs light and uses more energy (clean your light bulbs!).**

3. Do not use any punctuation before the opening parenthesis within a sentence. To decide whether any punctuation should

follow the closing parenthesis, imagine the sentence without the parenthetical material.

► **As he walked past/ (dressed, as always, in his Sunday best), I got ready to throw the spitball.**

► **He walked past (never noticing me behind the statue)/ on his way to the assembly.**

4. Quotation marks should never surround parentheses.

► **His first poem "("Eye")" was also his most famous.**

Exercise 55.2 Using parentheses

Insert parentheses where needed in the following sentences, and correct any errors in their use.

EXAMPLE **During leap year, February has twenty-nine (29) days.**

1. German meteorologist Alfred Wegener he was also a geophysicist proposed the first comprehensive theory of continental drift.
2. According to this geological theory, 1 the earth originally contained a single large continent, 2 this land mass eventually separated into six continents, and 3 these continents gradually drifted apart.
3. Wegener contended that continents will continue to drift. They are not rigidly fixed. The evidence indicates that his predictions are accurate.
4. The continents are moving at a rate of one yard .09144 meters per century.
5. The movement of the continents, (slow though this movement may be), occasionally causes earthquakes along fault lines such as the famous San Andreas Fault in California.

55i When quoting, use brackets to set off material that is not part of the original quotation.

Brackets set off information you add to a quotation that is not part of the quotation itself. Use brackets to add significant information that is needed to make the quotation clear.

► **Samuel Eliot Morison has written, "This passage has attracted a good deal of scorn to the Florentine mariner [Verrazzano], but without justice."**

In this sentence, the writer is quoting Morison, but Morison's sentence does not include the name of the "Florentine mariner." The writer places the name—Verrazzano—in brackets so that readers will know his identity.

Information that explains or corrects something in a quotation is also bracketed.

► **Vasco da Gama's man wrote in 1487, "The body of the church [it was not a church but a Hindu shrine] is as large as a monastery."**

Brackets are also used around words that you insert within a quotation to make it fit the grammar, style, or context of your own sentence. If you replace a word with your own word in brackets, ellipses are not needed.

► **At the end of *Pygmalion*, Henry Higgins confesses to Eliza Doolittle that he has "grown accustomed to [her] voice and appearance."**

To make the quote fit properly into the sentence, the writer inserts the bracketed word *her* in place of *your*.

If you change the first letter of a word in a quotation to a capital or lowercase letter, enclose the letter in brackets: *Ackroyd writes, "[F]or half a million years there has been in London a pattern of habitation and hunting if not of settlement."*

If you are adding ellipses to a passage that already contains ellipses, you can distinguish them from the ellipses that appear in the original by using brackets. (*See 55j on ellipses.*)

Note: Brackets may be used to enclose the word *sic* (Latin for "thus") after a word in a quotation that was incorrect in the original. If you are following MLA style, the word *sic* should not be italicized when it appears in brackets. The three other styles covered in this book (APA, Chicago, and CSE) put *sic* in italics.

► **The critic noted that "the battle scenes in *The Patriot* are realistic, but the rest of the film is historically inacurate [sic] and overly melodramatic."**

Sic should be used sparingly because it can appear pretentious and condescending, and it should not be used to make fun of what someone has said or written.

If you need to set off words within material that is already in parentheses, use brackets: (*I found the information on a Web site published by the National Institutes of Health [NIH].*)

55j Use ellipses to indicate that words have been omitted from a quotation or that a thought is incomplete.

If you wish to shorten a passage you are quoting, you may omit words, phrases (such as the one highlighted in the quotation that follows), or even entire sentences. To show readers that you have done so, use three spaced periods (. . .), called *ellipses* or an *ellipsis mark*.

FULL QUOTATION

> Just before noon on April 23, 1838, the *Sirius,* a small paddle-wheel steam packet nineteen days out of Cork, limped across the Upper Bay, its coal supply all but exhausted, and made landfall to the cheers of a great crowd gathered at the Battery. A scant four hours later, a second steamer, twice as big and half again as fast, hove into view, belching black smoke. This was the *Great Western,* fourteen days out of Bristol. She had been chasing *Sirius* across the Atlantic, and the sight of her churning toward the city touched off even more exuberant rejoicing, as it was now doubly clear that New York had established a maritime steam link to Europe.
>
> —Edwin G. Burrows and Mike Wallace, *Gotham: A History of New York City to 1898,* p. 649

EDITED QUOTATION

In their account of the boom in transatlantic trade in the mid-nineteenth century, Burrows and Wallace describe its beginning: "Just before noon on April 23, 1838, the *Sirius*, a small paddlewheel steam packet . . . made landfall to the cheers of a great crowd gathered at the Battery" (649).

Some instructors may ask you to use brackets to enclose any ellipses that you add, to indicate that the elision is yours and was not in the original source.

EDITED QUOTATION (ALTERNATE STYLE, WITH BRACKETS)

In their account of the boom in transatlantic trade in the mid-nineteenth century, Burrows and Wallace describe its beginning: "Just before noon on April 23, 1838, the *Sirius*, a small paddlewheel steam packet [. . .] made landfall to the cheers of a great crowd gathered at the Battery" (649).

The following guidelines will help you use ellipses correctly for the different kinds of omissions you may need to make. All quotations are cited in the style recommended by the Modern Language Association (MLA). (*For guidance in using MLA style, see Chapter 23; for guidance in using the APA, Chicago, and CSE styles to cite sources, see Chapters 24, 25, and 26.*)

1. If you are leaving out the end of a quoted sentence, the three ellipsis points are preceded by a period to end the sentence. (*See also item 4 on p. 776.*)

END OF A QUOTED SENTENCE OMITTED

In describing the arrival in New York of the first transatlantic steamers, Burrows and Wallace note that "four hours later, a second steamer, twice as big and half again as fast, hove into view. . . . It too was greeted with 'rejoicing'" (649).

Note that ellipses are not needed at the beginning of the quotation because the lowercase letter *f* makes it clear that the first part of the sentence has been left out.

To add a parenthetical reference after the ellipses at the end of a sentence, place it after the quotation mark but before the final period.

EDITED QUOTATION WITH PARENTHETICAL REFERENCE

In describing the arrival in New York of the first transatlantic steamers, Burrows and Wallace note that "four hours later, a second steamer, twice as big and half again as fast, hove into view . . ." (649).

2. If you are leaving out a sentence or sentences, use three ellipsis points preceded by a period.

ENTIRE SENTENCE OMITTED

Burrows and Wallace recount the arrival of the second steamer:

> A scant four hours later, a second steamer, twice as big and half again as fast, hove into view, belching black smoke. . . . She had been chasing *Sirius* across the Atlantic, and the sight of her churning toward the city touched off even more exuberant rejoicing, as it was now doubly clear that New York had established a maritime steam link to Europe. (649)

3. If you are leaving out the last part of one sentence and the first part of the next, use three ellipses points.

PARTS OF TWO ADJACENT SENTENCES OMITTED

Burrows and Wallace describe a joyful scene: "This was the *Great Western* . . . and the sight of her churning toward the city touched off even more exuberant rejoicing, as it was now doubly clear that New York had established a maritime steam link to Europe" (649).

Note that the comma after *Western* has been retained because it is needed before the coordinating conjunction *and,* which is joining two independent clauses. Commas and other punctuation marks that are not needed in the new sentence can be dropped.

4. If you are leaving out the last part of a sentence and one or more of the sentences that follow it, use three ellipsis points preceded by a period.

LAST PART OF ONE SENTENCE AND ONE OR MORE SUBSEQUENT SENTENCES OMITTED

"[A] second steamer, twice as big and half again as fast, hove into view. . . . She had been chasing *Sirius* across the Atlantic, and the sight of her churning toward the city touched off even more exuberant rejoicing . . ." (Burrows and Wallace 649).

Note that ellipses are not needed at the beginning of the quotation because the letter *A* in brackets indicates that the first part of the sentence has been omitted. At the end of the quotation, the sentence period follows the parenthetical citation, and the three ellipsis points represent the omission of the end of the quoted sentence.

Note: If the quotation begins with a capitalized word, rather than with a lowercased word or one starting with a bracketed capital letter, ellipses should precede the first word of the quotation so that readers will know that the first part of the sentence has been left out.

The arrival of the steamers in 1838 meant that ". . . New York had established a maritime steam link to Europe" (Burrows and Wallace 649).

5. Ellipses are usually not needed to indicate an omission when you are quoting only a word or phrase.

PHRASE QUOTED—NO ELLIPSES

According to Burrows and Wallace, the arrival of the two steamers caused "exuberant rejoicing" in the city (649).

6. To indicate the omission of an entire line or more from the middle of a poem or of a paragraph or more from a prose quotation, insert a line of spaced periods. (Otherwise, the rules for omitting words from a poetry quotation are the same as those given in items 1–5.)

Shelley seems to be describing nature, but what is really at issue is the seductive nature of desire:

See the mountains kiss high Heaven.
And the waves clasp one another:
. . . .
And the sunlight clasp the earth,
And the moonbeams kiss the sea:
What is all this sweet work worth
If thou kiss not me? (1-2, 5-8)

Ellipses should be used only as a means of shortening a quotation, never as a device for changing its fundamental meaning or for creating emphasis where none exists in the original.

You can also use ellipses to leave a thought or statement hanging or to suggest that a series continues.

INCOMPLETE THOUGHT

She glared at me and said, "If I have to come over there one more time . . ."

INCOMPLETE SERIES

The chores were seemingly endless. Feed the animals, make breakfast, wash the dishes, make the beds, sweep the floors . . . and then do it all over again the next day.

55k Use a slash to show line breaks in quoted poetry, to separate options or combinations, and in electronic addresses.

When quoting two or three lines of poetry within a sentence, use a slash to show where each line of poetry ends. Add a space before and after the slash.

QUOTATION WITH SLASHES

► **In "The Tower," Yeats makes his peace with "All those things whereof / Man makes a superhuman / Mirror-resembling dream" (163–65).**

Reproduce the capitalization and punctuation of the original poetry, but add a period if necessary to end your sentence. If you leave out the end of the last line you are quoting, add ellipses (*see 55j*). Do not use slashes in block quotations or extracts of poetry (*see 54d*).

You should also use slashes to mark divisions in Internet addresses (URLs) and in fractions

► **www.mheducation.com/college.html**

► **3/4, 1 2/3**

Note: There is a space, not a hyphen, between the *1* and the *2/3*.

Slashes are also used to indicate a choice or combination.

► **credit/noncredit** **owner/operator** **and/or**

> ***Note:*** Although this use of the slash is common in business writing, it is discouraged in academic writing, especially in the humanities.

Exercise 55.3 Using brackets, ellipses, and slashes

Insert brackets, ellipses, and slashes where needed in the following sentences, and correct any errors in their use. Refer to the following excerpts from a poem and an essay.

> The lights begin to twinkle from the rocks;
> The long day wanes; the slow moon climbs, the deep
> Moans round with many voices. Come, my friends.
> 'T is not too late to seek a newer world. (54-57)
>
> —from *Ulysses* by Alfred, Lord Tennyson

> Now when I had mastered the language of this water and had come to know every trifling feature that bordered the great river as familiarly as I knew the letters of the alphabet, I had made a valuable acquisition. But I had lost something, too. I had lost something which could never be restored to me while I lived. All the grace, the beauty, the poetry had gone out of the majestic river!
>
> —from "Two Views of the Mississippi" by Mark Twain

EXAMPLE **The speaker in the poem *Ulysses* longs to seek "/ / / a newer world" (57).**

1. Ulysses is tempted as he looks toward the sea: "The lights begin to twinkle from the rocks; The long day wanes . . ." (54-55).
2. In "Two Views of the Mississippi," Mark Twain writes that "I had mastered the language of this water. I had made a valuable acquisition."
3. Twain regrets that he "has lost something"—his sense of the beauty of the river.
4. In Tennyson's poem, "the deep the ocean / moans round with many voices" (55-56).
5. In *Ulysses* the ocean beckons with possibilities; in "Two Views of the Mississippi," the river has become too familiar: "All the grace had gone out of the majestic river!"

Exercise 55.4 Chapter review: Dashes, parentheses, and other punctuation marks

Edit the following passage by adding or deleting dashes, parentheses, brackets, ellipses, and slashes. Make any other additions, deletions, or changes that are necessary for correctness and sense. Refer to the following excerpt as necessary.

> This is a book about that most admirable of human virtues—courage.
>
> . . . .
>
> Some of my colleagues who are criticized today for lack of forthright principles—or who are looked upon with scornful eyes as compromising "politicians"—are simply engaged in the fine art of conciliating, balancing and interpreting the forces and factions of public opinion, an art essential to keeping our nation united and enabling our Government to function.
>
> —JOHN F. KENNEDY, *Profiles in Courage,* pp. 1, 5

John Fitzgerald Kennedy—the youngest man to be elected U.S. president—he was also the youngest president to be assassinated. He was born on May 29, 1917, in Brookline, Massachusetts. Kennedy was born into a family with a tradition of public service; his father, Joseph Kennedy, served as ambassador to Great Britain. (his maternal grandfather, John Frances Fitzgerald, served as the mayor of Boston.)

Caroline, John Fitzgerald Jr., and Patrick B. (Who died in infancy) are the children of the late John F. Kennedy. Kennedy's background, a Harvard education, military service as a lieutenant in the navy, and public service as Massachusetts senator—helped provide John F. Kennedy with the experience, insight, and recognition needed to defeat Richard Nixon in 1960.

Even before being elected U.S. president, Kennedy received the Pulitzer Prize for his book *Profiles in Courage* 1957. According to Kennedy, "This *Profiles in Courage* is a book about that most admirable of human virtues—courage" 1. "Some of my colleagues," Kennedy continues, "who are criticized today for lack of forthright principles / are simply engaged in the fine art of conciliating. . . ." 5.

During Kennedy's presidency, Americans witnessed 1 the Cuban missile crisis, 2 the Bay of Pigs invasion, and 3 the Berlin crisis. Most Americans—we hope—are able to recognize Kennedy's famous words—which were first delivered during his Inaugural Address: "Ask not what your country can do for you—ask what you can do for your country."

56 End Punctuation: Periods, Question Marks, and Exclamation Points

Periods, question marks, and exclamation points mark the ends of statements, commands, questions, and exclamations. Periods are also used in abbreviations.

www.mhhe.com/mhhb2
For information and exercises on end punctuation, go to
Editing > End Punctuation

End Punctuation and Grammar Checkers

Computer grammar checkers will catch a few errors in the use of end punctuation, such as use of a period instead of a question mark at the end of a question. For the most part, though, you cannot rely on your grammar checker to recognize these errors. You will need to check your writing carefully for problems with end punctuation.

56a Use a period after most statements, indirect questions, polite requests, and mild commands.

STATEMENT
There are more than one thousand periods in this book.

STATEMENT CONTAINING A QUOTATION
"What is the word count?" she asked.

STATEMENT CONTAINING AN INDIRECT QUESTION
She asked me where I had gone to college.

POLITE REQUEST
Please go with me to the lecture.

MILD COMMAND
Take a vitamin every day.

56b Use a period in abbreviations according to convention.

A period or periods are used with the following common abbreviations, which end in lowercase letters.

Mr.	Dr.	Mass.
Ms.	i.e.	Jan.
Mrs.	e.g.	a.m.

If an abbreviation is made up of capital letters, however, the periods are optional. Be consistent throughout your document.

RN (or R.N.)	BA (or B.A.)
MD (or M.D.)	PhD (or Ph.D.)

Periods are omitted in abbreviations for organizations, famous people, states in mailing addresses, and acronyms (words made up of the initial letters of their parts).

FBI	JFK	MA	NATO
CIA	LBJ	TX	NAFTA
NASA			

When in doubt, consult a dictionary. (*For more on abbreviations, see Chapter 58.*)

When an abbreviation ends a sentence, the period at the end of the abbreviation serves as the period for the sentence. If a question mark or an exclamation point ends the sentence, place it *after* the period in the abbreviation.

► **When he was in the seventh grade, we called him "Stinky," but now he is William Percival Abernathy, Ph.D.!**

56c Do not use a period at the end of a sentence within a sentence.

Omit the period when a sentence is contained within parentheses or quotation marks.

► **I rapped on Mai's door (she is usually home), but no one answered.**

► **"I'm not home," came the reply.**

56d Use a question mark after a direct question.

► **Who wrote *The Old Man and the Sea*?**

Occasionally, a question mark changes a statement into a question.

► **You expect me to believe a story like that?**

You can end a polite question with either a period or a question mark, but be consistent within your paper.

► **Will you please go with me to the lecture.**

► **Will you please go with me to the lecture?**

When questions follow one another in a series, each one can be followed by a question mark even if the questions are not complete sentences, as long as the meaning is understood. You begin each question in the series with a capital or a lowercase letter.

► **What will you contribute? Your time? Your talent? Your money?**

► **What will you contribute? your time? your talent? your money?**

Use a question mark in parentheses to indicate a questionable date, number, or word, but do not use it to convey an ironic meaning or to indicate that you are not certain of a fact.

► **Chaucer was born in 1340 (?) and lived until 1400.**

► **His yapping dog had recently graduated from obedience ~~(?)~~ training.**

► **Franklin Roosevelt was elected president four ~~(?)~~ times.**

> ***Note:*** Do not use a question mark after an indirect quotation, even if the words being indirectly quoted were originally a question.
>
> ► **He asked her whether she would be at home later~~?~~.**

56e Use exclamation points sparingly to convey shock, surprise, or a forceful command.

► **Stolen! The money was stolen! Right before our eyes, somebody snatched my purse and ran off with it.**

► **Watch out for the flying glass!**

> ***Note:*** Using numerous exclamation points throughout a document actually weakens their force. As much as possible, try to convey emotion with your choice of words and your sentence structure instead of with an exclamation point.
>
> ► **Jefferson and Adams both died on the same day in 1826, exactly fifty years after the signing of the Declaration of Independence~~!~~.**
>
> The fact that the sentence reports is surprising enough without the addition of an exclamation point.

Although you might use an exclamation point within parentheses (!) to convey an ironic or sarcastic meaning in your personal writing, this use is inappropriate in academic writing.

56f Place a question mark or an exclamation point within a sentence if your meaning requires it.

- ► **The wait seems endless (how long has it been?), but he will return.**
- ► **He has been gone so long—will he ever return?—that I have almost forgotten his voice.**
- ► **"Will you wait for me?" he asked.**
- ► **"Never!" I answered.**

(*For more on inserting questions and exclamations within sentences, see Chapters 54 and 55.*)

56g Do not add a comma or an additional end mark after a period, a question mark, or an exclamation point.

- ► **William earned a Ph.D./**
- ► **Is it you who asked, "Will he be home soon?"?**
- ► **"It isn't true!/ " she exclaimed.**

56h Make sure that the end mark concludes a complete sentence.

Punctuating a dependent clause or phrase as if it were a sentence results in a fragment. Make sure that your sentence has a subject and a complete verb and does not start with a subordinating word. (*For more on sentence fragments, see Chapter 32.*)

SENTENCE FRAGMENT	Although it was clearly marked on the label.
SENTENCE FRAGMENT	Driving all over town in search of a present?

Exercise 56.1 Chapter review: End punctuation

Insert periods, question marks, and exclamation points in the following passage. Delete any unnecessary commas.

Do you realize that there is a volcano larger than Mt St Helens Mt Vesuvius Mt Etna Mauna Loa is the largest volcano on Earth, covering at least half the island of Hawaii The summit of Mauna Loa stands 56,000 feet above its base This is why Native Hawaiians named this volcano, the "Long Mountain" Mauna Loa is also one of the most active volcanoes on the planet, having erupted thirty-three times since 1843 (most people do not think of a volcano as dormant) Its last eruption occurred in 1984 Most people associate a volcanic eruption with red lava spewing from the volcano's crater, but few people realize that the lava flow, and volcanic gases are also extremely hazardous Tourists like to follow the lava to where it meets the sea, but this practice is dangerous because of the steam produced when the lava meets the water So, the next time you visit an active volcano, beware

FIGURE 56.1 Tourists watching lava from Mauna Loa flow into the sea.

CHECKLIST

Editing for Sentence Punctuation

As you revise, ask yourself these questions:

- ☐ Are commas used appropriately to separate or set off coordinated independent clauses; items in a series and coordinate adjectives; introductory sentence elements; nonessential sentence elements; direct quotations; and the parts of dates, addresses, titles, and numbers? (*See Chapter 51: Commas, pp. 718–45.*) Are any commas mistakenly used with sentence elements that should not be separated or set off? (*See Chapter 51: Commas, pp. 740–45.*)

- ☐ Are semicolons used appropriately to join independent clauses and to separate items in a series when the items contain commas? (*See Chapter 52: Semicolons, pp. 745–51.*)

- ☐ Are colons used appropriately after a complete sentence to introduce a list, an appositive, or a quotation; after one independent clause to introduce a second that elaborates on the first; and in business letters, ratios, and bibliographic citations? (*See Chapter 53: Colons, pp. 752–55.*)

- ☐ Are quotation marks used appropriately with other punctuation to identify brief direct quotations, dialogue, and the titles of short works? Are single quotation marks used appropriately to identify quotations within quotations? (*See Chapter 54: Quotation Marks, pp. 755–66.*)

- ☐ Are brackets and ellipses used correctly to identify elisions and interpolations within quotations? Are dashes and parentheses used appropriately to insert or highlight nonessential information within a sentence? (*See Chapter 55: Dashes, Parentheses, and Other Punctuation Marks, pp. 766–79.*)

- ☐ Are periods used appropriately at the end of sentences and in abbreviations? Are question marks and exclamation points used appropriately at the end of sentences and within quotations? (*See Chapter 56: End Punctuation, pp. 780–84.*)

The great twelfth-century inventor al-Jazari designed many innovative, mechanical devices. This plan for a water–operated automaton documents the engineering behind one invention's design; each working part relies on the precise placement of others.

PART 11

It wasn't a matter of rewriting but simply of tightening up all the bolts.
—MARGUERITE YOURCENAR

Mechanics and Spelling

57 Capitalization

Many rules for the use of capital (uppercase) letters have been fixed by custom, such as the convention of beginning each sentence with a capital letter, but the rules sometimes change. As you revise your drafts, check to make sure you are using capital letters appropriately in the following types of words:

- Proper nouns (names), words derived from proper nouns, brand names, and certain abbreviations (*see 57a, pp. 789–91*)
- People's titles (*see 57b, p. 791*)
- Names of areas and regions (*see 57c, p. 792*)
- Names of ethnic groups and sacred things (*see 57d, pp. 792–93*)
- Titles of works of literature, art, and music; documents; and courses (*see 57e, p. 793*)

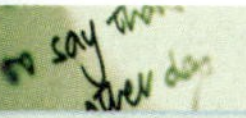

WRITING OUTCOMES

Part 11: Mechanics and Spelling

This section will help you answer questions such as:

Rhetorical Knowledge

- Should I write *15* or *fifteen*? **(59a, b)**
- Should I use contractions like *can't* or *don't* in my paper? **(61b)**

Critical Thinking, Reading, and Writing

- Should I capitalize names of religious and ethnic groups? **(57a)**

Processes

- Can my word processor's grammar checker help me edit for mechanics? **(57–62)**
- What should I remember when using my word processor's spelling checker? **(63)**

Knowledge of Conventions

- Should I capitalize titles like *Professor?* **(57b)**
- What is the difference between *its* and *it's?* **(61c)**

Self-Assessment: *Take an online quiz at www.mhhe.com/mhhb2 to test your familiarity with the topics covered in Chapters 57–63. Pay special attention to the sections in these chapters that correspond to any questions you answer incorrectly.*

- The first word of a sentence (*see 57f, p. 794*)
- The first word of a quotation (*see 57g, pp. 794–95*)
- The first word of an independent clause after a colon (*see 57h, p. 795*)

Capitalization and Grammar Checkers

Grammar checkers will flag words that should be capitalized or lowercased by convention, but they will not flag proper nouns unless the noun is stored in the program's dictionary, and they will not necessarily point out a noun that can be either proper or common, depending on the context. For example, a grammar checker flagged the capitalization error in the first sentence (should be *North America*) but not the second (should be *Buffalo*):

Maria is going to study the mammals of north America.

The Darwin Martin House, designed by Frank Lloyd Wright, is located in buffalo, New York.

Editing tip: The abbreviation *cap* indicates that a letter should be capitalized. (Professional editors and proofreaders also add three lines under the letter to mark it for capitalization.) The abbreviation *lc* indicates that a letter should be lowercased rather than capitalized. (Professional editors and proofreaders also add a slash mark through the letter to mark it as lowercase.)

✓ 57a Capitalize proper nouns (names), words derived from them, brand names, certain abbreviations, and call letters.

www.mhhe.com/mhhb2

For information and exercises on capitalization, go to **Editing > Capitalization**

Proper nouns are the names of specific people, places, or things, names that set off the individual from the group, such as the name *Jane* instead of the common noun *person.* Capitalize proper nouns, words derived from proper nouns, brand names, abbreviations of capitalized words (including *acronyms,* abbreviations that form words), and the call letters of radio and television stations.

PROPER NOUNS	Ronald Reagan, the Sears Tower, the Internet
WORDS DERIVED FROM PROPER NOUNS	Reaganomics, Siamese cat, *but* french fries, simonize
BRAND NAMES	Apple Computer, Kleenex

ABBREVIATIONS AND ACRONYMS	FBI (government agency), A&E (cable television network), NATO (international alliance)
CALL LETTERS	WNBC (television), WMMR (radio)

PROPER and COMMON NOUNS

People: John F. Kennedy, Ruth Bader Ginsburg, Albert Einstein

Nationalities, ethnic groups, and languages: English, Swiss, African Americans, Arabs, Chinese, Turkish

Places: the United States of America, Tennessee, the Irunia Restaurant, the Great Lakes, *but* my state, the lake

Organizations and institutions: Phi Beta Kappa, Republican Party (Republicans), Department of Defense, Cumberland College, the North Carolina Tarheels, *but* the department, this college, my hockey team

Religions, religious bodies, books, and figures: Islam, Buddhism, Jews, Christians, Baptists, Hindus, Roman Catholic Church, the Bible, the Koran *or* Qur'an, the Torah, God, Holy Spirit, Allah, *but* a Greek goddess, a biblical reference

Scientific names and terms: *Homo sapiens, H. sapiens, Acer rubrum, A. rubrum*, Addison's disease, Cenozoic era, Newton's first law, *but* the law of gravity

Names of planets, stars, and other astronomical bodies: Earth (as a planet) *but otherwise* the earth, Mercury, Polaris *or* the North Star, Whirlpool Galaxy, *but* a star, that galaxy, the solar system

Computer terms: the Internet, the World Wide Web *or* the Web, *but* search engine, a network, my browser

Days, months, and holidays: Monday, Veterans Day, August, the Fourth of July, *but* yesterday, spring and summer, the winter term

Historical events, movements, periods, and documents: World War II, Impressionism, the Renaissance, the Jazz Age, the Declaration of Independence, the Constitution of the United States, *but* the last war, a golden age, the twentieth century, the amendment

Academic courses and subjects: English 101, Psychology 221, a course in Italian, *but* a physics course, my art history class

CHARTING the TERRITORY

Capitalization Rules in the Disciplines

Different disciplines have their own guidelines for capitalizing specialized vocabulary. In scientific names, for example, the genus is capitalized, but the species is not: *Homo sapiens*. The names of higher divisions—phylum, class, order, family—are capitalized: *Felidae*. In musical chord notation, a capital *M* stands for "major"; a lowercase *m* stands for "minor." Consult a discipline-specific style guide when in doubt.

Note: Seasons, such as summer, and the days of the month are not capitalized when they are spelled out.

► **Why would *Valentine's Day*, the day representing love and romance, fall in *winter*—and in the coldest month of the year at that?**

► **She will be available to meet with you on Sunday, the *seventh* of March.**

57b Capitalize a person's title when it appears before a proper name but not when it is used alone.

Capitalize titles when they come before a proper name, but do not capitalize them when they appear alone or after the name.

Every Sunday, *Aunt Lou* tells fantastic stories.

My *aunt* is arriving this afternoon.

Everyone knew that *Governor Grover Cleveland* of New York was the most likely candidate for the Democratic nomination.

The most likely candidate for the Democratic nomination was Grover Cleveland, *governor* of New York.

Exceptions: Capitalize the name for a family relationship used alone (without a possessive such as *my* before it).

► **I saw *Father* infrequently during the summer months.**

Most writers do not capitalize the title *president* unless they are referring to the President of the United States: "The *president* of this university has seventeen honorary degrees." Usage varies, but be consistent. If you write "the President of the University," you should also write "the Chair of the History Department." A company may capitalize a reference to its own Board of Directors in internal communications.

For MULTILINGUAL STUDENTS

***Capitalizing the Pronoun* I**

Unlike other languages, English requires you to capitalize the first person singular pronoun (*I*). All other pronouns are lowercase, unless they start a sentence or are part of the title of a work.

► **When *I* get home, *I* will call my doctor for the test results and let you know what she says.**

English also is the only language to distinguish between common and proper nouns (capitalize the latter).

57c Capitalize names of areas and regions.

Names of geographical regions are generally capitalized if they are well established, like *the Midwest* and *Central Europe.* Names of directions, as in the sentence *Turn south,* are not capitalized.

CORRECT *East* meets *West* at the summit.

CORRECT You will need to go *west* on Sunset Road.

Note: The word *western* is capitalized only when it is part of the name of a specific region.

► **The river flows through the ~~Western~~ [western] part of the state.**

► **The ~~Western~~ [western] *High Noon* is one of my favorite movies.**

► **I visited ~~western~~ [Western] Europe last year.**

57d Follow standard practice for capitalizing names of races, ethnic groups, and sacred things.

The words *black* and *white* are usually not capitalized when they are used to refer to members of racial groups because they are adjectives that substitute for the implied common nouns *black person* and *white person.* However, names of ethnic groups and races are capitalized: *African Americans, Italians, Asians, Caucasians.*

Note: In accordance with current APA guidelines, most social scientists capitalize the terms *Black* and *White*, treating them as proper nouns.

Many religious terms, such as *sacrament, altar,* and *rabbi,* are not capitalized. The word *Bible* is capitalized (though *biblical* is not), but it is never capitalized when it is used as a metaphor for an essential book.

► **His book *Winning at Stud Poker* used to be the *bible* of gamblers.**

57e Capitalize titles of works of literature, works of art, musical compositions, documents, and courses.

Capitalize the first and last word of a title and subtitle. Capitalize all the words within the title or subtitle *except* articles (*a, an,* and *the*), the *to* in infinitives, and prepositions, as well as coordinating conjunctions. (However, if you are using APA style, capitalize any word that has four or more letters.) Capitalize all words in a hyphenated word unless the additional word is a preposition (*Hands-on*), a conjunction or an article (*Peaches-and-Cream, Dime-a-Dozen*), or a second number (*Twenty-five*). Capitalize the word that follows a colon or semicolon in a title.

Book: *Two Years before the Mast*

Chapter: "Capitalization"

Play or film: *The Taming of the Shrew*

Building: the Eiffel Tower

Ship or aircraft: the *Titanic* or the *Concorde*

Painting: the *Mona Lisa*

Article or essay: "On Old Age"

Poem: "Ode on a Grecian Urn"

Music: "The Star-Spangled Banner"

Document: the Bill of Rights

Course: Economics 206: Macro-Economic Analysis

TEXTCONNEX

Emphasis in E-Mail

Words or phrases in all capital letters are not always welcome in e-mails, chat rooms, electronic mailing list postings, and other online forums where they are equivalent to shouting. Also, strings of words or sentences in capital letters can be difficult to read. If you want to emphasize a word or phrase in an online communication, put an underscore before and after it.

► **That's a _very_ interesting point.**

57f Capitalize the first word of a sentence.

A capital letter is used to signal the beginning of a new sentence.

► **Robots reduce human error, so they produce uniform products.**

Sentences in parentheses also begin with a capital letter unless they are embedded within another sentence.

► **Although the week began with the news that he was hit by a car, by Thursday we knew he was going to be all right. (It was a terrible way to begin the week, though.)**

► **Although the week began with the news that he was hit by a car (it was a terrible way to begin the week), by Thursday we knew he was going to be all right.**

57g Capitalize the first word of a quoted sentence but not the first word of an indirect quotation.

► **She cried, "Help!"**

► **He said that jazz was one of America's major art forms.**

The first word of a quotation from a printed source is capitalized if the quotation is introduced with a phrase such as *she notes* or *he concludes.*

► **Jim, the narrator of *My Ántonia,* concludes, "Whatever we had missed, we possessed together the precious, the incommunicable past" (324).**

When a quotation from a printed source is treated as an element in your sentence, not a sentence on its own, the first word is not capitalized.

► **Jim took comfort in sharing with Ántonia "the precious, the incommunicable past" (324).**

If you need to change the first letter of a quotation to fit your sentence, enclose the letter in brackets.

► **The lawyer noted that "[t]he man seen leaving the area after the blast was not the same height as the defendant."**

If you interrupt the sentence you are quoting with an expression such as *he said,* the first word of the rest of the quotation should not be capitalized.

► **"When I come home an hour later," she explained, "the trains are usually less crowded."**

Many authors in earlier centuries and some writers today—especially poets—use capital letters in obsolete or eccentric ways. When quoting a text directly, reproduce the capitalization used in the original source, whether or not it is correct by today's standards.

► **Blake's marginalia include the following comment: "Paine is either a Devil or an Inspired Man" (603).**

57h Capitalizing the first word of an independent clause after a colon or in a series of short questions is optional.

If the word group that follows a colon is not a complete sentence, do not capitalize it. If it is a complete sentence, you can capitalize it or not, but be consistent throughout your document.

► **The question is serious: do you think the peace process has a chance?**

or

► **The question is serious: Do you think the peace process has a chance?**

In a series of one- or two-word questions that follow a complete sentence, you can capitalize the first word of each question or not, as long as you are consistent.

► **When are you available? Next week? Next month?**

or

► **When are you available? next week? next month?**

Note, however, that incomplete questions like these are not usually appropriate in academic writing.

57i Capitalize the first word of each item in a formal outline.

Capitalize the first word of each item in an outline, whether or not the item is a complete sentence. If the items are complete sentences, remember to add a period at the end of each one.

I. Evidence of the last Ice Age in New England and the Middle Atlantic States

- **A. Glacial deposits in Cape Cod**
- **B. Terminal moraines on Long Island**
- **C. The Finger Lakes in central New York**

57j Be consistent about the capitalization of the first word of items in numbered lists.

Lists can either run in with your text or be displayed. In either case, you are required to capitalize the first word of each item if the items are complete sentences. In run-in lists, do not capitalize the first letter of items in a list if they are not sentences. In displayed lists, capital letters are optional for items that are not sentences, but you need to be consistent. If the lead-in to the list is a complete sentence, it can end with a colon. If it is not, you should incorporate the list into your sentence.

RUN-IN LIST WITH PHRASES

There are three ways to register: (1) by mail, (2) by telephone, and (3) in person on the day classes begin.

or

The three ways to register are (1) by mail, (2) by telephone, and (3) in person on the day classes begin.

DISPLAYED LIST WITH PHRASES

There are three ways to register:

1. By mail
2. By telephone
3. In person on the day classes begin

or

1. by mail
2. by telephone
3. in person on the day classes begin

It is preferable to introduce a displayed list with a complete sentence ending in a colon. Items in a displayed list do not need to end in periods unless they are complete sentences.

Note that the items in each sample list are grammatically parallel. (*For more on parallel structure in lists, see Chapter 42: Faulty Parallelism, pp. 643–44.*)

57k Capitalize the first word in the greeting and closing of a letter.

Dear Mr. Morrison:

Sincerely,

Yours truly,

Exercise 57.1 Chapter review: Capitalization

Edit the following passage, changing letters to capital or lowercase as necessary.

Perhaps the most notable writer of the 1920s is F. Scott Fitzgerald. He was born on September 24, 1896, in St. Paul, Minnesota, to Edward Fitzgerald and Mary "mollie" McQuillan, who were both members of the catholic church. After attending Princeton university and embarking on a career as a writer, Fitzgerald married southern belle Zelda Sayre from Montgomery, Alabama. Together, he and his Wife lived the celebrated life of the roaring twenties and the jazz age. Fitzgerald wrote numerous short stories as well as four novels, *This Side of Paradise, The Beautiful and Damned, The Great Gatsby,* and *Tender is the night. The Great Gatsby,* which he finished in the Winter of 1924 and published in 1925, is considered Fitzgerald's most brilliant and critically acclaimed work. readers who have read this novel will remember the opening words spoken by Nick Carraway, the narrator in the story: "in my younger and more vulnerable years my father gave me some advice that i've been turning over in my mind ever since. 'Whenever you feel like criticizing anyone,' he told me, 'Just remember that all the people in this world haven't had the advantages that you've had.'"

FIGURE 57.1 The cover of the first edition of *The Great Gatsby*.

58 Abbreviations and Symbols

Abbreviations and symbols are used in the body of scientific and technical reports. Abbreviations are also used in lists of works cited or references for all types of academic papers. However, in nontechnical writing you should avoid using abbreviations or symbols, except in the situations explained in this chapter.

www.mhhe.com/mhhb2
For information and exercises on abbreviations, go to
Editing > Abbreviations

Editing tip: The abbreviation *abbr* indicates a problem with the use of abbreviations.

Abbreviations and Grammar Checkers

Computer grammar or spelling checkers may flag an abbreviation, but they generally can not tell you if your use of it is acceptable or consistent within a piece of writing.

58a Abbreviate familiar titles that precede or follow a person's name.

Some abbreviations appear before a person's name (*Mr., Mrs., Dr.*) and some follow a proper name (*Jr., Sr., MD, Esq., PhD*). Abbreviations that follow a person's name often indicate academic or professional degrees or honors.

Punctuation tips: Periods are used with most abbreviations that end in lowercase letters: *Mr., Ms., Jr.* If the abbreviation is made up of capital letters, however, the periods are optional: *RN* or *R.N.; PhD* or *Ph.D.; MD* or *M.D.* In most cases, when an abbreviation follows a person's name, a comma is placed between the name and the abbreviation. In the case of *Jr.*, however, the comma between the name and abbreviation is optional (*See Chapter 51: Commas, p. 738*).

TITLES BEFORE NAMES	Mrs. Jean Bascom Dr. Epstein
TITLES AFTER NAMES	Robert Robinson, Jr. Elaine Less, CPA, LLD

Do not use two abbreviations that represent the same thing: *Dr. Peter Joyce, MD.* Use either *Dr. Peter Joyce* or *Peter Joyce, MD.*

Spell out titles used without proper names.

► **Mr. Carew asked if she had seen the ~~dr.~~** *doctor.*

Academic titles such as *PhD* can appear by themselves, however.

► **Elena earned her PhD in biochemistry.**

For MULTILINGUAL STUDENTS

Reading Abbreviations in Standard American English

Learning how to read abbreviations in standard American English can be puzzling—to native speakers as well as multilingual students—because no universal logic governs the way they are pronounced. In general, however, they fall into five types.

1. **Acronyms**—abbreviations composed of the initial letters of words or syllables—**that are read as individual letters,** such as *ATM* (*automated teller machine*), *ID* (*identification*), *IBM* (*International Business Machines*), and *UN* (*United Nations*)
2. **Acronyms that are read as words,** such as *NATO* (*North Atlantic Treaty Organization*) and *AIDS* (*acquired immuno-deficiency syndrome*)
3. **Acronyms that are sometimes read as the phrases they represent and sometimes as individual letters,** such as *FYI* (*for your information*) and *AKA* (*also known as*)
4. **Abbreviations that are consistently read as full words,** such as *Dr.* or *Mr.*
5. **Clippings**—words used in a shortened form, usually informally—such as *lab* (for *laboratory*), *exam* (for *examination*), and *memo* (for *memorandum*)

To avoid confusion, identify an abbreviation for your audience word by word the first time you use it. For a list of common abbreviations, consult your English dictionary.

58b Use abbreviations only when you know your readers will understand them.

If you use a technical term or the name of an organization, a country, or a government agency in a report, you may abbreviate it as long as your readers are likely to be familiar with the abbreviation.

FAMILIAR ABBREVIATION	The EPA has had a lasting impact on the air quality in this country.
UNFAMILIAR ABBREVIATION	After you have completed them, take these forms to ~~HREC.~~ ^ *the Human Resources and Education Center.*

Write out an unfamiliar term or name the first time you use it, and give the abbreviation in parentheses.

► **The Student Nonviolent Coordinating Committee (SNCC) was far to the left of other civil rights organizations, and its leaders often mocked the "conservatism" of Dr. Martin Luther King, Jr. SNCC quickly burned itself out and disappeared.**

Note: In the body of a paper, you can use *U.S.* as an adjective (*U.S. Constitution*) but not as a noun (*I grew up outside of the United States*).

Punctuation tip: Periods are omitted in abbreviations for organizations, certain famous people, states in mailing addresses, and acronyms (words made up of initials): *FBI, CIA, APA, JFK, LBJ, TX, NASA, NATO, NAFTA, WWII*. The periods in the abbreviations for the United States of America are optional: *U.S.A. (U.S.) or USA (US)*.

TEXTCONNEX

Digital Age Abbreviations and Acronyms

CD	compact disc
CD-ROM	compact disc read-only memory
DVD	digital video disc (or digital versatile disc)
DVD-ROM	digital video disc read-only memory
FTP	file transfer protocol
GB	gigabyte
HTML	hypertext markup language
http	hypertext transfer protocol
KB	kilobyte
IM	instant message
MB	megabyte
MOO	multiuser domain, object-oriented
URL	uniform resource locator
WWW	World Wide Web

58c Abbreviate words typically used with times, dates, and numerals, as well as units of measurement in charts and graphs.

Abbreviations or symbols associated with numbers should be used only when accompanying a number: *3 p.m.*, not *in the p.m.*; *$500,* not *How many $ do you have?* The abbreviation *B.C.* ("before Christ") follows a date; *A.D.* ("in the year of our Lord") precedes the date. The alternative abbreviations *B.C.E.* ("before the Common Era") and *C.E.* ("Common Era") can be used instead of *B.C.* or *A.D.*, respectively.

6:00 p.m. *or* 6:00 P.M. *or* 6:00 PM

9:45 a.m. *or* 9:45 A.M. *or* 9:45 AM

498 B.C. *or* 498 B.C.E. *or* 498 BCE

A.D. 275 *or* 275 C.E. *or* 275 CE

6,000 rpm

271 cm

Note: Be consistent. If you use *a.m.* in one sentence, do not switch to *A.M.* in the next sentence.

In charts and graphs, abbreviations and symbols such as = for *equals, in.* for *inches, %* for *percent,* and *$* with numbers are acceptable because they save space.

58d Use abbreviations in mailing addresses.

Abbreviations such as *St.*, *Ave.*, and *Apt.* are used in mailing addresses on correspondence. The following list gives the postal abbreviations for states and territories in the United States and provinces and territories in Canada.

United States

AK Alaska
AL Alabama
AR Arkansas
AZ Arizona
CA California
CO Colorado
CT Connecticut
DC District of Columbia
DE Delaware
FL Florida
GA Georgia
GU Guam
HI Hawaii
IA Iowa
ID Idaho
IL Illinois
IN Indiana
KS Kansas
KY Kentucky
LA Louisiana
MA Massachusetts
MD Maryland
ME Maine
MI Michigan
MN Minnesota
MO Missouri
MS Mississippi
MT Montana

NC	North Carolina	SC	South Carolina	MB	Manitoba
ND	North Dakota	SD	South Dakota	NB	New Brunswick
NE	Nebraska	TN	Tennessee	NL	Newfoundland and Labrador
NH	New Hampshire	TX	Texas	NS	Nova Scotia
NJ	New Jersey	UT	Utah	NT	Northwest Territories
NM	New Mexico	VA	Virginia	NU	Nunavut
NV	Nevada	VT	Vermont	ON	Ontario
NY	New York	WA	Washington	PE	Prince Edward Island
OH	Ohio	WI	Wisconsin	QC	Québec
OK	Oklahoma	WV	West Virginia	SK	Saskatchewan
OR	Oregon	WY	Wyoming	YT	Yukon Territory
PA	Pennsylvania	**Canada**			
PR	Puerto Rico	AB	Alberta		
RI	Rhode Island	BC	British Columbia		

58e Become familiar with abbreviations used in research citations.

Depending on the documentation style they are using, writers of research papers may use the following abbreviations in the list of works cited or references at the end of the paper or in explanatory notes. Refer to Chapters 23–26 or to a discipline-specific style manual (*see p. 339 for a list*) for guidelines about using abbreviations for this purpose.

Names

anon.	anonymous	dir.	director, directed by
ed., eds.	editor(s), edited by, edition	illus.	illustrator, illustrated by
gen. ed.	general editor	trans.	translator, translated by
comp.	compiler, compiled by		

Parts of Publications

app.	appendix	fwd.	foreword
ch.	chapter	illus.	illustration
col., cols.	column, columns	introd.	introduction
cont.	contents	l., ll.	line, lines
div.	division	n, nn	note, notes
fig.	figure	no.	number
ff.	following (pages or lines)	n. pag.	no pagination
		p., pp.	page, pages

par., pars.	paragraph, paragraphs	pt.	part
pref.	preface	sec., secs.	section, sections

Types of Publications

bk.	book	rev.	revision, revised, *or* review, reviewed
bull.	bulletin	rept.	reprint *or* report
diss.	dissertation	ser.	series
ed.	edition	supp.	supplement
jour.	journal	vol., vols.	volume, volumes
mag.	magazine		
ms., mss.	manuscript, manuscripts		

Months of Publication

Jan.	January	Sept.	September
Feb.	February	Oct.	October
Mar.	March	Nov.	November
Apr.	April	Dec.	December
Aug.	August		

Publishers

P	Press	Soc.	Society
U	University	n.p.	no place of publication or no publisher
UP	University Press		
GPO	Government Printing Office		

Other Abbreviations

b.	born	esp.	especially
©	copyright	n.d.	no date of publication
c. *or* ca.	about (*circa*)	v. *or* vs.	versus
d.	died		

58f Avoid Latin abbreviations in formal writing.

Latin abbreviations can be used in notes or works-cited lists, but in formal writing it is usually a good idea to avoid even common Latin abbreviations (*e.g., et al., etc.,* and *i.e.*). Instead of *e.g.,* use *such as* or *for example.*

cf.	compare (*confer*)	i.e.	that is (*id est*)
e.g.	for example, such as (*exempli gratia*)	N.B.	note well (*nota bene*)
et al.	and others (*et alii*)	viz.	namely (*videlicet*)
etc.	and so forth, and so on (*et cetera*)		

58g Avoid inappropriate abbreviations and symbols.

Days of the week (*Sat.*), places (*TX* or *Tex.*), the word *company* (*Co.*), people's names (*Wm.*), disciplines and professions (*econ.*), parts of speech (*v.*), parts of written works (*ch., p.*), symbols (@), and units of measurement (*lb.*) are all spelled out in formal writing.

► **The *environmental* (not *env.*) engineers from the Paramus Water *Company* (not *Co.*) are arriving in *New York City* (not *NYC*) this *Thursday* (not *Thurs.*) to correct the problems in the *physical education* (not *phys. ed.*) building in time for *Christmas* (not *Xmas*).**

Exceptions: If an abbreviation such as *Inc., Co.*, or *Corp.* is part of a company's official name, then it can be included in formal writing: *Time Inc. announced these changes in late December.* The ampersand symbol (&) can also be used but only if it is part of an official name: *Church & Dwight.*

Exercise 58.1 Chapter review: Abbreviations and symbols

Spell out any inappropriate abbreviations in this passage of nontechnical writing.

In today's digital-savvy world, a person who has never used a computer with access to the WWW and a Motion Pictures Experts Group Layer 3 (MP3) player would be surprised to find that anyone can download and groove to the sounds of "Nights in White Satin" by the 1960s rock band the Moody Blues at 3 AM without ever having to have spent $ for the album *Days of Future Past.* However, music listeners should understand that such file sharing, commonly known as "file swapping," is illegal and surrounded by controversy. The Recording Industry Association of America (RIAA), which represents the U.S. recording industry, has taken aggressive legal action against such acts of online piracy, etc. E.g., in a landmark case in 2004, U.S. District Judge Denny Chin ruled that ISPs must identify those subscribers who share music online, at least in the states of NY, NJ, and CT. As the nature of music recordings changes with the proliferation of digital music services & file formats, this controversy is far from being resolved. In recent yrs companies such as Apple and Amazon as well as cellular phone carriers have set up online music stores. Consumers can buy downloadable music for very little $.

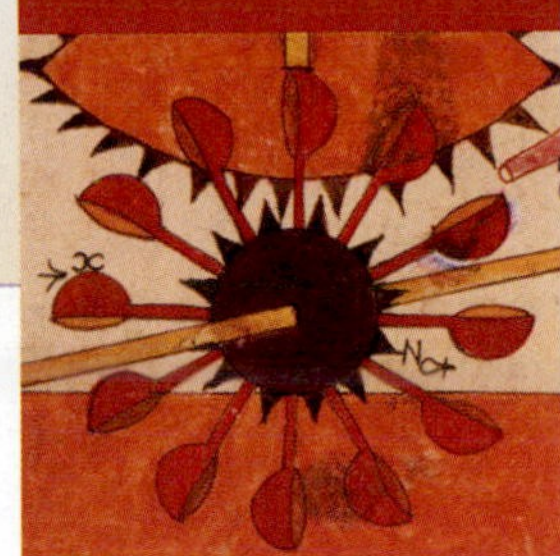

59 Numbers

Numbers appear in all types of academic writing but they are handled differently in a nontechnical context than in a technical context. Academic writing in the humanities is usually nontechnical; academic writing in the sciences and in business is often technical.

> ***Editing tip:*** The abbreviation *num* indicates a problem with the way a number is expressed in a sentence. (Professional editors and proofreaders sometimes circle a number that should be spelled out and write *sp* in the margin.)

59a In nontechnical writing, spell out numbers up to one hundred and round numbers greater than one hundred.

www.mhhe.com/mhhb2
For information and exercises on numbers, go to
Editing > Numbers

- **The principal announced that *twenty-five* students failed the exam, but more than *two hundred* passed.**

When you are using a great many numbers or when spelling out a number would take more than two words, use numerals.

- **This regulation affects nearly *10,500* taxpayers, substantially more than the *200* originally projected. Of those affected, *2,325* filled out the papers incorrectly and another *743* called the office for help.**

Round numbers larger than one million are expressed in numerals and words: *8 million, 2.4 trillion.*

Use all numerals rather than mixing numerals and spelled-out words for the same type of item in a passage.

- **We wrote to 130 people but only ~~sixteen~~ 16 responded.**

> ***Exception:*** When two numbers appear together, spell out one and use numerals for the other: *two 20-pound bags.*

When you are writing about more than one type of item, you can spell out numbers for one type and use numerals for the other, as long as you are consistent.

► **The two football teams battled to a 28-28 tie, so the game went into overtime. The Raptors won with a 3-point field goal and then went on to defeat the other three teams in the league.**

> ***Punctuation tip:*** Use a hyphen with two-word numbers from twenty-one through ninety-nine, whether they appear alone or within a larger number: *fifty-six, one hundred twenty-eight.* A hyphen also appears in two-word fractions (*one-third, five-eighths*) and in compound words made up of a spelled-out number or numeral and another word (*forty-hour work week, 5-page paper*).

59b In technical and business writing, use numerals for exact measurements and all numbers greater than ten.

► **The endosperm halves were placed in each of 14 small glass test tubes.**

► **A solution with a GA_3 concentration ranging from 0 g/ml to 10^5 g/ml was added to each test tube.**

► **With its $1.9 trillion economy, Germany has an important trade role to play.**

59c Always spell out a number that begins a sentence.

If a numeral begins a sentence, spell out the numeral or reword the sentence.

Twenty-five
► **~~25~~ children are in each elementary class.**

Each elementary class has
► **25 children. ~~are in each elementary class.~~**

Reword sentences that start with numbers to avoid mixing numerals and spelled-out numbers for the same type of quantities.

Boarding the vessel were 22
► **~~Twenty-two~~ men and 300 women. ~~boarded the vessel.~~**

59d Use numerals for dates, times of day, addresses, and similar kinds of conventional quantitative information.

Dates: October 9, 2008; 1558–1603; A.D. 1066 (*or* AD 1066); *but* October ninth, May first

Time of day: 6 A.M. (*or* AM *or* a.m.); but a quarter past eight in the evening; three o'clock in the morning

Addresses: 21 Meadow Road, Apt. 6J, Grand Island, NY 14072

Percentages: 73 percent; 73%

Fractions and decimals: 21.84; 0.05; 6½; *but* two-thirds (*not* 2-thirds); a fourth

Measurements: 100 miles per hour (*or* 100 mph); 9 kilograms (*or* 9 kg); 38°F; 15°Celsius; 3 tablespoons; 4 liters (*or* 4 l); 18 inches (*or* 18 in.)

Volume, chapter, page: volume 4 (or Volume 4); chapter 8 (or Chapter 8); page 44 (or p. 44)

Scenes, lines in a play: *Hamlet,* act 2, scene 1, lines 77–84

Scores and statistics: 0 to 3; 98–92; an average age of 35

Amounts of money: 10¢ (*or* 10 cents); $125, $2.25, $2.8 million (*or* $2,800,000)

Serial or identification numbers: batch number 4875; 1520 on the AM dial

Telephone numbers: (716) 555-2174

Note: In nontechnical writing, spell out the names of units of measurement (*inches, liters*) in text. You can use abbreviations (*in., l*) and symbols (%) in charts and graphs to save space.

Numbers and Grammar Checkers

Computer grammar checkers cannot help you decide if a number should be expressed in figures or spelled out. You need to learn and apply the rules of the discipline in which you are working.

For MULTILINGUAL STUDENTS

Dates and Decimals

In American English, the day usually follows the month in dates: *May 9, 2005; 5/9/05.* Decimals are preceded by a period (*one-tenth = 0.1*), and commas are used within whole numbers longer than four numerals (*twenty-two thousand three = 22,003*). In four-digit numbers, the comma is optional: *4,010* or *4010.*

Exercise 59.1 Chapter review: Numbers

Edit the sentences that follow to correct errors in the use of numbers. Some sentences are correct; circle their numbers.

EXAMPLE I have ~~five hundred forty-six dollars~~ $546 in my bank account.

1. The soccer team raised one thousand sixty seven dollars by selling entertainment booklets filled with coupons, discounts, and special promotions.
2. 55% of the participants in the sociology student's survey reported that they would lie to a professor in order to have a late assignment accepted.
3. In one year alone, 115 employees at the company objected to their performance appraisals, but only twenty-four filed formal complaints.
4. When preparing a professional letter, set the margins at 1 inch.
5. Eighty-five applicants hoped to win the four-year scholarship, but only one person was awarded full tuition and living expenses.
6. Four out of 5 children who enter preschool in Upper East County already know the alphabet.
7. The motorcycle accident occurred at a half past 4 in the morning on the interstate highway, but paramedics did not arrive until six thirty AM.
8. The horticulturist at the nursery raises more than 200 varieties of orchids.

60 Italics (Underlining)

To set off certain words and phrases, printers have traditionally used *italics,* a typeface in which the characters slant to the right. MLA documentation style requires italics instead of underlining. However, your instructor may prefer you to use underlining. (*See Chapter 23: MLA Documentation Style, pp. 342–90*).

TEXTCONNEX

Italics and Underlining

Italics may not be available in online environments. To indicate italics, put an underscore mark before and after what you would italicize in a manuscript: *Tom Hanks gives one of his best performances in _Saving Private Ryan_.*

On the Web, underlining indicates a hypertext link. If your work is going to be posted online, use italics for titles instead of underlining to avoid confusion.

► **Tom Hanks gives one of his best performances in *Saving Private Ryan*.**

► **Tom Hanks gives one of his best performances in <u>Saving Private Ryan</u>.**

www.mhhe.com/mhhb2
For information and exercises on italics, go to
Editing > Italics

Editing tip: The abbreviation *ital* indicates that italics are needed. (Professional editors and proofreaders also mark words to be italicized by underlining them.) The abbreviation *rom*, which stands for roman (or regular) type, indicates that an italicized word or words should not be italicized. (Professional editors and proofreaders also circle words to be changed from italics to roman.)

Italics and Grammar Checkers

Computer grammar checkers cannot help you decide if you have used italics or underlining appropriately. You will need to learn how to apply to your own work the rules found in this chapter or required by the discipline in which you are working.

60a Italicize (underline) titles of lengthy works or separate publications.

Italicize (or underline) titles of long works or works that are not part of a larger publication. The box on the next page provides a guide.

In titles of lengthy works, *a, an,* or *the* is capitalized and italicized if it is the first word, but *the* is not treated as part of the title in names of newspapers and periodicals in MLA or Chicago style: the *New York Times.* APA and CSE style treat *the* as part of the title.

Court cases may also be italicized or underlined, but legal documents are not.

► **In *Brown v. Board of Education of Topeka* (1954), the U.S. Supreme Court ruled that segregation in public schools is unconstitutional.**

► **He obtained a writ of habeas corpus.**

Do not italicize or underline punctuation marks that follow a title unless they are part of the title:

► **I finally finished reading *Moby Dick*!**

Exceptions: Do not use italics or underlining when referring to the Bible and other sacred books.

Quotation marks are used for the titles of short works, including essays, newspaper and magazine articles and columns, short stories, and short poems. Quotation marks are also used for the titles of unpublished works when they are referred to within texts,

WORKS THAT SHOULD BE ITALICIZED (or UNDERLINED)

Books (including textbooks)
The Color of Water
The Art of Public Speaking

Magazines and journals
Texas Monthly
College English

Newspapers
Chicago Tribune

Comic strips
Dilbert

Plays, films, and television series
Death of a Salesman
On the Waterfront
The American Experience

Published speeches
Lincoln's *A House Divided*

Long musical compositions
Beethoven's *Pastoral Symphony* (*but* Beethoven's Symphony no. 6—the title consists of the musical form, a number, and/or a key)

Choreographic works
Balanchine's *Jewels*

Artworks
Edward Hopper's *Nighthawks*

Web sites
The Motley Fool

ITALICIZED WORKS (continued)

Software
Microsoft PowerPoint

Long poems
Odyssey

Pamphlets
Gorges: A Guide to the Geology of the Ithaca Area

including student papers, theses, and dissertations. (*See Chapter 54, pp. 761–62, for more on quotation marks with titles.*)

60b Italicize (underline) the names of ships, trains, aircraft, and spaceships.

Italicize the name of a specific ship, aircraft, or spaceship, but do not italicize any abbreviations used with the name, such as HMS or SS. Model names and numbers (such as Boeing 747) are not italicized.

Queen Mary 2 *Orient Express* *Spirit of St. Louis* *Apollo 11*

60c Italicize (underline) foreign terms.

► **In the Paris airport, we recognized the familiar no smoking sign: *Défense de fumer*.**

Many foreign words have become so common in English that everyone accepts them as part of the language. Terms such as rigor mortis, pasta, and sombrero, for example, do not require italics or underlining.

60d Italicize (underline) scientific names.

The scientific (Latin) names of organisms, consisting of the genus and species, are always italicized. Although the whole name is italicized, only the genus is capitalized.

► **Most chicks are infected with *Cryptosporidium baileyi*, a parasite typical of young animals.**

60e Italicize (underline) words, letters, and numbers referred to as themselves.

For clarity, italicize words or phrases used as words rather than for the meaning they convey. (You may also use quotation marks for this purpose, but be consistent.)

► **The term *romantic* does not mean the same thing to the Shelley scholar as it does to the fan of Danielle Steel's novels.**

Letters and numbers used alone should also be italicized.

► **The word *bookkeeper* has three sets of double letters: double *o*, double *k*, and double *e*.**

► **Add a *3* to that column.**

60f Use italics (underlining) sparingly for emphasis.

An occasional word in italics helps you make a point. Too much emphasis, however, may mean no emphasis at all.

WEAK	You don't *mean* that your *teacher* told the whole *class* that *he* did not know the answer *himself*?
REVISED	Your teacher admitted that he did not know the answer? That is amazing.

Note: If you add italics or underlining to a quotation, indicate the change in parentheses following the quotation.

► **Instead of promising that no harm will come to us, Blake only assures us that we "need not *fear* harm" (emphasis added).**

Exercise 60.1 Chapter review: Italics

Edit the following passage, underlining the words that should be italicized and circling the italicized words that should be roman.

Today, thousands of people in the United States practice *yoga* for its physical, spiritual, and mental benefits. The word *yoga,* originating from the Sanskrit root yuj, means the union of the body, spirit, and mind. Although there are many styles of *yoga,* people who want a gentle introduction to *yoga* should practice Iyengar yoga, a style developed by B. K. S. Iyengar of India, which uses props such as blocks, belts, and pillows to help the body find alignment in asanas (poses) and pranayama (breathing). Those people who want to learn more about Iyengar yoga are encouraged to read the following books written by the master himself: *Light on Yoga, Light on Pranayama,* The *Art of Yoga,* The *Tree of Yoga,* and

Light on the Yoga Sutras of Patanjali. Those who want to learn about the general benefits of *yoga* can find numerous articles, such as "*Yoga and Weight Loss*," by doing a general online search. All forms of *yoga* promise the *diligent* and *faithful* practitioner increased *strength, flexibility,* and *balance.*

FIGURE 60.1 A yoga class.

61 Apostrophes

Apostrophes show possession (*the dog's bone*) and indicate omitted letters in contractions (*don't*). They are also used in such a wide variety of other ways that they can be confusing. Keep track of the uses that give you trouble, and when in doubt, consult this chapter.

Editing tip: The abbreviation *ap* indicates a problem with the use of apostrophes.

Apostrophes and Grammar Checkers

Spelling and grammar checkers can help you catch some errors in the use of apostrophes. For example, a spelling checker may sometimes highlight *its* used incorrectly instead of *it's* or an error in a possessive (for example, *Englands' glory*) but often gets it backwards. Spelling and grammar checkers also miss many apostrophe errors, so you should double-check all words that end in *-s* in your work.

www.mhhe.com/mhhb2
For information and exercises on apostrophes, go to
Editing > Apostrophes

61a Use apostrophes to indicate possession.

For a noun to be possessive, two elements are usually required: (1) someone or something is the possessor and (2) someone, something, or some attribute or quality is possessed.

POSSESSOR	PERSON, THING, ATTRIBUTE, QUALITY, VALUE, OR FEATURE POSSESSED	POSSESSION
woman	son	the woman's son
Juanita	shovel	Juanita's shovel
child	bright smile	a child's bright smile

Sometimes the thing possessed precedes the possessor.

thing possessed — possessor

► **The motorcycle is the student's.**

Sometimes the sentence may not name the thing possessed, but its identity (in this case, *house*) is clearly understood by the reader.

► **I saw your cousin at Nick's.**

> ***Note:*** You can also indicate possession using the preposition *of: the bright smile of a child.*

1. Deciding whether to use an apostrophe plus s or use only an apostrophe

Making singular nouns possessive To form the possessive of all singular nouns, add an apostrophe plus *s* to the ending: *baby's.* Even singular nouns that end in *s* form the possessive by adding *-'s: bus's.*

> ***Note:*** If a singular noun with more than two syllables ends in *s* and adding *-'s* would make the word sound awkward, it is acceptable to use only an apostrophe to form the possessive: *Socrates'*. Whatever your choice, be consistent.

Making plural nouns ending in s possessive To form the possessive of a plural noun that ends in *s,* add only an apostrophe to form the possessive: *subjects', babies'.*

Making plural nouns that do not end in s possessive To form the possessive of a plural noun that does not end in *s,* add an apostrophe plus *s* to form the possessive: *men's, cattle's.*

Making indefinite pronouns possessive To form the possessive of most indefinite pronouns, such as *no one, everyone, everything,* or *something,* add an apostrophe plus *s*: *no one's, anybody's.*

> ***Note:*** Adding *-'s* makes some indefinite pronouns sound awkward. In those cases, use *of* to form the possessive: *the wishes of a few, the parents of both.*

Forming Possessives

IF THE WORD IS A(N)	ADD	EXAMPLE
singular noun	-'s	horse's Moore's
plural noun ending in *-s*	-'	horses' Moores'
plural noun not ending in *-s*	-'s	children's
indefinite pronoun	-'s	everybody's

2. Using the apostrophe in tricky situations

Multiple possessors To express joint ownership by two or more people, use the possessive form for the last name only; to express individual ownership, use the possessive form for each name.

- ► **Felicia and Elias's report**
- ► **The city's and the state's finances**

Compound words To form the possessive of compound words, add an apostrophe plus *s* to the last word in the compound.

- ► **My father-in-law's job**
- ► **The editor-in-chief's responsibilities**

Proper names To form the possessive of proper names, follow the rules given above, with some exceptions. Some place or organizational names that include a possessive noun lack an apostrophe. In these cases, follow the established style rather than adding an apostrophe.

► **Kings Point** ► **Department of Veterans Affairs**

> ***Note:*** To form the possessive of buildings, machines, and other inanimate objects, use *of* if adding *-'s* sounds awkward: *the window of the house* (not *the house's window*).

Exercise 61.1 Using apostrophes to form the possessive

Write the possessive form of each word. The first one has been done for you.

Word(s)	Possessive
the press	*the press's*
nobody	
newspapers	
Monday and Tuesday classes (individual ownership)	
deer	
women	
someone	
Edward	
trade-off	
well-worn footpath	
United States	
this year and last year combined population (joint ownership)	

61b Use apostrophes to form contractions.

A contraction is a shortened word or group of words formed when some letters or sounds are omitted. In a contraction, the apostrophe serves as a substitute for the omitted letters.

we've = we have   weren't = were not   here's = here is

In informal writing, apostrophes can also substitute for omitted numbers in a decade: *the '90s.* It is usually better to spell out the name of the decade in formal writing, however: *the nineties.*

CHARTING the TERRITORY

Contractions in Academic Writing

The MLA and APA style manuals allow contractions in academic writing, but the MLA manual says they should be used rarely. Some instructors think that contractions are too informal, so check with your instructor before using them in an assignment.

✓ 61c Distinguish between contractions and possessive pronouns.

The following pairs of **homonyms** (words that sound alike but have different meanings) often cause problems for writers. Note that the apostrophe is used only in the contraction.

CONTRACTION	POSSESSIVE PRONOUN
it's (it is or it has) *It's* too hot.	its The dog scratched *its* fleas.
you're (you are) *You're* a lucky guy.	your Is that *your* new car?
who's (who is) *Who's* there?	whose The man *whose* dog was lost called us.
they're (they are) *They're* reading poetry.	their* They gave *their* lives.

*The adverb *there* is also confused with *their* and *they're: She was standing there.*

Exercise 61.2 Distinguishing between contractions and pronouns

Underline the correct word choice in each sentence.

EXAMPLE **Transcendentalists have had a strong influence on American thought; (there/they're/their) important figures in our literary history.**

1. In the essay "The Over-soul," Ralph Waldo Emerson describes the unity of nature by cataloging (it's/its) divine, yet earthly, expressions, such as waterfalls and well-worn footpaths.
2. Emerson states that you must have faith to believe in something that supersedes or contradicts (your/you're) real-life experiences.
3. (Who's/Whose) the author of the poem at the beginning of Emerson's "Self-Reliance"?
4. Emerson believes that (there/they're/their) are ways to live within a society without having to give in to its pressures.
5. According to Emerson, people should occasionally silence the noise of (there/they're/their) inner-voices and learn to listen to the world's unconscious voice.
6. Emerson also believes that, in the end, (it's/its) the individual—and the individual alone—who must decide his or her own fate.

61d An apostrophe can be used with *s* to form plural letters and words used as words, but it usually should not be used to form plural numbers and abbreviations.

If a letter or word is used as a letter or word rather than as a symbol of the meaning it conveys, it can be made plural by adding an apostrophe plus *s*. The letter or word should be italicized but not the *'s*.

- ► ***Committee* has two *m*'s, two *t*'s, and two *e*'s.**
- ► **There are twelve *no*'s in the first paragraph.**

MLA and APA style recommend against using an apostrophe to show the plural of a number or an abbreviation *(1990s, RPMs)*.

- ► **He makes his 2*s* look like 5*s*.**

Previously, use of the apostrophe was common in these circumstances (*he makes his 2's look like 5's*).

Because styles vary, consult the appropriate guide for your discipline and course, or ask your instructor.

61e Watch out for common misuses of the apostrophe.

Do not use an apostrophe with *s* to form a plural noun.

- ► **The ~~teacher's~~ *teachers* asked the girls and boys for their attention.**

(*See Chapter 63, pp. 827–28, for more on forming plural nouns.*)

Do not use an apostrophe with *s* to form the present tense of a verb used with a third-person singular subject (*he, she, it,* or a singular noun).

- ► **A professional singer ~~need's~~ *needs* to practice different vocal techniques.**

Do not use an apostrophe with the possessive form of a pronoun such as *hers, ours,* or *theirs.*

- ► **That cat of ~~our's~~ *ours* is always sleeping!**

(*See 61c for advice on distinguishing contractions* [it's] *from possessive pronouns* [its].)

Exercise 61.3 Chapter review: Apostrophes

Edit the following passage by adding and deleting apostrophes and correcting any incorrect word choices.

Transcendentalism was a movement of thought in the mid to late 1800s that was originated by Ralph Waldo Emerson, Henry David Thoreau, and several other's who's scholarship helped to shape the democratic ideals of their day and usher America into it's modern age. Emerson, a member of New Englands' elite, was particularly interested in spreading Transcendentalist notion's of self-reliance; he is probably best known for his essay "Self-Reliance," which is still widely read in todays' universities. Most people remember Thoreau, however, not only for what he wrote but also for how he lived: its well known that—for a while, at least—he chose to live a simple life in a cabin on Walden Pond. Altogether, one could say that Emerson's and Thoreau's main accomplishment was to expand the influence of literature and philosophy over the development of the average Americans' identity. With a new national literature forming, people's interest in they're self-development quickly increased as they began to read more and more about what it meant to be American. In fact, one could even say (perhaps half-jokingly) that, today, the success of home makeovers on television and the popularity of self-help books might have a lot to do with Emerson's and Thoreau's ideas about self-sufficiency and living simply—idea's that took root in this nation more than a hundred years ago.

62 Hyphens

Hyphens are used to form compound words and to indicate that a word is being broken at the end of a line. Unlike a dash (-- or —), which is used *between* words, a hyphen (-) is used *within* words.

Editing tip: The abbreviation *hyph* indicates a problem with the use of a hyphen. Professional editors and proofreaders usually indicate that a hyphen is needed with a caret and two lines (=) to distinguish the hyphen from a dash.

► **He was a self employed worker for most of his life.**

Hyphens and Grammar Checkers

Spelling and grammar checkers will generally not help you find problems in the use of hyphens. Your dictionary is your best guide.

www.mhhe.com/mhhb2
For information and exercises on hyphens, go to
Editing > Hyphens

62a Use hyphens to form compound words and to avoid confusion.

Think of hyphens as bridges. A hyphen joins two nouns to make one compound word. Scientists speak of a *kilogram-meter* as a measure of force, and professors of literature talk about the *scholar-poet.* The hyphen lets us know that the two nouns work together as one. As compound nouns come into general use, the hyphens between them tend to disappear: *firefighter, thundershower.*

A dictionary is the best resource when you are unsure about whether to use a hyphen. The dictionary sometimes gives writers several options, however. For example, you could write *life-style* or *life style* or *lifestyle* and be correct in each case, according to the *Random House Webster's College Dictionary.* If you cannot find a compound word in the dictionary, spell it as two separate words. Whatever spelling you choose, be consistent throughout your document.

62b Use hyphens to join two or more words to create compound adjective or noun forms.

A hyphen can link words to form a compound adjective.

accident-prone
quick-witted

Hyphens often help clarify adjectives that come before the word they modify. If you say, "She was a quick thinking person," you might mean that she was quick and that she was also a thinking person. If you say "She was a quick-thinking person," though, your meaning is unmistakable: she thought rapidly. Modifiers that are hyphenated when they are placed *before* the word they modify are usually not hyphenated when they are placed *after* the word they modify.

► **It was a *bad-mannered* reply.**

► **The reply was *bad mannered.***

Do not use a hyphen to connect an *-ly* adverb to the word it modifies. The fact that the word is an adverb makes the relationship between the words clear.

► **They explored the newly/discovered territories.**

Use a hyphen with most compound adjectives containing comparatives (*-er*) and superlatives (*-est*), but do not hyphenate *more/most* and *less/least*.

► **The new car runs on a *cleaner-burning* fuel.**

► **When buying a car, gas mileage is my *most important* consideration.**

Foreign phrases used as modifiers do not take hyphens.

► **The treasurer made most decisions and was the committee's *de facto* leader.**

Do not hyphenate possessive phrases: All in a *full day's work*.

Hyphens are also used in nouns designating family relationships and compounds of more than two words.

brother-in-law
stay-at-home
stick-in-the-mud

Note: Compound nouns with hyphens generally form plurals by adding *-s* or *-es* to the most important word.

attorney-at-law/attorneys-at-law
mother-in-law/mothers-in-law
court-martial/courts-martial

In a pair or series of compound nouns or adjectives, add suspended hyphens after the first word of each item.

► **The child care center accepted *three-, four-,* and *five-year-olds.***

Some proper nouns that are joined to make an adjective are hyphenated.

the Franco-Prussian War
of Mexican-American heritage

62c Use hyphens to spell out fractions and compound numbers.

Use a hyphen when writing out fractions or compound numbers from twenty-one through ninety-nine.

three-fourths of a gallon
thirty-two
twenty-five thousand

> ***Note:*** In MLA style, use a hyphen to show inclusive numbers: *acts 1-4*.

62d Use hyphens to attach some prefixes and suffixes.

Use a hyphen to join a prefix and a numeral or capitalized word.

un-American	pre-Columbian	pre-1900
mid-August	neo-Nazi	

A hyphen is sometimes used to join a capital letter and a word.

T-shirt	V-six engine

The prefixes *all-, ex-, quasi-,* and *self-* and the suffixes *-elect, -odd,* and *-something* generally take hyphens.

all-purpose	self-sufficient	thirty-something
ex-convict	president-elect	
quasi-scientific	fifty-odd	

Most prefixes, however, are not attached by hyphens unless a hyphen is needed to show pronunciation, avoid double letters (*anti-immigration*), or to reveal a special meaning that distinguishes the word from the same word without a hyphen: *recreate* (play) versus *re-create* (make again). Hyphens also join prefixes to open compounds: *anti-drunk driving*. Check a dictionary to be sure you are using the standard spelling.

62e Use hyphens to divide words at the ends of lines.

When you must divide words, do so between syllables, but pronunciation alone cannot always tell you where to divide a word. If you are unsure about how to break a word into syllables, consult your dictionary.

► **My writing group had a very fruitful *collab-oration*. [not *colla-boration*]**

Never leave just one or two letters on a line.

► **He seemed so sad and vulnerable and so *discon-nected* from his family. [not *disconnect-ed*]**

Compound words such as *hardworking, rattlesnake,* and *bookcase* should be broken only between the words that form them: *hard-working, rattle-snake, book-case.* Compound words that already have hyphens, like *brother-in-law,* are broken after the hyphens only.

> ***Note:*** Do not hyphenate an abbreviation or acronym (*CIA*) or a one-syllable word (*pitched*).

TEXTCONNEX

Dividing Internet Addresses

If you need to divide an Internet address between lines, divide it after a slash. Do not interrupt a word within the address with a hyphen; readers may assume the hyphen is part of the address.

Exercise 62.1 Chapter review: Hyphens

Edit the following passage, adding and deleting hyphens as necessary.

We need only to turn on the television or pick up a recent issue of a popular fashion or fitness magazine to see evidence of modern society's obsession with images of thinness. Few actors, models, or celebrities fail to flaunt their thinly-trimmed waist-lines, regardless of their gender. Not surprisingly, more than ten million females and almost one million males in the United States are currently battling eating disorders such as anorexia nervosa and bulimia nervosa. A person who is anorexic fears gaining weight, and thus en-gages in self starvation and excessive weight loss. A person who is bulimic binges and then engages in self-induced purging in order to lose weight. Although we are often quick to assume that those with eating disorders suffer from low self-esteem and have a history of family or peer problems, we cannot ignore the role that the media play in encouraging eating disorders, particularly when thinness is equated with physical attractiveness, health and fitness, and success over-all. We need to re-member the threat of these eating disorders the next time we hear a ten year old girl tell her mommy that she "can't afford" to eat more than one half of her peanut butter and jelly sandwich.

63 Spelling

Proofread your writing carefully. Misspellings creep into the prose of even the best writers.

Unfortunately, pronunciation is at best an unreliable guide to spelling in English. Words can have similar patterns of letters but be pronounced in different ways, or different patterns can be pronounced in the same way. For example, the following words, all containing the pattern *-ough,* are each pronounced differently: *thought, cough, through, bough.* On the other hand, these words, each with a different pattern, are pronounced in the same way in American English: *bite, fight, height.* In addition, word endings often get swallowed or mispronounced in everyday speech. *Supposed to* and *used to* come out sounding like *suppose to* and *use to*. Other difficulties come from common nonstandard pronunciations including *axe* for *ask* and *nucular* for *nuclear*.

www.mhhe.com/mhhb2
For information and exercises on spelling, go to
Editing > Spelling

Rather than relying on pronunciation, use the following strategies to help you improve your spelling.

- Become familiar with the major rules of spelling (*see 63a, pp. 825–28*).
- Learn to distinguish **homonyms**—words that are pronounced alike but have different meanings and spellings (*see 63b, pp. 828–31*).
- Be aware of commonly misspelled words, and keep your own list of words that give you trouble. Include tricks to help you remember how to spell particular words. For example, there is "a rat" in *separate,* and there are two double letters, "cc" and "mm," in *accommodate* (*see 63c, pp. 831–34*).
- Keep a good college dictionary at hand. If you are not sure how to spell a word, try looking up different combinations of letters until you hit the right one. You can also try typing a synonym for the problem word into your word-processing program's thesaurus to see if the word you are looking for is listed as an alternative.

Editing tip: The abbreviation *sp* indicates a spelling error. Check your draft for spelling errors after you are happy with its style and content. First, check any words that your computer software's spell-checker has highlighted, and then print out a draft to review slowly. Some people find it helpful to use a ruler to focus on one line at a time or to read the draft from the final sentence to the first as a way of making sure to pay attention to individual words. Circle each spelling that you are unsure of. Then, when you have checked the entire paper, look up each circled word in a dictionary.

Spelling Checkers

Computer spell-checkers are helpful tools. Some word-processing programs automatically correct obvious misspellings as you type them. Spell-checkers will also give you a list of possible substitutes for a highlighted word. All spell-checkers have limitations, however. They cannot tell how you are using a particular word. If you write *their* but mean *there,* a spell-checker cannot point out your mistake. Spell-checkers also cannot point out many misspelled proper nouns.

63a Learn the rules that generally hold for spelling, as well as their exceptions.

1. Placing *i* before *e*

Use *i* before *e* except after *c* or when the combination is sounded like *a,* as in *neighbor* and *weigh.*

I* BEFORE *E	believe, relieve, chief, grief, wield, yield
EXCEPT AFTER *C*	receive, deceive, ceiling, conceit
EI* SOUNDED LIKE *A	weight, freight, eight, rein
EXCEPTIONS	caffeine, codeine, foreign, forfeit, height, leisure, seize, weird

2. Forming plurals

Most plurals are formed by adding *-s.* Some others are formed by adding *-es.*

When to Form the Plural with *-es*

SINGULAR ENDING	PLURAL ENDING
-s, -sh, -x, -z,* "soft" *-ch bus, bush, fox, buzz, peach	***-es*** buses, bushes, foxes, buzzes, peaches
consonant + *o* hero, tomato	***-es*** heroes, tomatoes EXCEPTION: solo/solos
consonant + *y* beauty, city	**change *y* to *i* and add *-es*** beauties, cities EXCEPTION: a person's name—Kirby/the Kirbys
-f, -fe leaf, knife, wife	**change *f* to *v* and add *-s* or *-es*** leaves, knives, wives EXCEPTION: Words that end in *-ff* and some words that end in *-f* (staff, roof) form the plural by adding only an *-s* (staffs, roofs).

Most plurals follow standard rules, but some have irregular forms (child/children, tooth/teeth). Some words with foreign roots create plurals in the pattern of the language they come from, as do these words.

addendum/addenda
alumna/alumnae
alumnus/alumni
analysis/analyses
crisis/crises
criterion/criteria
datum/data
medium/media
phenomenon/phenomena
stimulus/stimuli
thesis/theses

Some nouns with foreign roots have both irregular and regular plural forms (*appendix / appendices / appendixes*). As in other cases where you have options, you should be consistent in using the spelling you choose.

Note: Some writers now treat *data* as though it were singular, but the preferred practice is still to recognize that *data* is plural and takes a plural verb.

► **The *data are* clear on this point: events have made the pass/fail course obsolete.**

Compound nouns with hyphens generally form plurals by adding *-s* or *-es* to the most important word.

attorney-at-law/attorneys-at-law
mother-in-law/mothers-in-law
court-martial/courts-martial

For some compound words that are spelled as one word, the same rule applies (*passersby*); for others, it does not (*cupfuls*). Consult a dictionary if you are not sure.

If both words in the compound are equally important, add *-s* to the second word: *singer-songwriters.*

A few words such as *fish* and *sheep* have the same forms for singular and plural. To indicate that the word is plural, you need to add a word or words that indicate quantity: *five fish, a few sheep.*

For MULTILINGUAL STUDENTS

American and British Spelling

Standard American spelling differs from British spelling for some words—among them *color / colour, canceled / cancelled, theater / theatre, realize / realise,* and *judgment / judgement.*

3. Adding suffixes

Although suffixes are simply added to the end of most words, sometimes a spelling change is required (*see the box below and on the next page*).

Words ending in *-cede, -ceed,* and *-sede* frequently cause spelling problems. Most words that end with this sound use the spelling *-cede* (*recede, concede, precede, intercede*); the following four words are the only exceptions:

exceed	succeed
proceed	supersede

> ***Note:*** Adding a prefix such as *re-, un-, de-,* or *anti-* does not change the spelling of the word the prefix is attached to (*reunion, unintended, destabilized, antidepressant*), although a hyphen may be needed for clarity (*recreate / re-create, anti-inflammatory*).

SPELLING CHANGES with SUFFIXES

***Adding suffixes to words that end in a silent* e**

If the suffix begins with a vowel (as in *-ed, -ing, -er, -est*), drop the final *e*, and then add the suffix.

force/forced   surprise/surprising   remove/removable

EXCEPTIONS: Keep the silent *e* if it is needed to clarify the pronunciation (*mile / mileage*), if the word would be confused with another word without the *e* (*dyeing*), or if the *e* is needed following *c* or *g* to keep the sound of the consonant the same (*manageable, traceable*).

In a few words the *e* is dropped when the suffix begins with a consonant.

true/truly	judge/judgment
argue/argument	acknowledge/acknowledgment

***Adding suffixes to words that end in a consonant* + y**

Change the *y* to an *i* and add the suffix.

happy/happiness   hungry/hungrier   apply/applied

EXCEPTION: Do not change the *y* to an *i* when adding the suffix *-ing* (*apply / applying, enjoy / enjoying, cry / crying*) or when adding *-s* to a proper name ending in *y* (*Ballys*).

(*continued*)

SPELLING CHANGES with SUFFIXES *(continued)*

Adding suffixes to words that end in one vowel + a consonant

Only when the consonant ends a one-syllable word or a stressed syllable (*refer,* not *glower*), double the final consonant and add the suffix.

stun/stunning refer/referred transmit/transmitted

EXCEPTION: bus/busing

***Adding the suffix* -ly *to words that end in* -ic**

Add *-ally.*

logic/logically terrific/terrifically static/statically

Exercise 63.1 Practicing spelling rules

Write the correct plural form for each of the following words. Consult the preceding rules or a dictionary, as needed.

Bentley	hoof	trophy
president-elect	potato	index
life	fungus	Sidney
box	brother-in-law	self
appendix	stereo	nucleus

Exercise 63.2 Practicing spelling rules

Some words in the following list are misspelled. Circle each of the misspelled words, and write the correct spelling next to it.

either	boxxing	hopping
hygiene	supplyed	nieghbor
dealer	neither	worried
buying	divorced	tring
exced	managable	receipt

✓ 63b Learn to distinguish words that are pronounced alike but spelled differently.

Homonyms are words that sound alike but have different meanings and different spellings. Many are commonly confused, so you should check them when you are proofreading your work. The box that begins on this page contains a list of common homonyms as well as words that are almost homonyms. For more complete definitions, consult the Glossary of Usage (*Chapter 50, pp. 707–16*) and a dictionary.

Exercise 63.3 Distinguishing homonyms

Review the list of common homonyms on pages 829–31, and highlight the words that give you trouble. Then write each word in a sentence.

COMMON HOMONYMS and NEAR HOMONYMS

accept (to take willingly); **except** (to leave out; but for)
adapt (to change); **adopt** (to take as one's own)
advice (an opinion); **advise** (to give an opinion)
affect (to influence; a feeling); **effect** (to make; a result)
aisle (passage between seats); **isle** (island)
all ready (prepared); **already** (by this time)
allude (to hint at); **elude** (to escape or avoid)
allusion (indirect reference); **illusion** (unreal image or faulty idea)
altar (a platform used in worship); **alter** (to change somewhat)
amoral (neither moral nor immoral); **immoral** (violating morals)
are (form of *be*); **hour** (sixty minutes); **our** (possessive of *we*)
ascent (the act of rising up); **assent** (to agree to)
assistance (help); **assistants** (helpers)
bare (to reveal; naked); **bear** (to carry; an animal)
belief (conviction); **believe** (to have faith)
beside (by the side of); **besides** (in addition, other than)
board (a piece of lumber; a group; to enter a vehicle); **bored** (uninterested)
brake (to stop); **break** (to separate into parts)
buy (to purchase); **by** (next to)
capital (punishable by death; uppercase letter; city); **capitol** (the building)
censer (incense container); **censor** (to remove objectionable material); **censure** (to blame)
choose (to select); **chose** (past tense of *choose*)
cite (to quote or refer to); **sight** (a spectacle; the sense); **site** (a place)
clothes (attire); **cloths** (fabric)
coarse (rough); **course** (a path; a series of classes)
complement (something that completes); **compliment** (praise)
conscience (knowledge of right and wrong); **conscious** (to be aware)
council (an advisory group or meeting); **counsel** (to give advice)

(*continued*)

COMMON HOMONYMS and NEAR HOMONYMS (*continued*)

descent (downward movement); **dissent** (to disagree, disagreement)
desert (a dry, sandy place; to leave); **dessert** (an after-dinner course)
device (a scheme; a piece of equipment); **devise** (to invent)
discreet (showing good judgment); **discrete** (distinct)
dominant (commanding, having influence); **dominate** (to control)
elicit (to bring forth); **illicit** (illegal)
emigrate (to move from a country); **immigrate** (to move to a country)
eminent (highly ranked); **imminent** (about to happen); **immanent** (inherent)
envelop (to surround); **envelope** (stationery)
fair (beautiful; lawful; acceptable); **fare** (payment for travel; to go; food or drink)
farther (related to geographical distances); **further** (in addition)
flaunt (to show off); **flout** (to ignore in a showy way)
forth (forward); **fourth** (numerical place)
gorilla (large primate); **guerrilla** (unconventional soldier)
hear (to perceive by listening); **here** (at this place)
hole (an opening); **whole** (complete, in one piece)
it's (it is, it has); **its** (possessive of *it*)
know (to be aware of); **no** (negative)
lay (to place); **lie** (to recline)
lead (to guide; a metal); **led** (past tense of *lead*)
lessen (to make less); **lesson** (something learned)
lightning (flashing light in a storm); **lightening** (to make lighter)
loose (not securely attached); **lose** (to misplace)
meat (flesh of an animal); **meet** (to come together, encounter)
moral (lesson); **morale** (attitude or mental condition)
of (derived from, coming from); **off** (opposite of *on*)
passed (past tense of *pass*); **past** (former time)
patience (self-control); **patients** (people under medical care)
peace (quiet; harmony); **piece** (part of)
personal (private); **personnel** (employees)
plain (simple); **plane** (aircraft; a tool for leveling wood)
practicable (can be done); **practical** (sensible)
precede (to go before); **proceed** (to go by; to carry on)
presents (gifts); **presence** (being at hand)
principal (chief); **principle** (a basic truth; a sum)
rain (precipitation); **reign** (to govern as a monarch); **rein** (leather strap that controls an animal)
raise (to lift something); **raze** (to tear down); **rise** (to go upward)

(*continued*)

COMMON HOMONYMS and NEAR HOMONYMS (*continued*)

respectfully (with respect); **respectively** (in the given order)
right (correct); **rite** (part of a ceremony); **write** (to compose)
road (street); **rode** (past tense of *ride*)
scene (part of or place in a story); **seen** (past tense of *see*)
sense (a meaning; to be aware of); **since** (after, because)
stationary (not moving); **stationery** (writing paper)
straight (unbending; honest); **strait** (a narrow channel)
than (used in comparisons); **then** (related to time sequence)
their (possessive of *they*); **there** (place); **they're** (they are)
threw (past tense of *throw*); **through** (from one end to another); **thorough** (complete)
to (indicating movement); **too** (also); **two** (number)
waist (body part); **waste** (discarded material)
weak (not strong); **week** (seven days)
wear (to use as clothing); **where** (place); **were** (past tense form of *be*)
weather (atmospheric condition); **whether** (if it is or was true)
which (what one); **witch** (sorcerer)
who's (who is); **whose** (possessive of *who*)
you're (you are); **your** (possessive of *you*)

63c Check for commonly misspelled words.

Words that are exceptions to standard spelling rules are commonly misspelled. The words in the following box (*pp. 831–34*) often give writers trouble.

COMMONLY MISSPELLED WORDS

A
absence
acceptable
accessible
accidentally
accommodate
accomplish
accuracy
accustomed
achieve
actually
address
admission
adolescent
aggressive
amateur
analysis
analyze
angel
anonymous
apology
apparent
appearance

(*continued*)

COMMONLY MISSPELLED WORDS *(continued)*

appreciate
appropriate
approximately
arguing
argument
arrest
assassination
atheist
athlete
audience
average

B
bargain
basically
beginning
belief
believe
beneficial
boundary
breath
bureaucracy
business

C
calculator
calendar
carrying
ceiling
cemetery
certain
changeable
changing
characteristic
chief
chocolate
chose
coarse
column
commercial
commitment
committee
competent
competition
conceive
concentrate
consistency
consistent
continuous
controlled
controversial
convenience
convenient
coolly
courteous
criticism
criticize
cruelty
curiosity
curious
curriculum

D
decision
definitely
descendant
description
desirable
despair
desperate
destroy
develop
difference
different
disappear
disappoint
disapprove
disastrous
discipline
discriminate
discussion
disease
dissatisfied
divide
divine

E
easily
ecstasy
efficient
eighth
embarrass
emphasize
enemy
entirely
environment
equipment
equipped
especially
essential
exaggerate
exercise
existence
experiment
explanation

F
familiar
fascinate
favorite
February
finally
foreign
fulfill

G
gauge
generally
government
grammar
guarantee
guard
guidance

H
happily
harass
height
heroes
humorous
hungry
hurriedly
hypocrisy
hypocrite

I
ideally
imaginary

COMMONLY MISSPELLED WORDS

imagine
imitation
immediately
incidentally
incredible
independence
individual
individually
influential
initiate
innocuous
inoculate
integrate
intelligence
interest
interference
irrelevant
irresistible
irreverent
irritable
irritated

J
jealousy
judgment

K
kindergarten
knowledge

L
laboratory
leisure
license
lieutenant
likelihood
livelihood
luxurious
luxury
lying

M
magazine
maintenance
manageable
marriage
mathematics
meant
medicine
miniature
mirror
mischievous
missile
misspelled
mortgage
muscle
mysterious

N
naturally
necessary
neighbor
niece
noticeable
noticing
nuclear
nuisance
numerous

O
occasion
occasionally
occur
occurred
occurrence
official
omission
omitted
opponent
opportunity
opposite
ordinary
originally

P
parallel
paralleled
parliament
particularly
peaceable
peculiar
perception
performance
permanent
permissible
personnel
persuade
physical
physiology
pitiful
playwright
poison
politician
possession
practical
practically
preference
prejudice
preparation
prevalent
privilege
probably
process
processes
professor
prominent
pronunciation
psychology
purpose
pursue
pursuing
pursuit

Q
quandary
questionnaire
quizzes

R
really
rebel
receive
recognize
recommend
referred
relief
relieve

(*continued*)

COMMONLY MISSPELLED WORDS (*continued*)

religious
remembrance
reminisce
repetition
representative
resemblance
restaurant
rhyme
rhythm
ridiculous

S
sacrifice
sacrilegious
satellite
scarcity
schedule
secretary
seize
separate
several
shining
significance
similar
sincerely
sophomore
specimen
sponsor
strategy
strenuous
studying
succeed
sufficient
summary
superintendent
supersede
suppress
surely
surprise
suspicious

T
technical
technique
temperature
tendency
thorough
together
tomatoes
tomorrow
tragedy
twelfth
tyranny

U
unanimous
unconscious
undoubtedly
unnecessary
usually

V
vacuum
vengeance
villain
visible

W
Wednesday
weird
wholly
woman
women
writing
written

Exercise 63.4 Commonly misspelled words

Highlight the words in the preceding list that give you trouble. In a list or spelling log, write down other words you often misspell. Try to group your errors. Do they fall into patterns—errors with suffixes or plurals, for example? Errors with silent letters or doubled consonants?

Exercise 63.5 Chapter review: Spelling

Edit the following passage, correcting any misspelled words. In addition to applying the spelling rules in this chapter, you may need to consult a dictionary.

> Most people will agree that scientists need to find cures for Alzheimer's and Parkinson's diseases, yet many individuals are opposeed to stem cell research because of it's controversal use of human embryoes. The procedure that many people, including many goverment officials and law makers, oppose is

somatic cell nucclear transfer, commonly known as therapeutic cloning. This tecnique involves creating and then harvesting embryoes for there stem cells. These cells can develop into any type of tissue in the body and perhaps regenerate mature organs. The results of this type of research might prove benefical.

Some people confuse therapeutic cloning with reproductive cloning, a procedure that creates embryoes for human reproduction rather than for medical research. People who oppose therapeutic cloning beleive that this procedure cannot be done ethicly because the embryo, an early stage of human life, is eventually destroyeed. Opponents argue on morale grounds that therapeutic cloning will lead to human cloning. Others assert that therapeutic cloning can produce genetic abnormalities, witch few people are willing to except. What position does your conscious allow you to support?

CHECKLIST

Editing for Mechanics and Spelling

As you revise, check your writing for mechanics and spelling by asking yourself these questions:

- ☐ Are words and letters capitalized according to convention and context? (*See Chapter 57: Capitalization, pp. 788–97.*)
- ☐ Are abbreviations capitalized and punctuated in a consistent way? Are Latin abbreviations and non-alphabetic symbols used appropriately? (*See Chapter 58: Abbreviations and Symbols, pp. 797–804.*)
- ☐ Are numbers either spelled out or represented with numerals according to the conventions of the type of writing (nontechnical or technical) you are engaged in? (*See Chapter 59: Numbers, pp. 805–8.*)
- ☐ Are italics (or underlining) used appropriately for emphasis and to identify the titles of works, foreign words, and words used as words? (*See Chapter 60: Italics and Underlining, pp. 808–13.*)
- ☐ Are apostrophes used appropriately to indicate possession and to form contractions? Are any apostrophes misused to make a noun plural? (*See Chapter 61: Apostrophes, pp. 813–19.*)
- ☐ Are hyphens used appropriately to form compound words, in spelled-out numbers, and with certain prefixes and suffixes? (*See Chapter 62: Hyphens, pp. 819–23.*)
- ☐ Have you learned the rules for spelling (and their exceptions) and checked a dictionary for any words whose spelling you are unsure of? (*See Chapter 63: Spelling, pp. 824–35.*)

Shinjuku's Skyscraper District in Tokyo—featured in the film Lost in Translation*—caters to an international, multilingual populace with signs in Japanese and English.*

PART 12

Language is a city to the building of which every human being brought a stone.

—Ralph Waldo Emerson

Guide for Multilingual Writers

64 English Basics

64a Learn the characteristics of English nouns and their modifiers.

1. Reviewing noun types

To use an English noun properly, you need to know its basic characteristics and how it functions in a sentence. English nouns fall into a variety of overlapping categories, including:

- count and noncount
- proper and common
- concrete and abstract

(*For a brief overview of these and other noun categories, see Chapter 30: Parts of Speech, pp. 482–84.*)

www.mhhe.com/mhhb2
For information and exercises on English for multilingual students, go to
Editing > Multilingual/ESL Writers

2. Recognizing the difference between count and noncount nouns

Recognizing the difference between count and noncount nouns can help you choose the correct article (*a, an,* or *the*) or quantifier (*some, many, three, a few,* for example) and verb form for each noun.

WRITING OUTCOMES

Part 12: Guide for Multilingual Writers

This section will help you answer questions such as:

Rhetorical Knowledge

- What is the difference between *He stopped to rest* and *He stopped resting*? **(64c)** How does *few* differ from *a few*? **(66b)**

Critical Thinking, Reading, and Writing

- How are verb tenses used with reported speech? **(66j)**

Processes

- How can I find and correct problems with subject-verb agreement? **(66g)**
- How can I check for mistakes in word order? **(66i)**

Knowledge of Conventions

- What are count and noncount nouns? How do their uses differ? **(64a)**
- Is it correct to say *I must to write my term paper*? **(64c)**

Count nouns **Count nouns**—nouns that name specific, countable things—can be either singular or plural. Plural forms can be regular or irregular. In regular nouns, the ending *-s* signals the plural form:

shoe	shoes
clock	clocks
grandmother	grandmothers
preference	preferences

Irregular plurals take a variety of forms:

man	men	knife	knives
woman	women	mouse	mice
child	children	deer	deer
ox	oxen	species	species
loaf	loaves	syllabus	syllabi

Because irregular plurals take so many different forms, always check a dictionary when you are unsure of the correct form for a particular word.

Noncount nouns **Noncount nouns** refer to categories of people, places, things, or ideas that cannot be counted. Because they cannot be counted, noncount nouns, even those that end in *s*, are always singular, never plural. However, some noncount nouns derived from adjectives take plural verbs (*the rich, the military*).

The most common noncount nouns fall into one of the following categories:

- Abstract nouns: *advice, bravery, capitalism, confusion, courage, fortitude, greed, patience, peace*
- Certain classes of concrete nouns:
  - Collections of individual items: *clothing, furniture, homework, jewelry, luggage, makeup*
  - Fields of study: *astronomy, chemistry, linguistics, physics*
  - Games: *baseball, chess, football, hockey, poker, soccer*
  - Diseases: *cholera, diabetes, pneumonia*
  - Natural substances and phenomena: *air, blood, cold, dust, heat, rain, weather*

Note: Many nouns can be either count or noncount depending on the context in which they appear.

► ***Baseball*** [the game: noncount] **is never played with two *baseballs*** [the object: count] **at the same time.**

► **The suspect's *hair*** [noncount] **is brown, and the two *hairs*** [count] **found at the scene of the crime are also brown.**

3. Using articles appropriately with count, noncount, and proper nouns

In English, articles must accompany nouns in many situations. Be aware of the conventions that govern the use of articles, especially if English conventions differ from those of your native language or if articles do not exist in your native language.

Articles in English express three basic meanings:

- Indefinite (indicating nonspecific reference)
- Definite (indicating specific reference)
- Generic (indicating reference to a general category)

Indefinite and definite meaning A noun has indefinite meaning, or nonspecific reference, when it is first mentioned. To express indefinite meaning with count nouns, use the **indefinite article** (*a, an*) for singular forms and no article for plural forms.

► **I bought *a* new computer. / I bought new computers.**

> ***Note:*** Noncount nouns *never* take the indefinite article.
>
> ► ~~A knowledge~~ Knowledge **is a valuable commodity.**

To express definite meaning, or specific reference, use the **definite article** (*the*) with noncount nouns and both singular and plural count nouns. A noun has definite meaning in a variety of situations:

1. When the noun identifies something previously mentioned

   ► **I was driving along Main Street when *a* car** [nonspecific reference] **pulled up behind me. *The* car** [specific reference to the previously mentioned car] **swerved into the left lane and sped out of sight.**

   ► **Knowledge** [nonspecific] **is a valuable commodity. *The* knowledge** [specific] **I gained in college, for example, helped me get a good job.**

2. When the noun identifies something familiar or known from the context

   ► **We could not play today because *the* soccer field was wet.**

3. When the noun identifies a unique subject

   ► ***The* moon will be full tonight.**

4. When the noun is modified by a superlative adjective

   ► **We purchased *the* most economical appliance.**

5. When information in modifying phrases and clauses makes the noun definite

   ► *The* goal *of this discussion* is to explain article use.

   ► *The* book *that we studied in this course* is about medieval art.

6. When the noun refers to a general category

   ► *The* hummingbird is native to the Americas.

Generic meaning A noun is used generically when it is meant to represent all the individuals in the category it names. Singular count nouns used generically can take either an indefinite or a definite article depending on context.

► *A student* can use the Internet to research *a topic* efficiently.

► *The university* is *an institution* with roots in ancient times.

Plural nouns used generically take no article.

► As *people* live longer, they need more medical services.

► *Psychologists* believe that *children* should reduce the amount of time they spend watching television.

Articles and proper nouns Most proper nouns take no article.

► ~~The~~ Arizona is a dry state.

Some proper nouns, however, do take the definite article.

► New York City has five boroughs: Manhattan, Staten Island, Brooklyn, Queens, and *the* Bronx.

► *The* Civil War was a watershed event in American history.

Some other exceptions are the names of structures, names that include the word *of*, and many countries with names that are two or more words long.

► *the* White House

► *the* Wizard of Oz

► *the* United States

4. Using quantifiers appropriately with count and noncount nouns

Because noncount nouns are singular only and refer to things that cannot be counted, they require different quantifiers than count nouns, which refer to countable entities and can be plural. Following is a list of some quantifiers for noncount and count nouns, as well as some quantifiers that can be used with both.

- **With noncount nouns only:** *much, a great deal of, a little, little* (note that *little* carries the negative connotation of "hardly any")

  ► We did not spend *much time* studying for the exam.

  ► *Little time* remains before the paper is due.

  ► The coach gave us *a little advice* before the game.

- **With count nouns only:** *many, several, a number of, a couple of, a few, few* (note that *few* means "hardly any" in contrast to *a few*)

  ► We did not spend *many hours* studying for the exam.

  ► *Few days* remain before the paper is due.

  ► The coach gave us *a few suggestions* before the game.

- **With either count or noncount nouns:** *all, a lot of, any, some, no, enough*

  ► *All homework* must be handed in by Monday.

  ► *All assignments* must be handed in by Monday.

  ► We don't have *any luggage*.

  ► We don't have *any suitcases*.

Exercise 64.1 Classifying nouns

Identify the category of each noun (common or proper, count or noncount) and give its singular or plural form, if applicable.

EXAMPLE

patience *(common, noncount, singular only)*

1. research
2. basis
3. luggage
4. fascination
5. idea
6. the Rocky Mountains

Exercise 64.2 Using quantifiers

In the following passages, choose the appropriate quantifiers from the options in parentheses. If there is more than one acceptable option, choose the one that best fits the context.

1. The airline industry has been facing (much/many) challenges lately. The high cost of fuel and services has left many companies nearly bankrupt. Major airlines are now turning to the government and even to their employees for (some/little/a little) help. They cannot expect to get as (many/much) understanding as they want, in either case.
2. Estate sales attract (many/much) bargain shoppers and collectors. Early arrivals can find (a great deal of/a number of) items, including, for example, (much/a lot of) jewelry, (some/many) furniture, and (much/many) antiques. The resale value of such items is unpredictable, however, so buyers cannot count on getting rich from their finds.
3. A recent United Nations report shows that the impact of natural disasters has increased dramatically in recent years. In the 1990s, three times as (much/many) people were affected by catastrophes as in the previous decade. One reason for the increase is that (many/much) more people than before now live in the cities and coastal areas that are vulnerable to storms and earthquakes.
4. Long road trips can be taxing on families with small children. Psychologists have (a little/a few) tips to make these trips easier. These tips include planning (much/plenty of) activities for the car, packing (a great deal of/several) toys, bringing (some/any/little/a little) music to listen to, and trying to leave early in the morning so the children can sleep through the first (few/little) hours of the trip.

Exercise 64.3 Using articles in context

Correct any misused or missing articles in the following passage.

In her novel *Like Water for Chocolate,* Laura Esquivel uses the magical realism to tell story of a family. Young Tita lives with her strict mother and two older sisters, Gertrudis and Rosaura, on the ranch near the Mexican border with the United States. Pedro, the admirer, comes to ask permission to marry Tita, but her mother refuses because of their family tradition. It is the youngest child's duty to stay with and take care of her mother until death. Pedro then marries Rosaura, telling Tita that it is because he wants to stay near her. Through years in kitchen, Tita develops unique and magical cooking skills. She pours her heart and emotions into dishes that she prepares, sometimes with the disastrous results. Gertrudis becomes affected by the Tita's culinary delights and runs off on back of a revolutionary fighter's horse.

> Tita eventually enters into the relationship with Dr. Brown, a kind man, and considers the marriage, but she cannot overcome her feelings for Pedro. At novel's end, Tita and Pedro are brought together in death. The heat of their spirits uniting sparks a fire that destroys ranch. Only thing left after a fire is Tita's cookbook.

---

5. Working with English adjectives

English adjectives do not change form to agree with the form of the nouns they modify. They stay the same whatever the gender or number of the noun.

► **Juan is an *attentive* father. Alyssa is an *attentive* mother. They are *attentive* parents.**

Adjectives usually come before a noun, but they can also occur after a linking verb.

► **We had a *delicious* meal.**

► **The food at the restaurant was *delicious.***

Be aware, however, that the position of an adjective can affect its meaning. The phrase *my old friend*, for example, can refer to someone with whom the speaker has had a long friendship (*a friend I have known for a long time*) or to an aged friend (*my friend who is elderly*). In the sentence *My friend is old*, in contrast, *old* has only one meaning—elderly.

When two or more adjectives modify a noun cumulatively, they follow a sequence—determined by their meaning—that is particular to English logic:

1. Determiner/article: *the, his, my, that, some*
2. Adjectives that express subjective evaluation: *cozy, intelligent, outrageous, elegant, original*
3. Adjectives of size and shape: *big, small, huge, tiny, tall, short, narrow, thick, round, square*
4. Adjectives expressing age: *old, young, new*
5. Adjectives of color: *yellow, green, pale*
6. Adjectives of origin and type: *African, Czech, Gothic*
7. Adjectives of material: *brick, plastic, glass, stone*
8. Nouns used as adjectives: *dinner* [*menu*], *computer* [*keyboard*]
9. Noun modified

Here are some examples:

DETERMINER	SUBJECTIVE EVALUATION	SIZE AND SHAPE	AGE	COLOR	ORIGIN AND TYPE	MATERIAL	NOUN AS ADJECTIVE	NOUN
your	cozy			red		brick	family	cottage
those			old		African			statues
the	ugly			orange		plastic	school	chairs
its	striking	arched			Gothic	stained-glass		window

Exercise 64.4 Working with English adjectives

Correct any errors in adjective placement or agreement in the following sentences. Some of the sentences may be correct as written.

EXAMPLE

huge brick
The houses in the development were all ~~brick huge~~ mansions.

1. House hunting can be a time-consuming activity and frustrating.
2. Prospective home buyers are bombarded with images of spacious, elegant houses.
3. Multiple bedrooms, bathrooms fully equipped, and gardens landscaped are becoming standard features of suburban new properties.
4. The kitchens are filled with shiny surfaces and high-tech numerous gadgets.
5. Many American young families cannot afford those expensives properties.

64b Learn the characteristics of English pronouns.

The pronoun system in English is less complex than those of many other languages. For instance, English has few pronoun case forms. Some features of English pronouns, however, may present problems for the multilingual learner.

- The second-person pronouns *you* and *your/yours* have only one form for both singular and plural referents.

- ***You*** **are my *friend.***
- ***You*** **are my *friends.***
- ***Your car*** **is parked in the driveway. The *car* is *yours.***
- ***Your cars*** **are parked in the driveway. The *cars* are *yours.***

■ In English, the gender and number of a pronoun is determined by the gender and number of the noun or pronoun it replaces (its antecedent). (In some other languages, possessive pronouns take the gender and number of the nouns they modify.)

- **Daria bought her daughter a red bike and ~~his~~ *her* son a yellow bike.**
- **The school is planning a bike tour in Vermont for ~~their~~ *its* students.**

Exercise 64.5 Reviewing pronoun usage and reference

Correct the errors in pronoun usage and reference in the following sentences.

EXAMPLE

This book is ~~her~~ *hers*, not mine.

1. The American college today often has a large international population and must deal with issues of ethnicity and national allegiance among their students.
2. Hoping to educate better citizens for an increasingly interconnected world, schools are emphasizing international relations in its programs.
3. Students should care about the future of the world, not just about the future of theirs careers.
4. That woman's mother is from Belgium and his father is from Mexico.

64c Learn the characteristics of English verb phrases.

English verbs require **auxiliary (helping) verbs** in many situations to provide information about time (tense) and the characteristics of an action.

1. Using helping verbs to form tenses

Many English tenses consist of a form of the helping verbs *have* or *be* combined with either the *-ing* or the *-ed* form of the main verb. In these tenses:

- The subject agrees with the helping verb, not the main verb.

  ► **She ~~have~~ has traveled to many places.**

- The helping verb should never be omitted.

  ► **She is traveling to South America next summer.**

- To make a negative statement, insert *not* after the helping verb.

  ► **She is *not* traveling to Europe.**

(*For a complete discussion of English tenses and how to form them, see Chapter 35: Problems with Verbs, pp. 562–69.*)

2. Understanding modal auxiliaries

In addition to those required for tense formation, English has a variety of helping verbs, known as **modals,** that express an attitude to the action or circumstances of a sentence:

can	must	will
could	ought to	would
may	shall	
might	should	

- These verbs do not change form to indicate person or number.
- They do not change form to indicate tense.
- They are followed directly by the base form of the verb without *to*.

  ► **We *must* ~~to~~ study now.**

- Sometimes they are used with *have* plus the past participle of the verb to indicate the past tense (*see the table on page 848*).

  ► **He *must* have studied hard to do so well.**

Some verbal expressions ending in *to* also function as modals, including *have to, be able to,* and *be supposed to*. These **phrasal modals** behave more like ordinary verbs than true modals, changing form to carry tense and agree with the subject.

Modals are used to express the following:

FUNCTION	PRESENT/FUTURE	PAST
Permission	**may, might, can, could** *May (Might/Can/Could)* I come at five o'clock?	**might, could** My instructor said I *could* hand in my paper late.
Polite request	**would, could** *Would* you please open the door?	
Ability	**can, am/is/are able to** I *can* (*am able to*) take one piece of luggage.	**could, was/were able to** I *could* (*was able to*) take only one piece of luggage on the plane yesterday.
Possibility	**may, might** She *may* (*might*) try to return this afternoon.	***may, might* + *have* + past participle** His train *may* (*might*) *have* arrived already.
Expectation	**should** I only have one more chart to create, so I *should* finish my project today.	***should* + *have* + past participle** The students *should have* finished the project by now.
Necessity	**must (have to)** I *must* (*have to*) pass this test.	***had to* + base form** She *had to* study hard to pass.
Prohibition	**must + not** You *must not* go there.	
Logical deduction	**must (has to)** He *must* (*has to*) be there by now.	***must* + *have* + past participle** You *must have* left early to make the noon bus.
Intention	**will, shall** I *will* (*shall*) go today.	**would** I told you I *would* go.
Specula-tion (past form implies that something did *not* happen)	**would, could, might** If she learned her lines, she *could* play the part.	***would (could/might)* + *have* + past participle** If she had learned her lines, she *might have* gotten the part.
Advisabil-ity (past form implies that something did *not* happen)	**should (ought to)** You *should* (*ought to*) water the plant every day.	***should* + *have* + past participle** You *should have* listened to the directions more carefully.
Habitual past action		***would (used to)* + base form** When I was younger, I *would* ride my bike to school every day.

3. Including linking verbs

In some languages, linking verbs (verbs like *be, seem, look, sound, feel, appear, remain*) may sometimes be omitted, but not in English.

look/seem/appear. . .
► **They ^ happy.**

am
► **I ^ Jonathan.**

Exercise 64.6 Using modals, other helping verbs, and linking verbs

Correct any errors in the use of modals, other helping verbs, and linking verbs in the following sentences.

EXAMPLE

had
We ^ been hoping that we could ~~to~~ visit California before we graduated.

1. Do you know where you and Erica will to go on vacation this summer?
2. We hoping to go to Europe, but it too expensive to travel there now.
3. You should to look online. You can to find great deals there.
4. I have been looking all over the Internet, but I not found any cheap hotels.
5. Have you thought about camping? My sister did able to save a lot of money by camping when she traveling around Europe last summer.
6. That is a great idea! Are there any campsites she can suggests in Spain and Portugal?
7. I am not sure if she went to Portugal, but she must been to Spain. Let me ask her.
8. That is excellent. I just hope I will not have buy too much camping gear.
9. I have a lot of gear, and I am sure Erica coulds borrow some of my sister's things.
10. Thanks so much! I have a feeling we going to have a great vacation after all.

Exercise 64.7 Using modal verbs with perfect tenses

Correct any errors in these sentences with modals.

EXAMPLE

The Civil War must have ~~was~~ ^been^ an important event in American history.

1. My history paper is giving me a headache. I should have start earlier.
2. I could had begun my research earlier, but I waited until just last week.
3. Because the subject is so complicated, I should not have chose to write about the Civil War.
4. My history professor must has been using the same essay topics for twenty years.
5. If the instructor had given us more choices, I might picked an easier topic.
6. I could have did better on the last paper, so I should have research it more.

---

4. Understanding verbals

Verbals are words derived from verbs that function as nouns or modifiers. They do not indicate tense and cannot function alone as complete verbs. There are three kinds of verbals:

- Past and present **participles** used as adjectives or in adjective phrases

  ► ***Reading as much as they could,* the students learned many new words.**

  The participial phrase *reading as much as they could* modifies *students.*

  ► ***Exhausted by the race,* the candidate withdrew.**

  The participial phrase *exhausted by the race* modifies *candidate.*

- **Gerunds,** or present participles used as nouns or in noun phrases

  ► **Intensive *reading* enriches your vocabulary.**

  The gerund *reading* is the subject of the sentence.

  ► **The conductor criticized his *singing* because it was off-key.**

  The gerund *singing* is the object of the sentence.

- **Infinitives** used as nouns or in noun phrases

► ***To graduate*** **on time became unlikely for her after she got sick.**

The infinitive *to graduate* is the subject of the sentence.

► **He managed *to complete* his dissertation in six months.**

The infinitive phrase *to complete his dissertation* is the object of the sentence.

Note: The present participle is the *-ing* form of a verb. In regular verbs, the past participle ends in *-ed*, but it takes many forms in irregular verbs. (*See the list of irregular verb forms in Chapter 35: Problems with Verbs, pp. 554–55.*)

An infinitive is the word *to* plus the base form of the verb: *to be, to learn, to graduate, to complete.*

Remember that English sentences require a complete verb that indicates tense. A participle alone cannot be a complete verb, so an expression that includes a participle but no helping verb or verbs is considered a fragment, not a complete sentence.

► **He ^*is* writing an essay.**

► **She ^*has* written an essay.**

Be aware of this strict rule, especially if your first language sometimes allows the omission of helping verbs. (*For more on fragments and how to avoid them, see Chapter 32: Sentence Fragments, pp. 512–23.*)

Gerunds after a preposition A gerund, not an infinitive, follows a preposition:

► **I look forward to ~~work~~ ^*working* on the project with you instead of ~~to do~~ ^*doing* it alone.**

Present versus past participle Although both present and past participles can function as adjectives, present-participle adjectives differ from past-participle adjectives in ways that can be difficult for multilingual writers to distinguish. To use these forms properly, keep the following in mind:

- Present-participle adjectives usually modify nouns that are the agent, or cause, of an action.

► **This problem is *confusing*.**

The present participle *confusing* modifies *problem*, which is the agent, or cause, of the confusion.

- Past-participle adjectives usually modify nouns that are the recipient of an action.

► **The students are *confused* by the problem.**

The past participle *confused* modifies *students*, who are the recipients of the confusion the problem is causing.

Here are some other present- and past-participle pairs that often cause trouble for multilingual writers:

amazing	amazed	frightening	frightened
annoying	annoyed	interesting	interested
boring	bored	satisfying	satisfied
depressing	depressed	shocking	shocked
embarrassing	embarrassed	surprising	surprised
exciting	excited	tiring	tired

Exercise 64.8 Choosing the correct participle

Underline the correct participle from each pair in parentheses.

EXAMPLE

The (tiring/tired) students celebrated the end of final exams.

1. I spent a busy week (preparing/prepared) for the art history final.
2. The review material is very (boring/bored).
3. The term paper I am writing for the class is on a (challenging/challenged) topic: twentieth-century painting.
4. I am especially (interesting/interested) in the paintings of Picasso.
5. I will be (relieving/relieved) when I have finished the paper and handed it in.
6. Most students have already submitted their (completing/completed) papers.
7. I am so (exciting/excited) that the semester is almost over.

Gerunds versus infinitives Verbs in English differ as to whether they can be followed by a gerund, an infinitive, or either. Some verbs, like *avoid*, can be followed by a gerund but not an infinitive.

► **We avoided ~~to climb~~ *climbing* the mountain during the storm.**

Other verbs, like *attempt*, can be followed by an infinitive but not a gerund.

► **We attempted ~~reaching~~ *to reach* the summit when the weather cleared.**

Others can be followed by either a gerund or an infinitive with no change in meaning.

► **We began climbing. / We began to climb.**

Still other verbs have a different meaning when followed by a gerund than they do when followed by an infinitive. Compare these examples:

► **She stopped eating.**

She was eating, but she stopped.

► **She stopped to eat.**

She stopped what she was doing, in order to eat.

Learn these obligatory verb-verbal combinations as you would any other aspect of new vocabulary. The lists here provide common examples of each verb type.

Some verbs that take only an infinitive

afford
ask
appear
attempt
choose
claim
decide
expect
fail
hope
intend
learn
manage
mean
need
offer
plan
prepare
promise
refuse
request
seem
tend
threaten
want
wish
would like

Some verbs that take only a gerund

admit
advise
avoid
consider
defend
deny
recommend
discuss
enjoy
feel like
finish
forgive
imagine
risk
look forward to
mention
mind
practice
propose
quit
tolerate

regret	suggest	understand
resist	support	urge

Some verbs that can take either a gerund or an infinitive

An asterisk (*) indicates those verbs for which the choice of gerund or infinitive affects meaning.

begin	like	start
continue	love	stop*
forget*	prefer	try*
hate	remember*	

Exercise 64.9 Using gerunds versus infinitives after verbs

Underline the correct choice—gerund or infinitive—in each pair in parentheses.

EXAMPLE

Most people hope (to work/working) in rewarding jobs.

1. In the past, people were expected (to stay/staying) at the same job for a long time, ideally for their whole career.
2. Today, people tend (to change/changing) careers several times before retiring.
3. People who are not happy with their careers attempt (to find/finding) other jobs that interest them more.
4. Others, who regret (not to get/not getting) undergraduate or graduate degrees when they were younger, go back to school.
5. Some people even look forward to (to change/changing) jobs every few years to avoid boredom.
6. So, if you do not like your job, stop (to complain/complaining) and do something about it.

65 English Sentence Structure

65a Learn the requirements of English word order.

English has strict rules of word order in sentences. These rules can present difficulties for multilingual students.

1. Understanding word order in declarative sentences

Declarative sentences provide information (declare something) about their subjects.

The English word order for declarative sentences with a transitive verb is subject–verb–object (or S–V–O). (*See the box "For Multilingual Students: English Word Order" in Chapter 31, p. 498.*)

FAULTY WORD ORDER	**Wrote** (V) **Clara Schumann** (S) **a piano concerto** (O)**.**
REVISED	**Clara Schumann** (S) **wrote** (V) **a piano concerto** (O)**.**

Stated, nondulicated subject All English sentences and clauses except commands (*see p. 857*) must have an explicitly stated subject.

► **The teacher told us to review sentence structure. ~~Said~~** *She said* **we would have a quiz on it next week.**

Unlike in some other languages, however, in English a pronoun cannot duplicate the subject.

► **The teacher ~~she~~ told us to review sentence structure.**

If the subject follows the verb, then the expletive *there* or *it* is needed in the subject position.

► **~~Is~~** *There is* **a new independent radio station in our city.**

There indicates existence or locality. The verb *is* agrees with the subject (*radio station*), which follows the verb.

> ***Note:*** The pronoun *it* (see the example on the next page) can also be the subject of a sentence about weather or environmental conditions (*It is cold in this house*), time (*It is three o'clock*), or distance (*It is five miles to the next filling station*).

It is
► ~~Is~~ hard to find doctors who are willing to move to rural areas.

Word order in verb phrases Helping verbs (hv) always precede the main verb (mv) in verb phrases.

► I have (hv) been (mv) sick lately.

The negative word *not* usually precedes the main verb and follows the first helping verb in a verb phrase.

not
► I have ^ been ~~not~~ sick lately.

Word order of indirect and direct objects Some transitive verbs—including *ask, bring, find, get, give, hand, lend, offer, pay, promise, read, send, show, teach, tell,* and *write*—can take an indirect object as well as a direct object. The **direct object** receives the action of the verb; the **indirect object** is the beneficiary of the action.

The indirect object usually precedes the direct object.

► The students sent [their parents] (ind obj) [an e-mail message.] (dir obj)

► The students sent them an e-mail message.

The indirect object can follow the direct object if it is introduced by a preposition such as *to* or *for*.

to
► The students sent an e-mail message ^ their parents.

Exception: If the indirect object is a noun and the direct object is a pronoun, the indirect object cannot come before the direct object.

to their parents
► The students sent ~~their parents~~ it ^.

Some verbs, such as *analyze*, *describe*, *mention*, and *say*, do not take an indirect object before the direct object.

to her friend
► She mentioned ~~her friend~~ the news ^.

for us
► The scientist analyzed ~~us~~ the compound ^.

2. Understanding word order in questions

Questions can take a variety of forms. In most of them the S–V word order of declarative sentences is reversed, and the verb, or part of it, precedes the subject.

- For simple forms of the verb *be*, put the subject after the verb.

She *was* on time for the meeting.	*Was* she on time for the meeting?

- For other simple verbs, begin the question with a form of *do* followed by the subject and then the main verb.

You *noticed* the change in the report.	*Did* you *notice* the change in the report?

- For verbs consisting of a main verb with one or more helping verbs, put the subject after the first (or only) helping verb. Place any one-word adjective after the subject.

He *is* not *pleased* with the results.	*Is* he not *pleased* with the results?
You *have been waiting* a long time.	*Have* you *been waiting* a long time?
The guests *have arrived*.	*Have* the guests *arrived*?

- Questions that begin with question words like *how, what, who, when, where*, or *why* follow the same patterns.

  When did the guests *arrive*?
  Where have you *been* hiding?

- When the question word is the subject, however, the question follows the S–V word order of a declarative sentence.

  What happened last night?
  Who spilled the milk?

3. Understanding word order in commands

In commands, or imperative sentences, the subject, which is always *you*, is omitted.

► **[you] Read the instructions before using this machine.**

► **[you] Do not enter.**

► **[you] Do not touch this chemical—it is hazardous.**

Exercise 65.1 Understanding word order in declarative sentences, questions, and commands

Find and correct the errors in the following sentences. Some sentences have more than one error.

EXAMPLE **Frodo ~~the ring~~ carries ^ to Mount Doom.** (*the ring* inserted after "carries")

1. J. R. R. Tolkien he wrote the three books of *The Lord of the Rings.*
2. You have read them yet?
3. What the books are about?
4. The books describe us the world of Middle Earth.
5. Gandalf gives to Frodo a magical ring.
6. The movies are good?
7. The movies won many Oscars?
8. You tell me your opinion of the movies after you see them.

4. Understanding word order in reported speech

Changing a direct quotation (someone else's exact words) to an indirect quotation (a report of what the person said or wrote) often requires changing many sentence elements. When the quotation is a declarative sentence, however, the subject-before-verb word order does not change.

DIRECT QUOTATION **The instructor said, "You have only one more week to finish your papers."** (S: You; V: have)

INDIRECT QUOTATION **The instructor told the students that they had only one more week to finish their papers.** (S: they; V: had)

Changing a direct question to an indirect question, however, does require a word order change: from the V–S pattern of a question to the S–V pattern of a declarative sentence.

DIRECT QUESTION **The instructor always asks, "Are you ready to begin?"** (V: Are; S: you)

INDIRECT QUESTION **The instructor always asks [us] if we are ready to begin.** (S: we; V: are)

In an indirect quotation of a command, a pronoun or noun takes the place of the command's omitted subject, *you*, and is followed by the infinitive (*to*) form of the verb.

DIRECT QUOTATION: COMMAND	The instructor always says, "[*you*] Write down the assignment before you leave."
INDIRECT QUOTATION: COMMAND	The instructor always tells *us* to write down the assignment before we leave.

In indirectly quoted negative imperatives, the word *not* comes before the infinitive.

DIRECT	The instructor said, "Do not forget your homework."
INDIRECT	The instructor reminded us *not* to forget our homework.

5. Placing adverbs

An adverbial modifier should never come between the verb and the direct object in a sentence.

► She finished ~~quickly~~ the exam. ^quickly

or

► She ^quickly finished ~~quickly~~ the exam.

► She presented ~~with great eloquence~~ the issue ^with great eloquence.

Adverbs can come after, but usually not before, the first helping verb in a verb phrase.

► They ~~gradually~~ are ^gradually moving into their new home.

Note that adverbs of frequency (*sometimes, often, never*) usually fall between the subject and the predicate.

► She *sometimes* writes articles for this magazine.

Adverbs of degree (*completely, absolutely*) fall immediately before the modified word.

► I *absolutely* agree!

Adverbs of manner (*quickly, well, poorly*) follow the verb.

► She sang *beautifully*.

When adverbs occur at the very beginning of a sentence, they usually show special emphasis.

► *Sneakily,* she hid the letter under her bed.

Certain adverbs—mostly negatives like *never, rarely,* and *seldom*—change the normal subject-before-verb word order when they appear at the beginning of a sentence.

► **Rarely ^is the weather ~~is~~ so cold in California.**

(*See the box "For Multilingual Students: Adverbial Modifiers and Subject-Verb Order" in Chapter 45, p. 665.*)

65b Use subordinating and coordinating words correctly.

1. Distinguishing the different functions of *that*

The word *that* can introduce a subordinate clause either as a relative pronoun or as a subordinating conjunction.

► **The house *that* they decided to buy needs a lot of renovation.**

The relative pronoun *that* replaces the noun *house*.

► **The Bakers said *that* their new house needed a lot of renovation.**

The subordinating conjunction *that* introduces a noun clause that is the direct object of the sentence.

2. Using either subordination or coordination

Do not use both subordination and coordination together to combine the same two clauses, even if the subordinating and coordinating words are similar in meaning. Some examples include the use of *although* or *even though* with *but* and the use of *because* with *therefore*.

FAULTY **_Although_ I came early, _but_ the tickets were already sold out.**

REVISED **_Although_ I came early, the tickets were already sold out.**

or

I came early, _but_ the tickets were already sold out.

FAULTY **_Because_ Socrates is human, and humans are mortal, _therefore,_ Socrates is mortal.**

REVISED **_Because_ Socrates is human, and humans are mortal, Socrates is mortal.**

or

Socrates is human, and humans are mortal; _therefore,_ Socrates is mortal.

3. Distinguishing *because* and *for*

The word *for*, when used as a subordinating conjunction, has the same meaning as *because*. *For* is more formal, however, and is used less frequently.

FORMAL SOUNDING	**He did not respond to the employment ad, *for* he knew he had little chance of getting the job.**
PREFERRED	**He did not respond to the employment ad *because* he knew he had little chance of getting the job.**

Exercise 65.2 Using English word order

Find and correct the errors in the following sentences. Some sentences have more than one error.

EXAMPLE	**Because they worry about food so much, ~~therefore~~ Americans may have more eating-related problems than people in other developed countries.**

1. As Michael Pollan in the *New York Times Magazine* writes, Americans have become the world's most anxious eaters.
2. Researchers have found that Americans they worry more about what they eat than people do in other developed countries.
3. Therefore, tend to enjoy their food less and associate a good meal with guilty pleasure.
4. Paradoxically, this worrying does not stop regularly many Americans from overeating.
5. The report also tells to readers that it is not uncommon for people to visit the gym after overeating.
6. The people of many other nations take pleasure in eating and turn often a meal into a festive occasion.
7. Although they relish their meals, but they are less prone to obesity or eating disorders than Americans.
8. Some scientists speculate that the people of these nations therefore are less obese because they cook with more healthful ingredients than Americans.
9. The question arises, however, whether might people's attitude toward eating be as important to good health as what they eat?

66 Identifying and Editing Common Errors

For multilingual students one of the main sources of errors in written English is native language interference, or the inappropriate transfer of usages from different languages into English. It helps to be aware of the similarities and differences between English and your native language (for example, in vocabulary, tense formation, word order, and article use) especially when you are editing your writing.

Interference can be both lexical (involving the meaning and structure of words) and syntactic (involving the structure of sentences).

66a Beware of misleading cognates.

Because English evolved from several different languages, you may find that some English words are very similar to words in your native language (and may indeed have a similar origin). Explore these **cognates,** but do not rely on them. You will find many to be false friends: you turn to them for support, but they let you down because they have a different meaning in English than in your native language.

Here are some examples:

ENGLISH WORD	MEANING IN ENGLISH	COGNATES IN OTHER LANGUAGES AND THEIR MEANINGS
assist	help	Spanish *asistir:* attend
attend	be present at	French *attendre:* wait for
demand	request forcefully, claim	French *demander:* request, ask a question of
fabric	cloth	German *fabrik:* factory
library	a place where books can be borrowed	French *librairie,* Spanish *librería,* Italian *libreria,* Portuguese *livraria:* bookstore
passionate	emotional	French *passionnant:* fascinating
sympathetic	compassionate	French *sympathique*, Spanish, *simpático,* Italian *simpatico:* nice, friendly

► **She ~~demanded~~ *asked* her instructor for an extension on her term paper.**

► **We bought our textbooks at the campus ~~library~~ *bookstore*.**

66b Express quantity and intensity appropriately.

As discussed in Chapter 64 (*section 64a*), some quantifiers can be used with count nouns only, some with noncount nouns only, and some with both count and noncount nouns. Certain quantifiers differ subtly in the quantity of a thing they designate. Here are some examples, arranged on a scale from small amount to large amount:

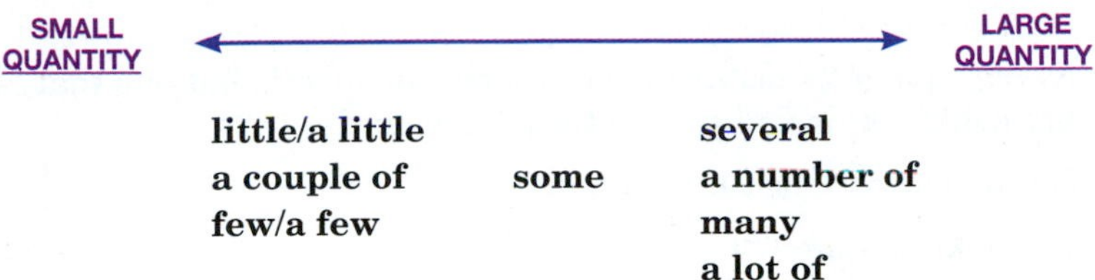

The quantifiers *a few* and *few* for count nouns and *a little* and *little* for noncount nouns all indicate a small quantity. In contrast to *a few* and *a little*, however, *few* and *little* have the negative connotation of "hardly any."

► **The problems are difficult, and we have *few* options for solving them.**

The outlook for solving the problems is gloomy.

► **The problems are difficult, but we have *a few* options for solving them.**

The outlook for solving the problems is hopeful.

► **We have *little time* to find a campsite before sunset.**

The campers might have to spend the night in the open by the side of the trail.

► **We have *a little time* to find a campsite before sunset.**

The campers will probably find a place to pitch their tent before dark.

Similarly, both *very* and *too* intensify adjectives, but *too* has a negative meaning.

► **The suitcase is *very* full.**

► **The suitcase is *too* full to close.**

66c Understand adverb formation.

The usual way to form an adverb is to add the ending *-ly* to the corresponding adjective. The adjective *quick*, for example, becomes the adverb *quickly*, and the adjective *happy* becomes the adverb *happily*.

However, there are exceptions to this rule.

1. Not all adverbs end in *-ly*.

Adjective	**Adverb**
good	well
fast	fast
hard	hard

> ***Note:*** Adding *-ly* to *hard* does produce an adverb, but one that has a different meaning than the adverb *hard*.
>
> *Hardly* means "almost not at all."
>
> ► **He *hardly* works.** (He is lazy.)
>
> *Hard*, in contrast, means "with great exertion."
>
> ► **He works *hard*.** (He works a lot.)

2. Some words that end in *-ly* are adjectives, not adverbs. Examples include *friendly, lovely,* and *manly*.
3. Adverbs such as *seldom* and *often* do not have corresponding adjectives.

When in doubt about the meaning or form of an adverb, consult your dictionary. (*For more on adverb usage, see Chapter 37: Problems with Adjectives and Adverbs, pp. 597–609.*)

Exercise 66.1 Avoiding lexical pitfalls: False friends, quantifiers, and adverb formation

Correct the errors in lexical usage in the following sentences. Note that to identify the errors in some of them, you will need to refer to Chapter 64 *(pp. 838–54)*.

EXAMPLE **Although the field hands work hard~~ly~~ all day, they make ~~a~~ little money.**

1. A great deal of reports in the press point out that the spread of infections in hospitals has reached almost epidemic proportions.

2. The best way for hospital staffs to prevent the spread of infections is to follow meticulous hygiene procedures.
3. Hospital workers are demanded to wash their hands often.
4. They should wash their hands after the interaction with every patients.
5. Otherwise, there is a little hope of stopping the spread of infections.
6. On the other hand, no matter how hardly they try, hospital workers cannot completely eliminate the risk of infection.
7. Hospital visitors also need to take few precautions to avoid health risks to themselves and patients.
8. To avoid contact with dangerous microbes, for example, visitors should touch as little surfaces as possible while in the hospital.
9. Visitors should also wash their hands carefully after all visit.
10. In the end, however, patients and visitors have to rely mostly on their immunity to ward off infection.

66d Manage English prepositions.

The relationship between prepositions and the words they accompany is often arbitrary. In standard English, for example, people ride *in* cars but *on* trains. They eat a romantic dinner *by* candlelight, but they cook it *on* a stove *with* gas. As a result, the use of prepositions is among the most difficult aspects of English for multilingual students to master.

Some of the most troublesome combinations are those with verbs and with adjectives. Whenever you learn a new adjective or verb, you should also learn the preposition or prepositions that are commonly used with it. Here are some examples:

SOME VERB-AND-PREPOSITION COMBINATIONS

approve of
base on
believe in
combine with
compare with/to
consist of
contribute to
depend on
distinguish from
focus on
insist on
prefer to

SOME ADJECTIVE-AND-PREPOSITION COMBINATIONS

afraid of
associated with
aware of
capable of
content with
familiar with
famous for
interested in
proud of
sorry for
tired of
worried about

The prepositions that indicate time and location are often the most idiosyncratic in a language. The following are some common ways in which the prepositions *at, by, in,* and *on* are used.

TIME

AT The wedding ceremony starts *at two o'clock.* [a specific clock time]

BY Our honeymoon plans should be ready *by next week.* [a particular time]

IN The reception will start *in the evening.* [a portion of the day]

ON The wedding will take place *on May 1.* The rehearsal is *on Tuesday.* [a particular date or day of the week]

LOCATION

AT I will meet you *at the zoo.* [a particular place]

You need to turn right *at the light.* [a corner or an intersection]

We took a seat *at the table.* [near a piece of furniture]

BY Meet me *by the fountain.* [a familiar place]

IN Park your car *in the parking lot* and give the money to the attendant *in the booth.* [on a space of some kind or inside a structure]

I enjoyed the bratwurst *in Chicago.* [a city, state, or other geographic location]

I found that article *in this book.* [a print medium]

ON An excellent restaurant is located *on Mulberry Street.* [a street, avenue, or other thoroughfare]

I spilled milk *on the floor.* [a surface]

I watched the report *on television.* [an electronic medium]

66e Master phrasal verbs.

In some cases, adding one or two prepositions to a verb changes the verb's meaning. These verb-preposition combinations are called **phrasal verbs.**

PHRASAL VERB	DEFINITION	EXAMPLE
turn away	avert, refuse	The refugees were *turned away* at the border.
turn off	disconnect, stop	Who *turned off* the lights?
turn on	connect, start	I overslept because I forgot to *turn on* the alarm.
turn down	reject	The company *turned down* her job application.

Phrasal verbs are of two kinds: separable and inseparable. A phrasal verb is **separable** if a direct object can come either between the verb and the preposition or after the preposition:

► *Put* your books *away.*

► *Put away* your books.

Note: If the direct object of a separable phrasal verb is a pronoun, it must come between the verb and the preposition.

► *Put* ^them *away* ~~them~~.

SOME SEPARABLE PHRASAL VERBS

ask out	give up	put off
call back	hand in	start over
call off	hand out	take off
cross out	pick up	throw away
fill in	put away	try on
fill out	put back	write down
give back	put down	

A phrasal verb is **inseparable** if no other word can come between the verb and the preposition:

► I *ran into* Mark on the street.

SOME INSEPARABLE PHRASAL VERBS

call on	get on	look out
come across	get out	pass out
drop in (on)	get over	run into
drop out (of)	get through	run out (of)
get back	grow up	speak up
get in	keep on	watch out (for)
get off		

66f Learn the meaning of idioms.

Idioms are expressions whose meaning cannot be understood from the meaning of the individual words they are composed of. They are usually phrases that may consist of several different categories of words. Learn the whole structure of an idiom as you would learn any other vocabulary word. In formal writing, avoid most idioms.

COMMON IDIOM	MEANING
be in seventh heaven	be elated
be on the ball	be alert
child's play	easy
get something off one's chest	confess
get the ball rolling	start a project
get to the point	do not digress
hit the sack	sleep
hold one's tongue	keep silent
make ends meet	live within one's income
odds and ends	miscellaneous things
on the tip of one's tongue	almost remembered
pain in the neck	aggravating
pay through the nose	pay a painfully large amount of money
push one's luck	risk losing what one has gained by trying too hard for something
scared stiff	terrified
talk nonsense	be illogical
be in a fix	be in difficulty
make headway	make progress
stir things up	provoke action

Exercise 66.2 Avoiding lexical pitfalls: Prepositions, phrasal verbs, and idioms

Fill in the missing preposition in each sentence.

EXAMPLE **High school students often worry *about* getting into the college of their choice.**

1. High school teenagers are aware _____ the difficulty of getting into a good college.

2. Not only do they have to excel _____ their studies, but they also have to have many extracurricular interests.
3. Students try to distinguish themselves _____ other students through their activities.
4. They participate _____ dance, language, or art clubs; they try out for sports teams; or they work on the yearbook.
5. Sometimes they insist _____ doing things they do not particularly enjoy, just to make their college applications look impressive.
6. The pressures of college applications combined _____ schoolwork, homework, and extracurricular activities can be very stressful.
7. Teachers feel sorry _____ students, who often become overworked and overextended.
8. Students need to find balance and realize that getting ____ a college cannot be their only focus.
9. They should enjoy high school and be content ____ their daily accomplishments.

66g Avoid errors in subject-verb agreement.

The subject and verb—in most cases adjacent to one another—are the core of an English sentence and must agree in person and number. The following steps will help assure subject-verb agreement in your sentences.

1. Identify the subject, which may be separated from the verb by another word group. Determine its person (first, second, or third) and number (singular or plural). Remember that in regular nouns the ending *-s* signals the plural form (*see 64a*). In other cases, identifying whether a subject is singular or plural can present problems:

   - Nouns with irregular plurals (*see 64a*)
   - Nouns without singular forms (*trousers, binoculars*)
   - Noncount nouns, which are always singular
   - Subjects accompanied by quantifiers
   - Indefinite pronouns, most of which are always singular, but some of which are always plural, and some of which can be singular or plural depending on context (*see Chapter 34: Subject-Verb Agreement, pp. 547–48*)
   - Gerunds and infinitives, which are always singular
   - The word *what*, which is always singular when it is the subject of a question

- The filler subject *there*, which can be either singular or plural depending on the subject it fills in for

► **There *are* some *tools* for this experiment.**

► **There *is* new *equipment* in the lab.**

► **There *is* no *tolerance* for discrimination in our society.**

2. Apply the general rules for subject-verb agreement.

- For the simple present tense of regular verbs, a third-person singular or noncount subject takes the base form of the verb with the ending *-s* or *-es*. All other subjects take the base form with no ending.

► **The *student writes* well.**

► **The new lab *equipment works* well.**

► **College *students write* frequently.**

► ***I/you/we/they write* frequently.**

- The verb *be* has three present tense forms (*am, are,* and *is*) and two past tense forms (*was* and *were*).

► ***I am* often early for class.**

► **The *student is* often late for meetings.**

► **The *teacher was* late yesterday.**

► **The *teachers/we/you/they were* never late for class.**

► **The *students/we/you/they are* never late for class.**

- In all tenses formed with auxiliary verbs, including all passive-voice verbs, the subject agrees with the auxiliary verb.

► **The *teacher has* graded all the papers.**

► **The *students have* completed the assignment.**

► **The *student is* applying for a scholarship.**

► **The *teachers were* grading papers all week.**

► **The *homework is/was* completed by the student.**

► **The *assignments are/were* submitted by all the students.**

(For a detailed discussion of subject-verb agreement, tense formation, and voice, see Chapter 34: Subject-Verb Agreement, pp. 536–52, and Chapter 35: Problems with Verbs, pp. 552–75.)

Exercise 66.3 Avoiding syntactic pitfalls: Subject-verb agreement

Find and correct the errors in the following sentences.

EXAMPLE **The price of digital cameras ~~are~~ is falling.**

1. Obesity in children and adolescents are becoming a major problem around the world.
2. Statistics reveals that more than fifteen percent of children and adolescents are obese.
3. There is several causes for obesity, some of which are subject to individual control and some of which are not.
4. Genetics are not subject to individual control.
5. The many controllable causes of obesity includes lack of exercise, sedentary behavior, and poor eating habits.
6. Socioeconomic status can trigger obesity because healthful food also tend to be relatively expensive.
7. The environment in which people live affect their diet and the amount of exercise they get.
8. Preventing obesity in children are not easy.
9. Collaboration between schools and families are needed to create an active and healthful environment for children.
10. Everyone agree that the consequences of obesity in adulthood can be deadly, so it is critical to diagnose and treat this problem early.

66h Avoid errors in pronoun reference.

In English, a pronoun must agree with its antecedent (the noun it refers to) in number and gender. In addition, the antecedent for the pronoun you are using should be clear and located close enough to the pronoun to avoid any ambiguity. (*For a detailed discussion of pronoun reference, see Chapter 36: Problems with Pronouns, pp. 592–96.*)

Exercise 66.4 Avoiding syntactic pitfalls: Pronoun reference

Find and correct the errors in the following sentences.

EXAMPLE **The computer has become ubiquitous since ~~their~~ its invention more than fifty years ago.**

1. Cafés are finding modern ways to attract its customers.
2. A coffee drinker no longer needs to bring their friends to a café to have a conversation.

3. Internet access allows customers to bring his computer instead.
4. Instead of hearing the conversations of other people, the customer hears their fingers clicking on keyboards.
5. Providing Internet access is a clever marketing idea because when someone is on the Internet, they are likely to stay at the café a long time and buy more coffee than they otherwise would.
6. In addition, comfortable couches provide the customer with a homey ambience that makes them reluctant to leave.
7. At cafés that offer free Internet access, one can expect to see a group of students working on their computer.
8. Students can get a cup of coffee, surf the Web, and pay for it online with a credit card.
9. So it is not surprising to see a person at a café laughing aloud while typing furiously on her laptop.
10. The computer probably cannot replace face-to-face interaction, but they can put people all over the world in instant communication with one another.

66i Avoid errors in word order.

When constructing a sentence, check for the following aspects of word order:

- The inclusion of a subject (obligatory) and, depending on the type of sentence, the order of subject and verb *(see 65a)*
- The logical placement of adjectives *(see 64a)*
- The correct placement of objects (direct and indirect) and modifiers (adverbs) *(see 65a)*

Exercise 66.5 Editing for word order

Correct any word order errors in the following paragraph.

the Tour de France

EXAMPLE Lance Armstrong won ^ seven times ~~the Tour de France~~.

During even good times, credit card debt is a burden heavy to carry. Financial advisers stress always that people should stop adding to their debt and begin rapidly paying it down while they have the option. When asked what would they do if they knew they would be laid off in six months, most people say they would start slashing expenses. Consuming less and buying less are both ways reasonable to reduce outflow. Every household needs a pool of money to keep it afloat during hard times when the income stream dries temporarily up. That fund needs to hold enough to pay the bills and keep on the table food for at least six months. Having enough money tucked away to survive for half a year can soften the blow of unemployment because buys precious time for a job search.

66j Understand tense sequence in reported speech.

As pointed out in Chapter 65 (*pp. 858–59*), changing a direct quotation to an indirect quotation often requires changes in many sentence elements. In addition to the changes in word order discussed in Chapter 65, these include changes in tense sequence.

If the verb that introduces the quotation is in the present tense, the tense of the indirect quotation is the same as the tense of the direct quotation.

DIRECT He says, "I believe you."

INDIRECT He says that he believes me.

However, if the introductory verb is in the past, the tense of the indirect quotation shifts in the following ways:

- The simple present becomes the simple past:

  DIRECT He said, "I believe you."

  INDIRECT He said that he believed me.

- The simple past and the present perfect become the past perfect:

  DIRECT She said, "We saw the movie."

  DIRECT She said, "We have seen the movie."

  INDIRECT She said that they had seen the movie.

- The future becomes future-in-the-past:

  DIRECT She said, "We will see the movie tomorrow."

  INDIRECT She said that they would see the movie tomorrow.

- The past perfect remains the same:

  DIRECT They said, "We had hoped the movie would be better."

  INDIRECT They said that they had hoped the movie would be better.

66k Avoid double negation.

In English, negative meaning is expressed either by negating the verb with *not* or by using another negative word like *no, nothing, never,* or *hardly*—but not both. Unlike many languages, standard English does not permit two negatives in one sentence.

► **The students ~~did not have~~ [had] no homework.**

or

► **The students did not have ~~no~~ [any] homework.**

Exercise 66.6 Understanding tense sequence in direct and reported speech

Change direct speech to reported (indirect) speech, and reported speech to direct speech.

EXAMPLE

DIRECT **Roosevelt said to the American people, "The only thing we have to fear is fear itself."**

REPORTED *Roosevelt told the American people that the only thing they had to fear was fear itself.*

1. "Today we will discuss Amy Tan's novel *The Joy Luck Club,*" said the professor.
2. Professor Hampton explained that it had taken Amy Tan several years to complete this novel because of the number of times she revised it.
3. "Although Amy Tan has written several other novels, *The Joy Luck Club* remains the most popular," said the professor.
4. The professor asked if anyone had read any of Tan's other novels, such as *The Kitchen God's Wife* or *Saving Fish from Drowning.*
5. "I'll wait for the movies to come out," one student answered.
6. A student asked if Tan's other novels had themes similar to those in *The Joy Luck Club.*
7. The professor replied that the themes of cross-cultural understanding and misunderstanding were prevalent in Tan's novels.
8. "From the opening pages of the story, have we seen hints of the conflicts to arise between cultures and generations?" asked the professor.

9. A student replied that Lena was a perfect example of someone caught between cultures.
10. "The author uses a lot of flashbacks to show contrast between past and present, China and the United States, old customs and new customs," another student added.

CHECKLIST

Self-Editing for Multilingual Students

As you edit, see if you can detect patterns in your mistakes—that is, recurring errors in sentence structure. This checklist will help you identify the types of errors that can confuse your readers. Check the rules for those items that you have trouble with, and study them in context.

As you edit a sentence, ask yourself these questions:

- ☐ Do the subject and verb agree? (*See Chapters 34: Subject-Verb Agreement and 35: Problems with Verbs, as well as 66g.*)
- ☐ Is the form of the verb or verbs correct? (*See Chapters 34: Subject-Verb Agreement and 35: Problems with Verbs, as well as the coverage of verb phrases in Chapter 64.*)
- ☐ Is the tense of the verb or verbs appropriate and correctly formed? (*See Chapters 34: Subject-Verb Agreement and 35: Problems with Verbs, as well as the coverage of verb phrases in Chapter 64 and tense formation in Chapter 66.*)
- ☐ Do all pronouns agree with their referents, and are the referents unambiguous? (*See Chapter 36: Problems with Pronouns, as well as the coverage of pronouns in Chapters 64 and 66.*)
- ☐ Is the word order correct for the sentence type (for example, declarative or interrogative)? Is the word order of any reported speech correct? (*See Chapter 65.*)
- ☐ Is the sentence complete (not a fragment)? Is the sentence contained (not a run-on or a comma splice)? (*See Chapters 32: Sentence Fragments and 33: Comma Splices and Run-on Sentences.*)
- ☐ Are articles and quantifiers used correctly? (*See Chapter 64.*)

(*continued*)

CHECKLIST *(continued)*

- ☐ Is the sentence active or passive? (*See Chapters 31: Sentence Basics, 35: Problems with Verbs, and 46: Active Verbs.*)
- ☐ Are the words in the sentence well chosen? (*See Chapters 48: Appropriate Language and 49: Exact Language.*)
- ☐ Is the sentence punctuated correctly? (*See the chapters in Part 10: Sentence Punctuation and Part 11: Mechanics and Spelling.*)

This fourteenth-century map features Mansa Musa, the greatest ruler of the Empire of Mali in West Africa. During his reign, Mali prospered as a hub of trade and learning.

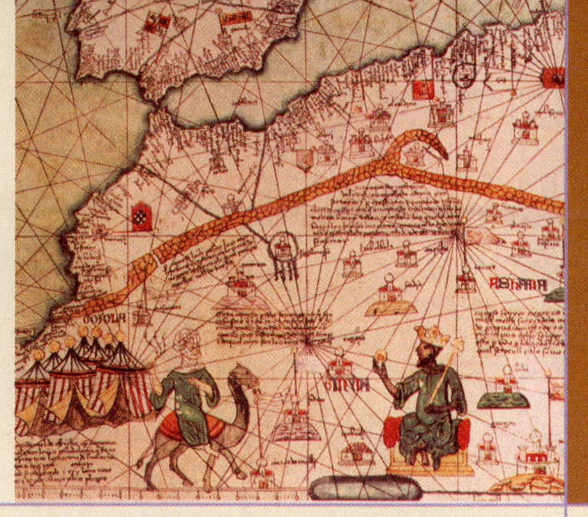

PART 13

The adequate study of culture, our own and those on the opposite side of the globe, can press on to fulfillment only as we learn today from the humanities as well as from the scientists.

—Ruth Benedict

Further Resources for Learning

Timeline of World History

3000

ca. 3000 BCE City of Babylon is founded; cuneiform script, the earliest known fully developed system of writing, emerges in ancient Mesopotamia.

ca. 2660–1640 BCE Old and Middle Kingdoms of Egypt. Pyramids and grand monuments such as the Great Sphinx of Giza are built as royal tributes and burial structures.

2500–2001 BCE Bow and arrow is first used in warfare; cotton is cultivated in Peru.

2000 BCE *Gilgamesh,* ancient Mesopotamian epic, is composed (fullest extant *written* text of this epic dates from **seventh century** BCE): theme is futile human quest for immortality.

2000

ca. 1950 BCE Irrigation systems are in use in Chinese agriculture.

ca. 1850 BCE Oldest surviving Egyptian mathematics text shows that decimal system was in use.

1792–1750 BCE Rule of Babylonian king Hammurabi produces an orderly arrangement of written laws—the Hammurabi Code—among the first in the ancient world.

1200 BCE Olmec culture flourishes in Mexico (until **ca. 400** BCE).

ca. 1000–80 BCE Varna system—precursor of caste system—evolves in India.

1000

776 BCE First recorded Olympic games are held at Olympia in Greece.

ca. 750 BCE *Iliad*—the earliest surviving example of Greek literature—and *Odyssey* are composed (ascribed to Homer).

700

Literary and cultural developments and events

Historical events

Advances in science and technology

Changes in everyday life

Break in timeline

600

ca. 560–480 BCE Life of Buddha (Siddhartha), founder of Buddhism.

551–479 BCE Life of Confucius, China's greatest philosopher.

508 BCE Athens becomes the world's first democracy.

500

ca. 500 BCE Many Old Testament books are transcribed.

ca. 500 BCE Greeks adopt Ptolemaic model of cosmos, in which the sun revolves around the earth.

461–429 BCE Reign of Pericles ushers in flowering of Athenian culture: Aeschylus, *Oresteia* (**458 BCE**); Sophocles, *Antigone* (**ca. 442–441 BCE**) and *Oedipus the King* (**ca. 429 BCE**); Euripides, *Medea* (**431 BCE**); Aristophanes, *Lysistrata* (**411 BCE**); Plato, *Republic* (**ca. 406 BCE**).

399 BCE Greek philosopher Socrates is tried and executed for corruption of youth.

400

404 BCE Golden age of Periclean Athens ends with fall of Athens to Sparta.

387 BCE Greek philosopher Plato founds the Academy.

356–323 BCE Life of Alexander the Great, king of Macedonia, who conquers the Persian Empire.

350 BCE Aristotle, student of Plato, writes *Poetics*, founds rival school, Lyceum; earliest portion of *Mahabharata* (Sanskrit heroic epic) is composed mid-century.

300

ca. 300 BCE Euclid writes *Elements*, seminal work of elementary geometry.

ca. 250 BCE Archimedes, founder of mathematical physics, writes *Measurement of the Circle* (includes concept of π).

ca. 250 BCE *Ramayana* (Sanskrit heroic epic) is composed mid-century.

215 BCE Construction of Great Wall of China begins.

200

ca. 200 BCE–500 CE Roman Empire encompasses the entire Mediterranean region.

100

27–19 BCE Roman poet Virgil composes the epic poem *Aeneid*.

23–13 BCE Roman poet Horace composes *Odes*.

0

8 Ovid composes *Metamorphoses*, a 15-volume poem based on Greek and Roman myths.

30 Jesus is crucified by the Romans in Jerusalem.

ca. 65–85 New Testament Gospels are composed.

300

ca. 300 Large towns exist in inland Niger Delta, later to develop into the Empire of Ghana in west Africa.

400

410 Visigoths sack Rome.

413–26 St. Augustine writes *City of God,* interpreting history in light of Christianity.

478 First Shinto shrine is built in Japan.

500

550–900 Mayan civilization reaches Late Classical phase: art, architecture, and writing flourish at Tikal and dozens of other city-states.

600

622 Mohammed, founder of Islam, flees from Mecca to Medina, transforms Islam into religious and secular empire.

ca. 650–750 *Beowulf,* Old English epic, is composed.

651–5 Koran or Qur'an, the holy book of Islam, is codified.

700

718 Muslims are in control of most of Iberian peninsula; some Muslim influence remains until Christian forces gain control in **1492** with taking of Granada.

900

960–1279 Song Dynasty in China: flowering of arts and scholarship.

1000

ca. 978–1026 Life of Lady Shikibu Murasaki, Japanese author of *Tale of Genjii*, considered by many to be the world's first novel.

1100

1096–1291 The Crusades, nine military expeditions in which European Christians attempted to reconquer the Holy Land (Palestine) from the Muslims, take place.

ca. 1100 *Song of Roland*, French epic poem, is composed.

1200

ca. 1200 Zen Buddhism travels from China to Japan, becomes influential in Japanese politics, painting, landscape, and culture, especially in the tea ceremony.

ca. 1290–1918 Ottoman Empire, Muslim Turkish state comprising Anatolia, modern southeastern Europe, and the Arab Middle East and North Africa, is established.

1300

ca. 1300–1650 Renaissance in Europe: "rebirth" of arts and culture.

1307–21 Dante Alighieri composes *La Divina Commedia,* an epic poem describing his imaginary journey through heaven and hell.

1312–27 Empire of Mali in West Africa reaches its height under Mansa Musa, builder of the Great Mosque at Timbuktu.

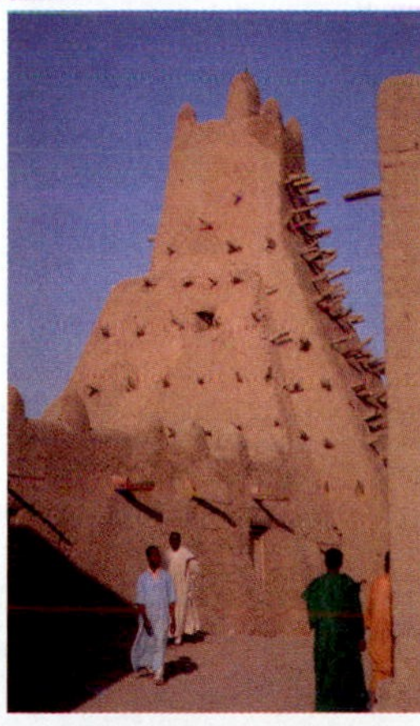

1347–51 "Black Death," an epidemic of the bubonic plague, rages in Europe, eventually claiming 25–50% of the population.

1350

ca. 1350–1400 Great Zimbabwe, a fabled stone city that controlled a large part of southeast Africa in medieval times, reaches its height.

ca. 1370–1400 English poet Chaucer composes *The Canterbury Tales*, a collection of 24 tales with dramatic links.

1400

1431 Joan of Arc, leader of French army against the British in the Hundred Years' War, is burned at the stake for heresy by the British.

ca. 1438–1532 Inca Empire, largest native empire of the Americas, reaches its height in Central and South America; expansion ends with the Spanish invasion led by Pizarro.

1450

1453 Constantinople falls to Ottoman Turks, marking the end of the Byzantine Empire.

ca. 1455 Gutenberg Bible set and printed; Gutenberg's invention of movable type leads to book printing boom in Europe.

1484 Botticelli paints *Birth of Venus* for the Medici family of Florence.

ca. 1492 Christopher Columbus lands in the Bahamas.

1500

1499 Amerigo Vespucci lands in South America.

1503 Leonardo da Vinci, painter, inventor, and scientist, paints *Mona Lisa*.

1508–12 Michelangelo paints the ceiling of the Sistine Chapel in Rome.

1513 Niccolo Machiavelli writes *The Prince*, arguing for pragmatism over virtue in a ruler.

1517 Martin Luther's *95 Theses* introduces the Protestant Reformation in Europe.

1520 Gold, silver, and chocolate are brought from the Americas to Spain.

1532 Sugar cane is cultivated in Brazil.

1593–99 Shakespeare's sonnets are published, followed by *Hamlet* **(1600–1)** and *Othello* **(1604).**

1599 Globe Theater is built in London.

1600

1603 Kabuki is first performed in Japan by female entertainer Okuni.

1605 Miguel de Cervantes Saavedra writes his masterpiece *Don Quixote.*

1608 Galileo Galilei invents astronomical telescope, provides evidence to support Nicolaus Copernicus's theory that the earth and planets revolve around the sun.

1609 Tea is first shipped to Europe from China.

1611 King James Bible is published, becomes most popular version for more than three centuries.

1614 Pocahontas, Native American princess, marries tobacco planter John Rolfe.

1619 African captives are brought to Jamestown, Virginia, to be servants; slave system develops over the next 80 years.

1620 Pilgrims sail for America and found Plymouth Colony.

1625

1631–48 Taj Mahal, premier example of Mogul architecture, is built in Agra, India.

1632 Rembrandt van Rijn, prolific Dutch painter, paints his first major portrait, *The Anatomy Lesson of Dr. Tulp.*

1637 René Descartes, called by some the founder of modern philosophy, writes *Discourse on Method* (from which comes "*Cogito, ergo sum*": "I think; therefore, I am").

1642–1648 English Civil War pits Parliamentary forces under Oliver Cromwell against Charles I: Charles I is defeated and beheaded in **1649.**

1650

1651 Thomas Hobbes writes *Leviathan,* portraying human life in a state of nature as "nasty, brutish, and short" and offering as a remedy a social contract in which the ruler's power—for the sake of expediency—is absolute.

1667 John Milton writes *Paradise Lost,* an epic poem describing man's "first disobedience" and the promise of his redemption.

1675

1687 Isaac Newton publishes *Principia,* in which he codifies laws of motion and gravity not modified until the twentieth century.

ca. 1688–1790 The Enlightenment, an intellectual movement committed to secular views based on reason, takes hold in Europe.

1690 John Locke publishes *Essay Concerning Human Understanding,* in which he espouses an empiricist view of philosophy (limiting true knowledge to what can be perceived through the senses or through introspection).

1700

ca. 1701 Peter the Great begins westernization of Russia.

1740

ca. 1740s Culmination of the Baroque era in music: Vivaldi, *The Four Seasons;* Bach, *Brandenberg Concertos;* Handel, *Messiah.*

Johann Sebastian Bach

1750

1755–73 Samuel Johnson publishes *Dictionary of the English Language.*

1760

1761 Jean-Jacques Rousseau publishes *The Social Contract,* in which he praises the natural goodness of human beings but insists on the need for society to attain true happiness.

1767–87 Sturm und Drang ("Storm and Stress"), a literary and intellectual movement in Germany that prefigures Romanticism (**ca. 1789–1825** in England).

1769 James Watt patents a steam engine.

1770

ca. 1770 Industrial Revolution begins, fueled by steam power: first steam-driven cotton factory (**1789**) and first steam-powered rolling mill open in England (**1790**).

1775–81 American Revolution: hostilities begin at Lexington and Concord, Massachusetts, in 1775, although the Continental Congress will not officially vote for independence until 1776.

1776 "Declaration of Independence" is approved by the Continental Congress on July 4.

Adam Smith publishes *Causes of the Wealth of Nations,* advocates regulation of markets through supply and demand and competition.

1780

1781 Immanuel Kant publishes *Critique of Pure Reason,* an attempt at reconciling empiricism and rationalism, and for many the single most important work of modern philosophy.

1780s–90s Height of the Classical era in music: Mozart writes the opera *Don Giovanni* (**1787**); Haydn establishes the form of the symphony with *The Clock Symphony* (**1794**).

1788 Bread riots occur in France

1789 William Blake's *Songs of Innocence,* followed by *The Marriage of Heaven and Hell* (**1790**) and *Songs of Innocence and Experience* (**1794**), ushers in early Romanticism in England; Olaudah Equiano's *The Interesting Narrative of the Life of Olaudah Equiano, or Gustaus Vassa, the African,* one of the first slave narratives, is published.

1789–99 French Revolution transforms France from a monarchy to a modern state.

1790

1792 Mary Wollstonecraft publishes *A Vindication of the Rights of Woman*, an early work of feminism.

1793 Queen Marie Antoinette and King Louis XVI of France are guillotined.

ca. 1795–1825 English Romantic poetry flourishes with the work of William Wordsworth (**1770–1850**), Lord Byron **(1788–1824)**, Percy Bysshe Shelley **(1792–1822)**, and John Keats (**1795–1821**).

1798 Thomas Malthus's *An Essay on the Principle of Population* stirs interest in birth control and concerns about overpopulation.

1799 Rosetta Stone is found in Egypt, making it possible to decipher hieroglyphics; perfectly preserved mammoth is found in Siberia.

1800

1800 Alessandro Volta produces first battery of zinc and copper plates.

1803 Beethoven composes *Third Symphony (Eroica)*, marking the start of his dramatic middle period.

1804–6 Lewis and Clark expedition from St. Louis to the Pacific fuels westward expansion in the USA.

1804 Napoleon becomes emperor of France.

1807 Hegel publishes *Phenomenology of Spirit,* which introduces the concept of "master-slave" dialectic.

1808 Goethe publishes Part 1 of *Faust,* a drama about a man who sells his soul for knowledge and power.

1810

1812 Noah Webster's *American Dictionary of the English Language* helps standardize spelling of American English.

1813 Jane Austen publishes her novel *Pride and Prejudice*.

1813 Mexico declares independence from Spain, becomes a republic in **1824.**

1815 Napoleon is defeated by British and Prussian forces at Waterloo.

1818 Mary Shelley publishes horror classic *Frankenstein.*

1820

ca. 1821 Cherokee leader Sequoya codifies the Cherokee alphabet.

1823 Monroe Doctrine closes Western Hemisphere to colonial settlements by Europe.

ca. 1825 Katsushika Hokusai, great Japanese printmaker, creates *Mt. Fuji on a Clear Day.*

1830

1830–42 Auguste Comte, founder of philosophical positivism, writes *The Course of Positive Philosophy,* advocates application of scientific method to social problems.

1830 Church of Jesus Christ of Latter-day Saints (Mormons) is founded by Joseph Smith.

1831 Nat Turner leads a group of fellow slaves in the largest slave revolt in North America.

1833 Charles Babbage designs an "analytical engine," prototype of the modern computer.

1836 Samuel Colt puts his revolver into mass production, revolutionizes manufacture of small arms.

1837 Ralph Waldo Emerson, American transcendentalist, delivers "The American Scholar," an address expressing American literary independence.

1837–1901 Queen Victoria reigns in England, Ireland, and India.

1838 Charles Dickens publishes *Oliver Twist,* the first of many novels that sharply criticize abuses brought on by the Industrial Revolution in England.

1839 Daguerreotypes, forerunners of modern photographs, are developed by L. M. Daguerre and J. N. Niepce in France.

1840

1840s Rise of Romantic movement in France, Germany, and Italy.

1841 First university degrees granted to women in USA.

1843 Søren Kierkegaard, Christian existentialist philosopher, publishes *Either/Or.*

1843 Richard Wagner composes *The Flying Dutchman,* an opera expressing his ideal of the *Gesamtkunstwerk* ("total work of art").

1844 Samuel Morse invents the telegraph.

1847 Charlotte Brontë publishes *Jane Eyre*; Emily Brontë publishes *Wuthering Heights;* Anne Brontë publishes *Agnes Grey.*

1848 Seneca Falls Convention for Women's Suffrage is held in USA; Karl Marx and Friedrich Engels write *Communist Manifesto*, a pamphlet exhorting workers to unite against capitalist oppressors.

1850

1855 Walt Whitman publishes first edition of *Leaves of Grass,* creates a new American style for poetry.

1857 French poet Charles Baudelaire publishes *Flowers of Evil,* one of the seminal works of modern poetry.

1859 Charles Darwin publishes *On the Origin of Species*, establishes theories of evolution and natural selection ("survival of the fittest").

ca. 1860 Louis Pasteur invents pasteurization process, advances germ theory of infection, discovers rabies and anthrax vaccines (**1880s**).

1860

1860–65 Emily Dickinson writes most of her poetry; creates a new rhythm and vernacular for American verse.

1861–65 US Civil War pits northern against southern states.

1863 "Emancipation Proclamation" frees all slaves in states rebelling against the federal government.

1865 US President Abraham Lincoln is assassinated.

1865–69 Leo Tolstoy publishes *War and Peace,* an epic of the Napoleonic invasion of Russia.

1867 Universal Exposition in Paris introduces Japanese art to the West.

1867–94 Publication of Karl Marx's *Das Kapital*, a political and economic treatise providing the theoretical basis of socialism.

1868 Overthrow of Tokugawa Shogunate, followed by the Meiji Restoration and establishment of a new government, signals emergence of Japan as a major world power.

1869 US transcontinental railroad is completed.

1870

1874 First exhibition of French Impressionism in Paris is held; notable exponents include Monet, Renoir, Pissarro, Degas, and Cassatt.

1875 Alexander Graham Bell invents the telephone.

1877 Thomas Edison invents the phonograph.

1878 In Boston, Mary Baker Eddy founds Church of Christ, Scientist, a religion emphasizing divine healing.

1879 Thomas Edison invents the light bulb.

1880

1883–85 Friedrich Nietzsche writes *Thus Spake Zarathustra*, which expounds on the concept of *Übermensch* (superman).

1890

1889 Eiffel Tower is built for Paris Exposition.

1893 Fabian Society, a socialist group that includes Irish playwright George Bernard Shaw, is established.

1893 X rays are discovered.

1895 Louis and Auguste Lumière project brief motion pictures on a screen to a paying audience in Paris; based on Thomas Edison's technology, their Cinématographe became the prototype of the movie camera.

ca. 1895 Charles "Buddy" Bolden, New Orleans cornet player and band leader, begins playing improvised music later known as jazz.

1898 Marie and Pierre Curie isolate radium and polonium.

1900

1903 Orville and Wilbur Wright make their debut power-driven flight near Kitty Hawk, North Carolina.

1907 Albert Einstein first publishes equation $E = mc^2$, deduced from his theory of special relativity, ushering in revolution in physics and astronomy.

1907 Pablo Picasso's *Les Demoiselles d'Avignon,* first Cubist painting, ushers in new artistic aesthetic.

1908 Henry Ford introduces the Model T; demand for cars induces the company to introduce assembly-line technique.

1910

1910 International Psychoanalytic Association is founded by Sigmund Freud and others; Freud's theories of the unconscious begin to gain popular recognition.

1913 *The Rite of Spring,* ballet with groundbreaking music by Igor Stravinsky and choreography by Vaslav Nijinsky, is first performed.

1914 Serbian nationalist assassinates heir to the Austro-Hungarian Empire in Sarajevo, sparking World War I.

1914–21 James Joyce writes *Ulysses,* a masterpiece of modernist literature; publication in USA is delayed until **1933** because of obscenity charges.

1915 Margaret Sanger opens the first birth control clinic in USA.

1915 British passenger ship *Lusitania* sunk by German submarine, fueling American sympathy for war efforts of Britain, France, and Russia.

1917 USA enters World War I; Russian Revolution: Bolsheviks led by Vladimir Lenin seize power.

1918 Romanian poet Tristan Tzara writes manifesto for Dada, avant-garde artistic movement established in part in reaction to the senseless slaughter of World War I.

1918 Treaty of Versailles ends World War I; death toll approaches 15 million worldwide; race riots rock major US cities.

1920

1918–19 Influenza epidemic kills 22 million worldwide.

1920 Nineteenth Amendment to the US Constitution grants women suffrage.

ca. 1920 Arnold Schoenberg invents 12-tone system of musical composition.

1922 First fascist government formed by Benito Mussolini in Italy.

1920s Harlem Renaissance: flowering of African American literature and the arts, particularly jazz, centered in New York City.

1924 Joseph Stalin succeeds Lenin as head of Soviet Union.

1927 Martin Heidegger publishes *Being and Time*, a founding work of existentialist philosophy; Martha Graham, pioneer of modern dance, opens a dance studio in New York.

1927 Charles Lindbergh makes first solo, nonstop transatlantic flight; Werner Heisenberg develops Uncertainty Principle, which, together with Theory of Relativity, becomes basis of quantum physics; first successful transmission of an image via "television" occurs.

1929 Virginia Woolf, central to the Bloomsbury literary group, publishes feminist work *A Room of One's Own.*

1930

1930s The Great Depression, precipitated by a stock market crash in **1929,** begins in USA and spreads abroad; in response, President Roosevelt introduces "New Deal" measures based on Keynesian economics.

1931 Incompleteness Theorem is developed by the mathematician and philosopher Kurt Gödel.

1933 Adolf Hitler becomes chancellor of Germany, gradually assumes dictatorial power.

1935 African American Jesse Owens wins four gold medals in track at the Berlin Olympics.

1936–39 Spanish Civil War.

1939 World War II begins shortly after Germany's invasion of Poland; Hitler's Nazis begin program of extermination of "undesirable" elements, including dissidents, homosexuals, Gypsies, and especially Jews; 6 million Jews die in the ensuing Holocaust.

1940

1941 Japan bombs Pearl Harbor, and USA enters World War II.

1943 Jean-Paul Sartre, existentialist philosopher, publishes *Being and Nothingness.*

1945 USA drops atomic bombs on Hiroshima and Nagasaki, Japan—World War II ends; United Nations is formed; Soviet Union occupies Eastern Europe.

1947 India and Pakistan gain independence from Britain.

1948 Mahatma Gandhi, Indian nationalist and spiritual leader, is assassinated; Pakistan-India wars ensue.

1949 Communists seize mainland China; Mao Zedong becomes first chairman of the People's Republic of China.

1949 Simone de Beauvoir publishes *The Second Sex,* a groundbreaking study of women's place in society.

1950

1950–55 Jonas Salk develops polio vaccine.

1950s–70s Height of the "Cold War," in which USA and Soviet Union face off—mutual military buildup and threat of nuclear annihilation create a "balance of power."

1953 J. D. Watson and F. H. C. Crick determine the structure of DNA, launching the modern study of genetics.

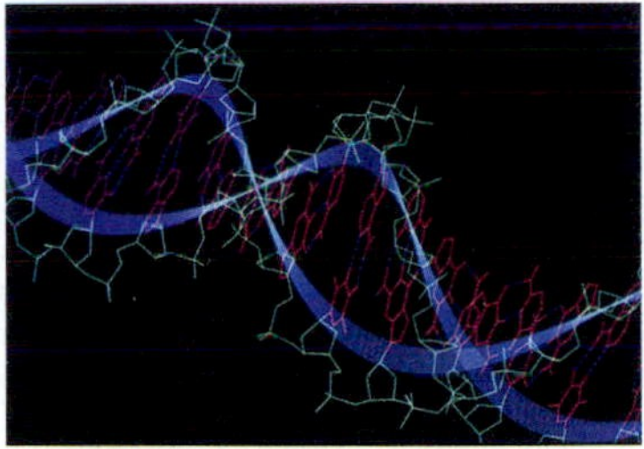

1956 Soviet Union crushes revolt in Hungary.

1959 Cuban Revolution: Fidel Castro overthrows Batista regime.

1960

1961 Berlin Wall erected; USA stages failed "Bay of Pigs" invasion of Cuba.

1962 Cuban missile crisis—Soviet missile-building in Cuba precipitates tense standoff with USA, ultimately resolved through diplomacy; César Chávez organizes the National Farm Workers Association (NFWA).

1963 Martin Luther King, Jr., delivers "I Have a Dream" speech to crowd of 250,000 at the Lincoln Memorial;

US President John F. Kennedy is assassinated in Dallas.

1964 US involvement in Vietnam War escalates with Tonkin Gulf Resolution; Malcolm X is assassinated in New York; Watts riots roil Los Angeles.

1966 Mao Zedong's Cultural Revolution begins, aiming to revitalize communist zeal; Black Panther Party is founded in Oakland, California.

1968 Martin Luther King Jr. is assassinated in Memphis, Tennessee.

1969 American astronaut Neil Armstrong becomes first man to walk on the moon.

1970

1971 East Pakistan (now Bangladesh) declares independence from West Pakistan.

1973 *Gulag Archipelego* by Alexander Solzhenitsyn is published in Paris; it is a massive study of Soviet penal system based on author's firsthand experience.

1974 US President Richard Nixon resigns as a result of the Watergate scandal.

1975 Bill Gates and Paul Allen build and sell their first computer product, creating Microsoft.

1975 Wave of former colonies—Mozambique, Surinam, Papua New Guinea—gain independence.

1975–79 Vaccination programs against smallpox eradicate the disease worldwide.

1979 Islamic revolution in Iran: Shah flees, Khomeini comes to power.

1980

1981 First cases of acquired immune deficiency syndrome (AIDS) in the USA are reported in New York and California.

1982 Benoit Mandelbrot publishes *The Fractal Geometry of Nature,* contributing to chaos theory.

1986 Chernobyl nuclear power plant disaster spreads fallout over Soviet Union and parts of Europe.

1989 Pro-democracy protests in Tiananmen Square, China, are quashed by government crackdown; Berlin Wall is demolished; Eastern Europe is democratized.

1990

1991 Soviet Union is dissolved, making way for looser confederation of republics.

1995 Internet boom hits—number of people online grows exponentially.

2000

2000 Initial sequencing of human genome completed.

2001 Hijacked planes fly into 110-story World Trade Center Towers in New York City and the Pentagon in Washington, D.C.—thousands die; USA invades Afghanistan in "war on terror."

2004 Massive Indian Ocean tsunami devastates coastal communities from Indonesia to Somalia.

2005 Voters in France and Holland reject the proposed constitution for the European Union.

2005 Hurricane Katrina overwhelms US Gulf coast and forces the evacuation of New Orleans.

2006 YouTube.com launches, enabling anyone with an Internet connection to view and post digital video files.

2008 Barack Obama becomes first African American to win US presidency.

Selected Terms from across the Curriculum

Here is a sampling of terms that commonly appear in academic ***discourse.*** *Each of the words printed in bold has its own entry.*

alienation Being estranged from one's society or even from oneself. First used in psychology, the term was adapted by Karl **Marx** (1818–1883) in his writings on the relationship of workers to the products of their labor. In the twentieth century, **existentialist** philosophers used the word to mean an individual's loss of a sense of self, his or her *authenticity,* amid the pressures of modern society. *See also* **Marxism.**

archetype A model after which other things are patterned. The psychoanalyst Carl Jung (1875–1961) used the term to denote a number of universal symbols—such as the Mother or the universal Creator—that inhabit the collective unconscious, the elements of the unconscious that are common to all people.

Aristotelian Relating to the writings of Aristotle (384–322 BCE), Greek philosopher and author of works on logic, ethics, rhetoric, and the natural sciences. Aristotle established a tradition that values **empirical** observation, **deductive reasoning,** and science. This tradition can be contrasted with **Platonic idealism.**

bell curve In statistics and science, a graph in which the greatest number of results are grouped in the middle. If a math test is graded on a bell curve, for instance, most students will receive B's and C's, whereas only a few will receive A's or F's. Plotted on a graph, the curve will evoke the shape of a bell.

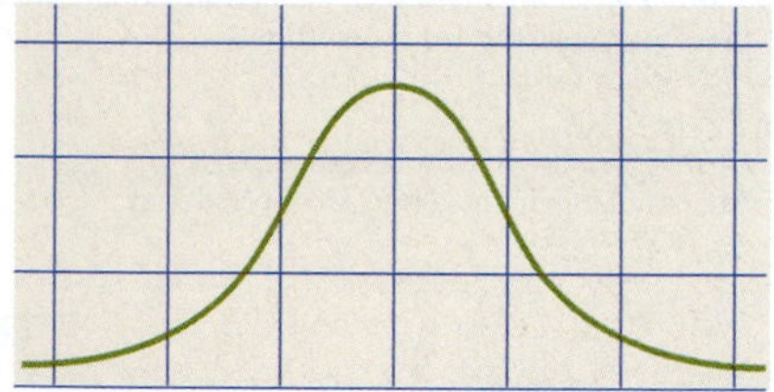

A bell curve.

binary oppositions Paired terms conventionally treated as stable and logical opposites, such as *light/dark* and *man/woman.* Certain **postmodern** trends in philosophy and literary theory, notably **deconstruction,** seek to expose the "artificiality" of these and other **constructs** that shape the way we see the world. *See also* **structuralism.**

black hole From astronomy, a region in space-time where matter is infinitely dense and dimensionless and where the gravitational field is so strong that nothing can escape from it. The term is often used metaphorically to indicate something that is limitless or unresolvable.

Boolean logic (after the English mathematician George Boole, 1815–1864) A specialized algebra developed for the analysis of logical statements, used extensively in the development of the modern computer. A computer performs everything from simple math to Internet searches by means of Boolean logic, which uses **variables** and operators such as AND, OR, NOT, IF, THEN, and EXCEPT.

bourgeois Of or relating to the middle **class.** The term is used in **Marxist** analysis to represent the capitalist class. *Bourgeois* commonly connotes an excessive concern with respectability and material goods.

canon Originally referring to a code of laws established by the church, the canon now typically refers to a collection of books deemed necessary for a complete education. Current debate tends to focus on the exclusion from the canon of works by and about women and people of color. *See also* **multiculturalism.**

capitalism An economic system that emerged during the Industrial Revolution of the nineteenth century and offered private individuals the ownership of industry as well as unregulated market freedom. Today capitalism includes Keynesian economic models that allow government to regulate industry, particularly regarding such concerns as the minimum wage, tariffs, and taxes.

case study An intensive investigation and analysis of a person or group; often the object of study is proposed as the model of a certain phenomenon. Originally used in medicine, the term is now also common in psychology and business.

chaos theory A branch of mathematics used to describe highly complex phenomena such as weather or the flow of blood through the body. Chaos theory starts with the recognition that minute changes in a system can have large and unpredictable results. The *butterfly effect,* for instance, states that the flap of a butterfly's wings in China could theoretically cause a hurricane in New York.

An image generated from the Mandelbrot set, an aspect of chaos theory.

class *See* **Marxism.**

classical Originally used to describe the artistic and literary conventions of ancient Greece and Rome. *Classical* (or *classicism/neoclassicism*) is also used for periods and products in the sciences, social sciences, philosophy, and music marked by straightforwardly rational models that describe the workings of the universe and human society as logical and ultimately harmonious. *See also* **modernism, postmodernism.**

colonialism A policy by which a nation extends and maintains political and military control over a territory, often reducing it to a state of dependence. Begun as a way of acquiring resources such as spices, precious metals, and slaves, later instances of colonialism—such as the US occupation of the Philippines from 1898 to 1946—have served mostly political or strategic purposes. *Postcolonial* refers to a state (or a cultural product or even a state of mind) that reflects former colonial occupation. *See also* **imperialism.**

constant In mathematics, science, and general usage, a factor that does not change. A mathematical or scientific constant is a quantity assumed to have a fixed value within a specific context. In physics, for example, the speed of light in a vacuum is 186,000 miles per second and is denoted by the constant *c*. Thus, in Einstein's famous equation $E = mc^2$, c is a constant and m, standing for any mass, is a **variable.**

construct (*noun*) Something that is shaped by culture ("constructed") but sometimes assumed to be "natural." For example, some might hold that the idea of gender ("maleness" and "femaleness") is a construct rather than the essential or inborn quality that past generations often assumed it to be.

contingent In logic, that which is true only under certain circumstances. In common usage, contingent often connotes that which has happened or can happen only as a result of a long, perhaps improbable sequence of events. Whenever you think, "It could easily have been different," you are feeling a sense of *contingency.*

correlation In statistics, a number that describes the relationship between two **variables.** In a *positive correlation,* the variables increase in tandem—for example, the higher a student's IQ, the better his or her scholastic performance. In a *negative correlation,* one variable increases while the other decreases—for example, the more green tea consumed, the lower the incidence of cancer.

counterculture *See* **culture.**

cross section A sample meant to be representative of a whole population. *See also* **longitudinal.**

culture Knowledge, beliefs, behavior, arts, institutions, and other products of work and thought that characterize a society. Within a dominant culture there may exist many *subcultures:* groups of particular ethnicity, age, education, employment, inclination, or other factors. A *counterculture* is a form of subculture whose values and lifestyle reject those of the dominant culture. *See also* **relativism.**

Darwinism British naturalist Charles Darwin's (1809–1882) theory of the historical evolution of species based on *natural selection,* or "the survival of the fittest." Where insects living within the bark of trees constitute a major food source, for instance, birds with longer, more pointed beaks tend to survive longer and produce more offspring, who then pass on longer, sharper beaks to ensuing generations.

deconstruction A method of literary criticism whose best-known theorist, Jacques Derrida (1930–2004), postulated that texts rest on **binary oppositions** such as *nature/culture, subject/object,* and *spirit/matter* that have been incorrectly assumed to be "true"; in exposing this fallacy, Derrida revealed the illogic of texts thought to be logical and coherent. Although often associated with **postmodernism** and the debate about the **canon,** deconstruction is in a philosophical sense a radical form of skepticism. In more common usage, to *deconstruct* something is to analyze it intensively, exposing it as (perhaps) something unexpected.

deductive reasoning Reasoning to a conclusion based on a previously held principle. *Inductive reasoning,* on the other hand, is the process of deriving a conclusion based on data. **Empiricism** holds that all knowledge is derived from sense experience by induction, whereas *rationalism* claims that knowledge can be deduced from certain *a priori* (presumptive) claims.

demographics (from the Greek *demos,* "people," and *graphia,* "writing") The quantitative study of human populations. A demographic study of a city might include the rate at which its population is growing, the size and distribution of its middle **class,** or the number of its families who have access to the Internet.

determinism In philosophy and science, the doctrine that every event is *determined,* or entirely shaped by earlier events, and that given complete knowledge of prior events and the laws that govern them, all future events can be predicted. Something described as *overdetermined* is thought to be shaped by more than one equally significant cause. Usually contrasted with free will, determinism is a feature of eighteenth- and nineteenth-century **classical** thought. In science, determinism has come to be opposed by the *indeterminism* of **quantum physics.**

dialectic In philosophy, history, and the humanities, the use of logical oppositions as a means of arriving at conclusions about ideas or events. *Dialectical reasoning* is most often associated with the philosophies of Georg Hegel (1770–1831) and Karl **Marx** (1818–1883). According to Hegel, any human idea or *thesis* (for example, the sun circles the earth) naturally gives rise to an opposing idea or *antithesis* (the earth circles the sun), and these ideas resolve into a new idea or *synthesis* (the earth revolves around the sun but in an ellipse). Hegel's famous *master/slave dialectic* describes a seeming paradox: a slave holds power over his master because the master could not hold power without the slave. Marx extended dialectical reasoning in his theory of dialectical **materialism,** which analyzes not opposing ideas but contradictory **class** interests.

discipline A field of study with common research methods, approaches to creating knowledge, and written genres: for example, sociology, chemistry, art history. Sometimes members of multiple disciplines (like ecology and sociology) come together to address a complex issue like global warming.

discourse *Discourse* is most often used in English to denote writing and speech. The term can also refer to habits of expression characteristic of a particular community or to the content of that expression ("The *discourse* of experimental science does not often allow the use of the personal pronoun *I*").

discourse community *See* the Charting the Territory box on p. 689.

ecosystem A principal unit of study in ecology, the science of the relationships between organisms and their environments. All parts of an ecosystem are interdependent, and even small perturbations of one part (such as might be caused by pollution) can have profound effects on all of the other parts—a phenomenon often studied in **chaos theory.**

empiricism (from the Greek *empierikos,* "experienced") A philosophical trend, developed in large part by the philosophers John Locke (1632–1704) and David Hume (1711–1776), that data derived from experience or the senses are the ultimate source of knowledge, as opposed to reason, tradition, or authority. *Empirical* data are data gained through observation or experiment. Especially in medicine and psychology, *empirical* is often contrasted with *theoretical.* In its emphasis on observation and experience, empiricism is a conceptual cousin of **inductive reasoning** and **Aristotelianism.**

Enlightenment An intellectual movement committed to secular views based on reason that established itself in Europe in the eighteenth century (ca. 1688–1790).

epistemology The study of the nature of knowledge, its foundations and limits.

ethos (Greek for "character, a person's nature or disposition") The spirit or code of behavior peculiar to a specific person or group of people—for example, "part of the college student ethos is to stay up late drinking cola and eating Captain Crunch." Ethos is one of the parts of Aristotle's **rhetorical triangle** (**ethos-logos-pathos**): in order to argue effectively, a speaker or writer must communicate a credible **persona** and a coherent perspective.

existentialism A strain in philosophy that emphasizes the isolation of the individual in an indifferent universe and stresses the individual's freedom (and responsibility) to determine his or her own existence. Having roots in the philosophies of Friedrich Nietzsche (1844–1900) and Martin Heidegger (1889–1976), existentialism was extremely influential in France after World War II, where French intellectuals like Jean-Paul Sartre (1905–1980) and Albert Camus (1913–1960) argued that by making conscious choices and taking responsibility for one's acts, one could overcome the otherwise absurd nature of the universe.

fascism (from the Italian *fascio,* "group") A name for the form of government established by Benito Mussolini (1883–1945) in Italy and Adolf Hitler (1889–1945) in Germany. Arising in response to economic and political upheaval in Europe after World War I, both governments centralized authority under a dictator, exerted strong economic controls, suppressed opposition through censorship and terror, and implemented belligerent nationalist and racist policies.

feminism The principle that women should enjoy the same political, economic, social, and cultural rights and opportunities as men. Mary Wollstonecraft's *A Vindication of the Rights of Woman* (1792) was a pioneering feminist work. The *suffrage movement,* which demanded that women be granted the right to vote, emerged following the first women's rights convention in Seneca Falls, New York, in 1848, and had achieved its goal in the United States and Europe by the early twentieth century. The *women's movement* that began in the 1960s initiated a new wave of feminism that focused on rectifying political, economic, social, and cultural inequalities between women and men.

Mussolini and Hitler.

Freudian Relating to the theories of Sigmund Freud (1856–1939), the Viennese neurologist who invented psychoanalysis. A Freudian interpretation focuses on the unconscious emotional dynamics that are played out in a particular situation; in the study of literature, a Freudian interpretation focuses on such dynamics as they are represented in the **text.** Freud identified three areas of personality. The ego is the conscious self; the id embodies desire and instincts; and the superego represents internalized social rules and curbs the id and ego. *See also* **repression** and **unconscious.**

game theory (also sometimes called *decision theory*) A mathematical method for analyzing situations of conflict or competition so as to determine a winning strategy. Game theory is useful not only in *true games* such as poker but also in business management, economics, and military strategy. *See also* **zero sum game.**

geometric progression A sequence of numbers determined by multiplying or dividing each number in succession by a **constant.** For example, *1, 4, 16, 64, 256* is a geometric progression with a constant multiplier, or coefficient, of 4. *Arithmetic progressions* proceed more slowly by adding or subtracting a constant: for example, *1, 4, 7, 10, 13* is an arithmetic progression with a constant *addend* of 3.

globalization The process by which communication and transportation technologies have made the world seem smaller and more interconnected. In economics, *globalization* refers to the way these advances have made national borders far less relevant in determining markets. The *antiglobalization* movement aims to protect workers from exploitation by multinational corporations, to prevent job loss among domestic workers, and to counter cultural homogenization. The presence of a McDonald's in Beijing is a good example of the effects of globalization.

hegemony Generally, the dominance of one nation or state over its neighbors. The Italian Marxist Antonio Gramsci (1891–1937) and his followers often used the term to refer to the dominance of the capitalists over the working class. *Hegemony* is now also used to describe a theory that has dominance in a particular field of study: "Dualism has long exercised hegemony in Western thought."

humanism (also *secular humanism*) A movement traditionally associated with Renaissance philosophers who deemphasized the role of religion or God in society while celebrating the achievements of human beings. There are *humanistic* branches of psychology, theology, and other disciplines that move the role of the human individual to the forefront of their studies.

hypothesis A statement that can be shown to be true or false either experimentally (in science) or through the use of logic (in other disciplines). For example, a simple hypothesis that light is necessary for the survival of a certain plant could be proved or disproved by trying to grow the plant in a dark closet.

icon In **semiotics,** a sign that looks like what it refers to. A picture of the globe used to signify the earth or a line drawing of a suitcase indicating where to go to get your luggage at an airport are icons. Historically, an icon was a small picture of a religious figure, usually Jesus or the Virgin Mary.

idealism In philosophy and psychology, the notion that the mind determines ultimate reality, an idea that can be traced to **Plato** (428–347 BCE).

ideology A set of beliefs about the world (and often how it can be changed) espoused by an individual, group, or organization; a systematized worldview. **Capitalism,** for example, is an ideology. In the work of the Marxist critic Louis Althusser (1918–1990), an *ideology* is that which allows the individual to find his or her place and sense of self-worth within a given society.

imperialism One country's imposition of political and economic rule upon other countries. The British annexation of several countries in Africa in the nineteenth century is an example of this brand of imperialism. Today the term has been broadened to include the exportation of dominant cultural products and values. For example, some people in Europe and other parts of the world see the influx of American films into their markets as a form of *cultural imperialism. See also* **colonialism.**

inductive reasoning *See* **deductive reasoning.**

laissez-faire (French for "allow to act") Generally, noninterference in the affairs or conduct of others. In economic and political theory, the idea that governments should not intervene in markets. The concept is based on the **classical** economic theory developed by Adam Smith (1723–1790) and others, which argues that an "invisible hand"—supply and demand, and competition—is sufficient to guide economic markets.

logos (Greek for "word") In Aristotle's **rhetorical triangle,** the topic of the argument or argument itself.

longitudinal A study in which the same group of subjects is examined over a long period of time. A *longitudinal study* could, for example, be conducted to test the rate of obesity over time among a certain group of schoolchildren.

Marxism The economic and political doctrine put forth by Karl Marx (1818–1883) and Friedrich Engels (1820–1895). It centers on the **class** struggle between the proletariat (the working class) and the **bourgeoisie** (capitalists, those who own the *means of production*). (*Class* refers to social and/or economic standing in society. Marx saw class as economically based, although many have argued that family, cultural background, and education affect it.) Marxism predicts that the working class will wrest the means of production from the bourgeoisie and cede them to the state, which will distribute goods equitably.

materialism In philosophy, the belief that physical matter is all that exists and that so-called higher phenomena—for example, thought, feeling, mind, will—are wholly dependent on and **determined** by physical processes. Since the **Enlightenment,** almost all scientists have been materialists. In history and economics, the dialectical materialism of Karl **Marx** (1818–1883) held that **cultural** phenomena are determined wholly by economic conditions.

mean (also *average*) The sum of a set of numbers divided by the number of terms in the set. For example, the mean of the set (1, 2, 3) is 2 because its sum (6) divided by the number of terms (3) equals 2.

median The middle term in an ordered set of numbers. For example, the median of the ordered set (2, 6, 10, 12, 15) is 10 because there are two numbers (2 and 6) below 10 and two (12 and 15) above 10.

meta- A prefix often used to suggest "moving beyond," "going up a level," or "transcending." Thus, *metaphysics* is the branch of philosophy that deals with questions that cannot be resolved by physical observation, such as whether God exists.

modernism Often used in opposition to classicism or neoclassicism when denoting periods in the sciences, social sciences, philosophy, and music, *modernism* as a trend in thought represents a break with the certainties of the past, among them a confidence that everything can be known. *Modern* science has been characterized by highly counterintuitive theories such as **relativity**—according to which there is no absolute way to measure time—and **quantum physics**—according to which you can know the speed or the position of a subatomic particle but never both. In literature, the **stream of consciousness** and/or *free association* style of *modernist* writers like Virginia Woolf (1882–1941) and James Joyce (1882–1941) broke decisively with the storytelling conventions of the late-nineteenth-century, or Victorian, novel. Thus, some critics believe that **postmodernism** is really only the development of a trend begun in the modernist era.

Virginia Woolf.

multiculturalism The view that many cultures, not just the dominant one, should be given attention in the classroom and in broader society. The debate on multiculturalism is related to the debate on the **canon.**

nature-nurture controversy A debate about whether genetic (*nature*) or environmental (*nurture*) factors have the upper hand in determining human behavior. Experimental studies involving fraternal and identical twins raised together and apart have been undertaken to investigate the issue, but fundamental questions about method and the small **samples** involved have left the question unresolved. This debate pervades countless topics studied in the social sciences, among them questions of gender difference, intelligence, poverty, crime, and childhood development.

object/subject In philosophy and psychology, the *subject* does the observing or experiencing, while the *object* is that which is observed or experienced. Throughout history, this philosophical dualism has been studied, refined, and debated extensively. In **Freudian** and post-Freudian psychology, an *object* is an external person or thing that gratifies an infant and is therefore loved.

objective Pertaining to that which is independent of perception or observation, as opposed to *subjective,* which pertains to that which is determined by perception or observation. The old philosophical puzzle—If a tree falls in the woods, and no one is there to hear it, does it make a sound?—plays upon the notions of philosophical *objectivity* and *subjectivity.*

Oedipus complex The psychological notion expounded by Sigmund **Freud** (1856–1939) that describes the unconscious sexual longing of a son for his mother and his unconscious wish to kill his father, his rival for possession of the mother. The name is a reference to Sophocles' play *Oedipus Rex.* Freud also wrote of the *Electra* complex, which describes the similar sexual longing of a daughter for her father.

ontology Generally, the study of being and human consciousness.

paradigm A theoretical framework that serves as a foundation for a field of study or branch of knowledge. Darwinian evolution, Newtonian physics, and Aristotle's chemistry are all examples of scientific paradigms. *Paradigm shifts* designate the transition from one paradigm to another, usually with a profoundly transformative effect. For example, the shift from Newtonian physics to quantum physics might be termed a *paradigm shift.*

pathos (Greek for "suffering, experience, emotion") In Aristotle's **rhetorical triangle,** the feelings evoked in the audience by an argument.

persona (Latin for "mask") An assumed or public identity (as distinct from the *inner self*); a character adopted for a particular purpose; in literature, the voice or character of the speaker.

Platonic Following the teachings of the Greek philosopher Plato (428–347 BCE), Platonic **idealism** is a system that attempts to show a rational relationship between the individual, the state, and the universe, governed by what is good, true, and beautiful. Only a reflection of the truth can be perceived, and the gap between the ideal and its reflection motivates human consciousness. It can be contrasted with the **Aristotelian** tradition, which values empirical observation and scientific reasoning. In common usage, a *platonic relationship* is a close friendship that does not have a sexual component.

pluralism In everyday language, a condition of society in which multiple religions, ethnicities, and subcultures coexist peacefully. *Pluralism* can also refer to any philosophical system that proposes that reality is made up of a number of distinct entities. The pragmatist William James (1842–1910) and the analytic philosopher Bertrand Russell (1872–1970) were prominent *pluralist* thinkers.

postcolonial *See* **colonialism.**

postmodernism A cultural trend that seeks to expose the artificiality of the **constructs** that defined earlier periods of cultural production while confessing—indeed, in some cases even boasting of—an inability to replace them with an authentic substitute. One of the hallmarks of *postmodern* cultural products is *pastiche,* or *collage,* a form that borrows from other trends and emphasizes the disjuncture between disparate elements. *See also* **modernism.**

praxis Often used as a substitute for *practice* in ordinary usage, and opposed to **theory.** In the work of Antonio Gramsci (1891–1937), the "philosophy of praxis" outlined the refinements to Marxism that were necessary to make it relevant in the twentieth century.

qualitative research: Research that focuses on observing what people say and do. Qualitative research methods include observation, interviews, surveys, and focus groups. In contrast, quantitative research measures numerical data. **Quantitative research** methods include counting, measuring, statistically analyzing, and reporting the results of research.

quantitative research: *See* **qualitative research.**

quantum physics A theoretical branch of physics that deals with the behavior of atoms and subatomic particles. The work of such pioneers as Max Planck (1858–1947), Niels Bohr (1885–1962), and later Werner Heisenberg (1901–1976) has had a profound impact on the way we understand such things as the relationships between matter and energy. *See also* **relativity.**

relativism The belief that the meaning and value of all things are determined by their *context*—their relationship to other things in that time and place—rather than that things have inherent or absolute meaning or worth. *Moral relativism* is the idea that different people, groups, nations, or cultures have differing ideas about what constitutes good and evil and that those differences must be respected. *Cultural relativism* is the position that there is no absolute point of view from which one set of cultural values or beliefs can be deemed intrinsically superior to any other. *See also* **culture, humanism.**

relativity In physics, the theory expounded by Albert Einstein (1879–1955), which states that all motion is relative and that energy and matter are convertible. The famous formulation $E = mc^2$ equates energy (E) with matter (m) multiplied by the speed of light (c) squared. Einstein's work directly challenged two cornerstones of **classical** physics—that motion is an absolute and that energy and matter are two completely different entities.

Albert Einstein.

repression In **Freudian** psychology, the process that keeps unacceptable desires, fears, and other troubling material (such as memories of traumatic experiences) from reaching (or returning to) consciousness. *See also* **unconscious.**

rhetoric In classical times, the art of public speaking. Currently, the term more broadly encompasses *language* or *speech,* often in a derogatory context (as in "The mayor's speech was so much empty *rhetoric*"), as well as the study of writing and the effective use of language.

rhetorical triangle Aristotle's description of the context of argument, consisting of **ethos** (roughly, the character of the speaker), **logos** (the topic of the argument or the argument itself), and **pathos** (the feelings evoked in the audience).

sample A subset or selection of a group from a population. In a *random sample,* each subject is chosen in ways that replicate pure chance, and all members of the population have an equal chance of being selected for the sample.

scientific method A process involving observations of phenomena and the conducting of experiments to test ideas suggested by those observations. The development of the scientific method, a specialized form of trial and error, ushered in the scientific revolution of the seventeenth century. Francis Bacon (1561–1626), René Descartes (1596–1650), and especially Galileo Galilei (1564–1642) are most often credited with developing its constituent procedures: (1) choosing a question or problem (for example, what causes yellow fever); (2) developing a **hypothesis** (the disease is caused by a bacteria or virus transmitted by mosquitoes); (3) conducting observations and experiments (noting **correlations** between mosquito populations and incidence of yellow fever); (4) examining and interpreting the data (high correlations exist between incidence of yellow fever and that of the *A. aegypti* mosquito); (5) affirming, revising, or rejecting the hypothesis; and (6) deriving further experiments and hypotheses from it (microscopically examining the bodies of *A. aegypti* and yellow fever victims to try to find a virus or bacteria present in both).

secular Not having to do with religion or the church; deriving its authority from nonreligious sources. *See also* **humanism.**

semiotics The theory and study of signs and symbols. According to semiotics, meaning is never inherent but is always a product of social conventions, and **culture** can be analyzed as a series of sign systems. *See also* **structuralism.**

skepticism The belief that nothing can be held true until grounds are established for believing it to be true. René Descartes (1596–1650), one of the founders of modern philosophy, expressed this attitude in his famous statement *"Cogito, ergo sum"* ("I think; therefore, I am").

Socratic method Repeated questioning to arrive at implicit truths, a teaching method used by the Greek philosopher Socrates (470?–399? BCE), who influenced **Plato.**

solipsism Philosophical theory that the self is the only thing that can be known and verified and therefore is the only reality.

standard deviation A measure of the degree to which data diverge from the **mean.** A high standard deviation means a greater range of results. Thus, in a **bell curve,** a tall, skinny curve represents a smaller standard deviation than does a wide, flat one.

statistical significance A value assigned to a research result as a measure of how likely it is that the result reflects mere chance. The higher the statistical significance, the less likely it is that chance determined the outcome. The results of studies employing large numbers of subjects typically have a higher statistical significance than do those from studies of a small number of subjects.

stream of consciousness A **modernist** literary technique in which the writer renders the moment-by-moment progress of a character's or narrator's thoughts. Among those writers who have used the technique are James Joyce (1882–1941) in *Ulysses,* Virginia Woolf (1882–1941) in *Mrs Dalloway,* and Marcel Proust (1871–1922) in *Remembrance of Things Past.*

structuralism An analytical method, today often subsumed under **semiotics**, that is used in the social sciences, the humanities, and the arts to examine underlying deep structures in a **text** by close investigation of its constituent parts (often termed *signs*). For example, in *narratology* (the study of narratives), myths, folktales, novels, paintings, and even comic books are reduced to their essential structures, from which are derived the rules that govern the different ways in which these narratives tell their stories. In *structural* approaches, the individual works under study are commonly considered less important than the universal structures that underlie them. This tendency has opened the approach to charges of anti-**humanism.** Michel Foucault (1926–1984) and other *poststructuralists* have challenged structuralists' belief in the possibility of revealing essential structures of knowledge and reality through this type of study. *See also* **semiotics, deconstruction.**

subculture *See* **culture.**

subjective *See* **objective.**

sublime Inspiring awe; impressive; moving; of high spiritual or intellectual worth. Michelangelo's painting on the ceiling of the Sistine Chapel is often cited as an example of the *sublime* in art; in nature, mountains such as Kilimanjaro have been described as *sublime.*

The ceiling of the Sistine Chapel.

symbiosis In biology, a prolonged association and interdependence of two or more organisms, usually to their mutual benefit. *Parasitism* occurs when one organism benefits at the expense of another. In general usage, *symbiotic* is used metaphorically to denote a mutual dependency and benefit between people, organisms, or ideas.

taxonomy Any set of laws and principles of classification. Originating in biology, taxonomy includes the theory and principles governing the classification of organisms into categories such as species and phyla. Today

Glossary of Key Terms

This glossary defines key terms used in this handbook to discuss learning, writing, researching, and editing. It includes all the terms that appear in the book in bold type. The references in parentheses that follow the term indicate the chapters or chapter sections in which the terms are discussed.

absolute phrase (31h) A phrase made up of a noun or pronoun and a participle that modifies an entire sentence: *Their heads hanging, the boys walked off the field.*

abstract and concrete (30b; 49c) An **abstract** word names qualities and concepts that do not have physical properties, such as *idea* or *beauty.* A **concrete** word names things that can be perceived with the senses, such as *chocolate* or *jacket.*

abstract noun (30b) See *noun.*

acronym (58a) An abbreviation composed of the initials of an organization and sometimes pronounceable as if it were a word, such as *NASA* (National Aeronautics and Space Administration) or *OSHA* (Occupational Safety and Health Administration).

active voice (31c.3; 35l; 41d, 46b) The form of a transitive verb in which the subject of the sentence is doing the acting. See *voice.*

adjective (30d; 37) A word that modifies a noun or pronoun with information specifying, for example, which one, what kind, or how many: *a delicious orange.*

adjective clause (or relative clause) (31i.1; 51e) A dependent clause that begins with a relative pronoun or adverb (such as *who, whom, whose, which, that, where*) and modifies a noun or pronoun (see *adjective*): *The house that I grew up in eventually sold for a million dollars.*

adjective phrase (51e) A phrase that begins with a preposition or verbal and modifies a noun or pronoun: *The game lasting 21 innings was by far the longest of the season.*

adverb (30e; 37) A word that modifies a verb, an adjective, or another adverb with information specifying, for example, when, where, how, how often, how much, to what degree, or why: *She was terribly unhappy.*

adverb clause (31i.2; 51e) A dependent clause, usually introduced by a subordinating word (such as *after, because,* or *when*), that modifies a verb, an adjective, or another adverb (see *adverb*): *After he lost the tennis match, Rodrigo went straight to the gym.*

agreement (34, 36) The appropriate pairing in number, person, and gender of one word to another. See *pronoun-antecedent agreement* and *subject-verb agreement.*

analogy (4d.6) A comparison that points out the similarities between two often very different things, such as a heart and a pump or an eye and a camera. A well-structured analogy can make something unfamiliar seem familiar and provide insight into difficult concepts.

analysis (7d) An aspect of critical reading that involves examining a work in detail, in particular by breaking it down into significant parts and examining how those parts relate to each other.

annotation (7d.1) The process of taking notes on the who, what, how, and why of a work while reading or examining it carefully.

antecedent (30c; 34i; 36k) The noun that a pronoun replaces. In the sentence *Katya, who was at the concert, saw her picture in the paper,* the antecedent of the pronouns *who* and *her* is *Katya.*

APA documentation style (24) The documentation style developed by the American Psychological Association and used in many of the behavioral and social sciences.

application letter (29c) A letter to a potential employer that usually accompanies an applicant's résumé and highlights the information on the résumé that demonstrates the applicant's suitability for the job he or she is seeking.

appositive (31g; 36e; 51e) A noun or noun phrase that appears next to a noun or pronoun and renames it: *My friend Max, the best dancer on campus, is a chemistry major.*

archive (19b) A cataloged collection of documents, manuscripts, or other materials, possibly including receipts, wills, photographs, sound recordings, and other kinds of media.

argument (2d; 10) An attempt to persuade others to accept a point of view or a position on a contentious issue through logic and the marshalling of evidence.

articles (30d; 64a) The words *a, an,* and *the. A* and *an* are *indefinite articles; the* is a *definite article.*

audience (2f) The intended readership for a piece of writing.

auxiliary verb (30a; 35f) See *helping verb.*

balanced sentence (42) A sentence that presents two clauses in parallel grammatical form: *Spare the rod and spoil the child.*

bias (10b.2) In argument, a sometimes unstated positive or negative inclination that affects and limits a writer's objectivity.

blog (1b.3, 14a, 14f, 16i) A Web site that can be continually updated, usually featuring time-stamped entries and a forum for readers to post comments.

body (3c) In writing, the middle section where the main idea is developed in a series of paragraphs, each making a point that is supported by specific details.

Boolean operators (16d) Terms used in search engines for refining keyword searches.

brainstorming (3a.3) A technique for developing ideas about a topic.

browser (14e) Software that allows users to view material on the Internet.

call number (16g) A number based on a classification system for shelving books in libraries. Books on the same topic have similar call numbers and are shelved together.

case (30c.4; 36a–f) The form of a noun or pronoun that determines the grammatical role it plays in a sentence. See *pronoun case.*

chartjunk (5h) Distracting visual details in a chart or graph.

chat room (3a.9, 16i) An online site, usually devoted to a specific topic, in which people can engage in real-time discussions.

Chicago documentation style (25) A style of documentation recommended by the *Chicago Manual of Style* and used in the humanities.

chronological organization (4c.1) In writing, the arrangement of information about events according to the sequence in which the events occurred.

citation (21a; 22c; 23; 24; 25; 26) The identification and acknowledgment of the source of information or ideas presented in a paper.

claim (10b.2) An assertion about a topic. In an argument paper, claims should be backed by reasons and evidence. See *Toulmin method.*

classical structure (10c.5) A traditional way to structure an argument (used in ancient Greece). It includes the following components: thesis, support, response to counterarguments, and conclusion (summary of argument and appeal to reader).

classification (4d.3) In writing, a method of organizing information by grouping it into categories.

clause (31d; 51e) A group of related words containing a subject and a predicate. An *independent (main) clause* can stand on its own as a sentence: *We can have a picnic.* A *dependent (subordinate) clause* cannot stand on its own as a sentence: *We can have a picnic if it doesn't rain.*

cliché (49f) An overworked expression or figure of speech.

clipping (58a) The use of a shortened form of a word, usually informally, such as *exam* for *examination.*

clustering or mapping (3a.4) A brainstorming technique for discovering connections among ideas by writing a topic in the center of a page and then clustering related topics and subtopics around the central term as they come to mind.

cognate (66a) A word in English that is similar to a word in another language and has a similar origin.

coherence (5g.3) The quality of a piece of writing that links ideas from sentence to sentence and from paragraph to paragraph clearly and logically.

collaborative learning (5a.1) A process in which classmates work together to review and make constructive suggestions on one another's work.

collaborative writing (2i) Writing coauthored by two or more people.

collective noun (30b.5; 34e) See *noun.*

colloquial (48b) Language that is appropriate to informal conversation but not precise enough for academic writing.

comma splice (33a) An error in which two independent clauses are joined by a comma without a coordinating conjunction.

common noun (30b.1) See *noun.*

comparative degree (37g) See *comparison.*

comparison (37g) The form of an adjective or adverb that indicates its degree or amount. The *positive degree* is the simple form and involves no comparison: *large, difficult* (adjectives); *far, confidently* (adverbs). The *comparative degree* compares two things: *larger, more difficult; farther, more/less confidently.* The *superlative degree* compares three or more things, indicating which is the greatest or the least: *largest, most difficult; farthest, most/least confidently.*

comparison and contrast (4d.9) In writing, an organizational strategy that involves pointing out similarities and differences among items. See *subject-by-subject* and *point-by-point comparison.*

complement (31c) A word or group of words that follow a linking verb to explain or define the subject of a sentence. See *subject complement* and *object complement.*

complete predicate (31c) See *predicate.*

complete subject (31b) See *subject.*

complete verb (32a; 35f) A main verb and any helping verbs needed to indicate tense, person, and number.

complex sentence (31j) See *sentence.*

compound predicate (31c.2; 32c.7) Two or more predicates connected by a conjunction.

compound sentence (31j) See *sentence.*

compound-complex sentence (31j) See *sentence.*

compound structures (36c) Words or phrases joined by *and, or,* or *nor.*

compound subject (31b.2; 34d) See *subject.*

concise (38) Of writing, employing as few words as needed to be clear and engaging.

conclusion (3c) The closing section of a paper. A good conclusion gives readers a sense of completion and often offers a final comment on the thesis.

concrete (30b; 49c) See *abstract and concrete.*

concrete noun (30b) See *noun.*

conjunction (30g) A word that joins words, phrases, or clauses and indicates their relation to each other. *Coordinating conjunctions* (such as *and, but, or, nor, for, so, yet*) join words or ideas of equal weight or function: *The night grew colder, but the boys and girls kept trick-or-treating. Correlative conjunctions* (such as *both . . . and, neither . . . nor, not only . . . but also*) link sentence elements of equal value, always in pairs: *She knew that either her mother or her father would drive her to the airport. Subordinating conjunctions* (such as *after, although, as if, because, if, when*) introduce dependent or subordinate clauses, linking sentence elements that are not of equal importance: *They waltzed while the band played on.*

conjunctive adverb (30e) A word or expression such as *for example, however,* or *therefore* that indicates the relation between two clauses. Unlike conjunctions, conjunctive adverbs are not grammatically strong enough on their own to hold the two clauses together, requiring the clauses to be separated by a period or semicolon: *The night grew colder; however, the boys and girls kept trick-or-treating.*

connotation (49) The secondary, or implicit, meaning of a word that derives from the feelings and images it evokes.

contraction (61b) A shortened word formed when two words are combined and letters are replaced with an apostrophe: *doesn't* for *does not.*

coordinate adjectives (51c) Two or more adjectives that act individually to modify a noun or pronoun: *Her speech was brief, clear, and engaging.*

coordinating conjunction or **coordinator** (30g.1; 42c) See *conjunction.*

coordination (44a–b) In a sentence, the joining of elements of equal weight. See also *subordination.*

copyright (20a) The legal right to control the reproduction of any original work—a piece of writing, a musical composition, a play, a movie, a computer program, a photograph, or a work of art.

correlative conjunction (30g.2) See *conjunction.*

count noun (30b.2) See *noun.*

counterargument (10c.4) In an argument paper, a substantiated claim that does not support the writer's position.

critical response paper (7e) A paper that synthesizes the writer's response to another work. A critical response paper typically begins with a summary of the work followed by a thesis that encapsulates the writer's response to the work and then an elaboration on the thesis.

critical reading (7) A process for systematically and thoughtfully approaching a text to understand its literal and implicit meaning and arrive at a judgment about it. The process typically involves previewing the text, reading and analyzing it, and synthesizing and evaluating it.

CSE documentation style (26) A style of documentation developed by the Council of Science Editors and used in the sciences.

cumulative adjectives (51c) Adjectives that act as a set and should not be separated by a comma. The first adjective modifies the following adjective or adjectives as well as the noun or pronoun: *world-famous American sculptor.*

cumulative sentence (45c) A sentence that begins with a subject and verb and then accumulates information in a series of descriptive modifiers: *The reporters ran after the film star, calling out questions and shoving each other aside.*

dangling modifier (43f) A modifier that confusingly implies an actor different from the sentence's subject: *Being so valuable, thousands of people flooded into California during the gold rush.*

database (16e.2) A collection of information available either in print or electronically.

deductive reasoning (10b.1; p. FR-20) A method of reasoning based on claims structured such that if the premises are true, the conclusion must be true: *All humans are mortal, and Socrates is a human, so Socrates must be mortal.*

definite article (64a) See *articles.*

definition (4d.5) In writing, an organizational strategy based on the explanation of concepts a reader must understand to grasp the ideas that follow.

degree (37g) See *comparison.*

demonstrative pronoun (30c.5) A pronoun such as *this, that, these,* and *those* that points out nouns and pronouns that come later: *This is the house that Jack built.*

denotation (49) The primary, or dictionary, definition of a word.

dependent or **subordinate clause** (31i) See *clause.*

description (4d.3) In writing, an organizational strategy based on the presentation of vivid details describing sight, sound, taste, smell, or touch.

descriptive adjective (30d) An adjective that names a quality or attribute of a noun or pronoun: *beautiful sunset.*

determiner (30d) A word that precedes and labels a *noun.* Determiners include *articles* (*a, the*), *quantifiers* (*one, some*), and possessives (*my, their*).

dialect (48a) A variant of a language that is used by a particular social, geographical, or ethnic group.

diction (49) Word choice.

direct address (51g) A construction that includes a word or phrase that names the person or group being spoken to: *Are you coming, Vinny?*

direct object (31c.3) See *object.*

direct question (41e) A sentence that asks a question and concludes with a question mark. Contrast with *indirect question.*

direct quotation (21c.5; 41e; 54a) The reproduction of the exact words someone else has spoken or written. In academic writing, direct quotations are enclosed in quotation marks or, if long, set off in a separate block of text.

discipline (1a.1) A specialized branch of academic study or area of inquiry.

discourse community (48a) A group of people who share certain interests, knowledge, and customary ways of communicating.

discussion list or **electronic mailing list** (16i) A group of people interested in a particular topic linked in networked e-mail conversation. A list can be open (anyone can join) or closed (only certain people can join).

division (4d.4) A form of classification that involves breaking a subject into its parts. See *classification.*

documentation (22c; 23–26) The acknowledgment in full citations in a paper of the source of any words or ideas that come from others.

document design (6) The arrangement of text and visuals in a paper or other document. The goal of good document design is to showcase the work effectively for its purpose and audience.

do/say plan (3c.2) An informal but detailed outline that lays out what the writer will introduce, support, and conclude.

doublespeak (48d) The deceitful use of language to obscure facts and mislead readers.

drafting (4) A stage of the writing process that involves developing and honing a paper through a series of versions.

editing (5) A stage of the writing process in which writers polish sentences and paragraphs for correctness, clarity, and effectiveness.

electronic portfolio (6d) See *portfolio.*

elliptical clause (31i.4; 38c) A clause in which one or more grammatically necessary words is omitted because their meaning and function are clear from the surrounding context: *I like New York more than [I like] Los Angeles.*

empty phrase (38b) A phrase that provides little or no information: *The fact is, the planets revolve around the sun.*

ethos (10b.3, 10c.6; p. FR-21) See *logos, ethos, pathos.*

euphemism (48d) An innocuous word or phrase that substitutes for a harsh, blunt, or offensive alternative: *pass away* for *die.*

evaluation (15a) A judgment about a set of facts or a situation.

evidence (10b.1) The facts, statistics, anecdotes, and expert opinions writers use to support their claims.

excessive coordination (44c) The use of coordination to string together too many ideas at once.

excessive subordination (44e) The use of subordination to string together too many subordinate expressions at once.

exclamatory sentence (31a) A sentence that expresses strong emotion and ends with an exclamation point.

exigence (2b) The occasion or situation that requires a written response.

expletive construction (38d) The use of *there, here,* or *it* in the subject position of a sentence, followed by a form of *be: Here are the directions.* The subject follows the verb.

extract or **block quotation** (54d) A long direct quotation that is not enclosed by quotation marks but is set off from the text.

fact (15a) Objective information that can be measured, observed, or independently verified.

fair use (20a) The provision of copyright law that permits the reproduction, in some circumstances, of limited portions of a copyrighted work for news reporting or for scholarly or educational purposes.

fallacies (10b.4) Mistakes in logic or reasoning.

faulty coordination (44c) The use of coordination to join sentence elements that aren't logically equivalent, or to join elements with an inappropriate coordinating word.

faulty parallelism (42a) An error that results when items in a series, paired ideas, or items in a list do not have the same grammatical form.

faulty predication (40b) An illogical, ungrammatical combination of subject and predicate.

field research (19c) Research that involves eliciting information through direct observations, interviews, or surveys.

figurative language or **figure of speech** (49e) An imaginative expression, usually a comparison, that amplifies the literal meaning of other words. See also *hyperbole, irony,* *metaphor, personification, simile,* and *understatement.*

focused freewriting See *freewriting.*

fonts (6c.2) The variations available in size and form (bold and italic, for example) of a particular typeface. See *typeface.*

formal outline (3c.2) An outline that classifies and divides the information a writer has gathered by organizing main points, supporting ideas, and specific details into separate levels of subordination.

fragment (32) See *sentence fragment.*

freewriting (3a.2) A method for developing ideas by writing down whatever comes to mind about a topic. Ideas that emerge from freewriting can become the subject of further exploration in *focused freewriting,* or freewriting that begins with a point or a specific question.

function word (42d) A word, such as an article, a preposition, or a conjunction, that indicates the relationship among other words in a sentence: *I called the company for days but never got through.*

funnel opener (4f) An introduction that begins with broad assertions and then narrows in focus to conclude with a statement of the writer's thesis.

fused sentence (33a) See *run-on sentence.*

gender (36j–m; 64b) The classification of nouns and pronouns as masculine (*he, father*), feminine (*she, mother*), or neuter (*it, painter*).

generalization A broad statement without details.

general word (49c) A word that names a broad category of things, such as *trees* or *students.*

generic noun (36m; 64a) A noun used to represent anyone and everyone in a group: *the average voter; the modern university.*

genre (2e) A category of writing. In literary writing, for example, genres include story, play, and poem; in nonfiction writing, genres include letter, essay, review, and report.

gerund (31f) The present participle (*-ing*) form of a verb used as a noun: *Most college courses require writing.* See *verbal.*

gerund phrase (31f.2; 34j) A word group consisting of a gerund followed by objects, complements, or modifiers: *Walking to the mailbox was my grandmother's only exercise.*

GIF (14e) See *JPEG.*

grammar (30) A description of the rules and conventions for combining the elements of a language into meaningful sentences.

grounds (10b.2) In argument, the reasons and evidence presented in support of a claim. See *Toulmin method.*

help sheets (16a) In libraries, documents that provide information about the location of both general and discipline-specific resources, both in print and online.

helping or **auxiliary verb** (30a; 35f) Verbs that combine with main verbs to indicate a variety of meanings, including tense, mood, voice, and manner. Helping verbs include forms of *be, have,* and *do* and the modal verbs *can, could, may, might, shall, should,* and *will.* See *modal verb.*

hit (16f) In online keyword searches, a link yielded by a search.

homonyms (63b) Words that sound alike but have different meanings and different spellings, such as *bear* and *bare.*

HTML/XML (14e) Hypertext markup language and extensible markup language used to code text so that it appears as a formatted Web page in a browser.

hyperbole (49e) Deliberate exaggeration. See *figurative language.*

hypertext essay (14c) A multimedia essay with embedded links that take readers to other files, including text, image, audio, and video files.

hypothesis (15d.4; p. FR-22) A proposed explanation for a particular set of observations or provisional answer to a research question that is subject to testing and revision during the course of research.

idiom (1c.2; 49d; 66f) An expression whose meaning is established by custom and cannot be determined from the dictionary definition of the words that compose it: *Boston Red Sox fans were in seventh heaven when their team finally won the World Series in 2004.*

image interpretation (14b) A paper that combines an image with the writer's interpretation of that image.

imperative mood (41d) Of verbs, the mood that expresses commands, directions, and entreaties: *Please don't leave.* See *mood.*

imperative sentence (31a) A sentence in the imperative mood.

indefinite article (64a) See *articles.*

indefinite pronoun (30c.7; 34f; 36m) A pronoun such as *someone, anybody, nothing,* and *few* that does not refer to a specific person or item.

independent clause (31d) See *clause.*

index (16e.2) A catalog of articles published in periodicals; an alphabetical list, usually appearing at the end of a book, that lists the topics covered in the book and the pages on which those topics are discussed.

indicative mood (35k; 41d) Of verbs, the most common mood, used to make statements (*We are going to the beach*) or ask questions (*Do you want to come along?*). See *mood.*

indirect object (31c.3; 65a) See *object.*

indirect question (41e) A sentence that reports a question and ends with a period: *My mother often wonders if I'll ever settle down.* Contrast with *direct question.*

indirect quotation (41e; 54a) A sentence that reports, as opposed to repeating verbatim, what someone else has said or written. Indirect quotations are not enclosed in quotation marks.

inductive reasoning (10b.1; p. FR-22) A method of reasoning that involves deriving a general conclusion from specific facts. When using inductive reasoning, a writer presents evidence (facts and statistics, anecdotes, and expert opinion) to convince reasonable people that the writer's argument is probably true.

infinitive (31f) A verbal consisting of the base form of a verb preceded by *to: to run, to eat.* See *verbal.*

infinitive phrase (31f.3) An infinitive, plus any subject, objects, or modifiers, that functions as an adverb, adjective, or noun: *When I was a child, I longed to be a famous soprano.*

informative report (2d; 8a) Writing that passes on what the writer has learned about a subject.

instant messaging (IM) (16i) An online medium for real-time communication.

intellectual property (20a) A work under copyright or some other legal protection, such as patent or trademark.

intensive pronoun (30c) A pronoun ending with the suffix *-self* or *-selves* that adds emphasis to the noun or pronoun it follows. It is grammatically optional: *I myself couldn't care less.*

interjection (30h) A forceful expression, usually written with an exclamation point: *Hey! Beat it!*

interpret (7d) To explain the meaning of something.

interpretation (15a) The determination of implications and meanings, for example, in a painting, a short story, or a political speech.

interpretive analysis (2d; 9) A kind of writing that explores the meaning of documents, cultural artifacts, social situations, and natural events.

interrogative pronoun (30c.6) A pronoun (*who, whose, whom, which, what, whatever*) used to ask questions.

interrogative sentence (31a) A sentence that poses a direct question.

in-text citation or **parenthetical citation** (23–26) Source information placed in parentheses in the body of a paper.

intransitive verb (31c.3; 35c) A verb that describes an action or a state of being and does not take a direct object: *The tree fell.*

introduction (3c) A paragraph or series of paragraphs that begins an essay.

invention techniques (3a) Prewriting strategies for exploring ideas about a topic.

inversion (45d) In sentences, a reversal of standard word order, as when the verb comes before the subject: *Up jumped the cheerleaders.*

irony The use of words to imply the opposite of their literal meaning: *Aren't you cheerful this morning!* (to a grumpy roommate). See *figurative language.*

irregular verb (35a) A verb that forms the past tense and past participle other than by adding *-ed.*

jargon (48c) One group's specialized, technical language used in an inappropriate context; that is, used with people outside the group or when it does not suit a writer's purpose.

journal (3a) A place to record one's thoughts in writing.

JPEG and GIF (14e) File formats for digitally coding photographs and other visuals that are recognized by Web browsers.

keyword (16b.1) A term entered into an online search engine to find sources—books, journal articles, Web sites—of needed information.

keyword search (16d) An online search conducted by entering keywords into a search engine.

limiting modifier (43c) A word such as *only, even, almost, really,* and *just* that qualifies the meaning of another word or word group.

limiting sentence (4c.2) A statement that seems to oppose a paper's main idea, allowing the writer to bring in a different perspective.

link (14c) A connection from one electronic file to another, or from one place to another in the same file.

linking verb (31c.3; 34h; 35f; 37f) A verb that joins a subject to its subject complement. Forms of *be* are the most common linking verbs: *They are happy.* Others include *look, appear, feel, become, smell, sound,* and *taste: The cloth feels soft.*

logos, ethos, pathos (10b.3, 10c.6; pp. FR-21–22, and FR-24) Greek words for the qualities of *thought, character,* and *feeling* that the writer of an argument paper conveys to the audience he or she is attempting to persuade.

main verb (30a) The part of a verb phrase that carries the principal meaning.

mechanics (57–62) Conventions regarding the use of capital letters, italics, abbreviations, numbers, and hyphens.

metaphor (49e) An implied comparison between two unlike things: *Your harsh words stung my pride.* See *figurative language.* Compare to *simile.*

misplaced modifier (43a) A modifier placed confusingly far from the expression it modifies, that ambiguously modifies more than one expression, or that awkwardly disrupts the relationships among the grammatical elements of a sentence.

mixed construction (40) A sentence with parts that do not fit together logically or grammatically.

mixed metaphor (49e) A confusing combination of two or more incompatible or incongruous metaphoric comparisons: *His fortune burned a hole in his pocket and trickled away.*

MLA documentation style (23) The documentation style developed by the Modern Language Association and used in the arts and humanities, especially in literature and languages.

modal verb (30a.3) A helping verb that signifies the manner, or mode, of an action: *You should get ready for your guests.*

modifier (37; 43) A word or group of words functioning as an adjective or adverb to describe or limit another word or group of words.

mood (35k) The form of a verb that reveals the speaker or writer's attitude toward the action of a sentence. The *indicative mood* is used to state or question facts, acts, and opinions: *The wedding is this weekend. Did you get your suit pressed?* The *imperative mood* is used for commands, directions, and entreaties: *Take your dirty dishes to the kitchen.* The *subjunctive mood* is used to express a wish or a demand or to make a statement contrary to fact: *If I were rich, I would travel the world by boat.*

multimedia writing (14) Writing that combines words with images, video, or audio into a single composition.

narration (4d.2) In writing, a strategy for developing a paragraph or essay based on the retelling of events, usually in chronological order.

navigation bar (14e.5) A grouping of links on a Web page that makes it easy to move to other pages and back again.

netiquette (1b.3) A new word, formed from a combination of *Internet* and *etiquette,* that refers to good manners in cyberspace.

networked classroom (1b.3) A classroom in which each student works at one of a group of linked computers.

noncount noun (30b.2; 64a) See *noun.*

nonrestrictive element (51e) A nonessential element that adds information to a sentence but is not required for understanding its basic meaning.

noun (30b) A word that names a person, place, thing, or idea: *David, Yosemite, baseball, democracy.* **Common nouns** name a general class and are not capitalized: *teenager, dorm, street.* **Proper nouns** name specific people, places, or things and are capitalized: *Shakespeare, London, Globe Theater.* **Count nouns** name specific items that can be counted: *muscle, movie, bridge.* **Noncount nouns** name nonspecific things that cannot be counted: *advice, air, time.* **Concrete nouns** name things that can be perceived by the senses: *wind, song, man.* **Abstract nouns** name qualities and concepts that do not have physical properties: *love, courage, hope.* **Collective nouns** are singular in form but name groups of people or things: *crew, family, audience.*

noun clause (31i.3) A dependent clause that functions as a noun: *They told me where to meet them.*

noun phrase (31e) A noun plus all of its modifiers.

number (30a.1) The form of a verb, noun, or pronoun that indicates whether it is singular or plural.

object (31c) A noun or pronoun that receives or is influenced by the action reported by a transitive verb, a preposition, or a verbal. A **direct object** receives the action of a transitive verb or verbal and usually follows it in a sentence: *Tom and I watched the sunrise together.* An **indirect object** names for or to whom something is done: *Tom promised me a pancake breakfast afterward.* The **object of a preposition** usually follows a preposition and completes its meaning: *We drove into town together.*

object complement (31c.3) A word or group of words that follows an object in a sentence and describes or renames it: *I call my cousin Mr. Big.*

object of a preposition (30f) See *object.*

objective case (36) See *pronoun case.*

objective stance (8b.3) The fair presentation of differing views without indicating a preference for one view or the other. Contrast with *subjective stance.*

paragraph (4b) A set of sentences that work together to develop an idea or example.

parallel construction (47d) See *parallelism.*

parallelism (42) The presentation of equal ideas in the same grammatical form: individual terms with individual terms, phrases with phrases, and clauses with clauses. The use of parallelism results in **parallel constructions.**

paraphrase (21c.3) The restatement of source material in different words and in a different form from the original, and usually more succinctly and in less detail.

parenthetical citation or reference (23–26) See *in-text citation.*

participial phrase (31f.1) A word group that consists of a participle and any objects or modifiers and functions as an adjective: *Jumping the fence, the dog ran down the street.*

participle (31f; 35a) The *-ing* (present participle) or *-ed* (past participle) form of a verb. (In regular verbs, the past tense and the past participle are the same.) Participles are used with helping verbs in verb phrases (*They are walking slowly.*) and as verbals (*Walking is good exercise.*). See *verb phrase* and *verbal.*

parts of speech (30) The eight primary categories to which all English words belong: verbs, nouns, pronouns, adjectives, adverbs, prepositions, conjunctions, and interjections.

passive voice (31c.3; 35l; 41d) The form of a transitive verb in which the subject of the sentence is acted upon. See *voice.*

pathos (10b.6; pp. FR-21, FR-22, and FR-24) See *logos, ethos, pathos.*

peer review (1b.4; 5a.1) A structured process in which students respond to each other's work at different stages in the writing process.

perfect tenses (35g.3) See *tense.*

periodic sentence (45c) A sentence in which the key word, phrase, or idea appears at the end: *Despite a massive investment, the assembling of a stellar cast, and months of marketing hype, the movie flopped.*

periodical (16e.1) A regularly published newspaper, magazine, or scholarly journal.

person (30a.1; 34) The form of a verb or pronoun that indicates whether the subject of a sentence is speaking or writing (*first person*), is spoken or written to (*second person*), or is spoken or written about (*third person*).

personal pronoun (30c.1; 36) A pronoun that stands for a specific person or thing. The personal pronouns are *I, me, you, he, his, she, her, it, we, us, they,* and *them.*

personification (49e) The attribution of human qualities to objects, animals, or abstract ideas. See *figurative language.*

phrasal verb (49d, 66e) A verb that combines with a preposition to make its meaning complete and often has an idiomatic meaning that changes when the preposition changes: *look out, dig into.*

phrase (31d) A group of related words that lacks either a subject or a predicate or both and cannot stand alone as an independent sentence. Phrases function within sentences as nouns, verbs, and modifiers.

plagiarism (20; 21) The use of someone else's words, ideas, or other original work without acknowledging its source. Plagiarism is, in effect, the theft of someone else's intellectual property.

planning (3) The early stage of writing, when a writer generates ideas, develops a thesis, plans a structure, and considers the use of visuals.

plural (30b.3) Referring to more than one. See *number.*

podcast (1b.3, 16i, 21b.4) Digital audio and video content distributed periodically via online syndication (see *RSS feed*) for playback. Subscribers receive automatic downloads to be played on a computer or personal media player.

point-by-point comparison (4d.6) The comparison of two items one feature at a time. A point-by-point comparison of two photographs might first discuss the subject of each, then the composition of each, then the use of color, and so forth. See *subject-by-subject comparison.*

portfolio (6) A collection of one's writing for presentation to others, such as potential employers. An **electronic portfolio** is a portfolio in electronic form and can include video, audio, and image files as well as text files.

positive degree (37g) See *comparison.*

possessive case (30b.6; 36) See *pronoun case.*

possessive noun (30b.6) A noun that indicates possession or ownership: *Jesse's, America's.*

possessive pronoun (30c.2) A pronoun that indicates ownership: *mine, ours.*

predicate (31c; 40b) In a sentence, the verb and its objects, complements, or modifiers. The predicate reports or declares (*predicates*) something about the subject. The verb itself, including any helping verbs, constitutes the **simple predicate.** The simple predicate together with its objects, complements, and modifiers constitutes the **complete predicate.**

prefix (47e) One or more letters that attach to the beginning of a word and change its meaning, such as <u>non</u>issue, <u>un</u>happy, and <u>extra</u>ordinary.

premise (10b.1) A statement or assertion that supports an argument's conclusion.

preposition (30f) A word that precedes a noun, pronoun, or noun phrase (the *object of the preposition*) and allows the resulting **prepositional phrase** to modify another word or word group in the sentence.

prepositional phrase (30f) A preposition and its object: *We went home <u>after completing our exams</u>.*

present tense (35a) See *tense.*

presentation software (14d) An electronic replacement for the traditional kinds of visual aids speakers have used to accompany oral presentations. Software like Microsoft's PowerPoint makes it possible to incorporate audio, video, and animation as well as text and still visuals into a presentation.

pretentious or stilted language (48b) Language that is overly formal or full of fancy phrases, making it inappropriate for academic writing.

previewing (7b) Scanning a text for basic information about its author, title, and contents in preparation for further critical examination.

prewriting activities (3a) See *invention techniques.*

primary research (15a; 19) Research that involves working in a laboratory, in the field, or with an archive of raw data, original documents, or authentic artifacts to make firsthand discoveries.

primary source (7b) A firsthand (primary) account of an event or research. Examples of primary sources include letters, contemporary newspaper accounts of events, a researcher's lab notes, and historical data like that found in census records.

progressive tense (35g.4) See *tense.*

pronoun (30c; 36) A word that takes the place of a noun.

pronoun-antecedent agreement (36) The appropriate pairing in number, person, and gender of a pronoun to its antecedent: *Judi loved her tiny apartment.*

pronoun case (36) The form of a pronoun that reflects its function in a sentence. Most pronouns have three cases: **subjective** (*I, she*), **objective** (*me, her*), and **possessive** (*my, hers*).

pronoun reference (36) The nature of the relationship—clear or ambiguous—between a pronoun and the word it replaces.

proofreading (5i) The process of checking the final draft of a piece of writing to make sure it is free of mistakes.

proper adjective (30d) An adjective formed from a proper noun, such as *Britain/British.*

proper noun (30b.1; 57a) See *noun.*

purpose (2c) A writer's goal: for example, to inform, to interpret, or to argue.

quantifier (64a) Words that tell how much or how many: *a few, some, many.*

questionnaire (19c.3) A series of questions structured to elicit information from respondents in a survey.

quotation (21c; 21e; 41e; 54a–e, h–i) A restatement, either directly (verbatim) or indirectly of what someone has said or written. See *direct quotation* and *indirect quotation.*

reciprocal pronouns (30c.8) Pronouns such as *each other* or *one another* that refer to the separate parts of a plural antecedent: *They helped one another escape from the flooded city.*

redundancy (38c) Unnecessary repetition.

reflexive pronoun (30c.3) A pronoun ending in *-self* or *-selves* that refers back to the sentence subject: *They asked themselves if they were doing the right thing.* Reflexive pronouns, unlike intensive pronouns, are grammatically necessary. See *intensive pronoun.*

regionalism (48a) An expression common to the people in a particular region.

regular verb (35a) A verb that forms its past tense and past participle by adding *-d* or *-ed* to the base form.

relative clause (31i.1; 51e) See *adjective clause.*

relative pronoun (30c.4) A pronoun such as *who, whom, which,* or *that* used to relate a relative (adjective) clause to an antecedent noun or pronoun: *The woman who came in second is a friend of ours.*

research journal or **research log** (21c.2) A tool for keeping track of your research.

research project (15b) A project that involves conducting research, evaluating the results of the research, and writing a paper in which sources are accurately cited and documented.

restrictive element (51n) A word, phrase, or clause with essential information about the noun or pronoun it describes. Restrictive elements are not set off by commas: *The house that Jack built is sturdy.*

résumé (29b) A brief summary of one's education and work experience.

review of the literature (8d) An informative report on the current state of knowledge in a specific area.

revising (5) A stage of the writing process in which the writer reviews the whole paper and its parts, adding, deleting, moving, and editing text as necessary.

rhetoric (p. FR-25) The study of the effective use of language as determined by a writer's or speaker's audience and purpose.

rhetorical question (45d) A question asked for effect, with no expectation of an answer.

Rogerian argument (10c.7) A style of argument, developed by Carl Rogers, that emphasizes the search for common ground with one's audience.

Rogerian structure (10c.6) A way of structuring an argument. It includes an emphasis on values shared with opponents, the sympathetic presentation of opposing positions, and a potential compromise. (See *Rogerian argument.*)

RSS feed (16i) *RSS* stands for "Really Simple Syndication." A real-time stream of content from a frequently updated Web site, delivered via *feed-reader software*.

run-on sentence or fused sentence (33a) An error in which two independent clauses are joined together without punctuation or a connecting word.

scientific method (10b.1) The method by which scientists gather data from experiments, surveys, and observations to formulate and test hypotheses.

scratch outline (3c.2) A simple list of points, without the levels of subordination found in more complex outlines.

search engine (16c) Software that searches for information on the Internet or online databases.

secondary research (15a; 19) Research that involves investigating what other people have learned and written about a field or topic. Contrast with *primary research.*

secondary source (7b) A source with information derived from the study of primary sources (or other secondary sources). Textbooks and encyclopedia articles are examples of secondary sources. Contrast with *primary source.*

sentence (31j) A subject and predicate not introduced by a subordinating word that fit together to make a statement, ask a question, give a command, or express an emotion. A **simple sentence** is composed of only one independent clause: *I am studying.* A **compound sentence** contains two or more coordinated independent clauses: *I would like to go to the movies, but I am studying.* A **complex sentence** contains one independent clause and one or more dependent clauses: *If you try to make me go to the movies, I'll be really annoyed.* A **compound-complex sentence** contains two or more coordinated independent clauses and at least one dependent clause: *I'm staying home to study because I'm failing the course, but I'd much rather go to a movie.*

sentence fragment (32) An incomplete sentence that is treated as if it were complete, with a capital letter at the beginning and a closing punctuation mark.

sentence outline (3c.2) A formal outline in which each topic and subtopic is stated in a full sentence.

sequence of tenses (35g) The choice of verb tenses within the clauses and phrases of a sentence to reflect the logical relationship in time among the actions each expresses.

server (14e) A computer that links other computers in a network.

sexist language (48e) Language that demeans or stereotypes women or men based on their sex.

signal phrase (21e.1) A phrase that indicates who is being quoted. *In his memoir, my grandfather wrote, "My father was the first to leave Romania."*

simile (49e) A comparison, using *like* or *as,* of two unlike things: *His eyes were like saucers.* See *figurative language.*

simple predicate (31c.1) See *predicate.*

simple sentence (31j) See *sentence.*

simple subject (31b) See *subject.*

simple tense (35e) See *tense.*

singular (30b.4) Referring to one. See *number.*

slang (48a) An informal and playful type of language used within a social group or discourse community and generally not appropriate for academic writing.

social-networking site (1b.3, 16i) Web site that allows users to build profiles, connect with one another, and form communities.

spatial organization (4c.1) The arrangement of details about a subject in a paragraph according to the way they appear to the viewer: from top to bottom, outside to inside, east to west, and so on.

specific word (49c) A word that names a particular kind of thing or item, such as *pines* or *college senior.*

split infinitive (43e) One or more words interposed between the two words of an infinitive: *The team hoped to immediately rebound from its defeat.*

squinting modifier (43c) A modifier misplaced such that it is not clear whether it describes what precedes it or what follows it. It should be repositioned for clarity.

standard English (48) The form of English characteristic of most academic discourse and expected in most academic writing.

stereotype (48e) A simplified image or generalization about the members of a racial, ethnic, or social group.

storyboard (14d) A comic strip–like sketch that outlines major changes of action in a film or video scene sequence.

subject (31b) The words that name the topic of a sentence, which the predicate makes a statement about. The **simple subject** is the pronoun or noun that identifies the topic of a sentence: *The dog was in the yard.* The **complete subject** includes the simple subject and its modifiers: *The big black dog was in the yard.* A **compound subject** contains two or more subjects connected by a conjunction: *The dog and cat faced each other across the fence.*

subject-by-subject comparison (4d.6) The comparison of two items as a whole, beginning with a description of the relevant features of one, followed by a discussion of the features of the other. See *point-by-point comparison.*

subject complement (30d; 31c.3; 34h; 36d; 37f; 40a) A word or word group that follows a linking verb and renames or specifies the sentence's subject. It can be a noun or an adjective.

subject directory (16f) In an Internet search, a hierarchical listing of subject categories, beginning with broad categories and branching to increasingly specific subcategories. Subject directories provide an alternative to keyword searches.

subject-verb agreement (34) The appropriate pairing, in number and person, of a subject and a verb: *The student looks confused; The students look confused.*

subjective case (36) See *pronoun case.*

subjective stance (8b.3) The presentation of an issue from a personal point of view or reflecting personal preference. Contrast with *objective stance.*

subjunctive mood (35k) Of verbs, the mood used to express a wish or a request or to state a condition contrary to fact: *I wish I were home.* See *mood.*

subordinating conjunction or **subordinator** (30g.3) See *conjunction.*

subordination (44a; 44d) In a sentence, the joining of a secondary (subordinate) element to the main element in a way that shows the logical relationship between the two: *Although we shopped for hours, we didn't find a dress for the party.*

suffix (47e) One or more letters that attach to the end of a word and change its meaning or grammatical role, such as *walker*, *kindness*, and *fortunately.*

summary (7d.2; 21c.4) A brief synthesis, in a writer's own words and form, of the main points of a source written by someone else.

superlative degree (37g) See *comparison.*

survey (19c.3) A research tool common in the social sciences in which subjects are asked to respond to a questionnaire.

synchronous communication (16i) Real-time online exchanges between individuals. See *chat room, instant messaging.*

synonyms (49b) Words with similar meanings, such as *scowl* and *frown.*

syntax (30) The rules for forming grammatical sentences in a language.

synthesize (7e) To bring together and make connections between things. Synthesis is an important element in critical thinking, reading, and writing.

tag sentence (51g) A sentence with a phrase or question attached at the end. *It's hot today, isn't it?*

template (14d.3) In presentation software, a predesigned slide format, usually provided with the software.

tense (35g) The form of a verb that indicates its time of action, whether present, past, or future. There are three **simple tenses:** present (*I laugh*), past (*I laughed*), and future (*I will laugh*). The **perfect tenses** indicate actions that were or will be completed by the time of another action or time: *I have spoken* (present perfect); *I had spoken* (past perfect), *I will have spoken* (future perfect). The **progressive forms** of the simple and perfect tenses indicate ongoing action: *I am laughing* (present progressive), *I was laughing* (past progressive), *I will be laughing* (future progressive), *I have been laughing* (present perfect progressive), *I had been laughing* (past perfect progressive), *I will have been laughing* (future perfect progressive).

thesis (3b) A paper's central idea.

thesis statement (3b) The statement that asserts a paper's central idea.

tone (2g) The writer's voice, communicated through content, style, and word choice.

topic (2c) The subject of a paper.

topic outline (3c.2) A formal outline in which each topic and subtopic is stated in words and phrases.

topic sentence (4b.2) The sentence that announces a paragraph's main idea.

Toulmin method (10b.2) A method of analyzing arguments based on **claims** (assertions about a topic), **grounds** (reasons and evidence), and **warrants** (assumptions that link the grounds to the claims).

transition (5f.3) The connection of one idea to another in writing.

transitional expression (5f.3) A word or phrase that links one idea to another.

transitional sentence (5f.3) A sentence that refers to the previous paragraph and at the same time moves an essay on to the next point.

transitive verb (31c.3; 35c) A verb that takes a direct object. *He bought a new bike last week.*

tree diagram (3c.2) A method of planning a paper's organization by showing the relationship between topics and subtopics (but not the sequence of topics) in a branching structure.

typeface (6c.2) A design established by printers for the letters in the alphabet, numbers, punctuation marks, and special characters.

understatement (49e) An exaggeratedly restrained comparison. See *figurative language.*

URL (14e) (uniform resource locator) A Web address.

Usenet news group (16i) An Internet news group in which messages are posted to a computer that hosts the group and distributes the postings to subscribers.

unity (5f) The clear relationship between the main idea of a paragraph and the evidence that supports it.

verb (30a) A word that reports an action, condition, or state of being. Verbs change form to indicate person, number, tense, voice, and mood.

verb phrase (30a; 31e) A main verb plus its helping verbs: *Louie is helping with the party preparations.*

verbal (31f; 35j; 64c) A word formed from a verb that functions as a noun, an adjective, or an adverb, not as a verb.

verbal phrase (31f) A verbal plus an object, complement, or modifier.

virtual classroom (1b.3) A class conducted entirely online so that students can participate wherever they are.

virtual world (1b, 3b, 16i) A Web-based simulated world in which users interact.

voice (31c.3; 35l; 46) The form of a verb used to indicate whether the subject of a sentence does the acting or is acted upon. In the **active voice,** the subject acts: *The crowd sang "Take Me Out to the Ballgame."* In the **passive voice,** the subject is acted upon: *"Take Me Out to the Ballgame" was sung by the crowd.*

warrant (10b.2) An unstated assumption that underlies an argument's claim and the grounds that support it. See *Toulmin method.*

Weblog (1b.3, 14a, 14f, 16i) See *blog.*

Web page (14a) A page on the World Wide Web.

Web site (14a) A site on the Web usually consisting of written work, links, and graphics.

white space (6c.1) The area of a document that does not contain type or graphics.

wiki (1b.3, 14a, 14f, 16i) Internet sites designed to allow participants to comment on and modify one another's work.

working bibliography (21a) A preliminary list of books, articles, pamphlets, Web sites, and other sources that seem likely to help answer a research question.

writing process (2a) The activities writers engage in as they undertake and complete a writing project. These activities include understanding the assignment, generating ideas, drafting, revising, and designing and producing the finished work.

writing situation (2b) The characteristics of a particular writing project, including its genre, topic, purpose, audience, tone, length, due date, and format.

Credits

Text Credits

p. 6: Adapted from Robert S. Feldman, *P.O.W.E.R. Learning: Strategies for Success in College and Life*, 2nd ed. Copyright © The McGraw-Hill Companies, Inc. Reprinted with permission; **p. 8:** Bottom graph: Copyright © 1998 from *Misused Statistics*, 2nd and Revised Edition by Herbert F. Spirer, Louise Spirer and Abram J. Jaffe. Reprinted by permission of Taylor and Francis Group, LLC, a division of Informa plc, and the author; **p. 18:** Definition of "pig out" and "academic" from *Random House Webster's English Learner's Dictionary*. Copyright © 1999, 2007 by Random House, Inc. Used by permission of Random House Reference and Information Publishing, a division of Random House, Inc.; **p. 24:** Sebastian Salgado/Amazonas/Contact Press Images. Reprinted by permission of Contact Press Images and Terra. Microsoft® Internet Explorer screen shot reprinted with permission from Microsoft Corporation; **p. 29:** From Dana Payne, *Keeper at Woodland Park Zoo*. Reprinted by permission of Dana Payne; **p. 40:** From Google.com. Microsoft® Internet Explorer screen shot reprinted with permission from Microsoft Corporation; **p. 41:** From Google.com. Microsoft® Internet Explorer screen shot reprinted with permission from Microsoft Corporation; **p. 52:** Gary Klass, "Presenting Data" http://lilt.ilstu.edu/gmklass. Reprinted by permission of Gary Klass; **p. 53:** From Clarke & Cornish, "Modeling Offenders' Decisions," in *Crime and Justice*, volume 6, Tonry & Morris, eds., 1985, p. 169. Copyright © 1985 University of Chicago Press. Used by permission of the publisher, University of Chicago Press; **p. 57:** Fast, J. D. From "After Columbine: How People Mourn Sudden Death." *Social Work*, Vol. 48, No. 4, 2003, **p. 485.** Copyright 2003, National Association of Social Workers, Inc., Social Work. Reprinted with permission from the National Association of Social Workers. All printed material is copyrighted; **p. 57:** Keys, David. "Rethinking the Picts," *Archaeology*, Vol. 57, Number 5, 2004. Copyright © 2004 by The Archaeological Institute of America. Reprinted with permission; **p. 58:** Suiter, J. Jill, Rebecca Powers, and Rachel Brown. From "Avenues to Prestige Among Adolescents." *Adolescence*, Summer 2004. Reprinted by permission; **pp. 58–59:** Chapell, Mark, et al. From "Bullying in College by Students and Teachers." *Adolescence*, Spring 2004. Reprinted by permission; **p. 59:** Guorong, Yang. From "Transforming Knowledge Into Wisdom." *Philosophy East and West*, Volume 52, Number 4, October 2002, pp. 441–458. © 2002 by University of Hawaii Press. Reprinted with permission; **p. 60:** Greene, Ross, et al. From "Are Students with ADHD More Stressful to Teach?" *Journal of Emotional and Behavioral Disorders*, Summer 2002; **p. 64:** Ducharme, Michelle M. From "A Lifetime in Production." *Newsweek*, September 9, 1996, p.17. All rights reserved. Reprinted by permission of the author; **pp. 65–66:** Reich, Robert. From "The Future of Work," *Harper's*, April 1989, 26+. Copyright © 1989 by Robert Reich. Reprinted by permission of the author; **p. 62:** China: Population Density, 2000. Copyright © 2005 Center for International Earth Science Information Network (CIESIN), Columbia University, and Centro Internacional de Agricultura Tropical (CIAT). Gridded Population of the World Version 3 (GPWv3). Palisades, NY: Socioeconomic Data and Applications Center (SEDAC), CIESIN, Columbia University. Available at: http://sedac.ciesin.columbia.edu/gdw. Reprinted with permission from CIESIN; **p. 65:** From Galle, *Business Communication: A Technology-Based Approach*, 1st ed., 1996, Fig. 8.4, p. 240. Copyright © 1996 The McGraw-Hill Companies. Reprinted with permission; **p. 67:** Chart: Morning News Viewership, All Networks: http://www.stateofthenewsmedia.org/narrative_networktv_audience .asp?cat=3&media=4>. Reprinted by permission of Nielson Media Research; **p. 68:** From Lahey, Benjamin, *Psychology: An Introduction*, 9th ed., 2007, Fig. 12.2, p. 466. Copyright © 2007 The McGraw-Hill Companies, Inc. Reprinted with permission. **p. 69:** From Schaefer, Richard T., *Sociology*, 10th ed., 2007, Fig. 2.1, p. 29. Copyright © 2007 The McGraw-Hill Companies, Inc. Reprinted with permission; **p. 73:** Hoffman, Ross N. from "Controlling Hurricanes." *Scientific American*, October 2004, p. 69. Copyright © 2004 Scientific American, Inc. All rights reserved. Reprinted with permission; **pp. 73–75:** Keys, David. "Rethinking the Picts," *Archaeology*, Vol. 57, Number 5, 2004. Copyright © 2004 by The Archaeological Institute of America. Reprinted with permission; **p. 75:** Belson, Ken. From "Saved, and Enslaved, by the Cell." *The New York Times*, October 10, 2004, p. 12. Direct quote by Kenneth J. Gergen reprinted by permission of Kenneth J. Gergen; **p. 80:** Screen shot reprinted with permission from Purdue Unversity OWL. Microsoft® Internet Explorer screen shot reprinted with permission from Microsoft Corporation; **p. 81:** Microsoft® Word screen shot reprinted with permission from Microsoft Corporation; **Fig. 5.4:** Draft from *Mathematics: Applications and Connections, Course 2*. Copyright © 1998 Glencoe/

McGraw-Hill. Reprinted with permission; **p. 105:** Screen shot of Microsoft® Word used by permission of Microsoft Corporation; **p. 117:** Screen shot from Process & Product: Reflections, © 2006 Ken Tinnes. http://www.students.niu.edu/~z120512/104.M70/eportfolio/Reflections/Process/process.html. Reprinted with permission; **pp. 126–128:** Hentoff, Nat. "Misguided Multiculturalism," *The Village Voice*, July 19–25, 2000, pp. 29–30. Copyright © 2000 by Nat Hentoff. Reprinted by permission of the author; **p. 147:** Canetto, Silvia Sara, et al. From "Love and Achievement Motives in Women's and Men's Suicide Notes." *Journal of Psychology*, Vol. 136, Issue 5, pp. 573–6, September 2002. Reprinted with permission of the Helen Dwight Reid Educational Foundation. Published by Heldref Publications, 1319 Eighteenth St., NW, Washington, DC 20036-1802. Copyright © 2002; **p. 149:** Elaine Maimon and Janice Peritz, *A Writer's Resource,* p. 116. Copyright © 2003 The McGraw-Hill Companies, Inc. Reprinted with permission; **p. 152:** Fig. 1: Illustration of a test tank used to study orientation behavior. *Tested Studies for Laboratory Teaching* Volume 6. Reprinted by permission of Jon C. Glase; **p. 155–156:** Berwick, Carly. "The Sample Life," *ARTnews*, November 2004, p. 134. Copyright © 2004 by Carly Berwick. Reprinted by permission of the author; **p. 163:** "Testimonial" from *On the Bus with Rosa Parks*, W.W. Norton and Co., © 1999 by Rita Dove. Reprinted by permission of the author; **pp. 174–175:** From Kottak, Conrad. "Ritual at McDonalds" in *Cultural Anthropology*, 9e. Copyright © 2002 The McGraw-Hill Companies, Inc. Reprinted with permission; **pp. 188–191:** Avoiding Fallacies from Elaine Maimon and Janice Peritz, *A Writer's Resource,* 3rd ed. Copyright © 2010 The McGraw-Hill Companies, Inc. Reprinted with permission; **pp. 198–199:** Using Visuals in Your Argument from Elaine Maimon and Janice Peritz, *A Writer's Resource*, 3rd ed. Copyright © 2010 The McGraw-Hill Companies, Inc. Reprinted with permission; **pp. 207–208:** Jamieson, Dale. "The Morality of the Species." Copyright © 1991 by The Hastings Center. Reprinted by permission. This article originally appeared in *The Hastings Center Report*, Vol. 21, No. 2 (1991); **pp. 209–212:** "Growing More Food" reprinted by permission of Council for Biotechnology Information. http://www.whybiotech.com/index.asp?id=1821; **pp. 213–214:** Daum, Meghan. "Virtual Love." Reprinted by permission of International Creative Management, Inc. Copyright © 1997 by Meghan Daum. First appeared in *The New Yorker*, August 25, 1997; **pp. 215–216:** Ladson-Billings, Gloria. From "The Dreamkeepers: Successful Teachers of African American Children," pp. 35–36. Copyright © 1994 by John Wiley & Sons, Inc. Reprinted with permission; **pp. 223–224:** From Elaine Maimon and Janice Peritz, *A Writer's Resource*, p. 126. Copyright © 2003 The McGraw-Hill Companies, Inc. Reprinted with permission; **p. 230:** "Musee des Beaux Arts," copyright 1940 & renewed 1968 by W.H. Auden, from COLLECTED POEMS by W.H. Auden. Used by permission of Random House, Inc. and Faber and Faber, Ltd. Copyright © The Estate of W.H. Auden; **p. 242:** Copyright © 1993 by The Vietnam Women's Memorial Foundation, Inc. Glenna Goodacre, sculptor. Microsoft® Internet Explorer screen shot reprinted with permission from Microsoft Corporation; **p. 243:** Screen shot of Governors State University Library. Reprinted with permission of Governors State University. Microsoft® Internet Explorer screen shot reprinted with permission from Microsoft Corporation; **p. 245:** Screen shot of blog for English course by Jason Tougaw, Queen's College. Reprinted with permission; **p. 260:** Screen shot of Governors State University Library. Reprinted with permission of Governors State University. Microsoft® Internet Explorer screen shot reprinted with permission from Microsoft Corporation; **p. 268:** Image published with permission of ProQuest-CSA LLC. © 2007, ProQuest-CSA LLC; all rights reserved. Further reproduction is prohibited without permission. Microsoft® Internet Explorer screen shot reprinted with permission from Microsoft Corporation; **pp. 269–270:** Image published with permission of ProQuest-CSA LLC. © 2007, ProQuest-CSA LLC; all rights reserved. Further reproduction is prohibited without permission. Microsoft® Internet Explorer screen shot reprinted with permission from Microsoft Corporation; **pp. 271, 273:** From Google.com. Microsoft® Internet Explorer screen shot reprinted with permission from Microsoft Corporation; **p. 283:** Map track of Tropical Storm Jeanne. www.skeetobiteweather.com. Reprinted by permission of Skeetobite Studios, Inc.; **p. 287:** From Google.com. Microsoft® Internet Explorer screen shot reprinted with permission from Microsoft Corporation; **p. 288:** Screen capture of Commons Deed from http://creativecommons.org. This work is licensed under the Creative Commons Public License and can be redistributed under that license. Microsoft® Internet Explorer screen shot reprinted with permission from Microsoft Corporation. Disclaimer of warranties: The licensor offers the work as-is and makes no representation or warranties of any kind concerning the work, express, implied, statutory, or otherwise, including, without limitation, warranties of title, merchantibility, fitness for a particular purpose, noninfringement, or the absence of latent or other defects, accuracy, or the presence of absence of errors, whether or not discoverable. Some jurisdicitions do not allow the exclusion of implied warranties, so such exclusion may not apply to the licensee; **p. 295:** Screen shot of WWF web page reprinted with permission. Microsoft® Internet Explorer screen shot reprinted with permission from Microsoft Corporation; **p. 296:** Screen shot from Gray Wolf page at http://bear-tracker.com/wolves. Reprinted with permission from Kim Cabrera. Microsoft® Internet Explorer screen shot reprinted with permission from Microsoft Corporation; **p. 321:** Screen shot reprinted with permission from NewOrleansOnline.com. Photos courtesy of the Louis Armstrong House Museum, Queens College. Used with permission; **pp. 325–326** Ephland, John. From "Down Beat Jazz 101: The Very Beginning," *Down Beat* Magazine, http://www.downbeat.com/default.asp?sect=education&subsect=jazz. Courtesy of Down Beat Magazine; **p. 348** Excerpt from "Trumpet Player," from *The Collected Poems of Langston Hughes* by Langston Hughes, edited by Arnold Rampersad with David Roessel, Associate Editor. Copyright © 1994 by The Estate of Langston Hughes. Reprinted by permission of Alfred A. Knopf, a division of Random House, Inc., and of Harold Ober Associates Incorporated; **p. 386** Illustration of Louis Armstrong and Joe Glazer. Courtesy of the Louis Armstrong House Museum, Queens College. Used with permission; **MLA Foldout:** Table of contents and introductory page from Hayes, Brent Edwards. "Louis Armstrong and the Syntax of Scat." Critical Inquiry 28 (2002): 618–49. Copyright © 2002 by The University of Chicago Press. Reprinted with permission from the publisher, The University of Chicago Press; "Heebie Jeebies" by Boyd Atkins. Copyright © 1926 Universal Music Corp. Copyright Renewed. All Rights Reserved. Used by Permission; From *Louis Armstrong: An Extravagant Life* by Lawrence Bergreen. Copyright © 1997 by Lawrence Bergreen. Used by permission of Broadway Books, a division of Random House, Inc.; Image published with permission of ProQuest-CSA LLC. © 2007, ProQuest-CSA LLC; all rights reserved. Further reproduction is prohibited without permission. Microsoft® Internet Explorer screen shot reprinted with permission from Microsoft Corporation; Screen shot from Reuters.com, "Companies seek alternatives to plastic chemical" by Will Dunham, Wed Sep 17, 2008 8:52pm EDT. Reproduced with permission from Reuters. Microsoft® Internet Explorer screen shot reprinted with permission from Microsoft Corporation; **p. 415:** Fig. 1 from Hamburger Connection Fuels Amazon Destruction: Cattle Ranching and Deforestation in Brazil's Amazon by D. Kaimonwitz, B. Mertens, S. Wunder and P. Pacheco, 2002. Center for International Forestry Research (CIFOR). Reprinted with permission from CIFOR; **APA Foldout:** Title page and copyright page from *Exploring Agrodiversity* by Harold Brookfield, 2001. Reprinted by permission of Columbia University Press; Screen shot of Wiley Interscience web site and abstract for: Soares-Filho, B., Alencar, A., Nepstad, D., Cerqueira, G., del Carmen Vera Diaz, M., Rivero, S., et. Al. (2004). Simulating the response of land-cover changes to road paving and governance along a major Amazon highway: the Santarém-Cuiabá corridor. *Global Change Biology* 10 (5), 745–764. Reprinted with permission of the publisher, Wiley-Blackwell. Microsoft® Internet Explorer screen shot reprinted with permission from Microsoft Corporation; Excerpt and table of contents page from *A Voice in the Wilderness* by Jack Epstein, 2001. Reprinted by permission of Latin Trade Magazine; The U'was Reject Consulation Process and Ecopatrol's Oil Project on Their Reserve in Columbia by Atossa Soltani/Amazon Watch, 10/23/2006, http://www.amazonwatch.org/newsroom/view_news.php?id=1240. Reprinted with permission. Microsoft® Internet Explorer screen shot reprinted with permission from Microsoft Corporation; **pp. 457–463:** Elaine Maimon and Janice Peritz, A Writer's Resource, 3rd ed. Copyright © 2010 The McGraw-Hill Companies, Inc. Reprinted with permission; **p. 663:** From Jerry Bentley and Herbert Ziegler, *Traditions and Encounters: A Global Perspective on the Past*, 2nd ed., p. 91. Copyright © 2003 The McGraw-Hill Companies, Inc. Reprinted with permission; **p. 679:** Definition of "compare" from *Random House Webster's Dictionary of American English*. Copyright © 1997 by Random House, Inc.; **p. 680:** By permission. From the *Merriam-Webster Online Dictionary* © 2008 by Merriam-Webster, Incorporated (www.Merriam-Webster.com); **pp. 687–88:** Bentley and Herbert Ziegler, *Traditions and Encounters: A Global Perspective on the Past*, 2nd ed., p. 91. Copyright © 2003 The McGraw-Hill Companies, Inc. Reprinted with permission; **p. 759:** "Short Story on a Painting of Gustav Klimt" (4 line excerpt). By Lawrence Ferlinghetti, from *Endless Life: Selected Poems.* Cpyright © 1976 by Lawrence Ferlinghetti. Reprinted by permission of New

Directions Publishing Corp; **p. 777:** Reprinted with the permission of Scribner, a Division of Simon & Schuster Adult Publishing Group, and of A P Watt Ltd on behalf of Gráinne Yeats, from *The Complete Works of W.B. Yeats, Volume I: The Poems,* edited by Richard J. Finneran. Copyright © 1928 by The Macmillan Company. Copyright renewed © 1956 by Georgie Yeats. All rights reserved; **p. 855:** Text from Elaine Maimon, Janice Peritz, and Kathleen Yancey, *A Writer's Resource*, 2e, **p. 625**. Copyright © 2007 The McGraw-Hill Companies, Inc. Reprinted with permission; **p. 866:** Elaine Maimon, Janice Peritz, and Kathleen Yancey, *A Writer's Resource*, 2e, **p. 616.** Copyright © 2007 The McGraw-Hill vCompanies, Inc. Reprinted with permission; Location from Elaine Maimon, Janice Peritz, and Kathleen Yancey, *A Writer's Resource*, 2e, **p. 617.** Copyright © 2007 The McGraw-Hill Companies, Inc. Reprinted with permission.

Photo Credits

Part Opener 1: © Visual Language; **p. 9:** Mario Tama/Getty Images; **p. 53:** *(top)* Frank Micelotta/Getty Images, *(middle)* Space Science and Engineering Center/University of Wisconsin–Madison, *(bottom)* www.adbusters.org; **p. 63:** © David Leeson/Dallas Morning News/Corbis Sygma; **p. 64:** ©2000 by Sebastiao Salgado/Amazonas Images/Contact Press Images; **p. 66:** © Bettmann/Corbis; **p. 103:** ©2000 by Sebastiao Salgado/Amazonas Images/ Contact Press Images.

Part Opener 2: © Philadelphia Museum of Modern Art/Corbis; **pp. 124, 131:** www .peacecorps.org; **p. 132:** © Lynsey Addario/Corbis; **p. 156:** Stephanie Berger for The New York Times; **p. 161:** Campbell's Soup Can, 1962 (screen print) by Andy Warhol (1930–87) Saatchi Collection, London, UK/The Bridgeman Art Library/ © 2008 The Andy Warhol Foundation for the Visual Arts/ARS, New York; **p. 171:** Public Domain; **p. 179:** © Irwin Thompson/The Dallas Morning News; **p. 192:** www.adbusters.org; **p. 202:** Karen Bleier/AFP/ Getty Images; **p. 220:** *(left)* © UPPA/Topham/The Image Works, *(right)* © Jacob Halaska/ Jupiter Images; **p. 229:** *(top)* © Thomas Hoepker/Magnum Photos, *(bottom)* © The Gallery Collection/Corbis; **p. 235:** University of Washington Libraries/Special Collections.

Part Operner 3: © Photo courtesy of NASA/Corbis; **p. 303:** Diego Goldberg/Sygma/Corbis.

Part Opener 4: © Nevros/Folio, Inc.; **p. 386:** Louis Armstrong Archives. Queens College City University of New York, Flushing.

Part Opener 5: Design Firm: Pentagram Design, NCY. Art Directors: John Klotnia and Woody Pirtle. Graphic Designers: Seung il Choi, John Klotnia, and Ivette Montes de Oca. Illustrators: Lori Anzalone, Dugald Stermer, and Kevin Torline. Printer: Sandy Alexander, Inc. Paper: Mohawk Vellum, 60 # Text Recycled. Client: National Audubon Society. © Pentagram.

Part Opener 6: © Will & Deni McIntyre/Photo Researchers, Inc.

Part Opener 7: © Mimmo Jodice/Corbis; **p. 534:** Réunion des Musées Nationaux/Art Resource, NY; **p. 583:** Portrait of Elizabeth Barrett Browning (1806–61) 1855 (oil on panel), Brett, John (1830–1902)/Private Collection/www.bridgeman.co.uk.

Part Opener 8: © Frank Lloyd Wright, American, 1867–1959. Tree of Life Window, from the Darwin D. Martin House, Buffalo, New York, designed 1904. Leaded clear and stained glass suspended in wood frame. Elvehjem Museum of Art, University of Wisconsin–Madison, Art Collections Fund and Alta Gudsos Fund purchase, 1982.7 and Artists's Rights Society; **p. 635:** Raymond K. Gehman/Getty Images; **p. 642:** © Burstein Collection/Corbis.

Part Opener 9: © Justin Kerr; **p. 698:** *(left)* © University of Pennsylvania/AP Photo, *(right)* Ryan McVay/Getty Images.

Part Opener 10: Royalty-Free/Corbis; **p. 725:** © Robert Harding/Getty Images; **p. 770:** © Bettmann/Corbis; **p. 784:** © Roger Ressmeyer/Corbis.

Part Opener 11: © Bridgeman-Giraudon/Art Resource, NY; **p. 797:** Matthew J. & Arlyn Bruccoli Collection of F. Scott Fitzgerald, University of South Carolina; **p. 813:** © Digital Vision/Getty Images.

Part Opener 12: © Jon Hicks/Corbis.

Part Opener 13: © HIP/Art Resource, NY; **FR-2:** *(top)* © Royalty-Free/Corbis, *(bottom)* Bettmann/Corbis; **FR-3:** © Royalty-Free/Corbis; **FR-4:** *(top)* © PNC/zefa/Corbis, *(bottom left)* © Corbis, *(bottom right)* © Burstein Collection/Corbis; **FR-5:** *(left)* © Nik Wheeler/Corbis, *(right)* © The Art Archive/Corbis; **FR-6:** *(left)* Hulton Archive/Getty Images, *(top right)* © Adalberto Rios Szalay/Sexto Sol/Getty Images, (bottom right) © Burstein Collection/Corbis; **FR-7:** *(left)* © Jacob Halaska/Jupiter Images; *(right)* © Bettmann/Corbis; **FR-8:** Library of Congress; **FR-9:** *(left)* © Bettmann/Corbis, *(right)* © Library of Congress; **FR-10:** *(left)* © Bettmann/Corbis, *(top right)* © Fototeca Storica Nazionale/Photodisc/Getty Images; *(bottom right)* © Historical Picture Archive/Corbis; **FR-11:** *(left)* © Pixtal/age Fotostock, *(right)* © Bettmann/Corbis; **FR-12:** *(left)* © Bettmann/Corbis, *(right)* © Philadelphia Museum of Art/Corbis; **FR-13:** *(top)* Royalty-Free/Corbis, *(bottom left)* © Underwood & Underwood/Corbis, *(bottom right)* © Frank Driggs Collection; **FR-14:** © Bettmann/Corbis; **FR-15:** *(left)* © Library of Congress Prints & Photographs Division [LC-USE6-D-007408], *(right)* © Will & Deni McIntyre/Photo Researchers, Inc.; **FR-16:** *(left)* © Photodisc/Getty Images, *(top right)* © Bettmann/Corbis, *(bottom right)* © Jack Star/PhotoLink/Getty Images; **FR-17:** *(top)* © Bettmann/Corbis, *(bottom left)* Coast Guard photograph by Petty Officer 2nd Class Kyle Niemi/Getty Images, *(bottom right)* Chad Baker/Ryan McVay/Getty Images; **FR-19:** © Philip Colla Natural History Photography; **FR-21:** © Bettmann/Corbis; **FR-23:** © Hulton-Deutsch Collection/Corbis; **FR-25:** © Bettmann/Corbis; **FR-26:** © Bettmann/Corbis.

Index

(continued)

(continued)

(continued)

(continued)

(continued)

(continued)

(continued)

(continued)

S

(continued)

(continued)

(continued)

Index for Multilingual Writers

BOXES FOR MULTILINGUAL STUDENTS

✓ IDENTIFYING AND EDITING COMMON PROBLEMS

Grammar Conventions (Parts 7)

Clarity and Word Choice (Parts 8 & 9)

Punctuation, Mechanics, and Spelling (Parts 10 & 11)